WORLD STUDIES

FIFTH EDITION

bju press
Greenville, South Carolina

Note: The fact that materials produced by other publishers may be referred to in this volume does not constitute an endorsement of the content or theological position of materials produced by such publishers. Any references and ancillary materials are listed as an aid to the student or the teacher and in an attempt to maintain the accepted academic standards of the publishing industry.

World Studies Student Edition
Fifth Edition

Writers
Jill Blackstock, MEd
John Seney, MA

Writer Consultants
Kirsten Alexander, MEd
L. Michelle Rosier

Biblical Worldview
William Ostrom, PhD
Bryan Smith, PhD

Academic Integrity
Jeff Heath, EdD

Academic Oversight
Rachel Santopietro, MEd
Michael Winningham, MA

Editor
Manda Kalagayan, MEd

Designer
Garison Plourde

Cover Designer
Elly Kalagayan

Design Assistants
Jullianna Eckardt
Kristiana Olson
Priscilla Smith

Illustrators
Peter Bull
Martín Bustamante
Samantha Chow
John Cunningham
Cynthia Long
Joey Macalle
Angeles Peinador (Beehive Illustration)
Riley Stark

Production Designer
Sarah Centers

Permissions
Maria Andersen
Sharon Belknap
Sarah Gundlach
Carrie Hanna

Project Coordinator
Chris Daniels

Postproduction Liaison
Peggy Hargis

Photograph credits begin on page 494.

The text for this book is set in Adobe Flood, Adobe Minion Pro, Adobe Myriad Pro, Aphrosine by Paratype, Arial MT, Calibri by Monotype, Candara, Concave Tuscan by Wood Type Revival, Flood by Joachim Müller-Lancé, Freight Sans by Joshua Darden, Gin by Mattox Shuler, Helvetica, Korolev by Rian Hughes, Liza by Underware, Luckiest Guy by Astigmatic, Modesto by Jim Parkinson, Montserrat by Julieta Ulanovsky, Mr Rafkin by Sudtipos, Nelson by Laura Worthington Type, Octin by Ray Larabie, Pentz by Fort Foundry, Roboto by Christian Robertson, Times, Times New Roman PS MT, UnifrakturMaguntia by j. 'mach' wust, and Wingdings 3.

ISBN 978-1-64626-053-9

15 14 13 12 11 10 9 8 7 6 5 4 3

Contents

Features of the Book

2 | EMERGENCE OF EUROPE

400 – 1450

ESSENTIAL QUESTIONS

- What were the characteristics of feudalism in Europe in the Middle Ages?
- How did nation-states develop in Europe?
- Why did power shift between groups in the Middle Ages?
- What was culture like in the Middle Ages?
- How did calamities of the late Middle Ages shape modern Europe?

RICHARD THE LIONHEART

Richard I of England seems at first glance to have been the perfect example of a medieval warrior and king. His outstanding military ability earned him the admiration and respect of contemporaries as well as future generations. Looking deeper below the surface, though, we see that Richard's story shows a world that was not always noble.

Richard was born on September 8, 1157, the third son of Henry II, king of England and great lord in France. Richard's family showed little respect for each other. Encouraged by their mother, Richard and two of his brothers revolted against their father in 1173–74. Later more conflict arose among the three brothers and (after the other two died) between Richard and his father again. Despite the conflict, though, Richard inherited his father's throne and some of his father's French territory when his father died in 1189.

Richard spent much of his time trying to hold on to his land in France, so he was only in England a few months out of the ten years he was king. Still his subjects appreciated his impressive military accomplishments. He was only sixteen years old when he led his first army. His skill and fierce determination on the battlefield earned him the name "Lionheart."

Like many other medieval warriors, Richard joined a crusade (a religious war between the Christians and the Muslim Turks). Together with the king of France and the emperor of the Holy Roman Empire (modern-day Germany), who drowned along the way, Richard planned to take Jerusalem back from the Muslim commander Saladin so Christian pilgrims could visit it again. Crusading was expensive, and Richard sold and taxed as much as he could in England to pay for the trip.

Richard won important victories outside the cities of Acre and Joppa in the Holy Land. At Acre he was sick but participated in the battle from a stretcher. Richard failed to take Jerusalem but signed an agreement allowing temporary access for Christian pilgrims.

Richard was in constant conflict with the other leaders of the crusade. On the way home he was captured and turned over to the new Holy Roman Emperor. England was asked for a huge sum of money, 150,000 silver marks, to ransom its king. Richard's mother worked to secure his release, and, despite an offer of 80,000 marks from the king of France to keep Richard in captivity, the Holy Roman Emperor released him.

Richard returned home to face more plots from his younger brother John and the king of France. Though he put these plots down, Richard continued to participate in warfare all his life. He died in 1199 of complications from a battle wound.

▲ Crusaders wore a cross as a symbol of the vow they took to defend Christianity and the Holy Land.

Emergence of Europe 27

The **chapter outline** lists the major topics that will be covered.

Opening stories engage interest with detailed, personal information about events.

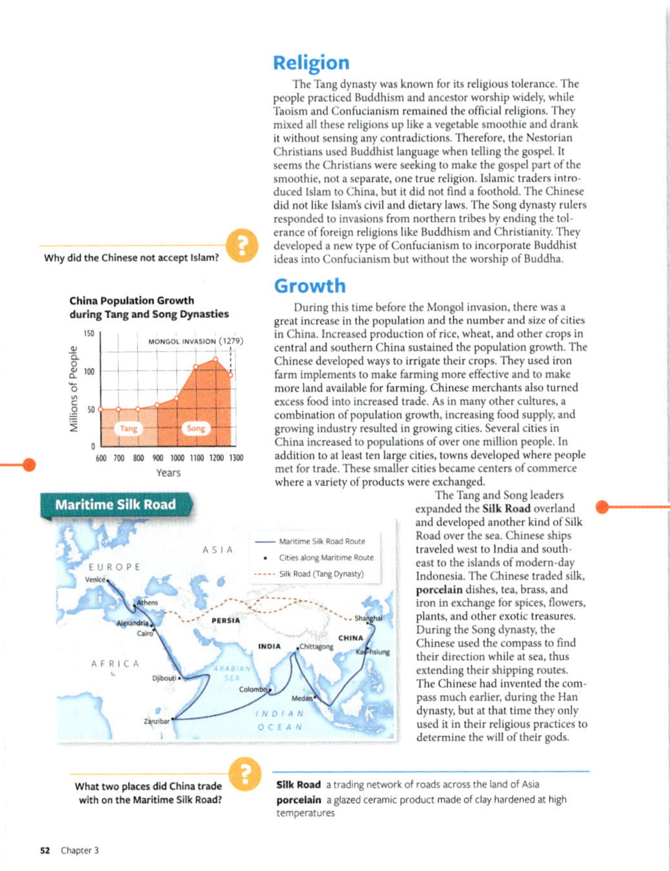

Religion

The Tang dynasty was known for its religious tolerance. The people practiced Buddhism and ancestor worship widely, while Taoism and Confucianism remained the official religions. They mixed all these religions up like a vegetable smoothie and drank it without sensing any contradictions. Therefore, the Nestorian Christians used Buddhist language when telling the gospel. It seems the Christians were seeking to make the gospel part of the smoothie, not a separate, one true religion. Islamic traders introduced Islam to China, but it did not find a foothold. The Chinese did not like Islam's civil and dietary laws. The Song dynasty rulers responded to invasions from northern tribes by ending the tolerance of foreign religions like Buddhism and Christianity. They developed a new type of Confucianism to incorporate Buddhist ideas into Confucianism but without the worship of Buddha.

Why did the Chinese not accept Islam?

Growth

During this time before the Mongol invasion, there was a great increase in the population and the number and size of cities in China. Increased production of rice, wheat, and other crops in central and southern China sustained the population growth. The Chinese developed ways to irrigate their crops. They used iron farm implements to make farming more effective and to make more land available for farming. Chinese merchants also turned excess food into increased trade. As in many other cultures, a combination of population growth, increasing food supply, and growing industry resulted in growing cities. Several cities in China increased to populations of over one million people. In addition to at least ten large cities, towns developed where people met for trade. These smaller cities became centers of commerce where a variety of products were exchanged.

China Population Growth during Tang and Song Dynasties

Maritime Silk Road

The Tang and Song leaders expanded the **Silk Road** overland and developed another kind of Silk Road over the sea. Chinese ships traveled west to India and southeast to the islands of modern-day Indonesia. The Chinese traded silk, **porcelain** dishes, tea, brass, and iron in exchange for spices, flowers, plants, and other exotic treasures. During the Song dynasty, the Chinese used the compass to find their direction while at sea, thus extending their shipping routes. The Chinese had invented the compass much earlier, during the Han dynasty, but at that time they only used it in their religious practices to determine the will of their gods.

What two places did China trade with on the Maritime Silk Road?

Silk Road a trading network of roads across the land of Asia
porcelain a glazed ceramic product made of clay hardened at high temperatures

52 Chapter 3

Maps and charts help students visualize concepts and geographic locations.

Terms in bold type draw attention to important facts, ideas, individuals, or definitions.

3.2 **The Rise of the Mongol Empire**

The Mongols were nomads who lived in tribes on the Mongolian plateau north of China. They traveled across the plains in search of grazing land for their large herds of horses. The Mongols lived in movable tent-like structures called **gers.** In the western Mongol lands, similar structures were called "yurts," a Turkic word. The difference between the two is that gers have interior poles holding up the center of the roof, but yurts do not.

These tribes often fought among themselves over grazing lands. However, two factors led these tribes to combine and become a great empire. First, the climate cooled over a vast region. Because of the cooling, the nomads had to travel farther in search of grassland for their herds. As they traveled farther from their homelands, they encountered different peoples whom they conquered. The second factor in the birth of the Mongol Empire was Temujin, a gifted Mongol boy during the twelfth century. He proved to be one of the world's greatest military commanders.

GUIDING QUESTIONS

- How did the Mongol Empire rise and expand?
- Who was Genghis Khan?
- How did the Mongol conquests affect the people of Asia and Eastern Europe?
- What was Mongol religion like?
- What was Pax Mongolica?

What kind of shelter did the Mongols live in?

Outside and inside of a ger

Kingdoms of Asia and the Mongol Empire 55

Guiding Questions help prepare students to read the material carefully.

Reading Check questions help students remember what they have learned.

Photographs, illustrations, and artwork assist students in "seeing" the sites, people, and events discussed in the text.

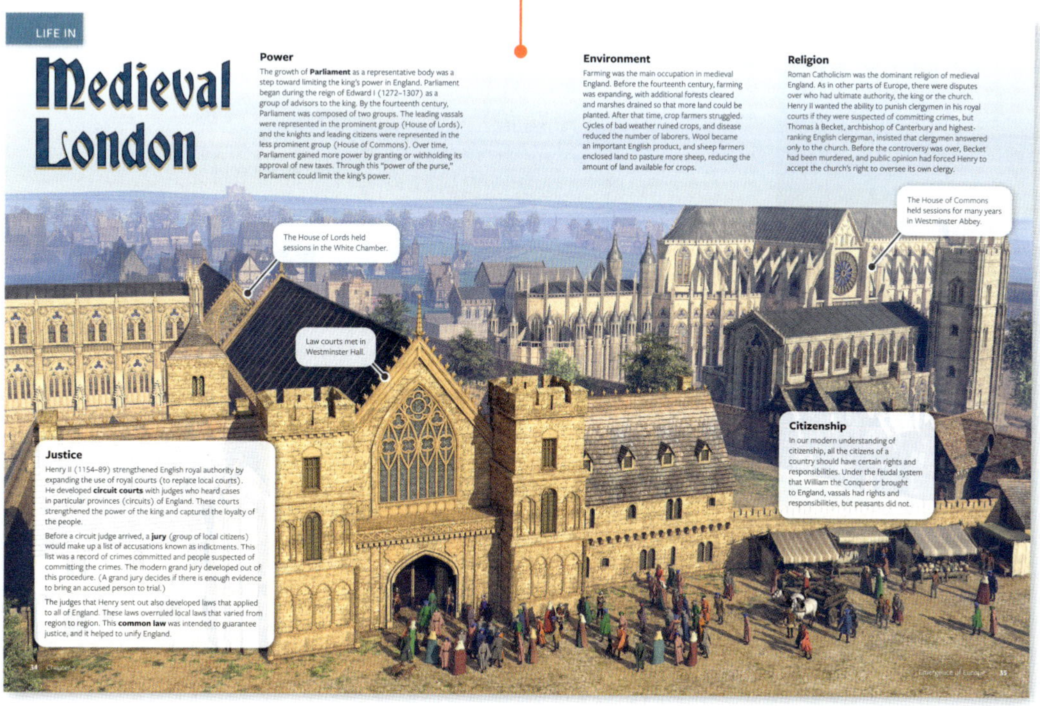

LIFE IN

Medieval London

Power

The growth of **Parliament** as a representative body was a step toward limiting the king's power in England. Parliament began during the reign of Edward I (1272–1307) as a group of advisors to the king. By the fourteenth century, Parliament was composed of two groups. The leading vassals were represented in the prominent group (House of Lords), and the knights and leading citizens were represented in the less prominent group (House of Commons). Over time, Parliament gained more power by granting or withholding its approval of new taxes. Through this "power of the purse," Parliament could limit the king's power.

Environment

Farming was the main occupation in medieval England. Before the fourteenth century, farming was expanding, with additional forests cleared and marshes drained so that more land could be planted. After that time, crop farmers struggled. Cycles of bad weather ruined crops, and disease reduced the number of laborers. Wool became an important English product, and sheep farmers enclosed land to pasture more sheep, reducing the amount of land available for crops.

Religion

Roman Catholicism was the dominant religion of medieval England. As in other parts of Europe, there were disputes over who had ultimate authority, the king or the church. Henry II wanted the ability to punish clergymen in his royal courts if they were suspected of committing crimes, but Thomas à Becket, archbishop of Canterbury and highest-ranking English clergyman, insisted that clergymen answered only to the church. Before the controversy was over, Becket had been murdered, and public opinion had forced Henry to accept the church's right to oversee its own clergy.

The House of Lords held sessions in the White Chamber.

The House of Commons held sessions for many years in Westminster Abbey.

Law courts met in Westminster Hall.

Justice

Henry II (1154–89) strengthened English royal authority by expanding the use of royal courts (to replace local courts). He developed **circuit courts** with judges who heard cases in particular provinces (circuits) of England. These courts strengthened the power of the king and captured the loyalty of the people.

Before a circuit judge arrived, a **jury** (group of local citizens) would make up a list of accusations known as indictments. This list was a record of crimes committed and people suspected of committing the crimes. The modern grand jury developed out of this procedure. (A grand jury decides if there is enough evidence to bring an accused person to trial.)

The judges that Henry sent out also developed laws that applied to all of England. These laws overruled local laws that varied from region to region. This **common law** was intended to guarantee justice, and it helped to unify England.

Citizenship

In our modern understanding of citizenship, all the citizens of a country should have certain rights and responsibilities. Under the feudal system that William the Conqueror brought to England, vassals had rights and responsibilities, but peasants did not.

Biographies provide details about significant people.

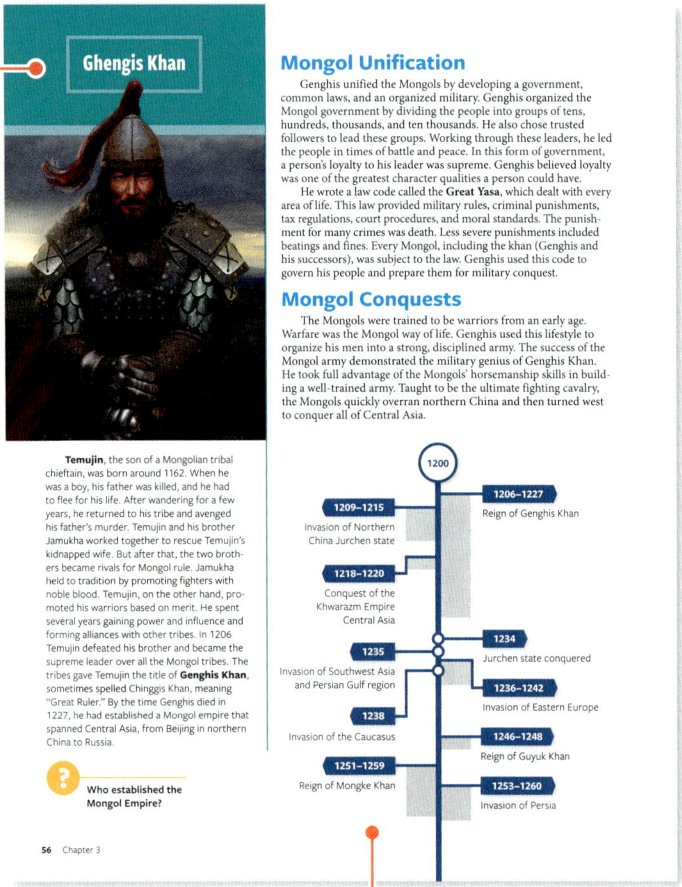
Ghengis Khan

Temujin, the son of a Mongolian tribal chieftain, was born around 1162. When he was a boy, his father was killed, and he had to flee for his life. After wandering for a few years, he returned to his tribe and avenged his father's murder. Temujin and his brother Jamukha worked together to rescue Temujin's kidnapped wife. But after that, the two brothers became rivals for Mongol rule. Jamukha held to tradition by promoting fighters with noble blood. Temujin, on the other hand, promoted his warriors based on merit. He spent several years gaining power and influence and forming alliances with other tribes. In 1206 Temujin defeated his brother and became the supreme leader over all the Mongol tribes. The tribes gave Temujin the title of **Genghis Khan**, sometimes spelled Chinggis Khan, meaning "Great Ruler." By the time Genghis died in 1227, he had established a Mongol empire that spanned Central Asia, from Beijing in northern China to Russia.

Who established the Mongol Empire?

Mongol Unification

Genghis unified the Mongols by developing a government, common laws, and an organized military. Genghis organized the Mongol government by dividing the people into groups of tens, hundreds, thousands, and ten thousands. He also chose trusted followers to lead these groups. Working through these leaders, he led the people in times of battle and peace. In this form of government, a person's loyalty to his leader was supreme. Genghis believed loyalty was one of the greatest character qualities a person could have.

He wrote a law code called the **Great Yasa**, which dealt with every area of life. This law provided military rules, criminal punishments, tax regulations, court procedures, and moral standards. The punishment for many crimes was death. Less severe punishments included beatings and fines. Every Mongol, including the khan (Genghis and his successors), was subject to the law. Genghis used this code to govern his people and prepare them for military conquest.

Mongol Conquests

The Mongols were trained to be warriors from an early age. Warfare was the Mongol way of life. Genghis used this lifestyle to organize his men into a strong, disciplined army. The success of the Mongol army demonstrated the military genius of Genghis Khan. He took full advantage of the Mongols' horsemanship skills in building a well-trained army. Taught to be the ultimate fighting cavalry, the Mongols quickly overran northern China and then turned west to conquer all of Central Asia.

1200
1206–1227 Reign of Genghis Khan
1209–1215 Invasion of Northern China Jurchen state
1218–1220 Conquest of the Khwarazm Empire Central Asia
1234 Jurchen state conquered
1235 Invasion of Southwest Asia and Persian Gulf region
1236–1242 Invasion of Eastern Europe
1238 Invasion of the Caucasus
1246–1248 Reign of Guyuk Khan
1251–1259 Reign of Mongke Khan
1253–1260 Invasion of Persia

56 Chapter 3

Infographics combine graphics and text to aid student comprehension and memory.

Timelines help students place events in historical context.

SYMPTOMS OF THE BLACK DEATH

Day 1
Large painful boils called "buboes" appear in the armpits and groin.

Day 2
Fever and vomiting set in.

Day 3
Bleeding under skin creates dark spots all across the body.

Day 4
Plague attacks the nervous system, causing spasms and severe pain.

Day 5
30–50% of Europeans die, usually within 5 to 7 days of the onset of symptoms.

Cities in Europe were especially vulnerable to the spread of the plague for several reasons. Open sewers and improper disposal of trash made the cities unsanitary. Rats and fleas thrived there. Houses were also often close together, and the people lived in crowded settings. These unhealthy conditions provided a breeding ground for disease and its spread.

Besides the obvious reduction of the population in Europe, there were several other consequences of the Black Death. The people quickly turned to the Roman Catholic Church for deliverance. Many made trips to Rome and made donations to the church in hopes of rescue from the plague. However, though some church officials selflessly served the sick and dying, the Catholic Church proved to be unable to stop the plague. When people saw priests and nuns dying as quickly as others, they lost faith in the claims of the church. In addition, many concluded that the plague was sent by God to punish the people for their sins. The Catholic Church lost much of the authority that church leaders had built up over the years as people began to look other places for help with their problems.

The wealthy left the cities and lived on secluded estates to avoid contact with the plague. Others gave themselves over to sinful living since they believed that death was imminent. Crime also became a serious problem. As previously mentioned, many blamed Jews for the plague, and thousands of Jews died as the people slaughtered whole Jewish communities for their imagined crime.

By 1350 the Black Death had run its course, but it took many years for Europe to recover. The Roman Catholic Church had lost much of its credibility during the crisis. On the other hand, the movement toward the development of strong nation-states continued to gain momentum.

How did the Black Death possibly begin and spread?

WORLDVIEW DILEMMA

What is a biblical response to the suffering of others?

A Identify the sin in their life that caused the suffering.

B Seek to ease their suffering with love and wisdom.

C Recognize that suffering is a part of life and we can do nothing about it.

Worldview Dilemmas help students develop biblical answers to foundational ethical questions.

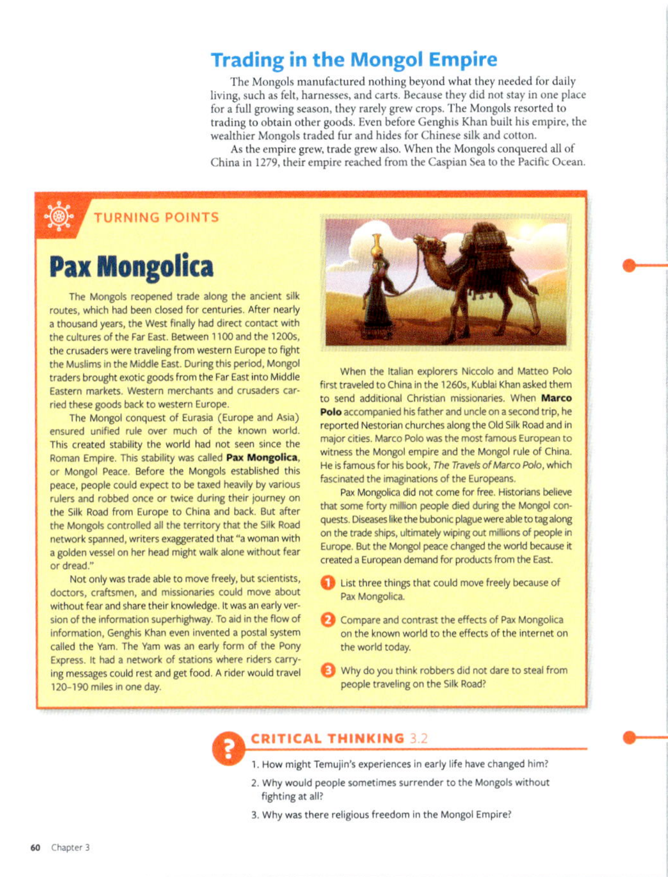

Trading in the Mongol Empire

The Mongols manufactured nothing beyond what they needed for daily living, such as felt, harnesses, and carts. Because they did not stay in one place for a full growing season, they rarely grew crops. The Mongols resorted to trading to obtain other goods. Even before Genghis Khan built his empire, the wealthier Mongols traded fur and hides for Chinese silk and cotton.

As the empire grew, trade grew also. When the Mongols conquered all of China in 1279, their empire reached from the Caspian Sea to the Pacific Ocean.

TURNING POINTS

Pax Mongolica

The Mongols reopened trade along the ancient silk routes, which had been closed for centuries. After nearly a thousand years, the West finally had direct contact with the cultures of the Far East. Between 1100 and the 1200s, the crusaders were traveling from western Europe to fight the Muslims in the Middle East. During this period, Mongol traders brought exotic goods from the Far East into Middle Eastern markets. Western merchants and crusaders carried these goods back to western Europe.

The Mongol conquest of Eurasia (Europe and Asia) ensured unified rule over much of the known world. This created stability the world had not seen since the Roman Empire. This stability was called **Pax Mongolica**, or Mongol Peace. Before the Mongols established this peace, people could expect to be taxed heavily by various rulers and robbed once or twice during their journey on the Silk Road from Europe to China and back. But after the Mongols controlled all the territory that the Silk Road network spanned, writers exaggerated that "a woman with a golden vessel on her head might walk alone without fear or dread."

Not only was trade able to move freely, but scientists, doctors, craftsmen, and missionaries could move about without fear and share their knowledge. It was an early version of the information superhighway. To aid in the flow of information, Genghis Khan even invented a postal system called the Yam. The Yam was an early form of the Pony Express. It had a network of stations where riders carrying messages could rest and get food. A rider would travel 120–190 miles in one day.

When the Italian explorers Niccolo and Matteo Polo first traveled to China in the 1260s, Kublai Khan asked them to send additional Christian missionaries. When **Marco Polo** accompanied his father and uncle on a second trip, he reported Nestorian churches along the Old Silk Road and in major cities. Marco Polo was the most famous European to witness the Mongol empire and the Mongol rule of China. He is famous for his book, *The Travels of Marco Polo*, which fascinated the imaginations of the Europeans.

Pax Mongolica did not come for free. Historians believe that some forty million people died during the Mongol conquests. Diseases like the bubonic plague were able to tag along on the trade ships, ultimately wiping out millions of people in Europe. But the Mongol peace changed the world because it created a European demand for products from the East.

1. List three things that could move freely because of Pax Mongolica.
2. Compare and contrast the effects of Pax Mongolica on the known world to the effects of the internet on the world today.
3. Why do you think robbers did not dare to steal from people traveling on the Silk Road?

CRITICAL THINKING 3.2

1. How might Temujin's experiences in early life have changed him?
2. Why would people sometimes surrender to the Mongols without fighting at all?
3. Why was there religious freedom in the Mongol Empire?

60 Chapter 3

Turning Points feature boxes highlight things or events that changed the direction of society.

Critical Thinking questions require students to establish connections or draw conclusions based on content.

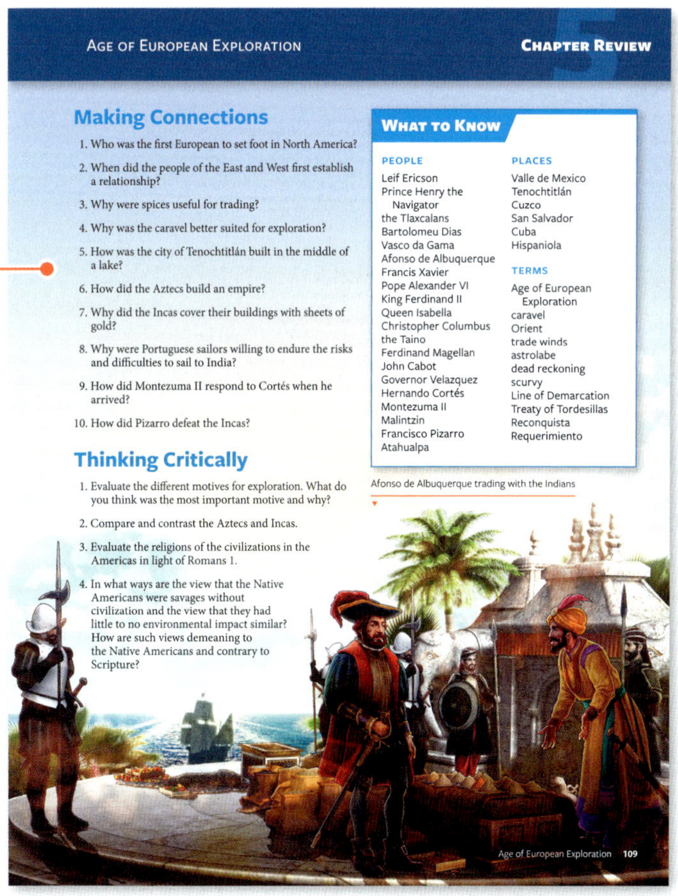

AGE OF EUROPEAN EXPLORATION — CHAPTER REVIEW

Making Connections

1. Who was the first European to set foot in North America?
2. When did the people of the East and West first establish a relationship?
3. Why were spices useful for trading?
4. Why was the caravel better suited for exploration?
5. How was the city of Tenochtitlán built in the middle of a lake?
6. How did the Aztecs build an empire?
7. Why did the Incas cover their buildings with sheets of gold?
8. Why were Portuguese sailors willing to endure the risks and difficulties to sail to India?
9. How did Montezuma II respond to Cortés when he arrived?
10. How did Pizarro defeat the Incas?

Thinking Critically

1. Evaluate the different motives for exploration. What do you think was the most important motive and why?
2. Compare and contrast the Aztecs and Incas.
3. Evaluate the religions of the civilizations in the Americas in light of Romans 1.
4. In what ways are the view that the Native Americans were savages without civilization and the view that they had little to no environmental impact similar? How are such views demeaning to the Native Americans and contrary to Scripture?

What to Know

PEOPLE
Leif Ericson
Prince Henry the Navigator
the Tlaxcalans
Bartolomeu Dias
Vasco da Gama
Afonso de Albuquerque
Francis Xavier
Pope Alexander VI
King Ferdinand II
Queen Isabella
Christopher Columbus
the Taino
Ferdinand Magellan
John Cabot
Governor Velazquez
Hernando Cortés
Montezuma II
Malintzin
Francisco Pizarro
Atahualpa

PLACES
Valle de Mexico
Tenochtitlán
Cuzco
San Salvador
Cuba
Hispaniola

TERMS
Age of European Exploration
caravel
Orient
trade winds
astrolabe
dead reckoning
scurvy
Line of Demarcation
Treaty of Tordesillas
Reconquista
Requerimiento

Afonso de Albuquerque trading with the Indians

Age of European Exploration 109

The **Chapter Review** asks students about terms, people, places, and concepts to help them think critically, improve understanding, and prepare for assessments.

WORLD STUDIES

FIFTH EDITION

1 PREPARING FOR WORLD STUDIES

3000 BC – AD 1000

ESSENTIAL QUESTIONS

- Why is it important to study history?
- How does a biblical worldview affect the way a believer interprets history?
- What were the ancient civilizations?

Amnesia

Imagine that you awaken in a hospital room and cannot remember how you got there. As you think further, not only do you not remember how you got there, but you do not even remember your name. You try to remember where you live, who your parents are—nothing! A nurse brings a tray of food, but eating is altogether unimportant; in fact, everything is secondary to the priority of remembering a single personal detail. If this were a movie, the villain would enter your room and try to deceive you about who you are in order to get you to do what he would like. But fortunately, your family and friends arrive, and you can see the honest love and concern in their eyes. After months of therapy, you finally regain your memory, but you never want to experience anything like that again.

Yet the ruler of this world (John 14:30) prefers that people live like this regarding their understanding of national and world history. If it is important to remember facts like your name, who your family is, and where you come from, it is also important to go further—to learn the history of your ancestors, your country, and your world.

1.1 Why Study History?

History is the inquiry into what happened in the past and why it happened. It is the study of the record of the past acts of God and man on earth from Creation to the present, based on the best surviving evidence. Since God alone sees the whole picture, down to the motivations that led people to act as they did, He alone knows perfectly what happened. History, as a subject matter that people research, is all about trying to understand what happened in the past through the study of writings, artifacts, and other records. Historians hope to get as clear a picture as possible of what happened and why it happened.

GUIDING QUESTIONS

- What is history?
- How does a knowledge of history help us make moral judgments?
- How does a knowledge of history develop a cultural identity?
- How do justice, power, citizenship, environment, and religion relate to the study of history?

? What is the definition of history?

Making Moral Judgments

One reason to study history is to improve our ability to make moral judgments. Study any civilization in the past, and you will discover something good and bad about it. A biblical worldview helps us understand why this is the case. Since every civilization is made up of people created in the image of God, we should expect to find them producing some good things in culture. At the same time, sin has damaged the image of God in human beings. Because of this, there are bad things in every culture. The way we distinguish between good and bad actions in world history is by reading the human story in light of God's standard for human behavior—the Bible. Christians can gain much wisdom by learning from both the mistakes and the successes of previous generations.

◄ An artist's rendering of Luke writing his Gospel

Developing a Cultural Identity

Like the person with amnesia, those who have little historical knowledge will not know who they are nor the contributions their ancestors made to give them their cultural identity. They become susceptible to whatever the latest trends are, even though they may not be best. They will not understand the failures, mistakes, and triumphs that have made them who they are. God understood the danger of this kind of deception. This is one reason He commissioned Moses to be Israel's first historian. This is also the reason He exhorted His people to remember. Repeatedly in Deuteronomy, God tells the Israelites to remember what He did for them and what their forefathers did. "Remember, and forget not, how thou provokedst the LORD thy God to wrath in the wilderness: from the day that thou didst depart out of the land of Egypt, until ye came unto this place, ye have been rebellious against the Lord." There are many more commands to remember in the Bible. Why did God command this? Psalm 78:7 gives us the answer: "That they might set their hope in God, and not forget the works of God, but keep his commandments." When we forget what God has done, we forget who we are and lose our way. Recorded history is filled with stories of what happens when nations and cultures forget God. But it is also filled with stories of hope and recovery. God is the prime actor on the stage of history, and He is moving history toward His ultimate goal.

Learning about Key Themes

History is not what many people think. It is not a simple matter of memorizing names, places, and dates on a calendar. It is so much more exciting than that. When we engage in history, we are investigating questions, controversies, and challenges that previous civilizations have faced. We do this investigation so we can develop wisdom for our own engagement with our culture. As we study, we will find that these challenges can be grouped into just a handful of categories or themes. For this book, we have identified five themes: justice, power, citizenship, environment, and religion. These are the areas where we will be making our moral judgments and learning about cultural identity. Every culture has its own take on these themes. Our concern will be to evaluate each culture based on how closely it aligns with the biblical standard.

Justice

A civilization cannot function without **justice**. *Justice* means to be treated rightly. Where there is no justice, chaos reigns. One of the most fundamental jobs of a society is to determine what is just and unjust and then to make laws and penalties that ensure justice is upheld. The Bible teaches that a society is just when people do right and respect each other's rights. The rights that people have are based on the image of God that each human bears. Because humans are made in God's image, it is wrong to murder or steal or commit any number of sins against other people. Instead, the Bible commands that people love others as they love themselves. Most civilizations base their understanding of justice on something other than the Bible. Much of the conflict in human history comes from opposing views of what is just or the ignoring of justice altogether.

Power

Power is essential to rule any civilization. For a civilization to grow and thrive, its leaders must have the power to provide order for the people who live there. Civilizations also need to exercise power over forces of nature that could threaten them. A Christian views the use of power as good and necessary. The command to exercise dominion over the earth is a command to exercise power in the world. But in a fallen world, power is often abused. Humans have used power to abuse others. The power that should have been used to cultivate creation has instead been used to damage it.

Citizenship

For most of world history, the common people were treated as subjects rather than citizens. A subject is one who is under the power of another. But the idea that people are citizens and not subjects became more common during the past six hundred years. A citizen has a status that gives him certain rights, privileges, and duties within his civilization. **Citizenship** gives individuals a say in how their community is run. It also imposes duties that require significant sacrifice. Christians need to evaluate what rights citizens should have and what duties should be required of them.

Environment

Every civilization is placed in a particular geographical location. Each location has special features. Many civilizations grew up along great rivers. Others learned how to flourish in harsh climates. Whatever the **environment**, God called mankind to rule over this world. Understanding how geography and the environment shape a civilization is important. Understanding how to manage the environment according to biblical wisdom is even more important.

Religion

Religion is the human response to God and His revelation. Humans cannot escape being religious because God made us to worship Him. Being religious is essential to being human. But what happens when the human heart turns away from the one true and living God of the Bible? Do humans cease to be religious? Not at all. They simply redirect their religious worship to something in creation. All religion, other than biblical religion, amounts to a rejection of the Creator in favor of imaginary gods. As we study world history, we will pay attention to the various ways the fallen culture has turned away from God and developed religions in opposition to God's Word.

?

What are the five themes of civilization?

? CRITICAL THINKING 1.1

1. How does the study of history help develop our cultural identity?
2. Why can Christians make moral judgments about people's actions in world history?
3. What is the difference between a subject and a citizen?
4. What is the difference between true religion and false religion?

GUIDING QUESTIONS

- Why is it possible to study history?
- What is the work of a historian?
- How are Christian and non-Christian approaches to history different?

1.2 The Work of the Historian

Why is it possible to study history? Many people do not appreciate how a biblical view of the world makes historical investigation possible. While non-Christians can be good historians, they cannot explain why history is knowable. The biblical view of history is that history unfolds according to God's plan and has a beginning and an end. The ancient peoples (outside of Israel) viewed time as cyclical, meaning that as time passed things kept repeating. This is understandable since we observe seasonal cycles every year and see generations follow the same pattern of birth, growth, and death. They thought it useless to try to understand what was happening since they were victims of the whims of gods and nature. With this view, history is not being directed toward God's conclusion. God revealed to the Israelites that time is linear, with a beginning and an end. Isaiah 46:9-10 says, "Remember the former things of old: for I am God, and there is none else; I am God, and there is none like me, Declaring the end from the beginning, and from ancient times the things that are not yet done, saying, My counsel shall stand, and I will do all my pleasure." Even though past events could resemble previous events, the world is not trapped in some never-ending cycle. History had a definite beginning and will one day have a definite end because God created the world, and He directs the unfolding of history.

Although we are not able to see how all of history fits together, we can know that it does indeed fit together because God holds it together. This wonderful truth is necessary to make the study of history possible. It is why non-Christians can study history, because even though they do not acknowledge God's direction of history, they still think about the past as if it has rhyme and reason. The Christian can explain these things. God made it possible to know history. He created a world where there are historical artifacts. He created us as rational people who can investigate the past.

? How did God make it possible to know history?

Investigating History

How do historians accurately describe what happened in the past? A historian is like a detective. A detective may arrive at a car accident a couple of minutes after the incident; he then tries to determine what happened and who should be held responsible. The detective gets the story from the two drivers involved, but they may not know what happened, or they may be lying. He interviews witnesses and asks them what they saw. Some witnesses may contradict each other because they had different perspectives. Finally, he will look at the evidence—the skid marks, the damage to the cars, and the damage to the area. After he has collected all the information, only then can he write a detailed narrative about what occurred. This is what a historian does except that instead of arriving a couple of minutes after the event the historian arrives one hundred, one thousand, or two thousand years after the event.

When the historian seeks to write the story of an event in the past, he goes first to the accounts of the people involved and the eyewitnesses. Those accounts are called **primary sources**. The most important primary sources are firsthand accounts that are written; for modern history, that may also include recordings. Historical writings come in many forms: diaries, journals, letters, or books. Most historians consider it impossible to write a reliable history of a period without using written records. Primary sources can also include **artifacts**. Artifacts are objects made by people. They may be small relics, towering monuments, or priceless works of art. Most artifacts are simple, everyday items like pottery, tools, weapons, furniture, clothing, coins, and jewelry unearthed by archaeologists. Historians can also study **secondary sources**, which are records that explain or interpret primary sources. This history book would be a secondary source; other examples are a Wikipedia article or a biography. A historian will seldom depend on secondary sources, but sometimes they are all that is available.

After the historian has collected, evaluated, and studied all sources, he writes down the story to the best of his understanding. He writes his account just as the detective would write the account of the accident. The detective would include only the facts; he would not include any assumptions or wishes. He would also discard all unnecessary information. The historian, unlike the detective, should not simply state what happened; he must also explain why it happened and how that explanation remains significant for people today.

The Christian Approach to History

All historians approach the study of the past with certain presuppositions—beliefs about the world and how it operates. For example, when **secular** historians seek to understand historical events and the motivations of past cultures, they are guided by secular presuppositions. They may see economic interests (a desire for money), ethnic conflicts (natives vs. Europeans), class struggles (rich vs. poor), or gender conflicts (men vs. women) as reasons for people's actions. Some of their observations may have some truth to them, but overall they leave out key truths for understanding history. These key truths, as provided by a biblical worldview, are: first, that God made the world and everything in it; second, the world has fallen into a sad and broken condition because of human sin; and third, God is working to redeem this world to Himself.

secular relating to the world, not specifically religious

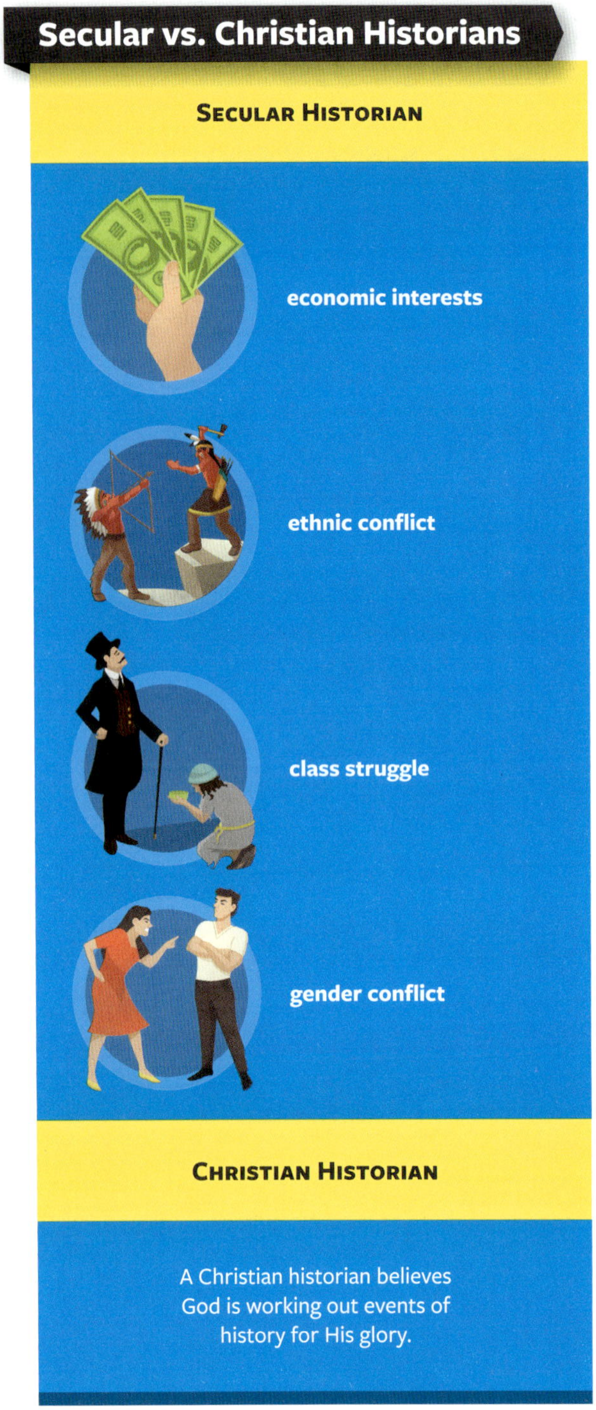

Some Christians may think that these key truths are only relevant for studying history in the Bible. But they are equally relevant for studying all of history because they help make sense of the past. When economic interests, ethnic conflict, class struggles, or gender conflicts are at play in a situation, the Christian historian will interpret these things within the context of the key biblical truths already mentioned.

Ethnic conflict, for example, is a real factor in certain historical events, but depending on their **presuppositions**, different historians will come to different conclusions about the nature of the problem and the appropriate solutions. So how might a Christian historian approach a matter like this? He or she begins with the understanding that ethnic diversity is part of God's good creation, that ethnic conflict is the result of living in a fallen world, and that ethnic harmony is possible through the gospel of Jesus Christ. We can say more about how all this works, but this example gives us a small glimpse into how biblical truths shape the thinking of the Christian historian at the level of presuppositions.

Christians study history with hope because they know how the story ends. But they need to be careful when attempting to discern God's role in history. When dealing with aspects of history where God has not revealed His providential purposes, the historian may only humbly suggest what God's intentions might have been. Events are often complex, and historians do not have access to all relevant information. Historians should avoid the temptation to declare that all calamities are God's judgments and that all victories prove that God is on the side of the victors. Believers, including historians, can rest in the knowledge that God's ultimate goal is to glorify Himself through redeeming a people.

presupposition a thing assumed beforehand at the beginning of a line of argument or course of action

CRITICAL THINKING 1.2

1. How do primary and secondary sources differ?
2. List several of the tasks of a historian.
3. Summarize the three truths a Christian historian uses to interpret history.
4. Where would we find what God's providential purposes are?

1.3 Ancient Civilizations

This book covers world history beginning about the thirteenth century AD. (The thirteenth century is the 1200s.) In this way, it picks up where the book *Heritage Studies 6: Ancient Civilizations* left off. The following pages review those ancient civilizations before continuing on with the study of world history.

GUIDING QUESTIONS

- What were the ancient civilizations?
- How is Jesus the central figure in world history?

EGYPT

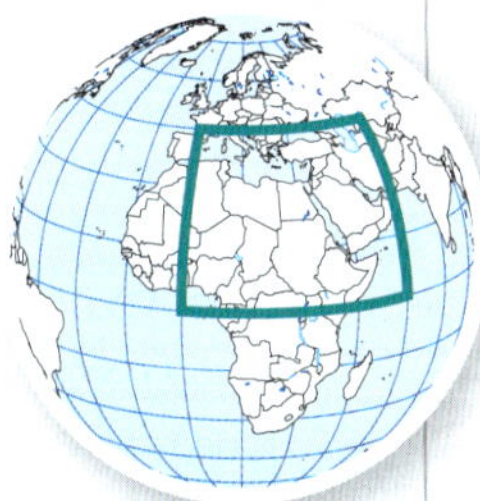

Egyptian civilization developed along the Nile River since the river created fertile land to grow crops. The desert geography protected Egypt from invasion.

RELIGION IN EGYPT

The Egyptians were polytheistic. Two of their more important gods were Ra, the sun god and creator, and Osiris, the god of the underworld and the judge in the afterlife.

Culture

Egypt's class structure was like a pyramid—farmers, merchants, servants, and slaves were on the bottom; on the next level were the priests, soldiers, scribes, and artisans; next were the highest-ranking officials; on the pinnacle was the pharaoh.

Egyptian Kingdoms

3000 BC

2700–2200 BC

Old Kingdom
The pharaohs had great power. The people believed the pharaohs were gods. The pyramids were built during this time.

2000 BC

2040–1650 BC

Middle Kingdom
This was a time of peace and stability. Pharaohs showed greater concern for the people.

1570–1075 BC

New Kingdom
The Hyksos ("foreign rulers") ruled during this time. The Hyksos taught the Egyptians how to make weapons of bronze and iron as well as horse-drawn chariots.

1000 BC

BABYLON

Babylon was in the Fertile Crescent between the Tigris and Euphrates Rivers in the area now known as Iraq.

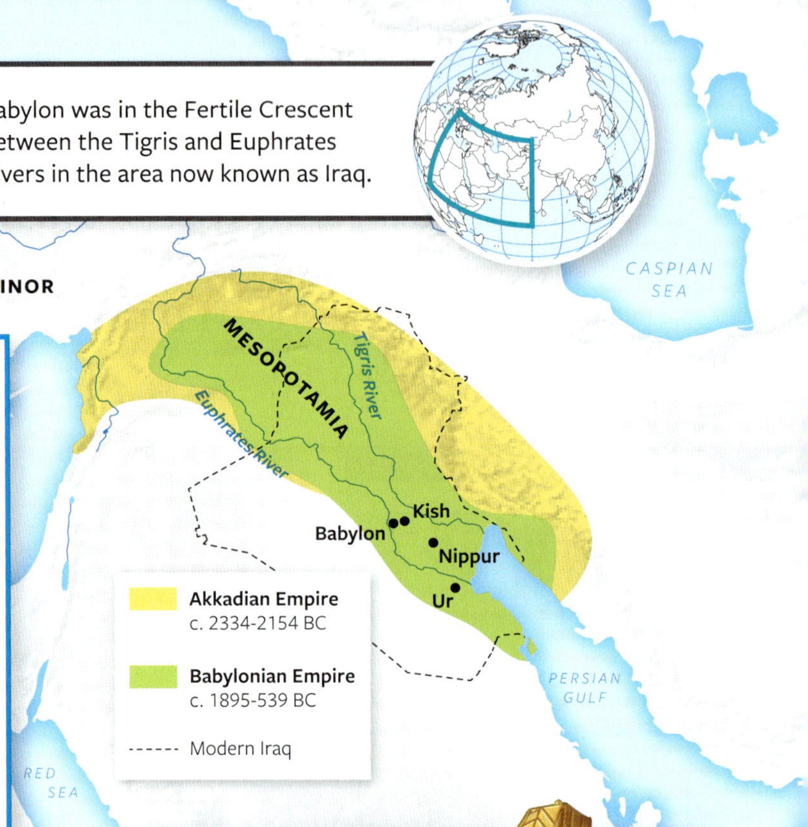

The Chaldeans

Shortly before 1000 BC, the Chaldeans began to settle around **Babylon**. They were constantly overrun by the Assyrian kings. In 612 BC the Chaldeans joined with the Medes and helped destroy Nineveh, the capital of the Assyrian Empire. Babylon became the capital city of the Chaldean Empire. During the reign of Nebuchadnezzar, the empire reached its height.

Nebuchadnezzar is remembered not only for his military accomplishments but also for building up Babylon. The city was surrounded by a brick wall so wide that two chariots could pass on the road on top of it. The Hanging Gardens of Babylon were one of the wonders of the ancient world. Despite the glories of the Chaldean Empire, it did not last even one hundred years. Nebuchadnezzar viewed his accomplishments with a heart of pride, so God's judgment fell upon him. The king lost his throne, and he became like a beast of the field. When Nebuchadnezzar recognized the foolishness of his pride and God's greatness, God restored him as king (Daniel 4:33–37).

The Hanging Gardens of Babylon were one of the original Seven Wonders of the Ancient World.

Neo-Babylon
605–539 BC

Medo-Persia
539–331 BC

Greece
331–168 BC

Rome
168 BC– AD 476

Divided Kingdom?
AD 476 – present?

Nebuchadnezzar's Dream

God revealed to Daniel the meaning of Nebuchadnezzar's dream of a statue, which outlined the future ruling kingdoms of the world.

PERSIA

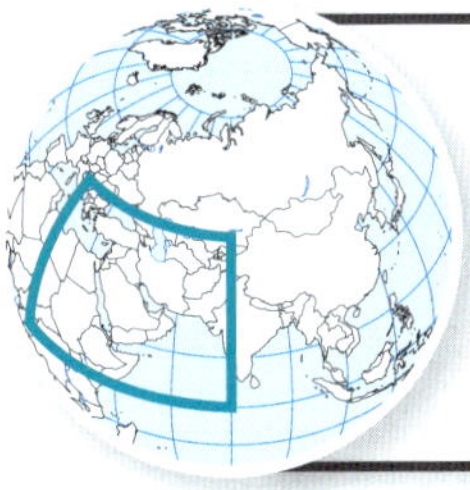

Persia was in a mountainous region of the Middle East, between the Persian Gulf and the Caspian Sea; it is called Iran today.

Persian Emperors & Wars

590 BC

547–530 BC

Cyrus II

Cyrus conquered the Chaldeans in 539 BC. Cyrus II was a wise ruler who treated his defeated enemies well. God used him to free the Israelites from Babylon and restore them to the land of Israel to rebuild their temple.

522–486 BC

Darius I

During Darius's reign, the Persian Empire reached its height. The lands Persia conquered were divided into provinces called satrapies. Darius built and maintained a good road system that people used for transporting a variety of goods. Darius had a strong, well-organized, and loyal military to keep his empire under control. Darius respected the God of the Israelites and played an important role in the rebuilding of the Jewish temple. Beginning in Darius's reign, Persia fought three major wars with Greece.

499 BC

Battle of Marathon

The Persians lost the battle and suffered heavy casualties.

486–465 BC

Xerxes

Xerxes became king following his father Darius's death. Persia remained a powerful empire for more than a century even after being defeated by Greece. Esther became queen during this time.

480 BC

Battle of Thermopylae

A Greek traitor showed the Persians a path through the mountains that they could use to surround the Greek army. The Greeks fought to the end but lost.

The Battle of Salamis

Themistocles, an Athenian general, planned to defeat the Persians on the sea by taking advantage of Greek ships' speed and maneuverability against the larger Persian ships. If he could trap the Persian ships in a tight space, the Greeks could win. They lured the Persians into the strait, and once the Persian fleet entered it the Greeks launched their ships, ramming and sinking many of the Persian ships and winning the battle.

465–424 BC

Artaxerxes

Xerxes was assassinated, and after a power struggle his son Artaxerxes became king. Artaxerxes I continued the building projects of his ancestors. He also showed kindness to the Israelites. It was during his reign that Ezra and Nehemiah returned to Jerusalem.

334–323 BC

Alexander the Great

In 334 BC Alexander the Great of Greece invaded and defeated the Persian Empire. Alexander ruled all the lands that had once made up the Persian Empire, continuing the Persian form of centralized government. He blended Greek and Persian culture. Alexander's reign over Persia was short. He died in his early thirties.

323 BC

Later Persian Dynasties

400 BC

334–63 BC

The Seleucids

The lands Alexander conquered were divided and given to four different generals. Persia came under the control of a family called the Seleucids. Greek culture continued to spread throughout Asia, including Persia.

247 BC–AD 224

The Parthians

The Parthians were Persians who regained control of their empire from the Greeks. Their art reveals a lasting Greek influence. The Parthians controlled part of the Silk Road and collected a toll from those traveling on it. The Parthians lacked a strong central government and were further weakened by war with the Romans.

A Parthian king's head carved out of limestone

AD 1

AD 224–651

The Sassanids

The Sassanid kings wanted to bring back all that was truly Persian and rid the culture of Greek influences. Some of the Sassanid kings built new cities, buildings, and canals. But the Sassanids also fought with the Romans and later with the Byzantines. The last Sassanid king was conquered by Arab invaders, who introduced Islam to Persia.

AD 400

A Sassanid silver horse head

RELIGION IN PERSIA

Zoroastrianism

Zoroaster lived during the sixth century BC. Through Zoroastrianism he tried to explain the existence of good and evil. He taught that a good god, Ahura Mazda, struggled with an equally powerful evil being, Ahriman. Ahura Mazda was believed to be the creator and the only god. Monotheism made Zoroaster's religion different from most of the other religions in the ancient world. Zoroaster taught that each person must choose between good and evil.

GREECE

Greece is a mountainous peninsula with valleys and natural harbors. It also includes thousands of tiny islands.

Greek Civilizations

2000 BC

ca. 2000–1400 BC

Minoans (Isle of Crete)
They built a beautiful palace in the city of Knossos and gained their wealth by trading with peoples of other lands.

Ancient ruins of Knossos palace on the island of Crete in Greece

ca. 1250 BC

Mycenaeans
They started the Trojan War, which according to the legend lasted ten years.

Depiction of the Trojan horse

500–146 BC

Athens and Sparta
Athens and Sparta were ruled by oligarchies. Athens became a democracy in 500 BC. Athenians were interested in the arts and sciences and government. Sparta kept its oligarchy. Spartan boys were raised to be soldiers.

AD 1

Religion in Greece

They believed in many gods; they made fanciful stories about the gods called **myths**.

Cultural Achievements

In philosophy, Socrates taught by asking questions. Plato taught that the ideal government was ruled by a few intelligent men and that there was a spiritual world superior to the physical world. Aristotle introduced the scientific method to solving questions. Greeks made contributions in mathematics (the invention of geometry), medicine (the work of Hippocrates), art, architecture, and sports.

ROME

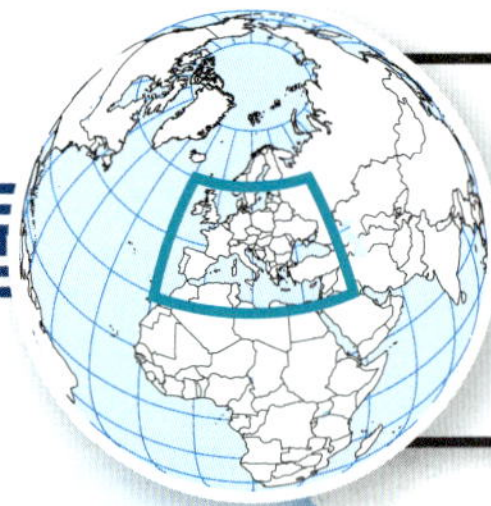

Italy is a mountainous, boot-shaped peninsula that extends into the Mediterranean Sea in southern Europe. Italy includes the islands of Sardinia, Sicily, and several other smaller islands.

Roman Eras

753 BC

753–509 BC

Early Rome

According to legend, Rome was founded in 753 BC by twin brothers Romulus and Remus near the Tiber River. Romulus built the city and named it Rome. The Latins had been living in Rome for over one hundred years when the Etruscans, an advanced civilization with Hellenistic culture from the north, conquered Rome. There were two classes of people; the patricians made up the ruling class, and the plebeians made up the working class.

509–31 BC

Roman Republic

The Latins drove the Etruscans from the city and established a republic, a government ruled by laws and representatives chosen by the people. The republic was divided into three governing branches—the consuls, the Senate, and the Assembly. Gradually, the plebeians gained more rights until they had equal say in the government. The republic worked very well for several hundred years. But eventually a long civil war followed which a general named Sulla won. Sulla declared himself the dictator and reorganized the Roman government. After restoring stability to the Senate, he stepped down as dictator.

100 BC

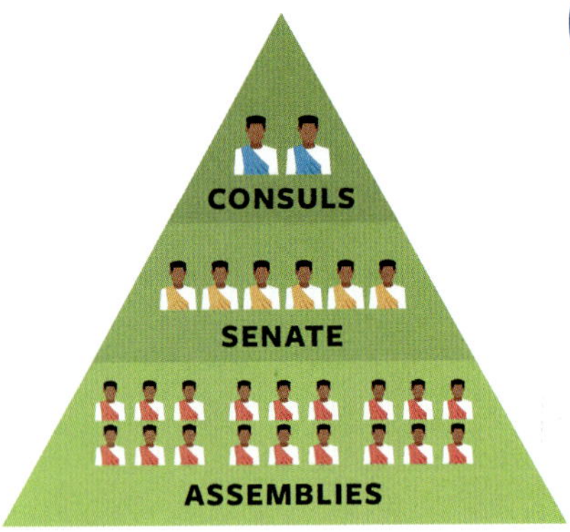

31 BC–AD 476

Roman Empire

Julius Caesar was popular with the common people; his popularity threatened the government leaders. Caesar marched to Rome and plunged it into a second civil war. After his victory, Caesar was proclaimed the dictator of Rome. Caesar made many reforms that helped to unify Rome and strengthen its bonds with its conquered peoples. Many Romans wanted the Senate to return to power. On March 15, 44 BC, the Ides of March, two of Caesar's friends led the group that assassinated Caesar in the Senate. But the republic would never return. Two men, Octavian and Mark Antony, took Caesar's place, each ruling half of the empire. They were too ambitious to share power. Antony and Octavian clashed in a naval battle off the coast of Greece. Octavian was victorious and became the sole ruler. He used the title princeps, meaning "first citizen." He was also commonly called *Augustus*, which meant "revered one." The reign of Augustus began a period of peace and prosperity that Rome enjoyed for the next two hundred years, called **Pax Romana.** During the Pax Romana, the culture of Rome was like Greek culture. Rome's greatest artistic achievements were in architecture. It was the first empire to use concrete. Roman emperors staged events to win public favor and to keep the unemployed entertained. Spectators enjoyed watching chariot races, gladiator contests, and wild animal fights. The emperor Diocletian divided the empire in half, keeping the eastern part under his control. During his reign, the persecution of Christians was widespread. When emperor Constantine took power, he unified the empire. In 313 Constantine issued a decree to legalize Christianity. A barbarian invasion along with the decline of Rome's government, economy, and society caused the collapse of the Western Roman Empire. The Eastern Roman Empire endured for another thousand years as the Byzantine Empire.

AD 476

A Roman aqueduct | ▶

ROMAN RELIGION

Epicureanism & Stoicism

The Romans adopted gods from many of the peoples they conquered. They had a polytheistic religion and honored their gods by building them temples and naming the planets after them. Two Greek philosophies were also practiced as religions in Rome—Epicureanism and Stoicism. The followers of Epicureanism believed that everything—including gods, man, and the earth—was only matter. Epicureans lived for pleasure alone. The Stoics believed that doing one's duty led to happiness. They emphasized virtues such as courage, justice, and obedience. Stoicism was popular among the Roman soldiers.

Roman Wars

300 BC

264–241 BC

First Punic War

Both Rome and the North African city of Carthage fought for control of the Mediterranean Sea. The Romans needed to defeat the powerful Carthaginian navy. The Romans designed a ship that dropped a plank that they could attach to an enemy ship, allowing Roman soldiers to board and capture the enemy. With these ships, Rome was victorious over the Carthaginian navy.

218–201 BC

Second Punic War

A brilliant Carthaginian general named Hannibal decided that to defeat Rome, he would first invade regions of the peninsula outside Rome and win support against the Romans. To avoid being seen by the Romans, he gathered his army in Spain and planned to march across the rugged, snow-covered Alps. Hannibal started with about forty thousand men and a herd of war elephants. Many of the soldiers and most of the elephants died in the Alps. By the time Hannibal's army reached the Italian Peninsula, it was much smaller than the Roman army. However, Hannibal's skill at planning made up for the size of his army. He won many battles, but he could not completely win the war. The turning point of the war came when Rome sent an army to attack Carthage. Hannibal immediately rushed home to protect his city. The Romans were victorious at the Battle of Zama.

149–146 BC

Third Punic War

Carthage decided to fight one of Rome's allies. This action angered the Romans. So Rome declared war on Carthage. After a three-year siege, Rome captured and destroyed Carthage. Rome went on to control the whole Mediterranean world.

100 BC

INDIA

India is a large peninsula in southern Asia. The Himalayas stretch across northeastern India, forming a natural barrier that separates India from the rest of Asia. For this reason, India is often called a subcontinent.

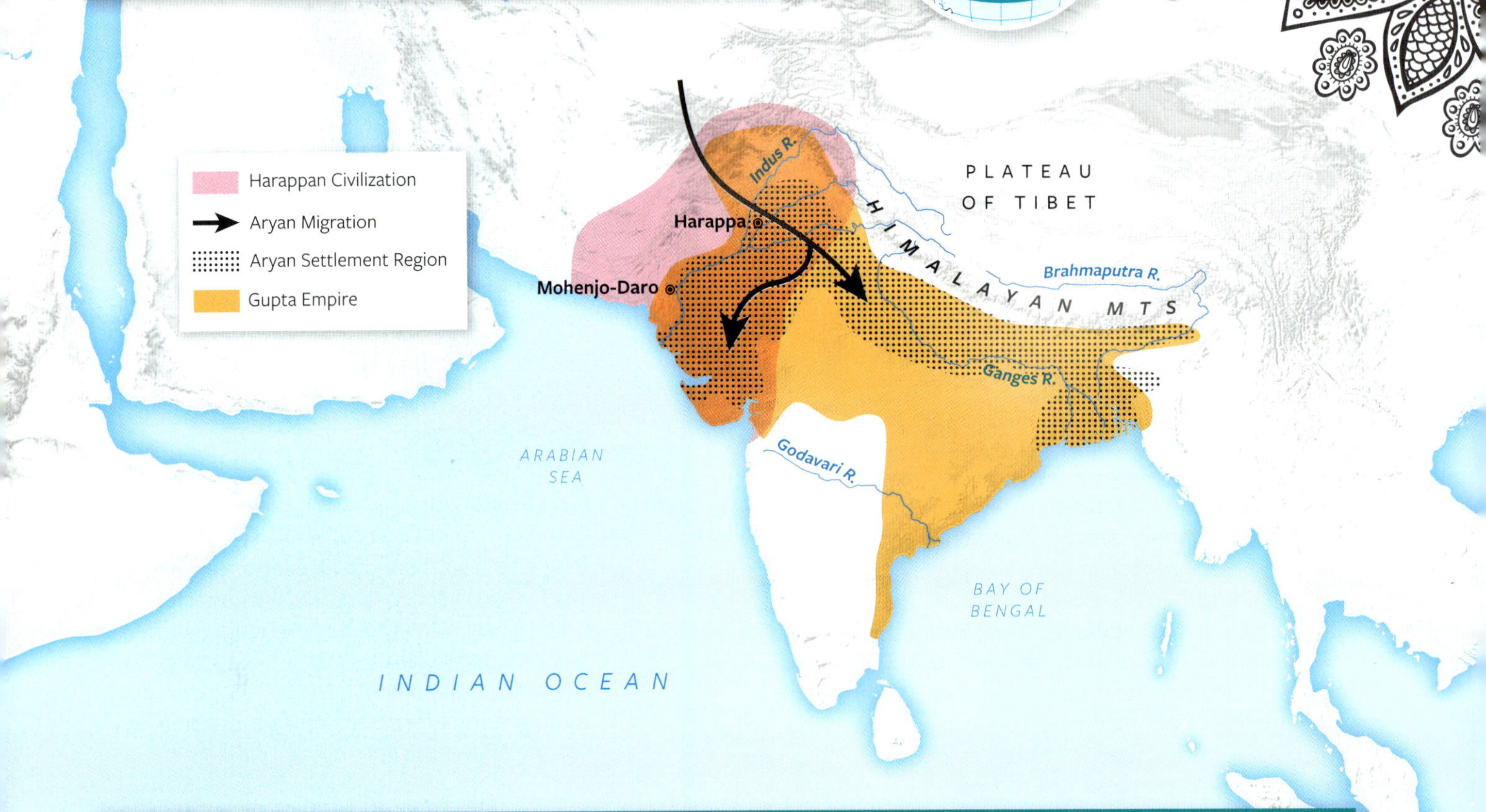

RELIGIONS IN INDIA

Hinduism and Buddhism

Hinduism is polytheistic. Hindus worship thousands of gods, but they consider three gods to be the most important: Brahma, the Creator; Shiva, the Destroyer; and Vishnu, the Preserver. Hindus believe that these three gods, as well as thousands of other gods, are different forms of the great god Brahman. He is not a personal being, so he is often called the great soul. The ancient Hindus left behind books called the Vedas. Veda means "knowledge." A later book, the Upanishads, describes the Hindu teachings in more detail. Hindus believe that everything in the world, including plants, animals, and gods, is part of Brahman. This belief is pantheism, the idea that everything in the universe is part of a supreme being.

Another part of Hinduism is reincarnation, the belief that a person lives more than once in different bodies—even in animals. A person's state in reincarnation depends on his karma, one's good or bad deeds. Hindus believe that the higher a person is in the caste system, the closer he is to reuniting with Brahman.

Siddhartha Gautama became dissatisfied with Hindu beliefs. He disliked the caste system and the priests who ruled the people. He changed his name to Buddha, meaning "Enlightened One." He introduced the Four Noble Truths. In these writings he proposed that suffering can be overcome if a person does good works and ignores his desires. The Eightfold Path was Buddha's list of good works. According to Buddhism, doing the things on the list is supposed to help a person achieve happiness and peace. Like Hindus, Buddha believed in reincarnation. He believed that people would have another chance to reach nirvana if they did not achieve it in the present life.

Indian Civilizations

2500 BC

2500 BC–1700 BC

The Harappans

The Harappans flourished in the fertile Indus Valley, which was good for farming and raising animals. Two of their cities have been discovered, Harappa and Mohenjo-Daro. They developed technology that allowed them to have running water and indoor plumbing.

Sheep herd grazing in Kashmir, India

ca. 1800 BC–1500 BC

The Aryans

Nomads from the north called Arya, meaning "noble," invaded and probably ended the Harappan civilization. The Aryan way of life became the characteristic culture of ancient and modern India. Much more is known about the Aryans than the Harappans because they had a written language called Sanskrit. Craftsmen produced artwork and sculptures that reflected their religious beliefs. The farmer depended upon the annual rains for success. The Aryans encouraged large families. Extended families lived together in compounds made up of several huts or houses. The oldest man in the family had complete authority over the other members. Another important social group was the caste. Castes were the classes of Indian society. Every person was born into a caste, which he would stay in for the rest of his life. The highest was the priestly caste. The next caste was made up of warriors and rulers. The caste below that was made up of farmers, traders, and artisans. Laborers and servants belonged to the lowest caste. Some Indians, called untouchables or outcastes, were outside the caste system.

1000 BC

Sanchi Stupa temple in India

322 BC–184 BC

The Mauryans

In 326 BC the army of the Greek leader Alexander the Great conquered portions of northwestern India. Alexander met Chandragupta Maurya, who modeled himself after Alexander. Chandragupta conquered most of the Ganges River Valley and became the first ruler in the Mauryan dynasty. Chandragupta established a centralized government and maintained a strong army. Asoka, a grandson of Chandragupta, came to the throne in 273 BC and was one of the greatest rulers of the Mauryan Empire. He united most of the Indian subcontinent. However, after years of great military successes, Asoka began to hate warfare; he lost his desire to conquer. Instead, he devoted himself to Buddhism and its teachings. He built thousands of dome-shaped shrines called stupas. Since Buddhism emphasizes doing good works and relieving suffering, Asoka also made many improvements to give his people better lives. Asoka had a major part in spreading Buddhism to other countries. After he died in 233 BC, his sons struggled for power, and invaders were able to overcome the last Mauryan king in 184 BC.

AD 319–467

Gupta

Nearly six hundred years after the Mauryan Empire, the Gupta Empire was established. This empire began a period called the Golden Age of India.

AD 500

CHINA

China was isolated from the world by great mountains, deserts, and the ocean. The Huang He (Yellow) and Yangtze Rivers provided fertile soil, food, fresh water, and transportation for the Chinese.

RELIGIONS IN CHINA

Confucianism and Taoism

Confucius taught that through proper behavior man could solve society's problems. Confucius expressed this belief in the proverb "What you do not want done to yourself, do not do to others." Lao Tzu was another influential teacher in China. His teaching, called Taoism, was second in importance to the teachings of Confucius. Tao meant "the way" and was the guiding force in nature. Lao Tzu encouraged men to find peace and happiness by living in harmony with nature. Confucianism guided the thinking of China's educational, social, and political systems. Taoism became the basis of magical and superstitious elements in Chinese culture.

Chinese Dynasties

1500 BC

1500 BC–1000 BC

Shang
Most of the common people were farmers. The people practiced ancestor worship and used oracle bones to predict the future. The ancient Chinese were skilled artists, particularly in bronze metalworking.

Bronze work from the Shang Dynasty

1000 BC–221 BC

Zhou
Zhou was the longest ruling dynasty. This was called China's classical age. Much of China's culture was established during this time. The Zhou believed that heaven, the supreme force of nature, gave the king his right to rule. This belief was called the **Mandate of Heaven**.

500 BC

221 BC–202 BC

Qin
The Qin dynasty was founded by Qin Shi Huang Ti, the "First Emperor." Under his rule, China became more unified. Qin set up a bureaucracy to run the government. Qin brought order and protection to China through harsh and ruthless measures. He unified China by demanding one writing system and building roads and canals. To help protect the country, the Chinese built the Great Wall in the north. Even though it was short, the Qin dynasty left a lasting monument—the name China comes from the name Qin.

202 BC–AD 220

Han
The Han dynasty was so popular that to this day some Chinese call themselves the "sons of Han." Confucianism became the government's official philosophy. The Han rulers developed a civil service system that included exams to determine a person's abilities. The Han made achievements in medicine, manufacturing, science, and literature. They developed trade routes with other regions. The main trade route was called the Silk Road, since silk was the most famous item traded. Confucianism divided people into four social classes that were more rigid. The Han believed in strong families. After the last Han rulers were overthrown, China suffered four hundred years of internal wars and invasions.

AD 500

The Great Wall of China

JAPAN

Japan is an archipelago, a group of islands. The four main islands of Japan are Hokkaido, Honshu, Shikoku, and Kyushu. The islands are mountainous. For centuries Japan was isolated from the rest of the world by the Sea of Japan and the North Pacific Ocean.

RELIGION IN JAPAN

Shintoism

Shintoism is a form of nature worship. It teaches that every object or creature in nature has a spirit that should be worshiped as a god. These gods, or nature spirits, are called kami. The most important kami is the sun goddess, Amaterasu. Shintoists also worship the emperor, whom they consider a god. The Japanese practice a mixture of Shintoism and Buddhism.

JAPANESE ERAS

AD 100

AD 250–710

Yamato Period

Japan was made up of different clans. The Yamato clan rose to power and formed strong military states. They developed organized cities, a government, social classes, and a written language. The Yamato clan was influenced by the Chinese. They chose an emperor who they claimed was a descendant of Jimmu Tenno, the mythical ancestor of Japanese emperors. They developed a constitution. In 645, during the Taika Reform or "Great Change," the leaders of Japan centralized the government. The clan chieftains lost their power to government officials who gathered the taxes for the emperor.

710–1185

Heian Period

The Heian period was named after the capital city at the time and was a time of peace and security. A group of nobles, known as the imperial court, served or advised the emperor. The court was the center of culture and learning and had strict rules of behavior. This was the golden age of the arts in Japan. To be accepted in Heian society, a person had to write poetry; haiku was one type. One characteristic of Japanese art was its use of brilliant colors. The nobles of Heian-Kyo worked to make their city beautiful; they surrounded buildings with elegant gardens and ponds. One family, the Fujiwara, gained power by marrying their daughters to emperors. A Fujiwara court official then ruled as regent for the infant emperor. The Fujiwara family controlled the Japanese government during much of the Heian period. By 1156 there was a civil war that resulted in the military ruling Japan. The emperor became ceremonial.

1000

1185–1868

Feudal Period

Feudalism is a system for organizing and governing society based on land and service. The ruler divided the land among the nobles, who then subdivided it among the peasants in exchange for loyalty and allegiance. The military leader, called the shogun, was chosen by the emperor and given supreme political power. In 1192 Yoritomo was appointed as the first shogun. This military government was known as a shogunate. Shoguns continued to rule for the next seven hundred years while the emperor had only ceremonial power. The samurai were warriors who served the shogun.

1900

MESOAMERICA

Mesoamerica extends from near the middle of Mexico to the central part of Central America. It includes the Yucatán Peninsula, the landmass extending into the Gulf of Mexico in present-day southern Mexico.

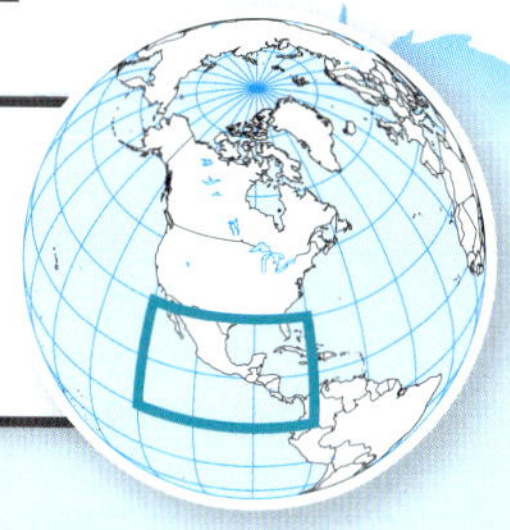

MESOAMERICAN CIVILIZATIONS

2000 BC

Olmec stone head statue

Mayan temple in Guatemala

1200 BC–400 BC

Olmecs

The Olmec civilization existed from 1200 BC to 400 BC and is considered one of the earliest Mesoamerican civilizations. It included large cities like Tenochtitlán and La Venta. These cities had avenues, water and drainage systems, and houses made of wood and clay. The name Olmecs means "rubber people" since they are believed to have been some of the first to use rubber. They were hunters, fishermen, and farmers. The most famous Olmec remains are gigantic stone heads carved from jade and basalt. Many of the Olmec beliefs and customs were passed on to other Mesoamerican civilizations. The calendar used for centuries in Mexico may have originated with the Olmecs.

1600 BC–AD 900

Mayas

For about twenty-five hundred years, the Mayas built farms and homes in the rainforests and high plateaus. As the Mayas prospered, their population increased, and their villages grew larger. By AD 250, Mayas dominated the region and built city-states. One of the largest and most magnificent city-states was Tikal, with an estimated sixty thousand people.

The Mayas made advances in art, architecture, and literature. They wrote hundreds of books, constructed huge palaces, and erected pyramid-shaped temples. They built irrigation systems, studied the stars, composed music, and played games. The Mayan calendar was based on the cycles of the moon and the sun. Their solar year had the same number of days as ours.

Mayan society had several levels of social classes. At the top was the king; the Mayas believed their king was descended from the gods and was to be obeyed without question. The priests and the nobles were second in importance. The priests practiced medicine and offered sacrifices. The nobles, both men and women, worked in the government. The nobles did not do manual work like farming, which was left to the common people. The lowest class was the slaves. Possibly a combination of famine, war, and internal rebellion ended Mayan society. Forms of the Mayan civilization continued in smaller towns.

AD 1000

RELIGION IN MESOAMERICA

Mesoamericans believed in many gods. They believed that the sun god was superior. They believed a blood sacrifice was necessary to please their gods, and so they sacrificed humans.

AFRICA

Africa is a large continent. It has large lakes, mountain ranges, mighty rivers, vast deserts, and lush rainforests. The Sahara is the single most important geographic factor in Africa. It divides the continent into two regions, North Africa and sub-Saharan Africa, all the land below the Sahara. Between the two regions is a belt called the Sahel that is two hundred miles wide and crosses the entire continent.

RELIGION IN AFRICA

Animism

Until Christianity and Islam were introduced to Africa, the people had beliefs that varied slightly from tribe to tribe. Most Africans had a concept of a god as a supreme being. They believed he could be reached through sacrifices and offerings. The belief in spirits who control natural forces for good or for evil was very common. Africans worshiped spirits that they believed lived in animals or things like trees and rivers and tried to make the spirits happy. They did not want the spirits to use their powers to harm them.

African Empires

330–600s

Aksum

Farmers settled eastern Africa and eventually built the empire of Aksum, a wealthy and powerful kingdom. It supplied precious stones, incense, gold, ivory, ebony, myrrh, and elephants to the Egyptian pharaohs and also traded with Arabs and Europeans. King Ezana ruled the empire of Aksum in the AD 300s. A Syrian Christian named Frumentius became a servant to King Ezana; probably through his influence Ezana became a Christian. Christianity became the official religion. Muslim armies conquered Egypt and cut Aksum off from its trade with the Mediterranean world. The kingdom disappeared, but the civilization continued as Ethiopia.

500

A gold nugget

700–1200

Ghana

The ancient empire of Ghana was located along the Niger River. The word *ghana* was the title the rulers used for themselves. Many Arabian merchants traveled back and forth to Ghana. Gold was traded for goods from merchants from all over the world. The main item traded for was salt. Along with gold, the Ghanaians traded cola nuts, honey, textiles, and slaves. The king of Ghana charged taxes on all trade. Ghana had a huge army that helped protect its trade. Eventually, wars with the Arabs began to interrupt trade and weaken Ghana's kings. When Mali attacked, Ghana could not fight back.

1000

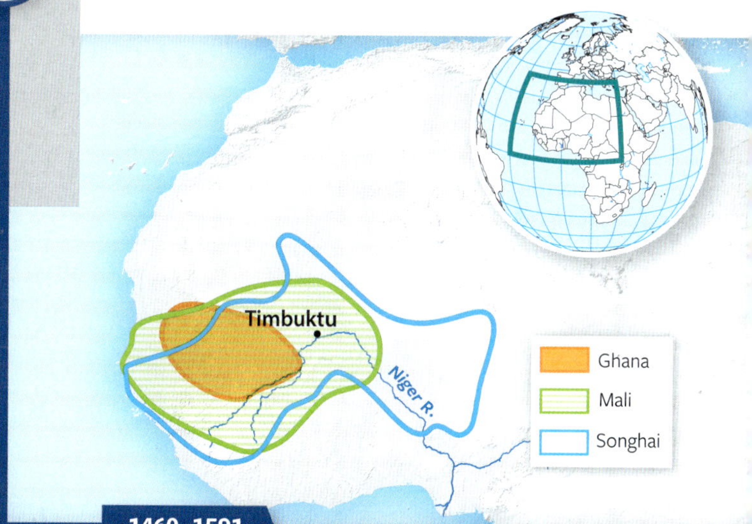

1235–1600s

Mali

The empire of Mali included all of Ghana and much more land as well. Mali had a strong ruler named Sundiata. Sundiata gained control of the gold and salt trade route across the Sahara. Sundiata and his successors were called by the title Mansa. The kings of Mali grew wealthy from the gold trade. Most of them adopted the religion of Islam. The Malians were characterized as loving justice and honesty. King Mansa Musa was famous for his immense wealth and his devotion to Islam. During his pilgrimage to Mecca, he gave away so much gold that the price of gold went down in that region for the next several years. He used his wealth to build many mosques, schools, and even a university in the city of Timbuktu. After Mansa Musa's death, there were no more strong kings in Mali. After four hundred years, Mali was once again a small village on the banks of the Niger River.

1460–1591

1500

Songhai

A ruler named Sunni Ali won independence for Songhai from Mali and established the empire. Sunni Ali was never defeated. The city of Timbuktu became Songhai's center of Islamic faith and learning. Songhai became larger than either Ghana or Mali had been. Songhai continued for more than a hundred years. But when Morocco attacked with better-trained soldiers armed with muskets, the Songhai army was defeated. Other enemies attacked Songhai, and soon the empire disappeared. In its place appeared many smaller kingdoms that frequently fought each other over land and trade.

TURNING POINTS

Resurrection of Christ

Throughout this book, we will feature various world events that were turning points. These events dramatically changed the course of world history. No event is more important than the resurrection of Christ Jesus. Time itself is divided by the date of His coming. Christianity is one of the few faiths that is dependent on its historical claims. Because religions like Hinduism or animism do not make specific historical claims, they cannot be disproven historically. But if the resurrection did not happen, being a Christian would be futile. The apostle Paul makes this point in Scripture: "And if Christ be not risen, then is our preaching vain, and your faith is also vain" (I Cor. 15:14). Because of its implications, many historians have tried to disprove the resurrection only to become believers. Scripture goes to great lengths to satisfy any honest skeptic and show that Jesus really did rise from the dead.

- Jesus was clearly dead. Luke, a physician, described the death in detail so no one could claim Jesus just passed out.
- Many historians claim the resurrection story grew over time from rumor to legend. But early accounts of the resurrection were solidified in creeds only a few months after the event.
- Jesus appeared to over five hundred people on eleven different occasions. This is important because for an event to be found true there must be witnesses.
- The character of the disciples was transformed following the resurrection. The disciples were in shock after the crucifixion. They were hiding out, not knowing what to do. Yet just a little while later they were forcefully proclaiming the gospel. Most died as martyrs, and none changed their story though they could have easily saved their lives by recanting.
- The Gospels recount how some of the disciples were initially very skeptical but were convinced of the truth. Thomas had honest doubts that were erased when he met Jesus. James, Jesus' half-brother, thought Jesus was mad and not the Messiah. Yet after Jesus died and rose again, James became the head of the Jerusalem church and died by the sword for his faith.
- The dramatic growth of the church in such a short time can only be explained by the truth of the resurrection.
- The conversion of Saul from the greatest persecutor of Christians to the most important apologist can only be explained by his encounter with the risen Christ.
- There were 351 Old Testament prophecies about the Messiah, and Jesus fulfilled them all.

1. Why is Jesus' resurrection so important to Christianity?
2. Why does the testimony of Thomas, James, and Saul hold greater weight?
3. What would the world be like if Jesus had not been raised from the dead?

CRITICAL THINKING 1.3

1. What civilization did Rome fight in the Punic Wars?
2. What one person was involved in the Greek, Persian, and Indian civilizations?
3. What did Confucius believe was the solution to society's problems?
4. What civilization had a very accurate calendar?
5. What is one thing all these empires have in common?

Making Connections

1. What are the five major themes of civilizations?
2. Would a biography of Abraham Lincoln be a primary or secondary source?
3. What are resources like relics, monuments, and works of art called?
4. Because Christians know the end of the story, when they study history they should have ___.
5. What type of religion did the Egyptians have?
6. How did God reveal to Daniel the future ruling kingdoms of the world?
7. What were the different eras of Rome, and what type of government did each have?
8. Which Chinese dynasty built the Great Wall?
9. What were two early civilizations in Mesoamerica?
10. What was the one empire in East Africa, and what was its official religion?

Thinking Critically

1. What are two reasons for studying history that you can give to your friend who says there is no reason to study history?
2. What are the main presuppositions Christians have when studying history?
3. What social structure do all the ancient civilizations have in common?
4. Compare and contrast Chinese and Japanese civilization.

What to Know

PEOPLE

Nebuchadnezzar
Alexander the Great
Julius Caesar
Qin Shi Huang Ti
Jimmu Tenno
Mansa Musa

PLACES

Egypt
Babylon
Persia
Greece
Rome
India
China
Japan
Mesoamerica
Africa

TERMS

history
justice
power
citizenship
environment
religion
primary sources
secondary sources
artifacts
myths
Pax Romana
Mandate of Heaven

2 EMERGENCE OF EUROPE

400 – 1450

ESSENTIAL QUESTIONS

- What were the characteristics of feudalism in Europe in the Middle Ages?
- How did nation-states develop in Europe?
- Why did power shift between groups in the Middle Ages?
- What was culture like in the Middle Ages?
- How did calamities of the late Middle Ages shape modern Europe?

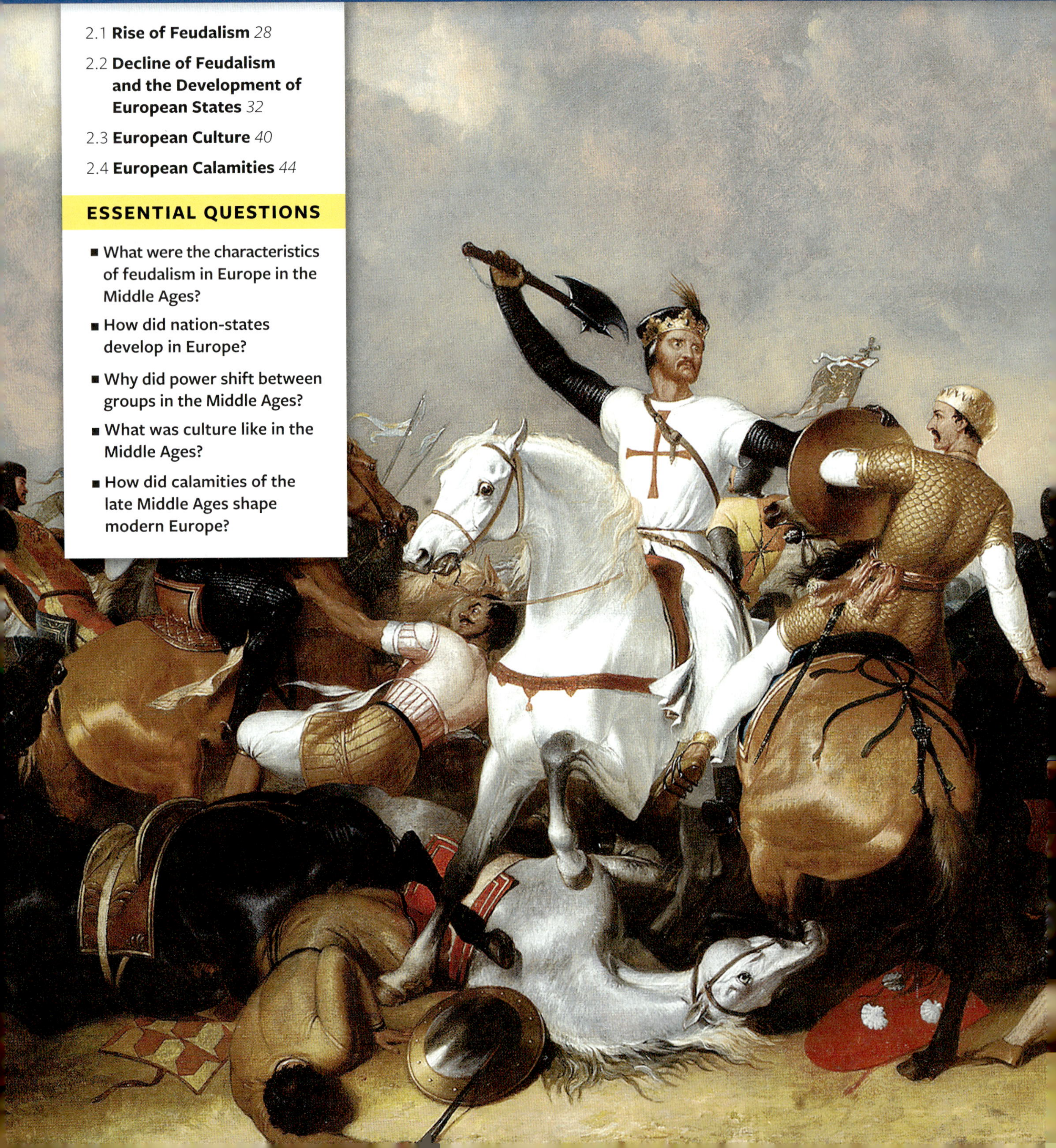

Richard the Lionheart

▲ Crusaders wore a cross as a symbol of the vow they took to defend Christianity and the Holy Land.

Richard I of England seems at first glance to have been the perfect example of a medieval warrior and king. His outstanding military ability earned him the admiration and respect of contemporaries as well as future generations. Looking deeper below the surface, though, we see that Richard's story shows a world that was not always noble.

Richard was born on September 8, 1157, the third son of Henry II, king of England and great lord in France. Richard's family showed little respect for each other. Encouraged by their mother, Richard and two of his brothers revolted against their father in 1173–74. Later more conflict arose among the three brothers and (after the other two died) between Richard and his father again. Despite the conflict, though, Richard inherited his father's throne and some of his father's French territory when his father died in 1189.

Richard spent much of his time trying to hold on to his land in France, so he was only in England a few months out of the ten years he was king. Still his subjects appreciated his impressive military accomplishments. He was only sixteen years old when he led his first army. His skill and fierce determination on the battlefield earned him the name "Lionheart."

Like many other medieval warriors, Richard joined a crusade (a religious war between the Christians and the Muslim Turks). Together with the king of France and the emperor of the Holy Roman Empire (modern-day Germany), who drowned along the way, Richard planned to take Jerusalem back from the Muslim commander Saladin so Christian pilgrims could visit it again. Crusading was expensive, and Richard sold and taxed as much as he could in England to pay for the trip.

Richard won important victories outside the cities of Acre and Joppa in the Holy Land. At Acre he was sick but participated in the battle from a stretcher. Richard failed to take Jerusalem but signed an agreement allowing temporary access for Christian pilgrims.

Richard was in constant conflict with the other leaders of the crusade. On the way home he was captured and turned over to the new Holy Roman Emperor. England was asked for a huge sum of money, 150,000 silver marks, to ransom its king. Richard's mother worked to secure his release, and, despite an offer of 80,000 marks from the king of France to keep Richard in captivity, the Holy Roman Emperor released him.

Richard returned home to face more plots from his younger brother John and the king of France. Though he put these plots down, Richard continued to participate in warfare all his life. He died in 1199 of complications from a battle wound.

GUIDING QUESTIONS

- How did Germanic kingdoms develop in Europe?
- Why did the Roman Catholic Church become powerful in the early Middle Ages?
- How did Charlemagne influence the political and intellectual development of Europe?
- What events contributed to the rise of feudalism?
- In what ways did lords control the lives of peasants?

2.1 Rise of Feudalism

Germanic Kingdoms

During the fifth century, Germanic tribes (tribes located north of the Rhine and Danube Rivers) began to migrate onto land governed by the Roman Empire, often fleeing more aggressive tribes. As the Western Roman Empire weakened, Germanic tribes increased in power. These tribes became the foundation of medieval Europe.

Theodoric, king of the Ostrogoths, moved into Italy in 493 at the request of the Byzantine emperor. The emperor of the Western Empire had been deposed in 476, and Theodoric was asked to restore Roman rule. Instead, Theodoric set up his own kingdom. However, he did allow the Roman inhabitants of Italy to continue to follow Roman law. Italy was reconquered during the time of Justinian, but it fell to the Germanic Lombard tribe in 568.

The Visigoths took control of Spain. They were like the Ostrogoths in that they kept elements of Roman tradition and law. They converted to Catholic Christianity to prevent unrest among their Roman subjects. Eventually, the Visigoths and the Romans intermarried and forged a common history. The Visigoths ruled Spain until the year 711.

The Franks inhabited modern-day France and parts of Germany, and the Angles and Saxons erected settlements in Britain. These tribes settled in their individual regions on a long-term basis and played an important role in the development of national culture.

Barbarians Invade and Roman Empire Divides

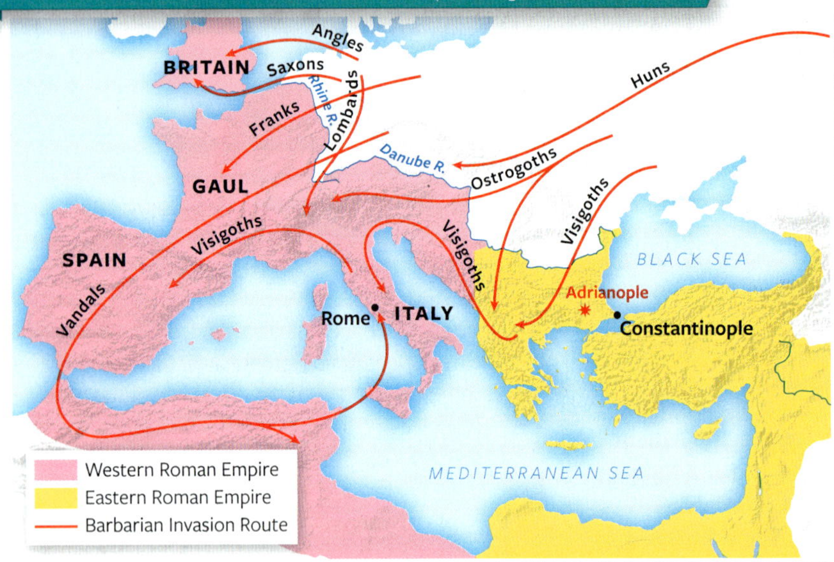

Who took political control of Europe after the collapse of the Western Roman Empire?

The Roman Catholic Church

As the Western Roman Empire declined and collapsed, the Roman Catholic Church began to develop. The weakening of political authority left the common people often without protection and order. Church officials stepped in to fill the void as political authority declined. This new role for the church helped meet immediate physical needs for the people of Europe but also distracted the church from its main mission of spiritual care.

The bishop of the city of Rome became an especially powerful member of medieval society. Bishops of Rome received the title of **pope**, or "papa." Leo I took part in negotiations in 452 to try to convince invaders, the Huns, not to destroy the city of Rome. Gregory I (pope from 590 to 604) was one of the first popes to claim authority over all Christians. Papal power increased further during the 800s when Nicholas I refused to grant the king of Lorraine (in modern France) the divorce he wanted. Gregory VII (pope from 1073 to 1085) confirmed papal power by forcing a German ruler to submit to him or lose his crown.

Why did the Roman Catholic Church grow in importance after the Western Roman Empire collapsed?

The Carolingian Empire

A man named Clovis became the leader of a Frankish kingdom in 481. He used military force and other means to combine several kingdoms. During an important battle, he cried out to God for victory and promised to be baptized. He won the battle and kept his promise. He also ordered three thousand of his soldiers to be baptized into the Roman Catholic Church. By embracing Catholic Christianity, Clovis won the support of church leaders in Rome.

When Clovis died, the kingdom was divided among his four sons. This royal line became known as the Merovingians. By the seventh century, the family had lost influence due to careless and immoral living. The mayor of the palace (the leading palace official) became the real power in the kingdom.

Near the end of the seventh century, Pepin II became the mayor of the palace in a strong Frankish territory. He conquered neighboring territories and united them under his rule. Charles Martel, Pepin's son, expanded the kingdom. Charles's son, Pepin the Short, received permission from the pope to take the title of king in 751. A new family now ruled the Franks. It would be named after its most famous member, Charlemagne.

After Pepin the Short died, his sons Carloman and Charles ruled together. Carloman soon died, and Charles became the sole ruler. Charles personally led his army and defeated many other tribes in Europe, including the Lombards and the Saxons. He organized his empire into districts. His government worked to increase central authority and maintain peace throughout his kingdom. The influence he extended over Europe resulted in his title **Charlemagne**, or "Charles the Great."

Charlemagne became a strong supporter of education. His royal court became a place of learning and scholarship. Under his influence, monasteries became centers of Western knowledge. Monks taught others to read and write. They also preserved Christian learning by storing and copying documents. Long after Charlemagne's death, monasteries continued to educate and preserve written works.

On Christmas Day in 800 an important event occurred. The pope placed a crown on Charlemagne's head and proclaimed him Roman emperor. Though this did not increase Charlemagne's power, it did raise an important question: who is more powerful—the state or the church? Later popes would point to this event and claim authority over kings.

How did monasteries promote education?

Charlemagne crushed a rebellion against Pope Leo III in late 800. Leo expressed gratitude for the service when he crowned Charlemagne emperor.

Feudal Society

Following Charlemagne's death, Europe was divided among his sons. The division of Europe and a lack of strong leadership caused a decline of central power. This decline, together with an increase in foreign invasions, led to the rise of a feudal system.

Feudalism in Europe solved needs both for support (food to eat) and for protection. Under feudalism, a landowner would grant use of a piece of land, called a fief, to a vassal. The vassal could support himself by growing crops on the land and, in exchange, would provide services for the landowner, often supplying military aid. The process of granting fiefs could go out several levels. Technically, kings were at the top of the feudal hierarchy, but they often had little real power over their vassals, the great lords of their kingdoms. The lords controlled large tracts of land, which they divided up as fiefs among lesser nobles. They also had their own soldiers, called knights, which maintained strong loyalty to them. Lesser nobles could, in turn, divide the land into smaller fiefs and have their own vassals. Knights, the warriors of the Middle Ages, were part of this system, receiving fiefs in exchange for their military service.

How did feudalism meet needs for support and protection?

Most people of the Middle Ages fit into one of three categories: those who worked, those who fought, and those who prayed.

Manorialism

Most of the people in the Middle Ages were peasants. They were not part of the feudal system. Many peasants were serfs. Serfs did not own land. Instead, they farmed or performed other duties that were useful to the nobles. In exchange for a portion of their produce or for services rendered, a noble allowed the serfs to live on his land. They were loyal to him and submitted to his authority. He acted as judge for their disputes, and in many cases they were restricted from leaving his estate.

The estate was known as a **manor**. Over time, the manor became largely self-supporting. It often had its own blacksmith, a mill to process grain, and skilled laborers to meet the needs of those living on the estate. It also had a church and priest.

Development of European Monarchies

Kings of the Middle Ages needed their nobles. They depended on them for financial and military support. As time passed, though, the kings worked to change this situation, seeking to strengthen their offices and increase their authority through strategies such as wars and marriage alliances.

? CRITICAL THINKING 2.1

How might it have been good or bad for the common people to have their disputes settled by their lord?

- Why did feudalism weaken in Europe?
- How did legal and constitutional reforms of England shape modern democratic governments?
- How was the development of central government in England and France different from its development in other parts of Europe?
- How did the political relationship between the Roman Catholic Church and nation-states change during the later Middle Ages?
- What were some causes and consequences of the Crusades?

2.2 Decline of Feudalism and the Development of European States

Growth of Towns

Manors had dominated Europe's landscape during the early Middle Ages, but starting around the year 1100 to about 1500, a change occurred. Although many people continued to live on lands controlled by nobles, more and more people moved to towns. These new townspeople came from many places for many reasons and started new towns or settled in old ones. Towns began to dominate the land.

One reason for the growth of towns was improved farming methods. Improved methods led to population growth as farmers could produce more and better crops to feed more people. Improved methods also allowed nobles to farm their lands with fewer people. Many people, no longer needed by their lords, bought their freedom and moved to towns. Younger children of nobles also moved to the towns since only the firstborn son would inherit the land.

Another reason for the growth of towns was the growth of trade. Places where trade routes or roads intersected became logical locations to build settlements. These settlements grew into towns and became centers of trade for all types of goods.

Towns became places of opportunity. Poor farmers, butchers, bakers, carpenters, and other craftsmen moved to towns and prospered. Nobles often owned or controlled the land on which towns developed, but over time the leading citizens of towns convinced nobles to give their towns charters. The town **charter** was a legal document listing the privileges of the townspeople. This freed the people from many feudal duties. The people still paid taxes to the lord, but they were now allowed to govern themselves. Kings also granted charters to towns. In granting a charter, a king redirected the loyalty of the people to himself and the taxes to his government. These were significant advances and contributed to the decline of feudalism.

Heavy wheeled plow

What were two reasons for the growth of towns?

Developing European States in the Middle Ages

Rise of Strong Monarchies

England

The conquest of **England** by William the Conqueror in 1066 laid the foundations for a strong monarchy in England. William was from the French region of Normandy, and he established a new royal dynasty, the Normans. This line was soon replaced by another dynasty, the Plantagenets, through William's great-grandson **Henry II**. Through war, marriage alliances, and government reforms, Henry II sought to increase the power of the king, setting England up to have a strong central government.

LIFE IN

Medieval London

Power

The growth of **Parliament** as a representative body was a step toward limiting the king's power in England. Parliament began during the reign of Edward I (1272–1307) as a group of advisors to the king. By the fourteenth century, Parliament was composed of two groups. The leading vassals were represented in the prominent group (House of Lords), and the knights and leading citizens were represented in the less prominent group (House of Commons). Over time, Parliament gained more power by granting or withholding its approval of new taxes. Through this "power of the purse," Parliament could limit the king's power.

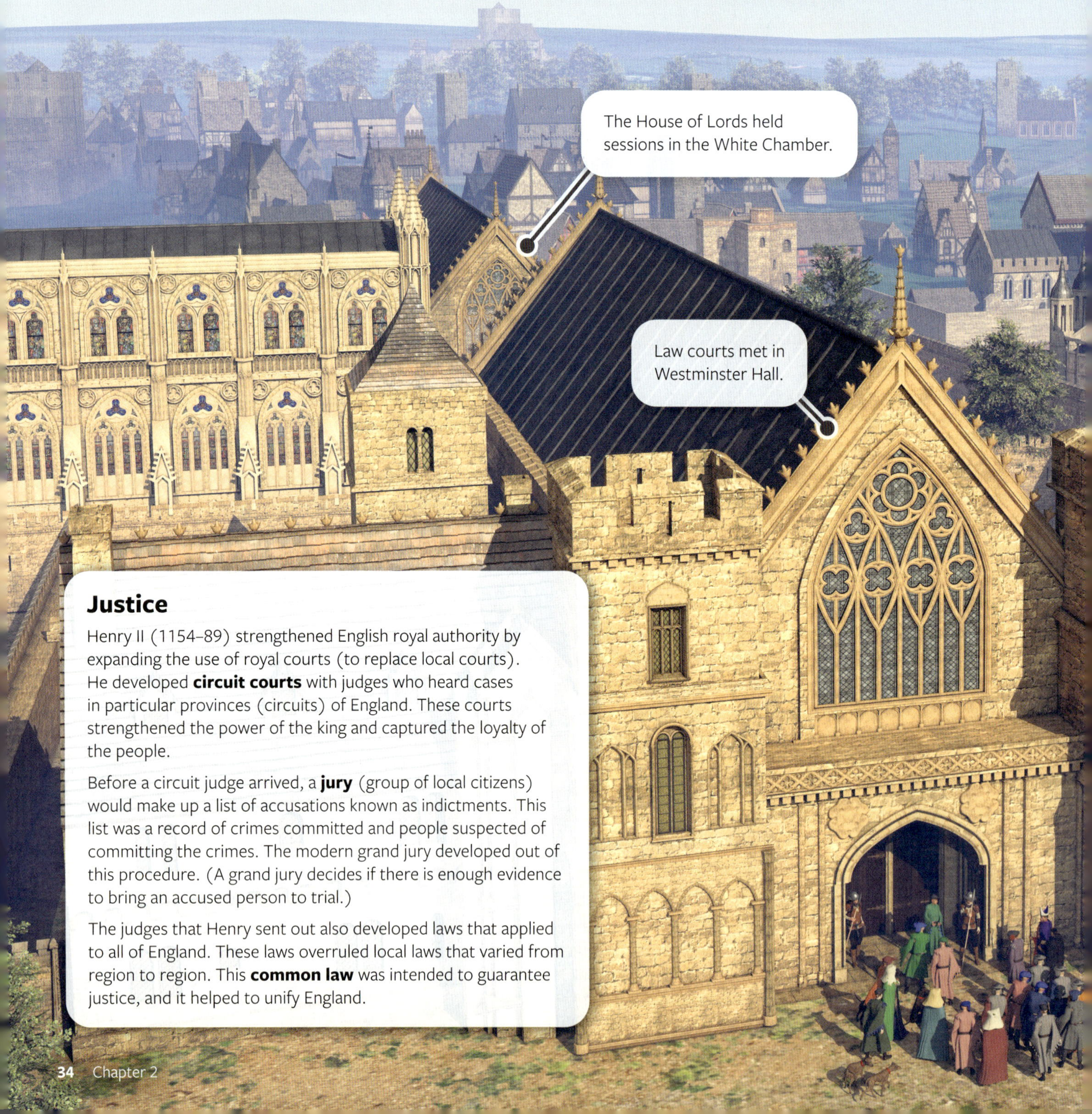

Justice

Henry II (1154–89) strengthened English royal authority by expanding the use of royal courts (to replace local courts). He developed **circuit courts** with judges who heard cases in particular provinces (circuits) of England. These courts strengthened the power of the king and captured the loyalty of the people.

Before a circuit judge arrived, a **jury** (group of local citizens) would make up a list of accusations known as indictments. This list was a record of crimes committed and people suspected of committing the crimes. The modern grand jury developed out of this procedure. (A grand jury decides if there is enough evidence to bring an accused person to trial.)

The judges that Henry sent out also developed laws that applied to all of England. These laws overruled local laws that varied from region to region. This **common law** was intended to guarantee justice, and it helped to unify England.

Environment

Farming was the main occupation in medieval England. Before the fourteenth century, farming was expanding, with additional forests cleared and marshes drained so that more land could be planted. After that time, crop farmers struggled. Cycles of bad weather ruined crops, and disease reduced the number of laborers. Wool became an important English product, and sheep farmers enclosed land to pasture more sheep, reducing the amount of land available for crops.

Religion

Roman Catholicism was the dominant religion of medieval England. As in other parts of Europe, there were disputes over who had ultimate authority, the king or the church. Henry II wanted the ability to punish clergymen in his royal courts if they were suspected of committing crimes, but Thomas à Becket, archbishop of Canterbury and highest-ranking English clergyman, insisted that clergymen answered only to the church. Before the controversy was over, Becket had been murdered, and public opinion had forced Henry to accept the church's right to oversee its own clergy.

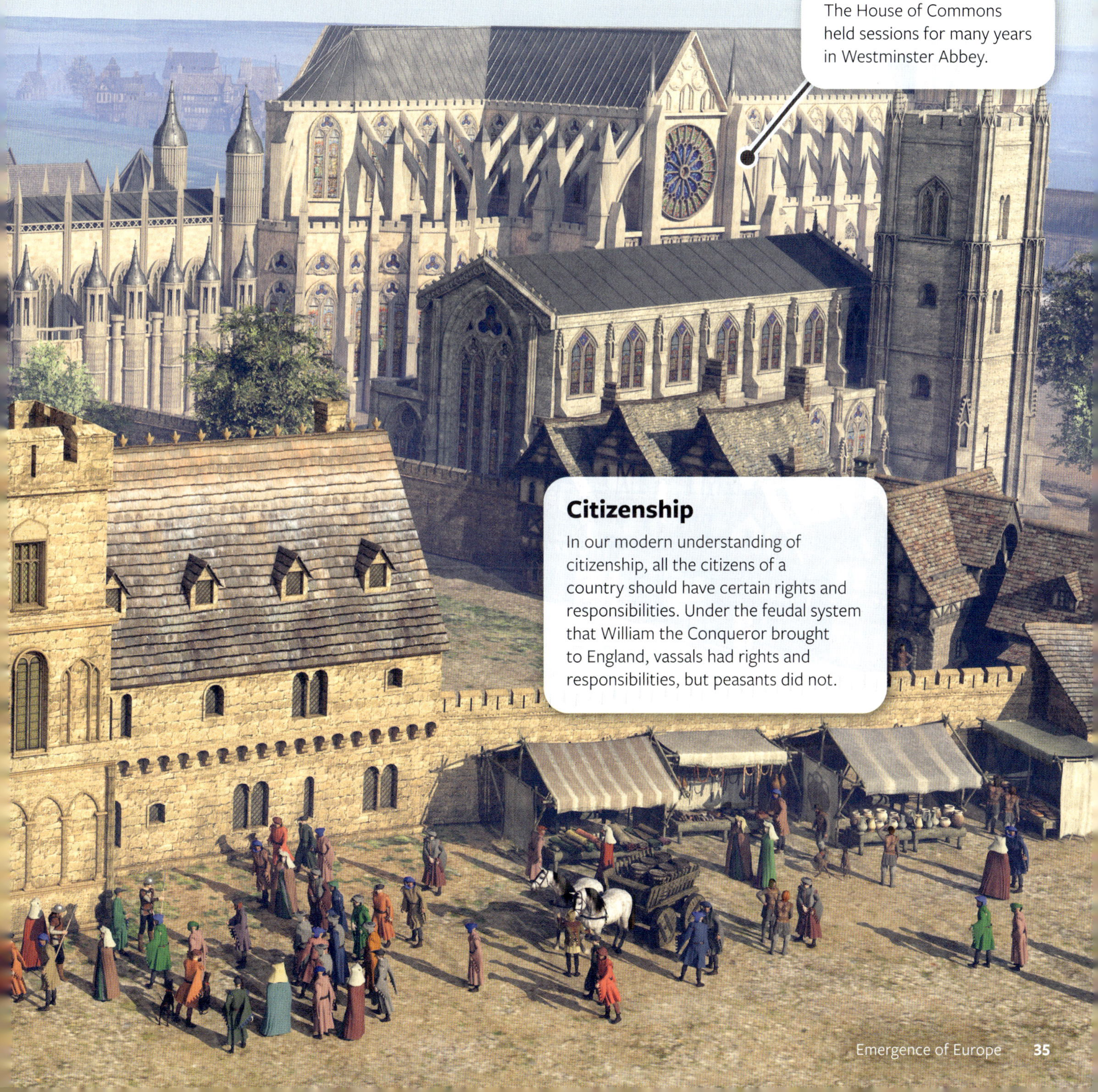

The House of Commons held sessions for many years in Westminster Abbey.

Citizenship

In our modern understanding of citizenship, all the citizens of a country should have certain rights and responsibilities. Under the feudal system that William the Conqueror brought to England, vassals had rights and responsibilities, but peasants did not.

TURNING POINTS

Magna Carta

One of the most influential events of the English Middle Ages was the signing of a document called the **Magna Carta**. Though the circumstances that prompted the signing were related to a specific king and his subjects, the impact of the document has been felt across the globe. Most significantly, many have seen the Magna Carta as an early expression of the revolutionary idea that a government is accountable to its people.

King John of England (1199–1216), brother of Richard I (and villain of the Robin Hood tales), continued many of the trends started by his family. He tried to hold on to his family's land in France and engaged in many costly military campaigns to do so. To carry out these campaigns, he looked to the nobles of England for both financial and military support.

Many English nobles objected to the way John treated them. They were not interested in his lands in France, and they resented the financial burden he placed on them and his refusal to acknowledge their legitimate rights.

Not long after John lost the Battle of Bouvines (1214) to King Philip of France, barons from the north and east of England organized a rebellion. They captured the capital of London as well as two other towns. John met with the leaders of the rebellion to try to work out peace. They gathered on June 15, 1215, in a meadow called Runnymede. Their negotiations ended with the signing of a document that became known as Magna Carta, the "Great Charter." Among the things the charter proposed were the guarantee of trial by peers, the promise of no taxation in excessive amounts or without consent, and the establishment of a council to verify that the charter was being followed.

The charter did not have a major impact in its day because neither side intended to follow its terms. Also, the rights that it was supposed to guarantee were for nobles and church officials, not for all the people of England. But many have seen the Magna Carta as an important historical precedent. The United States Constitution and several state constitutions looked to the Magna Carta and followed the principles they believed it established: rule by law, limited government, and guarantees of the rights of individual citizens. Modern democratic governments across the globe have been influenced by these types of principles.

1. Why did the nobles rebel against King John?
2. What reforms were proposed by the Magna Carta?
3. How did the Magna Carta influence the development of modern democratic governments?

France

France began as a fragmented piece of Charlemagne's empire. However, by the end of the tenth century, Hugh Capet, the count of Paris, founded a new royal line in France. The Capetian rulers gained territory by conquest and marriage alliances. They also developed an efficient centralized government. The Capetians supported the claims of the Roman Catholic Church and granted rights to towns in exchange for their support. These strategies increased royal power.

Philip II (1180–1223) made important contributions toward developing a strong monarchy in France. At that time the English controlled large areas of French land. Philip seized much of the English-controlled land in France during the reign of King John of England. In addition, he improved the effectiveness of the royal government by sending out royal officials called *baillis*, or bailiffs. These men collected taxes for the king and attempted to ensure justice in carrying out laws.

The Capetian family ruled France for over three centuries. During that time each ruler was able to pass the crown to a son, sparing France from revolts and major struggles for power. The resulting stability made possible a strong and powerful monarchy in France.

Other European Kingdoms

Holy Roman Empire

The region we now know as Germany failed to develop a strong, lasting monarchy in the Middle Ages as England and France did. When the last king of Charlemagne's line died in 911, local leaders called dukes began the practice of electing a king from among themselves. Whenever a king died, the dukes would elect a new king, frequently electing the king's son but not obligated to do so. This system of election helped keep the German kings to some degree weaker than kings who were born to their positions.

Another factor that ultimately weakened the German monarchy was its involvement in the Italian peninsula. Otto I, German king from 936 to 973, responded to pleas for military help first from Adelaide, queen of Italy, and later from the pope. For his aid, the pope crowned Otto Roman emperor (continuing the tradition of Charlemagne) in 962. This event marked the beginning of an association between the German and Italian states that came to be known as the "**Holy Roman Empire**," though it did not legitimately deserve any of those titles. Later German kings tried to increase their authority over the Italian peninsula, focusing especially on the northern and southern regions. They never could achieve the control they hoped for, though. The ultimate result of their efforts was that both Germany and Italy remained divided into a variety of smaller and weaker political units until the 1800s.

How was the method of choosing a new king different in the Holy Roman Empire from the method in France?

Through his military ability, Otto the Great suppressed rebellions and extended his kingdom.

In 1415 the Portuguese fought against the Muslims in the North African port city of Ceuta.

The Reconquista

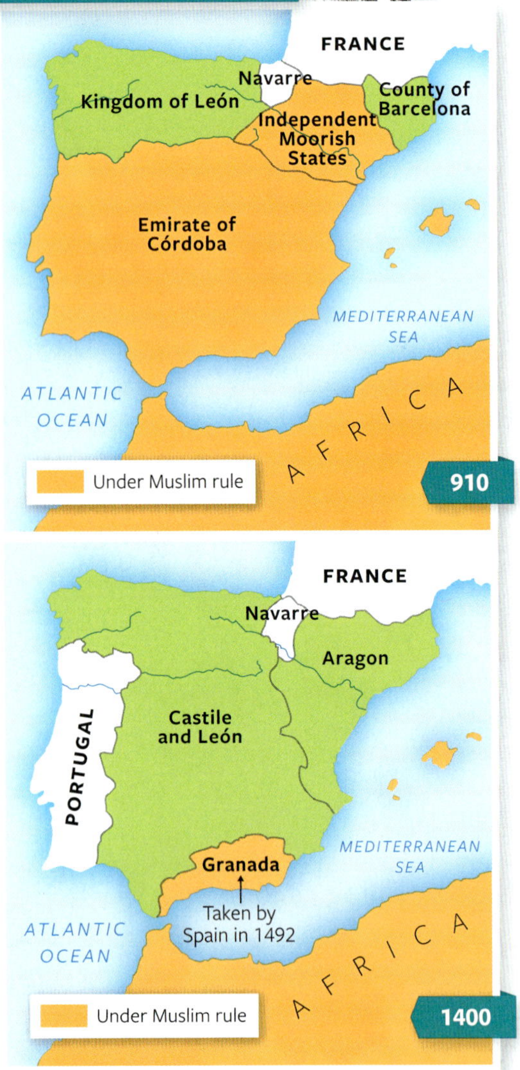

Iberian Peninsula

In the early 600s a new religion had developed along the western edge of the Arabian Peninsula. A man named Muhammad said that he had a vision when he was forty years old. This and later visions were compiled by his followers in a work known as the Qur'an. Muhammad taught that there was only one god, that he was single (not triune, like the Bible teaches), and that humans could not know him (they could only know his will). This new religion was called Islam, and its followers were known as Muslims. Through conversion and later military conquest, Islam spread throughout the Arabian Peninsula and then beyond. Leaders called caliphs established Muslim caliphates (empires) that built on the territorial gains of previous caliphates.

The Umayyad Caliphate began raids into **Spain** in 711. By 718 they had completely conquered the Iberian Peninsula (where Spain and Portugal are today). Starting in the 900s, Christian forces began to try to take the peninsula back. Their efforts became known as the *Reconquista*, or *"reconquest."* Christian and Muslim forces struggled for control of sections of this peninsula over the next five centuries. By the end of the 1200s, non-Muslim forces had regained control of most of the region. Only the Muslim kingdom of Granada remained. In 1492 Ferdinand II of Aragon and Isabella I of Castile took control of Granada, and Muslim rule came to an end. Their conquest of Granada freed up resources to support exploration, working to Christopher Columbus's advantage (see Chapter 5).

Northern and Eastern Europe

The Scandinavian kingdoms of Denmark, Norway, and Sweden began to develop politically starting in the late 900s. They were characterized by powerful nobles, political rivalries, and the national acceptance of Christianity. Political development was more difficult in eastern Europe as the people experienced brutal attacks from invaders such as the Mongols. In **Russia**, however, Alexander Nevsky, a local prince, worked with the Mongol state that had been established. He was designated "grand-prince," and his descendants eventually ruled Russia.

Relationship between Church and State

The power of the papacy peaked in the early 1200s under Pope Innocent III. He took the title "vicar of Christ" and claimed to have supreme authority over the church and state. To establish his claims, he sent armies and issued papal decrees to force rulers and nation-states to submit to his will.

Within a century, however, the political influence of Rome had almost disappeared. There were many reasons for this decline, including weak popes and frustration over abuses. Kings were quick to take advantage of Rome's loss of political power to increase their own power during this period.

?

Why did Rome's political influence decline?

Crusades

When Islam spread across the Middle East and North Africa, it pushed the Byzantine Empire out of the Holy Land (Israel of Bible and modern times). Still, Muslim caliphates periodically allowed Christian pilgrims to travel to the Holy Land to visit Christian sites. In 1073, however, the Seljuk Turks, a people from central Asia who had adopted Islam, took Jerusalem from the Fatimid caliphate, and the situation changed. The Byzantine Empire also found itself increasingly under attack by these new invaders.

Byzantine emperors appealed to popes to send military aid to Constantinople. In response to the first plea for help, Pope Urban II called for a **crusade** to liberate the Holy Land. This call was issued in 1095. Several armies traveled to the Middle East over the next two centuries, but only the First Crusade enjoyed a measure of success and gained control of a narrow strip of land. Other crusades failed, and the effort to free the Holy Land ended by the late 1200s.

Crusaders

Many crusaders were lords or knights. They faced several obstacles. Crusaders had to leave family behind, and many who went did not return. It was also expensive to go on a crusade, and the warriors had to pay their own way.

Motives of crusaders differed. Some viewed a crusade as exciting and an opportunity for adventure. Many were also motivated by religious fervor. By fighting in a holy war, crusaders believed they could earn forgiveness of sins.

Results

The most noticeable results of the Crusades were those experienced by the crusaders and the people who lived in the Holy Land. Thousands of warriors and civilians died. Property was destroyed. And despite all the violence and bloodshed, the Europeans failed to gain control of the Holy Land.

The contact that occurred between East and West did produce other results as well, though. For example, much of the knowledge that had been preserved by the Muslims and the Byzantine Empire found its way back to Europe. Information about science, diseases, astronomy, math, and many other subjects was gained. Greek and Arabic documents brought to Europe played an important role in the revival of education and the rise of universities in Europe.

Merchants filled their ships with spices, muslin, silk, and furs as they returned from taking crusading forces to the Middle East. These goods found a ready market in Europe and resulted in a great increase in trade. Merchants became very wealthy and formed part of a new economic class, a middle class. The middle class was composed of those who lived in towns and included merchants, bankers, craftsmen, and other skilled laborers.

In addition, manufacturing methods used by the Muslims were copied and taken back to be developed in Europe. New factories provided work for many poor Europeans and contributed to the growth of towns. New products and goods became available, and opportunities to make wealth abounded.

Critical Thinking 2.2

1. What strategies did England and France use for developing strong central governments?
2. How did the Crusades change the Middle East and Europe?

Crusades often involved sieges of walled cities.

GUIDING QUESTIONS

- What was medieval chivalry?
- What were contributions and challenges of Jewish communities in the medieval world?
- How did universities shape the modern world?
- What were key contributions of medieval art, architecture, music, and literature?

2.3 European Culture

Like every other period of history, the Middle Ages had its share of both positive and negative cultural elements. On the one hand were valuable contributions to the fine arts and important developments in education. On the other were destructive warfare and discrimination.

The Roman Catholic Church was one of the most dominant forces of the Middle Ages in Europe. Its influence could be seen clearly in the music and visual arts of the period and was also felt in many practical ways, even down to the regulating of war.

Chivalry

What were key elements of the code of chivalry?

Warfare was frequent and damaging during the Middle Ages. The Roman Catholic Church worked to improve the conduct of knights and to limit the destruction of warfare. The church decree known as the **Peace of God** placed church property out of bounds for fighting. This decree was also intended to protect those not directly involved in the fighting. The **Truce of God** restricted fighting to certain days of the week. For example, combat was not allowed from Wednesday evening through Monday morning. Though these decrees were not always followed, they did bring some improvement of conditions for the people of medieval Europe.

Another attempt to improve the behavior of knights was the development of a strict code called **chivalry**. *Chivalry* comes from a French word meaning "horseman." It is similar to the English word *cavalry*. Chivalry required knights to act with honor, generosity, and religious devotion. They had to be brave in battle and limit their fighting to other armed knights. A group of knights could not attack a single knight; instead, they were expected to fight him one at a time. Many of these ideals appeared most clearly in literature works like the stories of King Arthur and his knights of the Round Table.

Plate armor covered a knight from head to toe. It helped keep him safe but was hot and heavy.

Jewish Communities

Though most of the inhabitants of medieval Europe were Roman Catholics, there were pockets of minority populations scattered across the continent. Having been pushed out of their homeland by a variety of invasions, Jews had become a significant minority group in Europe. Jewish inhabitants of Europe made a variety of economic and cultural contributions. Many Jews became involved in trade and moneylending, at least in part because they were not bound by the prohibitions of the Catholic Church against charging interest. The services they provided were vital to the development of a growing economy in medieval Europe.

Jews also made important cultural contributions in places such as Spain (prior to being expelled in 1492). Contributions came in areas such as medicine, philosophy, and literature.

Despite their contributions, though, Jews faced periodic discrimination and sometimes severe persecution during the Middle Ages in Europe. In fact, some of the practices that are familiar to the world from Hitler's Nazi Germany, such as the required wearing of yellow badges, originated in the Middle Ages. Though political and religious leaders tried at times to stop unjust practices, they were not always successful. Jews were at various times forced to live in separate communities, wear identifying garments, or leave a region or country. Jews sometimes faced wild accusations, including poisoning the water of a town and making the people sick. In reality the Black Death had struck the community.

What contributions did Jewish communities make to the medieval world?

Universities

During the Middle Ages education was not available to most Europeans. However, learning was preserved in monasteries and cathedral schools for a privileged few. Students were trained in the liberal arts, which included grammar, rhetoric, logic, geometry, arithmetic, music, and astronomy. These studies were reserved for "free" (*liberei*) men (i.e., nobility) rather than "common" men. All subjects were taught in Latin.

The concept of a university became one of the unique contributions of European culture. Universities began to develop in the 1100s. Students gathered in places where well-known teachers instructed, and universities eventually formed in those locations. Muslim and Byzantine documents about medicine, science, and other subjects newly acquired through the Crusades, provided a wealth of information for instruction in the new schools.

Italy boasted two early universities in Salerno and Bologna, and Paris developed one soon afterwards. Over time, the universities became known for particular areas of study. For example, Salerno was known for medicine and Bologna for law.

Universities were organized in different ways. In Paris teachers regulated the university. In Bologna groups of students regulated the university; they hired teachers and set policy. Nations in Northern Europe tended to follow the Parisian pattern as they established universities. Nations in Southern Europe tended to follow the Bologna pattern.

▲ Early universities sometimes had older students, who wanted to advance in their professions. Eventually, many students entered universities as teenagers.

Students attending these universities often met in rented buildings, and some sat on straw as they listened to their teachers. Since paper was expensive and hard to find, the students often spent hours each day memorizing their lessons. The typical day for a student began at 4:00 a.m. and ended at bedtime about 9:00 p.m.

While Italy and France were the first regions to develop universities, schools had begun to appear in England, Spain, and Portugal by the end of the 1100s. By the 1300s Germany and other locations were establishing universities as well. More subjects were offered, and universities began to meet in permanent buildings.

Universities served a vital role in increasing literacy and advancing scientific discovery. They produced medical doctors, lawyers, theologians, and many other professionals. This system enriched European culture and spread knowledge throughout Europe. Kings and popes supported universities because they valued the services of graduates to promote their causes.

What kinds of professional occupations were produced by European universities?

Art, Architecture, Music, and Literature

Christian themes were at the center of European culture during the Middle Ages. These themes are evident in the art, architecture, music, and literature of the period.

Richard II (kneeling) is surrounded by his patron saints.

ART

THEMES

Christian teaching

SUBJECTS

Bible characters and saints of the Catholic Church

SYMBOLISM

Use of objects to represent ideas (for example, halos to represent holiness)

ARCHITECTURE

Construction of cathedrals (Romanesque vs. Gothic)

ROMANESQUE

- Rounded vaults (made by putting arches together)
- Thick stone walls
- Small windows, use of candles and torches
- Generally dark and cold

GOTHIC

- Flying buttresses (external supports)
- Higher ceilings and thinner walls
- Larger windows (use of stained glass) and doors
- Warmer and brighter than Romanesque style

Monks sing a requiem (a chant sung in honor of the dead).

MUSIC

GREGORIAN CHANTS

Monophonic music (just one melody line) that went along with the mass and daily prayer routines of the Catholic Church

BEGINNINGS OF POLYPHONY

- Harmony introduced to music.
- **Leonin** and **Perotin** of the Notre Dame school
- Development of written notation system for notes and rhythms

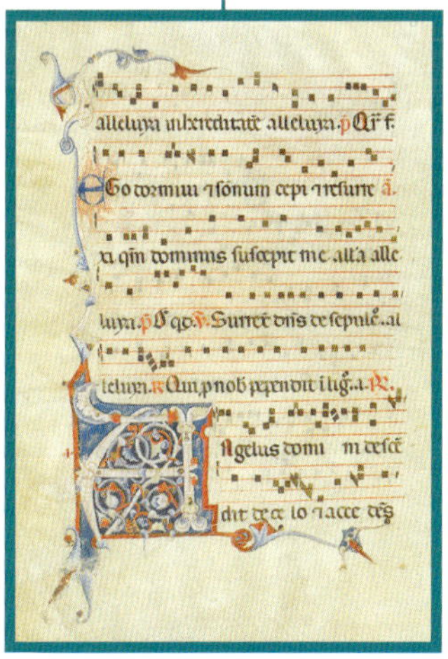

This music sheet is from an antiphonary, a songbook for the church that used responsive singing between voices.

CRITICAL THINKING 2.3

What does the artistic expression of the Middle Ages reveal about what was important during that period?

LITERATURE

CHANGE IN LANGUAGE

- **Latin**
  Language of the Roman Empire; used for government and education
- **Vernacular**
  Common spoken languages of the people; began to be used for popular writing (helped to develop and preserve local languages)

POPULAR WRITERS

- **Dante (Italian)**
  Divine Comedy (imaginary journey through hell, purgatory, and paradise; shows unrest and skepticism of late Middle Ages)
- **Chaucer (English)**
  The Canterbury Tales (group of pilgrims traveling to visit the tomb of a famous religious leader in England; gives glimpse of English life during the medieval period)

In *The Canterbury Tales*, the pilgrims tell several stories as they travel. These stories are used to analyze English society.

GUIDING QUESTIONS

- What were causes and consequences of the Great Famine of 1315?
- How did the Hundred Years' War shape France and England?
- How did the Black Death spread in Europe?
- What role did religion play in European responses to the Black Death?

2.4 European Calamities

A calamity can be defined as an event that causes dreadful loss, enduring suffering, or great misery. Famine, war, and plague are examples of calamities. Beginning in the fourteenth century Europe experienced all these calamities.

The Great Famine

The **Great Famine of 1315** was the first calamity to strike large areas of Europe during this period. It began with heavy and frequent rain over much of Europe starting in the fall of 1314. The spring and summer of 1315 remained cool, and crops rotted in the fields. Food for people and animals became scarce. Salt to preserve meat was also scarce because salt producers needed dry weather to extract the salt from salt water through evaporation. Eventually, food and salt became too expensive for most people to buy.

What conditions led to the Great Famine of 1315?

To survive, people slaughtered their farm animals for food and ate seed grain. Some parents abandoned their children because they could no longer feed them. This calamity resembled scenes from the Old Testament (2 Kings 6) as some resorted to cannibalism to survive. The frequent rain continued until 1317, and people were reduced to eating roots, grasses, and even tree bark to survive.

Many who survived the two years of rain and famine had been weakened by pneumonia and other illnesses. In addition, with the destruction of livestock and lack of seed for planting, the recovery was slow. Somewhere between 10 and 25 percent of the people died of starvation or illness between 1315 and 1322. While other calamities would take more lives, this one lingered for years and caused slow and agonizing deaths.

It is estimated that two-thirds of the people of Norway died as a result of the Black Death.

Hundred Years' War

Between 1337 and 1453 England and France fought a series of battles to settle the issue of English control of land in France. This became known as the **Hundred Years' War**. The French had steadily taken land away from the English for many years. However, the death of the last Capetian king without a male heir led to a crisis.

The English king Edward III was related to the French royal line through his mother and claimed the right to the French throne. However, the French nobles rejected this claim and selected Philip VI of the house of Valois as king. War was to be expected. This series of battles began as a contest between feudal nobles and ended as a rivalry between two emerging nations.

English forces started the war by crossing the English Channel. Although they were outnumbered, the English quickly won several key battles. They defeated the French by using new tactics and weapons. English longbows destroyed French forces from a safe distance. Thousands of French soldiers were slaughtered in these battles.

Although the English won most of the battles, the drain on English forces and resources was great. Over time the people of England tired of the cost of war, and political unrest occurred. Also, a plague killed many people in England. There were simply not enough soldiers to take advantage of English victories.

The French finally rallied to victory under the leadership of a peasant girl named **Joan of Arc**. She believed that she was being directed from heaven to drive out the English. Desperate for a leader, the French followed her and defeated the English. The English were able to capture her and burned her at the stake. However, her example strengthened the French to emerge as victors.

The Hundred Years' War had many short-term effects on France and England. New weapons and battlefield tactics helped shape the development of European warfare. And loss of life and destruction of property caused great suffering for the people of both countries. In the long term the end of the war permanently separated the two countries, leaving each to take its own course as an emerging nation-state.

Joan of Arc was officially tried for heresy. The church acquitted her of the charge several years after her death.

?

How did the Hundred Years' War shape France and England?

Black Death

Historians differ on how the plague known as the **Black Death** originated and was spread. However, there is no doubt that something like the bubonic plague killed millions of people throughout the world. Europe suffered a great loss of people as this plague spread from city to city and engulfed whole countries.

The plague may have begun in China and spread by trade ships to Europe by 1347. Rats and their fleas have been blamed for the spread of the bacteria that killed millions of people. Some estimate that between 30 and 50 percent of Europe's population died from the Black Death.

SYMPTOMS OF THE

BLACK DEATH

Day 1

Large painful boils called "buboes" appear in the armpits and groin.

Day 2

Fever and vomiting set in.

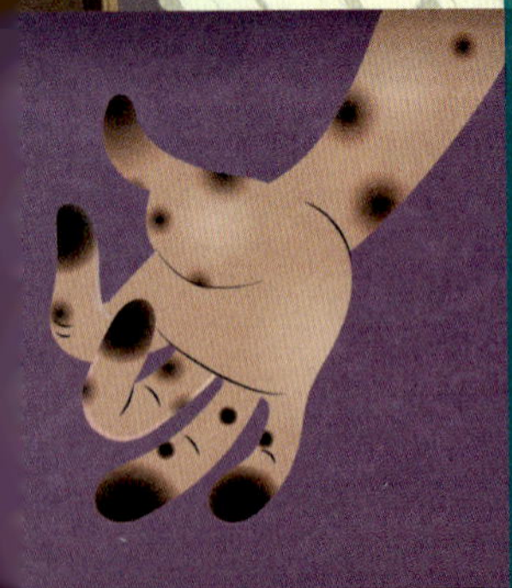

Day 3

Bleeding under skin creates dark spots all across the body.

Day 4

Plague attacks the nervous system, causing spasms and severe pain.

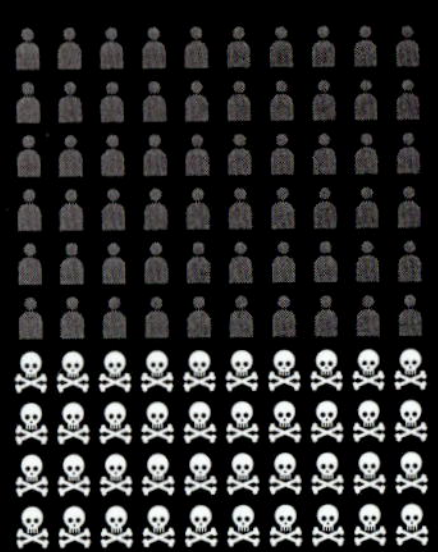

Day 5

30–50% of Europeans die, usually within 5 to 7 days of the onset of symptoms.

Cities in Europe were especially vulnerable to the spread of the plague for several reasons. Open sewers and improper disposal of trash made the cities unsanitary. Rats and fleas thrived there. Houses were also often close together, and the people lived in crowded settings. These unhealthy conditions provided a breeding ground for disease and its spread.

Besides the obvious reduction of the population in Europe, there were several other consequences of the Black Death. The people quickly turned to the Roman Catholic Church for deliverance. Many made trips to Rome and made donations to the church in hopes of rescue from the plague. However, though some church officials selflessly served the sick and dying, the Catholic Church proved to be unable to stop the plague. When people saw priests and nuns dying as quickly as others, they lost faith in the claims of the church. In addition, many concluded that the plague was sent by God to punish the people for their sins. The Catholic Church lost much of the authority that church leaders had built up over the years as people began to look other places for help with their problems.

The wealthy left the cities and lived on secluded estates to avoid contact with the plague. Others gave themselves over to sinful living since they believed that death was imminent. Crime also became a serious problem. As previously mentioned, many blamed Jews for the plague, and thousands of Jews died as the people slaughtered whole Jewish communities for their imagined crime.

By 1350 the Black Death had run its course, but it took many years for Europe to recover. The Roman Catholic Church had lost much of its credibility during the crisis. On the other hand, the movement toward the development of strong nation-states continued to gain momentum.

? **How did the Black Death possibly begin and spread?**

WORLDVIEW DILEMMA

What is a biblical response to the suffering of others?

- **A** Identify the sin in their life that caused the suffering.
- **B** Seek to ease their suffering with love and wisdom.
- **C** Recognize that suffering is a part of life and we can do nothing about it.

Making Connections

1. How did Germanic tribes replace Rome as the dominant influence on the European continent?
2. What actions did bishops of Rome take that strengthened the Roman Catholic Church?
3. How did Charlemagne contribute to the political and intellectual development of Europe?
4. Why did central power decline in Europe after Charlemagne's death?
5. What conditions weakened feudalism in Europe?
6. What modern political and legal practices originated in medieval England?
7. Why did the Catholic Church have less political power in the later Middle Ages?
8. What role did Jewish communities play in the medieval world?
9. How did universities affect the development of Europe?
10. List several new techniques used by artists and musicians of the Middle Ages.
11. What conditions led to the Great Famine of 1315, and how did the famine affect Europe?
12. List causes and consequences of the Crusades.

What to Know

Dates & Events

Great Famine of 1315
Hundred Years' War

People

Charlemagne
Henry II
King John
Dante
Chaucer
Leonin and Perotin
Joan of Arc

Places

England
France
Holy Roman Empire
Spain
Russia

Terms

pope
feudalism
manor
charter
Parliament
circuit courts
jury
common law
Magna Carta
crusade
Peace of God
Truce of God
chivalry
Romanesque
Gothic
Gregorian Chants
vernacular
Black Death

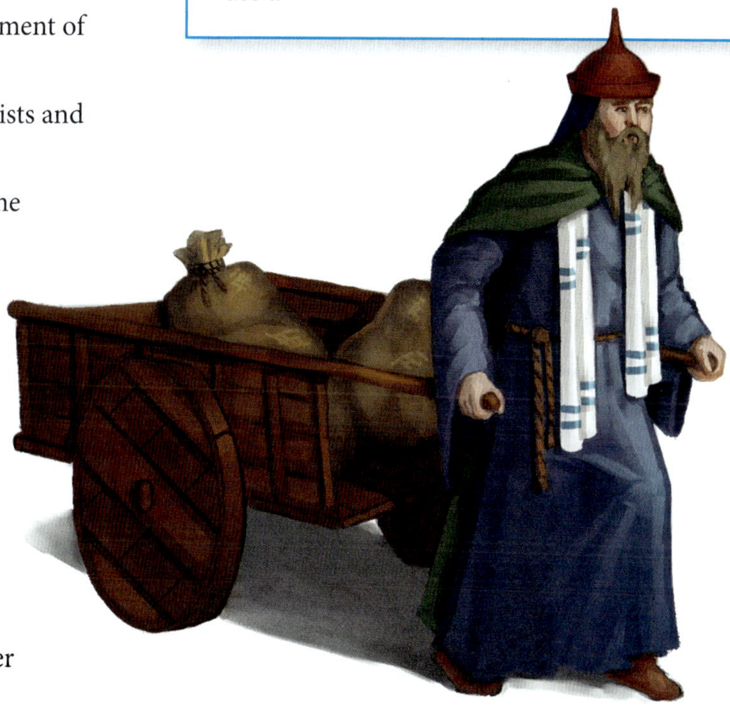

Jewish merchant

Thinking Critically

1. In what ways might medieval lords have made life better or worse for the peasants of Europe?
2. Why did England and France develop stronger central governments than other parts of Europe did?
3. How were France and England different after the Hundred Years' War than they were before?
4. How did the Black Death change the relationship of the common people of Europe to the Roman Catholic Church?

3 KINGDOMS OF ASIA AND THE MONGOL EMPIRE

AD 577 – 1480

ESSENTIAL QUESTIONS

- What was the Chinese civilization like during the period prior to the Mongol invasion?
- How did the Mongols conquer Asia and Eastern Europe?
- What were the achievements of the Mongol Empire?
- What were the early Southeast Asian and Russian civilizations like?
- How did the Mongol Empire decline and fall?

First Christian Missionaries to China

During the Tang dynasty, in the seventh and eighth centuries, China was more open to trade with the rest of the world than it had been before. The Chinese welcomed not only the trade but also the foreigners who brought the goods. The Chinese were tolerant of the foreigners' beliefs as well. Some of the foreigners were Nestorian Christians from Syria and Persia. The **Nestorian church** was named after Nestorius, a bishop (a person of high position in the Catholic or Orthodox churches) of Constantinople. He believed that Christ was two separate persons, one human and one divine (God), rather than the biblical belief that Christ was both God and human in one person (John 1:14; 8:58; 10:30). Nestorius's followers found refuge in Persia, and that is where the church grew up.

Tang emperor Taizong was interested in the Nestorian religion because he heard it was based on a book, and the emperor loved books. He had a library of over two hundred thousand volumes. In 635 the emperor welcomed a group of missionaries to the capital city. A man named **Alopen** led the group. The emperor most likely protected the missionaries during their journey to China from Persia. Taizong instructed Alopen to translate his Christian books into Chinese. Rather than directly translating the Bible, Alopen wrote two works to explain Christianity to the Chinese. These works were called *The Jesus Messiah Sutra and The Treaties on Monotheism.* Alopen tried to explain Christianity using Buddhist words. He sometimes replaced the word God with Buddha. While the introduction of Christianity to China was imperfect, it was the first recorded time they heard the name of Jesus. The emperor ordered the construction of churches, and many Chinese followed the faith until the end of the Tang dynasty.

An artist's depiction of Emperor Taizong greeting Alopen

GUIDING QUESTIONS

- What was the rule of the three pre-Mongol dynasties like?
- What were people's lives like during the three pre-Mongol dynasties?
- What was religion like in China during the Tang and Song periods?
- What were the cultural and technological achievements of the Tang and Song dynasties?
- How did China trade with the peoples of Southeast Asia and the lands on the edge of the Indian Ocean?

3.1 Three Chinese Dynasties

After the collapse of the Han dynasty, China went through a time of disunity and internal struggle followed by a long time of growth and cultural advancement. There were three influential dynasties during this time period preceding the Mongol invasion.

CHINESE DYNASTIES 581–1279

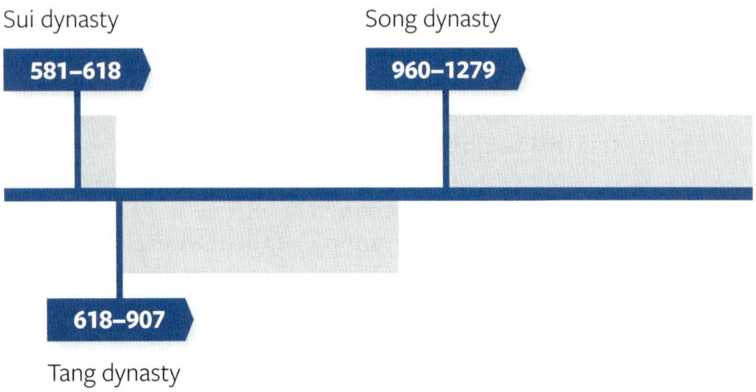

The Sui Dynasty

The **Sui dynasty** was short but left a big impact on China, much like the Qin dynasty. The preparations for reunification (the country had been divided into many regions) began in AD 577 when two northern Chinese states united. A general named Yang Jian seized power and put a child in place as emperor, but in 581 Jian convinced the child to make him emperor. Yang Jian took the name Emperor Wen. His son Yang followed him as emperor. Wen built the **Grand Canal** to connect the rich farmland in the south to the more arid lands in the north. The Chinese also repaired and extended the **Great Wall** during this time.

? **What was built to help farmers in the north?**

The Grand Canal

Yang advocated for Buddhism and a return to the examination system for those who worked in government. He also engaged in large military campaigns against Korea, Vietnam, and the western lands of Central Asia, near where the "stan" countries are today. The Chinese lost the war in Korea. They won in Vietnam, but the soldiers died of disease, so the victory was hollow. The war in the west was successful. But all the wars and building projects bankrupted the state treasury and resulted in the collapse of the dynasty.

The Tang Dynasty

The **Tang dynasty** was one of the longest Chinese dynasties following the time of Christ. It built upon the foundation of the Sui dynasty but was less harsh. The Tang period was a golden age for China. It was a prosperous time that included many cultural achievements.

There were two notable Tang dynasty rulers, **Emperor Taizong** and **Empress Wu Zetian**. Empress Wu was the only legitimate empress in Chinese history. She rose to power through political calculation and stabilized the Tang dynasty when it was close to collapsing. She opened opportunities for those who formerly had no chance of serving in government. Tang emperors expanded the civil service examination system that determined a person's ability to serve. Taizong was tolerant of foreign beliefs and created a long-lasting law code. The code had five hundred articles and prescribed specific punishments for various crimes. Although the law was revised heavily, it lasted until 1644. Natural disasters signaled the end of the Mandate of Heaven (heaven's permission to rule) for the Tang. A flood of the Grand Canal killed thousands in 858 and ruined farmland in the north. In 873 there was a famine. Millions starved to death. These calamities began a time of unrest among farmers that brought the dynasty to an end.

Empress Wu Zetian

What did Emperor Taizong create?

The Song Dynasty

The fifty-four years between the Tang and Song dynasties were a time of disunity called the five dynasties and ten kingdoms period. The first Song emperor, Taizu, took the throne of one of the five dynasties by force. He unified China through a 16-year-long military campaign. The **Song dynasty** is divided into two different eras, the Northern Song dynasty and the Southern Song dynasty. When the Jurchens, northern tribes who are the ancestors of the Manchus, invaded Song territory, the Song Chinese discovered they were seriously outmatched militarily by the Jurchens. The Song leaders moved south and reformed their dynasty. Confucian thought reigned supreme in the Song dynasty. A person had to know the Confucian classical books to work in the imperial government. The Song emperors built academies where the most gifted students could study literature, art, and science. Militarily they depended on superior weapons rather than a well-organized army. They invented rockets and mortars. The Song dynasty years are noted for economic growth, scientific advancement, and a return to uniquely Chinese religion and thought. The Mongols had great difficulty defeating the Song dynasty during their conquest of Eurasia.

Who invaded the Northern Song dynasty?

Religion

The Tang dynasty was known for its religious tolerance. The people practiced Buddhism and ancestor worship widely, while Taoism and Confucianism remained the official religions. They mixed all these religions up like a vegetable smoothie and drank it without sensing any contradictions. Therefore, the Nestorian Christians used Buddhist language when telling the gospel. It seems the Christians were seeking to make the gospel part of the smoothie, not a separate, one true religion. Islamic traders introduced Islam to China, but it did not find a foothold. The Chinese did not like Islam's civil and dietary laws. The Song dynasty rulers responded to invasions from northern tribes by ending the tolerance of foreign religions like Buddhism and Christianity. They developed a new type of Confucianism to incorporate Buddhist ideas into Confucianism but without the worship of Buddha.

Why did the Chinese not accept Islam?

Growth

During this time before the Mongol invasion, there was a great increase in the population and the number and size of cities in China. Increased production of rice, wheat, and other crops in central and southern China sustained the population growth. The Chinese developed ways to irrigate their crops. They used iron farm implements to make farming more effective and to make more land available for farming. Chinese merchants also turned excess food into increased trade. As in many other cultures, a combination of population growth, increasing food supply, and growing industry resulted in growing cities. Several cities in China increased to populations of over one million people. In addition to at least ten large cities, towns developed where people met for trade. These smaller cities became centers of commerce where a variety of products were exchanged.

China Population Growth during Tang and Song Dynasties

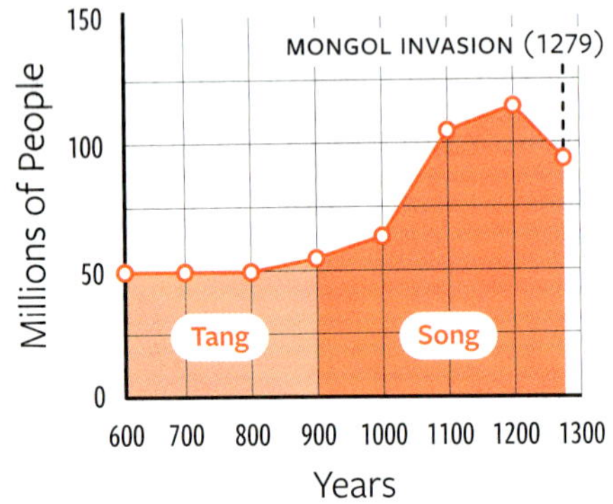

The Tang and Song leaders expanded the **Silk Road** overland and developed another kind of Silk Road over the sea. Chinese ships traveled west to India and southeast to the islands of modern-day Indonesia. The Chinese traded silk, **porcelain** dishes, tea, brass, and iron in exchange for spices, flowers, plants, and other exotic treasures. During the Song dynasty, the Chinese used the compass to find their direction while at sea, thus extending their shipping routes. The Chinese had invented the compass much earlier, during the Han dynasty, but at that time they only used it in their religious practices to determine the will of their gods.

Maritime Silk Road

What two places did China trade with on the Maritime Silk Road?

Silk Road a trading network of roads across the land of Asia

porcelain a glazed ceramic product made of clay hardened at high temperatures

Technological, Artistic, and Cultural Achievements

Scientific Discoveries

The Chinese made many scientific discoveries. They gained knowledge of how the physical and natural world behaved. For example, they discovered how to process iron ore, make paper, and make gunpowder. They also invented printing methods and the compass. These and many more discoveries, such as the development of silk fabric, became the basis for a long list of technological developments. Silk fabric is made from the fibers that certain moths produce to build their cocoons. Chinese emperors tried to keep the knowledge of how to develop silk a secret, but the technique was eventually smuggled into other lands.

Technological Advances

Technology, simply defined, is putting knowledge to effective use. Technology can be a concept (idea) or a technique (process). For example, when the proper ingredients were mixed to form paper, a recipe (concept) was developed. Over time, the Chinese built factories to make large quantities of paper.

Technology contributes to culture. The development of culture is a natural outgrowth of the **Creation Mandate**. God created mankind to "subdue" the earth and to "have dominion" over it. As the Chinese discovered new uses for God's creation, they were maximizing the usefulness of their resources. Even though the Chinese did not worship the Creator, they were demonstrating the truth of God's Word (Genesis 1:28).

Paper

China developed the earliest known paper, perhaps as early as a few years before the birth of Christ. They formed paper by combining fibers and rags with water. The mixture was pressed and then allowed to dry. The Chinese used paper for wrapping, padding, and writing. They folded and sewed paper into bags to protect the flavor of tea. During the Song dynasty, the Chinese issued the first known paper money for general use.

Gunpowder

For centuries, the Chinese mixed ingredients with saltpeter (potassium nitrate, used in fertilizer and explosives) to make items such as medicines. In the ninth century, the Chinese discovered gunpowder by accident. They were trying to create a substance that would give them eternal life. The Chinese quickly developed many weapons with gunpowder, including flame throwers, rockets, and crude bombs.

Iron

Iron smelting industries developed, and these industries employed many workers. The Chinese were also among the first to develop cast iron. This process would not be used in Europe for another thousand years. The sale of iron products brought great wealth to the rising merchant class in China.

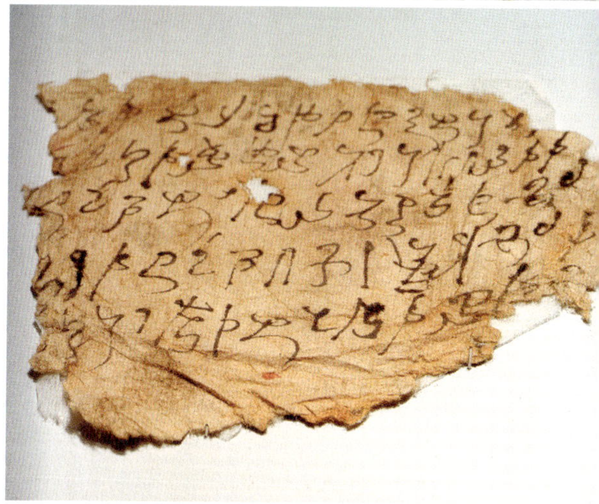

(top background) A Chinese woman modeling a traditional silk dress, (top inset) A silkworm, (second from top) Ancient Chinese paper, (third from top) An ancient Chinese cannon, (bottom) Cast-iron bells

Movable type used for a Chinese printing press

A painting done during the Song dynasty

An example of tri-colored glazed pottery

Printing

During the third century the Chinese became the first to develop woodblock printing. They carved images into a block of wood and then applied ink or paint. The woodblock was then pressed against paper or cloth. A reversed image of the carving would be imprinted on the material.

The Chinese also developed a method of printing that uses movable characters. This method, known as movable-type printing, was first developed in China around 1041. The characters were made of ceramic. Although the Chinese invented this technology, they made little use of it. The Chinese language is very complicated, and printing with this method involved a great amount of labor.

What was the Song dynasty first to use paper for?

Artistic and Cultural Advances

Poetry

The Tang dynasty period was known as the golden age for Chinese poetry. The subjects of the poems were nature, Confucian wisdom, and everyday life.

Deer-Park Hermitage

There seems to be no one on the empty mountain . . .
And yet I think I hear a voice,
Where sunlight, entering a grove,
Shines back to me from the green moss.

Art

The Song dynasty was known for its sophisticated landscape paintings. Later Song paintings include white space in the middle symbolizing the people's feelings of lostness after having to move south.

Tri-colored Glazed Pottery

The Chinese invented a new type of pottery during the Tang dynasty. It was called tri-colored glazed pottery, or Tangsancai. It was unique because they added metal oxides into the glaze to make the pottery shiny and create different colors. They made human and animal figurines with this method. These became valuable trade items. The tri-colored pottery was not practical for dishes because it leaked, and porcelain was already available for everyday use.

CRITICAL THINKING 3.1

1. Compare the different reasons each of the dynasties ended.
2. What did the Chinese hope to ensure by requiring people to pass examinations to work in government?
3. How did the invasion of the Northern Song dynasty affect its religion and art?

3.2 The Rise of the Mongol Empire

The Mongols were nomads who lived in tribes on the Mongolian plateau north of China. They traveled across the plains in search of grazing land for their large herds of horses. The Mongols lived in movable tent-like structures called **gers.** In the western Mongol lands, similar structures were called "yurts," a Turkic word. The difference between the two is that gers have interior poles holding up the center of the roof, but yurts do not.

These tribes often fought among themselves over grazing lands. However, two factors led these tribes to combine and become a great empire. First, the climate cooled over a vast region. Because of the cooling, the nomads had to travel farther in search of grassland for their herds. As they traveled farther from their homelands, they encountered different peoples whom they conquered. The second factor in the birth of the Mongol Empire was Temujin, a gifted Mongol boy during the twelfth century. He proved to be one of the world's greatest military commanders.

GUIDING QUESTIONS

- How did the Mongol Empire rise and expand?
- Who was Genghis Khan?
- How did the Mongol conquests affect the people of Asia and Eastern Europe?
- What was Mongol religion like?
- What was Pax Mongolica?

? **What kind of shelter did the Mongols live in?**

Outside and inside of a ger

Temujin, the son of a Mongolian tribal chieftain, was born around 1162. When he was a boy, his father was killed, and he had to flee for his life. After wandering for a few years, he returned to his tribe and avenged his father's murder. Temujin and his brother Jamukha worked together to rescue Temujin's kidnapped wife. But after that, the two brothers became rivals for Mongol rule. Jamukha held to tradition by promoting fighters with noble blood. Temujin, on the other hand, promoted his warriors based on merit. He spent several years gaining power and influence and forming alliances with other tribes. In 1206 Temujin defeated his brother and became the supreme leader over all the Mongol tribes. The tribes gave Temujin the title of **Genghis Khan**, sometimes spelled Chinggis Khan, meaning "Great Ruler." By the time Genghis died in 1227, he had established a Mongol empire that spanned Central Asia, from Beijing in northern China to Russia.

Who established the Mongol Empire?

Mongol Unification

Genghis unified the Mongols by developing a government, common laws, and an organized military. Genghis organized the Mongol government by dividing the people into groups of tens, hundreds, thousands, and ten thousands. He also chose trusted followers to lead these groups. Working through these leaders, he led the people in times of battle and peace. In this form of government, a person's loyalty to his leader was supreme. Genghis believed loyalty was one of the greatest character qualities a person could have.

He wrote a law code called the **Great Yasa**, which dealt with every area of life. This law provided military rules, criminal punishments, tax regulations, court procedures, and moral standards. The punishment for many crimes was death. Less severe punishments included beatings and fines. Every Mongol, including the khan (Genghis and his successors), was subject to the law. Genghis used this code to govern his people and prepare them for military conquest.

Mongol Conquests

The Mongols were trained to be warriors from an early age. Warfare was the Mongol way of life. Genghis used this lifestyle to organize his men into a strong, disciplined army. The success of the Mongol army demonstrated the military genius of Genghis Khan. He took full advantage of the Mongols' horsemanship skills in building a well-trained army. Taught to be the ultimate fighting cavalry, the Mongols quickly overran northern China and then turned west to conquer all of Central Asia.

1200

- **1206–1227** Reign of Genghis Khan
- **1209–1215** Invasion of Northern China Jurchen state
- **1218–1220** Conquest of the Khwarazm Empire Central Asia
- **1234** Jurchen state conquered
- **1235** Invasion of Southwest Asia and Persian Gulf region
- **1236–1242** Invasion of Eastern Europe
- **1238** Invasion of the Caucasus
- **1246–1248** Reign of Guyuk Khan
- **1251–1259** Reign of Mongke Khan
- **1253–1260** Invasion of Persia

1260–1294 Reign of Kublai Khan

1268 Renewed invasion of Song dynasty

1271–1370 Yuan dynasty

1275–1292 Marco Polo in China

1277–1292 Invasions of Southeast Asia

1322 Peace treaty with the Egyptian Mamluks

1335 Ilkhanate disintegrates

1363 Chagatai Khanate disintegrates

1370 Yuan dynasty ends

Mongol Army

The Mongol army was a splendid fighting force. It was organized into units of tens, hundreds, and thousands. The soldiers lived in the saddle and even slept while riding on a march to the next battle. They endured all types of hardships in their quest to build an empire. The Mongol horse was well suited for conquest and the extremes of the climate. Soldiers would often change horses several times a day, so vast numbers of them were needed for conquest.

Fast, ruthless, and deadly, the Mongol forces overwhelmed city after city. All who resisted were killed or used as human shields in future battles. The Mongol archer was skilled in battle. Trained to ride at a very young age, the archer learned to string his bow while riding and shoot his arrows when all the horse's hooves were off the ground. This ensured that his arrows would strike their target. Other Mongol weapons included lances and swords.

Mongol Armor

To protect themselves, Mongol horsemen wore stiff armor made from animal hides. Genghis also ordered his soldiers to wear a shirt made of raw silk because arrows could not easily penetrate the silk. Of course, if a man was shot, he was still hurt. But then his fellow soldiers gently pulled the shirt to remove the arrow from the wound. Protected from the arrow tip by the silk, the wound stayed cleaner and usually healed quickly.

? **When did the Mongol soldier shoot his bow?**

Mongol Tactics

How did the Mongol armies trick the peoples they attacked?

Genghis had to develop new fighting methods when his armies began to attack towns instead of other nomads. Many towns were surrounded by moats (trenches filled with water) and thick stone walls. These seemed to be unconquerable barriers at first. The Mongols forced captured engineers to teach them the art of siege warfare. In siege warfare, the Mongol soldiers fired arrows and flaming objects into the cities for weeks. They also kept food from going into the city until the people were starving. The Mongols borrowed rocket technology from the Chinese and fired gunpowder-filled bamboo rockets into the towns. These usually were not accurate but must have terrified those inside the towns.

Another effective tactic used by Genghis and his forces was known as the pretend retreat. The Mongol soldiers would pretend to be beaten and appear to leave their camp empty. When the townspeople came out to plunder the Mongol camp, the Mongols would suddenly reappear. The startled people were unprepared to defend themselves, and the Mongol forces would destroy them. When everything of value had been removed from the town, it too would be destroyed.

The Mongols were ruthless. They killed and destroyed wherever they went. As stories of Mongol cruelty spread, the very name Mongol struck fear in the hearts of their enemies. The Mongols took advantage of this fear and captured towns without a fight as people chose to surrender rather than face certain destruction. Many men who were captured in this manner were used to increase the size of the Mongol forces. Women and children often became slaves.

Mongol Religion

The Mongols worshiped many gods and believed that good and evil spirits controlled the world. They also believed in a supreme god who ruled all the spirits. They called him Tengri, meaning "the great god of heaven." The Mongols lived in fear of the spirits and hoped for blessings from them.

Every ger or yurt had small idols made of felt. The women made these idols at sewing parties. The Mongols believed that these idols protected their families and their animals. Before every meal, they spread food and drink on the lips of the idols. They also prayed to them. They believed that these idols had the power to bless them.

The Mongols also believed that certain men, called shamans, had power over the spirits. The shamans were the priests of the traditional Mongol religion, which is called shamanism. The shamans were medicine men and witch doctors who used a special language when performing their magical rituals. The Mongols often consulted their shamans before making important decisions.

The Mongols showed religious tolerance toward the peoples they conquered. It was partly because they viewed their religion as only for Mongols and partly because they did not want to further anger those they defeated. Some members of Genghis Khan's family even married Nestorian Christians. The later empire of the Mongols included people of many religions, including Christians and Jews. The time of religious liberty that came with the Mongol Empire would prove to be as short-lived as the empire itself.

Division of the Empire

Genghis Khan had four sons: Jochi, Chaghatai, **Ögödei**, and Tolui. He gave each a portion of the empire but wanted Ögödei to take his position as Great Khan. Genghis counseled them to hold the Mongol Empire together. Genghis believed that Ögödei had a better grasp of human nature. Therefore, Genghis thought Ögödei would prove to be the best one to rule. The territory each brother was given to rule was called a **khanate**. The Mongol conquests continued as each brother tried to enlarge his khanate.

Divided Khanate Empire

In 1258 Hülegü Khan, the son of Tolui, led the Ilkhanate and conquered Baghdad and the Abbasid **Caliphate** in the Middle East. Armies from Christian Armenia and Georgia joined the Mongols. There were many religious, political, and economic reasons for this alliance. The thirteen-day siege of Baghdad was an exceptionally brutal battle in which up to 800,000 civilians were killed along with 50,000 caliphate troops. Baghdad's defeat marked the end of the Islamic Golden Age. Mongol forces did not attempt to invade western Europe. Some believe it was because there were not enough open plains to supply food for their horses. Whatever the reason, western Europe was spared from conquest.

? Who was the second Great Khan?

caliphate an Islamic state ruled by a successor of Muhammad

Trading in the Mongol Empire

The Mongols manufactured nothing beyond what they needed for daily living, such as felt, harnesses, and carts. Because they did not stay in one place for a full growing season, they rarely grew crops. The Mongols resorted to trading to obtain other goods. Even before Genghis Khan built his empire, the wealthier Mongols traded fur and hides for Chinese silk and cotton.

As the empire grew, trade grew also. When the Mongols conquered all of China in 1279, their empire reached from the Caspian Sea to the Pacific Ocean.

TURNING POINTS

Pax Mongolica

The Mongols reopened trade along the ancient silk routes, which had been closed for centuries. After nearly a thousand years, the West finally had direct contact with the cultures of the Far East. Between 1100 and the 1200s, the crusaders were traveling from western Europe to fight the Muslims in the Middle East. During this period, Mongol traders brought exotic goods from the Far East into Middle Eastern markets. Western merchants and crusaders carried these goods back to western Europe.

The Mongol conquest of Eurasia (Europe and Asia) ensured unified rule over much of the known world. This created stability the world had not seen since the Roman Empire. This stability was called **Pax Mongolica**, or Mongol Peace. Before the Mongols established this peace, people could expect to be taxed heavily by various rulers and robbed once or twice during their journey on the Silk Road from Europe to China and back. But after the Mongols controlled all the territory that the Silk Road network spanned, writers exaggerated that "a woman with a golden vessel on her head might walk alone without fear or dread."

Not only was trade able to move freely, but scientists, doctors, craftsmen, and missionaries could move about without fear and share their knowledge. It was an early version of the information superhighway. To aid in the flow of information, Genghis Khan even invented a postal system called the Yam. The Yam was an early form of the Pony Express. It had a network of stations where riders carrying messages could rest and get food. A rider would travel 120–190 miles in one day.

When the Italian explorers Niccolo and Matteo Polo first traveled to China in the 1260s, Kublai Khan asked them to send additional Christian missionaries. When **Marco Polo** accompanied his father and uncle on a second trip, he reported Nestorian churches along the Old Silk Road and in major cities. Marco Polo was the most famous European to witness the Mongol empire and the Mongol rule of China. He is famous for his book, *The Travels of Marco Polo*, which fascinated the imaginations of the Europeans.

Pax Mongolica did not come for free. Historians believe that some forty million people died during the Mongol conquests. Diseases like the bubonic plague were able to tag along on the trade ships, ultimately wiping out millions of people in Europe. But the Mongol peace changed the world because it created a European demand for products from the East.

1. List three things that could move freely because of Pax Mongolica.
2. Compare and contrast the effects of Pax Mongolica on the known world to the effects of the internet on the world today.
3. Why do you think robbers did not dare to steal from people traveling on the Silk Road?

CRITICAL THINKING 3.2

1. How might Temujin's experiences in early life have changed him?
2. Why would people sometimes surrender to the Mongols without fighting at all?
3. Why was there religious freedom in the Mongol Empire?

3.3 The Yuan Dynasty (1279–1368)

The region in southern China that the Song Empire ruled was the last large area of Asia to fall to the Mongols. In 1260 **Kublai Khan**, one of Genghis's grandsons, came to power. His priority was to become the ruler of all China. Overcoming strong resistance, Kublai gained control of the Song Empire in 1279. This fulfilled his grandfather's dream of conquering China. Kublai established a new dynasty that he named the **Yuan** ("The Origin") **dynasty**. The Yuan was China's first foreign dynasty. However, Kublai was not content to stop with China. In 1274 he attempted to invade Japan but failed. In 1281 he assembled a larger force and attacked Japan from China and Korea. This attempt also failed. Despite great efforts, Kublai was unable to expand his empire beyond China.

Kublai tolerated the Chinese but staffed the government mostly with Mongols and other non-Chinese. The Yuan dynasty promoted Chinese culture without trying to change it. In the end, the Mongols had no lasting effects on China. By 1368 Mongol rule of China had ended.

GUIDING QUESTIONS

- How did Mongol rule affect the economy, society, and culture in China?
- How did Buddhism spread in Asia?

Kublai Khan

Kublai Khan's Yuan Empire

What country in East Asia did the Mongols fail to conquer?

Yuan Dynasty

Citizenship

The Yuan dynasty separated the people into a four-class system. The highest class belonged to the Mongolian people; in the second class were the Semu, a name for the many peoples from western and central Asia; the third class consisted of the Han people from northern China; and the peoples of the former Song dynasty were the lowest class. The Song Chinese were at the bottom because they were the last people to be defeated. This four-class system helped the Mongols, who were the minority, keep control of the majority.

Justice

The Yuan government offered unequal justice to the four classes. The third and fourth classes, made up of the Chinese, had to answer harder questions, and more of them, on the civil service examinations. For the same crime, different classes were given different punishments. The Mongols in the Yuan dynasty ruled from a law code that borrowed from Chinese and Mongol laws. It was more flexible than the earlier Chinese legal code.

Power

Power remained with the Mongols. But by settling in China, abandoning his nomadic ways, and distancing himself from the greater Mongolian empire, Kublai Khan set the Mongols up for their eventual loss of power in China.

Kublai Khan holding court in China

Religion

Religious freedom returned to China with Mongol rule. Buddhism and Christianity, the two popular foreign religions from the Tang dynasty, were able to flourish again. Buddhism grew dramatically in Yuan China. There was a rivalry between the Taoists and Buddhists. Teachers from the two argued their cases in court. The Taoists claimed that Buddha had converted to their religion. In the end they lost their case, and the khan sided with the Buddhists. Taoism declined, and Buddhism expanded greatly in China with the building of 42,000 monasteries. Kublai Khan favored Buddhism over other religions. But his mother claimed to be a Christian, and the khan was welcoming to Christians. Some Mongol rulers professed Christianity; still, it remained very much a minority religion in China.

Environment

The Mongols changed China by building new cities. Kublai Khan built a capital called Daidu at the site of present-day Beijing. He stopped living in gers, the symbol of nomadic life. Daidu was more accessible to traders than Khara Khorum, the Mongol capital deep in central Asia. When the Mongols conquered China, they destroyed the farmland and the related infrastructure. Kublai Khan sought to repair the farmland and the waterways that supplied the farms.

CRITICAL THINKING 3.3

1. How might Kublai's failure at conquest have caused him to act differently than other khans?
2. How did the Mongols keep control of the people in China?
3. Name the religious group and the people group that probably wanted to see an end to the Yuan dynasty and explain why.

GUIDING QUESTIONS

- What were the Southeast Asian civilizations like?
- How did Southeast Asia resist the Mongol Empire?
- What was the role of religion in Southeast Asia?
- What was the Golden Horde?

Vietnam Before 1471

3.4 Southeast Asian and Russian Civilizations

Vietnam

Champa and Dai Viet Kingdoms

Lying south of China is the land of Vietnam. The natural conditions of heavy rainfall, a hot/humid climate, and fertile soil made the land of Vietnam a superb location for growing rice, enabling a thriving civilization. Much of Vietnam's early history is unknown. However, there is evidence of two kingdoms in this region during this period. The kingdom to the north was called **Dai Viet**. The kingdom called **Champa** occupied the central and southern regions of modern Vietnam. Champa traded with and was influenced by India and China.

By the ninth and tenth centuries, the kingdom of Champa had developed into a thriving civilization. However, during the next five centuries, Dai Viet exerted increasing pressure on Champa. In 1471 troops from Dai Viet invaded and destroyed the capital of Champa. The people of Dai Viet came to be known as the Vietnamese. They gained complete control of the remaining Champa territories in 1832.

Culture and Religion of Vietnam

While the Vietnamese culture is very complex, we can briefly take note of two unique aspects. In early Vietnamese culture, both men and women wore the distinctive ao dai dress. The dress consists of a split tunic worn over trousers. Today only the women wear the ao dai. Another cultural element unique to Vietnam is its water puppetry. Water puppetry involves puppets that stand on water attached to bamboo poles. The water conceals the puppeteers' poles and strings. The puppeteers retell Vietnamese folk tales. The influence of India and China caused the Champa kingdom to import Hinduism and Buddhism. There are many remnants of Hindu temples today. Buddhism came to the north from China in the second century. Still, the Vietnamese retained much of their folk religion.

What crop flourishes in Vietnam?

Vietnamese girls wearing the traditional ao dai dress

A modern water puppet show in Vietnam

Angkor (Cambodia)

Cambodia has a long history that may be traced back as far as 1000 BC. During the AD 200s and beyond, Cambodia was influenced by India and China. An empire known as the **Khmer** developed in this region between the ninth and the thirteenth centuries. Angkor served as the Khmer's center of power. Many capitals were constructed in this area during the empire's peak. In addition, over one thousand temples, including Angkor Wat, were built in this area.

Over time, the Khmer engaged in a series of failed wars with its neighbors and steadily declined in power. In 1432 Angkor was pillaged by the Thai people, from Thailand to the west. The city was later abandoned. Over the next four centuries, the Cambodians were ruled by the Thai and the Vietnamese.

The Angkor Wat temple complex exhibits the influence of Hinduism and Buddhism on Cambodian civilization. The distinct towers represent mythical mountains from Hindu teaching. After Vietnam invaded Angkor in 1177, the Khmer people gave up Hinduism because those gods did not protect them. As the people accepted Buddhism, they then added Buddhist art to the temple.

▲ The Angkor Wat temple in Cambodia

Southeast Asian Resistance to Mongol Rule

Kublai Khan sent forces to conquer Vietnam, Burma, and Java (an island in Indonesia). The people of these countries resisted conquest by the Mongols in 1258, 1282, and 1288. In the final invasion the Mongols were soundly defeated at sea. Despite the Vietnamese success, historians consider these invasions a practical Mongol victory since the Vietnamese kingdoms agreed to submit and pay the Mongols tribute. During this time Kublai Khan also had to contend with another Mongol ruler for control of the empire. Kublai was forced to divert his soldiers to ensure his continued rule there. This diversion preserved Southeast Asia from Mongol domination.

? **What did the Southeast Asian kingdoms do after they defeated the Mongols militarily?**

The Golden Horde (Russia)

Batu Khan, another grandson of Genghis, led Mongol forces into Europe. Between 1237 and 1240 the Mongol forces (known in Europe as Tartars) smashed through Russian defenses. Hungary and Poland were also unable to stop the Mongol advance. A combined force of Poles, Czechs, and Germans tried to stop the Mongols at the **Battle of Liegnitz**. Accounts vary, but the Mongol forces seem to have destroyed this army. However, Batu pulled his soldiers back to the Volga River in Russia. He established an empire in Western Asia known as the **Golden Horde**.

The Mongols had a tremendous influence on the history of Russia. Mongol conquest isolated Russia from western Europe for over two centuries. Asian culture dominated Russia. Russian architecture from this period provides an example of this influence.

Where was the Golden Horde located?

During this time, Moscow developed from a small town to become the capital of Russia. As Moscow became more powerful and influential, the Golden Horde weakened. By 1480 Moscow had become strong enough to lead Russia in overthrowing Mongol rule.

CRITICAL THINKING 3.4

1. Compare and contrast the people, culture, and religion of Vietnam and Cambodia.
2. Compare the geography of Southeast Asia with the lands the Mongols were able to conquer. How might that have been an important factor to their success and failure?
3. How did the Mongols change Russia?

The onion domes on Russian cathedrals show the Asian influence on that culture.

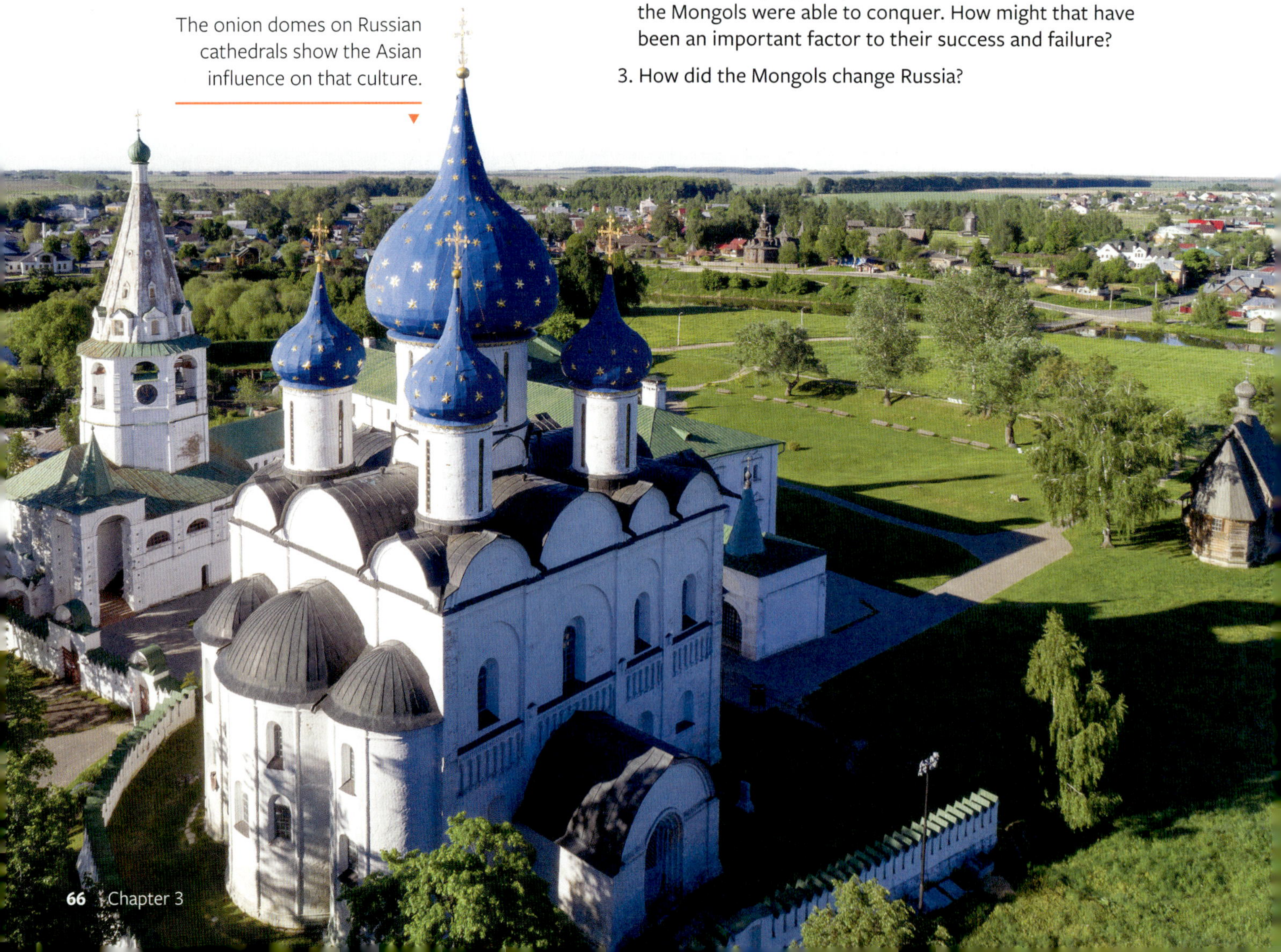

A depiction of the Battle of Ain Jalut

3.5 The Decline and Fall of the Mongol Empire

GUIDING QUESTIONS

- What were Timur's achievements?
- Why did the Mongol Empire fall?

Beginning of the Decline

In 1260 the Mongols were defeated at the **Battle of Ain Jalut**. This defeat proved to be the beginning of the end of the Mongol Empire. When Mongke Khan sought to expand the empire into Egypt, armies from Georgia and Armenia again joined the khan. They met and fought the Mamluks (Egyptians and Syrians) in Galilee north of Jerusalem. The Islamic soldiers took advantage of their knowledge of the territory and made hit-and-run attacks against the Mongols. Eventually, the Mongols committed all their forces and fell for a trap. The Mamluks defeated the Mongols using the same tactics the Mongols had perfected over the centuries.

As Islam was able to retain a homeland in Egypt, the religion spread throughout the Mongol Empire. The khan even converted to Islam. Once the religion became dominant, the Muslims often persecuted other religious groups. Christians and Jews were pressured to convert to Islam. Muslim rulers made Nestorians wear distinctive clothes, such as a yellow patch, marking them as Christians. They required Christians to wear special haircuts and even ride their horses sidesaddle so Muslims could easily identify them.

Timur (Tamerlane)

During the second half of the fourteenth century, another Mongol leader came to power in central Asia. **Timur** suffered from an accident during his youth and was lame. He was called Timur the Lame, or Tamerlane. Despite his physical limitation, Tamerlane became a powerful conqueror. He referred to himself as the "sword of Islam." He forced many to become Muslim. He desired to become the Great Khan, but that was impossible since he was not in the family tree of Genghis Khan. He demonstrated unusual cruelty as he extended his empire from Turkey to India. Tamerlane's forces captured Baghdad and Damascus and defeated the Ottoman Turks. He even invaded southern Russia and weakened the Golden Horde. However, rather than building a well-ruled empire, Tamerlane concentrated on collecting treasures taken in battle. The final blow to Christianity under Mongol rule came during the brutal reign of Tamerlane. He persecuted the Nestorians without restraint.

Tamerlane

Why was Timur called Tamerlane?

Collapse of the Mongol Empire

In the end, the Mongols had forgotten what got them their empire. They quickly developed a desire for the goods they saw. When the Mongols settled into towns and gave up their nomadic ways, they found their zeal for conquest faded. The Great Khans never set up a system for the peaceful transition of power. As a result, they fought each other for control every time a Great Khan died.

Because of this internal fighting, the Mongols' control of China weakened. The Chinese encouraged this fighting and viewed it as a way to break free from Mongol rule. By 1368 the Chinese were able to expel the Mongols from China. The Mongols retreated to their homeland in north-central Asia. The Chinese established the Ming ("brilliant") dynasty. They sought to remove all traces of Mongol rule. The Mughal Empire, a remnant of the southwestern Mongol Empire (mostly in India), lasted until the seventeenth century when the British arrived.

After a century of peaceful trade, the Muslims closed the Silk Road trade network and renewed their attacks on the remnants of the Byzantine Empire. Europeans, now familiar with the goods from the Far East, still wanted them. With the closing of the land routes, Europeans sought to find other ways to the East. As they searched for new routes, the Age of European Exploration began.

What was the last remnant of the Mongol Empire?

CRITICAL THINKING 3.5

1. What is one way Timur was different from the other Mongol conquerors?
2. What was the lasting effect of the Mongol Empire on the world?

Making Connections

1. Who was the first known Christian missionary to China?
2. Why did the Sui dynasty collapse?
3. Who was the only legitimate empress of China?
4. What religion was central to the Song dynasty?
5. What impact did the invention of the compass have for the Chinese?
6. What were the three areas of artistic advancement in the Tang and Song dynasties?
7. What type of lifestyle did the Mongols have?
8. What were the divisions of the Mongol Empire called?
9. What exceptionally bloody battle ended the Islamic golden age?
10. What did Kublai Khan do to improve the environment in China?
11. What was the central-southern kingdom of Vietnam called?
12. What happened at the Battle of Ain Jalut?

WHAT TO KNOW

EVENTS

Pax Mongolica
Battle of Liegnitz
Battle of Ain Jalut

PEOPLE

Alopen
Emperor Taizong
Empress Wu Zetian
Temujin
Genghis Khan
Ögödei
Marco Polo
Kublai Khan
Batu Khan
Timur

PLACES

Grand Canal
Great Wall
Dai Viet
Champa
Khmer
Golden Horde

TERMS

Nestorian church
Sui dynasty
Tang dynasty
Song dynasty
Silk Road
porcelain
technology
Creation Mandate
gers
Great Yasa
khanate
Yuan dynasty

Thinking Critically

1. What does the Bible say regarding the Mongol belief that good and evil spirits control the world? (Refer to Col. 1:17; Ps. 22:28; and Isa. 45:7.)
2. How is Pax Mongolica an example of the principle "peace through strength"?
3. Were the Mongol conquests valid since they brought religious freedom and peace afterward? Explain.
4. What examples from this chapter demonstrate how the main religion changed for political reasons?

A Chinese compass

4 Renaissance and Reformation

1294 – 1563

ESSENTIAL QUESTIONS

- What were the major causes and events of the Renaissance?
- How did the Renaissance influence European thought and culture?
- What were the major causes and events of the Reformation?
- How did the Reformation influence European thought and culture?
- How successful was the Roman Catholic Church in implementing reforms following the Reformation?

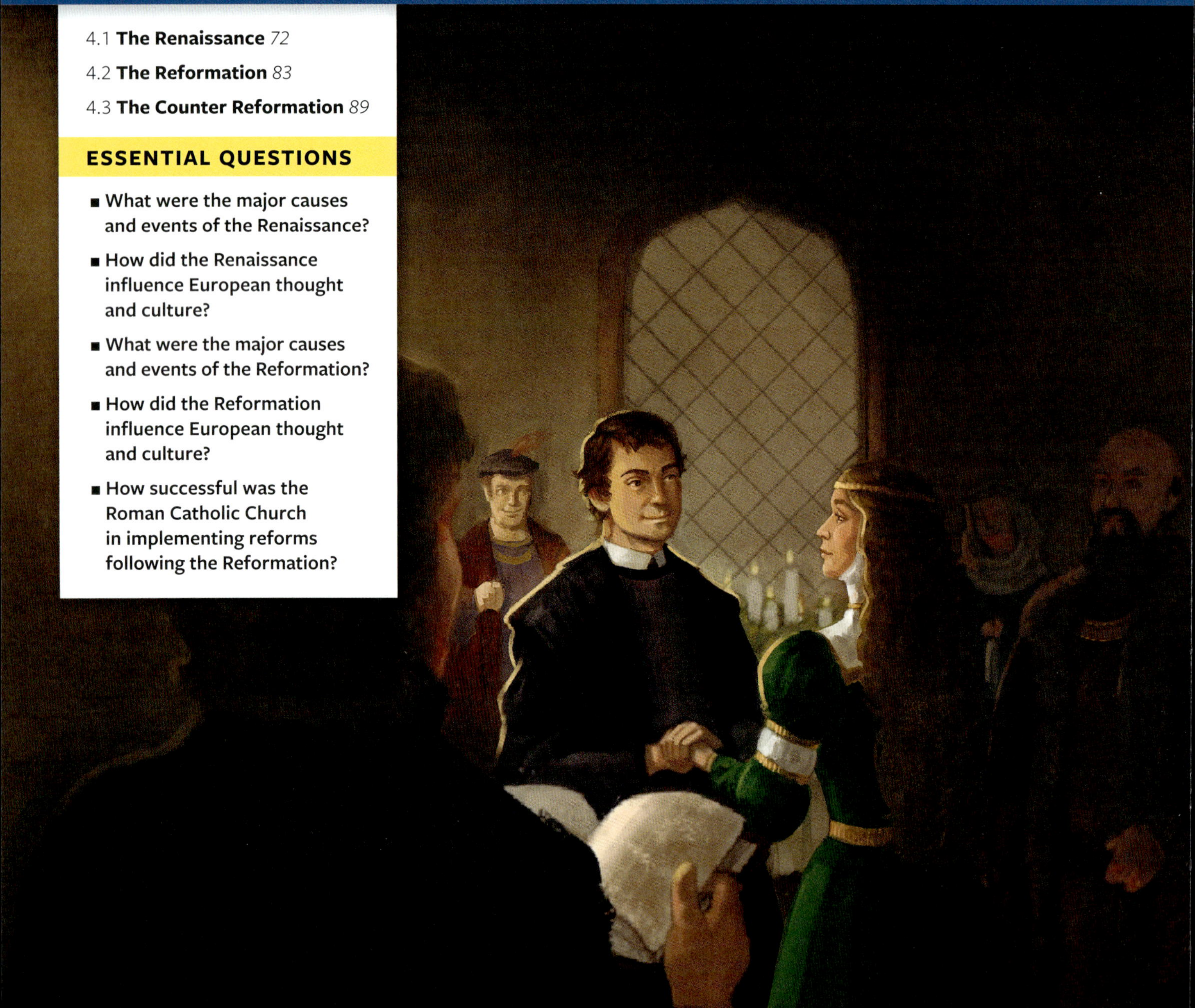

Katharina von Bora Luther

According to tradition, Katharina von Bora was born in 1499. When she was about five years old, Katharina's father sent her to be educated at a cloister (a place where religious groups live isolated from the rest of the world). A few years later she moved to a Cistercian monastery and eventually became a nun.

Katharina was a young adult when reformers began calling for changes in the Catholic Church. She and eleven other nuns became interested in the ideas of the reformers and decided to leave the monastery. That was easier said than done, though. According to Roman Catholic church law, it was illegal for a nun to give up her vows. If the women wanted to leave, they would have to sneak out. They asked a reformer named Martin Luther to help them, and he enlisted the aid of a merchant who delivered fish to the monastery each day. The twelve nuns hid in the merchant's cart and rode undetected out of the monastery grounds and back to the town of Wittenberg.

Once they were back in Wittenberg, the next question was where the women should go. Their families refused to let them come home, fearing trouble with the church, so Luther had to find a place for each woman to stay. In many cases that meant finding husbands for them. Eventually, only Katharina von Bora was left. Katharina was not interested in the first few marriage prospects she was offered. She stated that she would marry only Nicholas von Amsdorf, a university professor, or Luther. Luther hesitated at first but finally decided that marriage would be a good thing for him, and the wedding took place on June 13, 1525.

The leading nobleman in their territory gave Martin and Katharina a group of buildings called the Black Cloister. It was a former monastery that provided a huge place to live and a large farm to help with their support. While Martin preached, wrote, and taught the many students who were interested in the ideas of the reformers, Katharina managed the farm and household. She oversaw the garden and the livestock, cooked, and kept house for the many people who passed in and out of their home. Sometimes as many as thirty students and visitors boarded with them. This was in addition to the Luthers' own six children (four of whom lived to adulthood) and four adopted ones. It is no wonder that Katharina typically got up at 4:00 a.m. to get all her work accomplished!

While Martin was alive, the family prospered. After his death, the salary he received disappeared, and Katharina struggled financially. She also had to flee her home twice, once because of war and once because of bad crops and the Black Death. Still, to the end of her life at age 53, Katharina clung to her faith in Christ and the hope of her salvation through Him.

GUIDING QUESTIONS

- What were some major causes of the Renaissance?
- Did the Renaissance promote a biblical worldview?
- How did the Renaissance spread from Italy to northern Europe?
- How significant were the cultural and technological contributions of the Renaissance?
- How did life change for the people of Europe in early modern times?

4.1 The Renaissance

The **Renaissance** was a transitional period in Europe, bridging the gap between the Middle Ages and the modern world. Renaissance means "rebirth," and some saw the period as the start of something new. Others instead viewed it as the climax of gradual changes that had already been taking place during the Middle Ages. Either way, the Renaissance was notable for its interest in the classical world of ancient Greece and Rome. Scholars of the Renaissance believed that the classical period was superior to their own in its ideas and accomplishments. They wanted to study and imitate the masterpieces of the classical world. This led to an outpouring of literary, artistic, and architectural achievements. It also changed the way people thought about the world.

? **What period did Renaissance scholars look to for inspiration?**

Causes of the Renaissance

? **How did many classical documents reach Europe?**

In Chapter 2 you discovered that crusaders returning to Europe brought back many documents that had been preserved by the Byzantines and Muslims. These documents gave insights into the knowledge of the classical world. In 1453 the city of Constantinople fell to a Muslim people called the Ottoman Turks, causing many scholars from that city to flee to Europe. These scholars brought even more knowledge with them. This flood of information led to a revival of learning. Knowledge about science, medicine, and many other fields improved at an ever-increasing pace. The recovery of ancient knowledge led to more study and new discoveries.

During the Middle Ages life was difficult, and opportunities for education were limited. However, the growth of trade and the rise of towns had led to the expansion of a professional, or middle, class.

The wealth of this new class provided funds to support a revival of learning. Many students could now afford to hire private teachers. In addition, many towns started academies where boys could learn Latin and Greek.

How was the revival of learning funded?

Renaissance teachers encouraged their students to invent, explore, and discover. They also expected students to appreciate and create beauty through art. The goal of a Renaissance education was to make the student a well-rounded person, one who was educated and interested in many fields of study. Paintings, sculptures, and architecture of the period reflected this new spirit.

What was the goal of a Renaissance education?

Worldview of Renaissance Humanists

During the Middle Ages, people had focused mainly on the spiritual side of life. They emphasized their position as part of a group. For example, they were all members of the Roman Catholic Church. They thought much about the future and eternity. This emphasis on eternal things was reflected in their literature, art, and even architecture.

Scholars of the Renaissance began to view things differently. They showed a renewed interest in the practical details of the world around them. They emphasized the importance of people as individuals. Instead of thinking mainly about the future, they began to focus on the past and the present, glorying in man's achievements and potential.

How was the focus of the Renaissance different from the focus of the Middle Ages?

The philosophy that embodied the ideals of the Renaissance is known as **humanism** or **Renaissance humanism**. Humanists based their ideas on the writings of the classical world. They taught subjects that became known as the humanities. These subjects covered human interests and experiences. They included things like literature, philosophy, art, history, grammar, and speech.

Renaissance humanists believed that education could lead people to improve themselves. They wanted to prepare people to live full and virtuous lives, both in private and public.

What subjects did Renaissance humanists teach?

Spread of Renaissance Ideas

Italy

The Renaissance began in the **city-states** of northern Italy. Located strategically between Asia and the rest of Europe, these city-states were able to dominate international trade. They also developed into major centers for banking and manufacturing. Wealth from these activities was used to support the work of writers, artists, and architects.

Italian writers studied and imitated the works of ancient Greece and Rome. They were concerned with advancing human knowledge and promoting acceptable behavior. Three Italian authors stand out especially.

Petrarch

“Sweet air, that circlest round those radiant tresses, And floatest, mingled with them, fold on fold, Deliciously, and scatterest that fine gold, Then twinest it again, my heart's dear jesses.”

Castiglione

“For the courageous are often recognized even more in small things than in great.”

Machiavelli

“It should be observed here that men should either be caressed or crushed; because they can avenge slight injuries, but not those that are very severe. Hence, any injury done to a man must be such that there is no need to fear his revenge.”

Petrarch searched for ancient manuscripts and studied them. He composed poetry in Latin and followed the style of ancient Roman poets. Petrarch spread the ideas of the Renaissance and became known as the Father of Humanism.

Castiglione wrote a famous book on **etiquette**. Good manners were considered essential to members of the growing middle class, who were eager to behave properly. Castiglione's book, *The Courtier*, described proper conduct for the Renaissance man.

Machiavelli worked for the government in Florence, Italy, and observed political events in Europe. From his observations he wrote a book called *The Prince*. The political philosophy of the Middle Ages had been heavily influenced by the Bible and the Greeks, who wrote works on the virtues that a good prince should possess. But Machiavelli taught that those who lived by biblical and classical virtues might not always be able to gain or keep power. If a virtue helped a ruler gain power, the ruler should use it. If not, the ruler should disregard it. In this way Machiavelli represented the Renaissance trend of replacing religious tradition with human reason.

?

How did Petrarch, Castiglione, and Machiavelli shape the ideas of the Italian Renaissance?

city-state a city that forms an independent political unit
etiquette behavior that is considered acceptable within a society

Northern Europe

As citizens from the northern part of Europe traveled to Italy, they encountered Renaissance ideas. Northern Europe developed its own interest in the classical world. This interest took a slightly different focus, however. Writers of northern Europe tended to emphasize religious issues. They often gave more attention to Christian rather than classical sources. This trend led to a philosophy known as **Christian humanism**. Christian humanists wanted to return Christianity to the simple values they believed it emphasized in the early days of the church. To do this, they went back to biblical manuscripts and writings of the early church fathers. Two authors provide a good example of this trend.

Erasmus of Rotterdam (in Holland) was one of the most highly regarded and influential of the Christian humanists. He believed that people must have access to the Scriptures if they were going to live their lives according to its teaching. He mastered Latin and Greek and was the first to publish a Greek New Testament, using the earliest manuscripts he could find as his sources. He also published a new version of the Latin Bible.

Sir Thomas More was a close friend of Erasmus. He was both a devout member of the Catholic Church and an official in the court of King Henry VIII of England. His work *Utopia* (which means "nowhere") presented a view of an ideal country that would operate according to reason rather than self-centered motivations like greed.

? **How did writers of northern Europe differ from those of Italy?**

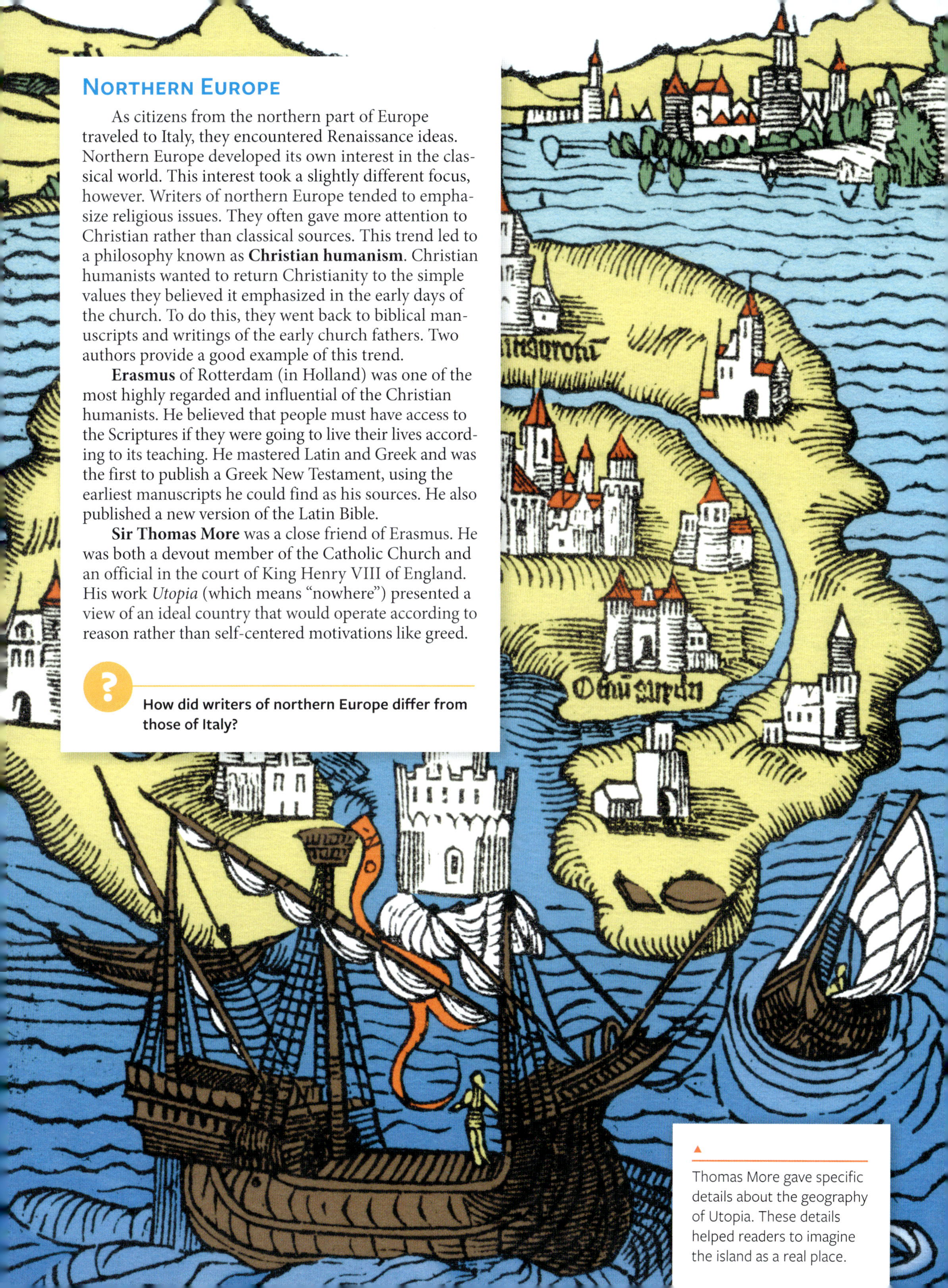

▲ Thomas More gave specific details about the geography of Utopia. These details helped readers to imagine the island as a real place.

Florence

Power

City-states like Florence faced civil war regularly as rival groups competed for power. Often one person (*signori*) or a few people (oligarchy) came out on top. Many rulers abused their power for personal gain. While pretending to enforce the law, they covered up their own corruption. Or they took complete control over making, enforcing, and interpreting laws, preventing any checks on their power.

Florence was known for its high-quality textiles, especially wool and silk.

Notaries recorded official transactions like property sales.

Citizenship

Citizenship was important in Florence. Only citizens had a say in the government. Most residents of Florence did not qualify to be citizens, though. Citizenship was determined by a person's property, length of residence, and social status.

Justice

The Ciompi Revolt was a rebellion of workers in the wool industry in Florence. Only workers who belonged to a **guild** could participate in the government. The *ciompi* (wool workers) wanted the right to establish their own guild so they could have a voice in the government. They also objected to the high taxes they were forced to pay. The *ciompi* had their demands met for a time, but they were eventually defeated.

guild people of the same occupation (e.g., cloth-makers) who work together to set up rules for their occupation and to protect themselves from competition

Religion

Renaissance humanism, although not rejecting Christianity, tended to emphasize humans rather than God. This emphasis led to the weakening of moral restraints. Instead of setting a righteous example, many Renaissance clergy lived in great wealth and immorality.

Environment

The location of Florence contributed to its development. The Arno River, together with streams that flow into it, provided an abundant water supply for the people of Florence. Among other things, the water supported their growing cloth industry.

Johannes Gutenberg

Johannes Gutenberg was born in the German town of Mainz in the late 1300s to an aristocratic family. We do not know a lot about his personal life apart from what shows up in some financial records. But we can determine that he was good at metal-working, that he sometimes borrowed money to fund his work as an inventor, and that he had some legal trouble with partners.

Gutenberg made a name for himself through his work on the movable-type printing press. Gutenberg's printing press was different from previous presses in at least three ways. Its type (blocks that contained letters or characters for printing) were made of a strong metal alloy, its ink was thick enough to transfer images from metal to paper, and its press had the strength to transfer images consistently.

Printing processes used before Gutenberg were slow and expensive. Books tended to be available only to the very wealthy. The printing press, however, made books available quickly and at a cost that many more people could afford.

Cultural and Technological Achievements of Renaissance Europe

Books

Books helped spread Renaissance ideas. This was true both because more people were reading books and because more books were available. During the Middle Ages, European writers had begun to write in the common languages of the people. This practice continued and expanded during the Renaissance. Works produced in the languages of the people captured a wider reading audience. In addition, as citizens became more prosperous, they had more time to read and discuss the new ideas.

Two technological developments aided the ability to publish books and, therefore, to make more books available. One was the production of paper during the thirteenth century. The other was the invention of the movable-type printing press by Johannes Gutenberg in the mid-1400s.

? **Why were books able to spread Renaissance ideas to many people?**

Art

The two paintings on this page show the same subject: the Madonna and Child (Mary and Jesus). The first one comes from a medieval church. The second was painted during the Renaissance. They clearly look different, but at first glance it may be difficult to tell why. A closer look reveals how the Renaissance artists made their paintings look different.

One key difference is that the people in the Renaissance painting look real, whereas the people in the other painting look flat. Renaissance artists had begun to study how bones and muscles work together. The artists learned about **anatomy**—the structure of humans, animals, and plants. Using this information, they could make their subjects appear more realistic. The change toward realism reflected the change away from the emphasis on purely heavenly things in the Middle Ages. Instead of painting flat people who were only symbols of the saints, Renaissance painters painted real people.

The Renaissance artist also added dimension to figures by **shading**. You can see that some parts of the faces, bodies, and clothes are darker. This shading makes these areas seem farther away. The Renaissance artist painted nearer areas lighter and farther areas darker to make objects and figures appear rounded. The gradually changing colors in the folds of cloth show this technique especially well.

In Renaissance painting, the background seems to be far away. The Renaissance artist gave depth to his background by painting faraway objects smaller than nearby objects. The ability to give depth to paintings was the result of the new study of **perspective**. The artist could figure out mathematically what size objects should be and at what angle they should be placed to give the appearance of reality. A Renaissance artist had to be a good mathematician as well as a painter.

?

How did Renaissance artists show that things were closer or farther away?

The *Last Supper* was painted on the wall of the dining room in the monastery of Santa Maria delle Grazie in Milan, Italy.

The *Mona Lisa* is likely a picture of Italian noblewoman Lisa Gherardini. It is considered perhaps the most valuable painting in the world.

Michelangelo painted more than 300 figures on the ceiling of the Sistine Chapel, many of them telling key stories from the Old Testament.

Two men stand out as Renaissance artists, both from Italy. **Leonardo da Vinci** painted *The Last Supper* and the *Mona Lisa*. **Michelangelo** is best known for his painting on the ceiling of the **Sistine Chapel** in Rome. He worked on this project for four years while lying on tall platforms.

What significant paintings were produced by Leonardo da Vinci and Michelangelo?

Sculpture

The sculptures of the Renaissance resemble the sculptures of the Greeks and Romans. The statues are lifelike, powerful, and stunning. The new knowledge of anatomy helped sculptors in forming human figures. Working with stone or bronze, they tried to make their figures as realistic as possible.

Much medieval sculpture was relief sculpture. That is, it was attached to a flat surface such as the wall of a cathedral or castle. This type of sculpture could not be viewed from all sides. Many Renaissance sculptors preferred to make freestanding statues. They followed the principles of classical art: balance, harmony, and realism. But even in relief sculpture, Renaissance works differed from medieval sculpture. By rounding the figures, showing anatomy, and following the rules of perspective, the artist brought flat sculpture to life. One of the greatest examples of Renaissance relief sculpture is the doors sculpted by Lorenzo Ghiberti for the baptistery of Florence.

Michelangelo's sculpture of David is one of the most famous works of the Renaissance.

Scenes from Ghiberti's doors to the baptistery in Florence

Ghiberti's self-portrait in one of the doors

Cathedral of Florence (Cathedral of Santa Maria del Fiore)

Architecture

Renaissance architecture rejected most of the Gothic style. Architects came to believe that pointed arches, tall towers, and flying buttresses were neither graceful nor beautiful. Instead, they wanted to return to the architectural style of the Greeks and Romans. Rounded arches, columns, and domes characterized Renaissance structures.

The Cathedral of Florence is a stunning example of Renaissance architecture. Filippo Brunelleschi designed the dome for this huge structure, solving several architectural problems to do so. The dome is eight-sided, double-walled, and made of over four million bricks. It weighs about thirty-seven thousand tons.

How did architectural features of the Renaissance differ from those of the medieval period?

The Renaissance Man

The ideal Renaissance man was one with a variety of accomplishments. Leonardo da Vinci was an excellent example of such a person. He excelled in sculpture, architecture, painting, music, and poetry. He also studied anatomy, botany, engineering, and mathematics. His notebooks were filled with sketches of inventions, including early versions of a tank, a submarine, a helicopter, and a machine gun.

What was the ideal Renaissance man like?

(Below left) The "Vitruvian Man" was intended to show ideal human proportions. Da Vinci based the drawing on an idea by the Roman architect Vitruvius, who stated that a human in different positions would fit perfectly within a circle and a square. (Below right) Da Vinci included designs for a giant crossbow in his notebooks. Da Vinci's notebooks were unusual in that notes were written backwards.

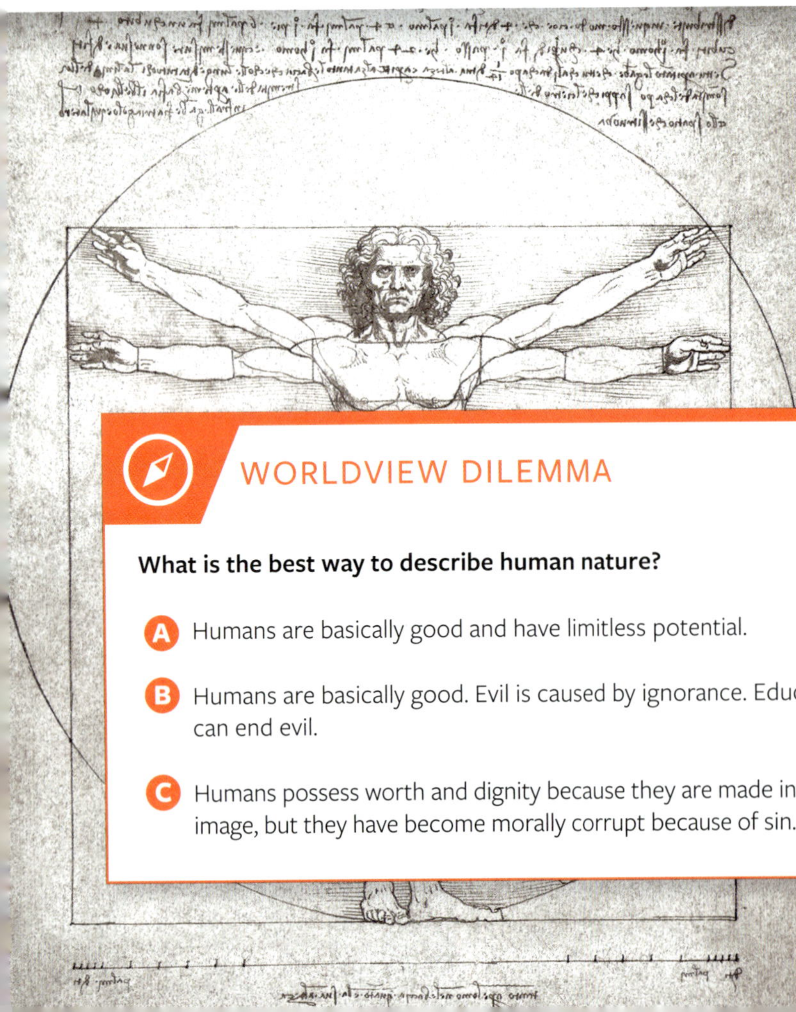

Worldview Dilemma

What is the best way to describe human nature?

A Humans are basically good and have limitless potential.

B Humans are basically good. Evil is caused by ignorance. Education can end evil.

C Humans possess worth and dignity because they are made in God's image, but they have become morally corrupt because of sin.

Changing Social Trends in Early Modern Europe

Society in early modern Europe continued to move away from the feudal structure of the Middle Ages. As more people moved to towns and cities, fewer remained on manors. Wealth became concentrated in trade and finance instead of agriculture. Many of the old landholding nobility married into wealthy urban families to keep their position in society, and a new class of nobles developed.

Life changed significantly for peasants also. Many were released from the obligations of serfdom as Europe adapted to a money economy. Peasants paid rent to live in their homes, and lords paid workers wages to work their fields. Many peasants died in the Black Death, and the labor of those who remained became more valuable.

How was wealth usually acquired by people of towns and cities?

4.2 The Reformation

GUIDING QUESTIONS

- What were some major causes of the Reformation?
- Who were the key reformers of the Reformation?
- How do the key ideas of the Reformation compare with biblical teaching?
- How did the Reformation spread through the countries of Europe?
- What political and religious changes did the Reformation cause?

Causes of the Reformation

Over the centuries writings of early church fathers, anonymous works, and traditions had become authoritative **doctrines** in the Roman Catholic Church. Some protested that these doctrines did not always match the teaching of Scripture. They also protested corrupt practices that they observed among some leaders in the church. Those who protested these things would later become known as **Protestants**.

What was a Protestant?

Doctrine

The most significant doctrinal difference of the Reformation was over the doctrine of salvation. The Catholic Church taught that salvation depended on God's grace but that human works were needed in addition to that grace. It denied that faith in Christ's atoning work was enough to receive salvation. Catholic teaching in this area influenced ideas such as **penance** (performing certain deeds to help earn forgiveness of sins) and **purgatory** (a place people go after death to finish atoning for sin before being allowed into heaven).

Another doctrine that some disagreed with was the church's practice of mass. The church taught that the wine and bread changed into the very blood and body of Christ each time the priest recited the Latin phrase *hoc est corpus meum* ("this is my body"). This teaching is known as **transubstantiation**, and it is still held by the Catholic Church today.

A third doctrine that was questioned was the need for believers to confess their sins to a human priest. The church taught that the priest was empowered to forgive sin. Therefore, church members were not encouraged to seek direct access to God.

What doctrines of the Catholic Church were disputed by Protestants?

doctrines basic beliefs of an organization

Practices

The Catholic Church had lost some of the people's confidence because of the Black Death. The behavior of many of the clergy and popes during the Renaissance further reduced respect for the church. Two events especially, the **Great Schism** and the sale of indulgences (see Turning Point on page 85), hurt the church's reputation.

Pope Boniface VIII (1294–1303) tried to strengthen the power of the Catholic Church by issuing a decree that everyone, including kings, had to submit to the pope to be saved. This was a bold statement, but Boniface did not have the power to enforce the decree. Instead, he was removed from office by an invading French force.

For the next seventy years, the French and Italians struggled for control of the papacy. Beginning in 1378 there was a French pope and an Italian pope at the same time, a division that became known as the Great Schism. To try to resolve this problem, a third man was chosen to become pope, but that only resulted in there being three popes. The problem was finally solved by the Council of Constance (1414–18). All three men were convinced to step down, and Martin V became the next pope. However, this struggle left many in the church shaken and doubting.

To try to repair the damage, church officials decided to use church **councils** to resolve any future issues. This would limit the power of the pope and seek to restore confidence in the Roman Catholic Church. However, this movement was short-lived as popes resisted limitations on their authority.

The French pope lived in the town of Avignon, while the Italian pope lived in the city of Rome.

What was the Great Schism?

Other Factors

Ongoing changes in European society prepared many for acceptance of the reformers' ideas. First, strong nation-states were developing, and their leaders sometimes clashed with church officials who claimed universal authority. Second, members of the new middle class were willing to embrace change, and they often stood in favor of the ideas proposed by the reformers. They also were becoming wealthy, and they opposed having to send money to Rome to support the Catholic Church. Third, the Renaissance interest in writings of the classical world led to a desire to find and study biblical manuscripts. In addition, the Renaissance emphasis on the individual fit well with the Reformation belief in a direct, personal relationship with God.

What prepared European society to accept the ideas of the Reformation?

Contributions of Reformers

Forerunners

John Wycliffe (1320–84) was a pastor, teacher, and theologian in England. He rejected the authority of the papacy and much of the authority claimed by the Roman Catholic Church. Wycliffe taught that an individual became part of the church of Jesus Christ through an invisible, miraculous work of the Holy Spirit. Once made a part of the body of Christ, a believer could not be excluded by anyone: pope, council, or bishop. Wycliffe produced the first Bible in the English language. His translation played a key role in a later English Bible known as the King James Version.

English reformer and scholar John Wycliffe

John Huss (c. 1372–1415) was a pastor in Bohemia (modern-day Czech Republic) who was influenced by Wycliffe's teachings. Huss also spoke out against the claims of the papacy and the corruption of the Roman Catholic Church. He was called to defend himself at the Council of Constance and was promised that he would be safe if he came. Instead, Huss was tried and burned at the stake for his teachings.

Bohemian reformer John Huss

Who were important forerunners to the Protestant Reformation?

councils meetings of top church officials

TURNING POINTS

Luther's Break with Catholicism

An **indulgence** is a paper that grants pardon from the punishment of sins. Indulgences had been granted for centuries to people in the Catholic Church who performed good works and prayers. However, Pope Leo X (1513–21) decided to use indulgences as a type of fundraiser. He needed money to finish building St. Peter's Basilica in Rome, so he allowed agents to sell indulgences. One agent, Johann Tetzel, sold them near Wittenberg, Germany, where a man named **Martin Luther** was a priest.

▲ St. Peter's Basilica is the largest church in the world, able to hold about 60,000 people.

Martin Luther had become a monk after a frightening experience during a thunderstorm. He studied the writings of the church fathers and prepared to be a priest. As he continued his studies, he began to read the Scriptures. Luther learned Greek and Hebrew so he could study the Scriptures in their original languages. He struggled with the fact that he was a sinner and often went to his superior to make confession. The head of Luther's monastery pointed him to the Bible. Eventually, Luther was appointed to preach at the church in Wittenberg.

When Luther learned that Tetzel was selling indulgences to his congregation, he became angry. Luther wanted to debate the value of indulgences and so followed the custom of the day, writing his arguments on a sheet of paper and posting it for debate on October 31, 1517. These ninety-five points of disagreement are commonly called Luther's Ninety-Five Theses. Although he wrote them in Latin, they were quickly printed in German and read by many citizens.

recant to officially reject an earlier position

“82. [The people ask] such questions as the following: Why does the pope not empty purgatory, for the sake of holy love and for the sake of desperate souls that are there, if he redeems an infinite number of souls for the sake of miserable money with which to build a church?”

The Catholic Church ignored Luther for a time but finally threatened to dismiss him from the church in 1520. This action, known as **excommunication**, denied him the possibility of salvation according to church teaching. By this time, though, Luther had discovered the truth found in Romans 1:17: “The just shall live by faith.” He concluded that salvation is a gift of God that cannot be earned.

At first Luther believed that he could reform the Catholic Church from within by debate. However, he eventually realized that his efforts were not going to be successful. When he was ordered to **recant** in 1521, he sealed his break with the Catholic Church, telling the assembly, “If, then, I am not convinced by proof from Holy Scripture . . . and if my judgment is not in this way brought into subjection to God's Word, I neither can nor will retract anything.”

Luther went on to translate the New Testament and then the whole Bible into German. This work was printed many times, and copies spread throughout Germany. He also wrote an official statement of beliefs called the Augsburg Confession. Through Luther's preaching and writings, the ideas of the Protestant Reformation spread far across Europe and took permanent hold in the hearts of many people.

1. What was Johann Tetzel doing in Wittenberg?
2. What were the Ninety-Five Theses?
3. How did Martin Luther help spread the ideas of the Protestant Reformation?

Swiss reformer Ulrich Zwingli

Reformers

Ulrich Zwingli

Ulrich Zwingli (1484–1531) was born in the German-speaking area of Switzerland. He became acquainted with Erasmus, who encouraged him to study the Bible. Zwingli became a priest in the Roman Catholic Church but was displeased with the corruption he found there. In 1519 he became the preacher at the largest church in Zurich, an important Swiss city-state.

Zwingli read some of Luther's writings, and he too realized that salvation comes by grace through faith. Just as Luther had written Ninety-Five Theses, Zwingli wrote Sixty-Seven Conclusions. Zwingli rejected Catholic doctrines such as the mass, celibacy (staying single) of the clergy, purgatory, and the supremacy of the pope.

Civil war broke out in Switzerland between city-states still loyal to Rome and ones that embraced the Reformation. Zwingli joined the conflict in 1531 as a chaplain. He was killed in battle as he attempted to help a wounded soldier. However, his work was carried on by his followers in Zurich.

Anabaptists

There was another group in Switzerland that followed Zwingli in the early days of the Reformation. However, by 1525 they had become impatient with Zwingli's slow reforms that were subject to approval by the magistrates (city rulers). They called themselves the Swiss Brethren, but their rejection of infant baptism soon earned them the name **Anabaptists** (those who baptize again). The Anabaptists spread throughout Switzerland, Germany, and the Netherlands. They fled from country to country and often were persecuted for their beliefs.

One distinct belief of Anabaptists was that state churches were unbiblical. Many rulers in northern Europe especially had embraced Protestantism and established official state churches based on the reformers' teaching. (For example, many German princes established "Lutheran" churches based on the reforms of Martin Luther.) Because everyone within a territory was officially a member of the state church, many congregations included both godly and ungodly members. Most Anabaptists refused to attend a state church. Instead, they insisted that true believers should be members of local churches that were free of state control.

Some Anabaptists also concluded that Christians should not serve in government. One Anabaptist writer noted that since Christ did not judge in worldly disputes, neither should Christians (Luke 12:14).

John Calvin

John Calvin (1509–64) was born in France and became a leading figure in the Reformation. Calvin ministered from Geneva, Switzerland, due to the hostility of the French government toward Protestant believers. Shortly after leaving France, Calvin wrote the first edition of his *Institutes of the Christian Religion*. He addressed the king of France in the preface. He wanted the king to understand that Protestants simply believed what the Bible taught. But his main purpose for writing the *Institutes* was to teach the basics of Christianity so that people, especially his own French people, would live godly lives. In the opening line of the *Institutes*, Calvin wrote that knowledge of God and knowledge of ourselves are mutually connected. If we are to know ourselves rightly, we must know God. As a pastor in Geneva, Calvin pursued this goal, the knowledge of God, in the sermons he preached and in the many commentaries he wrote.

For Calvin, knowing God meant living a life of godliness. When certain citizens of Geneva acted wickedly, Calvin would not let them participate in the Lord's Supper. This angered the leaders of Geneva. For a time they exiled Calvin from the city. Eventually, however, he was invited back.

Calvin's teaching was not free from controversy. His name is often associated with the doctrine of predestination. Calvin taught that no sinner would come to God on his own. Therefore, God chose to give grace to people of His choosing so that they would repent and believe. This doctrine was controversial then and continues to be so today.

Nonetheless, many persecuted Protestants found refuge in Geneva. Calvin saw the city as a missionary training center and founded a school there. Persecuted Christians would come to Geneva, receive training, and then return to evangelize their own people. Calvin especially wanted to see the gospel take root in his own homeland of France. He sent hundreds of missionaries into France to plant churches, and many died as martyrs. In addition, his written works were smuggled into France to educate and encourage the Christians who remained despite persecution.

? Who were key reformers in Switzerland?

French theologian and reformer John Calvin

While there were doctrinal and practical differences between Luther, Zwingli, Calvin, and other reformers, they all agreed on three key Reformation doctrines.

Key Doctrines of the Reformation

Scripture Alone

The reformers pointed out that Scripture and tradition often conflicted. However, God's Word is inspired, while man's traditions are not. Therefore, Scripture is the only reliable authority on anything it speaks of.

Faith Alone

As each reformer read the Bible, he discovered that salvation cannot be earned but is a gift received by faith. The sacraments of the Catholic Church had no power to save. The reformers taught that a person is saved by faith in Christ's shed blood alone.

Priesthood of the Believer

The reformers emphasized that people had to come to God as individuals. Upon receiving salvation through Christ, each person is made a priest. In other words, each believer has direct access to the saving benefits of Christ. The Roman Catholic Church taught that priests stood between individuals and God. However, the reformers said that Jesus was the only mediator people needed.

? What were three key ideas of the Reformation?

Christianity in Europe, c. 1600

Spread of the Reformation

The Reformation spread throughout Europe, including regions such as Germany, Switzerland, France, and England. The printing press made possible the rapid publication and spread of Reformation writings and Bibles. Protestants who were persecuted in one region fled to other regions and helped to spread the scriptural truths rediscovered during the Reformation. Despite political and religious opposition, the Reformation could not be contained.

Results of the Reformation

Freedom

The reformers opposed spiritual oppression. This prepared the way for a greater emphasis on freedom in many areas of European life. Limited religious freedom was given to those who lived under a prince who shared their religion. However, the Anabaptists sought full religious freedom—the right to worship according to one's own conscience no matter where one lived.

Citizenship

The reformers emphasized the role of Christians in society. They taught their followers that God desired servants who worked not for their own glory but for God's glory (1 Cor. 10:31). Christians are responsible to God for how they use their talents and abilities. Unlike the Renaissance humanists, the reformers said that a person should dedicate his talents to God, not himself.

The reformers also encouraged Christians to work hard at their occupations. They taught that everything a believer does is to honor God. They encouraged their followers to be a testimony of God's grace as they performed their daily tasks.

Family Life

The reformers knew families were a gift from God. Each member had an important role: a husband who loved his wife as Christ loved the church (Eph. 5:25), a wife who faithfully and lovingly followed her husband, and children who learned from their parents how to honor and serve the Lord.

Education

Many of the reformers were well-educated. They often knew Latin, Greek, and Hebrew, and some had read many ancient manuscripts. Therefore, the reformers placed a high priority on teaching everyone to read and to study diligently. Luther, Calvin, Zwingli, and many other reformers established schools and made education a priority.

Following Luther's example, many reformers also translated the Bible into the languages of the people. This enabled the people to read God's Word for themselves. In addition, books and pamphlets were printed, and the people learned about many subjects related to the Reformation.

Critical Thinking 4.2

In what ways might the Reformation have helped to influence culture in the modern world? (Think about the results of the Reformation that were stated in the text.)

4.3 The Counter Reformation

The Roman Catholic Church was slow to react to the initial development of the Reformation. However, as church leaders realized how quickly the Protestant movement was spreading, the reaction quickened. The Catholic reaction is officially known as the Counter Reformation, or sometimes the Catholic Reformation. It took a two-pronged approach: renew a spirit of religious devotion within the church and respond to challenges to church doctrine from Protestants.

GUIDING QUESTIONS

- How did the Roman Catholic Church respond to the Reformation?
- How do the key ideas of the Counter Reformation compare with biblical teaching?
- What were the wars of religion?

Reform of Church Practice

From popes to peasants, many realized that the Catholic Church of the Renaissance period needed reform. Attempts were made to abolish corrupt practices (like selling church offices for financial gain or collecting a salary for a church office without doing any work for it). In addition, reforming organizations inspired the founding of new religious orders (groups that live isolated from society and follow a certain set of rules). Three new orders, the Theatine, the Capuchin, and the Ursuline, focused on reform and physical care of the people and gained much good will for the church through their efforts.

The most influential reform effort was likely the founding of the Society of Jesus, or **Jesuits**, who were chosen especially for their preaching ability. The Jesuits sought to suppress heresy (Protestantism), promote Roman Catholic education, and spread the Catholic faith to other countries.

Jacques Marquette, well known for his explorations in the Great Lakes and Upper Mississippi Valley, was a Jesuit missionary to Native American tribes.

Inquisition

An **Inquisition** was an organization that was set up by the church or sometimes a government to find and remove what the Catholic Church defined as heresy. Following the pattern of the Spanish Inquisition of 1480 (which also targeted Jews and Muslims), Pope Paul III organized an Inquisition in 1542 to combat the gains of the Protestant Reformation. Courts that acted as agents of the Inquisition assumed that anyone who was accused of heresy was guilty. Many were arrested at night, taken before an inquisitor, and told to confess their errors. The accused were not allowed to know the charges or who had brought the accusation. Failure to confess could possibly lead to torture and being burned at the stake. Other members of one's family could also be arrested, and property might be taken.

Galileo Galilei appeared before the Roman Inquisition in April of 1633 to defend his scientific positions.

Index of Prohibited Books

What strategies did the Catholic Church use for stopping the spread of Reformation ideas?

When the Catholic Church realized the impact that printed materials were having on the spread of the Reformation, the church published a list called the **Index of Prohibited Books**. The church prohibited Catholics from reading anything that appeared on the list. Most versions of the Bible and all Protestant literature were prohibited.

Council of Trent

Another response to the challenges from Protestantism was the calling of a council. Known as the **Council of Trent**, it met several times over a twenty-year period.

The council wrote a statement of Roman Catholic beliefs and practices. This was the first written statement that contained all Catholic doctrines. The council members confirmed the authority of both Scripture and tradition. They insisted that both faith and works were necessary to receive justification (the act of declaring someone righteous). They also preserved the doctrine of a human priesthood that stood between God and the individual. Essentially, the church made no changes in its doctrine. Instead, the council ordered corrupt practices to stop, removed many corrupt clergy, and set stricter standards of discipline.

Catholic bishops met together in a series of council meetings to respond to challenges to the church's doctrine and practice.

Wars of Religion

Much of northern Europe had accepted Protestantism (although Poland and modern-day Belgium were brought back to Catholicism through the efforts of the Counter Reformation). Southern Europe, most especially Spain and Italy, remained strongly Catholic. Divisions in Europe over the Reformation led to a series of wars in the 1500s and 1600s that are sometimes collectively known as the wars of religion. The outcomes of these wars helped set the religious and cultural direction not only for each region of Europe but also for other parts of the world that Europeans colonized. (See Chapter 7 for a discussion of specific wars.)

Which regions of Europe embraced Protestantism, and which remained primarily Catholic?

CRITICAL THINKING 4.3

What did the Council of Trent show about the views of church officials on problems with the Catholic Church?

Making Connections

1. What caused the revival of learning that prompted the Renaissance?
2. What Renaissance ideas originated with Italian writers?
3. How did Renaissance thought influence northern Europe?
4. What role did books play in the spread of Renaissance ideas?
5. How did social patterns change for nobles and peasants during the early modern period?
6. What doctrines and practices of the Catholic Church did reformers protest?
7. How did Martin Luther help challenge the church's teaching on salvation?
8. How did the Reformation change European society?
9. What was the two-pronged approach of the Counter Reformation?
10. Identify which countries embraced Protestantism and which remained Catholic.
11. How did the Reformation affect interactions between European countries?

WHAT TO KNOW

PEOPLE

Petrarch
Castiglione
Machiavelli
Erasmus
Sir Thomas More
Leonardo da Vinci
Michelangelo
John Wycliffe
John Huss
Martin Luther
Ulrich Zwingli
Anabaptists
John Calvin
Jesuits

PLACES

Sistine Chapel

TERMS

Renaissance humanism
Renaissance humanism
city-states
etiquette
Christian humanism
guild
anatomy
shading
perspective
doctrines
Protestants
penance
purgatory
transubstantiation
Great Schism
councils
indulgence
excommunication
recant
Inquisition
Index of Prohibited Books
Council of Trent

Thinking Critically

1. How does biblical teaching about human nature compare with the Renaissance view?
2. How did the cultural achievements of the Renaissance reflect the Renaissance focus on humans?
3. How do the three key ideas of the Reformation compare with Scripture? (See Rom. 1:16–17, 2 Tim. 3:16, and 1 Pet. 2:5.)
4. How do the decisions of the Council of Trent compare with Scripture? (See verses above and Eph. 2:8–9, Rom. 5:1, Gal. 2:16, and 1 Tim. 2:5.)

One of the great achievements of Gutenberg's movable-type press was the printing of the Gutenberg Bible, completed around 1455.

5 AGE OF EUROPEAN EXPLORATION

1352 – 1541

ESSENTIAL QUESTIONS

- Why did Europeans decide to cross the oceans?
- What were the civilizations in Central and South America like?
- What resulted from European encounters with other civilizations?

Leif Ericson

In the late 800s the Vikings, men from Norway, Sweden, and Denmark, began to explore other lands. Some came to inhabited areas such as Ireland, England, France, Spain, and Italy, burning and pillaging as they went. Others settled peaceably within some of those lands. Still others discovered new lands to possess for themselves.

One land the Vikings inhabited was Iceland. The Vikings might have been content to stay in Iceland, but one Icelander, Erik the Red, was banished from his home for three years. So he traveled west in search of a new home. Erik found a new island and named this barren sheet of glacial ice Greenland to draw settlers whom he could lead. When his banishment was over, Erik went back to Iceland and enlisted one thousand people to come back to Greenland to settle. Erik the Red's son, **Leif Ericson**, traveled to Norway, where he became a Christian. He returned to Greenland to bring the Good News.

In 986 a trader named Bjarni Herjólfsson was sailing to Greenland to find his father. Storms blew him and his crew far off course. When they finally sighted land, it was green and heavily wooded, not at all like the descriptions of Greenland. Eventually, they found their way to Greenland and reported the land they had seen. What they had sighted were the islands off the east coast of present-day Canada.

Knowledge of this other land would send Leif Ericson to explore for himself in 1001. With thirty-five men, Leif set off for the western lands. He would be the first European to set foot in North America. He named these lands Helluland, meaning "flat rock land" (Baffin Island); Markland, or "forest land" (Labrador); and Vinland, "land of vines" (Newfoundland). Archeologists have found evidence of a Viking settlement at the L'Anse aux Meadows on the northern tip of Newfoundland. Leif and his men spent two winters in Vinland before returning to Greenland. Leif would never return to North America, spending the rest of his days teaching the gospel in Greenland.

In 1003 Leif's brother Thorvald and twenty-five men traveled back to Vinland. It was there that they met their first Skrælings, Native Americans. The first meeting was unfortunate. It is unclear who started the fight, but in the end, Thorvald and eight natives were dead. Leif's sister, Gudrid, sailed with her husband and at least sixty men, five women, and livestock to set up a permanent settlement in Vinland. The settlement lasted for only three years because of the continual onslaught from the Skrælings. Gudrid and her family were the last known Vikings to attempt to settle Vinland. The next settlers of this northeast corner of the New World would not come until over six hundred years later. They would come seeking refuge from religious persecution.

◂ | Columbus's ships, the *Santa Maria* (front), *Niña*, and *Pinta*

GUIDING QUESTIONS

- How did trading link the people of Africa, Asia, and Europe prior to European overseas voyages?
- Why did the Europeans seek to cross the oceans?
- What technology made exploration possible?

5.1 Motives and Technology for Exploration

Imagine a world without electricity, the internet, or even pizza. Most of the people who have lived on this earth prospered without these amenities. But we would prioritize getting those back if we lost one for just a short time. The fifteenth-century Europeans experienced something like this loss.

You will recall that during the Pax Mongolica, goods and information moved freely between the East and West. Italian explorer Marco Polo enlightened the Europeans about the products and culture of the Far East. He described the vast wealth of China in his book. Europeans were amazed by what they read. Polo spoke of a land of gold, silks, and spices. Spices like pepper, nutmeg, cloves, and cinnamon were found only in the East and were useful for making food tastier and preserving it over the long winters. Spices were also easy to transport and measure out for exchange. The flow of spices, tea, silk, and porcelain was steady until Mongol power slipped away.

Some trade with the East continued after the Pax Mongolica and the Crusades, but the goods passed through many agents, and the final cost was very high. During the Ming dynasty, the Chinese shipped goods across the Indian Ocean to Africa and India. But Europeans faced danger on the Mediterranean Sea because of Islamic Barbary pirates. Therefore, Europeans began to search for new trade routes that bypassed Muslims, local leaders, and Italian merchants. Many believed that a water route to the East could be discovered. With their expanded knowledge of foreign lands, Europeans spent the next several centuries finding alternative ways to get there. This period is known as the **Age of European Exploration**.

? **Why did goods from the East cost more after the Pax Mongolica?**

Motives for Exploration

The Europeans had many motives for overseas exploration. While the primary motivation was economic, other motives ranged from practical to noble.

Economic

Adventurers sailed south and west with the confidence that they could find another route to the wealth of the East. Motivated by dreams of shiploads of gold, silver, and spices, explorers risked their lives by sailing into uncharted waters.

Glory

Others explored to experience the thrill of adventure and receive the praise of men. Curiosity drove some explorers, while others were on a quest for glory. Explorers often wrote journals of their exploits, and some sent detailed letters back to their monarchs to document their activities.

Political

In addition to potential wealth, the prospect of political gains motivated European monarchs. As news of initial discoveries reached Europe, some rulers authorized exploration to lay claim to foreign lands. When empire-building became popular, the kings sent explorers to establish colonies and discover raw materials needed by the home country.

◂ | Examples of spices brought to Europe from the East

Religious

The continuing threat of Muslim invasions gave Europeans great concern. With the fall of Constantinople in 1453, the Ottoman Turks swept into what remained of the Byzantine Empire. Muslim forces also posed a serious threat to Italy because the Muslims had made several attempts to invade nearby Austria. Explorers sailed in search of a mythical king in Africa, Prester John, who was thought to be a Christian. Europeans hoped to get his help to defeat the Muslims and preserve Christianity. Some explorers went out to spread the gospel to peoples that had never heard it. Since most of the early explorers were Roman Catholic, their converts became followers of the Catholic Church.

? What were the four European motivations for overseas exploration?

Technology for Exploration

Technological advances made exploration possible. Newer and better ships that could cross the open seas, tools like compasses and maps for navigation, and schools to train the sailors were essential for travel across the ocean.

Shipbuilding

Europeans had ships that were built to sail only along the coastlines of the continents. They were not capable of traveling on long journeys on the open sea. The ships only had one mast and one square sail. The ships would also continue to depend on rowers. In the open sea the current quickly overpowered these ships. Advances in shipbuilding resulted in the **caravel**. The caravel utilized a combination of previous designs. It could travel on the open sea and sail upriver in the shallow coastal waters. This ship had three or four masts and used triangular sails combined with one or more square sails. The triangular sails enabled the caravel to maneuver in port and travel swiftly over shallow water. The square sail allowed the ship to catch more wind and travel quickly on the open sea.

? How was the caravel more advanced than previous ships?

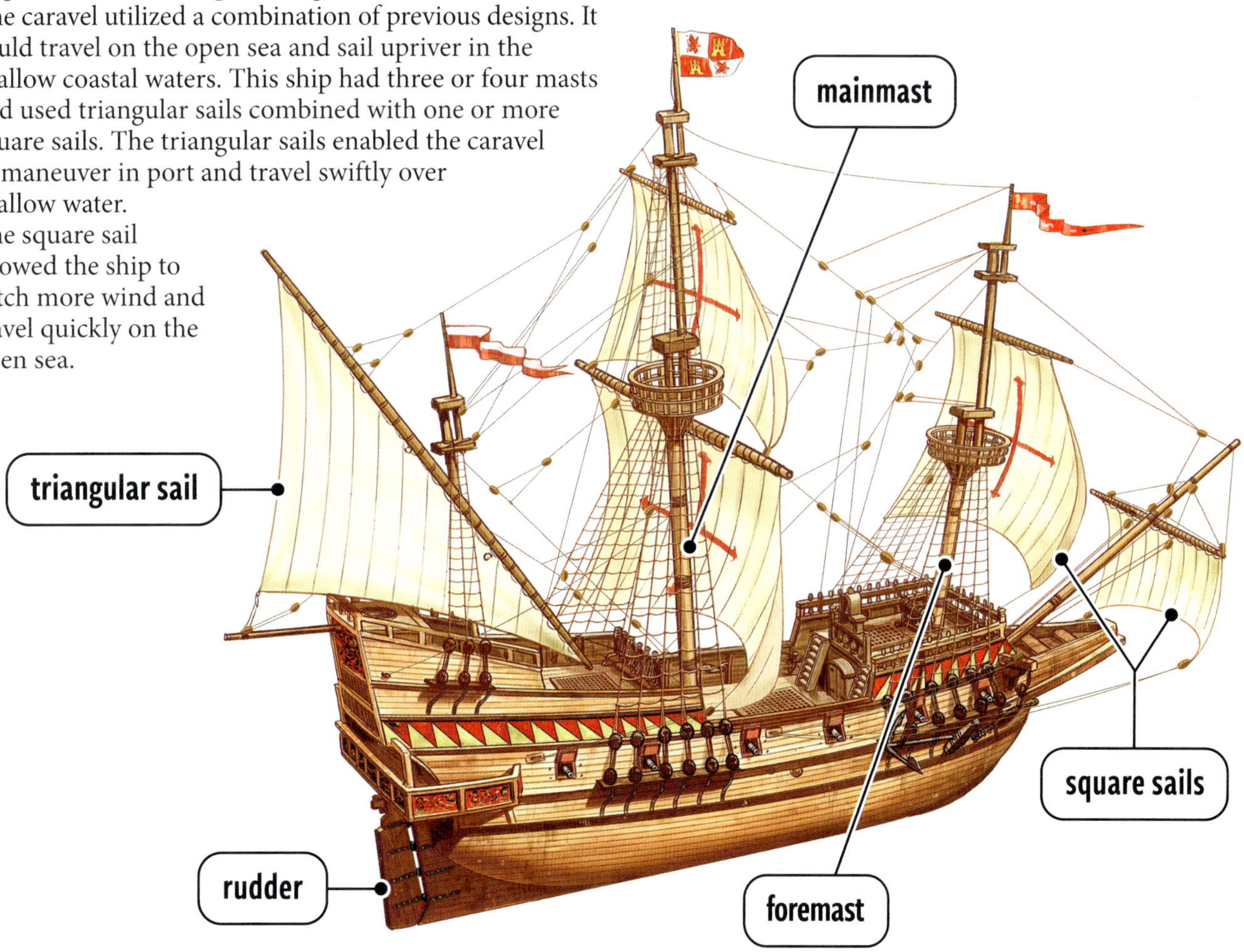

Ships played a central role in exploration, trade, and defense. Since the Muslims had cut off the land routes to the **Orient**, water routes were the only other option. The caravel and other ships carried spices, silk, and other treasures back to Europe. Eventually, nations would realize the importance of a navy, both to defend trade routes and to enable the establishment of colonies. Ships would also play a key role in wars between nations.

Navigation Tools

As Renaissance scholars learned more about their world, they provided explorers with new inventions. Other navigational information came to Europe through contact with the Islamic world.

Maps

Maps of the areas familiar to Europeans became more and more accurate during the fifteenth century. Italians excelled at making maps and improved them with input from traders and fishermen. However, for areas beyond the Mediterranean Sea or the coast of Europe, little or no information was available. Those who sailed in search of trade routes to the Orient traveled in uncharted seas. With each journey, they gained more knowledge, so they were able to update their maps. The invention of the printing press made rapid reproduction of maps possible and reduced the cost of making them.

Over time, these maps would include valuable information about wind patterns. Winds that were especially important to the early explorers were the **trade winds**, belts of consistent winds that blow from east to west. These fast-moving, favorable winds blew the explorers across the Atlantic Ocean.

Trade Winds

Instruments

A sailor's most useful instrument was the compass. The compass allowed him to set a course and follow its direction faithfully. The European sailors found the compass to be essential for navigating the open sea with no landmarks. By the fifteenth century, they had an improved compass composed of a needle spinning on a pin over a base. Several points of direction were marked on the base, making it possible to set and maintain an accurate course.

Orient the countries of Asia, especially East Asia

The **astrolabe** proved to be another helpful instrument. Sailors used it to measure the angle between the sun or a star and the horizon at a specific time of day or night. From this measure, the sailor could determine his latitude. However, the astrolabe had limitations. For example, measuring the angle on a tossing ship was difficult or impossible. Since time was measured by an hourglass, the captain rarely knew the exact time of his astrolabe reading. Eventually, the astrolabe was replaced with more accurate measuring devices.

Most early seamen navigated by **dead reckoning**. They decided what they thought their location was, estimated their speed, looked at the map, and aimed for a compass heading that they believed would get them to their goal. The difficulty was determining the effect of the winds and currents to move the ship in other directions. There is an old saying that it is called dead reckoning because "if you do not reckon right, you are dead." With the aid of the astrolabe, sailors were able to improve their accuracy by traveling north or south to get to the desired latitude. Then they would sail east or west on that latitude until they came to land.

Education

Prince Henry of Portugal sent out sailors and ships to explore the western coast of Africa in the fifteenth century. For these explorers, the sea contained many unknown dangers. They heard stories of sea monsters, deadly heat at the equator, and violent storms. Despite these dangers, some men, supported by their kings, set out to find and explore distant lands.

To prepare his sailors for these dangerous voyages, Prince Henry set up a navigation school. Portuguese sea captains learned how to use new methods and instruments. For his emphasis on training, Henry became known as **Prince Henry the Navigator**.

What was Prince Henry's key contribution toward the exploration effort?

Naval Warfare

As more countries built navies and explored, they depended on improved weapons to protect trade routes. Naval warfare is ancient and can be traced back to battles like those between the Greeks and the Persians in the fifth century BC. During the Age of European Exploration, the sailors attached a new weapon to ships: the cannon. The Venetians were among the first to use cannons onboard their ships. They used their fleet both to carry on trade and to defend against piracy. Later, the Portuguese developed fighting vessels to escort their ships along their many trade routes. Soon the use of cannons on ships became common as Europeans discovered how to use them effectively at sea and in coastal attacks on their enemies.

Critical Thinking 5.1

1. Why did the Europeans want to trade with the people of the East?
2. List and briefly describe two navigational improvements that made exploration possible.
3. List motives for exploration that were inconsistent with a Christian worldview and explain why they were inconsistent.

(top) Sailors used an astrolabe to find their location; (middle) Prince Henry the Navigator teaching future explorers; (bottom) A Spanish warship

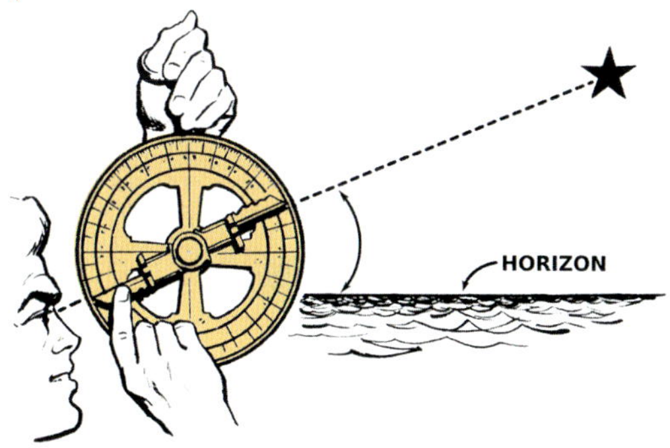

- What was the Aztec civilization like?
- How did the Incan Empire expand?
- What was the Incan civilization like?

5.2 Aztec and Incan Civilizations

While the Europeans were trying to find new sea routes to the East, in the empty space on their maps between the East and West existed two vast continents populated by advanced civilizations.

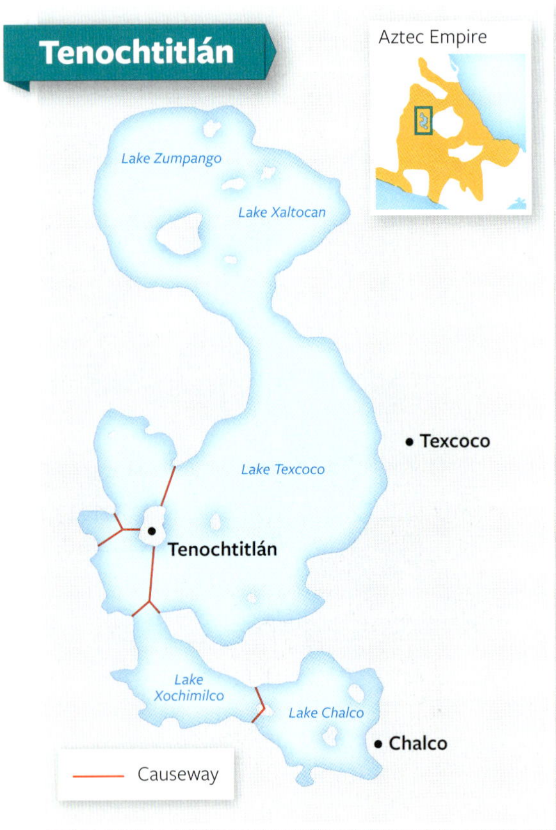

The Aztecs

The **Aztecs** were the people who ruled central and southern Mexico during the fifteenth and sixteenth centuries. *Aztec* is the name historians have given to these people, but they called themselves *Mexica* and would not have recognized the word *Aztec*. They flourished following the collapse of the Mayan and Toltec civilizations. The Aztecs had wandered in the wilderness for many years before entering an already-occupied fertile valley called the **Valle de Mexico**, where Mexico City is today. The Aztecs were an illiterate, warlike people before they settled down. They were not welcomed because they were viewed as barbarians, but they did find employment as mercenaries, soldiers for hire.

Dissatisfied with their status, they claimed a disregarded, unoccupied, swampy lake area for their city. Around 1325 they built their capital, **Tenochtitlán**, on an island in the middle of the lake. They first made floating islands from mounds of water plants and put them in the middle of the lake. When these had rooted, the Aztecs filled the roots with soil and built on them. The finished city had many islands that they accessed by boats and bridges. Several long causeways connected the islands of Tenochtitlán to each other and the mainland. The Aztecs were able to use the land to their advantage. They grew crops of peppers and flowers and extracted the salt from the water. The lake also provided them an abundant supply of fish and birds, which they hunted. The city was also very defensible because they could raise the bridges to keep out invaders.

Over time the Aztecs defeated and enslaved the other city-states. The area they conquered was large, with a population of five million people, who were required to pay tribute (taxes). Tenochtitlán allied with two other large cities, Texcoco and Tlacopan, to form the Triple Alliance. With the crowning of Montezuma I as emperor in 1440, an Aztec golden age began.

Montezuma I

How did the Aztecs make a city in an already-occupied valley?

Aztec Society

Aztec society was characterized by war and warriors. Every Aztec man who was able to fight had to serve in the army. Aztec warriors used terror and military skill to conquer many tribes around them. They tried to capture their enemies rather than killing them on the battlefield. The Aztec men would fight when they were not needed to work on the farm.

The Aztec people were governed by an elected king, the tlatoani. The tlatoani was assisted by a council of four who were usually his brothers, sons, or nephews. Upon the tlatoani's death the council would elect the next one. Once elected, the monarch lived in great splendor.

The Aztecs also developed a judicial system with a chief judge for each of the major cities. Aztec law was recorded in picture writing. The crimes considered most serious were punishable by death. For example, the punishment for adultery was death by stoning because marriage was recognized as a vital part of Aztec culture.

A representation of the Aztec god Quetzalcoatl

Aztec Religion

The Aztecs worshiped many gods and built large temples to honor these gods. Part of their worship included human sacrifice, during which they cut out the hearts of living people and offered them to the gods. The Aztecs sacrificed those they captured in war. When they dedicated the Great Pyramid of Tenochtitlán, they sacrificed eighty-four thousand people in four days. This emphasis on human sacrifice would come to be the civilization's undoing. The **Tlaxcalans**, people living on the eastern side of the valley, were the Aztecs' most frequent victims for sacrifice.

What did Aztecs believe their gods required for worship?

The Incas

The Incas built upon earlier cultures and developed their civilization in the 1200s. Their ancestors migrated from Asia. They settled on the desert coast of Peru, most likely because the waters off the coast are some of the most fertile fishing grounds in the world. The Andes Mountains and the Amazon jungle blocked their migration to the east. The Incan civilization was one of the few civilizations to grow in a narrow area along the coast and into the mountains; usually civilizations spread in every direction from a central point. At the empire's peak from 1438 to 1533, the territory under Incan rule extended three thousand miles in length and up to three hundred fifty miles in width.

The Incas accomplished a rapid expansion by making alliances and building relationships with heads of individual tribes. Tribute poured into the capital city in the form of food, copper, gold, silver, and alpaca wool. The Incan people did not use gold for money, so they used it to make such items as ornaments, vases, and temple vessels.

LIFE IN THE INCAN EMPIRE

Religion

The Incas were polytheistic, but the ruler retained the title of "Inca" and served as the empire's living god. He owned the land, and authority resided in him. The people sacrificed animals during four great festivals. Upon the death of the Inca or another major calamity such as an earthquake or volcanic eruption, hundreds of people were sacrificed. The Incas did not practice human sacrifice to the same extent as the Aztecs, but they did practice it. They sacrificed those captured in war or children raised specifically for the purpose of sacrifice. They believed the children would go to a better world and intercede for them. Recently, archaeologists uncovered the graves of 140 children in northern Peru. They are thought to have been killed in sacrifice. Unlike sacrifices in the Aztec and Incan religions, Jesus' sacrifice was voluntary and based on His substitutionary work. Instead of asking humans to sacrifice other humans for their sins, God became a man and laid down His own life for the sins of humanity.

Power

Many people groups made up the empire. The total population was ten million people who spoke over thirty different languages. At the highest level was the Inca who had all the power, which he delegated to the *panaqa*, a second level of up to ten groups of nobles. The Inca and the *panaqa* made all significant decisions for the people. The *panaqa* ruled a third level of ten more groups. The third level governed a fourth level of leaders who had some authority but were not of Incan blood. Finally, there were the *kurakas*, who governed the *ayllu*, the most local group in Incan society. Women could fill the role of the *kuraka*. In the *ayllu*, a village made up of an extended family, the members worked the land and supported each other. Because the Inca held the power in the society, the people became passive followers. Conquest by a foreign power would be easy if the Inca were captured or killed.

Justice

The Incan people had three moral precepts that governed their behavior: ***Ama sua***—do not steal, ***Ama llulla***—do not lie, and ***Ama quella***—do not be lazy. Punishments for breaking the law could be harsh, so the crime rate was low. Lawbreakers could lose their hands for stealing or be thrown off a cliff for murder. The Incas also could punish a whole village for one person's crime.

Citizenship

Those who spoke the Incan language, Quechua, had a special status and were able to govern the many tribes in the empire who were not of Incan descent. Quechua speakers were a small minority. The Incas were called "children of the sun." They believed that in ancient times they were uncivilized, living like animals, but the sun god, Inti, sent his two sons to teach them how to live.

A depiction of Machu Picchu in Peru

Environment

The capital of the Incan Empire was **Cuzco**, built at an elevation of over two miles. It served as both the political and religious capital of the empire and had a population of over 150,000. Here the Incas built large buildings out of stone with great precision. Without using mortar, they constructed buildings with such accuracy that even today a knife blade cannot fit between the stones. The buildings were said to be covered with sheets of gold to reflect the sun and remind the Incan people of their sun god. To make travel, communication, and trade possible, the people constructed two major highways that ran the length of the empire. They built long bridges to cross the steep valleys and ravines. While the peoples of the Americas did not usually use animals, the Incas were an exception. They used llamas and alpacas for pack animals and wool. They were able to use these animals because, even in the wild, the llamas and alpacas acted tame.

CRITICAL THINKING 5.2

1. How did the Aztecs expand their empire?
2. Compare and contrast Tenochtitlán and Cuzco.
3. Compare and contrast the Aztec and Incan civilizations with your civilization.

GUIDING QUESTIONS

- What European explorations took place from 1415 to 1532?
- How did the Portuguese expand their reach into Africa, India, and Southeast Asia?
- What happened when the Spanish met the Aztecs and Incas?
- How did the Aztec and Incan Empires collapse?
- How did the Europeans treat the native peoples of other lands?

5.3 European Expeditions

Prince Henry the Navigator died in 1460, but the work he started continued as Portuguese sailors explored farther and farther down the African west coast. Spain also pursued overseas exploration early on. These two nations had several advantages that enabled them to take the lead in European exploration. Spain and Portugal were bordered by the Atlantic Ocean and the Mediterranean Sea. They had a long history of shipbuilding and navigating these bodies of water. They had experienced sailors who had acquired navigational and mapmaking skills from the Moors (Spanish Muslims). Finally, Spain and Portugal were motivated by a strong crusading spirit that had enabled them to forcibly remove the remnants of Muslim influence in their region. They went out to spread the doctrines of the Roman Catholic Church and to continue the struggle against Muslims in other lands. They established the Roman Catholic Church everywhere they explored and in every colony they established. Spain sent explorers west and Portuguese sailors traveled south to find a new water route to the East.

? Which European nations were the earliest to lead overseas expeditions?

Portuguese Exploration

King Afonso of Portugal granted a contract to Fernao Gomes that required him to explore the African coast 345 miles farther each year for five years. Gomes hired a group of explorers, and they were able to outperform the contract requirement. In 1473 Lopo Gonçalves crossed the equator. In 1487 **Bartolomeu Dias** finally turned the corner that would open sea trade with India. Caught in a bad storm, Dias's ships rounded the tip of Africa without his realizing it. When Dias did become aware of where he was, he turned back and saw land. He wanted to continue to explore, but his frightened crew insisted on returning to Portugal. The Portuguese had proved that they could reach the East by sailing south around Africa.

Ten years later in 1497, **Vasco da Gama** led a fleet of four ships on a one-year journey to India. Instead of following the African coast as others had done in the past, he sailed west and then south in a broad sweep. This maneuver allowed him to take advantage of favorable winds and currents. By the time his ships reached the southern tip of Africa, he had sailed out of sight of land for fourteen weeks. In future explorations, wind-driven ships would often use this maneuver. After rounding the Cape of Good Hope (southern tip of Africa), Vasco da Gama and his crew sailed up the east coast of Africa. They stopped at trading cities, where they met both African and Arab traders. Landing on the southwest coast of India, da Gama and his men were surprised to find an advanced people.

? Who was the first Portuguese explorer to reach India?

When they tried to trade, the Portuguese were surprised that the Indians rejected the items they had brought. The Indians were not impressed by the Portuguese goods of cloth, honey, and oil. Muslim merchants also opposed da Gama's efforts to trade with the Indians. Eventually, the Portuguese did sell enough to buy spices and return to Portugal. To pay for the expedition, they sold the spices they bought in India. They had enough money left over to finance more voyages. This profit ensured that the Portuguese would make many more trips and extend their exploration even farther east.

Less than half of Vasco da Gama's crew returned. The rest died on the journey. Because they were out at sea so long, the men came down with a disease called scurvy. **Scurvy** is caused by not getting enough vitamin C. This disease would disable and kill sailors for hundreds of years. Finally, in the mid-1700s, the British discovered that drinking the juice of lemons and other citrus fruits kept the sailors from getting scurvy.

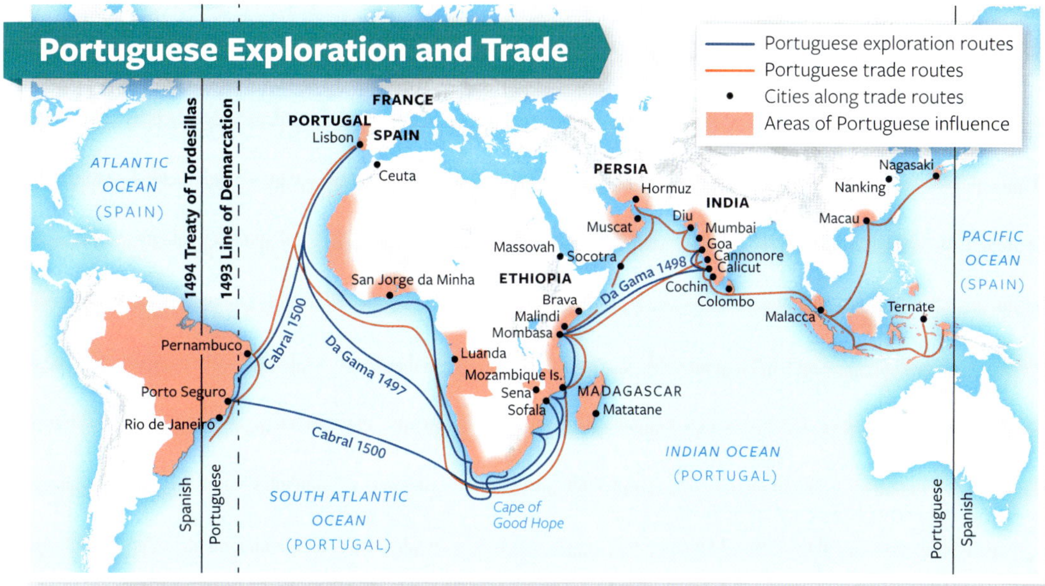

Portuguese sailors soon made regular voyages to the port cities of East Africa and India. Heavily armed Portuguese ships easily defeated Muslim efforts to block Portuguese trade. The Portuguese sent a fleet of twenty-two ships to India in 1505 to establish settlements and to protect their growing trade.

Early in the sixteenth century, the Portuguese became the first Europeans (after Marco Polo) to trade directly with the Chinese. Direct trade with China further weakened the Muslim and Italian monopolies on goods from the East and resulted in great wealth for Portugal. **Afonso de Albuquerque**, an explorer, admiral, and statesman, made several expeditions to India and one as far as the Persian Gulf. He became the governor of India, and from India he set up a trading center at Malacca in what is now Malaysia. From Malacca, the Portuguese could expand their influence further into Southeast Asia.

On May 4, 1543, the Portuguese landed on Tanegashima, a small southern Japanese island. A few years later, the Jesuit missionary **Francis Xavier** arrived in Japan and sought to convert the people to Roman Catholicism.

Where did the Portuguese regularly sail in the sixteenth century?

Line of Demarcation

Spain and Portugal were the leaders in early exploration. They were also both Roman Catholic nations. Some influential Roman Catholics believed that the pope, as the Vicar (representative) of Christ, was given the right to rule the whole world. It seemed logical, therefore, to appeal to the pope to decide who could settle where. Queen Isabella and King Ferdinand called on **Pope Alexander VI**, a Spaniard, to decide which country, Spain or Portugal, could explore and lay claim to certain areas. The line the pope decided on was called the **Line of Demarcation**.

Portugal could claim everything east of the line, while Spain could claim everything west of the line. The Portuguese were not pleased with this arbitrary division. The route they followed to catch favorable winds for their voyages around Africa often took them into Spanish waters and put them at risk for conflict. In a final agreement in 1494 called the **Treaty of Tordesillas**, the line was moved.

The new line was six hundred miles west of the original line. If the Spanish had understood what they were giving up, they probably would not have signed this treaty. Without realizing it at the time, the Portuguese gained a vast territory now known as Brazil. In 1500 the Portuguese accidentally discovered the "island of Brazil," as they called it, when one of their ships was blown off course on its way to Africa. Of course, the Reformation emerged shortly after the Treaty of Tordesillas. The pope's power was weakened by the refusal of Protestant nations to recognize the authority he claimed.

Who created the Line of Demarcation?

Portuguese Exploration 1400s–1500s

1487 Bartolomeu Dias sails around the southern tip of Africa

1492 Ferdinand and Isabella complete Reconquista

Columbus sent by Spain to find a western route to India

1497 Vasco da Gama reaches India

1500

1505 Portugal begins to trade with India

1519–22 Magellan's crew sails around the world

Hernando Cortes discovers and destroys the Aztec Empire

1531 Francisco Pizarro discovers and destroys the Incan Empire

c. 1550 Portugal begins to trade with Japan

1571 Battle of Lepanto

1577–80 Sir Francis Drake sails around the world

1600

TURNING POINTS

1492

The year 1492 was a pivotal year, which is something that civilizations sometimes experience. It was an eventful year for Europeans, Muslims, and Native Americans alike, comparable to the years of 2001 or 2020 for the United States and the world.

On January 2 **King Ferdinand II** and **Queen Isabella** of Spain completed the **Reconquista** when the city of Granada, in southern Spain, fell to their forces. Granada was the last remaining Muslim kingdom on the Iberian Peninsula. With its defeat, the Roman Catholic king and queen could now focus on expanding their power outside the peninsula.

On January 15 Ferdinand and Isabella met with **Christopher Columbus**. The Portuguese monarchs had been sending their ships to the East by sailing south. Columbus, an Italian explorer, believed he could get to the East by sailing west. By sailing west, Columbus hoped to discover a shorter route to China and the Indies (the islands near China, now known as Indonesia).

After other kings rejected his ideas, Columbus went to the Spanish king and queen, his last hope. He convinced them to finance his exploration. With all the important decisions they had to make, it is significant that one of those decisions involved sending Columbus on a voyage to discover a route to the East. Given the expense and risk of this voyage, it was a remarkable choice, especially since they had rejected Columbus a couple of times before.

On August 3, Columbus set sail with three ships, the *Niña*, the *Pinta*, and the *Santa María*. When he and his crew landed on the Caribbean island of **San Salvador** on October 12, he thought they were in the Indies. So he called the **Taino** people they encountered there Indians. It was the first of many misunderstandings and tragedies that would continue between the two cultures for years to come.

The most consequential difference between the Europeans and the peoples of the New World was their use of domesticated animals. The Europeans depended heavily on domestic animals such as pigs, horses, and cows, while the peoples of the Americas had never lived with these animals. The domestic animals carried diseases, like smallpox, to which the Europeans had gained some immunity. But the rapid introduction of these animals to the Americas was devastating to the native peoples. It seems that Columbus and other explorers did not understand that they were bringing disease.

Columbus landed in **Cuba** on October 28 and on the island of **Hispaniola** on December 5. Although Columbus was right about sailing west to get east, he did not sail far enough. The Caribbean islands did not yield the gold and spices sought by the explorers. Yet Columbus did discover a new continent that would influence the course of Western civilization. In 1519 **Ferdinand Magellan** sailed west from Spain to sail around the world. His ships rounded the tip of South America and crossed the Pacific Ocean. Tragically, Magellan was killed in the Philippines. The surviving members of his crew continued the voyage and returned to Spain. This journey lasted three years, but it proved that Columbus's theory was correct: it was possible to reach the East by sailing west.

1. Contrast the year 1492 for the Spanish, the Muslims on the Iberian Peninsula, and the Taino people.
2. Why might Columbus have had a hard time convincing a king to sponsor him?
3. What was significant about Columbus's expedition?

Columbus's Voyages

Malintzin

Some people play huge behind-the-scenes roles in the progress of world events. **Malintzin** was one of these persons. It seems she was born to nobility in an eastern Aztec city-state. Between the ages of 8 and 12, she was either sold or kidnapped into slavery. Her mother may have been the one to sell her as a slave. She became very bitter and angry for being made a slave. She learned to speak many different Mayan and Aztec languages. When Cortés landed on the Mexican coast, he quickly defeated the natives he first encountered. As a peace offering, they presented him with gifts of food, gold, and twenty slave women; one of them was Malintzin.

When the conquistadors discovered Malintzin's linguistic ability, they gave her an elevated status. Jeronimo de Aguilar, one of Cortés's men, shared fluency in one Mayan language with Malintzin, so he could translate what she said into Spanish. Montezuma spoke to Malintzin, then she translated for Aguilar, and then he translated for Cortés. Understanding the language gave Cortés a distinct advantage. Since Malintzin was loyal to the Spanish for freeing her from enslavement, she would provide valuable insight into Aztec thinking and strategy. Without her, the Spanish could not have formed an alliance with the Tlaxcalans. But Montezuma had to depend on his foolish magicians for advice. Following the defeat of the Aztecs, Malintzin married a conquistador and moved to Spain. She was accepted into Spanish high society.

? How did Malintzin help Cortés?

Early English Exploration

When the pope gave Spain and Portugal rights to all newly discovered lands in 1493, the other European nations objected. The English began exploring the New World soon after Columbus's first expedition. King Henry VII hired an Italian sailor named **Giovanni Caboto** (**John Cabot**) to lead the first English expedition to North America. Cabot was already an experienced sailor, having sailed to the Middle East. After a six-week voyage across the Atlantic, Cabot dropped anchor off the coast of Canada. He landed in the same area the Vikings had tried to settle centuries before. Like Columbus, Cabot thought he was in Asia. In 1498 he made a second voyage to the New World, accompanied by his son Sebastian; they explored the northern coast of North America. Though they did not find gold or spices, they found rich fisheries off the Newfoundland coast. The two expeditions to the New World were the basis for England's claim on America.

Spanish Conquest of the Americas

Columbus always believed that America was the Indies, a land of gold. Although later explorers realized America was not the Indies, they continued to think that America was a land of gold. Spain sent out several men to find this gold, conquer the people, and convert them to Roman Catholicism. **Conquistadors** discovered and brutally destroyed the native civilizations in Central and South America.

Conquest of the Aztecs

The Spanish set up colonies in Cuba and Hispaniola and soon heard rumors of a magnificent kingdom in the west. The Spanish made an ill-fated expedition from Cuba to Mexico in 1517. In 1518 Juan de Grijalva led another expedition to Mexico, but he was late in returning. So in 1519 **Governor Velazquez** of Cuba ordered **Hernando Cortés**, who had come from Spain in 1504, to embark on a larger mission. In the meantime, de Grijalva showed up and confirmed the rumors of riches in Mexico. The Europeans were startled to find highly developed native societies with towns and political structure. Christians should remember that humans were created in the image of God and given dominion over the earth. God enabled humans to develop complex cultures. Rather than be startled to find complex cultures, we should expect to discover them all over the world.

Cortés set sail for Mexico against the orders of Governor Velazquez, who had changed his mind about Cortés leading the expedition. Upon landing on the coast of Mexico, Cortés and his men met some Aztecs. They discovered the emperor's name was Montezuma. In his palace in Tenochtitlán, **Montezuma II** was trying to understand the new arrivals. Early accounts by conquistadors claimed the Aztecs mistook Cortés for their god Quetzalcoatl. This probably was not the case, and if it was, it only lasted for a brief time since hostilities between the two groups quickly broke out.

Since Cortés was on an illegal mission, he was also concerned about his men turning on him, so he had ten of his eleven ships destroyed to keep the men from trying to return to Cuba. The remaining ship he sent to Spain to try to gain favor with the king and undercut his commander, Governor Velazquez.

? How did Cortés disobey the governor?

Montezuma sent a delegation to meet Cortés; during the meeting, Cortés learned that the Aztecs possessed a lot of gold, and it was probably then that Cortés decided to conquer them. He also learned that Montezuma had enemies, particularly the Tlaxcalans. Cortés later wrote that once he understood the situation, he knew he would defeat the Aztecs because he remembered Mark 3:24, which says, "If a kingdom be divided against itself, that kingdom cannot stand." The Tlaxcalans did not join the Spanish immediately but fought them in a fierce three-day battle. Following the conflict, Cortés was able to ally with them. He gained tens of thousands of Tlaxcalan warriors to help conquer Tenochtitlán. News of this alliance filled Montezuma with fear and dread. Cortés destroyed cities in his march toward Tenochtitlán but also gained more allies.

When Cortés entered Tenochtitlán, Montezuma greeted Cortés rather than attacking him since Montezuma understood the conquistador had superior weapons. The emperor showed Cortés samples of Aztec wealth. The Spanish soldiers who had been to the great cities of the world said none of them compared to Tenochtitlán. After a few days, Cortés put Montezuma under house arrest and burned alive seventeen Aztec nobles. Montezuma submitted to Cortés's demands and urged the people to cooperate with the Spanish.

Meanwhile, Governor Velazquez sent seventeen ships to Mexico, led by Pánfilo de Narvaez, to arrest Cortés and bring him back to Cuba. It seems that Montezuma and Narvaez were able to communicate through secret messages passed along by native runners. Narvaez let Montezuma know that Cortés was not acting with the king's permission. Cortés left Tenochtitlán, and in a surprise attack, he quickly defeated Narvaez, despite being outnumbered. In the end, the soldiers the governor sent joined Cortés.

While Cortés was gone, the Aztecs rebelled, and the rebellion continued upon his return. When Cortés told Montezuma to speak to the people to get them to submit to the Spanish, the people stoned Montezuma to death. Cortés and his men were forced to fight their way out of the city, dropping the gold in the lake as they left.

Cortés was not going to leave Mexico in defeat. He regrouped, and in 1521 he began a four-month siege of Tenochtitlán. The Aztecs starved and were forced to eat leather and the dust from adobe bricks. Finally, in the central marketplace, Cortés defeated the last resisters. Cortés destroyed Tenochtitlán. In its place he built Mexico City. Over the temple of the Aztecs, Cortés built a Roman Catholic cathedral. The Spanish compelled the Indians to outwardly submit to the Church of Rome while allowing them to retain many aspects of their pagan worship.

A painting depicting Cortés's final conquest of Tenochtitlán

How did Montezuma II die?

The conquistadors used the Aztec practice of human sacrifice as the reason for destroying the empire, yet the Spanish treated the Aztecs' former victims as cruelly as they treated the Aztecs. It seems their priority was not in punishing the Aztecs for the blood they had spilled but in taking the Aztec gold and treasure.

Conquest of the Incas

A conquistador named **Francisco Pizarro** proved to be even more brutal than Cortés. He traveled to the New World to find gold, and he used violent methods to seize it at every opportunity. Pizarro heard of an Indian nation in South America—the Incan people—that had much wealth. He led a small group of men and sailed from Panama to Peru in 1531. Pizarro and his men worked their way through jungles for six months and attacked villages along the way. When they reached the Incan Empire, they took the Incan king, **Atahualpa**, captive. The Incas offered to fill the room where the Spanish held the king prisoner with gold and silver in exchange for his release. Over the next few weeks, the Incas delivered about thirteen thousand pounds of gold ($400 million today) and almost twenty-six thousand pounds of silver ($12 million). However, Pizarro brutally murdered Atahualpa anyway and made himself ruler of the Incan Empire.

Pizarro destroyed Cuzco and founded the city of Lima along the coast. However, he did not live to enjoy the treasures he had violently taken from the Incas. In 1541 a group of Spaniards stormed Pizarro's palace and killed him.

Pizarro taking King Atahualpa captive

Conclusion

The Spanish were able to make conquests in Central and South America because of the power their technology gave them. The use of this power was defended in a document called the **Requerimiento**, which said that God made Saint Peter and his heirs, the popes, rulers over all the earth. Therefore, if the natives did not convert, the Spanish had the right to conquer their lands and make them slaves. In the end, this model of empire building failed Spain—and Portugal as well. They were wealthy in gold and silver but never developed industrially (building factories) as the other European nations did, so Spain and Portugal eventually lost power. The British, like the Spanish and Portuguese, initially hoped to find gold and treasures in the Americas, but as colonists arrived with other purposes, the British colonies became successful.

CRITICAL THINKING 5.3

1. Why do humans, wherever they live and whatever their environment, develop cultures?
2. How did Portuguese conquests and Spanish conquests differ?
3. Compare and contrast the rule and character of Cortés and the Aztec kings.
4. In contrast to the Requerimiento, what does Romans 13:1–7 say about those whom God appoints to rule over nations?

Making Connections

1. Who was the first European to set foot in North America?
2. When did the people of the East and West first establish a relationship?
3. Why were spices useful for trading?
4. Why was the caravel better suited for exploration?
5. How was the city of Tenochtitlán built in the middle of a lake?
6. How did the Aztecs build an empire?
7. Why did the Incas cover their buildings with sheets of gold?
8. Why were Portuguese sailors willing to endure the risks and difficulties to sail to India?
9. How did Montezuma II respond to Cortés when he arrived?
10. How did Pizarro defeat the Incas?

What to Know

PEOPLE

Leif Ericson
Prince Henry the Navigator
the Tlaxcalans
Bartolomeu Dias
Vasco da Gama
Afonso de Albuquerque
Francis Xavier
Pope Alexander VI
King Ferdinand II
Queen Isabella
Christopher Columbus
the Taino
Ferdinand Magellan
John Cabot
Governor Velazquez
Hernando Cortés
Montezuma II
Malintzin
Francisco Pizarro
Atahualpa

PLACES

Valle de Mexico
Tenochtitlán
Cuzco
San Salvador
Cuba
Hispaniola

TERMS

Age of European Exploration
caravel
Orient
trade winds
astrolabe
dead reckoning
scurvy
Line of Demarcation
Treaty of Tordesillas
Reconquista
Requerimiento

Thinking Critically

1. Evaluate the different motives for exploration. What do you think was the most important motive and why?
2. Compare and contrast the Aztecs and Incas.
3. Evaluate the religions of the civilizations in the Americas in light of Romans 1.
4. In what ways are the view that the Native Americans were savages without civilization and the view that they had little to no environmental impact similar? How are such views demeaning to the Native Americans and contrary to Scripture?

Afonso de Albuquerque trading with the Indians

6 AFRICA AND THE RISE OF THE SLAVE TRADE

1220 – 1729

ESSENTIAL QUESTIONS

- What are some broad observations about African culture and religion?
- What were African civilizations like during the thirteenth through the eighteenth centuries?
- What was the role of trade and religion in the development of African empires?
- What did European powers do in Africa during the thirteenth through the eighteenth centuries?
- What was the transatlantic African slave trade?

Tuareg tribesmen of North Africa

The Man Who Never Lied

Africans depended on storytellers to pass on their history and traditions. One story is a lesson to children about a man who never lied.

Once upon a time there lived a wise man by the name of Mamad. He never lied. All the people in the land, even the ones who lived twenty days away, knew about him.

The king heard about Mamad and ordered his subjects to bring him to the palace. He looked at the wise man and asked, "Mamad, is it true that you have never lied?"

"It's true."

"And you will never lie in your life?"

"I'm sure in that."

"Okay, tell the truth, but be careful! The lie is cunning, and it gets on your tongue easily."

Several days passed, and the king called Mamad once again. There was a big crowd; the king was about to go hunting. The king held his horse by the mane. His left foot was already on the stirrup. He ordered Mamad, "Go to my summer palace and tell the queen I will be with her for lunch. Tell her to prepare a big feast. You will have lunch with me then."

Mamad bowed down and went to the queen. Then the king laughed and said, "We will not go hunting, and now Mamad will lie to the queen. Tomorrow we will laugh on his behalf."

But the wise Mamad went to the palace and said, "Maybe you should prepare a big feast for lunch tomorrow, and maybe you should not. Maybe the king will come by noon, and maybe he will not."

"Tell me will he come or will he not?" asked the queen.

"I do not know whether he put his right foot on the stirrup or he put his left foot on the ground after I left."

Everybody waited for the king. He came the next day and said to the queen, "The wise Mamad, who never lies, lied to you yesterday."

But the queen told him about the words of Mamad. And the king realized that the wise man never lies, and he says only that which he saw with his own eyes.

This story was more effective in teaching African children not to lie than the teachers just saying, "Do not lie."

GUIDING QUESTION

- What were some general characteristics of African culture and religion during this period?

6.1 Overview of African Culture

Africa is the second-largest continent and the home to over a billion people who are divided into thousands of different people groups. Yet we can identify some general characteristics of African society before expanding on the individual African kingdoms that followed the Songhai Empire.

Oral History

Much of African history has been overlooked; one reason for this is the lack of written records. Because Africans did not have written languages, they could not read or write books about their history. Instead, the people learned the history of their clan and tribe from storytellers. The storytellers, called **griots** in western Africa, memorized the long ancestry of their people. They knew stories or folktales about important heroic family members as well as bad ones. Children grew up learning these stories. When a child came to the age of initiation (usually in the early teen or preteen years), he heard his family's entire history. Much of what we know about African history and culture comes from these oral histories, which some Africans can still recite today.

A new chief listens to the history of his line given by a "griot," or storyteller.

A savanna in Kenya

Agriculture

Just like other people around the world, Africans adapted to changing conditions and lived on the natural resources around them. Some were able to blend growing crops with raising livestock to meet their dietary needs. Others learned to thrive on either crops or livestock, depending on the available resources.

Over the centuries, the soil became less productive, and the food for livestock decreased. The people often had to move to survive. Eventually, the depleted soil would again become able to support crops and sustain life. When the Africans found better ways to fertilize the soil, they built groups of more permanent dwellings that grew into cities.

Improved efficiency in farming resulted in greater yields. As the Africans produced more food than was needed, the excess provided an opportunity for trade. Increased trade and permanent settlements supported the continued development of civilization.

(top) Sorghum; (middle) Wheat; (bottom) A South African breed of cattle

Crops

Africans grew crops that would flourish in their region. In the rainforests, inhabitants gathered roots such as yams. On the **savanna** (flat grasslands), the people developed grain crops such as millet, sorghum, and wheat. Crops of cotton and watermelon began to appear in West Africa and the **Sahel**, while peas, flax, and millet (a cereal like oats) took hold in Ethiopia.

Livestock

Africans raised a variety of animals, including sheep, goats, and cattle. However, they prized these animals and seldom killed them. The animals provided milk and other benefits (such as wool) for their masters. Cattle especially were considered a sign of wealth. Therefore, to kill an animal meant the loss of wealth. Rather than kill their livestock, the Africans added to their diets by hunting or fishing.

Sahel a three-hundred-mile-wide band of grass-covered plains in Africa between the Sahara and the tropical forests

? **Why did the people of Africa have to move?**

This family in Kenya belongs to the Masai tribe.

Families

The family was the most important element of traditional African culture. An individual's family not only provided a person with history and traditions but also offered guidance throughout life. The family leader decided where members lived and how they earned their living. Family leaders also told them how to behave and what to believe. Often, Africans evaluated a person according to his position in a family rather than as an individual.

Africans believed that children were important. A man would often have several wives to rear many children. As was true in other ancient cultures, love was rarely the motivation for marriage in Africa. The parents of the children arranged the marriage for money and political benefit. Love was expected to follow marriage rather than precede it. One of the primary reasons for marriage was the rearing of children, which made the survival of family traditions possible. Marriage and large families also led to increased family honor and wealth.

Because a man had several wives, rivalries were common between the different wives and different children for their husband's/father's favor. Keeping the peace at home was a difficult job for the husband. Usually, each wife had a dwelling in the family compound. Daughters and sons lived in separate huts as well. This arrangement helped to prevent many quarrels.

The typical African family had other members besides parents and children. African families often included grandparents, uncles, aunts, and cousins. When a young woman married, she left her family group to join her husband's family group. These extended family groups tended to live together. Sometimes a whole community consisted of people belonging to the same family.

What was the primary reason for marriage in Africa?

The extended family provided security for all the members as well as a pool of wisdom and skills. Older members of the family could pass on life experiences and provide a connection to the past. The extended family was a building block for African civilization.

What was a clan?

The largest family group in Africa was the **clan**. A clan included everyone who could trace his ancestry to a common relative. The clan gave the individual his history and culture. In Africa, single families belonged to clans and lived under the authority of the clan elder or chief. The clan, not families or individuals, often owned and controlled the land used by the clan members. The chief decided where the clan lived, divided the land, and determined its use. A small clan might live together in a single community, while larger clans lived in several communities. On important occasions, the whole clan met together to celebrate.

Even larger than the family and clan was the tribe, which consisted of two or more clans that shared the same language, beliefs, and customs. Some tribes were small, while others had thousands of members. Africa's traditional clans and tribes formed the basis for later African states and kingdoms.

Dwellings

Africans used the materials that were available to them to house their families. Existing materials varied from region to region. Where stone was plentiful, they built their houses of stone. In other areas wood was available in sufficient supply to construct their houses. Some regions had a plentiful supply of clay, and the people baked bricks to use in building. Where no other resources were available, the inhabitants used a combination of sticks, leaves, grass, and clay to build their homes.

Indigenous Religions

Almost all Africans believed in a Supreme Being or High God. Some African accounts of Creation often bore an amazing resemblance to the biblical account in Genesis. Some Africans believed that the High God was a spiritual being who walked with men until something caused him to separate himself from the people. The Dinka tribe of Ghana told the story that the High God walked with people until a selfish woman made him angry, so he left. The Sudanese told a story that a woman was so noisy that the High God went into heaven to get away from her. Africans saw the High God as kind but generally unconcerned with the affairs of humanity.

In addition to a Supreme Being, many Africans also believed in lesser gods who had authority over different aspects of life. In many ways, African deities loosely resembled the gods of the Greeks and Romans. However, there were exceptions. The Kikuyu clan did not worship many gods but believed in one god, Ngai. The Kikuyu story of creation includes the creation of a male (Kikuyu) by the god Ngai. Kikuyu was given a wife (Mumbi), and they had nine daughters. When the daughters were old enough to marry, they met nine young men from a distant land. Their descendants became the Kikuyu clan in modern Kenya.

The family also played a key role in traditional African religion. Knowing that the High God was a spirit, Africans also believed that those who left this life continued to live in spirit. Thus, the family included not only living members but also those dead and unborn. Like the Chinese, Africans believed that their dead ancestors influenced their present lives. They also believed that their actions affected their yet unborn children.

Many Africans believed that when the High God left, he left both spirits and humans in the world to run its affairs. This belief resulted in most Africans living in fear of vengeful spirits. These many spirits, not the Creator God, became the object of African worship. Many Africans believed that some spirits lived in trees, rocks, rivers, or mountains, while others simply lived in the air. This belief is called animism. By praying and sacrificing to these spirits, the Africans hoped to receive blessings. They treated the spirits of their ancestors the same as spirits in nature. They believed that all spirits had the power to affect a person's life.

What were the two general characteristics of the High God worshiped in Africa?

African men practicing their animistic religion

CRITICAL THINKING 6.1

What traditional views of the African family departed from scriptural truth? What views upheld truth?

GUIDING QUESTIONS

- What were North and West African civilizations like?
- How did Islam expand in North and West Africa?

6.2 Northern and Western Africa

North Africa

Islam spread across northern Africa, from **Egypt** to **Morocco**. Arabic, the language of Islam, became the dominant language of this region. Muslim culture also replaced or mingled with the cultures of these African countries. Less than a century after the death of Muhammad, Islam controlled all this region north of the Sahara.

Egypt

From 1250 to the late 1800s, Egypt was ruled by two empires—the Mamluk Sultanate and the Ottoman Empire, with a brief seven-year period of French rule in the early 1800s.

Mamluk Sultanate

Who were the Mamluks?

You were introduced to the **Mamluks** in Chapter 3 when they defeated the Mongols at the Battle of Ain Jalut. That battle was just ten years after the founding of the Mamluk kingdom. *Mamluk* means "one who is owned." The Mamluk **Sultanate** was a unique kingdom ruled by slave soldiers. These men had been captured and enslaved as youths, taken from areas now known as Turkey, Armenia, Georgia, and the Balkan peninsula. These slaves were treated well, so they were loyal. They were warriors—well-trained cavalrymen (horse soldiers) and archers.

sultanate Islamic kingdom

They came to power almost by accident. In June 1249 the Egyptian **sultan** was fighting King Louis IX of France in the Seventh Crusade. The Egyptians were losing, and the sultan died, but his wife Shajar al-Durr, took over as the leader. Although she was not a soldier, her origins were the same as the Mamluks, so when she became sultana, it put the Mamluks in power.

A statue of Baibars

Mamluk soldiers defeated the French and kidnapped the king of France. Their commander was a man named Al-Malik al-Zahir Rukn al-Din Baibars al-Bunduqdari, but he went by **Baibars**. The Mamluks demanded a ransom of 400,000 livres (about $22,000,000 today), a huge amount of money for the country of France. The French paid the ransom, and the king was released after he promised never to return to Egypt. Shajar al-Durr married a Mamluk man, and he became the sultan since it was against Islamic tradition for a woman to lead the nation. After Baibars led the Mamluks to victory over the Mongols, it seems he assassinated the Mamluk sultan to become the sultan himself.

Mamluk soldiers kidnapping King Louis IX

Baibars accomplished much during his reign. He was described as energetic, shrewd, intelligent, and foresighted. He fought many wars to grow and solidify the Mamluk empire. The Mamluks extended their power across what is now Israel, Lebanon, Syria, Libya, Sudan, Egypt, and more. Baibars was also able to negotiate treaties with the Byzantine Empire. He traveled between Egypt and Syria to manage the empire.

The Mamluks built roads and canals. Their economy was based on trade, as they followed in the footsteps of Muhammad, who was a trader. They had trade agreements with the Italians. Farming was important but secondary. They grew cotton and sugar along the Nile River. The Mamluks built mosques, madrasas (Islamic schools), and hospitals. They repaired the Al-Aqsa Mosque (Dome of the Rock) in Jerusalem. It is the third-most holy place in Islam, after Mecca and Medina. Slavery continued in the kingdom despite the leaders being former slaves.

Like other empires before and after it, the Mamluk Sultanate faced pressure from all sides and from inside. Tamerlane and later the Ottomans attacked them in Syria. The Mamluks had internal challenges as different regional leaders rebelled. When the Portuguese arrived and started competing with them for trade, the Mamluks were further weakened as they lost income. The population decreased greatly because of famines and the Black Death. So in 1515 they were ripe for the taking by the Ottomans. Led by Selim I, the Ottomans invaded. The Mamluks fought for two years, but the Mamluk cavalry was no match for the Ottoman cannons. Finally, in 1517 Selim marched into Cairo (the capital of Egypt).

How did the Mamluks gain most of their wealth?

Egypt Eyalet

Under the rule of the Ottoman Empire, with its capital at Constantinople, Egypt became just the southern section of the empire. It was called the **Egypt Eyalet**. Egyptian culture declined during the Ottoman years. An example of this is that there are significantly fewer written works from this era. Ironically, the Mamluks retained their role as government officials during the Ottoman years.

What was the Egypt Eyalet?

sultan Muslim king

A fort in the city of Fez, Morocco

Marrakesh, Morocco, the "red city"

What were the two great cities of Morocco during this time?

Morocco

Morocco was the other powerful empire in North Africa. It became the power in northwest Africa following its victory over the Songhai Empire at the Battle of Tondibi in 1591. It won because its soldiers had better rifles than the Songhai soldiers. In 1549 an Arab Islamic government pushed out of power the native Berbers (desert nomads). The Arab leaders claimed to be descendants of Muhammad. The first Arab dynasty was the Saadi dynasty; it lasted until 1659. The second Arab dynasty was the Alaouite dynasty, and it is still in power in Morocco today.

Two cities exemplified the wealth and power of Morocco—**Marrakesh** and **Fez**. These two cities were at various times the capital of Morocco. Marrakesh is known as the "red city" because the buildings are made of red clay. It includes many large mosques with sweeping courtyards. The city also has many parks with olive and palm groves. Fez is in the middle of hills that are covered with orchards and olive trees. There are stone towers that were built to protect the city during an attack.

West Africa

The states of West Africa developed around the year 500. Starting as small city-states headed by a clan or tribal chief, these tribal kingdoms conquered other city-states and clans, thus growing into empires. Gold production in these nations became so prominent that the period between 500 and 1500 is called the Golden Age.

Central-West African Trade and Religion

West Africa is located in the savanna and Sahel regions that lie between the Sahara and tropical forests. As previously mentioned, crops ranged from grains and roots to cotton. However, this region became one of the first to combine a farm-based economy with a trade-based economy. West Africans developed iron production and turned this ore into many useful products. They also learned to work with camels and soon became involved in trade across the Sahara. In addition to cultivating food, the West Africans produced valuable trading items such as iron, cotton cloth, and gold.

Trans-Saharan Caravan Trade

Caravans traveled from oasis to oasis to survive the hazardous journey across the Sahara. Often the distance between oases took several days to travel. Camels were one of the few animals that could survive these journeys.

Camels are uniquely suited for harsh, sand-covered terrain for many reasons.

These traits made the camel a vital tool in hauling goods across a desolate and arid region where water is very scarce. Trade across the Sahara would have been greatly reduced, if not impossible, without the use of camels.

THE ANATOMY OF A CAMEL

SPECIALLY DESIGNED DESERT SURVIVOR

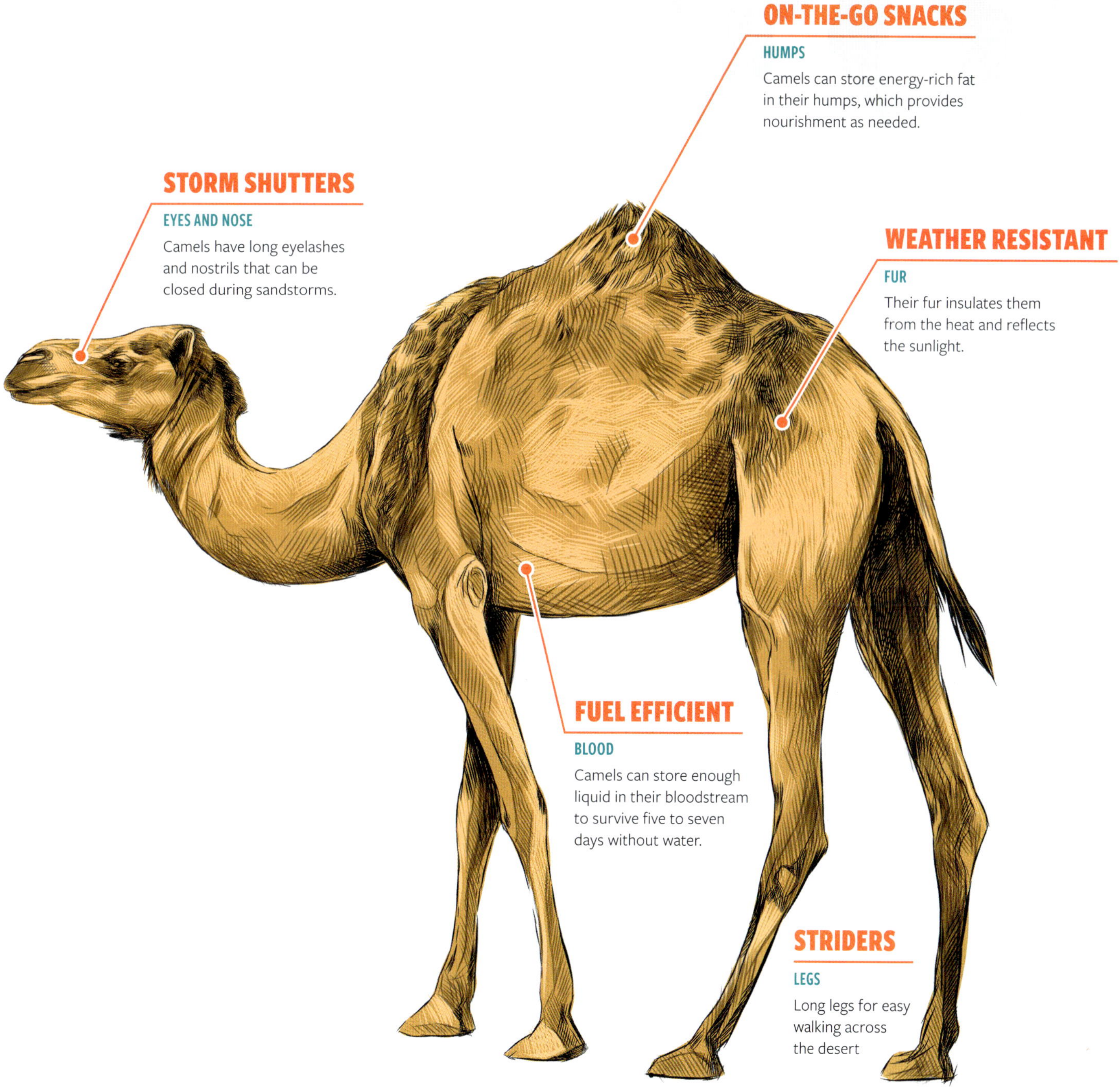

Expansion of Islam

The expansion of Islam to western Africa by way of Muslim traders led to an increased Islamic influence on African culture. Over time, the number of Muslims in this region increased to the point that Islam became the most influential religion in North and West Africa from the Sahel northward. The Muslims did not have as much success south of the Sahel. There would often be a great effort to convert rulers to Islam. Their conversion would ensure the security and influence of this religion. However, the conversion of a ruler seldom led to the conversion of average citizens. The people were generally free to practice whatever religion they desired. Some blended Islam and traditional religion, praying to Allah and offering sacrifices to their gods.

In addition to their beliefs, the Muslims brought a written language. Islamic scholars traveling in Africa taught the people to read and write Arabic. The same scholars recorded what they saw in Africa and gave us the first written history of the continent. Slowly, the ability to read and write changed the culture of Africa, which previously had known only oral recording of history and tradition.

Expansion of Islam, 630–1700

Who brought Islam to Africa?

Sub-Saharan West Africa

The region that lies south of the vast desert known as the Sahara is called **sub-Saharan Africa**. There were two significant people groups in sub-Saharan West Africa at this time, the Akan and the Kongolese.

The Akan People

The **Akan** lived in the area now known as Ghana. They thrived through a combination of farming and mining for gold. They traded with tribes from the Sahel and the Ivory Coast. Their diligent labor produced wealth and power as they gained control of trade. The Akan also exchanged gold for products from distant lands through the Portuguese traders at coastal settlements. The abundance of gold mined in this region led Europeans to refer to it as the **Gold Coast**.

King Otumfuo Nana Osei Tutu II is the traditional ruler of the Kingdom of Ashanti, which was part of the Akan empire from 1701 to 1957.

What was the source of Akan wealth?

Kongo (1390-1857)

The **Kingdom of Kongo** was located in an area encompassing present-day northern Angola and part of the Republic of the Congo and the DRC. Kongo was mostly independent from 1390 till 1857. The kingdom's capital, Mbanza, was a well-developed city in the middle of the jungle about 128 miles from the ocean and 100 miles from the Congo River. By the 1600s, one-fifth of the population of Kongo lived in Mbanza. Kongo depended heavily on trade for its wealth. It traded ivory and made copperware and pottery.

In 1483 the Portuguese explored up the Congo River and made contact with the Kongolese. Eventually, the king of Kongo and several nobles converted to Catholicism. After **King Afonso** of Kongo saw a vision of St. James and Mary, he was victorious in a battle over a rival. So he made Christianity the official religion. King Afonso studied church beliefs to the point that he knew more than the Portuguese missionaries teaching him. The king worked to develop a Roman Catholic Church in Kongo by incorporating pagan Kongolese beliefs into the church. It was Kongolese tradition for nobles to elect the king, but Afonso changed it so that the king's heirs followed him to the throne.

As the Portuguese increased their presence, conflicts increased, and in 1622 the first Kongo-Portuguese war broke out. The Kongolese were victorious over the Portuguese and looked to alliances with the Dutch to maintain their independence. Throughout the 1600s, Kongo and the Dutch fought many wars against the Portuguese. Kongo continued to be weakened by conflicts, civil war, and the slave trade but maintained its independence until 1857.

Kongo pottery

? How did Afonso create a Kongolese church?

? CRITICAL THINKING 6.2

What were at least two ways the Kingdom of Kongo responded to the Portuguese?

A painting depicting the king of the Kongo welcoming European soldiers, possibly in 1650

North and West Africa 1200–1700

1200

1235 The empire of Mali is established.

1250 Mamluk slaves begin their reign in Egypt.

1260 Egypt, under the Mamluk dynasty, halts the Mongol invasion at the Battle of Ain Jalut.

1324 Mansa Musa, emperor of the Kingdom of Mali, makes a pilgrimage to Mecca.

1366 Mamluks invade Nubia during a period of unrest.

1390 The Kingdom of Kongo is established in central Africa with its capital, Mbanza Kongo.

1434 Portuguese establish trading outposts along the West African coast.

1441 Antão Gonçalves of Portugal buys slaves in what is now Senegal and transports them to Lisbon, beginning direct European involvement in the African slave trade.

1462 Pope Pius II signs a papal bull which forbids enslavement of Africans recently converted to Christianity.

1470 The Portuguese begin trading along the Gold Coast of West Africa.

1483 Portuguese explorers land in the Kingdom of Kongo.

1517 Egypt becomes part of the Ottoman Empire.

1591 Morocco invades Songhai and holds control of the region until the 17th century.

1603 Morocco is split into two sultanates, Fez and Marrakesh.

1672 Alaouite dynasty is founded in Morocco.

1700

6.3 Eastern and Southern Africa

Sub-Saharan eastern and southern Africa blossomed with the growth of cities, the expansion of empires, and an explosion of trade.

GUIDING QUESTIONS

- What was the Ethiopian civilization like?
- How did Ethiopia resist Islam and seek to connect itself to the Christian world?
- How did commercial towns rise on the coast of Eastern Africa?
- How were Islam and Arab settlement important in East Africa?
- Why was Great Zimbabwe important?

Ethiopia

The **Zagwe dynasty** rose in **Ethiopia** roughly two hundred years after the Aksum Empire fell. The Aksum kingdom ceased in the later 700s because of droughts, overgrazing, and disease. The Zagwe dynasty lasted until 1270, but we know little about it. King Lalibela reigned during this time and left behind magnificent memorials: churches carved out of stone. The king commissioned the Coptic Church to build eleven churches. These churches were carved out of solid bedrock below ground level. A person standing on ground level can look down to view these remarkable structures. The churches have windows and have been sculpted inside and out. St. George's Church, the most famous of these churches, is shaped like a cross. The **Coptic Church**, founded in Alexandria, Egypt, in AD 42, has teachings about Christ's nature that are similar to those of the Nestorians. The Coptics sent missionaries south along the Nile River to establish churches in Nubia and Ethiopia. The Coptic Church remains the official church of Ethiopia today. After the Zagwe dynasty ended, another Christian kingdom took over called the **Solomonic dynasty**.

The Church of St. George in Lalibela, Ethiopia

ETHIOPIA

Justice

The Ethiopian kings adopted a Christian law code that the Egyptian Coptic Christians had imported from the Byzantines. It was called The Law of the Kings. The first part of the law outlined rules for the church; the second part concerned family and civil law. The law was based on principles found in the Old and New Testaments and was in effect until the 1970s.

Power

Ethiopian kings claimed their right to rule as descendants of Menelik, the supposed son of the Queen of Sheba and King Solomon. The Ethiopians even use the imperial title "The Conquering Lion of the Tribe of Judah." The kings also claimed their power as the keepers of the original ark of the covenant, which they say is on the altar in the cathedral at Aksum, a city in northern Ethiopia.

Religion

The Ethiopian church has retained many of its beliefs and traditions that began in Bible times. The leaders of the church are called patriarchs. The patriarchs claim that Ethiopians accepted Judaism long before they accepted Christianity. It is probably true since, in Acts 8, we find the Ethiopian eunuch, a royal official, traveling back from worshiping in Jerusalem. He had never heard of Jesus but was following the Old Testament law. Philip told the eunuch about Jesus; he believed and was baptized. The eunuch must have gone back and told the Ethiopian ruling class about Jesus. In 1441 the Roman Catholic Church hoped to unify with the Ethiopian church and thus gain a strong ally in Africa. But after years of effort, the union failed because Ethiopians would not abandon their understanding of the nature of Christ, that he had two distinct persons, divine and human. Catholics held to the view that Jesus was fully God and fully man, with the natures united.

Environment

Ethiopia was one of the first sub-Saharan African countries to use the ox-drawn plow. Therefore, there was a long tradition of farming since it enabled them to be self-sufficient. They held firmly to their traditional ways of farming. A Portuguese missionary observed that Ethiopian farmers would rather be wrong than change their ways. Because they did not adjust their farming practices to changing conditions, they suffered.

Our Lady Mary of Zion church in Aksum, Ethiopia, believed by Ethiopians to be the home of the ark of the covenant

The ruins of Kilwa

Ethiopia's Resistance to Islam

When Islam began to spread across North Africa in the seventh century, **Nubia**, present-day Sudan, blocked its spread to the south. After defeating Muslim invaders, the Nubians negotiated a peace that lasted six hundred years. At times Nubia was strong enough to send its troops as far north as Alexandria to protect Christian interests in Egypt. But by the early fourteenth century, the Mamluks from Egypt were able to appoint a Muslim king over Nubia. After this, Ethiopia struggled to defend itself from the onslaught of Islamic invaders. It fought an Islamic army that came from the region now known as Somalia. The Ethiopian-Adal War lasted from 1529 to 1543. The Christian kingdom survived, but the Muslims established a foothold in Harar, Ethiopia.

The Swahili Coast Cities

Around the twelfth century, the earliest trade cities appeared along the coast of East Africa. Cities such as Mapungubwe, Manda, and Shanga thrived on the trade of products such as gold, slaves, and ivory. However, within a century, these cities declined in importance as other cities arose to take their place. Muqdisho (modern Mogadishu on the Somali coast) and **Kilwa** rose in prominence during the thirteenth century. Kilwa is known for its impressive buildings made of coral. In the 1200s, a large palace was built there. It was considered by some to be one of the most beautiful cities in the world at that time.

Africans from the interior brought gold, ivory, and precious stones to these cities. They would walk hundreds of miles across the continent to coastal cities while carrying goods balanced on their heads. Merchants from Arabia, India, and even China sailed to these cities to trade. Eventually, these goods from Africa went to markets throughout Asia.

In July, traders from Asia and the interior of Africa came to the East African coastal cities to exchange their goods. The summer monsoon winds carried the ships loaded with African products east. In October, the winds reversed direction and carried the ships back to the ports in Africa. If this trade was protected, commercial prosperity was ensured. Empires developed, in part, to protect this profitable trade.

? **Where did the Africans and Asians trade their goods?**

Significance of Swahili

The language of these cities reflects the meeting of many cultures. The people spoke a common trade language known as **Swahili**. Swahili is built on the Bantu language and has served as the native tongue of various groups living along the southeast African coastline. About 35 percent of Swahili words are Arabic in origin. This Arab influence resulted from centuries of contact between Arab traders and many different Bantu-speaking peoples living along Africa's Indian Ocean coast. Swahili also uses words from many other languages, including English. This foreign influence was caused by the migration of many nationalities to this region and by contact through trade with different groups of people. This common language enabled many tribes and nationalities to carry on trade.

? **What was the trade language of East Africa?**

The ruins of Great Zimbabwe ▸

▲ The walls of Great Zimbabwe were made of carefully cut stone fitted together without mortar.

Islam in Sub-Saharan Africa

The spread of Islam to regions of sub-Saharan Africa was more gradual than its spread in northern Africa. Islamic merchants traveled to East Africa from Arabia and Persia. Islam came to South Africa in yet another way—with slaves brought in from Indonesia and Southeast Asia. These Muslims brought their religion with them. Over time, some of the Muslim merchants settled in West and East Africa and established communities. Initially, Islam and Coptic Christianity coexisted peacefully. However, Islam eventually became dominant and, to varying degrees, imposed its beliefs on the people.

Great Zimbabwe (1220–1450)

In the mid-1200s, the city of **Great Zimbabwe** was established on the Zimbabwe Plateau near the Sabi River. This city grew to a population of 15,000 to 20,000 citizens in the 1300s. The empire that developed was located in southeastern Africa between the Limpopo and Zambezi Rivers. Zimbabwe thrived on raising cattle and exporting gold, slaves, and ivory to the coast. Trade from India and China also passed through this empire.

For at least two hundred years, Zimbabwe expanded and built massive stone buildings and enclosures. The most famous structure is the Great Enclosure, which still stands thirty-five feet high with a base about fifteen feet thick. Perhaps even more impressive is that these great buildings were built without mortar. The stones were carefully cut and fitted together with precision. Many of the structures have survived for over seven hundred years.

This empire lay about two hundred miles from the East African coast. Therefore, it relied on coastal cities to receive and transport goods. Kilwa became a key port through which Zimbabwe's gold was transported north.

Zimbabwe means "great house of stone" or "place of stone houses." This city-state grew into a great empire over two centuries. The ruins cover eighteen hundred acres and include an area more than one hundred miles in diameter. In addition, bone fragments show that thousands of cattle were killed for meat. The vast eating of beef indicates a large wealthy class that could afford such luxury. For reasons unknown, this empire fell into rapid decline during the early fifteenth century. By the 1450s, Great Zimbabwe was abandoned by most of its occupants.

? **What does Zimbabwe mean?**

Mutapa Kingdom (1430–1693)

The **Mutapa Kingdom** came after Great Zimbabwe and controlled roughly the same territory of inland southern Africa as Great Zimbabwe. The people of Mutapa depended mostly on farming and livestock trade for their livelihood. There were gold mines that the king tightly controlled. The king and the ruling class gained wealth from the gold, ivory, copper, and slave trades. The kingdom was highly organized; the king had several advisors that he depended on to help him rule. Mutapa did not leave any stone structures as Great Zimbabwe did. Not until the early 1600s did the Portuguese explore the interior where the Mutapa Kingdom was located. Around 1633 they attacked the kingdom in hopes of getting the gold. But they did not find great amounts of gold and were soon victims of the many tropical diseases in the interior. The Portuguese left, but Mutapa was permanently damaged and fell to a rival kingdom in 1693.

? **Why did the Portuguese attack the Mutapa Kingdom?**

? CRITICAL THINKING 6.3

How might Ethiopia have been considered a Christian kingdom? How might it not?

South and East Africa 1200–1750

1220

The kingdom of Zimbabwe is established.

1300

1430

Mutapa Empire emerges in Southern Africa.

1431

Ming admiral Zheng He reaches the East African coast and begins a period of trade between the Swahili city-states and China.

1441

Act of Union is signed in Rome between the Church of Ethiopia and the Church of Rome.

1450

Great Zimbabwe is abandoned.

1500

1585

The Luba Kingdom is established in central Africa.

1628

Following a battle, the Portuguese replace the leadership in Mutapa with a lord under their control.

1652

The Dutch establish a permanent settlement at Table Bay in what is now South Africa.

1700

1729

Portuguese presence and authority is removed from the Swahili coast with the help of Omani Arabs.

6.4 The African Slave Trade

A slave is a person who is owned by another and forced to obey his or her owner. Since ancient times slavery has existed in the world, including in Africa. You may recall the Genesis account of Joseph being sold into slavery. Slavery continues today. Although the percentage of those in slavery compared to the world population is at its lowest, there may be as many as forty million people in slavery, some say the largest number in history.

GUIDING QUESTIONS

- How did African slavery compare to slavery in other parts of the world?
- What was the transatlantic slave trade?
- How did the transatlantic slave trade affect the Africans?
- How did African leaders and elites participate in the sale of slaves?

Early Islamic Slave Trade and European Serfdom

Slavery existed in Arabia before Islam, but it continued after the religion was founded. As the sources for slaves in Arabia lessened, the traders looked further and further. Once a people group accepted Islam, they could not be enslaved. Because Muslim traders were not allowed to enslave Muslims, they had to look for slaves in Africa and Europe. It seems they traded them in the same way they traded spices and gold. Early on, the slave trade was conducted at the Swahili coast and in North African trading cities. Women were enslaved at much higher numbers in the early Islamic slave trade than the later European slave trade.

North African Barbary pirates from the area now known as Libya and Tunisia enslaved Europeans. Most of the slaves were English and Italian women that were kidnapped from coastal cities. Slaves in the Islamic world were not used in large groups on plantations as they were later used in the New World. The Arabs experienced large revolts when they tried plantation slavery. Instead, they used slaves in small numbers as servants, cooks, and in other roles.

? How did the Muslims use slaves?

There were others in slavery in other parts of the world in the 1400s. In Eastern Europe up until the mid-1800s, there were people called **serfs** who were required to farm the land. They were different from slaves since they were attached to the land and could not be sold to others except with the land. However, they were like slaves in that they had no freedom to leave and no way to better their situation.

Portuguese African Slave Trade

In 1441, two Portuguese captains bought twelve African slaves from slave traders in the area now known as Mauritania, beginning a European practice that would continue until the early 1800s. In 1452 the Portuguese started growing sugar on the island of Madeira, off the African coast. Because sugarcane was such a labor-intensive crop, the Portuguese required many workers, a demand they fulfilled through obtaining African slaves.

Pope Nicholas V gave the Portuguese authority to put pagans and unbelievers into perpetual servitude in a declaration he gave on June 18, 1452, called the ***Dum Diversas***. By the 1470s the Spanish had joined the Portuguese in trading for African slaves.

? Why did the Portuguese want slaves?

African slaves harvesting sugar cane in the Caribbean

Countries Responsible for Transporting Slaves to the Americas 1501–1866

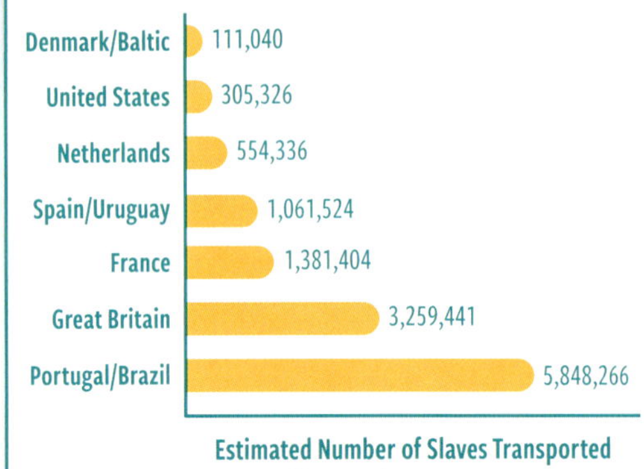

Source: slavevoyages.org

Captured slaves being taken to the port

The Transatlantic Slave Trade

In 1502 a Spanish merchant named Juan de Córdoba was the first recorded person to have shipped an African slave across the Atlantic to the Americas. African kings saw great profit in selling slaves to the Portuguese. Before the Europeans arrived, these kings were already putting people from rival tribes into slavery. They had slave markets where they sold debtors and prisoners of war. In the beginning, the slave trade helped kings solidify their rule. As the demand for slaves increased, King Afonso of Kongo accused the Portuguese of taking slaves illegally.

Prior to the transatlantic slave trade, people taken in slavery had been an outcome of war but not the purpose for going to war. With the increased European demand, gaining slaves became the purpose for going to war with other tribes. Ultimately the practice of slavery greatly weakened Kongo and other kingdoms. Some have claimed that the Africans who sold the people into slavery did not understand the ultimate conditions the slaves would face, but the African slave traders at least understood the Africans were destined for very bad conditions. In the end, the Africans cared more about freedom for themselves, their families, clans, and tribes than the well-being of those they were selling into servitude. Because the Europeans preferred male slaves, the population of West Africa quickly became imbalanced, with more women than men. It is estimated that some twelve million Africans were taken across the Atlantic. Many of those captured and enslaved in the interior died on the long journey to the coast, and many more perished on the ocean voyage.

The Europeans built castles on the west coast of Africa where they kept the slaves until the ships arrived. Hundreds of Africans were crammed into small rooms in the castles and shackled. They could spend up to three months in these rooms. The castle door-way that faced the sea was called the "door of no return."

CRITICAL THINKING 6.4

How should those who justly condemn the transatlantic slave trade respond to the slavery that goes on today?

A castle in West Africa built for imprisoning slaves destined to cross the Atlantic

Making Connections

1. How did Africans pass on their history and traditions?
2. How was the family important in early African culture?
3. How did most Africans use their livestock, and how did that differ from the use of livestock in Great Zimbabwe?
4. How did the Mamluks come to power in Egypt?
5. What did the Mamluks build?
6. Why was the west coast of Africa referred to as the Gold Coast?
7. Why were camels so vital in Africa?
8. What did the Kongolese nobles do after encountering the Portuguese?
9. On what basis did Ethiopian kings claim their right to rule?
10. How did the development of Swahili enhance trade?
11. How did Islam spread to sub-Saharan Africa?
12. Where did Great Zimbabwe get its wealth?
13. What is the definition of a slave?
14. Why did Africans sell other Africans?
15. Who were the first Europeans to buy slaves in Africa?

Thinking Critically

1. How does the Africans' avoidance of killing their livestock show wisdom in managing their resources?
2. What would life have been like in Africa without the camel?
3. Why did the Muslims and Catholics have to blend traditional African beliefs with their religion?
4. Why was Ethiopia more effective at resisting Islam than other places in Africa?
5. What does the development of trade reveal about the level of East African civilization?
6. When Europeans discovered Great Zimbabwe, they claimed that Africans could not have built this structure. Use verses such as Genesis 4:17 and 11:1-4 to evaluate this claim.
7. How did the transatlantic slave trade change Africa?

WHAT TO KNOW

PEOPLE

Mamluks
Baibars
King Afonso

PLACES

Egypt
Morocco
Marrakesh
Fez
Kingdom of Kongo
Ethiopia
Nubia
Kilwa
Great Zimbabwe
Mutapa Kingdom

TERMS

griots
savanna
Sahel
clan
sultanate
sultan
Egypt Eyalet
Gold Coast
Swahili
serf
Dum Diversas

7 COLONIZATION OF THE AMERICAS

1524 – 1763

ESSENTIAL QUESTIONS

- How did European economics and religion shape the colonization of the Americas?
- What strategies did European powers use to settle and govern Latin America?
- How did colonial governments in Latin America treat the people they governed?
- In what ways did the Spanish, French, and English patterns of colonization differ in North America?
- What role did religion play in the development of colonial empires?

The Passengers on the *Mayflower*

In 1608 two Separatist groups left England. Separatists believed the state church of England had unbiblical practices. They wanted to separate from the state church and worship God as they saw fit. These groups traveled first to the Netherlands, which had a reputation for religious freedom. But after twelve years some decided to look for a new home, hoping for relief from hardships, separation from ungodly influences, and opportunities to spread the gospel.

This small group of Separatists decided to move to America. They raised money, received a charter to establish a colony in northern Virginia (now part of New York) from a trading company called the Virginia Company, and hired two ships, the *Mayflower* and the *Speedwell*. Several non-Separatist passengers joined the group. They had valuable skills that could help the new colony. In addition, there were indentured servants (people who worked in exchange for the cost of the trip) and crew members.

The ships sailed in August of 1620, but the *Speedwell* had a leak. After two attempts to leave and six weeks of wasted good weather, the leaders transferred everyone to the *Mayflower*.

The *Mayflower* finally left on September 16. Violent storms caused seasickness for the passengers and prevented the ship from using its sails. After sixty-six days, the group sighted Cape Cod (today in Massachusetts). Though they had planned to settle farther south, they chose not to risk the stormy sea again. However, the Virginia Company had no authority on this part of the coast, so their charter was useless. They wrote a new agreement of self-government, now known as the **Mayflower Compact**, and signed it on November 11, 1620.

The *Mayflower* had 102 passengers: 41 Separatists (who called themselves "Saints") and 61 non-Separatist passengers and indentured servants (called "Strangers" by the Separatists). In addition, there were approximately 30 crew members. Below you can read about five of the people who made this historic voyage.

William Bradford was a Separatist leader. He began worshiping with a Separatist congregation as a teenager. He moved with the congregation to the Netherlands in 1608 and then to America in 1620. Bradford was governor of the new colony for more than thirty years. His journal, *Of Plymouth Plantation*, is an important record of the colony's history. Bradford was the first to use the term "pilgrim" for the Separatist colonists, a reference to Hebrews 11:13–16. Many years later, the colonists would be commonly known as Pilgrims.

Stephen and Elizabeth Hopkins were non-Separatist passengers. Stephen had visited America before. In 1609 he joined an expedition to help the struggling colony of Jamestown. His ship wrecked off the coast of Bermuda, and he spent time there as well as in Jamestown. Having received word that his wife had died, Stephen returned to England to take care of his children and eventually married Elizabeth Fisher. The Hopkins family agreed to join the Separatists in 1620. Stephen provided knowledge of the land and skill as a tanner and merchant. Elizabeth was the only woman to give birth on the voyage across the ocean. The baby was named Oceanus.

John Howland was an indentured servant. His *Mayflower* voyage almost ended in tragedy. During one storm he fell overboard and was saved only because he grabbed a rope while falling. Howland eventually held several important positions in the colony. His many famous descendants include Franklin Roosevelt, George H. W. Bush, and George W. Bush.

Christopher Jones was the captain of the *Mayflower*. Jones had a merchant business, but he needed new financial opportunities. He agreed to transport the Separatists. Many of Jones's crew got sick and died during the winter that followed their landing.

GUIDING QUESTIONS

- What is *mercantilism*?
- What is *capitalism*?
- How are the goals and methods of mercantilism and capitalism different?
- What happened during the wars of religion?
- How did the wars of religion affect European unity?

7.1 European Economics and Religion

European overseas exploration was frequently followed by the establishment of colonies. To understand how and why colonies developed as they did, it is helpful to know what was going on in Europe. New economic philosophies and conflicts over religion both played an important role in European colonization trends.

Economic Philosophies

Mercantilism

From around 1500 to 1800, Europe was dominated by an economic philosophy known as **mercantilism**. Under mercantilism, a country was considered wealthy if it had a large supply of gold and silver. The way to keep that supply was simple: make more money than you spend. For a nation, that meant there should be more **exports** (goods that are sold to other countries) than **imports** (goods that are bought from other countries).

Governments that followed mercantilist theory actively regulated economic activity. They encouraged exports by strategies like giving money to new industries and building roads, bridges, and canals to make travel easier for traders. They discouraged imports by putting **tariffs** (taxes) on goods coming into the country, thereby raising prices for consumers.

Mercantilism vs. Capitalism

	Mercantilism	Capitalism
Goals	 To have a large supply of gold and silver	 To provide goods and services through competition in a marketplace
Methods	exports / imports Encourage exports (give money to new businesses; build roads, bridges, and canals) discourage imports (put tariffs on foreign goods)	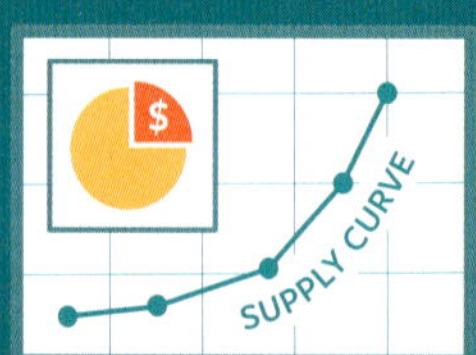 Use the buying decisions of customers to guide decisions about production.

What must a country have to be considered wealthy under mercantilism?

Capitalism

Many modern countries follow an economic philosophy called **capitalism**. Under capitalism, businesses are owned by individuals or **corporations** as opposed to being owned by the government. Businesses try to make money as they compete in a **marketplace**. What goods (or services) to make, how many to make, and how much to charge for them are based on what customers will buy. Capitalism in its modern form was popularized by a book called *The Wealth of Nations*, written by Adam Smith (see Chapter 9) and published in 1776.

Who owns businesses under capitalism?

corporation a business that receives a legal charter and sells stock to individual investors

marketplace a location where goods and services are bought and sold

Effects on Colonization

Mercantilism motivated many countries to establish colonies. Under mercantilist theory, colonies existed for the financial benefit of their mother countries (countries that establish colonies). Colonies helped manufacturers in the mother country by providing them with raw materials at relatively low prices and by buying their finished goods. In this way, mercantilist nations supported their goal of accumulating as much gold and silver as possible.

Capitalism, though not as prominent during this period, did influence colonization through the development of the **joint-stock company**, an early version of the corporation. Many merchants wanted to share in the profits that could be gained through trade with colonies, but few could afford to finance a colony by themselves. So joint-stock companies were created. With this arrangement multiple people invested money in a colony and received profits if the colony did well. The Virginia Company, which gave a charter to the English Separatists, was one of the earliest joint-stock companies.

Coat of arms of the Virginia Company of London

Which economic system involves active government participation in the economy?

Conflicts over Religion

Religion was another important factor in the development of colonies. Many areas of the world continue to show a strong Catholic or Protestant influence today based on the European countries that colonized them. The religion that each colonizing country embraced was affected not just by the Protestant and Catholic Reformations but also by various wars of religion of the 1500s.

France

Most of France remained Catholic after the Protestant Reformation; however, a small, determined minority, known as **Huguenots**, accepted a Calvinist form of Protestantism. Conflict eventually broke out between those who wanted to return all of France to Catholicism and those who wanted freedom to worship as Protestants. Politics complicated the situation because some thought the royal Valois family (which remained Catholic) had too much power and supported the Huguenots for political reasons.

Fighting began in 1562 and continued periodically for the next several years. One of the worst incidents was the Saint Bartholomew's Day massacre in 1572. King Charles IX's sister, a member of the Catholic Valois family, married **Henry of Navarre**, a member of the Huguenot Bourbon family, in Paris. It could have been a time of reconciliation for the two sides; instead, the Guise family, a noble family who passionately defended the Catholic Church, talked the king into attacking the Huguenots. Approximately three thousand Huguenots were murdered in Paris, while thousands more were attacked in other parts of France.

Later conflicts led eventually to the defeat of the Guise family, the death of a Valois king (Henry III), and the choosing of the Huguenot noble Henry of Navarre as king. Henry converted to Catholicism to avoid future troubles but issued the **Edict of Nantes**, which granted limited religious toleration to the Huguenots. Under a future French king, however, the edict would be revoked, and the Huguenots would be forced to flee France.

Artist's depiction of the St. Bartholomew's Day massacre

How did Henry of Navarre try to end religious warfare in France?

Philip II of Spain

Philip II was the son of the Habsburg ruler Charles V and Isabella of Portugal. He ruled over a global Spanish empire that included extensive territory in Europe as well as possessions on four other continents and many island territories (for example, the Philippine Islands were named for Philip). Philip was married four times (Mary I of England was his second wife) and had children with three of his wives.

As ruler of an enormous empire, Philip worked diligently but not always wisely. He liked to know every detail possible about an issue before deciding on it, so he spent hours poring over reports. He had a hard time ignoring unimportant details, even correcting spelling in correspondence he received. Too much attention to detail and a failure to make decisions promptly kept his government from ruling efficiently.

Philip was known especially as a champion of Catholicism. From Spain and Italy in the south of Europe to France, the Netherlands, and England in the north, Philip sought either to keep Protestantism from gaining ground or to reverse the process where it had already taken hold. In addition, as Spain explored and colonized areas across the globe, it took Catholicism with it, so Philip's empire was directly responsible for the spread of Catholicism to many areas of the world where it still has influence today.

The German States

Beginning in 1273, the emperors of the Holy Roman Empire were chosen from a family named Habsburg. The **Habsburgs** became one of the most powerful families in Europe, and they were strong supporters of the Catholic Church. The Habsburg ruler **Charles V** was named emperor in 1519, just as Martin Luther's ideas were starting to have an impact in the German states.

As religious disagreements began dividing the empire, Charles called various meetings of the Diet (German legislative body) to try to resolve the problem. Then in 1531 he issued a decree outlawing Lutheranism. This led to an alliance of Protestant German princes, determined to fight for the right to choose their own religion. Charles was distracted for many years with threats from foreign powers, but starting in 1549 he engaged in a series of wars with the Protestants and their allies. These wars were finally settled with the **Peace of Augsburg** (1555), which gave each German prince the right to choose the religion for his territory.

? **What right was granted by the Peace of Augsburg?**

Spain and the Netherlands

The Habsburgs controlled much territory. As Holy Roman Emperors, they officially ruled over the German states and a section of the Italian states. Through war and marriage alliances, they had gained control over Spain, Spain's overseas colonies, the Netherlands, and parts of Central Europe. When Charles V stepped down from ruling the Habsburg possessions in 1556, his authority was split between his brother Ferdinand (grandson of the Ferdinand who commissioned Christopher Columbus), who became Holy Roman Emperor, and his son Philip, who became the king of Spain. Following a strong tradition of Spanish religious zeal, **Philip II** (1556–98) became one of the strongest defenders of Catholicism in Europe.

Part of the territory that Spain controlled in the 1500s was the Netherlands (today the countries of Belgium, the Netherlands, and Luxembourg). Philip introduced several changes that the people of the Netherlands disliked: he tried to increase Spanish authority, he used their tax money to help Spain, and he tried to get rid of Calvinism. In response to unrest among Calvinist nobles, Philip sent troops to the Netherlands under the leadership of the Duke of Alva. The duke's harsh tactics created further bad will.

The seventeen provinces of the Netherlands tried to work together under the leadership of William the Orange to oppose Spanish control, but religious differences kept the alliance from working effectively. Eventually, the seven northern Protestant provinces went their own way, becoming known as the United Provinces or the **Dutch Republic.** The ten southern Catholic provinces remained under the control of Spain as the Spanish Netherlands.

? **How were the Netherlands split along religious lines?**

England

England became a Protestant nation through an unusual set of circumstances. King **Henry VIII** (ruler from 1509 to 1547), a devoted Catholic, asked the pope for a divorce from his wife, Catherine of Aragon, who had not produced any male heirs who lived past birth. Henry needed the divorce so that he could marry another woman, Anne Boleyn. Because the pope did not want to offend Charles V, Catherine's nephew, he refused. As a result, England eventually passed the Act of Supremacy, which identified the king as "the only supreme head on earth of the **Church of England**," and Henry got his divorce.

Though England was no longer officially under the Roman Catholic Church, it was uncertain how much change would be made in the doctrine and practice of the new church. Under Henry's son, **Edward VI**, the Church of England took a strong Protestant direction, but Edward died after only six years as king. His half-sister **Mary I**, daughter of Catherine of Aragon, and her husband, Philip II of Spain, were devout Catholics and made strong efforts to return England to the Catholic Church, including the persecution of Protestants. But Mary, like her brother, died without an heir after only a few years as monarch.

Elizabeth I, Mary's half-sister and queen for almost forty-five years, took a middle ground. Under Elizabeth, the Church of England was Protestant in its doctrine and practice, but it took steps to avoid offending Catholics. It also tried to avoid identifying too closely with the ideas of one group of Protestants over others. Elizabeth's moderate approach kept England relatively peaceful during her reign.

Burning Protestants at the stake earned Mary the nickname "Bloody Mary" and turned many English against Catholicism.

What was involved in Elizabeth I's moderate approach to religion?

Spread of Reformation in the Mid-1500s

TURNING POINTS

Spanish Armada

Elizabeth I of England seemed at first glance to be as moderate in foreign policy as she was in religion. She did not want war, and she avoided open conflict with her European neighbors. However, secretly she supported Protestant minorities in France and the Spanish Netherlands against their Catholic governments. She secretly encouraged English privateers (privately-owned ships that were used in war, especially for capturing enemy goods), which stole gold and silver from Spanish ships. Philip II of Spain eventually decided to invade England, both to stop these troublesome activities and to restore the country to Catholicism.

Sea captain Francis Drake was the first Englishman to circumnavigate the globe. He stole much Spanish treasure along the way.

The invasion strategy involved two groups: a fleet of Spanish ships and the Spanish army that was based in the Netherlands. The plan was for the army to cross the English Channel to attack England. The fleet would protect them from English ships while they made the crossing. A fleet of this type is known as an *armada*, so the invasion is commonly called the **Spanish Armada**.

As the Spanish and English anticipated war at sea, each side had a strategy that fit its strengths. Spain had experienced soldiers, so it hoped to get its ships close enough to English ships to allow its soldiers to board and fight the English directly. England, on the other hand, had many mounted cannons, so it hoped to keep away from Spanish ships and destroy them from a distance.

The Armada left Spain in July of 1588 and anchored off the coast of northern France in early August, engaging in three small battles with English ships along the way. Having to wait a few days for the soldiers to arrive from the Netherlands, the motionless Armada was an easy target. England sent fire ships (ships that were loaded with explosives and set on fire) against the fleet, drawing them back out into the open waters. Another battle and strong winds kept the Armada from its mission of escorting the soldiers across the Channel. Instead, the fleet had to return home by going up and around Scotland and down the coast of Ireland. Less than half the ships that started the voyage returned; the rest were lost due to battles, bad weather, lack of supplies, or human error.

Though Spain rebuilt ships and would experience additional conflicts with England in the future, the defeat of the Spanish Armada had a significant impact. Spain, with one of the most powerful militaries of the day, had been defeated. The Church of England remained independent. And English colonies established in North America in the next century would be chiefly Protestant.

1. Why did Philip II decide to invade England?
2. What was the basic strategy for the Spanish Armada, and why did it fail?
3. What was the significance of the Spanish defeat?

CRITICAL THINKING 7.1

How did the wars of religion permanently change the religious unity Europe had experienced before the Reformation?

7.2 Colonization of Latin America

South America was settled mainly by Spain and Portugal. Their similarities enabled them to establish a single Latin American culture. Once the boundaries dividing their holdings were set by the Line of Demarcation and the Treaty of Tordesillas (see Chapter 5), the Spanish and Portuguese rarely had conflict, although one major disagreement did occur in the area now known as Uruguay. The Portuguese had claimed the land down to the Uruguay River, but Spanish settlements were established on the Portuguese side of the river. The Spanish agreed to give up these settlements but then established other Spanish settlements in disputed lands. The conflict continued until a treaty was signed in 1777.

Other European nations established small claims in the South American continent. The French explored the Brazilian coast from 1503 to 1509. Their explorations made the Portuguese nervous enough to send a fleet of ships to protect Portuguese claims. However, the Portuguese soon gave up this effort, and in 1604 the French established a settlement in the northern region of South America. This territory later became known as French Guiana.

The Dutch and English also established settlements by the name of Guiana in the northern region of South America. Oddly enough, in 1581 the Dutch settled what later became British Guiana, and the British settled the area that later became Dutch Guiana. The Dutch lost their original territory to the English after several battles, and the English traded their Guiana to the Dutch for New York. Later, the names of both areas changed. British Guiana became Guyana, and Dutch Guiana became Suriname.

GUIDING QUESTIONS

- How were the Spanish and Portuguese colonial empires in the Americas similar and different in their development?
- How were indigenous people and slaves treated?
- Did the actions of the Catholic Church improve government in Latin American empires?
- How did the introduction of new plants, animals, and diseases affect the people of both the New and Old Worlds?

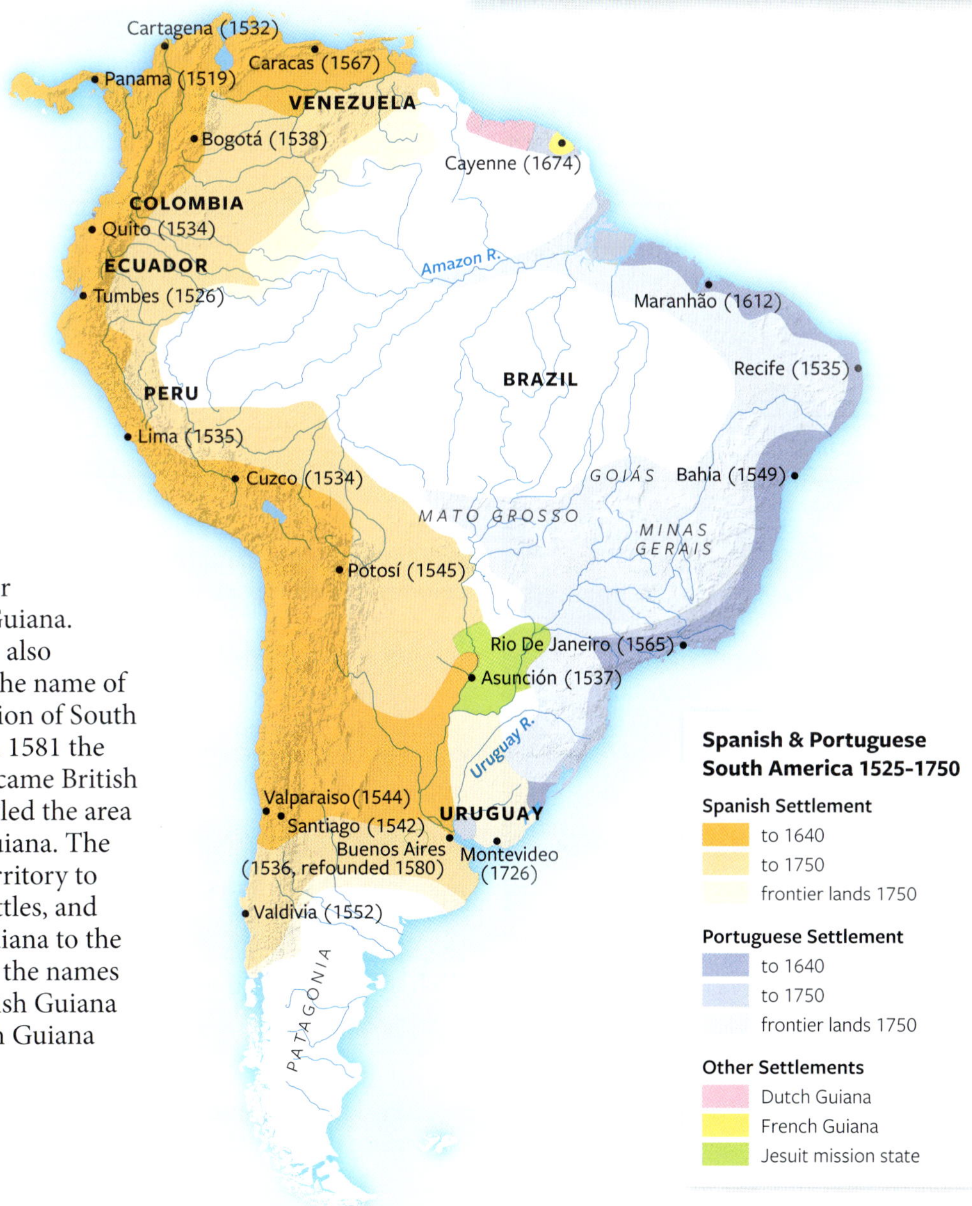

In addition to defending the colonies, colonial officials generally filled one of the following roles: promote religion, regulate trade, ensure justice.

Ruling the Colonies

Common Trends

Though Spanish and Portuguese rule in South America developed along different lines, there were some common trends. First, the Spanish and Portuguese to some degree ignored the **Creoles** (people of pure Spanish or Portuguese descent born in the Americas). The kings of Spain and Portugal instead often gave governing duties to those born in the mother country.

Second, both countries strictly managed the production of goods in the colonies, following the policies of mercantilism. They determined the price, quantity, and types of goods that could be produced and sold in the colonies. They placed high taxes on goods being exported and charged high prices on goods being imported. This practice severely restricted personal as well as colonial economic growth.

What similarities were there between Spanish and Portuguese rule of their colonies in the New World?

Portuguese Colonial Development

The system of government initially used by the Portuguese proved to be ineffective. Instead of retaining most of the power for itself, Portugal granted great authority to twelve nobles. These nobles received the title of **donatário**. The Portuguese government gave them total control of individual sections of land, and the donatários determined how the land would be divided among colonists. They were responsible to colonize, defend, and promote the religious and economic welfare of their territory.

Though these officials seemed to have great power, they often had trouble controlling the settlers, keeping other European countries out of their territory, and finding people to cultivate the land. In 1549 King John of Portugal began a process that put Portugal in more direct control of the colonies in Brazil. Conditions improved for a time, but the Portuguese officials also proved unable to govern well. Despite these problems, the tiny country of Portugal was able to maintain control of a colony eighty times its size for three hundred years.

Spanish Colonial Development

All laws and policies for the Spanish colonies came directly from Spain. This included all religious and economic policies. The Catholic Church became the official church in all Spanish colonies. Spanish officials had significant control over church affairs, having been granted authority by the pope in exchange for Spanish efforts to spread the Catholic faith. Economically, Spain took advantage of its colonies' resources, taking, for example, a percentage of their mined gold and silver.

In 1524 Spain established the Council of the Indies to oversee its colonies. The colonies were divided into large units called *viceroyalties*. Each was ruled by an official called a **viceroy**. Viceroys were expected to ensure that colonies operated efficiently and profitably and that inhabitants of the colonies were treated fairly. **Audiencias** were another important institution. They were high-level courts, and they also helped to carry out laws coming from Spain. Unlike viceroys, members of the *audiencias* often held their positions for life.

viceroy colonial ruler who represented the monarch of the mother country

Viceroys were almost always from Spain. In the 1600s the *audiencias* had many Creole members who were born in the Americas. However, in the mid-1700s the Spanish government changed its policy and restricted membership to **peninsulares**, Spaniards born in Spain. The Creoles resented this removal of their opportunity for influence. They eventually became involved in movements for independence.

? How did Portugal and Spain differ in who directed policy in their colonies?

Treatment of Indigenous Peoples and African Slaves

Indigenous Peoples

The relationship between the Spanish and the indigenous, or native, peoples of the Americas was often controlled by a system called **encomienda**. Under this system, the native peoples paid tribute to the Spaniards and provided physical labor for farming, mining, or manufacturing. In turn, the Spanish were supposed to provide protection, wages, and spiritual care.

This system would have favored the Spanish even if it had worked correctly. But because Spain was so far from its colonies, it could not ensure that Spanish colonists were doing their part. As a result, the native peoples were often mistreated for the financial benefit of the colonists. Many died from harsh conditions and sickness.

Encomienda

	The Plan	The Reality
Spaniards	Provide protection, wages, and spiritual care	Mistreated native peoples for their own financial benefit
Native Peoples	Pay tribute Provide labor for farming, mining, and manufacturing	Often died from harsh conditions and sickness

African Slaves

In the previous chapter you read about the capture of slaves in Africa. You learned that slaves were taken to the island of Madeira by the Portuguese to work on sugar plantations. Europeans discovered that sugar grew well in the climate and soil of the Americas. The Portuguese and Spanish set up sugar plantations in islands of the Caribbean and along the coast of Brazil. Initially these plantations used native peoples as laborers. But as native populations declined, slave traders began bringing Africans to the Americas.

? How was the encomienda system intended to work?

The Portuguese and Spanish dominated the early years of the slave trade, but as the trade increased, other European nations began to participate. The Dutch were heavily involved in portions of the 1600s, while the French and English became active in the 1700s. The trade in slaves was one section of a **triangular trade** pattern that developed between Europe, Africa, and the Americas. The triangle involved guns, textiles, and wine from Europe being sold in Africa, slaves from Africa being sold in the Americas, and crops like sugar and coffee from the Americas being sold in Europe. Because the slave trade was the middle section of the triangle, the trip the captives were forced to take between West Africa and the Americas is sometimes called the **Middle Passage**.

The Middle Passage was a brutal experience. Often hundreds of Africans were crammed, frequently chained, into a ship for the five-thousand-mile voyage across the ocean. To prevent revolts, crews forced the captives to spend most of their time below deck, where ceilings and oxygen levels were extremely low, temperatures were high, and sanitation was nonexistent. Possibly around 15 percent of captives died during the crossing.

Estimates suggest that well over ten million Africans survived the Middle Passage and were sold as slaves in the New World, most of them in Brazil and other Latin American colonies. A few hundred thousand Africans are estimated to have been taken directly as slaves to the colonies in North America.

This model of a slave ship was built for an exhibition at the Smithsonian National Museum of American History. Why do you think the ship has cannons? What positions are the Africans forced to remain in? What types of supplies do you think the ship might have been carrying in its lower deck?

Describe the Middle Passage.

Activities of the Catholic Church

Interactions with Indigenous Peoples

Friar Bartolomé de Las Casas

The Catholic Church gained great influence in Latin America as the clergy worked with the native peoples. The church sent friars and priests to the colonies to convert the native peoples to Catholicism. While they evangelized, many of the priests also promoted European culture. Therefore, the clergy played a key role in pressuring the native peoples to adapt quickly as the colonies grew.

The church often represented the native peoples during labor disputes and defended them against ill treatment. Dominican friar **Bartolomé de Las Casas** spoke out against the terrible treatment of native peoples. Through his efforts the **New Laws of 1542** were passed. The New Laws set up a government system in which courts were established to protect the native peoples from some of the abuses they suffered. The laws also prohibited the enslaving of native peoples and outlawed the passing on of government-awarded estates to later generations. Sadly, the landowners used their political influence to overturn many of these reforms.

Jesuits in South America

The Jesuits established missions soon after initial settlement in the Americas. In those missions they worked toward converting the native peoples. They learned the people's languages and taught them to read and write. Over time Jesuit control over the native peoples resembled that of the Spanish and Portuguese. While the Jesuits spoke out against abuse of the native peoples and supported their rights, they often used them as workers at mission facilities. This apparent contradiction angered the other landowners. Eventually, the Portuguese and Spanish governments acted to correct this problem.

Some Jesuits with their native helpers controlled large tracts of land and the agricultural production on the land. They operated sugar mills and slaughterhouses. Because they did not have to pay taxes and received additional income from tithes, they were often able to monopolize an industry. The tradesmen who did not have these advantages could not compete. Jealousy over profits and power led to the expulsion (forced removal) of the Jesuit order. The Jesuits were expelled by the Portuguese in 1759 and by the Spanish in 1767.

What did the New Laws of 1542 accomplish?

LIFE ON A HACIENDA

Power

The Spanish government gave large grants of land in Latin America to conquistadores and other Spaniards. From these grants, the landholders made large estates called **haciendas**. The purpose of the hacienda was to make money for the **hacendado**, or landholder. This might be done through mining, manufacturing, farming, or ranching.

Native peoples provided most of the labor for the estates. Many landholders took advantage of their laborers. They paid them low wages and charged high prices for goods at the company store. In this way, many laborers ended up in debt. They could not leave the hacienda until their debt was paid, so they became tied to the land as serfs in Europe were.

Environment

One of the most important resources of South America was the land itself. Development of the land occurred as the immigrant population increased. Overcrowding and lack of available land in Europe made people willing to move to the colonies, where they could make a new life for themselves and their children.

The main house became known for its distinct architecture: stucco walls and a red tile roof.

Religion

As the Catholic Church spread throughout the world, its practice frequently intermingled with the culture of the native peoples of a region, as with the Virgin of Guadalupe. Catholic tradition states that Juan Diego, an Aztec who had converted to Christianity, had two visions of the virgin Mary. In the first vision, she asked that a shrine be built for her. The spot for the shrine would be Tepeyac Hill, near Mexico City. In the second vision, she told Juan Diego to gather roses. These, together with an image of Mary that appeared inside his coat, would be a sign to the local bishop that he should build the shrine Mary asked for. The Virgin of Guadalupe, the name for Mary associated with this vision, became an important national symbol to the people of Mexico, who shared a common devotion to her. She was declared the patroness (protector) of all Latin America in 1910.

Justice

European countries had long been under the influence of Christian teaching (though many European Christians were Christian in name rather than in heart), so Europeans knew how people were supposed to be treated. They understood that native peoples were being mistreated through the labor systems of the Latin American colonies. That is why the protests of Las Casas and others led to the passing of the New Laws of 1542. Nonetheless, greed is a strong motivator for people to find a way around laws that seek to establish justice.

A hacienda might include living quarters for the family and their servants, a general store, a chapel and school, and stables and corrals.

Hacienda crops varied between regions. Some common plants were sugar and sisal (used for rope).

The Columbian Exchange

The interactions between the Old World (Europe, but also Africa and Asia) and the New World of the Americas changed life practically in both regions. This change came through the exchange of plants, animals, and diseases between regions. Because this exchange was prompted by the voyage of Christopher Columbus in 1492, it is often called the **Columbian Exchange**.

European explorers brought several new plants to the New World. Some examples are citrus fruits, bananas, grains like wheat and rice, sugar, and coffee. Many of these were found to thrive in the soil and climates of the Americas. For example, coffee is one of the most profitable exports in South America today. Foods from the New World were also taken back to the Old World. Potatoes, sweet potatoes, corn, cassava, tomatoes, chili peppers, cacao, peanuts, and pineapples were all contributions of the Americas. Some of these foods, such as corn, became staple crops of the regions they were introduced to.

In addition to plants, animals were exchanged. Turkeys were one of the few animals that were brought from the Americas to Europe, but several animals were brought from Europe to the Americas. These included cattle, horses, pigs, goats, sheep, and chickens. The horse proved to be the most beneficial animal to the native peoples. Before the arrival of horses, all hunting and travel was on foot. Horses were a welcome addition for their speed and strength. They made it possible to hunt more effectively. They also made it easier to carry loads and travel. Some scholars believe that pigs were the most destructive animals brought with the explorers. They often ran wild and tended to eat many of the plants used by native peoples for food.

Finally, various diseases were exchanged, with most diseases going from the Old World to the New. Some diseases may have come from animals like pigs. Others would have been carried by people. Diseases that were brought over from Europe and Africa included measles, smallpox, influenza, mumps, typhus, whooping cough, malaria, and yellow fever. Large percentages of the native population of the Americas, possibly 50 to 95 percent depending on the region, were killed, having no previous exposure to these diseases and therefore no immunity.

How did horses improve life for native peoples?

CRITICAL THINKING 7.2

Did the Catholic Church promote the biblical principle of loving one's neighbor through its interactions with the native populations of Latin America?

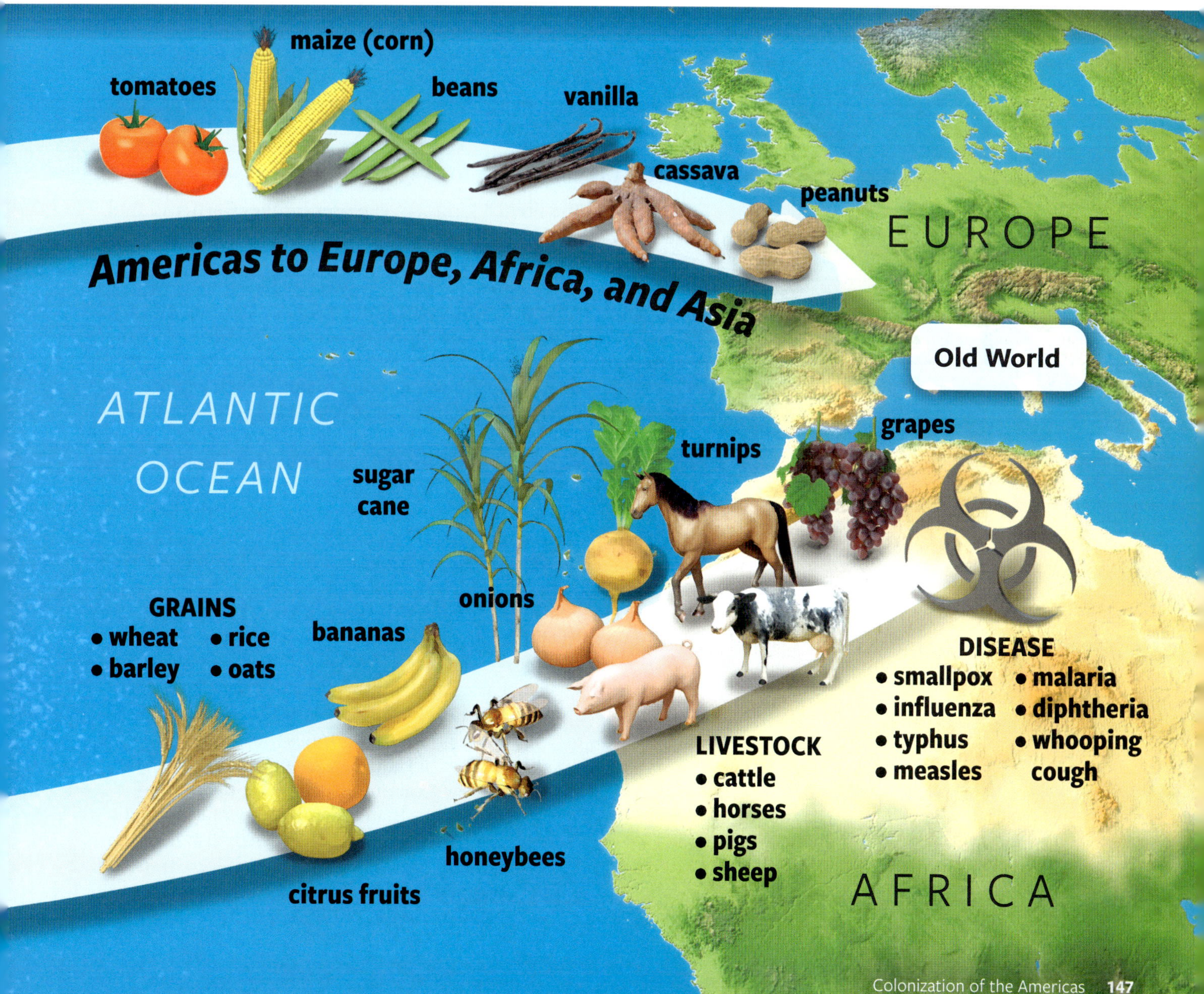

GUIDING QUESTIONS

- How were patterns of Spanish, French, and English settlement in North America different from each other?
- What religious, political, and cultural differences were there among the settlers of North America?
- How did religious differences affect the development of North America?
- What happened in conflicts between European powers in North America?

7.3 Colonization of North America

To many Europeans, the New World was more attractive than the Old. Many of these Europeans became so attracted to the New World that they left Europe for the growing settlements in North America. From the early period of North American settlement up to 1780, the greatest number of Europeans came from Spain, France, and England.

Patterns of Settlement

Spanish in the South

Because Spanish exploration began in the Caribbean and Gulf of Mexico, the Spanish tended to settle the southern portions of the North American continent. In the portion that today is the United States, they built settlements and outposts along the coasts of Florida, Georgia, South Carolina, and Virginia's Chesapeake Bay. They also established a presence farther west, among the Pueblo peoples in the area now known as New Mexico. The Spanish tended to exploit the land rather than develop it. They also forced native populations to follow their harsh policies. Conflict with native populations and lack of economic growth prevented Spain from becoming firmly established in North America.

French in the Far North

In 1534 the French king sent explorer Jacques Cartier to find riches in the New World and a water route to China. While he did not find riches or a route to China, Cartier made several trips and discovered the St. Lawrence River. He also made contacts with several native tribes with whom the French would later establish trade. Cartier traveled farther into modern Canada and built a settlement in modern Montreal.

Samuel de Champlain was another major French explorer. He discovered two of the Great Lakes (Ontario and Huron) and Lake Champlain, but his greatest legacy may have been his love for frontier areas. He was given the title Father of New France.

For many years, the French presence in the New World was little more than a scattered string of outposts. But by the late 1600s, the French determined to build an empire that would challenge the English presence in North America. In 1682, Robert de LaSalle explored the Mississippi River. At the river's mouth, he named the region Louisiana in honor of the French king, Louis XIV. LaSalle claimed all the surrounding territory for France.

However, the French discovered that it was easier to claim than to colonize. The French territory in the New World never had a large population. In the 1660s the number of French settlers in Canada was approximately 3,000. It grew to about 80,000 by 1750, but there were more than one million people living in England's colonies. The French also failed to develop the land. Many French were traders and trappers who took products like furs out of the New World but put little into it.

In exchange for furs, traders gave Native Americans items such as guns, tools, and beads.

English along the Atlantic Coast

The English began to settle the New World after the Spanish and French had already claimed regions of it. English nobles and private companies sponsored settlements ranging from the Carolinas to Massachusetts. Many of the early settlers were not properly equipped to carve out settlements from the wilderness, and others were not willing to work and help make the ventures a success. As a result, early efforts often met with failure. However, ships continued to bring colonists to the New World, and settlements began to survive. Strong leadership by men such as John Smith and Sir Thomas Dale of the Jamestown settlement aided this process.

In addition to fishing and farming, the colonists developed cash crops (crops which could be sold for cash or supplies) with the introduction of tobacco in 1614 and indigo, a plant used to make blue dye, in 1744. These crops enabled settlers to pay off their debts in England and develop a thriving economy in the New World.

The English settlements differed from Spanish and French settlements in three significant ways. Most of the English colonists came under private investors, not government sponsorship. The English colonists brought their families with them and established roots in America. And most English colonists were Protestants. However, the English settlements were like the French and Spanish in that they found a hostile and unfamiliar environment filled with dangers, challenges, and adventures.

?

In what three ways were English settlements different from French and Spanish settlements?

Jamestown was the first permanent English settlement in North America.

Differences among Settlements

Religious Differences

Puritan minister Richard Mather helped translate the Psalms for use in a hymnal, the *Bay Psalm Book*.

Many English traveled to the New World for religious reasons. Besides the Pilgrims, who established the Plymouth Colony in 1620, there were also the **Puritans** (Protestants who wanted to purify the Church of England of all Catholic practices), who settled the Massachusetts Bay Colony in 1630.

The earliest English colonies had established churches that were recognized and supported by the colonies' governments. Because the Puritans had a vision for creating a pure church in a pure society, they wanted every aspect of life to be lived in conformity to God's Word. They believed that they, like Israel, were a nation in covenant with God. Their nation was therefore bound to obey His will. As a result, the colonists were expected to attend church and live by its teachings. Those who openly refused were often expelled from the colony. This approach caused two problems. First, when the children did not follow the faith of their parents, the church began to be populated with unbelievers. Second, Christians who held different beliefs about issues such as baptism or church government were often treated harshly.

Roger Williams was expelled from the Massachusetts Bay Colony for his opposition to the established church. He founded the colony of Rhode Island and refused to allow an established church there. Soon other colonies were set up that encouraged religious pluralism, which allowed many different religions to be practiced freely. Pennsylvania was the largest of these colonies.

In the parts of Canada ruled by France and in the Spanish colonies, the Catholic Church controlled all religious life. Protestantism was not allowed in these lands, and church and state were intertwined as they were in the mother countries.

Political Differences

The level of political control in North America differed from region to region. Each English colony in the New World had some control over its own government. Every colony had a governor. Some were appointed by the king, but most were elected by the colonists. The governor ruled with the help of a legislature. The citizens of the colony had the right to elect members of the legislature, although citizenship was limited to free, white men who owned some property or paid taxes. The king and governor reluctantly granted more rights and privileges when the colonial legislatures withheld money. The English colonists' heritage of self-rule helped to prepare them for independence.

In contrast to the English colonists, the French colonists had little voice in their government. The French king believed he should have absolute rule over his colonies just as he had over France. He appointed governors who ruled without a legislature, giving no opportunity to develop a heritage of self-rule. The king also controlled the colonies' trade and taxation. The colonies' wealth supported the king's court in France rather than developing the colonies.

The Virginia House of Burgesses was the first representative assembly in the American colonies.

Cultural Differences

In the English New England colonies in particular, education was considered very important. The settlers in Massachusetts believed that education was necessary for reading Scripture, learning about God, and understanding His will. Initially, parents taught their children at home. Many parents recognized their God-given responsibility to teach their children (Deut. 6:7; Prov. 22:6).

As villages and towns developed, one of the first buildings the settlers constructed was a one-room school. The local pastor often taught the students at first. In time a teacher was hired, and the students learned the basics of reading, writing, speaking, and mathematics. Colleges were established to promote biblical learning and to train preachers to minister to the people. Harvard and Yale were founded during these early years to prepare men for the ministry.

Outside of New England, education did not receive the same emphasis. This was true for religious reasons: not every colony stressed personal knowledge of the Scriptures as the New England colonies did. It was also true for practical reasons: other colonies focused more on practical skills or did not have time or resources to prioritize education.

?

How was the religion of English settlements different from that of Spanish and French settlements?

Conflicts between European Powers

European powers engaged in several conflicts in the North American continent and on the seas surrounding it. Often these conflicts were part of larger European wars (see Chapter 9), and settlements reached between the major powers of Europe affected their colonies as well.

England and Spain

One war that England and Spain fought was the **War of Jenkins' Ear**. The merchant ship of Captain Robert Jenkins was boarded by Spanish coast guard officials in the Caribbean in 1731, a time of peace. In the fighting that broke out, his ear was cut off. Some years later, members of the English Parliament used this incident to provoke a war, wanting to protect English trading opportunities (part of which involved the slave trade). The war eventually became part of the European War of the Austrian Succession and was settled by the Treaty of Aix-la-Chapelle. England's trading rights in the Americas were protected by the terms of the treaty.

?

Why did Parliament want to start a war with Spain?

In 1739 six British ships under the command of Admiral Edward Vernon attacked the Spanish settlement of Puerto Bello, Panama, an important stopping point for ships carrying treasure to Spain.

England and France

Conflicts between England and France in the Americas were both more frequent and more severe than those between England and Spain, breaking out along the western frontier and the Canadian border. France had some major advantages going into these conflicts. It had several important alliances with native tribes (although not with the powerful Iroquois). The English frontier consisted of isolated farms and small communities. And the English colonies resisted working together to meet the French threat.

Four wars were fought between the English and French between 1689 and 1763. They were all part of European wars, but the colonial portions of the wars have their own names. King William's War (1689–97) was fought along the frontiers and ended with the return of all captured territory to its previous owners. Queen Anne's War (1702–13) was fought on the frontier and along the coasts and ended with the transfer of much of eastern Canada to English control. King George's War (1744–48) caused no real change for the colonies.

The **French and Indian War** (1754–63), part of the European Seven Years' War, was the most significant conflict between the two nations. The war started over a land dispute. The French constructed several forts in a disputed region. The governor of Virginia sent Lieutenant Colonel George Washington to remove the French. In the resulting conflict, the French forced Washington to sign a surrender note blaming England for what happened. The English denied the note, and war began.

For the first few years of the war, the French delivered decisive victories. They and their Native American allies fought with guerrilla warfare tactics (surprise attacks by small groups) and devastated the English frontier. However, a new English leader, **William Pitt**, introduced new strategies. The English used their navy to keep France from helping its colonies, and they appointed young, energetic commanders. The **Treaty of Paris**, which ended the war, required France to give England its Canadian land and to surrender its claims to the Mississippi and Ohio River valleys. The treaty also affected Spain, which had been part of the war in Europe. It had to give Florida to the English but gained the French lands west of the Mississippi River.

?

Where were most conflicts between English and French forces fought?

? CRITICAL THINKING 7.3

How did religious differences between European settlements in North America affect opportunities for education?

Making Connections

1. Identify the goals and methods of mercantilism and capitalism. How are they different?
2. Identify regions of Europe where Catholicism remained dominant or Protestantism gained acceptance due to the wars of religion.
3. How were the Portuguese and Spanish similar and different in the way they treated their colonies?
4. Identify effects of the Columbian Exchange that were beneficial and effects that were harmful for the people of the Americas. Using verses such as Proverbs 4:25–27 and Romans 13:10, assess whether the colonizing nations acted wisely in their side of the exchange.
5. How did the English settle North America differently from the French and Spanish?
6. How did English colonies differ from the French and Spanish in their religious beliefs and in the relationship between government and religion?
7. What were the causes and outcomes of the War of Jenkins' Ear?
8. What were the four wars fought between England and France over their North American territory?
9. Summarize the advantages that France had in the French and Indian War and the strategy that brought victory to the English.

Thinking Critically

1. How did the wars of religion weaken the unity of Europe?
2. Did European nations treat native peoples and African slaves justly? Explain your answer. Consider verses such as Genesis 1:26–27, Genesis 9:6, Exodus 21:6, Leviticus 19:13, and Matthew 7:12.
3. Did the Catholic Church improve conditions for native peoples? Explain your answer. Consider verses such as Proverbs 31:8 and Matthew 7:12.
4. How did the religious differences of North American colonies affect their political and cultural (educational) ideas? Consider verses such as 2 Timothy 3:16–17 and Acts 17:11.

What to Know

Dates & Events

Spanish Armada
Columbian Exchange
War of Jenkins' Ear
French and Indian War

People

Huguenots
Henry of Navarre
Habsburgs
Charles V
Philip II
Henry VIII
Edward VI
Mary I
Elizabeth I
Creoles
Bartolomé de Las Casas
Puritans
William Pitt

Places

Dutch Republic

Terms

Mayflower Compact
mercantilism
exports
imports
tariffs
capitalism
corporations
marketplace
joint-stock company
Edict of Nantes
Peace of Augsburg
Church of England
donatário
viceroy
audiencias
peninsulares
encomienda
triangular trade
Middle Passage
New Laws of 1542
haciendas
hacendado
Treaty of Paris

8 EMPIRES OF EURASIA

1300 – 1750

ESSENTIAL QUESTIONS

- How did empires rise and fall in Eurasia from the fourteenth to the eighteenth centuries?
- What did Eurasian empires achieve politically, economically, and culturally?
- What would the Bible say about the actions of Eurasian empires?

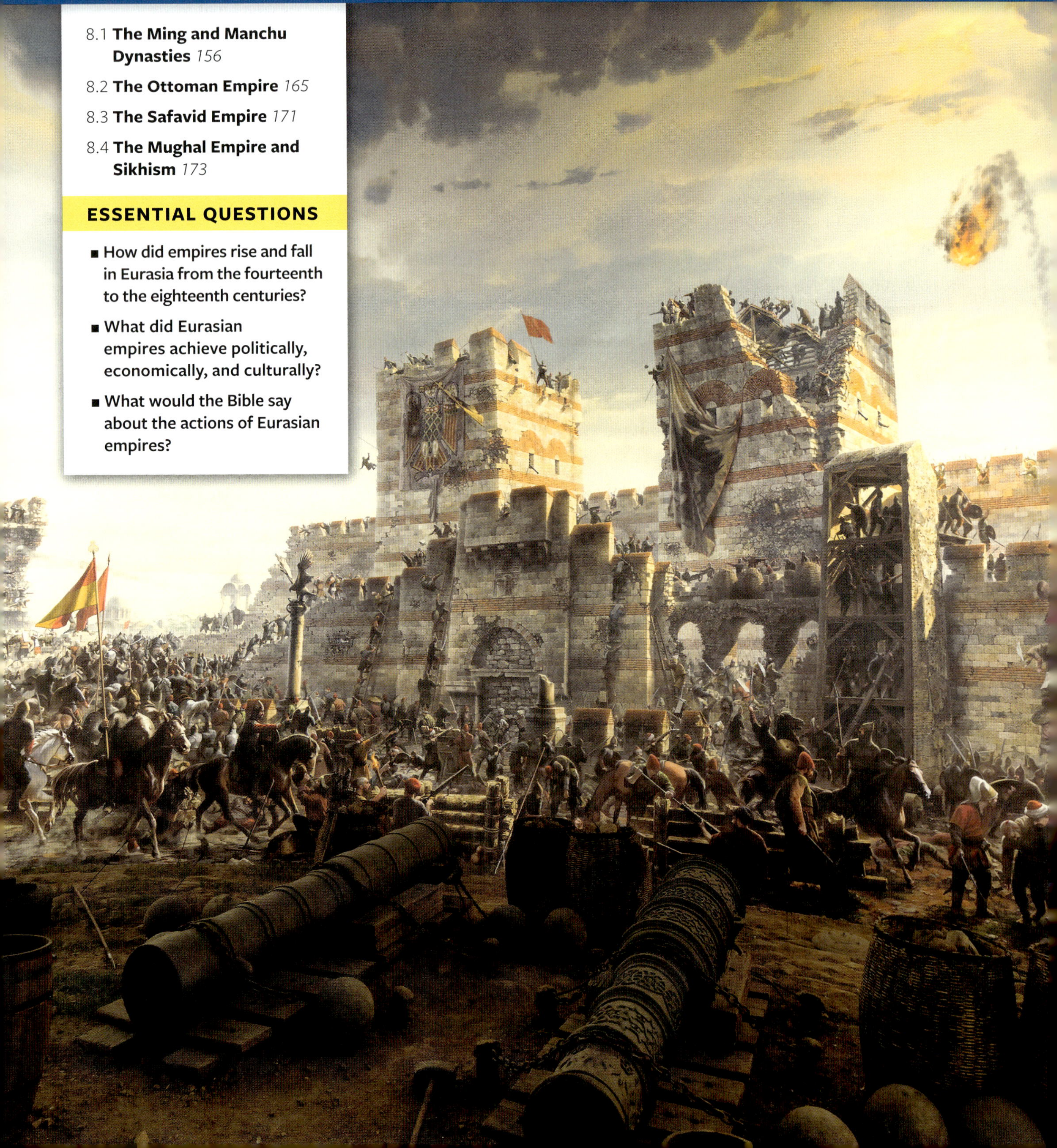

The Fall of Constantinople

Constantinople was the capital of the Roman Empire (later the Byzantine Empire) from the completion of the city's construction in AD 330 to its fall in 1453. Constantinople had great symbolic and strategic significance for the people of Europe. It was viewed as a continuation of the Roman Empire centuries after the western half of the empire collapsed. It was also valued as a last line of defense against the looming threat of the Ottomans, an Islamic empire that originated in the region of modern Turkey and was pushing into southern Europe.

Constantinople had a crucial location. Bordering the Bosporus Strait, it was situated at an important crossroads of trade between Asia and Europe. The city had impressive defenses. It was surrounded by a series of stone walls and fortifications. The walls that bordered the land entrances to the city were built two walls deep, with the taller wall measuring up to forty feet high and sixteen feet across. A moat further discouraged invading armies. The section of the city that faced the sea was also protected by walls, on average about twenty feet high. This system of walls was so strong and thick that it had protected the city from invaders for a thousand years.

The Ottomans had conquered many of the former lands of the Byzantine Empire, but the city of Constantinople held out. Sultan **Mehmed II** was determined to capture it. The year was 1453. Byzantine forces were seriously outnumbered, with only 6,000 to 7,000 professional soldiers to the Ottomans' 60,000 to 80,000.

The Byzantines' strategy had two parts: (1) to concentrate their troops in the weakest section of the city and (2) to stretch iron chains across the entrance to their harbor, the Golden Horn, guarding the chains with the small number of ships available to them. They had appealed to Europe for help, and they hoped to hold out until more soldiers arrived. (The Italian city-states of Venice and Genoa had already supplied some aid.)

The Ottomans had previously occupied a fort on one side of the Bosporus Strait; they built a second fort on the other side of the strait. Using these forts, they tried to prevent ships from coming to defend Constantinople. They planned to surround the city and overwhelm its outnumbered defenders. The success of their plan rested mainly on the work of a cannon builder named Orban. Orban was confident that he could make a cannon big enough to break through the walls of Constantinople. (Ironically, Orban had first offered his services to the city of Constantinople, but they could not afford to pay what he was asking.) He worked on location so that the cannon would not have to be moved. The completed cannon was twenty-six feet long and could shoot cannonballs that weighed as much as twelve hundred pounds.

The attacks began on April 6, 1453. At first the Byzantines were able to repair damages and repel the invaders. Some relief ships even arrived to help them. But two events changed the situation. First, the Ottomans broke into the Golden Horn harbor. While concentrating their firepower on the ships guarding the chains, they built a ramp so they could move their own ships across the land and into the harbor, bypassing the chains. Second, a key leader of the Byzantine forces, Giustiniani of Genoa, died. Without his direction, the Byzantines were unable to stop the Ottoman surge. The death of the Byzantine ruler, Constantine XI, made an Ottoman victory certain.

With the Ottomans in control of the city, several changes took place. Many churches were replaced with mosques. People from across the Ottoman Empire moved to the city. The job of keeping the Ottomans from conquering Europe was transferred farther north. And scholars fleeing the city contributed to a renewed interest in classical learning in Italy.

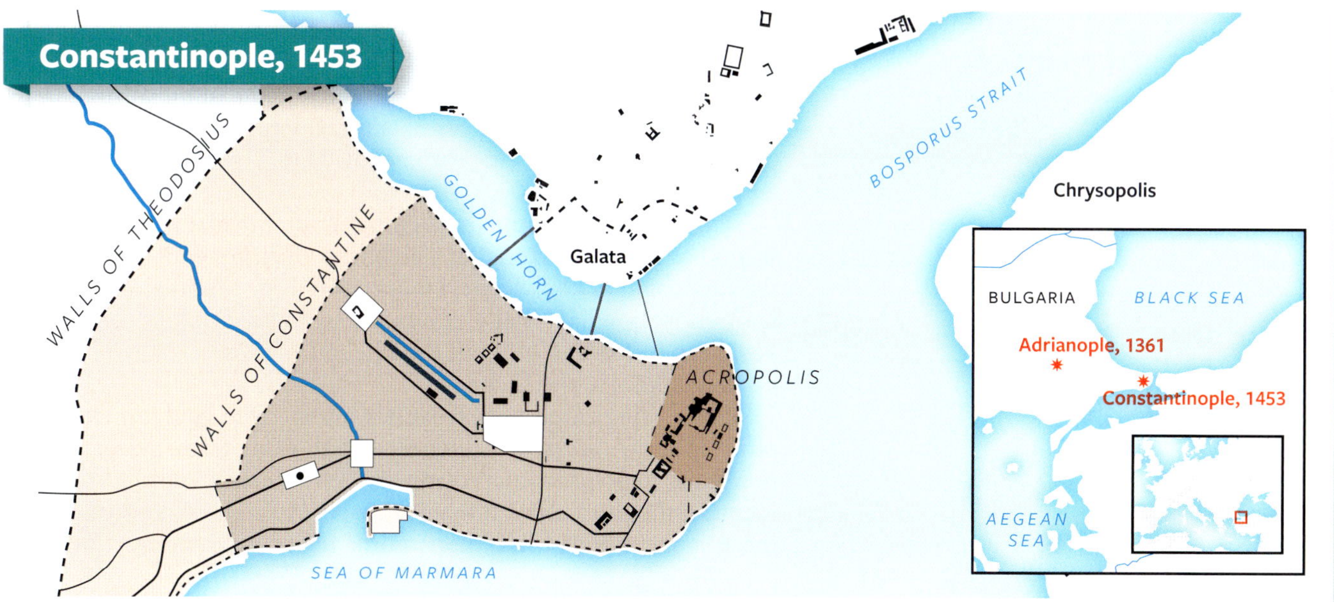

GUIDING QUESTIONS

- How did Ming rulers implement absolutism?
- In what ways was Chinese culture advanced during the Ming period?
- What were the purposes, events, and outcomes of the Zheng He naval expeditions?
- Did Ming rulers interact wisely with their citizens and with other nations?
- What led to the decline of the Ming dynasty and the rise of the Manchu dynasty?

8.1 The Ming and Manchu Dynasties

You learned in Chapter 3 that China was briefly ruled by a foreign power, the Mongols. After a little more than a hundred years, Chinese forces overthrew the Mongols and established a new dynasty called the **Ming dynasty** (1386–1644).

The Ming dynasty restored native Chinese rule. A renewed national pride caused the Chinese to look down on all foreigners, including European traders. The Ming rulers turned their attention to rebuilding the grandeur of China, and the people enjoyed an era of peace and prosperity under this dynasty. The Ming tried to maintain a government based on **absolutism**. In addition, they concentrated on the arts, reconstruction, and exploration.

Taizu claimed a divine right to rule China, an idea known as the Mandate of Heaven.

Imperial Absolutism

Taizu founded the Ming dynasty and established a pattern of absolute rule that his successors followed for the next three centuries. He was a harsh ruler and demanded that his ministers kneel before him. This was a contrast to previous dynasties, during which ministers had been allowed to sit or stand in the emperor's presence.

Chengzu became the third emperor after defeating the second emperor, Huizong, in a civil war. Chengzu encouraged the expansion of knowledge. He sponsored the production of a huge encyclopedia. He also reversed Taizu's policy of preventing naval expansion and sent out the Zheng He voyages that will be discussed later in the chapter.

Later Ming emperors gave much authority to government officials known as grand secretaries. In the long term, delegating power led to political corruption and a weakened central government. In the short term, it freed the rulers to explore interests in the arts, including porcelain, painting, poetry, and bronze work.

absolutism ruling without any limits on one's authority

Cultural Achievements

Literature

As in Europe during the Renaissance, increased wealth in China during the Ming dynasty provided the opportunity for increased learning and expanded literature. Bookshops sold samples of the examinations that all students had to pass to gain government employment. Novels and short stories also became popular. Men who did not pass the rigorous exams for government employment often developed literary careers to support themselves. Many oral stories were written down and sold in collections.

Porcelain

Artisans during the Ming dynasty perfected the art of making porcelain. They used it for a variety of products, including vases, plates, cups, tiles, and false teeth. These products were exported around the world.

Blue and white was a classic color combination in the decoration of porcelain products. Later, the development of overglaze enamels (polishes added after the object had been heated in the kiln a first time) allowed for more variety in colors, as some colors did not do well when subjected to extreme temperatures.

Ming vase with fish and foliage, 16th–17th century

Ming jar with dragon, 15th century

Ming painting of fishing beside a brook, 16th century

Drama

Drama in the Ming dynasty consisted of long and complex plays. Language, form, and music joined together to produce plays that often lasted for hours and contained more than forty scenes. Over time, selected scenes from various plays were combined to shorten performances.

Painting

During the Ming dynasty, painting **landscapes** (nature scenes) became a popular form of expression. Some painters drew the trees and other natural scenes in a way that invited the imagination of the viewer. Poems were written about the paintings that described imaginary creatures such as dragons and giant birds in conflict.

Architecture and Engineering

The Ming rebuilt broken portions of the Great Wall and extended it even farther. They repaired roads and bridges and rebuilt their capital (pronounced Peking by the English at that time but now pronounced Beijing) into a magnificent city. They also completed the restoration of the Grand Canal.

What were some achievements of Ming architects and engineers?

Ming painting on silk, 14th century

Hall of Prayer for Good Harvests, Temple of Heaven complex, Beijing

Stele Pavilion, Sacred Way, Ming Tombs, Beijing

LIFE IN

PEKING (BEIJING)

Power

The Ming emperor Taizu tried to manage every aspect of Chinese society, including households. He used a secret police force to discover any who opposed his controls. Officials who ignored or resisted imperial control were publicly beaten, sometimes resulting in their death. Such abuse of power results from a faulty worldview, one in which the leader has an exalted view of himself and denies the human dignity of his citizens.

Justice

The **Censorate** was an office of the Ming government that watched over the activities of government officials. Special investigators in the office reviewed things like government correspondence, building projects, and court cases. Their stated purpose was to prevent inefficient or corrupt government. But if they criticized something the emperor liked, they were reprimanded. Therefore, they were not always successful at promoting good government. This is why it is important, from a biblical worldview, for leaders to realize that they have limitations and accept wise counsel from government officials.

Peking contained sections for members of the government as well as regular citizens. Walls surrounded by moats protected the different sections.

Members of the secret police patrolled the city on horseback.

Religion

Confucianism during the Ming dynasty continued a process begun during the Song dynasty of trying to formulate a complete Confucianist worldview. Scholars considered questions related to origins, morality, ethics, and right behavior. Though Confucianism is considered to be an ethical system more than a religion, it functions in many ways as a religion because it addresses the same basic questions that religion does. Confucianism's emphasis on good moral character, however, is not rooted in the grace of God available in Christ, as biblical Christianity teaches.

Environment

During the Ming dynasty, improvements were made to deepen certain sections of the Grand Canal. In addition, new locks and reservoirs enabled the canal to maintain the water level needed to transport goods.

Workers wore conical hats as protection from both sun and rain.

Admiral Zheng He

Zheng He, previously named Ma He, was born around 1371 to a Chinese Muslim family. When the Ming conquered his province in 1381, the young Ma He was forcibly enlisted in the army. Early on he showed both military and diplomatic ability.

Ma He came under the authority of a prince who was over the Chinese state of Yan. The prince showed Ma He special favor. When the prince led a revolt and became the new emperor in 1402, Ma He rose in influence. The new emperor changed Ma He's name to Zheng He. He chose Zheng He to lead several naval expeditions.

Zheng He was well prepared for the expeditions. Several of his crew were skilled in languages. In addition, he had charts that helped him to gauge travel times and to be aware of prominent geographical features and landmarks. The most interesting thing about his voyages is the ships he took. Though not verified, some accounts say that his largest ships had four decks, carried hundreds of crew members, and were possibly twice the length of other known wooden ships.

Zheng He led seven expeditions, but nine years went by between the sixth and seventh voyage. It is believed that Zheng He died on the last expedition.

Naval Expeditions

Purposes

During a thirty-year period in the early 1400s, Ming emperors sent out seven naval expeditions. Around sixty large ships and over two hundred smaller ships were sent out to represent a renewed China. The emperor desired to gain control over trade, collect tribute, and demonstrate Chinese superiority over countries along the Indian Ocean. This fleet also reduced the ever-present threat of piracy.

Events

Zheng He was made the admiral of this great convoy, with an army and crew that may have numbered almost twenty-eight thousand. These ships sailed to many countries, including Arabia, East Africa, India, Indonesia, and Siam (Thailand). Zheng presented gifts of gold, silver, porcelain, and silk to foreign rulers.

The treasures he brought back to China included unusual animals such as ostriches, camels, and giraffes. On these voyages, Zheng used diplomacy when possible, and his large army when necessary, to enhance China's reputation and bring countries into submission. On his fourth voyage, Zheng brought envoys from several nations to China. These officials came to honor the Ming court. Over the course of these journeys, Zheng and his fleet traveled more than thirty thousand miles.

Outcomes

The naval voyages ended with the death of Ming emperor Xuanzong in 1436. There is some debate as to how much the voyages accomplished. They were not the start of a great trading empire for China. On the other hand, China did have more political influence in its region as a result. Also, because of increased interactions with other civilizations, Chinese citizens emigrated to nations of Southeast Asia, increasing Chinese trade through their influence.

? **What were some purposes of the Zheng He naval expeditions?**

Artist's conception of one of Zheng He's huge ships alongside a ship used by Columbus

Decline of the Ming and Rise of the Manchus

Decline of the Ming

While the Ming directed their attention to the south and east, foreign invaders from the north slowly gained control. The last four emperors became distracted with matters not related to governing China. One emperor even spent his life building furniture rather than attending to government. As a result, the power of the emperors diminished, and local officials ruled without fear of royal hindrance. Infighting and corruption further weakened the Ming dynasty. Seizing upon this opportunity, Manchurians from a region north of China steadily gained access to and then control of the Imperial City.

?

How did the last Ming emperors contribute to the decline of the dynasty?

Manchu Dynasty

Rise of the Manchus

In 1644 the **Manchu dynasty** seized power from the failing Ming dynasty. They had previously been invited into China to help the Ming government defeat a group of rebels. Once invited into the country, however, the Manchus steadily took power from the weak Ming rulers. The Manchus established the second foreign dynasty in Chinese history. The Manchu (Qing) dynasty ruled from 1644 to 1911, when dynasty rule ended in China.

?

How was the Manchu dynasty able to take control of China?

Inclusive Rule

The Manchu rulers worked hard to build a good relationship with the people of their newly conquered empire. They knew that to retain power and succeed in governing, they needed the support of the people. The Manchus tried to become Chinese rather than make the Chinese become Manchurian. The Manchus allowed the Chinese to have a part in the government. At the higher levels of government, a Chinese and a Manchu often shared the same office. At the local level, almost all government officials were Chinese.

Chinese actors recreate a Manchu religious ceremony.

Imperial Absolutism

The Manchu government differed little from the early Ming government. The emperor still held supreme power and could order any policy to be enforced throughout the empire. Scholars continued to receive positions in government by receiving a high score on civil service examinations. Many Chinese scholars held important positions at the imperial court in Peking. In addition, each level of government was responsible to the next higher level so that local governors had little control over their own affairs. This process enabled the Manchus to successfully govern their Chinese subjects for nearly two centuries without major discontent.

The Middle Kingdom

Throughout much of their history, the Chinese had an attitude of superiority toward other countries. They called themselves the Central Nation or the **Middle Kingdom** because they considered themselves to be the center of the world. In many ways China truly was much more advanced than other countries. For example, during the Middle Ages in Europe, China had a period of great achievement. Before Europe entered the modern age, China was the most technologically advanced region in the world.

The Manchus continued to promote this attitude of superiority. They especially tried to keep China from having any contact with the West through trade. All but one or two Chinese ports were closed to Western trade during the 1700s. This policy of isolation created problems for China. It not only kept the West from receiving quantities of desirable Chinese goods but also prevented the Chinese from receiving the new inventions and learning of the West. While the Western world moved rapidly into the modern age, the Chinese refused to change their traditional culture. Isolation caused the Chinese to fall behind in many areas, including technology and the military.

CRITICAL THINKING 8.1

1. How did Taizu's treatment of his ministers demonstrate his belief in the absolute authority of the emperor?
2. Why is it valuable for cultures to try to learn from each other?

8.2 The Ottoman Empire

The **Ottoman Empire** developed during the beginning of the 1300s in the land called **Anatolia** (the Asian portion of modern-day Turkey). Anatolia had experienced a period of upheaval as the empire of the Seljuk Turks fell apart and Mongol warriors invaded the land. One who emerged from the chaos was the leader of a small Turkish kingdom in the northwestern corner of Anatolia named Osman I. The inhabitants of Osman's kingdom, who became known as the Ottomans, were mostly Turkish and followers of Islam. The Ottomans were in a good geographical location to try to increase their territory; over the next century they wrestled with Byzantine forces for control of the Anatolian and Balkan Peninsulas. They also endured civil wars. When the Ottoman Empire emerged from internal strife under a ruler named Mehmed II, the goal became the conquest of Constantinople.

GUIDING QUESTIONS

- How did the decline of the Byzantine Empire contribute to the expansion of Ottoman power?
- Why did Ottoman military campaigns succeed?
- What political and economic strategies did the Ottomans use?
- Did Ottoman rulers treat the peoples of their empire with justice?
- What did the Ottomans achieve in art, architecture, and literature?

Decline of the Byzantine Empire

The Byzantine Empire had survived many wars and assaults over its thousand-year history. However, by the 1400s its age was showing. As is often the case with empires, weak leadership and internal strife had weakened the once-mighty Byzantine Empire. European crusaders had attacked Constantinople in 1204 and had severely weakened the city. Byzantine emperors regained power but concentrated on building defenses west of the city rather than rebuilding aging defenses in the eastern provinces. The Ottomans captured one Byzantine city after another. Final defeat of the remaining Byzantine forces was only a matter of time.

On May 29, 1453, Ottoman forces breached a section of the walls of Constantinople and poured into the city. They killed the defenders and pillaged (looted) the city for three days. Later, Constantinople was rebuilt, and the name was changed to **Istanbul**. This city became the permanent capital of the Ottoman Empire.

Modern Istanbul

What ancient empire grew smaller as the Ottoman Empire expanded its territory?

Ottoman Military Successes

After the defeat of Constantinople, the Ottomans swept north into eastern Europe, south into northern Africa, and east across the Anatolian Peninsula. The Ottoman navy turned the Mediterranean and the Black Seas into Muslim-controlled waters.

The Ottoman army became an advanced fighting force. They were among the first to use small cannons, called falconets, and muskets on the battlefield. The Ottoman cavalry developed techniques like those used by the Mongols. They used bows and short swords and advanced on fast Arabian horses to attack their enemies. When necessary, they pretended to retreat, drawing enemy forces forward while secretly surrounding them.

The European nations struggled against repeated Ottoman attacks for the next two centuries. The Ottoman threat finally ended when European forces were able to repel the Ottoman attack on Vienna in 1683. After this defeat, Europe continued to improve militarily, and the Ottoman army fell behind European forces.

What weapons and techniques contributed to Ottoman successes in battle?

THE ANATOMY OF AN OTTOMAN JANISSARY

ELITE INFANTRY SOLDIER OF THE OTTOMAN EMPIRE

BÖRK HAT

MADE OF FELT, FELL BELOW THE SHOULDERS

A metal plate on the front of the börk could hold a spoon. The spoon symbolized the unity of the Janissaries, who did everything together, including eating.

MUSKET

DEADLY ON THE BATTLEFIELD

The Janissaries were the first Ottoman soldiers to use firearms regularly. Muskets replaced earlier firearms in the 1500s. The first muskets were longer and heavier than previous firearms, so they could pierce through armor better.

YATAGAN SWORD

USEFUL FOR HAND-TO-HAND COMBAT

Yatagan swords had a special curved design. They were smaller than some swords, so they could be worn at the waist without hindering movement on the battlefield.

LAYERED CLOTHING

PRACTICAL FOR A SOLDIER

Ottomans generally dressed in layered clothing, which could easily be put on or taken off to adjust to the weather. Sashes secured clothing and provided a place to hang items such as a soldier's sword and powder horn.

TURNING POINTS

Siege of Vienna

From the 1300s to the 1600s, Ottoman forces fought for territory in southeastern and central Europe. Their main rival for control in that region was the Habsburgs (rulers of the Holy Roman Empire). The area surrounding Vienna, Austria, was significant both politically, to establish dominance over southern Europe, and economically, to control trade routes that crossed the center of Europe and Asia. The Ottomans had tried to take Vienna in 1529 but failed. Though warfare continued periodically in the region, the Ottomans did not make another attempt to capture the city for well over a hundred years. Then in 1682 Grand Vizier Kara Mustafa, an important political and military leader in the Ottoman Empire, convinced Sultan Mehmed IV to attack Vienna again. The main motivations for the attack seem to have been Habsburg strikes on Ottoman-controlled Hungary and requests for help from Hungarian Protestants, who were struggling against the Counter Reformation efforts of the Catholic Habsburgs.

The Ottomans began to mobilize (get forces ready for battle) in January of 1682 and declared war on the Habsburgs in August of that year. However, a siege would take some months to successfully implement, and it was too close to winter to start a siege in 1682. As a result, the siege was delayed until 1683, a problem for the Ottomans because it gave the Habsburgs time to form a defensive alliance with the pope, Venice, and Poland.

The siege finally began in July of 1683. The Habsburg emperor and several thousand troops evacuated. Left behind to defend the city were approximately 15,000 troops and 8,700 volunteers with 370 cannons. Against them were approximately 150,000 Ottoman troops with 130 field guns and 19 cannons.

The city of Vienna was surrounded by a series of walls and fortifications. The Ottomans dug trenches that would give them cover as they approached the city for an attack. They also dug tunnels under the walls that they could fill with explosives. All this took time, and the Viennese further slowed the process by putting up barricades of large tree trunks.

The delays gave the Habsburgs time to form an alliance force to challenge the Ottomans. The force included troops from several German states (all officially part of the Holy Roman Empire) and Poland. John III Sobieski, ruler of Poland and brilliant military commander, led the allied army of approximately 80,000 troops. The allied army took several villages surrounding the city while the Ottomans were still tied up with siege operations. Then they attacked the main concentration of Ottoman troops outside the city.

Winged Hussars

The key event of the battle was the charge of the allied cavalry. With 18,000 horsemen, it was the largest cavalry charge ever. The famous "Winged Hussars" of Poland took part in the charge. They were protected by breastplates and armed with lances (long wooden sticks with metal ends used for knocking down opponents). They looked intimidating, wearing cloaks of leopard skin and having wooden frames with feathers attached to their breastplates (their "wings"). The cavalry charge was the beginning of the end for the Ottoman forces, many of whom died or were captured during the battle.

The allied victory was significant for the future of Europe. An Ottoman victory could have meant the continued surge of Ottoman forces deeper into Europe and the dominance of Islam on the continent. Instead, the Habsburgs began pushing back in eastern and southeastern Europe, and Christianity remained the primary religion.

1. Why did the Ottomans try to take Vienna?
2. What was the key event of the battle?
3. What was the result of the Ottoman defeat for Europe?

Political and Economic Strategies

The Ottomans built a strong, powerful, and wealthy empire that endured for six centuries. Strategies that the Ottomans used for ruling and directing economic activity contributed to the early success of the empire.

Political Organization

The Ottomans developed a two-dimensional form of government: military and civil. The sultan held the highest civil position; however, he delegated his authority to advisers and ministers who governed the various areas of the empire.

What qualities did the Ottomans look for when choosing people to help manage their empire?

During the period when the Ottoman Empire was quickly expanding, loyal and skilled subjects from many nationalities were appointed to administer the affairs of the empire. Albanians, Hungarians, Greeks, Jews, and others were recruited to help manage this vast empire. This preference for qualified, talented officials strengthened the government and resulted in a stable empire during the early years of its development.

Economic Strategies

The leaders of the Ottoman Empire concentrated economic development in key cities like Adrianople and Istanbul. These cities were transformed into important trading and manufacturing centers. The Ottomans viewed merchants and artisans as essential to the economic success of the empire. They limited the amount of taxes they asked these groups to pay, instead allowing them to keep more of their own money and invest it in their businesses.

In addition, the Ottomans welcomed Jews who fled other parts of Europe due to persecution. The Jews brought skill and diligent labor in fields such as medicine, trade, and banking to the Ottoman Empire. Their economic success contributed to Ottoman economic success.

Why did the Ottomans limit taxes on merchants and artisans?

Key military conquests had placed the Ottoman Empire between the West and the East. Thus spices, silk, porcelain, and other Eastern treasures had to pass through Ottoman lands. Ottoman merchants made an immense profit by buying these goods and then selling them to the West at a much higher cost. However, this strategy of wealth had negative consequences for the Ottoman Empire. You learned in Chapter 5 that European nations responded by seeking water routes to India and China to bypass the Ottomans. The success of European nations at finding alternate routes to the East led to a significant decline in the Ottoman Empire.

The Ottomans played an important role in land trade between Asia and Europe but were left out of sea trade.

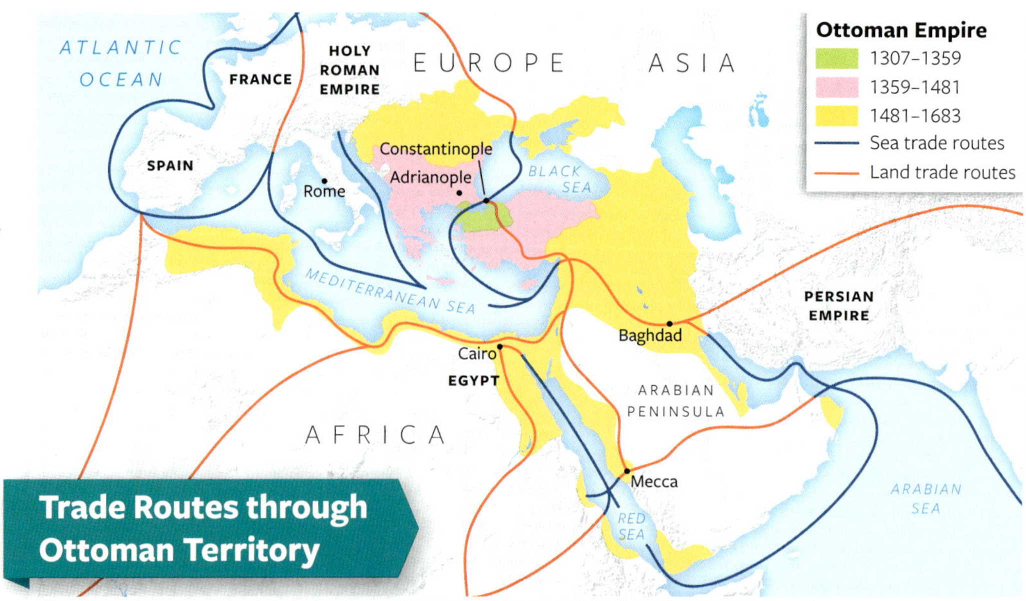

Trade Routes through Ottoman Territory

Treatment of Diverse Populations

The Ottoman Empire grew into a vast and varied state which ruled many conquered peoples. Within the empire a variety of religions, cultures, languages, and nationalities existed. The Ottomans used this diversity to their advantage.

Religious Mixture

Since the Ottoman Empire was Islamic and Islam is a monotheistic religion, those who practiced polytheism were not tolerated. Christians and Jews, as monotheists, were allowed limited and monitored opportunities to worship in exchange for paying the government an annual tax.

Restrictions on Christians included a prohibition on sharing the gospel with Muslims. Consistent with the teaching of Islam, conversion by a Muslim to Christianity was not allowed. In addition, no Orthodox or Armenian church building could be larger than the local mosque. As a result, many large cathedrals were destroyed or converted into mosques. The Muslim authorities even regulated the size and ringing of the bells in Orthodox churches.

Religious persecution of Christians and Jews occurred from time to time. As the Ottoman Empire began to disintegrate in the 1800s, persecution increased and intensified.

? **What restrictions were put on Christians and Jews in the Ottoman Empire?**

The Hagia Sophia church in Constantinople was converted to a mosque when the Ottomans conquered the city in 1453.

Cultural Variety

The Ottoman Empire began as a Turkish-dominated state. However, as the empire expanded through conquest, it gained control of territory on three continents. As a result, the Ottoman Empire became a collection of many cultures and languages. The Ottomans made provision for this variety and turned it into a means of strengthening the empire. Careful treatment of the various cultures and minorities enabled the Ottoman Empire to remain strong for several centuries.

Cultural Achievements

The cultural achievements of the Ottomans reflect the diversity of their empire. Byzantine, Mamluk, Persian, Turkic, Arabic, and European influences all played a part in the development of the Ottoman artistic and literary style.

Some of the most significant Ottoman cultural achievements were in the field of architecture. Three periods are notable for their architectural developments. The first was the period right after the conquest of Constantinople, when Ottoman architects took examples of Byzantine architecture and added Islamic elements. For example, the Hagia Sophia cathedral had four minarets (prayer towers) added to it. The second notable period was the reign of Sultan Suleiman the Magnificent. This period is often referred to as the Golden Age of the Ottoman Empire. The noted architect **Mimar Sinan** designed hundreds of buildings and other structures across the empire during this period. Many of his projects were mosques or other religious buildings, but he also designed public buildings like hospitals and infrastructure like aqueducts and bridges. The last notable period was the Tulip Period of the early 1700s, which got its name from the popularity of tulips with the people of the court. Architecture of this period combined existing Ottoman features with the current European style.

Art forms that were popular in the Ottoman Empire included illustrated calligraphy (ornamental writing), geometric designs, ornamental ceramics, and silk and rug weaving. Sometimes these forms had religious significance, as in the use of calligraphy to inscribe quotations from the Qur'an on the walls of mosques.

Literature of the Ottoman Empire differed depending on whether it was for the common people or the members of the Ottoman court. The folk literature of the common people was usually oral; it told a story and was often composed in quatrains, or sections of four lines. Court literature was written as well as oral; it focused on the culture of the court and was often composed in couplets, or sections of two lines. Both forms could be set to music.

▲ (top) Mimar Sinan designed the Suleymaniye Mosque, a famous landmark in Istanbul. (bottom) Calligraphy is often displayed inside mosques, as it is here in the Hagia Sophia in Istanbul.

What were some key areas of Ottoman artistic achievement?

WORLDVIEW DILEMMA

What is the best way to interact with people of other faiths?

- **A** Respectfully discuss their beliefs in light of biblical truth.
- **B** Criticize their faith with an attitude of superiority.
- **C** Accept their beliefs as equally valid as all other beliefs.

8.3 The Safavid Empire

In the region that lay between the Ottoman Empire and India, the Persians reemerged in a new empire. Remarkably, this empire grew out of a boy's desire to avenge the murder of some of his family members.

GUIDING QUESTIONS

- How did Persia unify under the Safavids and Ismail I?
- How was the Safavid Empire connected to the Shi'ite form of Islam?
- What are the similarities and differences between the Shi'ite and Sunni forms of Islam?
- What Safavid political, economic, and cultural achievements occurred under Shah Abbas?
- What led to the decline of the Safavid Empire?

Shah Ismail I

Ismail and his family belonged to the Safavid clan. A rival clan killed his father and older brother, making Ismail the head of his family at the age of seven. To survive, he went into hiding until he was twelve. Then he began his military career by leading forces to take revenge on those who murdered his father.

Once he had carried out his vengeance, Ismail's fame quickly spread, and he began to gain followers. Ismail had embraced the Shia form of Islam (see explanation on page 172), and the support of Shiites from various regions contributed to his rise in political prominence.

Ismail took territory and laid the foundations for a new state. With the conquest of the city of Tabriz in 1501, his empire was established. He became **Shah Ismail I** and founded the **Safavid dynasty** (1501–1722). He built this fledgling state into a growing economic and political power. He formed a strong centralized government and brought stability to his region. He also attempted to develop diplomatic relationships with neighboring states. Working with nearby countries was essential because of the region's location along the trade routes between the East and the West.

The Safavids often struggled with the Ottomans, Uzbeks (to the north), and even Portuguese forces for control of disputed territories and to determine which group would dominate this region. Ismail had developed a reputation for being invincible. However, this reputation was shattered in 1514 when the Safavid forces were defeated by a much larger Ottoman force. Ismail withdrew from an active role in governing, and the empire became vulnerable to internal struggles and attacks from neighboring states.

Safavid Dynasty

Shah Ismail I

What form of Islam did Ismail embrace?

Shah Abbas

During a time of weakness in 1587, a rival family leader installed his own sixteen-year-old son, Abbas, in place of the current Safavid ruler. **Shah Abbas** proved to be a strong leader and is regarded as the second founder of this empire.

The Safavid Empire experienced a period of political, economic, and cultural renewal under Abbas. Abbas rebuilt centralized authority. He reorganized the army and conquered land that had been taken from the Safavids by the Ottomans and others. He regained control of Baghdad and allied with the British to capture the Strait of Hormuz to enhance trade. He moved the capital of the empire to Isfahan and made it a great center for trade and manufacturing. He built an abundance of mosques, royal palaces, and public buildings, many of them in his new capital city. Under his leadership, a new style of architecture developed that was both grand and beautiful.

Shah Mosque, an example of Safavid architecture in Isfahan, Iran

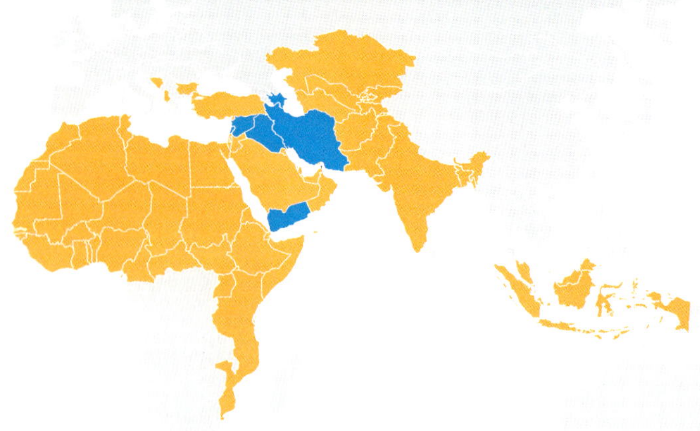

Decline

As with most empires, the Safavid Empire declined due to a lack of qualified successors. Neighboring states, including the Ottomans, invaded and took away territory. Internal strife led to revolts. In 1722 the empire was overthrown. However, the foundation of the modern state of Iran had been laid.

Shia vs. Sunni Islam

In AD 632 Muhammad, the founder of Islam, died. Following his death, a controversy arose over who should be the next leader of the Islamic faith. This controversy led to the splintering of Islam into two branches: **Shia Islam** (whose followers are known as Shiites) and **Sunni Islam** (whose followers are known as Sunnis).

Ismail's choice to follow the Shia form of Islam had some immediate consequences. It provided him with a group of supporters. It also put him at odds with the Ottomans, who were Sunnis. Possibly more significant, though, were the long-term consequences of Ismail's choice for the Middle East. The modern state of Iran continues to be the dominant Shiite power in the region. Many conflicts have arisen over the years between Iran and its neighbors that were at least partially due to the long-standing quarrel between the two main branches of Islam.

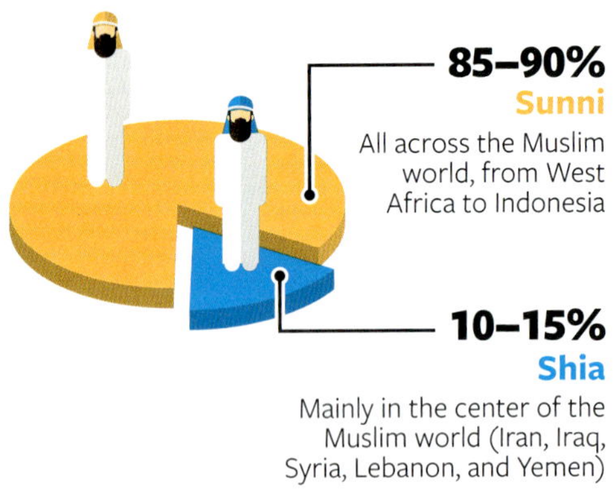

What problems led to the overthrow of the Safavid Empire?

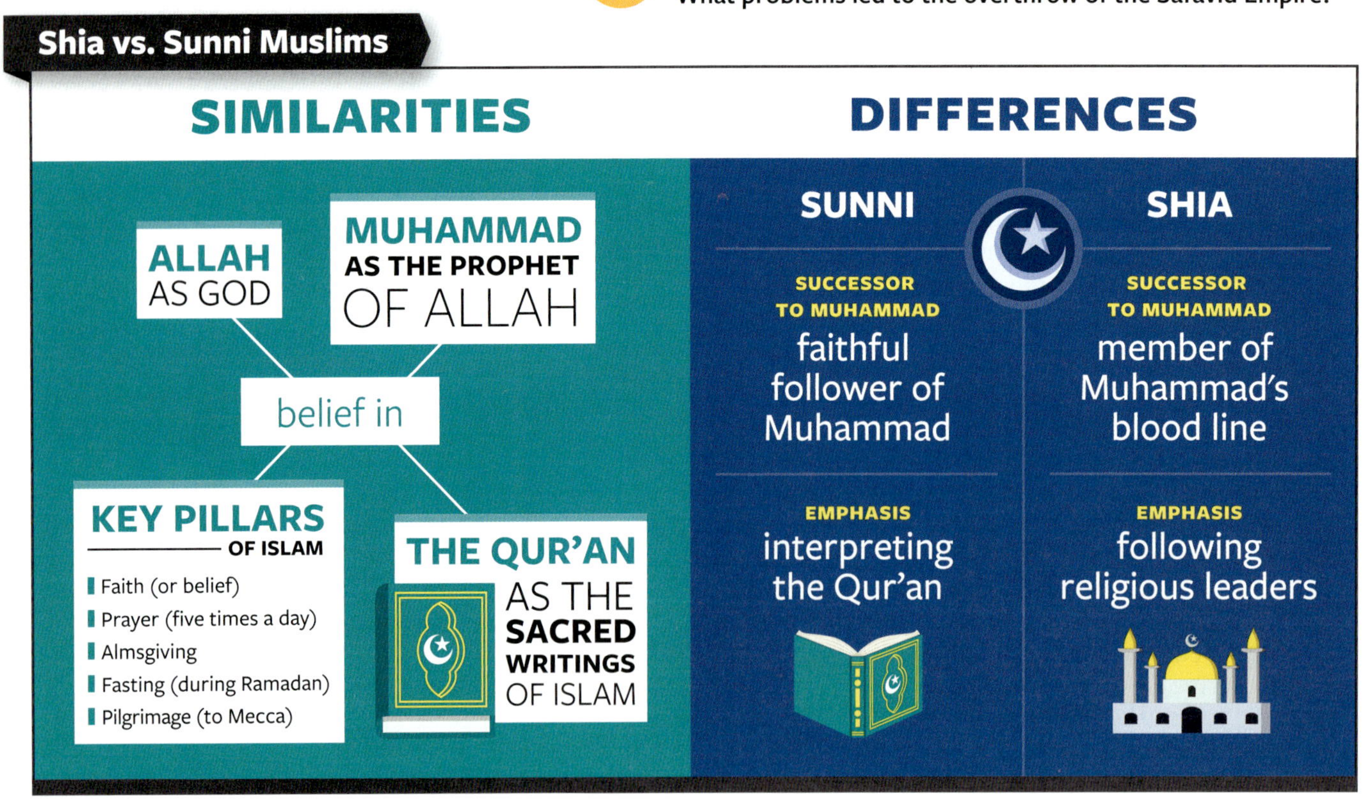

CRITICAL THINKING 8.3

Were the differences between Shia and Sunni Islam based on the main beliefs of Islam or on the way Islam was practiced? Explain your answer.

8.4 The Mughal Empire and Sikhism

The Mongols had attempted to conquer India for centuries. Despite many attempts and the terrible slaughter of Indians by Tamerlane, the Mongols had only been able to retain control of northern India. During the 1500s, a descendant of the Mongols and Turks finally gained control of most of India.

Conquests of the Mughals

The Muslim leader **Babur**, "the Tiger," became the leader of the Turkish-Mongol tribes of modern Afghanistan. In 1526 he invaded northern India with an army of twelve thousand men and overthrew the Muslim government. Babur was a descendant of two great Asian conquerors, Genghis Khan (Mongol) and Tamerlane (Turk). He established the **Mughal dynasty** (from *Mongol*) and conquered a large region in northern India.

Following the brutal example of his predecessors, Babur directed his forces to practice Muslim jihad by slaughtering their way into control of northern India. When they had destroyed the opposition, the Mughal rulers rebuilt their new territory in northern India according to Islamic law and acquired great wealth. Over time, the Mughal culture experienced a renewal of the arts, including a distinct type of architecture.

How did Babur gain control of northern India?

GUIDING QUESTIONS

- How did the Mughal dynasty develop in the subcontinent of India?
- How were Akbar's governing practices similar to and different from those of other Mughal rulers?
- What does Sikhism teach?
- Do the beliefs of Sikhism match the teaching of the Bible?
- What led to the decline of the Mughal Empire?

Mughal Dynasty

The Taj Mahal, built for the tomb of a ruler's wife, is the most famous example of Mughal architecture.

The most effective Mughal ruler came to power at the age of thirteen following the death of his father. **Akbar**, the grandson of Babur, continued the brutal conquest of India begun by his grandfather. Under Akbar's military leadership, the Mughal Empire expanded to the west, east, and south to central India.

Reforms of Akbar

How was Akbar's method of ruling similar to and different from Babur's method?

Having conquered central India through military conquest, Akbar gradually began to institute reforms in Indian society. He is said to have abolished the tax on non-Muslims and to have begun including Hindus in government, although he continued to endorse periodic slaughter of non-Muslims.

Teachings of Sikhism

Rulers of the Mughal dynasty had to contend with a new religion that was founded in the late 1400s, not long before they came to power. It became known as **Sikhism**. Sikhs believed in just one god, so the religion was monotheistic as was Islam. But it also was like Hinduism in that it was pantheistic. It taught that god was in everything and everything was in god, although it did acknowledge that god was greater than the material world.

The founder of Sikhism was Guru Nanak. He lived in the northwestern region of India called Punjab. A guru is a teacher. Guru Nanak was followed by nine other human gurus, the last of which, Guru Gobind Singh, declared that from then on, the sacred writings of Sikhism would be the guru. The writings are known as Guru Granth Sahib.

Sikhism rejects the possibility of absolute truth. Some of its key ideas are the value of meditating on god's name, the unity of god (there is only one god who is the same in all religions), the equality of all people, the need to serve others and pursue justice, and the importance of good conduct.

Mughal rulers tried to get Sikh followers to convert to Islam. They persecuted them when they refused to do so.

Sikh man praying in the lotus position (legs crossed)

Decline of the Mughal Empire

The last effective Mughal ruler, Aurangzeb, consumed most of the Mughal Empire's resources in conquering lower India. His death in 1707 ended the expansion of the empire and was followed by rapid decline. Successive rulers had little power and were dominated by rising warlords (leaders of local regions who maintained control by raising personal armies). Persian and Afghan forces frequently invaded and carried off treasures from Indian cities.

CRITICAL THINKING 8.4

Based on John 14:6, how would you answer the charge that there is no absolute truth?

Making Connections

1. How did the ruling practices of the Ming rulers demonstrate absolutism?
2. Describe the literature, art, and architecture of the Ming dynasty.
3. Tell why Zheng He led naval expeditions, what happened during the expeditions, and how the expeditions affected China.
4. How was the Manchu dynasty able to replace the Ming dynasty as rulers of China?
5. How did the weakening of the Byzantine Empire lead to the expansion of the Ottoman Empire?
6. What strategies helped the Ottoman army win battles?
7. How did the Ottomans promote wise government and economic growth in their empire?
8. Describe the literature, art, and architecture of the Ottoman Empire.
9. How did Ismail I bring together the people of Persia?
10. How did the Safavid Empire become associated with Shia Islam?
11. How did Shah Abbas strengthen the Safavid Empire politically, economically, and culturally?
12. What factors weakened the Safavid Empire and led to its eventual overthrow?
13. How did the Mughal dynasty establish control over northern India?
14. Were Babur and Akbar similar in how they treated the people of India? Explain your answer.
15. What are the key ideas of Sikhism?
16. What happened in the Mughal Empire after the death of Aurangzeb?

Thinking Critically

1. How should Christians treat people of other faiths? Consider verses such as Matthew 5:16. Compare your answer with the Ottomans' treatment of religious minorities within their empire.
2. Is the disagreement between Shiite and Sunni Muslims generally about the main beliefs of Islam? Explain your answer.
3. Does Sikhism agree with the Bible about the possibility of knowing truth and the unity of God? Consider verses such as Psalm 96:5 and Isaiah 45:22.

WHAT TO KNOW

PEOPLE

Mehmed II
Taizu
Chengzu
Zheng He
Mimar Sinan
Shah Ismail I
Shah Abbas
Babur
Akbar

PLACES

Anatolia
Istanbul

TERMS

Ming dynasty
absolutism
landscapes
Censorate
Manchu dynasty
Middle Kingdom
Ottoman Empire
Safavid dynasty
Shia Islam
Sunni Islam
Mughal dynasty
Sikhism

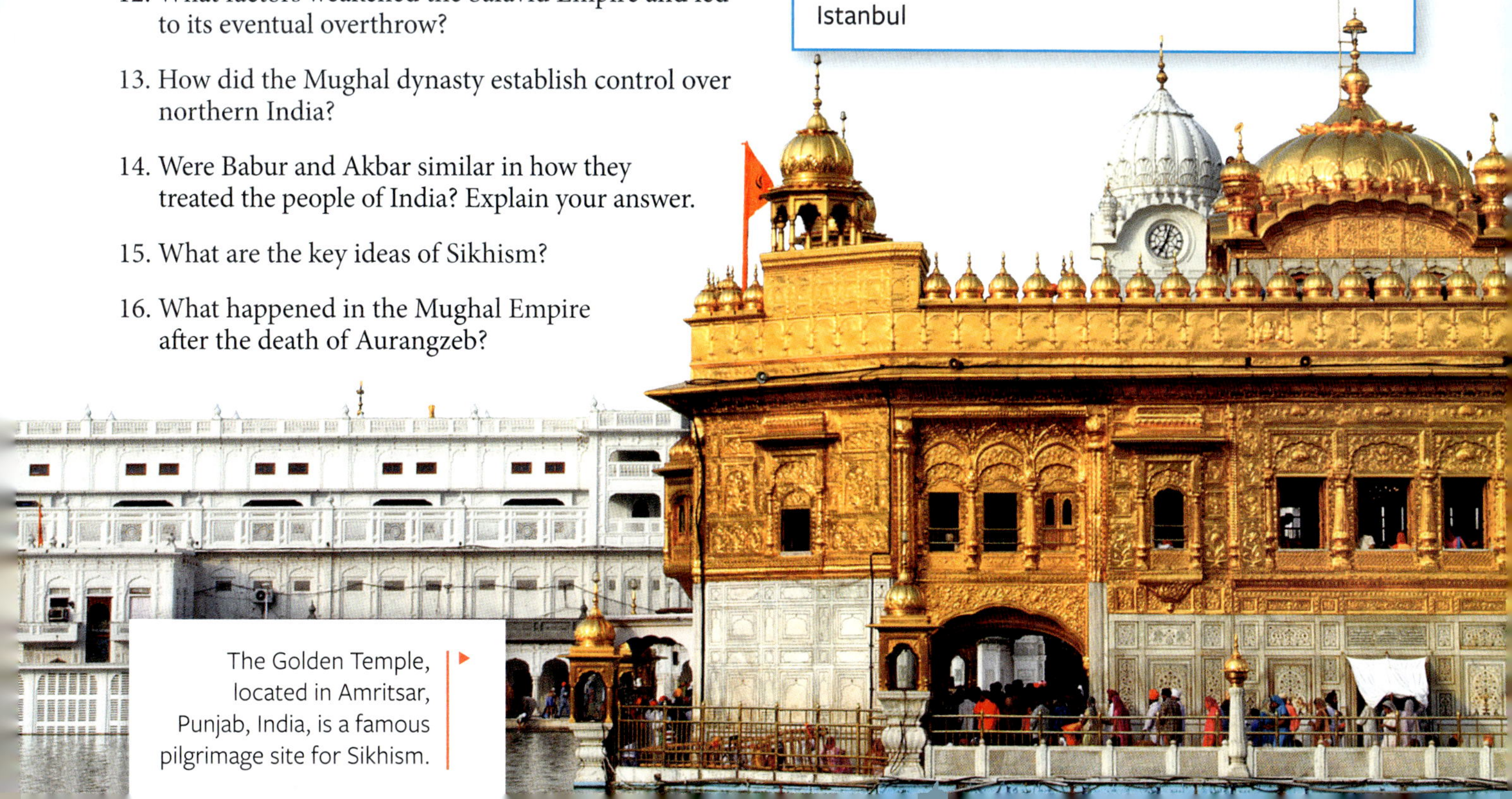

The Golden Temple, located in Amritsar, Punjab, India, is a famous pilgrimage site for Sikhism.

9 CHANGES IN EUROPEAN POWER AND THOUGHT

1600 – 1789

ESSENTIAL QUESTIONS

- Why did military and political power increase in some countries, and how were some countries exceptions to this trend?
- What major scientific advances were made during the Scientific Revolution?
- What was the significance of the Enlightenment?

Sir Robert Boyle

Robert Boyle was the fourteenth child of Richard Boyle, the first Earl of Cork, and Catherine Fenton. Boyle was sent to Eton College (a boarding school for boys) at eight years old. Then, like many young people from aristocratic families, he traveled on the continent of Europe for a few years, starting at age twelve, as a way of continuing his education.

Upon his return home, Boyle became involved with the Hartlib Circle. This informal group wrote about topics ranging from science to philosophy to religion. In the mid-1650s he moved to Oxford, where he joined the Oxford Philosophical Club. One of this group's activities was scientific experimentation. Boyle worked with other group members to conduct experiments with air. He discovered an idea that has become known as Boyle's law; it says that, all other things being constant, the pressure of a gas within a container is inversely proportional to its volume. In other words, as the volume decreases, the pressure of the gas increases. The opposite is true as well. This idea helps to explain what happens when you squeeze a balloon.

Boyle was a devoted Christian who disliked the trend of placing faith in science and human reason instead of God. He gave money to support Christian education and missions. He also wrote many works that explained how science and faith worked together. On the title page of his book *The Christian Virtuoso*, Boyle described his purpose for writing as "showing that by being addicted to experimental philosophy, a man is rather assisted, than indisposed, to be a good Christian." A better understanding of the workings of God's world, Boyle believed, should increase one's faith.

Boyle was an early member of the Royal Society, a British organization devoted to the promotion of scientific knowledge. Still in existence today, the society works to maintain knowledge of scientific inquiry of the past and to assist continued learning.

▲ Sketch of pump used by Boyle in his experiments with air

9.1 The Rising Power of European States

Thirty Years' War

Though the Peace of Augsburg (1555) had given German princes the right to choose the religion for their territories, tensions continued to simmer between Catholics and Lutherans and Catholics and Calvinists (who had not been mentioned in the treaty). The formation of the Protestant Union, a defensive military alliance by Protestant princes, was answered by the formation of the Catholic League by Catholic princes. Open conflict seemed inevitable, especially because other countries were likely to get involved.

The Habsburg rulers of the Holy Roman Empire (of which the German states were all officially a part) were Catholic and in agreement with the Catholic League. They could count on support from their relatives who ruled Spain and its territories. France, on the other hand, opposed the power of Spain and the Habsburgs in Europe; ironically, the French would support the Protestants even though France was Catholic.

Guiding Questions

- How did the Thirty Years' War and the Peace of Westphalia affect Europe?
- In what ways did the development of absolute governments in Europe differ from the development of limited governments?
- What was the significance of Peter the Great's reforms in Russia?
- How did the Dutch Republic emerge as a powerful European state?
- How did the English Civil War and the Glorious Revolution affect English society?

Gustavus Adolphus leads his troops to victory at the Battle of Breitenfeld in 1631.

What empire was weakened after the Thirty Years' War?

The conflict, known as the **Thirty Years' War**, can be divided into four stages. In the first stage (1618–25), a member of the Habsburg family and the head of the Protestant Union fought for control over the state of Bohemia. The Habsburgs won this stage, and Catholicism was named the official religion of Bohemia. In the second stage (1625–29), the Lutheran monarch Christian IV of Denmark tried to help the German Protestants. Christian lost to both the Catholic League and the army of the Habsburg emperor. In 1630 another Lutheran, Gustavus Adolphus of Sweden, took up the Protestant cause. A brilliant military commander, he defeated the emperor's army at the Battle of Lützen (1632). However, he died in the battle, and his troops began to struggle. They were defeated at the Battle of Nördlingen (1634). In the final stage of the war (1635–48), France came to the aid of Sweden. France defeated Spain, the Catholic League, and the Habsburg emperor.

The Thirty Years' War officially ended with the signing of the Peace of Westphalia in 1648. Some territory was exchanged, but the most significant effects of the treaty were religious and political. All German princes, including Calvinists, were free to choose the religion for their states. They could also carry out their own foreign policy. As a result, the Habsburg emperors had little authority left in the Holy Roman Empire.

The Thirty Years' War was the last major war fought over religion in Europe. After this point, conflicts tended to focus on political power.

Weakening the Holy Roman Empire

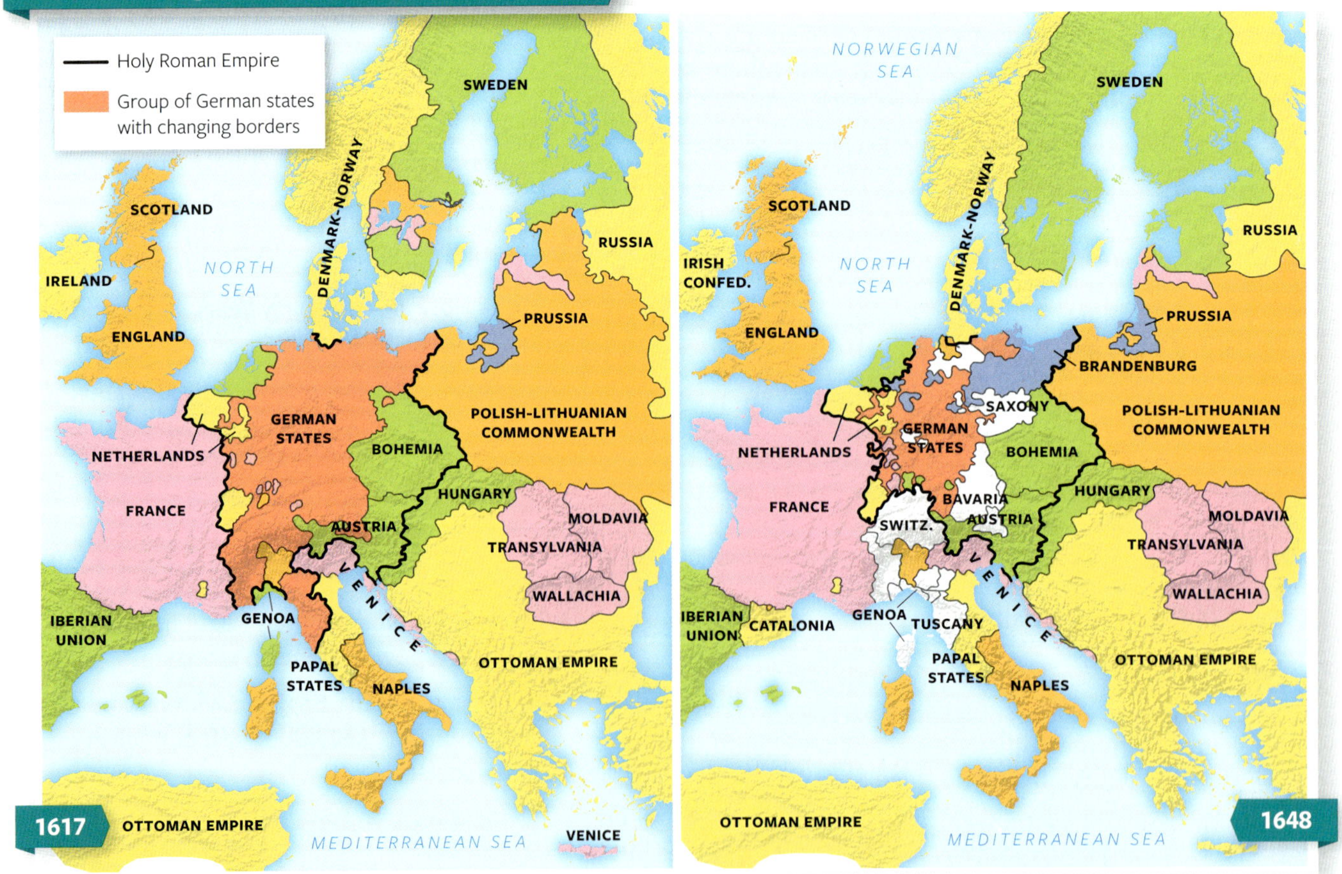

Development of Absolutism

During the 1600s, some rulers began to claim absolute power. They said that their authority came from God and that they answered only to God. This idea is sometimes known as the divine right of kings. In claiming this kind of absolute power, however, rulers were going beyond the boundaries that God places on human governments. Though monarchy is a legitimate form of government in the Bible, absolute power belongs only to God.

France

Of all the rulers who tried to become absolute monarchs, the French king **Louis XIV** was one of the most successful. Though local officials still controlled many of the daily activities of the common people, Louis succeeded brilliantly in dominating the national government.

Louis knew that the wealthiest nobles of the land were his main competition for power. He had a huge palace constructed in the town of Versailles, a few miles outside Paris. The palace became the seat of government as well as Louis's home. Louis arranged for top nobles to stay with him at Versailles, but he did not allow them to participate in government. Instead, he kept them busy with constant entertainment and elaborate rituals. For instance, when Louis got up in the morning, nobles assisted him in getting ready for the day. Wealthy and powerful men were willing to perform humble tasks like handing Louis a shirt because they could ask for special favors for themselves or their relatives while they were close to the king. As a result of this system, the nobles were relatively peaceful.

The Hall of Mirrors is the most famous room at the Palace of Versailles. The hall is 240 feet long, with 357 individual mirrors facing 17 large windows.

In policy decisions, Louis often showed a lack of wisdom and long-term thinking, though he built France into a dominant power. Louis removed religious toleration for the Huguenots, causing many of them to flee the country. He also spent lavishly on his own personal expenses at Versailles and on wars in Europe. Though his financial advisor, Jean-Baptiste Colbert, brought in money through mercantilist policies, Louis spent much of what came in. Ultimately, the entire country suffered financially.

How did Louis XIV keep his nobles from revolting against him?

Frederick the Great (ruled 1740–86) strengthened the Prussian bureaucracy and military. He provoked the War of the Austrian Succession by seizing Austrian territory.

German States

As the Holy Roman Empire weakened after the Thirty Years' War, two states, carved out of parts of the Empire, became powerful. They were called Brandenburg-Prussia, or just Prussia, and Austria.

Brandenburg-Prussia

Brandenburg-Prussia was a combination of three German territories, all ruled by the **Hohenzollern family**. There was Brandenburg in the northeast of the Holy Roman Empire, part of the Rhine valley in the west, and Prussia outside the Holy Roman Empire's eastern boundary. Because their territories were scattered and vulnerable to attack, the Hohenzollern rulers believed a strong military was necessary. Their army became known for both its efficiency and its domination of their state.

The Hohenzollerns had a deal with the Junkers, the nobles of their territory. The Junkers would not challenge the authority of the Hohenzollerns. In exchange, the Junkers had full authority over the peasants on their land, did not have to pay taxes, and got the best jobs in the army and bureaucracy.

Austria

Austria was a personal possession of the Habsburg family. Though the Habsburgs had little influence left as Holy Roman Emperors, there were many territories in central and southeastern Europe that they ruled personally (because of wars or alliances). The Habsburgs continued to be a powerful force on the continent through their control of these territories. Austria was one of the first territories the Habsburgs controlled, and several of their other central European territories are now part of the modern nation of Austria. The name *Austria* is sometimes used generically to refer to many of the Habsburg possessions. The Habsburgs could never establish tight control over all their territory because there were so many people groups, languages, and legislative bodies represented.

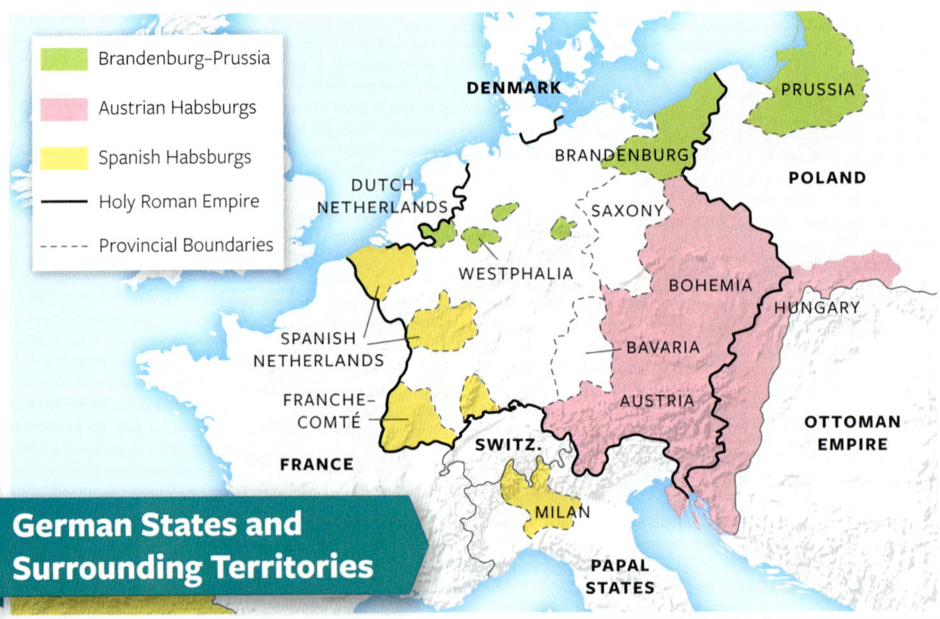

German States and Surrounding Territories

RUSSIA

The modern state of Russia developed around the region of Moscow. Moscow's rulers eventually took the title of *czar* (taken from "Caesar") and began expanding their territory. The **czars** fought for power with the boyars, Russia's top nobility. The boyars were finally put down when Michael Romanov became the czar in 1613; the Romanov dynasty lasted until 1917.

Russian society was designed to favor those at the top: the czar, who claimed absolute authority over the state, and the nobles, who owned large amounts of land. All others were tightly regulated by the government. This included the peasants, who were often tied to large estates as serfs, and the people of towns.

Czar Peter I, known as **Peter the Great**, introduced changes that eventually transformed Russia into a great state. Peter was interested in learning, especially about new technologies. He took a tour of Western Europe in 1697–98 and gained firsthand knowledge of Western innovations. He believed that becoming more like the West would strengthen Russia. His goal was to create a strong military and use it to build Russia's power and prestige in Europe.

Peter the Great

? **How did Peter I plan to make Russia a great state?**

Merchant Kuzma Minin challenged the people of the city of Nizhny Novgorod to raise an army to defend Russia against the Polish.

ST. PETERSBURG

Power

Peter I had a strong, forceful personality. He determined to make Russia like the West, whatever it took. He built a large army by requiring military service for both nobles and peasants. He started the first Russian navy. He copied Western governing and economic practices. He even tried to force the Russian people to abandon their traditional culture and act like Westerners, requiring men, for example, to shave their beards.

Justice

Peasants had a difficult life in Peter's Russia. They carried out all heavy labor, whether it was on farms, in the army, or on construction projects. They also bore the burden of financing Peter's massive military spending. When his economic policies failed to bring in the money he needed, Peter simply raised the peasants' taxes.

Estimates suggest that 20,000 to 40,000 people participated in the construction of St. Petersburg.

Environment

To advance trade with the West, Peter directed the construction of a new Russian capital on the Gulf of Finland, an extension of the Baltic Sea. It was named St. Petersburg. Peter was determined to make the site work, though the location was not ideal, being windy, cold, and wet, with marshy soil. Forced peasant labor was used to build the city, and thousands died under the harsh conditions.

Peter planned every aspect of the city. He ordered people to move there and told them how to build their houses. He arranged for the construction of many public buildings and gave directions for the infrastructure (things like roads and canals). He even planned for landscaping.

Citizenship

Peter created the Table of Ranks. Through service in the military, government, or court, people of slightly lower status could become part of the nobility. There were fourteen ranks in the table. If people succeeded in their positions at one rank, they could move up to the next.

Religion

As with everything else in Russia, Peter wanted to control the Russian Orthodox Church. He replaced the traditional church leader, the patriarch, with a group called the Holy Synod. The leader of the group, known as a procurator, was not a church official. Instead, he provided a voice for the czar in the development of church policy.

The architecture of St. Petersburg reflected Peter's desire for the city to look European.

The city of St. Petersburg was built across several islands, with bridges connecting sections of land.

Early stock exchange at Amsterdam

Denmark and Sweden

Denmark and Sweden had similar stories in the 1600s. Both wanted more power in the Baltic Sea region. Both had struggles between monarchs and nobles, with monarchs making efforts to establish their own absolute authority. Both had ambitions of increasing their territory through war. Sweden had success for a time, but eventually both states lost much of their potential influence through military defeats.

Steps toward Limited Government

While absolutism thrived in some European states, others adopted a more limited approach to government. Many Christians today advocate for limited government because humans are sinful. A system of checks and balances, often seen in limited governments, can help prevent government officials from acting selfishly.

Poland

Poland was a monarchy, but its kings were elected by the Polish nobility. The nobles purposefully chose kings who would not threaten their own power. As a result of this system, Poland failed to establish a strong central government. Its political weakness made Poland an easy target for invasion.

Dutch Republic

During the 1600s the Dutch Republic stunned everyone by building a vast economic empire. The state had no strong monarchy to direct economic policy. Instead, Dutch merchants played a major role in world trade. They sent out a huge fleet of ships to establish a large colonial empire and bring great wealth to the Dutch Republic.

The Dutch established a modern stock market to raise funds and finance trade. They also developed a banking system to manage wealth and provide loans for businesses. Other countries, such as England, adopted the Dutch banking system, and their economic productivity expanded as a result.

How did the Dutch Republic become powerful in the world?

England

In Chapter 2 you learned that Parliament gained the power to approve taxes. This power of the purse forced the king to work with Parliament to raise funds. However, **James I**, the Scottish cousin of Elizabeth I and first of the Stuart line, refused to work with Parliament and created strong resentment.

James's son **Charles I** followed in his father's footsteps. He asserted the divine right of kings and struggled to defeat Parliament's efforts to deny him absolute power. Frustrated at having to work with Parliament, Charles refused to call its members into session for eleven years (1629–40). Since he could not get new taxes approved without Parliament's consent, Charles looked for old laws that he could use to raise funds. For example, ship money was a tax from the Middle Ages that coastal towns had paid to help cover the cost of their defense. Charles brought this tax back and used it as a general means of raising money. Many opposed these attempts to get around Parliament. Charles's religious leanings caused controversy as well, given that he had married a Catholic and seemed to be trying to bring more ritual back to the Church of England.

The final straw came when Charles tried to force the Scottish church to use the English **prayer book**. The Scots rebelled, and Charles had to call Parliament into session since he could not raise enough money on his own to fund an army. With eleven years of collected complaints, Parliament came prepared to push the king for change.

English Civil War

In January 1642, Charles entered Parliament with several hundred soldiers and tried to arrest five members who he believed were plotting against him. They had already escaped, but this move caused both the king and Parliament to hire soldiers and prepare for battle. The **English Civil War** resulted. After the king's forces won the first battles, Parliament reorganized its forces, and **Oliver Cromwell** took an important role of leadership in its army. Parliament defeated the king's forces, and Charles was tried and executed in 1649. Cromwell filled the resulting power vacuum and ruled until his death in 1658.

prayer book a book that sets a pattern for worship services to follow

Charles I was executed on January 30, 1649, just outside the Palace of Whitehall.

Oliver Cromwell

Oliver Cromwell was born on April 25, 1599, to Robert and Elizabeth Cromwell. Cromwell attended grammar school, completed one year at Cambridge University, and studied law for a year. Although he struggled spiritually as a young person, Cromwell became a devoted Puritan. He married Elizabeth Bourchier in 1620, and they had nine children.

Cromwell won a seat in Parliament in 1628 and again in 1640 as tensions were rising with Charles I. When Parliament began preparing for armed conflict with the king, Cromwell organized and led a cavalry force from his hometown. He was a capable and successful commander. The discipline that he instilled in his men served them well on the battlefield.

There were two stages to the civil war. Cromwell was heavily involved in both, having been promoted to a high position in the army. His leadership was critical to winning several major battles.

Following the king's execution, there were three experiments in government. The third was basically a military dictatorship under the leadership of Cromwell, who was known as Lord Protector. Cromwell made some wise reforms during this time, but he also created bitter enemies through some of his actions, such as his brutal suppression of a rebellion in Ireland. Cromwell died of malaria on September 3, 1658.

Restoration and Revolution of 1688

Shortly after Cromwell's death, the English invited **Charles II**, son of Charles I, to become their king. Charles II continued the policies of his father and grandfather; however, he was often able to ignore Parliament by getting funds from the French king Louis XIV. In exchange for French support, Charles promised to convert to Catholicism at some point and to promote French foreign policy. When Charles died in 1685, his brother **James II** became king. James was openly Catholic, but the English tolerated him due to his advanced age. However, when his wife gave birth to a son, the English feared that they would be ruled by Catholic monarchs for many years to come. They invited James's daughter and son-in-law, both Protestants, to come to England and receive the throne.

In June 1688 the Dutchman William of Orange and his wife, Mary, landed in England with a small army, and James fled the country. This change of power without resorting to war became known as the **Glorious Revolution**.

William and his army sail for England in October 1688.

William and Mary

In exchange for the throne, **William and Mary** agreed to sign the **English Bill of Rights**. This document set limits on royal power, provided the English people with basic civil liberties, and prevented future rulers from being Roman Catholic.

Cabinet Government

During the time of the Stuart monarchs and their successors, a cabinet system of government began to develop in England. A **cabinet** is a body of officials who give advice to a government leader and oversee the departments that implement government policy. The cabinet system strengthened when George I, a cousin from the German state of Hanover, took the British throne in 1714. (The country became officially known as Great Britain after it joined together with Scotland under the Acts of Union of 1707.) George rarely attended cabinet meetings, so his officials became more than just advisers. They began to make policy for the government. This was another important step in limiting the power of the British monarchy.

What changes were made in England as a result of the English Bill of Rights?

European Wars of the 1700s

The European states fought several wars in the 1700s that strengthened or weakened governments and reshaped the map. Below are a few highlights.

* Associated North American wars are italicized.

War*	Purpose	Sides	Outcome
Second Northern War, 1700–21	To establish dominance in the Baltic Sea region	Russia, Denmark-Norway, and Saxony-Poland vs. Sweden	Russia gained power and influence.
War of the Spanish Succession, 1701–14 *Queen Anne's War*	To determine who would take the throne of Spain after Charles II, the last Spanish Habsburg, died	Austria, England, the Netherlands, and Prussia vs. France and Spain	Philip V, grandson of Louis XIV of France, became the king of Spain but could never be king of France. Spain kept its empire abroad but had to give up most of its European territory. (Austria gained the Spanish Netherlands and some territory in Italy as part of this agreement.)
War of the Austrian Succession, 1740–48 *King George's War*	To establish Maria Theresa as the rightful ruler of Austria and to determine the ownership of Silesia, an Austrian province stolen by Prussia	Austria, Britain, and the Netherlands vs. Prussia, France, and Spain	All territory taken during the war was returned to its original owner except Silesia.
Seven Years' War, 1756–63 *French and Indian War*	To settle territorial disputes in Europe, India, and North America	France, Russia, Sweden, Austria, and Saxony vs. Prussia, Hanover, and Britain	Prussia kept Silesia permanently. Great Britain became the dominant colonial power in India and North America.

CRITICAL THINKING 9.1

1. What was the main obstacle to the power of European monarchs who tried to adopt absolutism?
2. How did the English Civil War and the Glorious Revolution limit the power of the monarchs in England?

GUIDING QUESTIONS

- What were the key causes of the Scientific Revolution?
- Why was the scientific method important?
- Who were the significant contributors to the Scientific Revolution?
- Why were the advances in medicine, mathematics, and chemistry important?
- How did early modern scientific thinking differ from medieval scientific thinking?

9.2 The Scientific Revolution

People have been interested in the world around them since the beginning of time. Genesis 4 says that Tubal-cain, one of Cain's descendants, worked with brass and iron, so the process of extracting and purifying ore to produce metals preceded the Flood. This activity demonstrates humans' God-given ability to take parts of God's creation and develop them. The instinct to fulfill the Creation Mandate given by God in Genesis 1:28 appears in every time period and civilization.

Medieval Science

The 1600s and 1700s in Europe are often called the **Age of Reason**. The implication is that people before this time were guided not by reason but by superstition and religion. This is a popular view, but it is not accurate. Scholars in the Middle Ages observed the world around them and read the observations of others. They reasoned from these observations to general principles about the way they believed the world worked. Sometimes they drew incorrect conclusions. But given the knowledge they had, some of their assumptions and conclusions seemed to make good sense at the time.

The scientific thinking of medieval scholars was shaped by the writings of Aristotle, but these scholars knew that Aristotle was not right about everything. For instance, Aristotle taught that the world was eternal. Medieval scholars, however, believed the Bible's teaching that God created the world from nothing. In this and other areas, these scholars modified Aristotle's thought.

Medieval scholars built on the knowledge of the Muslim world, having gained access to Muslim documents through the work of men like **Albert the Great**, a Dominican friar. Some scholars made important new contributions of their own. For example, **Roger Bacon** made significant advances in physics, geography, and optics.

Some of the work of these scholars prepared the way for the **Scientific Revolution**. However, the most important scientific contribution of the medieval world was the development of the university as a place where people learned and wrote about the natural world.

What was the most important contribution of the medieval world to the development of scientific knowledge?

Renaissance Humanism

Several trends of the Renaissance period also encouraged the development of scientific knowledge. Interest in the classical world led to the translation of more ancient texts. The desire for realism led artists to practice careful observation. They also used geometry to get correct perspective. And the belief that a Renaissance man should have a variety of skills led many to become mathematicians. These Renaissance contributions built on medieval knowledge. They led to an outpouring of European scientific activity beginning in the 1500s.

What Renaissance trends came from the desire to achieve realism in art?

Astronomical Discoveries and Innovations

Discoveries in astronomy during this period changed people's understanding of nature as well as the way they thought about themselves and the world. In 1543 **Nicolaus Copernicus** presented his view that the earth revolved around the sun, not the sun around the earth as many formerly thought. He relied on mathematics to develop his theory. Another astronomer, **Galileo Galilei**, made observations using the newly invented telescope. His results supported Copernicus's theory (though his support for that theory led to a major controversy with the Catholic Church).

Nicolaus Copernicus

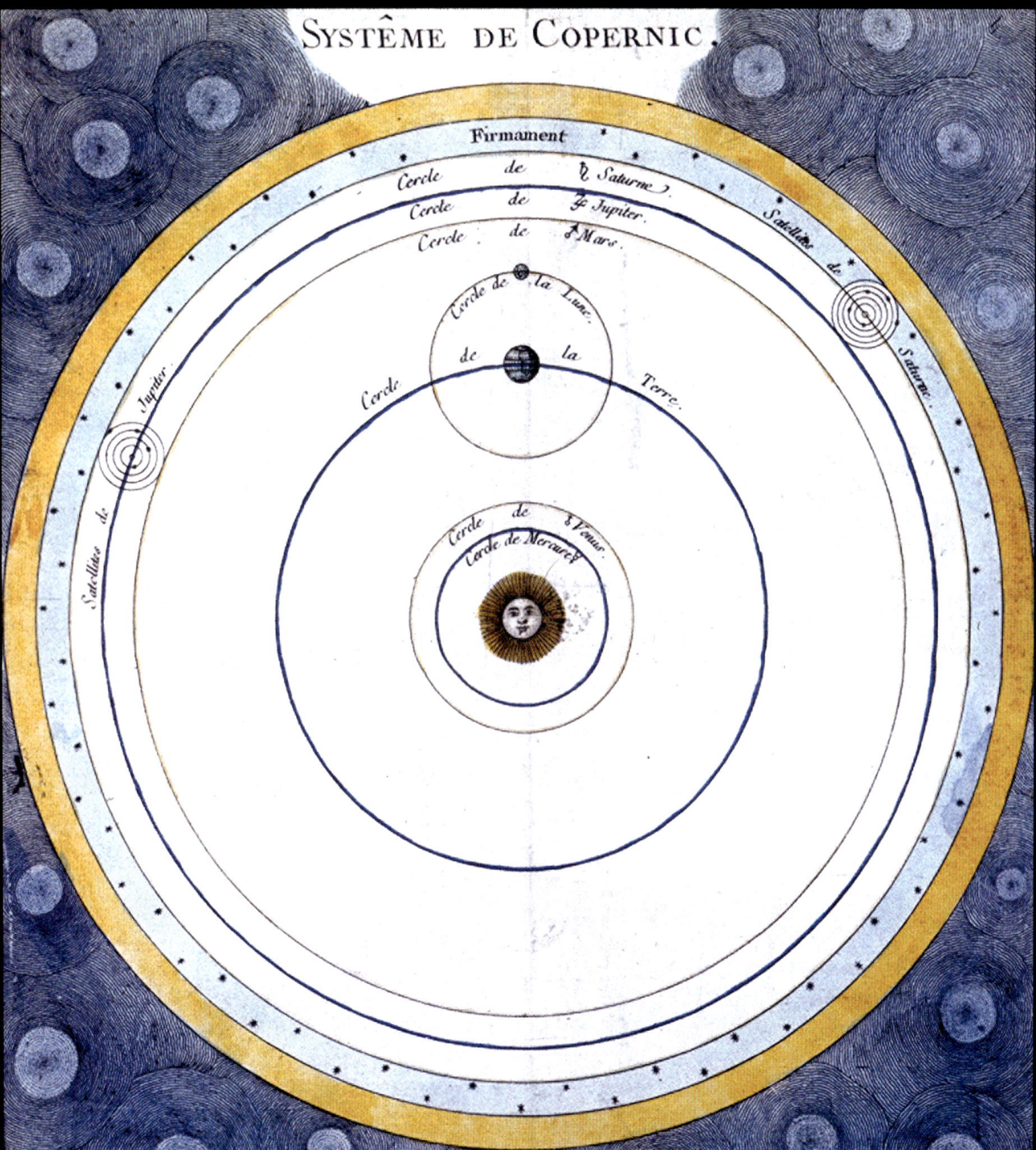

Copernican diagram of a heliocentric universe

Newton's reflecting telescope

How did the work of Copernicus and Galileo challenge earlier views about the movement of the universe?

Sir Isaac Newton discovered concepts that have become known as the **laws of gravity and motion**. According to these laws, gravity keeps the planets in their orbits. Among his many other accomplishments, Newton developed an advanced form of calculus (method of calculating) and invented the reflecting telescope. These contributions enabled an improved use of mathematics and a more-detailed observation of the universe.

English astronomer **Edmond Halley** recorded the position and motion of hundreds of stars. He also developed a theory about the orbit of comets. Halley accurately predicted that a comet which appeared in 1682 would return to our solar system seventy-six years later. This comet was later named Halley's comet.

Sir William Herschel made many discoveries, including the planet now known as Uranus. In 1784 he began to build telescopes to sell, and many wealthy men purchased them. His large telescopes enabled men to look farther out into the universe and view sights that previously could not be seen. Between 1787 and 1789, Herschel built a massive forty-foot-long telescope. With this telescope he could see several of the moons around Saturn.

Herschel's telescope

Discoveries in Other Fields

While some were looking to the heavens to find new worlds, others were looking through newly invented microscopes or expanding ancient knowledge. Advances were made in many areas, including medicine, mathematics, and chemistry.

Medicine

Rejecting superstitious remedies of the past, scientists began to investigate the body and treat its diseases. One scientist, **Paracelsus**, stated that the body is mostly chemicals and should be treated with chemicals. Other scientists studied anatomy. By learning the positions of bones, muscles, and organs, they were able to give better diagnoses and treatment. **Andreas Vesalius** developed his knowledge of human anatomy by dissecting human bodies. The Englishman **William Harvey** also made important contributions to medicine by discovering that blood is pumped by the heart, travels through the body in blood vessels, and returns to the heart in the circulatory system. Another Englishman, **Edward Jenner**, discovered a way to prevent people from getting a disease known as **smallpox**. This disease killed or terribly scarred many people until Jenner developed a **vaccine** to protect against it. The vaccine used a weakened form of a similar disease known as cowpox. Jenner's research led to the practical elimination of smallpox.

▲ Edward Jenner administers a smallpox vaccination.

? **How did Andreas Vesalius and William Harvey advance knowledge of the human body?**

Mathematics

Interest in business and science encouraged improvements in mathematics. Three improvements that occurred around the time of the Renaissance were the more common use of Arabic numerals, the introduction of the decimal point, and the use of symbols to simplify mathematical equations. Prior to this time, equations were written in standard form (every number word written out), making them enormous and difficult to read.

During this period great advances were made in both the theory and the practical application of mathematics. For example, it was vital to understand mathematics in order to explain the orbit of planets or to predict when asteroids would return to our solar system.

Chemistry

Muslim scholars had laid the foundation of modern chemistry. They introduced careful observation and controlled experimentation. Over time, these scholars discovered many chemicals. Chemistry became important in Europe as a result of diseases like the Black Death. Europeans experimented with various substances to develop medicines that would prevent or cure diseases.

vaccine a substance injected into the body to help it fight off a disease

Antoine Lavoisier is known as the Father of Modern Chemistry. His many contributions include naming oxygen and hydrogen and working to develop the metric system. Lavoisier formulated the law of conservation of matter. This law states that matter cannot be created or destroyed; it can only change form. Lavoisier also assembled the first-known list of elements.

Lavoisier's laboratory

THE
Scientific Method

1. Formulate a theory.
2. Experiment to test the theory.
3. Collect information.
4. Revise the theory.
5. Experiment to test the revised theory.

Scientific Methodology

The **scientific method** is a series of steps scientists use to answer questions about the physical world. These steps may vary, and their order may differ depending on the circumstance. However, they are designed to produce accurate and provable answers to the questions that scientists encounter.

The Muslim scientist Alhazen was one of the first to develop a scientific methodology in his research on light. He demonstrated this process in his *Book of Optics*. Many of the people already mentioned in this chapter developed their own procedures to answer questions and prove their theories through observation and experimentation.

?

What are the five steps of the scientific method?

Significance of the Scientific Revolution

The Scientific Revolution is sometimes described in terms of Europeans casting off the shackles of religion and tradition and instead embracing reason and science. However, this description is not entirely accurate. Though myth and superstition did have some influence (particularly in medicine), not all medieval scholars were bound by tradition and superstition. In addition, many scientists of the Scientific Revolution claimed to be Christians. They believed scientific investigation brought glory to God.

The Scientific Revolution did have some negative effects on Europeans' worldview, though. Before this time, reason was seen as a tool. It was a tool that could help a person understand the Bible. It could also help a person understand the world. But with the Scientific Revolution, reason came to be seen as an authority and not just a tool. Instead of seeking to understand Scripture as God's authoritative Word, some people began to decide which parts of Scripture they would accept and which parts they would reject based on what seemed reasonable to them.

TURNING POINTS

Leeuwenhoek's Work with Microscopes

Tools like microscopes helped to advance knowledge during the Scientific Revolution. Some of the most significant discoveries using microscopes came from a surprising source. **Anton Van Leeuwenhoek** was born on October 24, 1632, in Delft, Holland. Both he and his family made their living as craftsmen. He had no formal university training, but he was a hard and talented worker, and he wanted to know everything he could about the world around him.

Starting in the late 1500s, advances began to be made in the development of microscopes. The compound microscope, which contained more than one lens, was invented around 1595. Robert Hooke and other scientists used compound microscopes to learn more about the composition of living things. These early microscopes could magnify an object about twenty to thirty times its normal size.

Having read Hooke's book *Micrographia*, Van Leeuwenhoek became interested in building a microscope of his own. His microscope had just one lens, unlike the compound microscopes. The object to be observed was placed on a spike in front of the lens. There were two screws for adjusting the position of the object. Van Leeuwenhoek's microscope could magnify an object more than two hundred times its normal size. It also produced better images than the early compound microscopes.

Van Leeuwenhoek built more than five hundred microscopes of this style. The secret to his success seems to have been his attention to detail, from the carefully ground lens to the finely adjusted lighting. Van Leeuwenhoek looked at a wide variety of interesting and unusual things using his microscope, including plaque from his teeth. Because his microscopes had so much more magnifying power than other microscopes of his day, he made many important discoveries using them, including bacteria, protozoa, and blood cells.

Model of a Van Leeuwenhoek microscope

Van Leeuwenhoek frequently wrote the Royal Society of London to tell them about his observations. They eventually elected him as a member, though he never attended their meetings. Van Leeuwenhoek's findings launched the new scientific fields of bacteriology (the study of bacteria) and protozoology (the study of protozoa).

1. How were Van Leeuwenhoek's microscopes different from early compound microscopes?
2. What discoveries did Van Leeuwenhoek make using his microscopes?
3. What new fields came out of Van Leeuwenhoek's discoveries?

CRITICAL THINKING 9.2

How can scientific advances bring glory to God?

GUIDING QUESTIONS

- What were the principal ideas of the Enlightenment?
- How did Enlightenment ideas impact the development of modern governments?
- How did the Enlightenment influence the American Revolution?
- How does Enlightenment thought align with Scripture?

9.3 The Enlightenment

The very name *Enlightenment* shows how the philosophers and scientists of this period viewed the previous eras. To them, earlier periods were covered in darkness and urgently needed the new ideas of this new era. Those ideas came from the belief that human reason and careful observation were the only sure ways to know the truth. Freed from devotion to the past, Enlightenment thinkers reexamined the values and religious beliefs of Europe.

Principal Ideas of the Enlightenment

While a student, **René Descartes** read many of the classics recovered by the Renaissance, but he found them weak. Descartes noted that philosophy settled nothing; every philosophical point was debated. And though Descartes professed to be a good Catholic, he realized that the Reformation showed that even theology was a matter of great dispute. Descartes also concluded that people can be deceived by what they observe through their senses and through experiments. He decided that only mathematics led to certainty. This belief motivated Descartes to develop a method for knowing truth that was based on mathematics. He proposed doubting everything except basic axioms (statements about which there can be no doubt). Working from the axiom, a person should then reason through all the issues until truth is established.

Descartes's approach was a form of **rationalism**, the use of human reason as the best way to establish truth. This approach to truth was very different from previous attitudes in Europe. For example, Reformation churches considered Scripture the supreme authority. Reason was necessary for understanding both Scripture and the world, but it was not the authority that decided what was true and false.

John Locke insisted that the ideas Descartes found axiomatic (obvious) were not implanted by God in the human mind (as Descartes had claimed) but were developed through careful observation of the world. Locke argued in favor of **empiricism**, the belief that the best way to find true knowledge was through experience. Instead of arriving at truth through a sequence of careful reasoning, the empiricist observes the world around him to determine truth.

Descartes had insisted that he was not trying to attack Christianity. But the Dutch philosopher **Benedict de Spinoza** applied Descartes's approach to the foundation of the Christian faith, the Bible. Spinoza said that the Bible was written by humans at particular times in history. Since different people wrote portions of the Bible at different times, readers of the Bible should expect to find disagreements among the authors. The careful reader, Spinoza said, would use reason to distinguish what was true in the Bible from what was false. Spinoza believed the point of reading the Bible was not to learn how to live—reason taught that. It was simply a historical investigation. Spinoza read the Bible as a historical artifact rather than a revelation from God.

? **How did rationalism and empiricism differ in their views on finding truth?**

While philosophers like Spinoza were challenging confidence in the Bible as God's inspired Word, others were rejecting the idea that God is personally involved in the world that He created. They adopted a view known as **deism**. Under deism, God is viewed like a clock-winder, who made the world but left it to run according to the natural laws that He set up for it. Deists did not believe God gave individual attention to humans or had actively intervened to provide salvation through His Son, Jesus Christ. The Frenchman **Voltaire**, a key figure of the Enlightenment, was a well-known deist.

Influence of the Enlightenment

Democratic Thought and Government

Despite their disagreements about truth and other issues, Enlightenment thinkers shared a democratic urge. Their ideas helped to shape many practices and principles of modern democratic societies. The Enlightenment was especially influential in France. French Enlightenment philosophers, known as **philosophes**, proposed ideas for changing society that reflected their experience in a state ruled by absolutism. They often praised the English, who seemed to have more freedom than the French had. Voltaire wrote about the freedom of the English government, press, and religious life. The Baron de **Montesquieu** used the English government as an example of how governmental power should be restrained. He stated that the English had set up a system in which legislative powers (making laws), executive powers (enforcing laws), and judicial powers (interpreting laws) were each held by different groups of people. He believed that a **separation of powers** such as this would allow the three parts of government to put helpful checks on each other's power.

The desire to limit the power of government influenced the economic theory of the Enlightenment period as well. **Adam Smith**, a Scotsman, challenged the ideas of mercantilism, which promoted active government involvement in the economy. Smith believed that countries should trade freely with each other, that a country's greatest asset was the labor of its people, and that governments should not interfere in the economic activities of their people.

Some philosophers of the Enlightenment tried to put together a philosophy of government: why government exists and what should be expected of it. Though their ideas differed significantly, they can all be generally described by the term **social contract**. A social contract is an agreement by a group of people to place themselves under the authority of a government. **Thomas Hobbes** believed that without government, people would hurt each other; therefore, they should agree to be governed by an absolute ruler who had enough power to protect them. John Locke, on the other hand, believed that all humans have certain natural rights, things like life and property, that their government should protect. According to Locke, if a government failed to protect its citizens' natural rights, the citizens were entitled to replace the government. **Jean-Jacques Rousseau** believed that humans were happy in their primitive condition, but they needed government once private ownership was introduced to society. He believed people should be governed by their general will. In other words, all should abide by the decisions of the majority.

? **What is the advantage of having a separation of powers in government?**

The colonists fought for their liberty in clashes such as the Battle of Long Island (1776).

The Declaration of Independence and the US Constitution reflect Enlightenment ideas such as natural rights and a separation of powers.

How did Locke's idea about natural rights apply to the situation of the American colonists?

The American Revolution

Leading American colonists were familiar with the ideas of the Enlightenment. They believed, as Locke said, that they had certain natural rights that their government should preserve. They also knew that the English Bill of Rights had guaranteed many rights to the people of England. When the king and some members of Parliament decided to impose several taxes on the American colonies, the colonists resisted. Most taxes had been collected by colonial legislatures for many years. This intrusion by the king and Parliament threatened the Americans' independence. The king responded by sending troops to force the colonists into submission. However, the quartering of troops in the homes of the colonists was also illegal according to the English Bill of Rights. The colonists insisted on having the same civil liberties as those found in the English Bill of Rights. When British forces invaded the colonies, the colonists fought to preserve their liberty.

The constitution that was established for the new American nation in 1789 borrowed from the idea of a separation of powers. Three separate branches of government were created, and each was given functions that could check the power of the other branches when necessary.

Overall Effects

The Enlightenment introduced many political and social changes that were important to democratic societies. Its political influence was felt even across the ocean in the American colonies. But the Enlightenment also challenged the central role of Christianity in the culture of Europe. In doing so, it produced a shift in worldview that has affected Europe to this day.

Critical Thinking 9.3

Is deism true according to John 3:16?

Making Connections

1. What political and religious changes occurred in Europe as a result of the Thirty Years' War?
2. Choose one absolute state in Europe and one state whose government was limited in power. Explain what happened in each state to increase or decrease the power of the monarch.
3. What is the main problem with absolutism from a biblical worldview?
4. What is the biblical basis for some Christians' support of limited government?
5. How did the Dutch Republic become a powerful European state?
6. How did the English Civil War and the Glorious Revolution limit the power of the English monarchs?
7. What contributions did the medieval and Renaissance worlds make to the development of the Scientific Revolution?
8. What is the scientific method, and how did it advance knowledge during the Scientific Revolution?
9. Describe the philosophies of rationalism, empiricism, and deism.
10. How did Benedict de Spinoza view the Bible and its role in society?
11. How did the idea of a social contract help to prompt the American Revolution?

Thinking Critically

1. How did Europeans' view of religion change after the Thirty Years' War?
2. How did Peter the Great's westernization of Russia change Russia's influence in Europe?
3. How did the biblical view of the world make it possible for new discoveries to be made in medicine, mathematics, and chemistry?
4. How did early modern scientific thinking compare with medieval scientific thinking in its worldview?
5. What evidence can you see of Enlightenment influence on modern governments and economies?
6. How did the Enlightenment differ from the Reformation in its understanding of human reasoning?

What to Know

EVENTS

Thirty Years' War
English Civil War
Glorious Revolution
Age of Reason
Scientific Revolution

PEOPLE

Robert Boyle
Louis XIV
Hohenzollern family
Peter the Great
James I
Charles I
Oliver Cromwell
Charles II
James II
William and Mary
Albert the Great
Roger Bacon
Nicolaus Copernicus
Galileo Galilei
Sir Isaac Newton
Edmond Halley
Sir William Herschel
Paracelsus
Andreas Vesalius
William Harvey
Edward Jenner
Antoine Lavoisier
Anton Van Leeuwenhoek
René Descartes
John Locke
Benedict de Spinoza
Voltaire
Montesquieu
Adam Smith
Thomas Hobbes
Jean-Jacques Rousseau

TERMS

czars
prayer book
English Bill of Rights
cabinet
laws of gravity and motion
smallpox vaccine
scientific method
rationalism
empiricism
deism
philosophes
separation of powers
social contract

10 OCEANIA

1000 – 1900

ESSENTIAL QUESTIONS

- What physical characteristics define the region of Oceania?
- What were the original inhabitants of Oceania like?
- What were the interactions between European explorers and the indigenous peoples of Oceania like?
- How and where did European settlements develop in Oceania?
- How did the work of missionaries benefit the peoples of Oceania?

King Tupou I of Tonga

In his 1875 speech to the parliament of Tonga **King Tupou I** said, "If Tonga will remain as it is now, I will not say that it is because of our intelligence or our knowledge or whatever it is that we can do, but only because we are with God. As I have said before I will say again, Tonga is dedicated to God."

During the 1700s and 1800s, Europeans discovered and colonized the islands of Oceania in the Pacific Ocean. But one island kingdom remained independent: Tonga. Tonga is a small kingdom consisting of thirty-six inhabited islands lying south of Samoa and east of Fiji in Polynesia.

Tonga kept its independence because of one man, King Tupou. In 1826 Tahitian Christian missionaries brought the gospel to Tonga; British missionaries followed. Before he came to the throne, Tupou declared his desire to accept Christ and be baptized. His conversion set off a conflict between those loyal to Tupou and the other chiefs who wanted to keep the old religion.

Tupou was baptized and was a powerful evangelist, but a civil war broke out because of his decision. By 1852 Tupou finally defeated the other chiefs and united the islands. The war had caused a dilemma for the missionaries; they sided with Tupou and his goal of ending idolatry, yet he was shedding blood to gain victory.

Tupou established a government based on biblical values. He officially abolished serfdom, which the Tongans had practiced for centuries. Tupou established a parliament in 1862, and in 1875 the Tongan Parliament approved a constitution. The king was of such formidable character that European leaders viewed him as an equal. Tupou had a vision that if the people dedicated themselves to righteousness both in their public and private lives, the nation would find success and remain as a nation. He finished his 1875 speech by saying, "You are aware I am not boastful. If I have achieved anything then it is because the Lord is with me. For I am nothing but dust that God has heaped to build up Tonga. Glory be to Him."

10.1 Geography and People of Oceania

The vast Pacific, dotted with islands, was one of the last inhabitable regions to be discovered on earth. Early travelers navigated hundreds of miles across oceans to discover and settle these scattered lands formed by volcanoes. Civilizations developed, and generations of people traveled between these islands before European explorers stumbled upon them. When the Europeans discovered the islands, they found a wide variety of cultures and peoples living there. They also found plant and animal life that was unique to this region.

Guiding Questions

- Where are the islands of Oceania located, and what are they made of?
- What are the different theories for the origins of the indigenous peoples?
- What were the cultural practices of the indigenous peoples of Oceania?
- How did the political and cultural practices of the indigenous peoples fit with biblical principles?

◂ A member of a Papua New Guinean tribe

The Geography of Oceania

Oceania has four subregions—Australasia, Polynesia, Micronesia, and Melanesia. **Australasia** includes the continent of **Australia**, the island of Tasmania, and the smaller islands to the north and south of the continent. Australia is the largest landmass in Oceania. **Polynesia**, the largest region of Oceania, is triangular-shaped; its three corners are **New Zealand**, **Hawaii**, and **Easter Island**. Not including the continent of Australia, there are two types of islands in Oceania—high islands and low islands. **High islands** have a mountain or mountains, while **low islands** are flat and rise just slightly above sea level. **Micronesia** has thousands of low islands, also called **atolls**, spread across the ocean; Micronesia has no large islands and only a few high islands. **Melanesia** contains many large high islands, including New Guinea, New Britain, and Bougainville.

What is the largest landmass in Oceania?

atoll a chain of low islands formed from coral

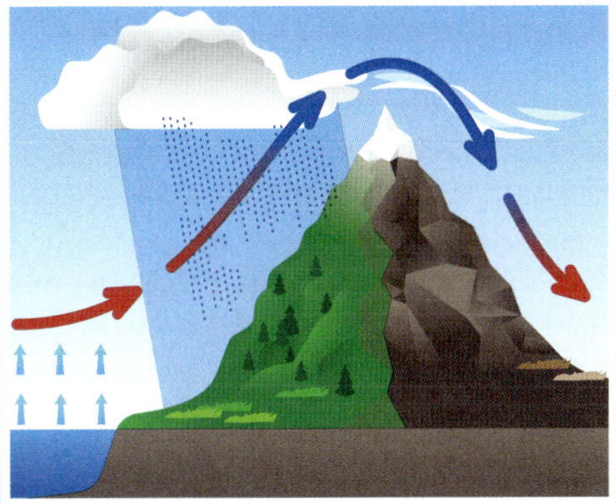

high islands

High islands tend to be better for people and agriculture. The high altitude of volcanic mountains allows the islands to capture moisture from the warm ocean breezes. As the air travels across the island, it rises over the mountains, cools, and then releases its moisture in rain or snow. Consistent moisture makes it easier to grow crops, and mountain streams provide plentiful drinking water. High island soil is fertile volcanic soil that makes plants more productive. This steady agricultural supply provides a stable economy for the people.

Moorea, French Polynesia

low islands

Low islands are composed of coral remains that developed on submerged volcanoes. Low islands tend to be drier than high islands because they do not have mountains to help create moisture. Coral sand lacks the nutrients needed to grow most crops. Therefore, people living on these islands are more dependent on fishing as a food supply. Low islands also tend to suffer greater damage from tropical storms and high waves.

A low island in Yap State, Micronesia

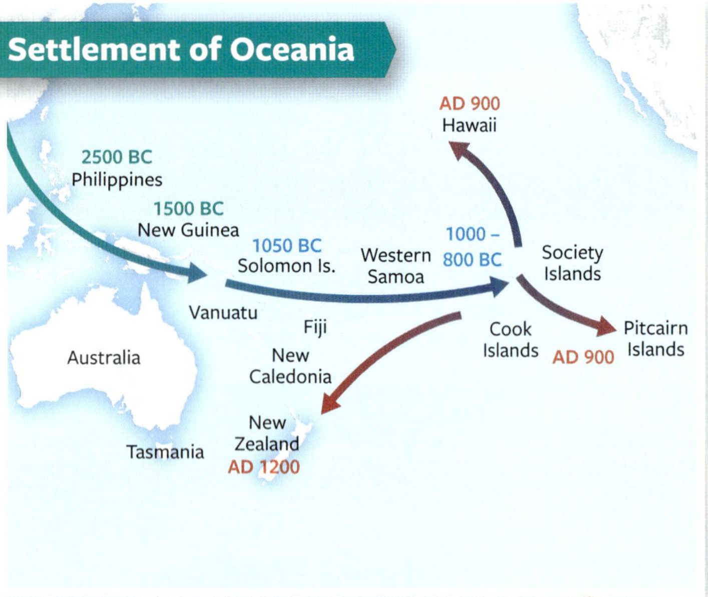

The People of Oceania

Creationists theorize that the early Australians came there via a land bridge. They were cut off from the rest of the world when the land bridge was covered by the ocean following an ice age. Both Christian and secular scientists agree that Australia was inhabited before the islands of the Pacific, but they disagree on the timing. Creationists believe that Australia was populated more recently.

The timing of when people came to Polynesia, Micronesia, and Melanesia is more certain. East Asians made their way to New Guinea and then "island hopped" across the Pacific. The Hawaiian Islands were settled around AD 900. New Zealand was settled last, around AD 1200.

Dingoes came to Australia from Asia in ancient times via sailing ships.

Early Polynesians brought taro plants to the various islands they settled.

? **Why were Australians separated from the rest of the world?**

Four pieces of evidence support this theory. First, the archaeological record (remains of buildings) of New Guinea shows earlier civilizations than the other Pacific islands. Second, the languages of the island peoples resemble Indonesian and Asian languages. Third, many of the plants and animals on the islands are also found in Indonesia and Asia. Fourth, the DNA of the Polynesians, Melanesians, and Micronesians has similarities to that of East Asians, while the indigenous Australians' DNA suggests they originated from Africa.

The people were able to settle different islands because they had developed exceptional navigation skills to sail across the great distances of the open ocean. They followed pathways in the vast ocean using the stars, planets, clouds, and ocean currents. For these sailors, the ocean was not empty and uncrossable but a place to journey in as one would on land.

Offering a different theory about Polynesians' origins, Norwegian explorer **Thor Heyerdahl** proposed that the first Polynesians came from South America rather than Asia. To substantiate his theory, he constructed a boat from balsa logs and other materials found in Peru. In 1947, Heyerdahl proved that it was possible to travel in a balsa boat from Peru to the island of Tuamoto in the Pacific. Despite the other substantial evidence that the islanders came from Asia, Heyerdahl did demonstrate that his theory was possible.

Australians

Indigenous Australians include the many tribal peoples who first lived on the continent. They were among the most isolated people groups in the world. They were separated not only from other countries but also from each other within Australia by the rugged and dry terrain. On a continent the size of the United States, the small population of the indigenous Australians was spread far and wide.

DNA a nucleic acid that carries genetic information of a living thing

Farming and Hunting

Many believed that indigenous Australians were primarily hunter-gatherers. That conclusion has come into question after an evaluation of the early European settlers' journals and the archaeological evidence. The first Europeans did not meet many indigenous Australians, whom they called **Aborigines** (from a Latin word that means "origin" or "original"). But the Europeans did record descriptions of planted trees and planned fields, evidence of farming. It seems the people of Australia grew millet and yams. They depended on unique plants that the Europeans thought were weeds but were actually useful, such as bush tomatoes and old man's weed. The Aboriginal Australians practiced fire-stick farming. They would deliberately set fires to clear brush and reinvigorate the soil. The indigenous Australians produced a crude form of flour that they baked inside hollowed-out trees. They created fishponds by stacking rocks to enable the farming of fish, an early form of **aquaculture**. They hunted with spears and throwing sticks that returned to the thrower. One tribe called the sticks **boomerangs**; that name has stuck with English speakers.

How did the Aboriginal Australians get food?

Society

The members of the extended family shared the role of raising the children, so much so that a child may have referred to multiple relatives as his mother or father. Ancestral laws governed what people could eat, what their religious duties were, and whom they could marry.

Religion

Aboriginal Australians refer to the time of creation as dreamtime, when their ancestor beings went back and forth across the earth making plants and animals. They believe that they are descendants of these beings and that dreamtime was the beginning of knowledge and laws. They do not distinguish between the Creator and the creature. We know, however, that created beings cannot also be the Creator because a creator is, by definition, more powerful than the things he creates. The true God is distinct from His created world, yet He is involved in the lives of His creatures.

Music, Art, and Sport

The early indigenous Australians developed forms of music as part of their worship. They used pieces of eucalyptus wood that had been hollowed out by termites to make an unusual musical instrument, the **didgeridoo**. While this instrument produces a single note, the person blowing through it can add his own vocal sounds to vary the final sound. The length of the didgeridoo determines the pitch of the sound, with longer instruments making a deeper sound.

Another reflection of the early Australians' religious expression is found in their art. They painted their bodies, rocks, and pieces of bark. The paintings often depicted religious stories, including accounts of creation.

Some indigenous peoples in western Australia developed a game called Marn Grook. This game has elements of football and soccer and is played with a ball shaped like a football and made from possum hide. Australian Rules football may have developed from this Aboriginal sport.

(top to bottom) An Aboriginal home; The Aborigines piled rocks to trap fish; A boomerang; An Aboriginal didgeridoo player

What is a didgeridoo?

old man's weed a plant used to treat everything from eye infections to tuberculosis
aquaculture growing aquatic animals and plants for food

POLYNESIANS

There are four notable Polynesian subgroups. The **Rapa Nui**, **Maoris**, and **Hawaiians** reside roughly in the corners of the Polynesian triangle, while the **Tahitians** live in south-central Polynesia.

Rapa Nui

The Rapa Nui were the people who lived on Easter Island. It is a high volcanic island located by itself out in the ocean, the Polynesian island closest to South America. The Rapa Nui were a mysterious people who disappeared but left behind nearly nine hundred huge stone statues.

The Rapa Nui moving their "moai" statues into place

Maoris

The Maoris were the first people to inhabit the islands of New Zealand. They came to the island sometime between AD 1200 and 1300. They were known for being fierce. The haka dance exemplifies this ferocity. Haka dancers make fierce faces, stick their tongues out, stand with bent knees, and chant angrily to repel any attacker.

Tahitians

The islands of French Polynesia sit alone out in the ocean in the center of Polynesia. Around the year AD 400, Samoans journeyed across the Pacific and settled on the islands now known as Tahiti and Bora Bora. They developed a more sophisticated culture than the other people of Oceania. The Tahitians exported their culture to Hawaii and the surrounding islands.

Hawaiians

The first people to settle the Hawaiian Islands traveled from the Marquesas Islands; they were later pushed aside by settlers from Tahiti. While each island in the Hawaiian group shared a common culture, they were not united. Kamehameha the Great fought for fifteen years to unify the island group by force. In 1810, he completed that effort using rifles and gunpowder that he bought from the Europeans.

? **Which Polynesians were known for being fierce?**

Micronesians

Micronesia is the least populated region of Oceania since the islands are small. The largest group of people is the Chamorros, who live on Guam and the Mariana Islands. They migrated to the islands from Taiwan and Indonesia during the time of Christ. Their culture and language resemble those of Polynesia.

? **What people group lives in Guam?**

Melanesians

The name *Melanesia* is derived from the Greek language and means "black islands." As with the indigenous Australians, little is known about Melanesian history prior to European contact. The people of **New Guinea** were extremely isolated from each other and remain that way to this day. Anthropologists speculate that this may have been because of constant war or disease. Cannibalism was a common practice. Whatever the case, they were so isolated that their languages do not even resemble each other. There are more language families in New Guinea than any other place in the world. For perspective, Greek, German, Spanish, and English are all in the same language family, Indo-European. Yet in New Guinea one can travel a relatively short distance to find different language families.

? **What are there more of in New Guinea than anywhere else?**

(top) Maori chief; (middle) A Yapese girl from Micronesia; (bottom) A woman in Papua New Guinea, which is part of Melanesia

POLYNESIA

Justice

Polynesians had a detailed system of laws called **kapus**, meaning "forbidden." The kapus regulated every activity—where to sleep, where and what to eat, what to wear, and how to worship. The kapus changed for each season. The seasons were tied to the religion; the people enjoyed more freedom during the season devoted to the god of peace, while the season for the worship of the war god was a dark time. The kapus particularly restricted women. Women could not eat foods like bananas or poi (taro root paste), nor could they eat with men. Because the kapus were so strict, it was not hard to break them. To remedy this, the Polynesians built places of refuge where the guilty person could find safety.

Citizenship

Everyone fit into three classes--the Ali'i, Maka'aina, and Kaua. The Maka'aina were the working people; the Kaua were the outcasts. Each member of the Maka'aina had a specific job which they learned from childhood. They might be fishermen, canoe-makers, craftsmen, farmers, or some other type of laborer. The Maka'aina paid taxes to the Ali'i, but they could move to another place if the Ali'i were overly harsh. The Kaua lived separately and were forced to survive on what food they could find.

Power

The chiefs, or Ali'i, were the most powerful people in the society; some were rulers, and others were priests. They had the most rights and responsibilities. The Polynesians believed in mana, or power. They thought certain people had more mana than others. The Ali'i had mana, and the most powerful Ali'i had the most mana. When a very powerful chief died, his bones would be hidden so no one could gain his mana.

Environment

The idea that the tribal peoples around the world lived in harmony with the environment is often exaggerated. Ancient peoples around the world probably used the land as recklessly as future generations, but their numbers were too small to make a big impact. The Polynesians, on the other hand, were distinctly aware of the limited land and resources of their islands. Polynesians depended on farming for their survival and developed many innovative farming techniques. They directed mountain streams to irrigate their taro fields, made fabric—called kapa—from certain tree barks, and built fishponds to ensure a constant supply of fish.

Religion

The Polynesians were animists and worshiped many gods. There was Kane, the creator god; Kanaloa, the god of the sea; Lono, the god of peace; Ku, the god of war; and others. The people believed that all plants and animals were forms of their gods. They worshiped their gods by offering sacrifices, building temples (called heiaus), and following the kapus. During the season devoted to Ku, human sacrifice was common. When a society worships multiple gods that govern different aspects of life, such as seasons of peace and seasons of war, it is impossible to have a consistent and coherent system of justice. By contrast, a biblical worldview provides a consistent and coherent system of justice because it is rooted in God, who is perfectly just and whose justice never changes.

CRITICAL THINKING 10.1

1. Was it right for King Tupou I to fight against those who opposed him? Explain your answer.
2. Why is it better to live on a high island than a low island?

GUIDING QUESTIONS

- How did the Europeans discover the islands of Oceania?
- What kinds of interactions occurred between European explorers and indigenous peoples?

10.2 European Exploration of Oceania

Europeans did not stop exploring when they discovered the Americas. Within one hundred years of Columbus's discovery, Europeans began directing their attention to the lands across the Pacific Ocean and the supposed wealth of these lands.

They also believed a great land existed at the southern pole of the earth. Mapmakers called this land the unknown southern land. They found support for this idea in the writings of the early Greek astronomer Ptolemy, who proposed that there must be a land in the Southern Hemisphere equal in size or mass to Europe and Asia to keep the world from toppling over. The Europeans pictured a huge continent, probably as large as Asia, overflowing with riches and treasures. Each European country sought to be the first to find the mythical southern land.

Alvaro de Mendaña had his men fire shots at the Solomon Islanders.

Spanish Exploration

Magellan was the first European explorer to discover some of the islands of Oceania. In 1521 he landed on the Micronesian island of Guam. Some Chamorros stole some items from the Spanish, so Magellan sent men on shore to recover the items. The crew killed some natives, so Magellan and his crew left the island for the Philippines. This same story would happen almost every time the European explorers landed on a new island.

The Incan people told their Spanish conquerors of a great Inca who had traveled west over the ocean and discovered a land filled with riches. Whether it was true or the Incas just wanted to draw attention away from themselves, Spanish interest was aroused.

In 1567 the viceroy of Peru commissioned an expedition into the Pacific to find this great land. The first expedition, led by **Alvaro de Mendaña**, included two ships. This expedition sailed west for two and a half months before discovering land in Melanesia. The island at which they arrived appeared fruitful at first, and hopes ran high that they had found the mythical Incan land. They named the island chain the **Solomon Islands** after King Solomon since he was famous for his great riches. After an initially friendly welcome and a brief time of peace, the Spanish offended their hosts. Rather than trying to trade with the islanders, the Spanish used force to get food. They fired shots and wounded or killed several islanders, so the Spanish left the islands and returned to Peru. No Europeans visited the Solomon Islands again for one hundred years.

Mendaña was not discouraged by this failure to find the mythical land. He led another expedition in 1595 with a young navigator named Pedro Fernández de Quirós. This time the expedition had four ships and carried settlers, including women and children. Among the passengers were Mendaña's wife, Doña Isabel, and her three brothers. They were aristocrats and brought their own supplies of animals, water, oil, and wine for their personal use.

The expedition charted a course for the Solomon Islands but miscalculated. Instead, they came to a new set of islands in Polynesia that they named the Marquesas. The islanders were friendly, and Mendaña invited them aboard. When the islanders began to steal supplies, the Spanish crewmen shot and wounded several people. Sadly, the Spaniards continued to deal brutally with the islanders.

Mendaña and de Quirós continued to search for the Solomon Islands. They came to islands southeast of the Solomons and called them the Santa Cruz Islands. They settled there, but fever soon spread and many died, including Mendaña. De Quirós took over the command and set sail for the Philippines. He rationed supplies, but Doña Isabel and her brothers would not share their provisions.

Two ships were destroyed by shipworms. After three months, the one remaining ship of the expedition arrived at Manila Bay. The Spanish authorities were shocked to find almost one hundred men, women, and children starving to death while two of Doña Isabel's pigs rested on the deck. The authorities ordered the pigs to be slaughtered to feed the starving travelers.

Why was de Quirós forced to sail to the Philippines?

Dutch Exploration

The Dutch authorities in Batavia, present-day Jakarta, Indonesia, called on one of their best captains, **Abel Tasman**, to search for the mythical southern land. In 1642 Tasman took two ships and began his voyage. He started in southern India and sailed east. This way, Tasman thought, he could not miss the huge landmass that he believed to be the southern land.

Tasman sailed on, vainly looking for the unknown land. He sailed south of Australia and landed on the island now named for him—Tasmania. The Dutch sailors found signs of life on the island but could not find the shy islanders.

Abel Tasman

Tasman soon realized that this island was not the continent that he sought, so he sailed even farther east and discovered another set of islands that we now call New Zealand. Tasman and his men discovered that the islanders were not friendly. The tall, fierce Maoris resisted Dutch attempts to land. As the Dutch sailors explored one of the bays, the Maoris killed four sailors and drove the others back to the main ships.

On a second expedition in 1644, Tasman mapped out parts of the western coastline of Australia. Even though the western coastline looked uninviting, the Dutch knew that in such a sizeable land there might be better places for settlement. However, the Dutch lacked the manpower and the money to explore and colonize. To avoid drawing attention to the area, the Dutch East India Company suppressed many of Tasman's findings. They claimed the land they found and named it New Holland. Tasman retired in 1652, having discovered three new and important islands—Australia, Tasmania, and New Zealand.

What three islands did the Dutch discover?

French Exploration

During the sixteenth and seventeenth centuries, the English and French stayed busy developing territory in the American colonies. However, when circumstances changed in their colonies in the 1700s, the French and British renewed efforts to explore. Several French and British explorers sailed the Pacific during the 1700s, but only one man from each country will be examined.

During his training to become a lawyer, **Louis Antoine de Bougainville** became bored with his studies and decided to pursue the challenge of a military career. He served with the French in Canada and witnessed the loss of Quebec to the British.

Hoping to regain power and respect for France, Bougainville organized an expedition to settle the Falkland Islands off the coast of Argentina. With thirteen colonists from Nova Scotia, he set sail for the Falklands in the fall of 1763. Due to English and Spanish claims on these islands, Bougainville was ordered to close his settlement. The French sent him in search of the mythical unknown land to the south. Bougainville brought two scientists on the voyage. A naturalist was brought along to describe and classify the new animals and plants, and an astronomer sought to work out new ways to determine longitude. This became the common practice of explorers since the scientific contributions were significant. On his journey across the Pacific, Bougainville claimed several islands for France, including Tahiti.

What idea did Bougainville develop that became a custom for other explorers?

English Exploration

Captain James Cook became the most famous explorer of the Pacific. His fame is especially amazing since he came from a working-class background and had little formal education. He rose in rank during a time when the wealthy and well-educated were usually the only ones to achieve high-ranking positions such as captain.

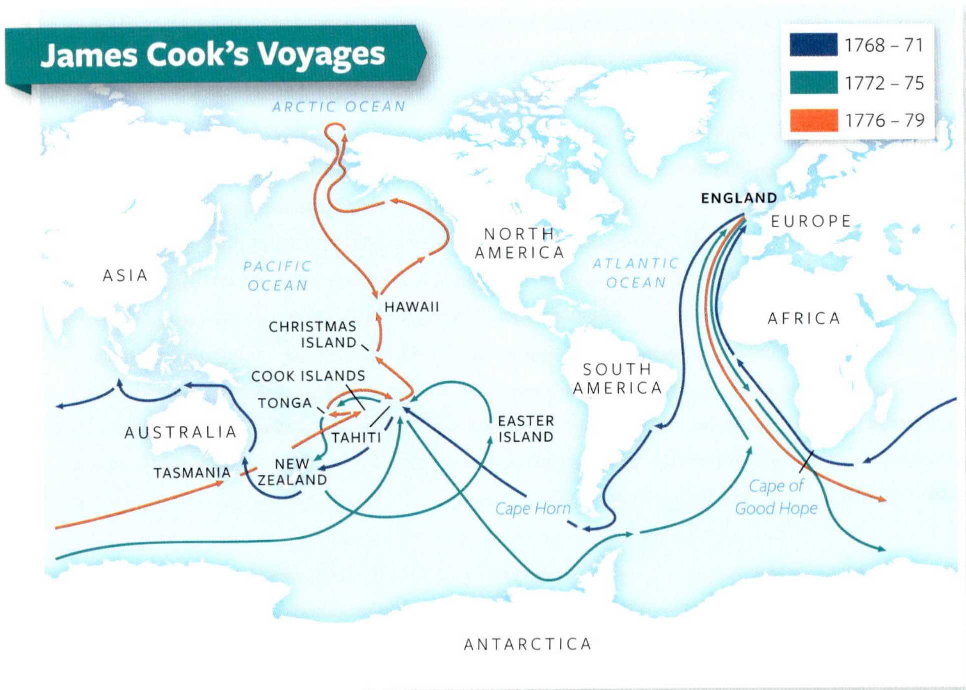

Cook was one of the best sailors and explorers of his time. His mission for the British was to discover the truth about the unknown southern land and to discover the elusive northern passage across the Arctic—a shortcut to Asia. In three voyages he crisscrossed the Pacific. First, Cook sailed in a westward direction around the world, passing New Zealand and Australia. On his second voyage he traveled east around Africa, spending much more time exploring Oceania and nearly reaching Antarctica. On his third voyage he sailed to Tasmania; then he went on to discover Hawaii and then traveled north between Alaska and Russia, in search of the Northwest Passage, before returning to Hawaii. Cook and his crew became the first men to sail completely around Antarctica, although they never actually saw that continent. Information gathered during his voyages proved that there was no great southern land the size of Asia.

During Cook's voyages, danger was often present. Once while sailing along the Great Barrier Reef off the coast of Australia, Cook's ship grounded on a reef. Cook ordered his men to lighten the ship, hoping that the tides would lift it off the reef. When the ship broke free, a large piece of coral broke off as well, plugging the hole until the ship could be repaired.

In his travels, Captain Cook discovered many islands in the Pacific, notably the Hawaiian Islands. He differed from other explorers by treating the island peoples fairly and generously. Cook often noted in his diaries the good characteristics and abilities that he observed in the islanders. He treated people with respect, tried to make friends, and avoided violence whenever possible. He understood how contact between his crew and the natives could introduce the natives to dangerous diseases and so restricted contact. Cook became one of the first white men to make peaceful contact with the Maoris.

Cook and his crew were welcomed by the Hawaiians during their first arrival. The Hawaiians may have viewed Cook as the god Lono since the ships resembled what Lono supposedly looked like. When Cook and his crew left Hawaii and sailed east in search of the Northwest Passage, they ran into storms and had to turn around. They were not greeted warmly upon their return to Hawaii.

Usually, if islanders stole an item from the English ships, Cook would capture a chief or other important person. Then he would announce that the captive would not be freed until the thief returned the stolen items. This method worked well until he tried it in Hawaii in 1779. After some Hawaiians stole tools and a canoe, Cook tried to take an old chief hostage. However, a mob of angry Hawaiians attacked Cook and his men. Cook's men escaped, but he did not. The furious Hawaiians beat Cook to death with their war clubs.

? **What was Cook looking for on his third voyage?**

? CRITICAL THINKING 10.2

Critique the interactions between European explorers and indigenous peoples.

The death of Captain Cook on the island of Hawaii

European Exploration of Oceania 1521–1778

1500

Spain and Portugal Explore Micronesia

- **1521** Ferdinand Magellan of Spain discovers many of the islands in Oceania
- **1525** Diogo da Rocha finds the Caroline Islands
- **1529** Alvaro de Saavedra Ceron lands on the Marshall Islands

Spain Explores Melanesia and Polynesia

- **1568** Alvaro De Mendaña finds the Solomon Islands
- **1595** Alvaro De Mendaña finds Marquesas Islands

1600

- **1606** Vanuatu discovered by Pedro Fernández de Quirós

Dutch Explore Polynesia and Australasia

- **1616** Dirk Hartog sails to western Australia
- **1643** Abel Tasman becomes the first European to visit Fiji

British Explore Polynesia and Australasia

- **1688** William Dampier arrives on west coast of Australia

1700

- **1770** Captain James Cook lands on the east coast of Australia, claiming it for Britain
- **1778** Captain Cook discovers the Hawaiian Islands

GUIDING QUESTIONS

- How did missionaries benefit the peoples of Oceania?
- How did the islands of Oceania come under European control?
- How did the Europeans settle Oceania?
- How did Hawaii go from a pagan land to a Christian land and back to a pagan land?

10.3 European Settlement of Oceania

Of the many lands in Oceania claimed by European countries, only a few were heavily colonized. The three places where settlement took place to the greatest extent were Australia, New Zealand, and Hawaii. As in other endeavors, colonization brought positive and negative consequences.

Missionaries to Oceania

The exploration and settlement of Oceania came at a time in world history when Britain and the United States were growing in power. Since both were Protestant nations and had large numbers of people who believed and obeyed the Bible, exploration provided an opportunity to demonstrate what a biblical missionary movement looked like. Earlier chapters discussed the Nestorians and the Roman Catholic missionaries who brought a gospel that included unbiblical beliefs. In some cases, Catholics used the sword to force conversion. Could the Protestant missionaries to Oceania follow the model of the apostles, preach the gospel, and bring true voluntary converts to Christ?

British missionaries arrived in Tahiti in 1797. Not until the conversion of a chief in 1819 did the missionaries have much success. The first British missionaries to Melanesia were killed and eaten by cannibals not long after they landed; the islanders drove away other missionaries. But more came to share the gospel with the islanders.

John Paton

John Paton holding the Vanuatu Bible translation he produced

One remarkable missionary was a Scottish man named John Paton. His father was a man deeply devoted to God. He set an example by praying continually, and he impressed on John the need to evangelize the world. John pledged in his heart to never dishonor his father. Before he was twelve years old, John had "committed his soul to God," and after college, when he heard of the plight of the South Pacific islanders, he committed to minister there.

John left Scotland with his new bride, Mary Ann, and sailed for the South Pacific in March 1858. They landed on the Melanesian island of Tanna in November. Their child, Peter Robert, was born three months later. Nineteen days after the birth, Mary Ann died of a tropical fever. A few days later, the baby died as well. Despite these overwhelming losses, John Paton continued his ministry among the hostile islanders. His life was constantly in danger, and the natives tried many times to kill him. He had a Scottish terrier, named Clutha, that would bark whenever there was danger. John could sleep, knowing the dog was standing guard. After four years he had to leave Tanna; at one point he was surrounded by the natives, who dared each other to strike John and his helper, Abraham. But Paton understood an important biblical truth: "I realized that I was immortal until my Master's work with me was done."

Despite these threats, he endured, married again, and developed a thriving ministry on Aniwa Island, a smaller island north of Tanna. Maggie, John's second wife, held classes with the women and taught them to sew, make hats, and read. The Patons built a church, two houses for orphans, and a printing house to produce a printed New Testament in the language of the people. More than thirty years of ministry by the Patons on Aniwa led to the professed conversion of everyone on that island. By 1899 the Aniwa New Testament was printed, and missionaries had been established on twenty-five of the thirty islands of Vanuatu, the group of islands that Tanna and Aniwa are part of.

? **Who warned Paton of danger?**

James Chalmers

James Chalmers, also from Scotland, arrived in Papua New Guinea in 1877 with his wife, Jane, and worked tirelessly to establish a ministry among the Papuan peoples. Those who accepted Christ were carefully nurtured in the faith. Chalmers was careful to baptize only those who demonstrated a genuine transformation and a growing desire to know the Word of God.

In 1901 Chalmers attempted to contact an isolated tribe that had been especially hostile toward outsiders. He and his assistant, Oliver Tomkins, accompanied some of the Papuans. Later, the Papuans returned without Chalmers and Tomkins. British investigators found that the Papuans had killed and eaten Chalmers and his assistant. Chalmers died as he had lived, striving to meet the spiritual needs of the indigenous peoples of New Guinea.

? On what island did James Chalmers minister?

The most important thing these missionaries brought was the good news of salvation through Jesus. But they also benefited the islanders in many other ways. By putting the languages in writing, they ensured the survival of the languages and the cultures. They brought medicine and were the only ones who were partially effective in treating and preventing the many foreign diseases that came to the islands. Some missionaries began to despise the islanders, but most continued to show Christ's compassion, despite experiencing many hardships. They were the only people standing in the way of foreigners who wanted to overtake the islands and destroy the natives there.

? What did the missionaries bring to the islands?

British Settlement of Australia

Captain Cook and his men landed in Botany Bay on August 23, 1770, and then surveyed the entire eastern coastline. He claimed the eastern half of the continent for Britain and called it **New South Wales**. The Dutch claimed the western half and called it **New Holland**. Neither country considered the people that were already living there. Nor did they do anything about their claims for many years.

The First British Settlers

The British had used the American colony of Georgia as a place to send prisoners, but after the colonies gained their independence, the British no longer had a place to send convicts. The English decided to rid themselves of many of the occupants of the overflowing British prisons and poorhouses by relocating those people to the land Cook had claimed in Australia.

The **First Fleet** was the name given to the first group of eleven ships to sail from England to Australia in May of 1787. Of the more than one thousand people on these ships, over eight hundred were convicts.

After traveling for about eight months, the fleet's captain, **Arthur Phillip** (later the colony's first governor), sighted Australia. He had sailed ahead intending to prepare a small settlement before the other ships arrived. However, the remaining ships arrived two days after he had sailed into Botany Bay. Phillip soon realized that this bay was too shallow and exposed to the open ocean to provide protection for the fleet. He found a more suitable port a few miles to the north with a deep harbor and protected coves. Phillip chose a sand-fringed harbor with a freshwater stream (Sydney Cove). The fleet arrived on January 26, 1788, now celebrated as Australia Day.

? Who made up the majority of the first Europeans to settle in Australia?

Arthur Philip raises the British flag in Sydney Cove.

The future of the colony depended on building homes and cultivating the land. However, there were no skilled laborers among the crew or convicts. In addition, the eucalyptus and other gum trees that were in abundant supply were very hard and quickly ruined the axes. To survive, the settlers resorted to building houses from cabbage trees covered with wattle and daub (sticks and mud plaster).

Another problem soon surfaced. On the long voyage Phillip had kept his crew and the convicts healthy, but much of the transported grain and flour was ruined. Without flour or grain the settlers would have no bread. In addition, many settlers began to show signs of scurvy. In desperation, they resorted to eating plants that they found around them to survive.

Phillip carefully rationed the remaining flour while the settlers waited for the supply ship that was scheduled to arrive within the first year. Unknown to the colonists in Australia and authorities in England, the supply ship struck an iceberg during the voyage and sank. The colonists had to survive for two years before they received any news from England. By that time, the colony faced famine.

Finally, the news came that an English ship had been sighted, and the settlers were excited when they received this report. However, their excitement soon turned to disappointment when the ship was found to be another transport ship with over two hundred convicts and few supplies. Providentially, a well-stocked supply ship soon arrived. The famine ended, and the colony became firmly established.

? **What did the first colony in Australia lack?**

Expansion and Establishment

For several years, the colonists remained near the coast. The Great Dividing Range, with its steep rock faces and giant gorges, effectively confined the colonists to living along the ocean. However, settlements continued to be established. Many convicts finished serving their prison terms and became profitable members of the colony. Not all convicts were in prison for what we would consider a crime today. Many were debtors who could not pay back their debts.

Settlers soon learned how to live entirely off the land. Using crop rotation and fertilizer, more and more farmers established successful farms on land grants from the colonial authorities. For the colonists to receive this land, they had to accept convict laborers to work the farms. The greatest problem with this arrangement proved to be thievery by the convict laborers.

The crossing of the Great Dividing Range provided a great opportunity for expansion into the interior of Australia. In May 1813 Gregory Blaxland and two companions started out from Blaxland's farm at the foothills of the mountains. After three weeks of exploring, these men looked down from a cliff edge and saw a stream running through the center of a valley. Further exploration revealed a passage to the western plains that enabled the exploration and colonization of the outback (the remote, dry region located in the center of the continent).

What were the second and third British colonies in Australia?

In 1836 explorers traveled southwest from Sydney around the coast and founded a new colony called South Australia. In 1852 sheep farmers in search of more pasture traveled south overland and discovered a river that they named the Murray. South of this river they founded the town of Melbourne and called the colony Victoria in honor of Queen Victoria of England.

Impact of British Settlement on the Indigenous Australians

Although the indigenous Australians were often involved in tribal conflict, they were very rarely hostile to the early settlers. As the flow of the English settlers increased, especially after gold was discovered, their settlements became well established and pushed into Aboriginal territory and hunting grounds. When the native population tried to resist, they were no match for the weaponry of the English. Gradually the Aborigines lost more and more of their land and rights. The Aboriginal Australians died in large numbers from the new diseases the Europeans introduced. Later, the government tried to force the native Australians to assimilate.

Why did the indigenous Australian population decline?

A New Nation Is Born

All the Australian colonies were under the rule of England when gold was discovered in New South Wales, and a gold rush resulted in 1851. Around that time the convict transports to the east coast stopped, and with the rush of gold-hungry immigrants, the percentage of free citizens increased dramatically. About four hundred thousand people lived in the Australian colonies in 1850. Within ten years the population had increased to over one million.

These new colonists wanted more freedom to govern themselves. In 1856, England responded by granting self-government to most of the colonies. However, England still protected the colonies and intervened in foreign affairs.

In 1901, after intense discussions, Australia became the Commonwealth of Australia, made up of six states—Queensland, New South Wales, Victoria, Tasmania, South Australia, and Western Australia—and two territories. Instead of each colony governing independently, the Commonwealth formed a single capital. By 1927 the government buildings in the new capital of Canberra were ready for use.

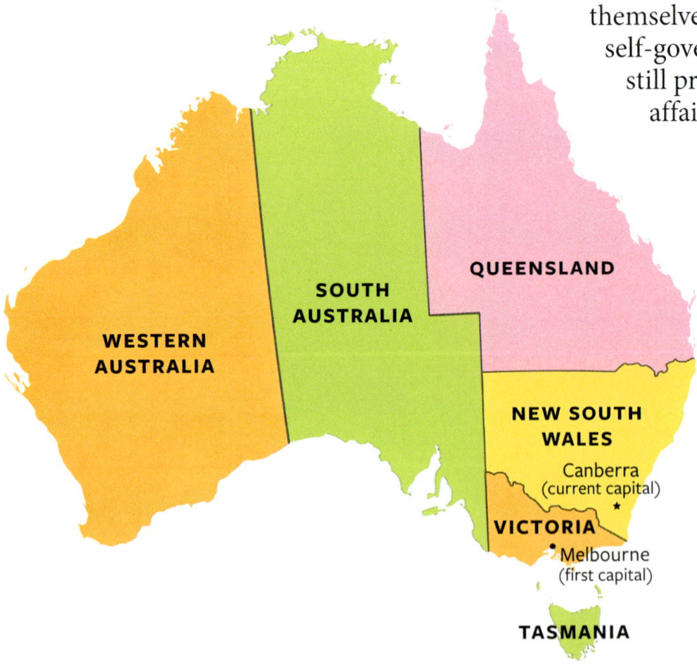

What brought a large number of free citizens to Australia?

British Settlement of New Zealand

Whalers, seal hunters, and traders set up trading stations in New Zealand. They were known for being lawless and for abusing the Maoris. British missionaries arrived in 1814. By 1835 the missionaries had put the Maori language into writing and were printing a Maori Bible. The Maoris slowly took over the leadership of the church, and the gospel spread through the islands. British settlers followed the missionaries and bought land from the Maoris, but the two groups misunderstood each other; the Maoris had no concept of land ownership.

In 1839 the British began plans to create a more formal colony in New Zealand. They wrote the **Treaty of Waitangi** to get the Maoris to give up their sovereignty and place the islands under the rule of the king of England. The problem was that the concepts in the treaty could not be translated into Maori since the ideas of sovereignty and land ownership were foreign to them. Many Maori chiefs thought signing the treaty would end the lawlessness of the British traders and settlers, who sold guns and rum and caused wars among the Maoris. But other chiefs refused to sign it. The treaty gave the Maoris all the rights of British citizens but took away their ability to govern themselves.

The Maori chiefs signing the Treaty of Waitangi

The second governor of New Zealand, Robert Fitzroy, worked to act justly toward the Maoris; he listened to both sides of disputes and in his first act found the colonists had broken the treaty. The governor also worked to make sure the Maoris were paid fairly for their land. But later governors often sided with the colonists. At first the Maoris far outnumbered the settlers, but more settlers came, and many Maoris died of disease. So the numbers quickly reversed. Generally, the relations between the British and the Maoris were peaceful, but there were some small conflicts after the Maoris understood what the treaty meant.

In 1852 the settlers were allowed some self-rule with the establishment of a General Assembly. New Zealand became one of the most prosperous places in the world at the time as the settlers farmed the fertile land and raised sheep. In 1861 gold was discovered, and the population doubled as many came to look for gold. In 1907 New Zealand became a separate country within the British Commonwealth, like Australia and Canada.

? **Why did many Maori chiefs sign the Treaty of Waitangi?**

TURNING POINTS

Hawaii

The settlement of Hawaii was closely linked to the missionary movement there. Hawaii is a micro example of the process Western nations have followed concerning Christ and Christianity. But rather than taking hundreds of years, Hawaii went through the steps in less than one hundred. In 1818 it was a pagan nation with no knowledge of Christ. In 1820 it was the first island group to wholeheartedly accept Christ. But by the 1900s, church attendance was in steep decline, and today Hawaii is largely a pagan land.

Queen Kaʻahumanu

In 1807 Henry Opukaha'ia, a Hawaiian man, escaped from murderers who killed his family, stowed away on an American ship, and was able to study at Yale. He desired to bring the gospel to his fellow Hawaiians and called on New Englanders to help him. But Opukaha'ia never saw his homeland again; he died of typhus at age 26. In 1819 seven American missionary couples set off for Hawaii in response to Opukaha'ia's call.

While the missionaries were sailing, the king of Hawaii, Kamehameha the Great, died, leaving Hawaii ripe for revolution. **Kaʻahumanu**, the king's favorite wife became the regent. She saw an opportunity to end the religion and laws that had governed the islands for over a thousand years.

Kaʻahumanu convinced **Keōpūolani**, the mother of the new king, twenty-two-year-old, Liholiho (Kamehameha II), to join her. Keōpūolani ate coconuts and dined with men, an act that should have resulted in her death according to their law. Some days later, Kaʻahumanu proclaimed Liholiho king. Keōpūolani looked at her son and put her hand to her mouth, indicating that men and women should be allowed to eat together. When the young king obeyed his mother, he effectively abolished the old law and religion. The missionaries arrived nine months later. They were astonished by the developments; they would not have to convince the Hawaiians to get rid of their old religion since that had been done already.

The missionaries won the trust of Queen Kaʻahumanu and Keōpūolani, and both became strong Christians. During the next thirty years, Hawaii would go from not knowing Christ to having the largest Protestant church on the earth at that time. The gospel spread from those islands across the Pacific. Despite many hardships, including diseases, economic upheaval, and foreign invasion, the Hawaiian church flourished with Hawaiians leading it. The missionaries were advisors to the king. The first kings took the missionaries' advice and created a representative government. Kamehameha III adopted the official motto for Hawaii, "The life of the land is perpetuated in righteousness."

Missionaries teaching the children of the Hawaiian royalty

But the grandchildren of the missionaries did not have the same godly perspective as their elders. They prioritized the economic progress of the islands over serving the native population. They also accepted evolutionary ideas, which they had learned when they were sent back to study in New England universities. They saw themselves as more evolved than the native Hawaiians. These Christians did not see a contradiction between a biblical worldview and evolutionary thought.

The later rulers of Hawaii rebelled against the teaching and advice of the descendants of the missionaries because they saw them as seeking profit for themselves. The king and queen made very poor decisions, which brought down the wrath of the Missionary Party (politicians who were descendants of the original missionaries). They forced the king to give up most of his power.

▲ Queen Lili'uokalani

After the king died, **Queen Lili'uokalani** came to power. She was determined to restore the power of the monarchy. Despite believing that the overthrow of the queen was wrong, most historians agree that Lili'uokalani was ill-suited for her role as queen. Lili'uokalani tried to pass a lottery bill and the legalization of other vices (immoral practices), and she wanted to abolish the constitution in favor of one that guaranteed more power to herself. The Missionary Party viewed this as a revolution. They overthrew her, charged her with treason, and placed her under house arrest.

These actions bitterly divided the Protestant churches in Hawaii. The missionary directors of the church defended the decision to overthrow the queen, but they recognized it had caused many to leave their churches. They believed the drop in church attendance would be temporary and that native Hawaiians would eventually understand the soundness of what they had done. They excommunicated (kicked out) pastors who sided with the queen and even ridiculed the calls of native pastors for prayer and fasting following the overthrow of the queen.

The new Hawaiian government quickly tried to become part of the United States. President Cleveland's representative arrived in Honolulu to sort out the facts. His goal was to discover the role, if any, of the US government in the overthrow of the queen and whether he should recommend Hawaii becoming part of the US. The representative opposed Hawaii becoming part of the US and specifically called out the missionary children: "It may be remarked as a significant fact, that with two exceptions, the children of the missionaries neglected to enter the chosen field of their fathers, seeming quite content to let the souls of the gentle Islanders take their chances, while for themselves they generally preferred lives which gave promise of more tangible rewards for thrift and energy."

A missionary grandchild who was an editor of the newspaper replied, "If some of our missionaries' sons have reaped large rewards in secular industry, it cannot be denied that they also contributed to the work of the gospel and education far more liberally than Christians do in America." In the end, the white Hawaiians got their republic but lost the native Hawaiians for the kingdom of heaven.

1. Recall the information about Polynesian justice and religion from earlier in the chapter. Why might Queen Ka'ahumanu and Keōpūolani have wanted to end the laws and religion of Hawaii?
2. What worldview did the descendants of the missionaries accept? How did this affect what they did?
3. What was President Cleveland's representative's major criticism of the descendants of the missionaries?

? CRITICAL THINKING 10.3

1. What impact did Europeans have on the Pacific islands?
2. Why did Australian colonists remain along the coast for several years?

European Settlement of Oceania 1788–1906

- **1788** Ships of the First Fleet from England reach Botany Bay, south of Sydney, to begin a penal colony
- **1800**
- **1815** British missionaries arrive in New Zealand
- **1840** British law established in New Zealand and the Maori people rebel against British rule
- **1865** European settlers begin to arrive on Vanuatu Islands
- **1875** Fiji becomes a British crown colony
- **1884** Britain establishes protectorate over southeast New Guinea; Germany annexes the northern part
- **1885** Spain asserts claim to Palau and annexes the Marshall Islands
- **1893** Britain declares protectorate over southern Solomon Islands
- **1898** Caroline Islands (Micronesia) come under German colonial control
- **1899** Germany buys Palau from Spain and annexes Western Samoa while giving over Eastern Samoa to the US.
- **1900**
- **1901** Commonwealth of Australia established
- **1906** Australia gains control of British New Guinea and renames it Territory of Papua

Making Connections

1. What is the difference between high and low islands?
2. Why do scientists believe indigenous Australians came from Africa?
3. What theory did Thor Heyerdahl propose?
4. How did Mendaña treat the island peoples during his visit to the Solomon Islands?
5. How did Doña Isabel and her brothers avoid suffering from starvation like the others on the Spanish ship?
6. Who was the most famous explorer of the Pacific? On what chain of islands did he die?
7. What were the two main missions of the most famous British explorer?
8. Why did John Paton not fear death?
9. Who was the first colonial governor of New South Wales?
10. What did the Europeans bring to Australia that proved lethal to the native population?
11. What did the colonies of Australia become in 1901?
12. Compare how the British settled Australia and New Zealand.

Thinking Critically

1. Evaluate the themes of justice and power in indigenous culture based on a biblical worldview.
2. Why were the places of refuge important in Polynesia? How might you witness to a Polynesian using this illustration?
3. How should the Europeans have related to the native peoples of Oceania?
4. Did the missionaries help the islanders? Explain.

What to Know

PEOPLE

King Tupou I
Thor Heyerdahl
Aborigines
Rapa Nui
Maoris
Tahitians
Hawaiians
Alvaro de Mendaña
Abel Tasman
Louis Antoine de Bougainville
Captain James Cook
John Paton
James Chalmers
Arthur Phillip
Queen Ka'ahumanu
Queen Keōpūolani
Queen Lili'uokalani

PLACES

Oceania
Australasia
Australia
Polynesia
New Zealand
Hawaii
Easter Island
Micronesia
Melanesia
New Guinea
Solomon Islands
New South Wales
New Holland

TERMS

high Islands
low islands
atolls
aquaculture
boomerangs
didgeridoo
kapus
First Fleet
Treaty of Waitangi

◄ Doña Isabel and her brothers feasting while the others starved

11 THE ATLANTIC REVOLUTIONS

1770 – 1871

ESSENTIAL QUESTIONS

- What were the causes and key events of the French Revolution?
- How did Napoleon rise to power and lose power in France?
- How did the Latin American nations gain independence?
- How did nationalism develop in mid-nineteenth-century Europe?
- How did German unification differ from Italian unification?

General José de San Martín at the Battle of Chacabuco, Chile, February 12, 1817

Charlotte Corday

In 1793 France was in the midst of a revolution that had started almost four years earlier. Some people lived in fear that they would be considered the next enemy of the state and be executed. Other people wanted their opponents' heads removed from their bodies. Two groups supported the revolution, the Girondins and the Jacobins. The Girondins preferred the revolution to progress nonviolently, while the Jacobins preached the use of the **guillotine** (the machine used to behead people) on all the revolution's opponents.

Charlotte Corday, a young French woman, was in favor of revolution but was deeply troubled by the violence. She sided with the Girondins. Corday was not in favor of the king's execution. She thought a newspaper publisher, **Jean-Paul Marat**, was the main instigator of the violence against the king and others. Corday believed if Marat was allowed to live there would be a civil war.

On July 9 Corday left her home in Caen and journeyed to Paris, 150 miles to the east. She planned to kill Marat in front of a crowd with a six-inch kitchen knife. But Corday had to change her plan after she learned he no longer left his home. Corday planned to get into Marat's home by telling him she had a list of Girondins who had escaped capture earlier that year. On July 13 Corday knocked on Marat's door, and Marat's fiancée's sister answered the door and did not let Corday in. She tried again in the evening; this time Marat allowed her to enter. It seems he spent most of his time in a bathtub to ease his irritation from a skin disease. After she gave him the list of names and he started copying them, she pulled the knife and stabbed him. He cried out, "Help me, my dear friend!" and died.

The women there immediately detained Corday. At her trial, she said, "I knew that he was perverting France. I have killed a man to save a hundred thousand." On July 17 Corday was executed by guillotine.

The murder of Marat caused the very thing Corday was trying to stop, more violence. Marat became a martyr, and just two months later the Reign of Terror began, the most violent time of the revolution when hundreds of people were beheaded every day.

11.1 The French Revolution

Certain plants deeply disappoint when they finally flower or produce fruit. As you water and feed the plant, it grows a strong green stem, and you think a beautiful flower or fruit will result. But when the flower finally blooms, it is ugly and produces a stink, like the *Helicodiceros* (dead horse arum lily) from Corsica (a French island). How can this plant disappoint so thoroughly? It could do nothing less; it was destined to turn into a stinking flower from the moment you planted the seed, and the result will be the same every time a *Helicodiceros* seed is planted. Such was the case with the French Revolution. The seeds were ideas that sounded good, but the French rejected a biblical worldview that constrained the extremes in these ideas. Therefore, the fruit of these ideas was the destruction of the individuals and the society that accepted them.

Guiding Questions

- How did Enlightenment thinking influence the French Revolution?
- What were the factors that contributed to the French Revolution?
- How did the French Revolution progress?
- How did the French and American Revolutions differ?

Causes of the Revolution

The spread of Enlightenment ideals, a vast difference between the social classes, continued mismanagement of the government, and a refusal to modify the existing system provided an opportunity for violent social turmoil.

The Seed for Revolution: Enlightenment Ideas

Thinkers like Voltaire and Rousseau spread Enlightenment ideas throughout France, beginning some fifty years before the revolution. Voltaire produced over twenty thousand letters, up to two thousand books, and many pamphlets. This flood of literature from Voltaire and other Enlightenment philosophers inspired the French to demand equality, civil liberties, and religious freedom—in this case, the separation of the Catholic Church from the state. They wrote about ideals like discovering truth from reason alone and assuring happiness to all men through progress. Some of the ideas sound good on the surface, but in this instance their goal was to put human reason in place of God.

Enlightenment thought encouraged freedom, but it was not a freedom tempered by responsibility and accountability to a higher power. Enlightenment philosophers had taken God and His Word out of the equation.

? What Enlightenment ideals did the French demand?

The Ground for Revolution: A Divided Society

Louis XIV claimed the divine right to rule, which to him meant that he had absolute power and that everyone in French society was below him. The people were separated into three groups, called estates. Each estate held different rights, responsibilities, and privileges.

The First Estate

The **First Estate** belonged to the leaders of the French church. The archbishops and bishops were a small minority of the First Estate. They managed the land of the Roman Catholic Church, which amounted to about 10 percent of the country. They also owned valuable properties in the cities. Under French law, these wealthy churchmen and their properties were exempt from most taxes. Their luxurious lifestyle differed drastically from that of the poor priests and monks who interacted with the French population. These common clergymen struggled to survive and supported the revolution when it finally swept across France.

The Second Estate

The **Second Estate** was composed of about 350,000 nobles and other aristocrats who owned or controlled about 20 percent of the land. They too were exempt from many taxes. Members of this class gained their wealth by charging rent to the peasants who farmed their land and charging fees for the use of their mills, winepresses, and bakeries. Given their enviable financial and social standing, they opposed any changes to the system.

? **Who were the members of the Second Estate?**

The Third Estate

The great majority of French men and women were confined to the **Third Estate**, on whom the nation placed a terrible financial burden. This group of at least twenty-four million people contained a wide variety of citizens, including the middle class, artisans, townsmen, and peasants. The middle class, which accounted for a small minority of the Third Estate, owned about 20 percent of the land. The vast majority of the Third Estate consisted of peasants, and they owned or rented up to 50 percent of the nation's land.

Economic Results of the Three Estate System

In the French society, those who were wealthy produced little or no wealth and were protected from most of the tax burden. Ironically, many of those who produced the nation's wealth were not allowed to benefit from their earned prosperity. Under this imbalanced system, the government oppressively taxed and the nobility charged rents and other fees to the Third Estate. This system reduced many people to poverty and limited opportunities for economic growth. At the same time, those who paid the most in taxes, rents, and fees were denied basic freedoms and political representation in the governing of France. Such injustice could not be sustained indefinitely.

◂ | Louis XVI and Marie Antoinette

The Fertilizer for Revolution: Political Incompetence

In 1770 sixteen-year-old **Louis XVI** married fifteen-year-old **Marie Antoinette**, and French citizens celebrated this union as the hope for the future of France. Upon the death of Louis XV in 1774, Louis XVI became king. Initially the royal couple enjoyed great popularity. But the king quickly demonstrated that he was weak and incapable of making difficult choices. Marie Antoinette convinced Louis to dismiss his father's administrators. The tax reforms that Louis XV had started near the end of his reign to restore financial stability ended with this unfortunate decision. Louis XVI and Marie Antoinette quickly became unpopular. Before long, their unpopularity gave way to hatred as the French people saw the monarchs' lavish but ineffective rule. Although the king had inherited many of France's problems from previous monarchs, he did nothing to solve them.

? How did the French people feel about King Louis XVI and Marie Antoinette?

The Versailles Palace

The Water for Revolution: Natural Disasters and an Economic Crisis

A food crisis was another cause of the revolution. There were three elements to this crisis. First, a volcanic eruption in Iceland in 1783 blocked the sun for eight months, causing crops to fail. Second, long before, the Black Death had reduced the population of France. A smaller population made it easier for the farmers to feed the people, but by the 1780s France was gaining 100,000 people every year, and farmers found it hard to produce enough food for the growing population. Third, the percentage of those living in the cities, and therefore not producing food, was rapidly increasing.

The economic crisis was the result of the French kings' lavish spending since the reign of Louis XIV. The cost of frequent wars and the building and maintenance of the Palace of Versailles had drained France of much wealth. Louis XV continued to drain French resources during the Seven Years' War with England. French support of the American War for Independence also placed French finances under a great strain. During the reign of Louis XVI, the French government borrowed its way into near bankruptcy. Payments for just the interest on the national debt consumed nearly half of France's annual income. By 1787 the French government faced a major economic crisis.

? Why was there a food shortage in France?

The Gardener for the Revolution: The Estates-General

? What was the Estates-General?

In 1789 after much delay and hesitancy, Louis XVI convened the **Estates-General**, an assembly of representatives from the three estates. In 1302 the first assembly of the Estates-General had been held because the king recognized the need for an assembly to represent the people and provide counsel. Until the 1500s, representatives of the First and Second Estates were selected by the king, while representatives of the Third Estate were elected by the people.

The Estates-General had not been convened since 1614 due to the rise of absolute monarchs and the ability of French kings to bypass the assembly. But now France faced a financial crisis, and nothing less than a meeting of the Estates-General would suffice to get popular support for reforming the tax system.

Course of the Revolution

On May 5, 1789, the Estates-General met to approve the king's proposed tax reforms. But from the outset, Louis humiliated the representatives of the Third Estate and gave preference to the members of the First and Second Estates. Traditionally, each estate had one vote. However, the representatives of the Third Estate demanded one vote for each representative. This voting method would provide a clear advantage for the Third Estate, which represented most French citizens.

The Tennis Court Oath on June 20, 1789

First Phase: Tennis Court Oath

The representatives of the Third Estate left the meeting in anger after the First and Second Estates refused to change the number of votes each estate had. Members of the Third Estate formed a new group, the **National Assembly of France**. They invited members of the First and Second Estates to join them, and many did. But the king locked the assembly out of its meeting room, so the members met in a nearby indoor tennis court where they signed the **Tennis Court Oath**. In the oath, they pledged to continue meeting until a constitution that would guarantee basic rights to all French citizens and limit the power of the government was written and accepted.

At this point the members of the National Assembly had no intention of transforming France into a democracy or ending the monarchy. By late June, the king seemed to be giving in. He instructed the remainder of the Estates-General to join the National Assembly and draft a constitution.

? What did the king do in response to the Third Estate forming the National Assembly?

The storming of the Bastille prison

Second Phase: Storming of the Bastille

In early July things took a turn. Rumors spread that the king was ordering troops to Paris and that he was going to starve the city. When he dismissed his popular finance minister, Jacques Necker, the people thought there must be truth to the rumors. Necker was popular with the people because he had opened the books of the king's treasury for everyone to see.

In response to these rumors, the citizens began to panic. They searched for weapons to defend themselves. On July 14 a crowd gathered at **the Bastille**, a fortress-prison formerly used to house political prisoners. When they encountered resistance, possibly even gunfire into the crowd, the mob stormed the building and killed those assigned to guard it. July 14 has since been celebrated as France's day of independence, **Bastille Day**.

Riots and demonstrations continued and grew increasingly violent. Rioters attacked government buildings and destroyed documents that recorded debts and rents due to members of the First and Second Estates. But the king remained passive and failed to use troops to end the violence.

? What happened on Bastille Day?

Phases *of the* **French Revolution**

1 **Tennis Court Oath**

2 **Storming of the Bastille**

The execution of Louis XVI

Third Phase: Destruction of the Old Government

On August 26, 1789, the National Assembly signed the **Declaration of the Rights of Man**. The declaration demanded the end of many of the abuses suffered by the French people and advocated ideals that included innocence until guilt is proven and liberty to do anything that does not injure another. The will of the people became the basis for law. There was no acknowledgement of a higher authority. The chief proponent of the declaration was **Maximilien Robespierre**, who went on to become the face of the revolution and the leader of the radicals, called **Jacobins**.

The king delayed signing the declaration, so on October 5, a crowd of women marched to his palace in Versailles to bring him to Paris and make him sign the document. The women were successful at getting the king to sign the declaration. But the king and queen felt trapped and planned to escape to the east to a territory ruled by Austria. They attempted to flee the country on June 20, 1791, but were captured and returned to Paris.

The National Assembly confiscated all the lands owned by the Roman Catholic Church to pay off the massive national debt. This move resulted in a verbal attack from the pope and great concern among many loyal Catholics in France. Many conservatives and nobles fled France and settled in neighboring countries. They labored from afar to overthrow the revolutionary government and regain their privileged positions.

The National Assembly demanded that Austria and other countries send these citizens back to France. Austria refused to comply with this demand. In April 1792 the Assembly declared war on Austrian King Francis II, Marie Antoinette's brother. King Louis XVI and Marie Antoinette thought the revolutionaries would lose the war and they would get their power back. Despite receiving no call from the king to mobilize the army, French citizens volunteered to defend France. On August 10 they assembled in Paris and imprisoned the king and queen, officially ending the monarchy. Prussia entered the war as Austria's ally, and their armies marched into France. But the volunteer army was able to push out the Austrians and Prussians. From this point on, the revolution became very violent. In September, a new assembly, the **National Convention**, took over the ruling of France. King Louis XVI was tried and executed by guillotine on January 21, 1793.

Why did the National Assembly declare war on Austria?

3

Destruction of the Old Government

Fourth Phase: Reign of Terror (September 5, 1793–July 28, 1794)

With the mounting problems of dealing with internal and international strife, the French leaders appointed committees to manage the government. The most important of these, the **Committee of Public Safety**, soon gained absolute authority in France.

To maintain control, this group of radicals called for the imprisonment or execution of all opponents to the revolution. This time was called the **Reign of Terror**. The Committee of Public Safety sent at least twenty-five thousand men and women to the guillotine, including Marie Antoinette. France was also engaged in wars with Italy, Spain, Portugal, Britain, Prussia, Austria, Switzerland, and the Netherlands. One historian likened these French soldiers to armed missionaries for the Enlightenment. They wanted not only to defend revolutionary France but to spread its system across Europe.

When Robespierre called for one last round of executions to rid the nation of traitors, the members of the Convention feared for their own lives and arrested and beheaded Robespierre instead. While Charlotte Corday had not been able to prevent the terror by killing Marat, the National Convention was able to end the terror by killing Robespierre.

Following the rejection of the existing government, a new government was formed that was headed by a five-man committee known as the **Directory**. This government quickly made peace with Prussia and Spain but remained at war with Austria and Britain. The leaders came to rely more and more on the army for support since they lacked the support of most of the French people. These circumstances created a rare opportunity for one man to seize power and rule France.

? What event ended the Reign of Terror?

4

Reign of Terror

TURNING POINTS

Revolutions Compared

Though many try to compare the American Revolution with the French Revolution, there are more differences than similarities. One notable similarity is that the two resulting systems of government have become the model for much of the world. Most governments today follow either the American (republic) or French (oligarchy, rule by a small group of people) form of government.

Different Foundation

France had rejected the Protestant Reformation and persecuted the Huguenots (French Protestants) two hundred years earlier. In stark contrast, the American colonies had been founded and populated to a large degree by Protestants who fled persecution in Europe. Enlightenment ideas influenced both France and the American colonies. But the French accepted these ideas without the biblical restraints recognized by many American colonists.

The French Revolution also opposed religion and established a secular state. In America, colonial religious leaders typically supported the war effort. In addition, the American colonies experienced a great spiritual awakening prior to the war and an extended period of revival following the war. French revolutionaries, however, exalted Reason and elevated Enlightenment philosophy to a religion.

Different Goals

These differing views of religion and reason led to different goals for the French and American Revolutions. The American colonists insisted on the same liberty won by the British in the Glorious Revolution. They sought to preserve the economic, political, and religious liberties that American colonists had enjoyed for more than a century. While both revolutions opposed a history of tyranny, the Americans had greater concerns about human sinfulness, which limited their aims. The French revolutionaries, by contrast, were attempting to overthrow a tradition of social, political, and economic inequality.

These differing goals led to different approaches to revolution. The American colonists were led by local elected leaders. Though they were seeking to free themselves from the oppression of the British crown, the Americans were seeking to preserve their own local forms of government. By contrast, the French citizens rushed to sweep away the existing government and replace it with an entirely new one of their creation.

Different Course

In America, elected leaders were influenced by a biblical viewpoint. They balanced liberty with responsibility. Rather than massive rejection of local authority and unrestricted violence, the American colonists limited their resistance to repelling the British and defending their freedom. The American Revolution did not lead to mass executions and anarchy. Rather, it led to the birthing of a nation that would be governed by laws and a constitution with a bill of rights to protect its citizens. The American Revolution tempered Enlightenment ideals with scriptural principles.

The French were led by students of the Enlightenment who sought liberty without responsibility. The French leaders were humanists who had rejected the scriptural view of mankind's fallen nature. Believing that man was perfectible, the leaders were confident that they could reshape the entire society.

Different Result

While both America and France were revolting against the old powers, America had a distinct advantage the French did not have. The leadership that the Americans were revolting against had ties to a different and separate land (Britain), while the French king and nobility were from the same land, France. When the American Revolution was over, the defeated foes returned to England. But while some of the French nobility went away, the majority did not. Therefore, the revolutionaries were always in fear that the nobility would come back to power. The cost of the unrestrained idealism mixed with fear in France was terrible in terms of loss of life. The result was anarchy and an opportunity for a dictator to seize control.

1. How might France be different today if it had not expelled the Huguenots?
2. How do the events of July 14, 1789, and July 4, 1776, differ?
3. Considering what happened in the French Revolution, what may be the result if the United States government and society give up all connection to a biblical worldview?

CRITICAL THINKING 11.1

How did France pursue a society based on the ideas of liberty and equality?

11.2 Napoleon

Napoleon Bonaparte took advantage of the chaos in France and used his power to take control of the government. He had risen through the military ranks, becoming a general in 1793. Napoleon had led French forces to many victories by using unusual battle tactics that included marching his troops all night and launching surprise attacks on unprepared enemy troops. He was victorious in Italy and almost took over Egypt for France. However, his ambitions extended far beyond defeating France's enemies.

GUIDING QUESTIONS

- How did Napoleon rise to power?
- What were Napoleon's military successes?
- What reforms did Napoleon implement?
- How was Napoleon defeated?

Rise

In 1799 Napoleon supported the overthrow of the unpopular Directory. Three consuls led the new government. Napoleon served as one of the three, but he quickly pushed the others aside to become the First Consul. He then turned this position into that of dictator of France when he became emperor in 1804.

Napoleon Bonaparte

Rule

Napoleon set about to win the support of the French people. He began by signing peace treaties between Britain and France. To stabilize the currency and enhance trade, Napoleon founded the Bank of France. He developed an improved tax system and stabilized the national debt, problems that had long plagued France. Napoleon also established a public education system and placed it under the guidance of the University of France.

Napoleon was a brilliant military organizer and strategist. Militaries today continue to follow the model of organization Napoleon invented. He came up with the **corps system** for organizing the army. Rather than the nation having one large army, the corps system divided the army into smaller self-contained armies. Each corps had its own artillery (cannons), infantry (foot soldiers), cavalry, supplies, and doctors. In this way, the whole army was able to maneuver quickly. The speed with which the French armies moved continually surprised their enemies.

The **Battle of Austerlitz** of 1805 was one of Napoleon's greatest victories. In the battle, he defeated the combined armies of Austria and Russia. Over a decade, Napoleon conquered several nations in Europe and, initially, played the role of liberator by dethroning the kings. By 1809 he had taken Italy, most of Spain, and the countries of Central Europe.

How did Napoleon come to rule France?

How was the organization of Napoleon's army different from other countries' armies?

A reenactment of the Battle of Austerlitz

Napoleon's Empire

Religion

During the revolution, France had gone through a time of de-Christianization. In the Reign of Terror, the Jacobins instituted a new religion, the Cult of Reason. They even changed the calendar so that there were ten days in a week and ten months in a year. One reason for doing this was to prevent people from knowing what day Sunday was. Part of Napoleon's appeal was that he was going to end all the radical change. Unlike the leaders of the revolution, who championed atheism, Napoleon understood that most of the people were still part of the church. Napoleon sought to gain the church's favor. He also understood that the church provided a moral compass for the society, which the worship of reason had failed to do. But he did keep much of the church's material wealth that had been taken during the revolution.

Power

Over time Napoleon gained all the power of the state. He took the title of emperor and effectively ended all the representative assemblies in France. But the country retained the name French Republic. Napoleon borrowed the old systems of power from the French kings. But unlike the most recent kings, who had displayed incompetence and indifference, Napoleon identified the problems of the country and tried to solve them. He did not hesitate to fire officials who criticized him, but if the officials were exceptionally skillful, Napoleon could look past a critical comment from them.

Justice

Napoleon came up with a new law code rightly called the **Napoleonic Code**. The inspiration for the Napoleonic Code did not come from earlier French laws. Instead, he modeled the law after Justinian's law code (the law of the Byzantine empire). The code made the law clear and available for everyone to read. The code was written in the current language of the day so that everyone could understand it. The law was much like the constitutional system the United States has enjoyed for over two hundred years. Everyone was supposed to be equal under the law, and the accused was presumed innocent until proven guilty.

Citizenship

The French people retained the rights found in the Declaration of the Rights of Man if those rights did not infringe upon the activities of Napoleon's regime (government). The declaration proclaimed equal rights for all citizens but did not say the rights were inalienable (or unremovable) because they were granted by the Creator. Therefore, the declaration included wordings that permitted any French government to abolish one or all of the rights. Article V said, "The law has the right to forbid only actions harmful to society." Napoleon used this principle to greatly limit the freedom of the press.

Environment

Paris under Napoleon was more orderly. The emperor prioritized a well-organized police department to fight crime and lawlessness. Napoleon organized a fire department for the city after he and the empress escaped a fire at the Austrian Embassy. Many of the great cities of the day were burning down because they lacked organized fire protection. He organized a hospital system by putting all the city's hospitals under the leadership of one person. Napoleon built new roads and bridges to improve traffic congestion. He built canals that provided free water to the Parisians.

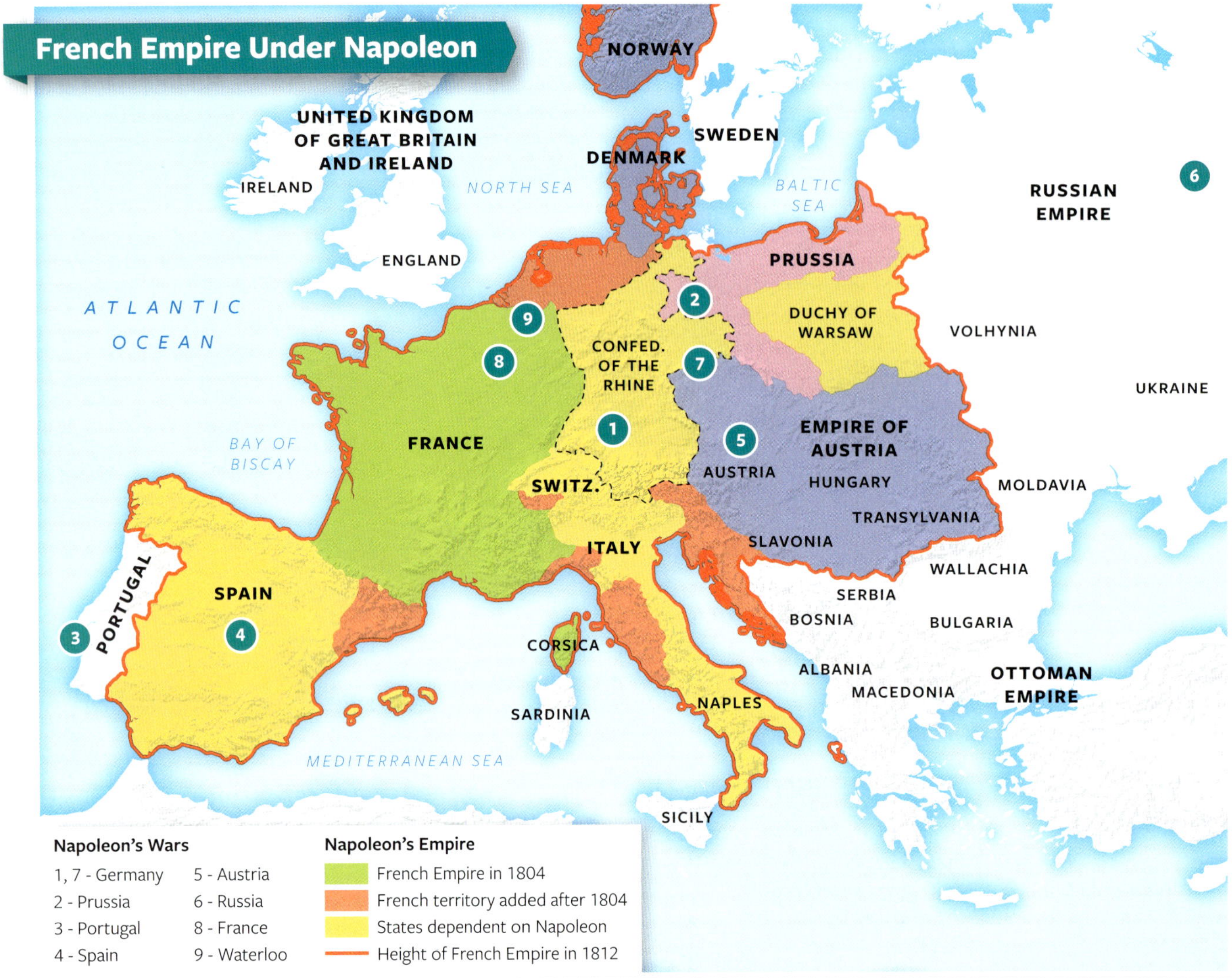

Fall

Napoleon took much of the wealth of the nations he invaded. He also placed one of his relatives on each of the thrones of these nations, revealing his true intention, to rule Europe rather than liberate it. French abuses stirred national pride within the conquered nations, and Napoleon faced mounting resistance. His treaty with Britain lasted only a year, and the British government declared war on France in 1803 because of what Napoleon was doing on the continent of Europe.

Napoleon's two failings as a military commander led to his final defeat. First, he knew how to lead an army but not a navy. Because of his ego, he failed to put a strong leader over the navy. In late 1805 at the **Battle of Trafalgar** off the coast of Spain, the French suffered a crushing naval defeat by the British. Even though he was outnumbered, the British commander, Lord Nelson, defeated the French admiral Villeneuve and achieved British dominance over the seas that lasted for over one hundred years. Napoleon's second failing was that his answer to any foreign problem was invasion with the army, even when diplomacy (talking with the enemy) or economic pressure through blockade would have been more successful.

What happened at the Battle of Trafalgar?

Invasion of Russia

Because of his defeat at Trafalgar, Napoleon could not invade Britain. So he was forced to try to strangle them economically with a blockade. He needed other nations to help, but Russia and other nations ignored Napoleon's economic blockade. This defiance led Napoleon to invade Russia. Napoleon entered Russia in 1812 with about six hundred thousand troops. The outnumbered Russians refused to engage Napoleon's forces. Instead the Russian army withdrew and lured the French deep into Russian territory. When the Russians did stand and fight, the French defeated them. The French occupied a burned and abandoned Moscow and waited for Czar Alexander, the ruler of Russia, to surrender, but he never did. When the French finally retreated, the Russian forces and the Russian winter destroyed the French army. Fewer than one hundred thousand French soldiers made it safely out of Russia.

? Why was Napoleon defeated in Russia?

Napoleon in Exile

Napoleon suffered another defeat in 1813 at Leipzig, in the German states. An alliance of European leaders forced Napoleon to step down as ruler of France and go into exile on Elba, an island just off the western coast of Italy. However, while the European leaders met to restore order in Europe, Napoleon escaped early in 1815 and returned to France to raise another army.

? Where was Napoleon first exiled?

The Final End of Napoleon Bonaparte

On June 18, 1815, the armies of Prussia and Britain confronted Napoleon and his forces at the **Battle of Waterloo** in what is now known as Belgium. Napoleon launched a surprise attack on the Prussian forces and separated them from the British army. Following thunderstorms and a delay while the ground dried, Napoleon sent his forces directly into the British line. However, the British forces held their position, and the Prussians regrouped and trapped the French forces. Napoleon's army collapsed. All in all, Napoleon had kept Europe at war for some fifteen years; the wars left millions of people dead, the countryside scorched, and cities burned. Napoleon was sent into exile on the island of Saint Helena in the South Atlantic, where he lived until his death in 1821.

CRITICAL THINKING 11.2

In what ways did Napoleon change France?

Napoleon on Saint Helena

GUIDING QUESTIONS

- What were the reasons for Latin American discontent?
- Who were the key figures in the Latin American independence movement?

11.3 Latin American Independence

The wave of enthusiasm for self-rule crossed the Atlantic from the countries in Europe to their colonies in Central and South America. Napoleon's invasion of Spain and Portugal had destabilized those countries so much that it gave an opportunity for the Creole leaders in the Americas to fight for their independence. The Creoles had grown to resent their lack of power in the government. They saw an opportunity to gain independence while the Iberian nations fought in Europe.

Part of the colonies' dissatisfaction with Spanish rule was the control exerted by the mother country. Until the 1700s the Spanish colonies could trade only with Spain. They could not even trade with each other. The Spanish did not limit their control to physical goods. They also tried to limit the sharing of new ideas. The Spanish government had no desire for their subjects (people whom they ruled) to accept the teachings of English and French philosophers. The Spanish wanted to keep their colonies isolated from European influence. But tight control only made the colonists want more information and freedom. European ideas were smuggled in, and discontentment spread from person to person. This quiet network of information spread seeds of revolution. The desire for independence grew stronger in Latin America. The only missing element was effective leaders to unite the various classes and defeat the Spanish.

In what two ways did Spain limit freedom in Latin America?

Haiti

The first independence movement in Latin America started in Haiti in 1804. Ninety percent of the half million people living in Haiti were slaves. During the French Revolution, the government abolished slavery. However, Napoleon revived this practice when he became the First Consul. He sent troops to put down slave rebellions in various colonies, including Haiti.

For the Haitians, the cost for independence in human lives (200,000) was immense, but they did not give up. Thousands of French soldiers died in a failed effort to subdue the Haitians. In 1804 Haiti became one of the first French colonies to gain independence and to end French-imposed slavery.

José de San Martín

Argentina and Chile

Buenos Aires, Argentina, declared its independence from Spanish control in 1810, and the independence movement quickly spread across the country. The Argentine government then chose **José de San Martín** to take independence to Peru.

San Martín was born to a prominent Argentine family in 1778. At age nine he crossed the ocean to study in Spain and went on to serve in the Spanish army. In 1812 San Martín resigned from the army to help in the independence movement in South America. He chose as his troops the gauchos (cowboys in Argentina). Although they were not disciplined, they proved to be faithful fighting companions and fought fiercely for independence. Prior to following San Martín, the gauchos had been little more than outlaws. However, their role in the fight for independence caused the people to respect them. Many of them began herding cattle for the wealthy landowners.

San Martín studied the strategies of great European generals as he made decisions about the best methods to defeat the Spanish. San Martín decided that instead of attacking the Spanish in Peru as ordered, he would cross the Andes Mountains and free Chile first. In 1817 his troops crossed the Andes and forced the Spanish from one city after another. With Chile free, San Martín turned to liberating Peru.

? Whom did San Martín choose for his troops?

Gran Colombia

Gran Colombia included the Spanish colonies in northwestern South America: Venezuela, Colombia, and Ecuador. Beginning in 1813 Bolívar led his troops to push the Spaniards out of Venezuela from the south, east, and west. Bolívar's men followed him through plains, deserts, swamps, and rivers. On several occasions Bolívar led his men through the Cordillera de Mérida, part of the Andes Mountains. This part of the Andes range rises to sixteen thousand feet in some places.

In 1816 the final move toward independence began with Venezuela and then spread to Colombia. Bolívar determined that the only way to free Venezuela was to free the entire continent of foreign rule. His greatest victories came in 1819 at a battle in Boyacá, Colombia, and in 1821 at the battle for Carabobo, Venezuela, with the support of his faithful general Antonio José de Sucre. In 1822 Sucre went on to free Ecuador from Spanish dominion.

Peru

In August of 1820 San Martín packed troops onto ships and set sail for Pisco, Peru. It was there that San Martín received a letter from Bolívar offering his assistance in Peru's struggle for independence. San Martín's forces moved up from the south, and Bolívar's troops came down from the north. Through these combined assaults, Peru was liberated from Spanish control.

? What were Bolívar's greatest victories?

Simón Bolívar

Born in 1783 in Caracas, Venezuela, **Simón Bolívar** was the fourth child of Juan Vicente and Doña María Bolívar. Both his parents had died by the time Bolívar was nine. Bolívar and his brother and sisters were left in the care of an uncle.

As a boy, Bolívar learned Latin, Greek, Spanish, and French from a tutor. His tutor introduced him to the teachings of several eighteenth-century philosophers. Bolívar came to believe that freedom was the source of men's happiness. This conviction stirred the spirit of independence in his heart.

In 1810 Bolívar was sent to England as an ambassador. Despite his objections to being sent to this country, he gained valuable insight that would help him later when he wrote constitutions for the emerging Latin American nations. He returned to South America and led many countries to independence.

What happened in Spain to end the revolutionary stalemate in Mexico?

(top) Gabino Gaínza signing an independence treaty for the Kingdom of Guatemala; (bottom) Pedro I declaring independence for Brazil

Mexico

Mexico went through a thirteen-year-long struggle for independence. Many individuals led the fight for a free Mexico. One notable figure was a priest named **Miguel Hidalgo y Costilla**. He declared independence for Mexico at his church. Hidalgo led many people and engaged in terror attacks against the Spanish, but he was caught and executed in 1811. The fighting continued; there was an insurgency (internal small attacks) from 1815 to 1820, with neither the Spanish nor the insurgents gaining an advantage. But back in Spain Enlightenment ideas were taking hold, which caused the king to lose some of his power. Therefore, the revolutionaries in Mexico saw an opportunity.

A Mexican officer, **Agustín de Iturbide**, allied with an insurgent leader, Guerrero, to take over the country. Their goal was to bring equality to all Mexicans and start a Mexican monarchy. They were victorious and signed a treaty with the viceroy of Mexico (the representative of Spain in Mexico) that granted Mexican independence. Agustín declared himself emperor in 1822, but his rule did not last long. He was overthrown in 1823; that year the Mexican leaders established the Republic of Mexico.

Central America

A Spanish-born general named **Gabino Gaínza** led the **Kingdom of Guatemala** to independence. This kingdom included Costa Rica, El Salvador, Honduras, Nicaragua, and Guatemala. Gaínza was a complicated person who wavered between loyalty to Spain and support for the rebels. It seems he committed atrocities against natives in Peru and Chile. In 1820 he was sent away to Central America and given the title of Captain-General of Guatemala. But others were critical of the move since they suspected him of having sympathies with the rebels. Gaínza had perfect timing; just after he took power, Mexico earned its independence. Since Guatemala was under the dependency of Mexico, it also was in line to gain its freedom. Gaínza could have challenged the revolutionaries by siding with the wealthy Spanish landowners. Instead, he supported independence, and thus Central America gained its independence without bloodshed. On September 15, 1821, the Kingdom of Guatemala was declared independent of Spain.

Brazil

Brazil gained its independence at the same time as the other Latin American nations but without violence. There were early stirrings of revolution supported by the upper class. However, the plans were discovered in the early stages, and the leaders were executed.

Oddly, independence came because Napoleon captured Portugal. In 1807 the Portuguese royalty fled to Brazil and declared it the center of the Portuguese empire. King João (John) then adopted economic reforms to make Brazil a proper environment for the monarchy. He repealed an earlier ban on factories, introduced a trade treaty with England, established a printing press, and declared Brazil equal to, instead of a colony of, Portugal. All these actions contributed to Brazil's independence.

In 1820 Portugal demanded that King João return. He left his son Pedro as regent of Brazil. In 1822, when Pedro was to return to Portugal, he refused. On September 7, 1822, Pedro shouted, "Independence or death!" and tore the symbol of Portugal from his military uniform. He was crowned emperor of an independent Brazil as **Pedro I**.

How did Central America gain independence?

CRITICAL THINKING 11.3

Compare the American Revolution with the Latin American revolutions.

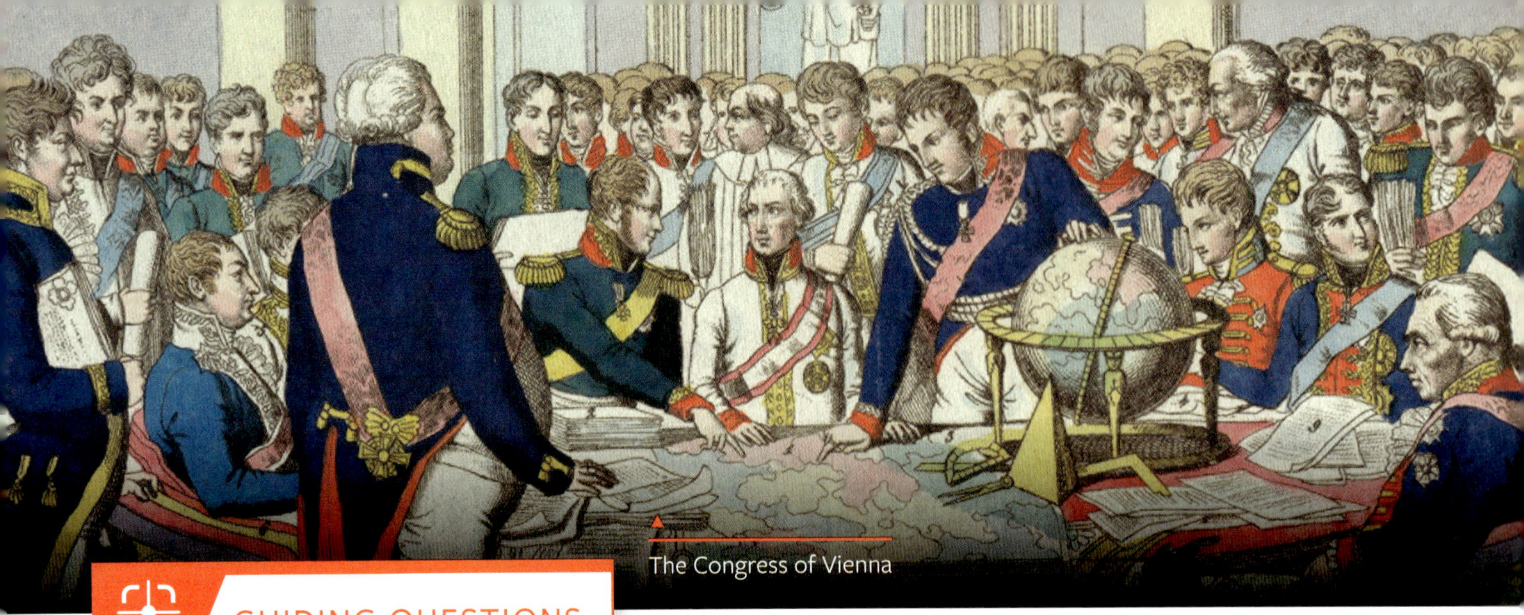

The Congress of Vienna

GUIDING QUESTIONS

- What were the causes of European revolts in the 1830s?
- What were the principles of conservatism, liberalism, and nationalism?

11.4 European Revolutions

Following Napoleon's defeat, European leaders had a meeting called the **Congress of Vienna**. The purpose of the meeting was to restore Europe to the condition it had been in before the French Revolution. Napoleon had stolen the European kings' lands, and now they met to hand back the lands to whomever the nobility considered the rightful owners, without any regard for the people who lived there. The European leaders were motivated by a belief in **conservatism**, which in this case referred to a desire to maintain the old institutions of the kings and the church to ensure social stability. But their desires faced the strong headwinds of **liberalism**, a belief that had spread via the French. Liberalism stressed freedom and equality for all.

What was the purpose of the Congress of Vienna?

The kings and church leaders did not understand that their time had passed. Rather than being loyal to a king who most likely was born in another country than the one he ruled, the people were giving loyalty to their own nation. The term for this is **nationalism** (an intense devotion and loyalty to one's people). Revolts against the old regimes soon broke out all over Europe.

The revolts came in three waves, the first in the 1820s, the second in the 1830s, and the third in 1848. Many of these revolts failed, but some succeeded. Greece and Belgium gained their liberty, while Poland and Hungary suffered a crushing defeat.

The longing of a group of people to form a nation may be a positive desire, depending on the motivation. Some groups pursued nationalism to escape the control of an oppressive power and seek equality for citizens. Others sought nationhood to combine regions with a common language or culture. Some can take nationalism too far when they view their nation as the greatest and seek to rule other nations.

What two European countries gained their independence in the waves of revolutions?

Ireland

Inspired by the French and American Revolutions, the Irish revolted against the British in 1798. The Society of United Irishmen led the revolution. The society was a unique alliance of Presbyterians and Catholics who both opposed the Church of England. They had early success, but when the British got organized and responded, some thirty thousand Irish were killed. The French landed to assist the rebels, but the British defeated them.

Who tried to help the Irish in their revolution?

Greece

Greece came under Ottoman control following the conquest of Constantinople in 1453. The Greeks repeatedly sought to break free from the Ottomans over the next three centuries. In 1819 the Greeks renewed their struggle. Finally, in 1829, the Greek forces received support from Russia, Britain, and France. The combined navies of these nations destroyed the Ottoman fleet. French troops then assisted Greek forces in their struggle to drive the Ottomans out of Greece. In 1832 Greece gained recognition as an independent state.

Belgium

This small nation was formed out of the southern provinces of the United Kingdom of the Netherlands. Due to differences in religion and language, this region had little in common with the rest of the Dutch kingdom. The people from this region were Roman Catholic and spoke French, while most in the Netherlands were Protestant and spoke Dutch. This region also suffered from high levels of unemployment and unrest within the working class. These differences and the resulting discontent led to uprisings in 1830. Some Belgian leaders took advantage of this strife and supported the idea of secession (becoming independent). Despite intense fighting, efforts to settle the question of Belgian independence on the battlefield were unsuccessful. The king of the Netherlands appealed to the Great Powers (major European nations) for a peaceful resolution. A conference of European powers met in London and recognized Belgian independence in 1831. However, the Dutch continued to resist Belgian independence until 1835.

? **Why did Belgium want independence from the Netherlands?**

Poland

This country endured many foreign invasions and partition attempts by neighboring countries. The Poles often rallied against the invaders and tried to expel them. This cycle was repeated in the nineteenth century. In 1807 Napoleon invaded a partitioned Poland and established a Polish state. Although Napoleon liberated the Poles from other European powers, he merely placed Poland under his own rule. In 1815, following the defeat of Napoleon, the Congress of Vienna partitioned Poland among its neighboring countries. Russia controlled the eastern portion of Poland and soon annexed this region. The Russians steadily reduced the freedoms of the Poles and installed a brutal regime. In November 1830 some Polish cadets revolted and led an armed rebellion against Russian oppression. As the resistance spread, many Polish citizens joined the uprising. Initially, the Poles succeeded on the battlefield. But Russia sent a large army and crushed the Polish forces in 1831. Poland did not regain its independence until after World War I.

? **What country did the Poles revolt against?**

The Polish Revolution of 1831

Hungary

Hungary had been under the control of Austria for centuries. In 1848 the Hungarians carried out mass demonstrations and demanded rights such as freedom of the press, trial by jury, and religious liberty. Initially, the Austrian ruler had to accept these demands due to internal problems. However, a new Austrian ruler rejected the Hungarians' demands and sent an army to subjugate them. Hungarian forces won the first few battles. The Austrian ruler then enlisted Russia's support, and the combined forces overwhelmed the Hungarians. Many Hungarian leaders were executed, and the rest escaped into exile. Like Poland, Hungary finally gained independence after World War I.

CRITICAL THINKING 11.4

How did religious differences contribute to Belgium's revolt against the Netherlands?

GUIDING QUESTION

- Why did the unification movements in Germany and Italy succeed?

11.5 German and Italian Unifications

Unification in Germany and Italy grew out of the surge of nationalism. German intellectuals attempted to revolt against the dominant powers in 1848, but other factors would eventually lead to the formation of the German state. Italy's efforts at unification began with the growth of patriotic societies. In both nations, strong leaders used diplomacy and military strategy to work toward unity.

German Unification

Initial progress toward German unification resulted from an economic union called the **Zollverein**, which was formed to enhance trade between the German states. Prior to this agreement, trade was limited between the German territories. This union reduced the cost of selling goods and greatly increased the volume of trade among the member states. Enhanced economic cooperation helped build support for political union.

In 1862 King Wilhelm I appointed **Count Otto von Bismarck** as the chancellor of Prussia. Bismarck became the driving force behind political unification of the German states. He used diplomacy, propaganda, and military might to unite the Germans.

? **What was the first step in German unification?**

Second Schleswig War

Bismarck's first opportunity to promote German unification came in 1864. He provoked a war with Denmark over a dispute regarding the two small territories of Schleswig and Holstein. These regions lay between Denmark and Prussia. Bismarck convinced Austria to side with Prussia against Denmark, and the Danes were easily defeated. Austria took control of Holstein, and Prussia gained control of Schleswig.

Austro-Prussian War

Bismarck convinced Russia and France to remain neutral while he tricked the Austrians into declaring war on Prussia. This war lasted only seven weeks, with Prussia emerging as the clear victor. As a result, Austria surrendered control of Holstein to Prussia. In addition, Prussia gained a dominant influence over the newly formed North German Confederation.

With Austria and Denmark neutralized, one nation lay between Prussia and a unified German state. Bismarck planned carefully to use France as a tool to complete German unification.

Franco-Prussian War

Though Prussia had gained dominance in northern Germany, the southern German territories remained fragmented and independent of Prussian control. Bismarck believed that a war between the German states and France would convince the southern territories to align with Prussia.

The Franco-Prussian War resulted from a controversy over the next king of Spain. At first, Leopold, a man related to the Prussian ruling family (Hohenzollern), was invited to become the next Spanish king. France felt threatened by this action and protested loudly. Even though Leopold declined the offer, the French were not satisfied. The French sent an ambassador to meet with the Prussian king and demand a promise that no member of the Hohenzollern family would ever rule Spain since it would bring Spain under Prussian influence.

The Prussian king refused to make such a promise and sent a dispatch (report) of this meeting to Bismarck. Bismarck carefully changed the wording to imply that the Prussian king and the French ambassador had insulted each other. Then he published the revised dispatch. Both nations were furious, and the French declared war on Prussia.

Bismarck's plan worked, and the southern German states sided with Prussia in the war against France. The German forces invaded France and trapped the French forces within two months. Ten days before the French surrendered, Kaiser Wilhelm I was declared ruler of the German Reich (empire) in the Palace of Versailles, near Paris. German unification had been accomplished.

French soldiers seek cover in a trench in the Franco-Prussian War.

What methods did Bismarck use to unite the German states?

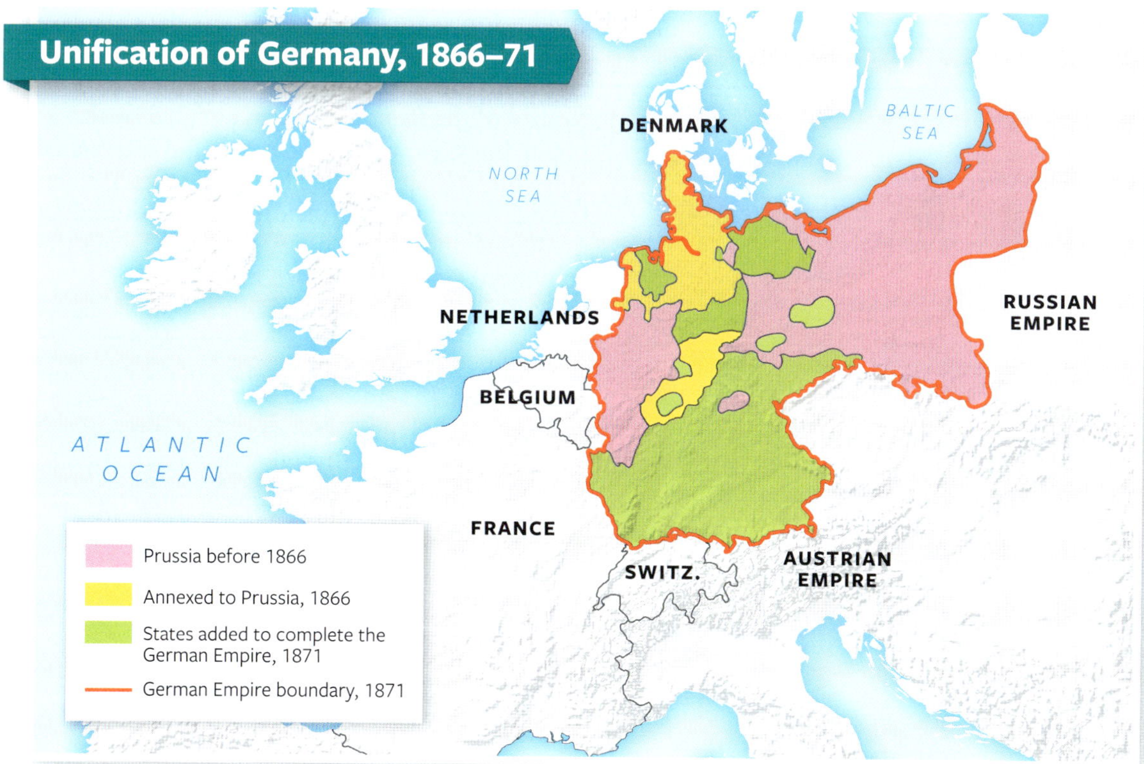

Italian Unification

For centuries, the Italian peninsula had been divided into many small kingdoms and controlled by foreign powers. But the drive toward nationalism surged in Italy as it had in other countries. A movement called the Risorgimento ("resurgence") contributed to the movement for nationalism.

Giuseppe Mazzini

In 1832 an Italian named **Giuseppe Mazzini** formed a group called Young Italy for the purpose of accomplishing Italian unification. The struggle proved to be slow and frustrating, but men like Mazzini persisted in their efforts.

Count Camillo di Cavour

Count Camillo di Cavour proved to be the most successful at uniting Italy. He was the prime minister of the Kingdom of Sardinia. Much like Bismarck in Germany, Cavour used whatever means necessary to promote Italian unification. He sent troops to support Britain and France in wars against Russia. While his support was largely symbolic, Cavour used these alliances to build support for unification. On another occasion Cavour supported Napoleon III, the nephew of Napoleon Bonaparte and emperor of France, against Austria to remove Austrian control of regions in Italy. Cavour's efforts were frustrated when Napoleon III abruptly made peace with Austria to prevent Cavour from gaining too much power.

? How did Cavour build support for unification?

Unification of Italy, 1859–71

Giuseppe Garibaldi

While Cavour unified the regions of northern Italy, a disciple of Mazzini, **Giuseppe Garibaldi**, formed an army known as the "Red Shirts" and conquered the island of Sicily in 1860. Garibaldi and his forces then moved to the Italian Peninsula and captured the city of Naples. Garibaldi planned to capture Rome and gain control of the Papal States (areas ruled by the pope), but Cavour traveled south and intervened. Since the French supplied forces to protect Rome, Cavour feared that Garibaldi's assault would draw the French into this conflict. Instead, Cavour convinced Garibaldi to turn his conquered territory over to Victor Emmanuel II, the king of Sardinia. In the spring of 1861, an Italian parliament declared the formation of the Kingdom of Italy. They named Victor Emmanuel II as the first king. By 1870 the Papal States and Rome were added to the Italian kingdom despite furious papal opposition. In 1871 Rome became the national capital.

? CRITICAL THINKING 11.5

Compare the German unification movement with the Italian unification movement.

Making Connections

1. What did Charlotte Corday hope to accomplish?
2. Why did the French turn from loving Louis XVI to hating him?
3. How did the National Assembly get money for France?
4. Why was Robespierre executed?
5. Why was Napoleon successful at defeating one army after another for more than a decade?
6. What contribution did Napoleon make to French law?
7. Why did Napoleon lose at sea?
8. Why were the people in Latin America discontent?
9. Who liberated Gran Colombia?
10. Were revolutionaries in the various European countries generally conservative or liberal?
11. How did religious differences contribute to Belgium's revolt against the Netherlands?
12. What European nation assisted Austria in subduing the Hungarian revolt?
13. What role did Count Cavour play in accomplishing Italian unification?
14. Why were Greece and Belgium able to achieve independence while Poland and Hungary were not?
15. Why did Bismarck publish an altered dispatch of a discussion between the king of Prussia and the French ambassador?

Thinking Critically

1. What lessons can be learned from the social, political, and economic problems in France prior to the revolution?
2. Compare and contrast the world in 2022 with 1780s and 1790s France.
3. Why was the French Revolution unable to build a stable society based on Enlightenment ideals?
4. Did Napoleon do more good than bad? Explain.
5. You are an editor of a German newspaper watching the events of the Franco-Prussian War unfold. Write an editorial explaining the pros and cons of nationalism.

WHAT TO KNOW

EVENTS

Bastille Day
Battle of Austerlitz
Battle of Trafalgar
Battle of Waterloo
Congress of Vienna

PEOPLE

Charlotte Corday
Jean-Paul Marat
Louis XVI
Marie Antoinette
Maximilien Robespierre
Jacobins
Napoleon Bonaparte
José de San Martín
Simón Bolívar
Miguel Hidalgo y Costilla
Agustín de Iturbide
Gabino Gaínza
Pedro I
Count Otto von Bismarck
Giuseppe Mazzini
Count Camillo di Cavour
Giuseppe Garibaldi

PLACES

Bastille
Gran Colombia
Kingdom of Guatemala

TERMS

guillotine
First Estate
Second Estate
Third Estate
Estates-General
National Assembly of France
Tennis Court Oath
Declaration of the Rights of Man
National Convention
Committee of Public Safety
Reign of Terror
Directory
corps system
Napoleonic Code
conservatism
liberalism
nationalism
Zollverein

12 THE INDUSTRIAL REVOLUTION

1700 – 1850

ESSENTIAL QUESTIONS

- What were some causes and developments of the Industrial Revolution?
- How did the Industrial Revolution impact society?
- How closely did nineteenth-century reform movements align with biblical teaching?

The Great Exhibition of 1851

The Industrial Revolution began in Great Britain in the mid-1700s. It was a time of great technological advancement, with many inventions focused on improving work processes. As a result of these improvements, manufacturing rather than farming became the focus of the British economy (a trend known as industrialization). This trend gradually spread to other parts of the world as well.

A British organization called The Royal Society for the Encouragement of Arts, Manufactures and Commerce held small shows starting in 1844 to demonstrate different inventions of the period. One of its members, Henry Cole, wanted to host a much larger show that would showcase the worldwide accomplishments of the new industrial age. He enlisted the help of another society member: Prince Albert, the husband of the British monarch, Queen Victoria. Albert saw great possibilities in the event, both for promoting British manufacturing and commerce and for establishing goodwill between countries. He played a key role in planning the Exhibition.

A special exhibition hall was constructed in Hyde Park, London. Joseph Paxton, who had built some early greenhouses, was the designer. The building was called the Crystal Palace because it was made mostly of glass stretched between thin iron rods. The building covered approximately eighteen acres. It was 1,848 feet long, 408 feet wide, and 108 feet high at its tallest point. Its huge size allowed the builders to keep some of the trees from the park and enclose them inside the building.

The Great Exhibition officially opened on May 1, 1851. Approximately 14,000 people set up displays. Britain and its colonies were assigned to one side of the exhibition hall, and exhibitors from the rest of the world were given the other side. Many of the most popular displays demonstrated machines that produced goods in factories. For example, the process of producing cotton cloth was shown from start to finish. However, there were many other exhibits as well. There were things displayed for their beauty, from artwork and sculpture to the Koh-i-noor diamond, the largest in the world at the time. There were scientific devices, ranging from barometers to electric telegraphs to surgical instruments. There were musical instruments, weapons, and raw materials from Britain's empire. There were even novelties such as the first voting machine and a bed that was designed to tip the sleeper out when it was time to get up.

The Exhibition sold around six million tickets. There were visitors from all levels of society, from wealthy factory owners and famous literary people to members of the working class. The Exhibition officially ended on October 15, 1851. The exhibition hall was taken down and reassembled (with some modifications) at Sydenham Hill in southeast London. It continued to be used as an exhibition site until it burned down in 1936. Proceeds from the Exhibition were used to build several museums and to support continuing education in the sciences and the arts. The Exhibition is often considered the first world's fair.

GUIDING QUESTIONS

- What factors helped to aid industrialization in Great Britain?
- What were some important technological developments of the Industrial Revolution?
- How did work patterns vary in the nineteenth century?

12.1 Industrialization in Great Britain

In the beginning Adam and Eve cared for the garden that God had entrusted to them under the Creation Mandate. Succeeding generations continued to farm and carry on basic industry (production of goods). Methods remained largely unchanged for centuries. Most farming was done with wooden tools and human or animal power. It involved pulling a crude device through the ground to loosen the soil in order to plant seed. Crops were harvested by hand or with a sharp tool. The labor was intense, and the harvest varied from season to season.

Most industry also remained primitive. Producing items required for daily life required a strong back and long hours. Shoes, clothing, tools, and other items were made by hand, and each piece that was made was slightly different from the rest.

Starting in the 1700s, people pressed the Creation Mandate forward by developing improved ways of farming the land and producing goods. Because of these developments, life in Europe entered a period of monumental change. Eventually, this change would affect people around the world.

Factors That Promoted Industrialization

Great Britain led the way in the early stages of the **Industrial Revolution**. This was true for several reasons. First, Britain had workers. The British population grew from six and one-half million in 1750 to nine million in 1800. Unlike earlier periods when the population had grown, Britain was able to maintain the growth and feed the extra people mainly from crops grown by British farmers. Food production was significantly increased through practices like rotating crops to replace nutrients in the soil, creating more planting space by draining marshes, and increasing the level of nitrogen (an important nutrient) in the soil using natural and artificial fertilizers. As Great Britain's population continued to grow, its farms increased not only their production but also their efficiency. With new timesaving machines and processes, farms needed fewer workers. Many people moved to the cities and found work in the developing industries.

Great Britain had other advantages as well that helped industry thrive. It had natural resources like iron ore and coal, which were needed to make and power the new machines of the Industrial Revolution. It had a stable government that supported economic freedom. And it had a huge empire that provided a market for the goods it was manufacturing.

Industrial Revolution period of change in the machines and processes used for farming and manufacturing

Besides all this, Great Britain had people who were willing to lead the new industries. They had the vision to see the possibilities of new ideas and the skill and dedication to carry them out, often at their own financial risk. We call these types of people **entrepreneurs**. **Richard Arkwright** was a famous inventor and entrepreneur. Arkwright invented machines for the new textile (cloth) industry; he also built and operated factories that produced cloth using his machines. Arkwright got the government to protect several of his inventions with a **patent**. A patent is a set of special rights that a government gives to an inventor for a certain period. During this time no one else can legally copy and sell the invention. This protection gives the inventor time to recover the cost of developing the invention and to make a profit. Once the patent expires, anyone can make and sell the product without breaking the law.

Men like Arkwright developed contacts with banks and wealthy persons, who provided the needed **capital**, or money, to fund a new industry. Any investors received a share of the profits made by a thriving business. However, they also shared in the losses if the business failed.

Some may conclude that this combination of factors was merely an accident of history. However, Christians can see the hand of God in arranging all these details and making possible the Industrial Revolution in Great Britain. We refer to this as divine providence.

Arkwright's plan for his spinning machine

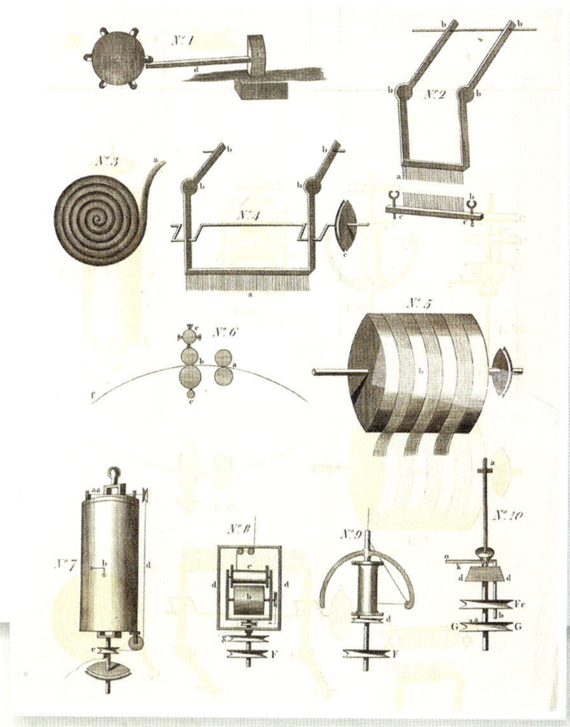

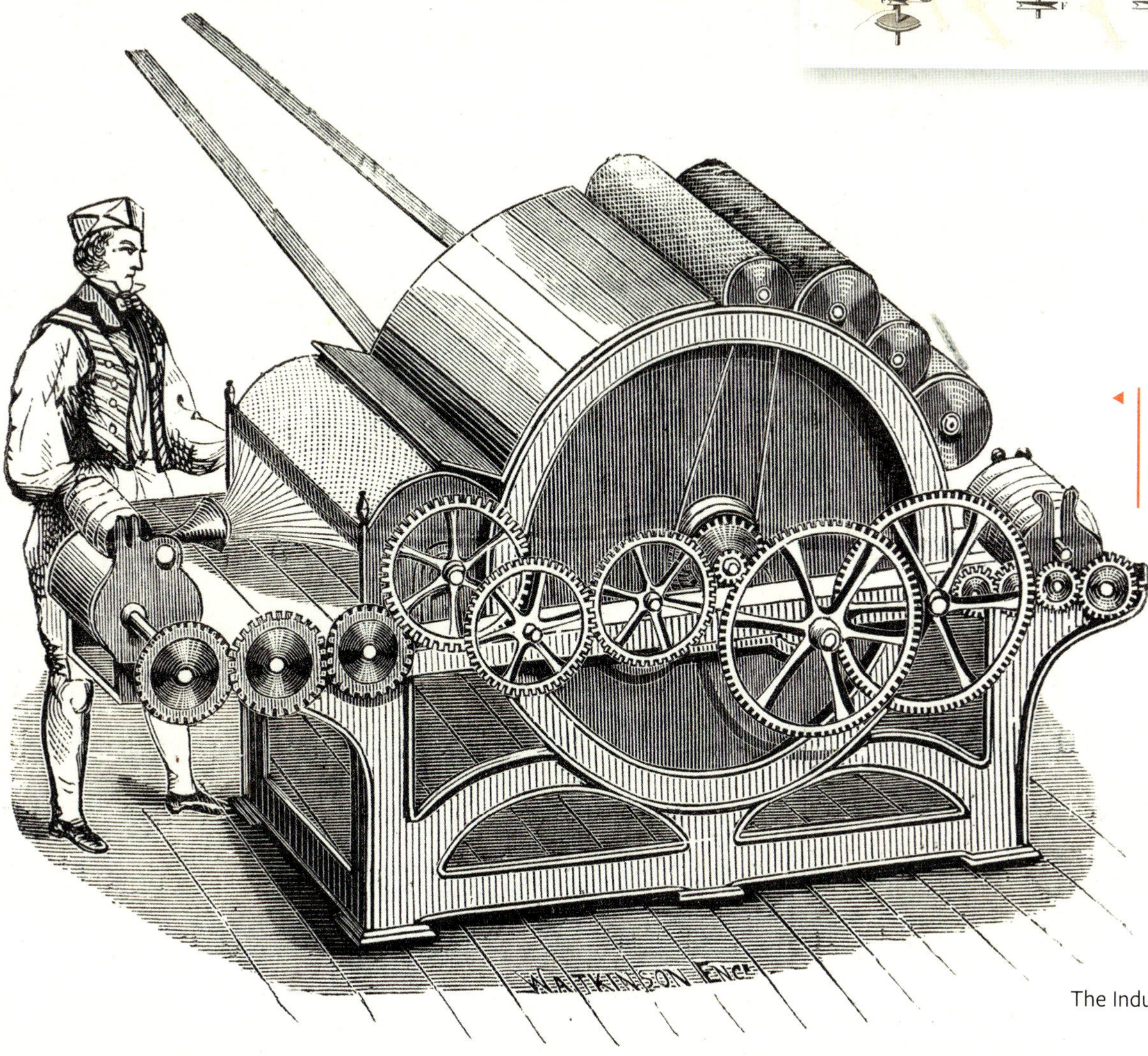

Arkwright's carding machine, used to untangle fibers for spinning

New Technologies

Many new technologies increased the productivity of both farms and industry during this time. A few key developments will be briefly examined.

BUILDING MATERIALS

IRON

- refined by using coke (a product of coal) to heat the ore and separate the metal
- further strengthened by the puddling process developed by **Henry Cort**, which removed impurities and produced wrought iron

STEEL

- combined iron with carbon and other elements
- produced a material that was stronger and cheaper than wrought iron

MACHINES

AGRICULTURE

Seed drill

- invented by **Jethro Tull** in 1701
- placed seeds in rows
- produced more crops using less seed

Improved plows in 1730 and 1763

Threshing machine

- invented by **Andrew Meikle** in 1786
- automatically separated wheat from husks

INDUSTRY

Flying shuttle

- invented by **John Kay** in 1733
- allowed rapid weaving of cloth

Spinning jenny

- invented by **James Hargreaves** around 1764
- quickly spun many strands of cotton into thread

SOURCE OF POWER

STEAM ENGINE

- channeled steam to move mechanical parts
- refined by **James Watt** in the 1760s
- used in factories, on farms, and for transportation
- provided consistent and reliable power for the Industrial Revolution

TRANSPORTATION

BETTER ROADS AND CANALS

RAILROADS

- originally used around mines and powered by humans or animals
- carried more weight and went faster when pulled by steam-powered locomotives
- made common in Great Britain by **George Stephenson**

George Stephenson

George Stephenson was born on June 9, 1781, in Wylam, Northumberland, England. Stephenson had no formal schooling as a child but learned to read and write as a young adult. He married three times. His only surviving child, Robert, was born in 1803. He and Robert worked closely together throughout their lives.

Stephenson began working with steam engines as a young man. Most early steam engines were stationary; they were part of machines that did not move. But after Richard Trevithick successfully tested a steam-powered locomotive in 1804, Stephenson became interested in building his own locomotive. He finished his first attempt in 1814. One big problem with early locomotives was their weight. They were too heavy to travel on wooden rails, and early cast-iron rails broke easily. Stephenson redesigned the rails and added more wheels to the locomotive to spread out its weight.

In 1821 Stephenson designed the Stockton and Darlington Railway, which was the first public railway line to use a steam-powered locomotive. In 1823 Stephenson and his son, together with some other associates, established a company to build steam locomotives. With a growing reputation, Stephenson was asked to build a forty-mile railroad line between the manufacturing city of Manchester and the port of Liverpool. Stephenson faced two major obstacles in building this line. The first obstacle was people whose living was threatened by the steam-powered locomotives (for example, farmers who grew oats to feed horses). They strongly opposed Stephenson's work, even to the point of violence. A second obstacle was not having flat ground. Going uphill strained a train's engine, and going downhill strained its brakes. Stephenson tried to make the ground as level as possible. Sometimes that meant building the ground up, cutting it back, or even digging a tunnel. Stephenson's locomotive company won a race to determine who would build the locomotives for the new Manchester-Liverpool line. His entry amazed everyone with a top speed of thirty-six miles per hour.

Stephenson deserves much credit for his role in the development of railroads. He identified and proposed solutions for many practical problems that railroads would face. For example, he anticipated that individual railroad lines would likely be joined together at some point and would need to have a standard rail width. Though other railway engineers surpassed Stephenson in some areas, he laid the foundation for their work.

Toy model of George Stephenson's Rocket locomotive

Development of the Factory

Before the Industrial Revolution, most laborers worked on farms or in **cottage industries**. Cottage industries were small-scale businesses, usually owned and operated by one family. Many early cottage industries produced cloth, especially wool cloth. Early spinning wheels and looms could fit in a home or shop and provided income for the family.

The invention of new machines for spinning and weaving led to a change in industry. The machines were large and expensive. Homes and shops were too small to hold the machines, and families could not afford them. This led to the construction of large buildings called **factories** by entrepreneurs who brought together machines and workers to produce goods on a large scale.

Factories were like farms and cottage industries in that they required many hours of hard work. But the pattern of work was much different in a factory. Working times might vary on a farm or in a cottage industry, but they were absolutely fixed in a factory. Tasks were different also. Farm laborers especially might do a variety of jobs. But factory workers had one task that was performed repeatedly. To maximize their profits, factory owners needed workers to operate as efficiently as possible. They used a variety of tactics, including the threat of firing, to get workers to conform to the new patterns of factory work.

Why were cottage industries replaced by factories?

Spinning wheel in a home

Textile production in a factory

CRITICAL THINKING 12.1

What differences might owners of cottage industries have experienced when they became employees at factories?

Expansion of Industrialization and the Rise of Social Reform

GUIDING QUESTIONS

- How did industrialization spread to the continent of Europe and to the United States?
- What changes did industrialization bring to people of the nineteenth century?
- Did the Industrial Revolution benefit or hurt society?
- How were efforts at social reform similar to or different from each other?
- What role did Christianity play in promoting the just treatment of workers?

Spread of Industrialization

The Industrial Revolution began in Great Britain. At first, the British tried to prevent knowledge of new technologies from spreading beyond their borders. However, they soon realized that this was impossible, so they decided to make money by exporting their inventions.

British machinery was sent to other European countries and to North America. British laborers traveled to these countries and helped factory owners set up and operate the machines. British investors helped to finance industrial growth in European countries such as France. Many nations profited from the spread of industry, and Great Britain played a leading role in this growth.

Following the pattern of Great Britain, American inventors looked for ways to simplify and speed up work processes. For example, in 1793 **Eli Whitney** invented the **cotton gin**. This device enabled one worker to process fifty pounds of cotton per day, whereas only one pound per day could be processed by hand. Because of inventions such as this, raw materials for factories could be processed at a much faster rate.

Another American, **Cyrus McCormick**, invented a horse-drawn **reaping machine** in 1831. Prior to his invention, many laborers were needed to cut the harvest by hand, and the process was very slow. With McCormick's reaping machine, more acres could be harvested in less time. This device, along with Meikle's threshing machine, led to increased wheat production while reducing the number of farm laborers needed.

What American inventions sped up work processes?

The cotton gin removed the seeds from cotton.

The early reaping machine cut the corn and left it on the ground. Workers had to gather the corn and tie it into bundles.

Effects of Industrialization on Society

Great Britain struggled to meet the problems and challenges that accompanied the Industrial Revolution. Workers endured dangerous and unhealthy working conditions. Crowded cities offered a poor quality of life. Every member of society was affected by the growing pains of an economy that was undergoing large-scale transitions.

Most modern historians focus on these negative aspects of the Industrial Revolution and minimize any positive contributions. A few may reverse this emphasis. The truth lies somewhere in between. New inventions did make work easier and ultimately brought more prosperity to people. In this way, the Creation Mandate continued to be carried out. On the other hand, the problems of industrial growth and lack of concern for workers showed evidence of the Fall.

Growth of Cities

Villages became towns and towns became cities as the British population increased and industry expanded. Fewer workers were needed on the farm, and families moved in order to find work. This migration supplied much-needed labor for the factories and other industries that abounded in the urban areas.

Towns and cities tended to grow quickly. However, adequate housing, roads, and sanitation did not keep pace with the rapid growth. As a result, multiple-story tenement buildings that housed many families were built quickly and crowded together. Traffic congested roads. Industrial waste corrupted water supplies, and smoke from coal-fired furnaces polluted the air.

Cheapside was a busy commercial street in London.

Social Classes

Class distinctions had existed for centuries in Great Britain and other European countries. Though social classes continued to exist, the Industrial Revolution prompted the development of new classes and began to break down the barriers that kept people in the same class their whole lives.

The middle class expanded during the Industrial Revolution and separated into upper and lower parts. Factory owners and wealthy investors composed the upper middle class. Merchants and small business owners composed the lower middle class. Poor laborers, whether on farms, in workshops, or in factories, continued to compose the lower class.

What new social classes came out of the Industrial Revolution?

The Industrial Revolution provided an environment that made social change possible. Families that had endured poverty for generations worked, saved, and improved their lives. Men like Cyrus McCormick and James Watt rose from humble beginnings and became very wealthy through their inventions and hard work. The opposite was also true, however. Children or grandchildren could waste inherited wealth and slide into poverty, highlighting the importance of carefulness in managing resources.

Those who had recently become wealthy tended to reject the widely held view that poverty and ignorance were acceptable. They built libraries and schools to make learning more widely available. Some wealthy industrialists donated up to half of their annual earnings to improve the standard of living for others. This access to learning continued to break down the distinctions between the classes and provided opportunities for more people.

(top) Boys began to work in factories at an early age; (bottom) Luddites attacked machines, such as the spinning jenny.

How was the Luddites' attempt to force change different from that of the trade unions and the Chartists?

Changes to Family Life

Life changed dramatically for families who moved to industrial cities. At first, several members of the family worked in factories. Wages in the factories were low, and everyone (including women and children) had to work long hours to meet financial needs. Family members often had to work different shifts and seldom had time together. This pattern was much different from life on a farm or in a workshop, where families worked hard but were usually together. In addition, the cities were crowded, a situation that brought its own challenges, including the rapid spread of disease by human contact or impure water.

Movements for Social Reform

As the Industrial Revolution progressed, the miserable living and working conditions of industrial workers eventually led to cries for reform. Often these cries came from the workers themselves. Sometimes they came from upper- or middle-class reformers. In time, Parliament passed legislation to protect workers and their families. A major spiritual awakening in the 1700s contributed to the desire to see society changed.

Cries for Reform

From Workers

Workers formed organizations to seek change. **Trade unions** consisted of people who worked in the same industries. They wanted to protect themselves from competition and to convince their employers to raise wages and improve working conditions.

A political movement called **Chartism** expressed the desire of workers to have more say in the government. The members of this movement published a list of goals called the People's Charter. It had six main points: (1) all males should be able to vote, (2) members of Parliament should be paid (so they did not have to try to get money in other ways), (3) members of Parliament should not be required to own a certain amount of property, (4) elections should be held every year, (5) each **electoral district** should include about the same number of people, and (6) voting should be secret.

Trade unions and Chartists were generally peaceful, though trade unions sponsored some disruptive strikes. The **Luddites**, on the other hand, pursued change violently. They were skilled craftsmen who had lost business as a result of the Industrial Revolution. They responded by physically attacking the machines they felt had taken their place. Not surprisingly, their efforts brought no change.

From Reformers

People outside the working class also wanted to help workers. Some were factory owners. Some were members of Parliament or in other ways influential. They pushed for reform legislation.

Government Action

With mounting pressure to act on behalf of workers, Parliament passed several reform measures starting in the early 1800s. These measures gradually reduced the number of working hours and completely prohibited women and children from some types of work. They also attempted to promote education for children.

electoral district section of the country that voted for one or more members of Parliament to represent it

Role of Religion

During this period God sent an evangelical revival to Great Britain. British pastors and evangelists spent countless hours preaching all over England. Factory owners, managers, and government officials responded to the preaching of God's Word. Every level of society changed as people were converted. Owners and managers determined to better care for their workers. Government officials passed laws that improved working conditions and addressed many of society's problems.

Nor were the workers forgotten in this revival. Evangelists preached to coal miners and factory workers. As laborers turned to Christ, they not only worked with a new sense of purpose but also abandoned habits that would have prevented them from improving their lives.

John Wesley became one of the greatest preachers in Britain during the 1700s. He traveled throughout the country on horseback and preached about forty-two thousand sermons. He organized his converts into **Methodist** societies, with laymen (church members other than pastors) serving as leaders.

Thousands from all walks of life were converted under the preaching of Wesley and the witness of many of his followers. Wesley and his followers also supported many reforms, including improved prison conditions and better working conditions.

George Whitefield, another influential preacher, had an international ministry. He preached throughout England, Wales, and the American colonies. Whitefield introduced Wesley to the practice of preaching outdoors to masses who did not attend church. It is estimated that Whitefield preached to as many as twenty thousand people at a time. He often preached thirteen times a week to both large and small groups. Thousands of people trusted Christ during his ministry.

The gospel transformed Great Britain as large numbers of men, women, and children came to Christ. Crime rates dropped. Movements for industrial reform remained largely peaceful. There was a decline in the drunkenness that plagued Great Britain. And the British nation was spared much of the violence that tore apart other European nations during this time.

John Wesley

George Whitefield

How did revival change the behavior of owners and managers, government officials, and workers?

MANCHESTER

Justice

In the early stages of the Industrial Revolution, the working class in Great Britain found itself in a desperate situation. Many could not survive in the cities unless they worked in a factory. But factory equipment tended to maximize production rather than worker safety. Conditions in many early factories were dirty and dangerous. Workers often became sick or were injured. Concerned with profits and having many potential employees to choose from, factory owners at first did not try to make conditions better for their workers.

Power

During the 1830s and 1840s, Parliament began to pass laws to help workers. For example, the 1833 Factory Act placed limits on child labor. Children under nine could not work in a textile factory. Children from nine to thirteen could not work more than eight hours a day and were required to attend school for two hours a day. The Mines Act (1842) banned women and girls as well as boys under ten from working in mines. The Ten Hours Act (1847) prohibited women and young people from working more than ten hours a day in any British industry. Parliament appointed inspectors to check the factories and enforce owner cooperation.

Canals reached Manchester in 1762, helping the city access resources and get goods to market.

Environment

Some mills and factories dumped their waste into rivers and polluted the water supply of industrial cities. Factories burned coal to fuel the steam engines and created terrible air pollution. People complained to their elected officials about the diseases that resulted from these conditions.

Religion

Christian philanthropists (people who give money or time to help improve others' lives) led by journalist Robert Raikes wanted to help children who were working in the factories and had no opportunity for education. Children worked Monday through Saturday but had nothing to do on Sunday, so reformers started "Sunday schools." The schools taught skills like reading and writing (using the Bible as their textbook) and gave religious instruction.

Citizenship

With the coming of each new generation, British citizens in the industrial age began to find themselves in a better position. The wages of the average worker gradually improved. In time, children no longer had to work to help support their families. The mass-produced goods from factories improved the lives of rich and poor alike. Clothing, shoes, and various household items were available at prices most people could afford. In addition, children had greater access to a free education than their parents had. Even higher education became possible for more people than ever before. British society benefited from these changes.

Besides factory workers, industrial cities needed people to build buildings, fix equipment, transport goods, and care for citizens' daily needs.

Need for Other Reforms: The Corn Laws

In this age of reform, the working class had one other major complaint: the price of bread. During the time of Napoleon, Great Britain had refused to trade with the European continent as part of its strategy to defeat the French ruler. After Napoleon was defeated, however, British landowners continued to push for restrictions on foreign cereal grains like corn and wheat to keep the prices of their own crops high. This benefited British agriculture but was devastating to the working class, who could barely afford to eat. Eventually, Parliament would address this issue as well.

The Struggle in Other European Countries

You learned in Chapter 11 that France endured a terrible revolution as the people sought reform. In the middle of the 1800s, Paris again became the scene of several riots over issues such as poor working conditions and low wages.

Labor unrest and a desire for freedom characterized several western European countries in 1848. Workers in France, Hungary, the German territories, and Russia resorted to armed resistance during these disputes. Few if any improvements resulted. Government oppression or indifference continued, and conditions for the laborers did not improve.

WORLDVIEW DILEMMA

What is the proper role of a Christian in making the world a better place?

- **A** Promote government control over industry.
- **B** Look out for your own personal interests.
- **C** Use your talents to improve your society.

12.3 End of the Slave Trade

GUIDING QUESTIONS

- How did abolitionists work to end the slave trade and abolish slavery?
- To what extent did Christianity impact the abolition movement?
- In what ways did the slave trade violate biblical principles?

The transatlantic slave trade was responsible for forcibly transporting well over ten million people from their homes in Africa to the New World (more died along the way). Extending from the 1500s to the 1800s, the slave trade not only subjected Africans to the horrors of the voyage and the injustice of slavery but also seriously weakened the continent they left behind, having removed many of its strong, capable citizens. Over time, especially as news leaked of atrocities onboard ships, more Europeans were confronted with the terrible realities of the slave trade. In response, a growing number found slavery to be a wicked abuse of fellow human beings and began to speak out against it.

The British were among the first to seek an end to slavery. After decades of debate, the practice of slavery ended peacefully in Great Britain. Many in America opposed slavery as well. However, Americans were divided over the issue, and slavery ended only after a civil war had been fought.

Britain

John Newton

William Wilberforce

Olaudah Equiano, a former slave who became a leading British advocate for the abolition of slavery

Quakers were the first known religious group to challenge slavery. Initially, Quakers owned slaves and did not oppose the practice. However, some Quakers began to question the right of one person to own another person. By the 1750s many Quakers rejected slavery and supported **abolition**.

About the same time, John and Charles Wesley also promoted the abolition of slavery. Under their influence, many Methodist laymen became involved in a growing abolitionist movement in Great Britain.

Best known for writing the words to the hymn "Amazing Grace," **John Newton** (1725–1807), a former slave-ship captain, became a Christian in 1748. He had firsthand knowledge of the horrible conditions of the slave trade and became an outspoken critic of slavery. In addition, Newton played a key role in encouraging a promising young member of Parliament to remain in politics.

William Wilberforce (1759–1833) first won election to a seat in Parliament in 1780. When he became a Christian around 1785, he struggled over whether he should remain in politics. Newton and others convinced Wilberforce to remain in Parliament and serve the Lord and the people of Great Britain. He worked to improve conditions for many in his country. However, Wilberforce's greatest achievement was leading the effort to abolish slavery in the British Empire.

Quakers members of an English religious movement that began in the 1600s; known for their belief in an "Inner Light" (God within each person), their informal meetings, and their emphasis on spiritual equality for males and females

abolition officially ending the institution of slavery

While the Quakers were the first to oppose slavery, they had no voice in Parliament. Quakers and Anglicans united their efforts with the formation of the **Committee for the Abolition of the Slave Trade** in 1787. Wilberforce supported this committee but did not officially join until 1791.

From 1791 to 1807 Wilberforce overcame setback after setback in Parliament as he sought to end British involvement in the slave trade. In 1807 Parliament finally passed a bill to end the slave trade in the British Empire. This did not free slaves throughout the British colonies, but it did lay a foundation for the eventual abolition of slavery.

Who led the effort in Parliament to abolish slavery in the British Empire?

TURNING POINTS

Slavery Abolition Act of 1833

The practice of slavery continued to exist in the British Empire for another twenty-six years after the slave trade was officially outlawed. During that time, changing circumstances in the Empire helped the cause of abolitionists in Parliament, who were pushing for a complete end to slavery. First, economic patterns were changing. Sugar plantations in the West Indies, the major location of slave activity in the British Empire, lost some of their economic importance as new trading opportunities opened in other parts of the world. Second, the number of people speaking out against slavery was increasing. They came from a variety of backgrounds: some black and some white, some young and some old, some wealthy and some working class. In 1823 Christian reformers helped to organize the Anti-Slavery Society, which worked to build public support for the abolitionists' cause. Third, opposition to slavery from slaves themselves was becoming both more vocal and more radical. In 1831, for example, a strike in Jamaica that was peaceful at first turned violent. Much property was destroyed; and in the conflict with plantation owners that followed, many slaves were killed.

In July 1833 Parliament considered legislation proposed by abolitionists for a third time. The legislation's official name gives a good summary of its provisions: "An Act for the Abolition of Slavery throughout the British Colonies; for promoting the Industry of the manumitted Slaves; and for compensating the Persons hitherto entitled to the Services of such Slaves." It was passed and then approved by the king on August 28, 1833, just a few weeks after Wilberforce's death. Its provisions, which took effect on August 1, 1834, included the following: (1) The territory of the East India Company and two islands were excluded from the act. (2) Only children under the age of six were immediately freed. Older slaves had to transition to freedom by working as apprentices for a few years. (3) Former slave owners in the Caribbean (but not slaves) were given money to make up for lost income.

Meeting of the British House of Commons

Though the Slavery Abolition Act did not immediately make right all the wrongs Africans had suffered as a result of the slave trade, it did signal a new era for Great Britain. Slavery had been seen for the moral evil that it was. Many people had worked together to pressure for reform, and their efforts had succeeded. And the British Empire had accomplished a significant social change through legislation instead of war.

1. What factors convinced Parliament to abolish slavery in the British Empire?
2. What provisions did the act make for former slaves and former slave owners?
3. What was significant about the way the British Empire accomplished the abolition of slavery?

America

In America, as in Great Britain, Quakers were among the first to speak out against slavery. Organized as the Society of Friends, the Quakers became a consistent voice in early America in opposition to slavery.

Thomas Paine published the first known article in the American colonies that supported the freeing of slaves. He titled the article "African Slavery in America," and he advocated the abolition of slavery by the emerging nation. Two students of Jonathan Edwards, an important figure in the Great Awakening, also published their support for abolition. Some slave owners shared this desire but chose to make provision in their wills for their slaves' freedom.

Even political opponents often agreed to cooperate to abolish slavery. For example, the New York Manumission (freedom from bondage) Society was composed of Federalists John Jay and Alexander Hamilton and Democratic-Republican Aaron Burr.

Congress banned the importation of slaves beginning on January 1, 1808. Authorities did not consistently enforce this ban, but slavery seemed to be declining. However, one laborsaving invention changed the course of American history and ended the trend to abolish slavery.

As you read earlier, Eli Whitney invented the cotton gin. Although he did not personally profit from his invention, this machine turned cotton into a highly profitable crop. Slave labor in the cotton fields aided southern prosperity. The majority of slaves were owned by about one percent of southern landowners. However, that one percent controlled large plantations and exerted a great influence over government officials. America did not abolish slavery until the end of the Civil War in 1865.

Leading American Abolitionists

William Lloyd Garrison and **Frederick Douglass** became two of the most famous American abolitionists. Garrison was the editor of the newspaper *The Liberator*. Through his writing, he influenced many to support abolition. Douglass, a former slave, was a persuasive spokesman for abolition through his dynamic speeches.

Harriet Tubman and **Levi Coffin** were important figures in the Underground Railroad, a secret organization that helped runaway slaves. Tubman escaped slavery herself and led thirteen trips to help other slaves escape. Levi Coffin offered shelter to fleeing slaves and helped more than two thousand get to freedom.

William Lloyd Garrison

Frederick Douglass

Harriet Tubman

Levi Coffin

How did William Lloyd Garrison and Frederick Douglass promote the cause of abolition in America?

CRITICAL THINKING 12.3

Why do you think there were many Christians involved in the abolition movement?

Making Connections

1. Why did the Industrial Revolution begin in Great Britain?
2. Identify important technological developments of the Industrial Revolution in building materials, machinery, power, and transportation.
3. Describe work patterns on a farm, in a cottage industry, and in a factory. Tell how the patterns were similar to or different from each other.
4. How did Great Britain aid the spread of industrialization to other countries?
5. Describe the effects of British industrialization on social classes and on the living conditions and family life of the working class.
6. Compare and contrast the reform efforts of trade unions, Chartists, Luddites, and people outside the working class in the following areas: types of reforms they wanted, whom they wanted to achieve the reforms, and whether they pursued reform peacefully.
7. Describe the role of early abolitionists in opposing slavery.
8. How was Parliament persuaded to end the slave trade?
9. What important pieces of legislation were passed by Parliament in 1807 and 1833?

What to Know

EVENTS

Industrial Revolution

PEOPLE

Richard Arkwright
Henry Cort
Jethro Tull
Andrew Meikle
John Kay
James Hargreaves
James Watt
George Stephenson
Eli Whitney
Cyrus McCormick
Luddites
John Wesley
George Whitefield
John Newton
William Wilberforce
William Lloyd Garrison
Frederick Douglass

TERMS

entrepreneurs
patent
capital
seed drill
threshing machine
flying shuttle
spinning jenny
steam engine
cottage industries
factories
cotton gin
reaping machine
trade unions
Chartism
electoral district
Methodist
abolition
Committee for the Abolition of the Slave Trade

Thinking Critically

1. Did the Industrial Revolution affect the quality of life for the people of Great Britain? Defend your answer.
2. Imagine that a friend tells you that Christians played no role in promoting a just treatment of workers in the 1800s. How would you respond?
3. What evidence suggests that Christianity was a major influence behind the abolition movement?

13 AGE OF RADICALS AND REFORMERS

1831 – 1911

ESSENTIAL QUESTIONS

- What was the impact of new belief systems on nineteenth-century Europe?
- What were the social reform movements of the latter 1800s?
- What were the Western cultural, intellectual, and educational trends during this period?
- What were the challenges to Christianity, and how did Christian leaders respond?
- What were the developments in science and technology during this period?
- How were Latin America and Canada transformed politically, economically, and socially during this period?

The Thames Iron Works, London, England

George Mueller

A radical is a person who favors extreme changes in things like culture, government, school, and religion. During the nineteenth century, there were many radicals devoted to changing the world according to their unbiblical philosophies, but **George Mueller** was a radical devoted to God. He was born on September 27, 1805, in Prussia. As a child, he was a liar and a thief. His father wanted him to become a pastor, not because he wanted George to serve God but because pastoring a church was a prestigious occupation. While training to be a pastor, Mueller was saved after attending a home Bible study. He changed his goal and pursued missionary service. When he went to England to interview with the London Missionary Society, God used illness to divert him. He became a pastor at a small church in Bristol, a busy industrial port city. The city was experiencing the positives and negatives of the Industrial Revolution. It was fast-growing but also full of crime, poverty, dirty streets, and many homeless children.

How was Mueller a radical? He decided to take what God said in His Word seriously. He was disheartened to see Christians acting like the world and even ministries not trusting God but taking loans from the bank. Mueller wanted to demonstrate what it looked like to trust God completely. He made the decision to never ask anyone to meet the needs of the ministry since God had promised to provide for those who were doing His will—in this case, His clear will found in Psalm 82:3, "Defend the poor and fatherless: do justice to the afflicted and needy."

The plight of orphans in England was severe. Many children were put in prison because there was no one to care for them. Even orphanages built expressly to help such children were often managed by cruel, unconcerned people. Many people called attention to this unhappy situation and demanded changes. Christians especially felt compassion toward the orphans and tried to help them.

In 1834 Mueller started the Scripture Knowledge Institute for Home and Abroad. The institute first educated children and adults in the Bible. Secondly, it distributed Bibles, Christian books, and tracts. It also supported missionaries, and the institute's final purpose was to "board, clothe and scripturally educate destitute children who have lost both parents by death."

By the time of his death in 1898, Mueller had built five large orphanage buildings and had cared for 10,024 orphans. He asked God alone for his needs, not making them known to others. Mueller saw about fifty thousand answers to prayer during his life; he kept track of them in a journal. Often, he would go to bed not knowing where the next day's food would come from. Yet God graciously rewarded his faith and supplied his needs. Because of God's faithful provision, thousands of orphans benefited from the work of George Mueller. In addition to helping the orphans, Mueller's life of faith is an example for us today.

Orphan boys on gymnastic equipment at one of George Mueller's orphanages

GUIDING QUESTIONS

- What are the main ideas of Marxism?
- Does Marxism align with biblical teaching?
- How did Darwin's philosophy challenge Christianity?

13.1 Radical Movements

The French Revolution was born of a worldview that attempted to put man on God's throne. Therefore, it left death and destruction in its wake. The only effective remedy for the idea that man can make a perfect world apart from God is the widespread acceptance of the gospel and biblical teaching. Unfortunately, the negative aspects of the Enlightenment that became evident during the French Revolution were able to survive in two ideologies (belief systems), Marxism and Darwinism.

The Industrial Revolution disrupted society as people struggled to adjust to new inventions and ways of life. These dramatic societal changes provided the ground for new unbiblical philosophies to take root and grow.

Marxism

Marxism is a political, economic, and religious theory invented by **Karl Marx**. The goal of Marxism is global, stateless (no countries) **communism**. Marx taught that the world must proceed through five stages before attaining full communism and that most of the world had already gone through the first three. The five stages are primitive communism, feudalism, capitalism, socialism, and finally communism.

Socialism

Socialism is the second-to-last stage of Marxism. Socialism emphasizes the welfare of the group over the individual's right to act freely. At its core, socialism is the government ownership of business. Socialism was a reaction against capitalism. It saw the capitalism that emerged from the Industrial Revolution as unjust because a small number of men controlled the wealth. The solution, as socialists saw it, was to press for social equality by restructuring the system so that workers controlled the wealth they produced. The socialists also emphasized harmony and cooperation throughout society. Instead of a society developed through competition, they sought a classless community where everyone cooperated for the common good. That is why socialism is so attractive. Yet if you have ever worked in a group or played on a team, you realize how difficult it is to get everyone to participate. If the team members will gain no personal reward, usually it is hard to motivate them to do their best for the group.

British Socialists

One of the first advocates for socialism was **Robert Owen**, a British textile manufacturer. He built small factory towns around the mills that he owned. In these towns, child labor and corporal punishment were not allowed. Owen provided every worker with housing, healthcare, and education. He was able to offer these benefits voluntarily from the income of the business.

---

communism the final stage of Marxism, when all property is owned by the government and a country has achieved a supposedly classless society

In 1825 Owen left England and moved to the United States, where he built a socialist community called New Harmony in Indiana. The townspeople did not use money. Instead, they got labor tickets, which represented the number of hours they worked. The experiment failed dramatically from the beginning, and after two years, the socialist community was no more. People lacked any incentive to do the hard jobs, like farming or building houses. They still argued over property even though private property was not allowed. There was no harmony. Unfortunately, Owen did not understand that the socialist model was at the heart of the failure. Instead, he blamed the character of the people for New Harmony's demise.

▲ Historic cabins of New Harmony, Indiana

What is the emphasis of socialism?

French Socialists

Charles Fourier was a French utopian socialist. A utopia is a perfect place, but the word *utopia* actually means "nowhere" since there is no perfect place on earth. Fourier proposed building agricultural communities in which everyone would work for the common good and where wealth would be distributed evenly. He lived on his mother's farm and wrote about his theories but died in 1833 before seeing his ideas tested.

His followers thought the United States would be the best place to test Fourier's socialist theories. In 1855 they founded a community called La Réunion near Dallas, Texas. Most of the residents of La Réunion were French. The Texas land was far less developed than New Harmony, so the challenges were far greater. Like New Harmony, no one owned anything for themselves. The leaders dreamed of a place with beautiful buildings and manicured gardens like Versailles, where people could stroll and discuss philosophy. What they found instead was a barren prairie with one building built by hired help. For a year, they worked together. They cleared 430 acres and built various buildings, including a store and a community office. But in the end, the individuals got no personal reward for their efforts, so the community dissolved.

Christian Socialists

Christian socialists tried to combine Christianity with socialism. They rightly criticized abuses against workers. But like all socialists, they tended to abandon the biblical teaching that all people are born sinners. They also mistook the roles of the church and the state. The church, not government, was commanded in the Bible to help and provide charity to people.

What biblical doctrine did Christian socialists ignore?

Karl Marx

▲ Karl Marx, Friedrich Engels, and Marx's daughters

Karl Marx was born on May 5, 1818, in Prussia. Although Marx's family was ethnically Jewish, they were all baptized and joined the state Evangelical Church of Prussia. Early in his youth Marx wrote a paper about abiding in Christ based on John 15. He wrote, "Thus the union with Christ means a most intimate and vital companionship with Him, keeping Him before our eyes and in our hearts, and being imbued by the highest love for Him."

Marx's high school had humanist teachers that taught and distributed literature about revolution, which prompted the authorities to raid the school. This early exposure to radical thinking started to change Marx's mind. He attended the University of Bonn and the University of Berlin. He wanted to study philosophy and literature, but his father wanted him to study law. In Berlin, he came under the influence of Bruno Bauer, a theology professor who taught that the Bible was not a record of history but mere fantasies written by men. From then on, Marx was a devoted atheist. He joined a radical poetry group and produced some very dark poetry. In a poem called "The Pale Maiden," he wrote,

> Thus Heaven I've forfeited,
> I know it full well.
> My soul, once true to God,
> Is chosen for Hell.

In another poem, "The Fiddler," he wrote,

> With Satan I have struck my deal.
> He chalks the signs, beats time for me,
> I play the death march fast and free.

Marx married Jenny von Westphalen on June 19, 1843. The marriage was controversial since she was a member of the nobility. They had seven children. His son and three daughters died in childhood, while three daughters lived to adulthood. Marx did not earn enough money from his writing to support his family, but he refused to pursue other means of employment. The family depended on the charity of others. His closest friend, Friedrich Engels, worked in a factory and generously supported Marx. Marx also depended on inheritance money from extended family for support. The Marx family lived in poor conditions. Engels claimed that those conditions caused the deaths of Marx's three young daughters.

A letter Marx wrote to Engels offers a glimpse of his family life, "Every day my wife says she wishes she and the children were safely in their graves, and I really cannot blame her." Of the three daughters who lived to adulthood, two committed suicide, and the other died of cancer.

Between 1843 and 1849, Marx was kicked out of Belgium, Prussia, and France because he supported revolution. Prussia and France had to expel him twice during those years. The family finally settled in London, England. Marx died on March 14, 1883, thirty-four years before seeing his theories implemented in Russia.

Communism

Communism Explained

Marx and Engels outlined their philosophy in the book ***The Communist Manifesto***. In this work, they insisted that there are two classes: the oppressor class (the **bourgeoisie**, or owners) and the oppressed class (the **proletariat**, or workers). They claimed that history is a series of struggles between these two classes and that these struggles would end when the proletariat united and violently revolted against the bourgeoisie. Then the workers would be able to establish a classless society. In this society the proletariat would rule, and there would be common ownership of property.

Marx believed that private ownership of property and private control of wealth were evil. Like other socialists, he believed that a small number of men controlling most of the wealth was wrong. He advocated for the ending of inheritance. Marx thought that an item's value came from the cost of materials plus the cost of the work that went into making it. He thought that a business owner who took the profits from sales was unjust because the owner did not work for those profits. Marx did not consider the costs of imagining, building, and running factories. In 1867, Marx produced his second significant work, *Das Kapital*, which was a critique of capitalism and expanded upon the same ideas of *The Communist Manifesto*.

Marx was a materialist; he believed that only matter was real. Rejecting belief in spiritual things, he claimed that belief in God, sin, and salvation through Jesus Christ kept the proletariat in bondage, blinding them to their real needs and their power to change society. Marx famously claimed that religion was the "opium of the people." It drugged people and kept them from seeing reality as they needed to see it. Marx rejected the idea that a sovereign God superintended the course of history. Instead, history moved forward as classes and societies struggled with each other in the pursuit of material gain.

But history has shown when a nation follows the Marxist path and the proletariat takes power, they transform into the bourgeoisie themselves. Since they do not earn that status by productive accomplishment but through theft, they become the most ruthless oppressors of all. With communism the new bourgeoisie uses government power to take property and control the public.

Marx holding a page of the newspaper that he and Engels printed in Cologne from 1848 to 1849

In Marxism, what two groups struggle against each other?

Biblical Response to Communism

The Bible has a lot to say about the Marxist worldview. Firstly, every material thing requires work to produce it. God worked six days to create everything we see around us. While your parents may provide for your material needs without charging you, they had to work to supply those things. In the same way, our salvation is not free; Jesus paid for it on the cross. But Marxists view material things as just being there. They think everyone should have equal material goods regardless of the effort they put forth (or did not put forth) to gain those goods. But someone exchanged something of value for every material object ever created. It is human nature to try to exchange a small amount of effort for a large value. We are always looking for "a deal." Socialism always results in fewer material goods and leads to rationing (a limit on each person's amount). In a free-market economy, the buyer and seller are free to negotiate a price, so it is a win-win.

Work is a blessing, not a curse (Gen. 2:15). A free-market system rewards the hard worker, but a socialist economy punishes him. Paul wrote about the two principles of work, "If any would not work, neither should he eat" (2 Thess. 3:10) and "The labourer is worthy of his reward" (1 Tim. 5:18). It seems that God put in our nature a sense of justice that we should receive a reward for work we perform (1 Cor. 3:12–15). With communism, different levels of work and even failure to work are treated equally, which is unjust. In a free market, the market determines the value of our work, and in heaven, God determines the value of our work.

The Bible prohibits theft (Deut. 5:19). Imagine you avoid socializing with your friends and study hard to get a good grade in your most challenging class. Your goal is to gain admission into a prestigious college. You get an A+, but other students who spent time with friends instead of studying earn a D. Your teacher, however, believes inequality is wrong and decides to take some of your points and give them to another student, raising his grade to a C. This also lowers your grade to a B. This is

what Marxism teaches: "From each according to his ability, to each according to his need." Would you or the other students study hard next time? Probably not. In this case, the teacher is stealing your reward and redistributing it.

In a free-market economy, people can do as they please with their property. If they want to share it with the needy, they have that freedom. But in Marxism, the government decides where the wealth goes. In Marxism, there is no incentive to do the more difficult jobs that take years to master, such as being a doctor or plumber. Why would you work so hard if you knew you would get paid the same amount as those who did not? The Russians living under Soviet communism had a joke: "They pretend to pay us, so we pretend to work."

A common word in the *Manifesto* is "abolition," the abolition of the bourgeoisie, the state, the family, and ultimately the individual. It seems the goals of Marx and Satan were aligned. In the poem "Feelings" Marx wrote, "Worlds I would destroy for ever, / Since I can create no world."

Charles Darwin

Charles Darwin was born on February 12, 1809. His parents were members of the Unitarian Church (a church that does not believe the Bible is God's Word). As a child, Darwin became very interested in nature. At the University of Edinburgh, he studied medicine, and in his free time, he learned about nature. His classes, however, bored him, and his father then sent him to Cambridge to study to be a pastor. Darwin eventually gave up becoming a pastor as well. In 1831 Darwin sailed on a five-year voyage as a naturalist on the HMS *Beagle*. His discoveries led him to start considering theories that all animals descended over time from common ancestors. When he returned to England, he was a celebrity among scientists who had read the reports of his discoveries. Darwin suffered ill health for most of his life, spending many long periods sick in bed. He became the secretary of the Geological Society in 1838.

On January 29, 1839, Darwin married Emma Wedgwood. They had ten children. Darwin struggled with the question of how a good God could design and sustain a world filled with pain and suffering. He concluded that God had little or nothing to do with creating or maintaining this world. The death of his beloved ten-year-old daughter, Annie, in 1851 seemed to him to prove his point. Darwin's ideas evolved. Initially, he did not plainly teach that humans were related to animals; he only suggested it could be true: "Light will be thrown on the origin of man and his history." Darwin died on April 19, 1882, at the age of 73.

Darwinism

Few people have influenced modern thought more than Charles Darwin. His most significant books were *On the Origin of Species* and *The Descent of Man*. His theory that life on earth developed through a series of gradual changes over millions of years led to fundamental changes in the direction of science and its influence on society. As scientists applied this theory, they excluded God and the Bible from consideration as sources of reliable information. Both Darwin's evolutionary theory and creationism (the biblical understanding that God spoke and made all things in six days) are belief systems, not science, because neither can be proven true using scientific methods.

Darwin's Galapagos Island finches, which he believed helped proved his theories

Darwin's observations and conclusions provided the foundation for an evolutionary theory to explain the origin and changes of life. His theory assumed a natural explanation for man's origins. His premise also assumed that spontaneous generation (the idea that life is generated from nonliving materials) was possible. Darwin's observations led him to believe that all living things had developed from a single life form.

His conclusion that humans are not special but just another organism led him to concur with Thomas Malthus that something needed to be done about the overpopulation of humans on the earth. Malthus wrote that overpopulation would eventually cause the food supply to disappear. Therefore, some form of population control was necessary. These are logical conclusions when people are considered part of the animal world. Darwin's theories also allowed for judging people based on their ethnicity, since certain people groups were thought to be more evolved than others.

Many Christians have felt pressured to fit the biblical Creation narrative into the evolutionary story told by the Darwinists. They think that in doing so they remove a great scientific objection to belief in Christianity. But in making this concession to Darwinism, Christians fail to answer the objection that Darwin himself raised against Christianity: how a good God could design and sustain a world filled with pain and suffering. The Bible's answer to this question is that death and suffering are a result of the Fall (Rom. 5:12; 8:20–21). Any attempt to fit the Bible and the theory of evolution together places death and suffering before human sin. It deprives the Christian of the answer to the question that Darwin struggled with. Instead of attempting to fit the Bible into evolutionary theory, Christian scientists should work to show the errors in the theory of evolution and develop alternative scientific explanations that are consistent with Scripture.

? What are Darwinism and creationism?

CRITICAL THINKING 13.1

According to Marx, what would end the cycle of class struggle?

TURNING POINTS

The Acceptance of Darwinism and Marxism

The theme in many of the turning points highlighted in this textbook is the pursuit or attainment of spiritual, economic, or political freedom. Spiritual freedom is a gift from God, which He provided to us through Christ. But the consequences of pursuing freedom *from* God, as Satan did long ago, is death. Marx and Darwin denied the existence of God; by leading the people away from God, they were following Satan.

The cultures of the past one hundred and fifty years have had Darwinism and Marxism as their cornerstones. While Christians have opposed these philosophies over the years, the world system that was already opposed to Christ has continued to embrace them. In the following chapters, you will learn how billions of people experienced horrors, deprivation, and death because they and their leaders accepted Darwinism and Marxism.

How do Darwinism and Marxism relate to each other? Darwinism was the key that opened the door to a Marxist worldview. Darwin allowed for a worldview in which God did not exist; therefore, people could follow Marxism and ignore the principles God established at Creation. Marx and Darwin were like-minded, and when Marx read Darwin's book, he immediately understood the significance. Marx offered to dedicate *Das Kapital* to Darwin, and they corresponded extensively. While they both despised Christianity, Darwin thought religion was temporarily useful in providing people with a moral framework until something could replace it. They both saw struggle as central to how the world worked, the "survival of the fittest."

1. How did Darwin and Marx view the spiritual world?
2. How did Darwin's theory make Marxism easier for people to accept?
3. Why might both theories make the individual unimportant?

GUIDING QUESTIONS

- How did the women's suffrage and temperance movements progress in the West?
- What were the major political reforms in Britain and France during the late nineteenth century?
- Why did anti-Semitism rise during the late nineteenth century?

13.2 Reform Movements and European Anti-Semitism

During the nineteenth century, various groups pressed for societal reform. Two popular movements centered on women's suffrage and the problem of drunkenness. Politicians responded slowly but deliberately to the pressure for reform. As people experienced the pains of rapid change, they found it easy to blame the Jews for their problems.

Women's Suffrage Movement

The right to vote, or **suffrage**, became a popular movement in English-speaking countries during the nineteenth and twentieth centuries. Men who had not previously gained the right to vote demanded this privilege. At the same time, women worked to share this freedom. Middle-class men in England soon found supporters in Parliament to represent their demands. However, women struggled to overcome decades of resistance and reluctance on the part of British officials. Even when women found a measure of support in Parliament, the majority refused to grant them suffrage. Women in America encountered the same resistance from their elected officials.

What right did British and American women pursue in the nineteenth century?

British women established suffrage committees beginning in the 1860s. By 1879 these committees had merged to form the National Union of Women's Suffrage Societies. They presented a united front and relentlessly pressured Parliament. In 1918 Parliament voted to allow British women who were over thirty to vote. Due to the persistence of reformers, all British women over the age of twenty-one received this privilege in 1928.

British women protesting in 1912 for the right to vote

The Temperance Movement

The drinking of beer and other alcoholic beverages was a central issue in nineteenth-century America and Britain. Doctors were just beginning to understand the power of addiction, but everywhere the symptoms of alcoholism were evident. Men, especially, chose alcohol as their drug to escape the troubles of the industrial era. Workers would be absent or would show up drunk. Worse yet they would abuse their wives and children when they were drunk.

British and American Christians along with some concerned non-Christians became deeply troubled by the increased abuse of alcohol. They formed societies to battle drunkenness by supporting **temperance** (drinking in moderation). Other groups thought the best policy was abstinence (no drinking of alcohol).

A political cartoon supporting the Prohibition movement

Temperance in Britain

Two temperance groups in Britain were the British Association for the Promotion of Temperance and the Band of Hope, which sought to protect working-class children from becoming alcoholics.

A division within the British temperance movement occurred over proposed laws to ban drinking. Some preferred to use moral persuasion rather than make drunkenness a legal matter. Legal efforts lost ground when restrictions on beer sales led to rioting. Parliament overturned laws that limited or prohibited the sale of alcohol, and additional efforts to regulate alcohol were met with stiff resistance.

While legal options proved elusive, efforts to reduce drunkenness continued. In 1873 a Catholic abstinence group formed the League of the Cross. Concerned women also formed the British Women's Temperance Association in 1876 to convince men to stop drinking alcohol.

? **What was the result of legal efforts to stop alcohol drinking in Britain?**

Temperance in America

Temperance societies began to form in America during the eighteenth century and continued to multiply through the nineteenth century. Concerned women in America formed the Women's Christian Temperance Union in 1880 to educate the public regarding the evils of alcohol. They worked with students to warn them before they began drinking. The American temperance groups ultimately wanted an amendment to the Constitution that would make the manufacture, sale, and transportation of alcohol illegal. They eventually did achieve that goal, when the Eighteenth Amendment was ratified in 1919.

? **What law did the American temperance groups hope to get passed?**

Economic and Political Reform in Western Europe

Britain and France provide two examples of economic and political reform in Europe during this period. Some of the decisions that preserved Britain from unrest and revolution continued to bless that nation. Likewise, some of the decisions that led France into revolution and political instability continued to plague that nation.

British Reforms

Before the middle of the nineteenth century, the British government had maintained high tariffs on products such as imported grain. These taxes protected those who produced these items in Britain. However, the high prices also burdened the British people.

In 1846 Parliament removed one of these tariffs by repealing the Corn Laws. This decision allowed merchants to import cheaper grain and lowered the cost of food for everyone. By repealing laws that had protected a segment of the market, Britain began to shift toward a free-trade economy. This transition resulted in a dramatic increase in trade and brought great prosperity to Britain.

Benjamin Disraeli giving his first speech in Parliament

While most of the British population had moved from the country to the cities, representation in Parliament did not reflect this change. The growing middle class began to demand a voice in government. They persisted, and the Reform Bill of 1832 entitled the middle class to vote. However, members of the working class remained excluded.

Following the Reform Bill of 1832, additional reform was met with stiff resistance. Finally, **Benjamin Disraeli**, a powerful member of the British Parliament who later became prime minister, supported a bill that doubled the number of men who could vote. In the **Reform Act of 1867**, Parliament granted voting privileges to all male homeowners. This act increased the number of voters to two million out of a population of around five million men. Later reforms provided more representation for those who lived in rural communities.

What government action increased trade for Britain?

Disraeli and Gladstone shaking hands as Gladstone retires, only to return later as prime minister

Two men represented the two sides of the reform arguments in Britain. Disraeli, a conservative, argued for limited reform while his chief opponent, **William Gladstone**, a liberal, stressed expansive domestic reform during his terms as prime minister. Disraeli was prime minister in 1868 and from 1874 to 1880. He sought to manage reform while he defended the power of the king and the church. He was also a strong advocate for the British Empire. Gladstone was prime minister off and on for four different terms between late 1868 and 1894. Gladstone helped to establish a national court system and voting by secret ballot. In addition, he labored to improve public education. Gladstone believed an educated public would produce informed voters.

Throughout this period in Britain, the House of Lords (representatives who are appointed from the nobility) struggled to retain power over the House of Commons (representatives who are elected by the people). However, the Parliament Bill of 1911 changed the balance of power. The House of Lords could no longer veto laws passed by the House of Commons. This bill established the supremacy of the House of Commons over the House of Lords.

French Reforms

France suffered political instability because of Napoleon I's failed attempts to control Europe. European leaders placed Louis XVIII, the brother of Louis XVI, on the French throne. He ruled for nine years until his death. Five kings followed Louis XVIII; most had short reigns. In 1830, following riots, a new populist king took the throne, Louis Phillipe. But the French became unhappy with his rule as well and overthrew Louis Phillipe's government in the Revolution of 1848. That year they elected Louis Napoleon Bonaparte as president of the newly formed Second Republic. In 1852, Louis followed his uncle's example and declared himself president for life, giving himself the title **Napoleon III**, emperor of France.

During Napoleon III's reign, France experienced growth in several areas. Industry developed, and many French families moved from the country to the cities. The French economy expanded as France finally reaped the benefits of the Industrial Revolution. Napoleon III also allowed freedom of the press and the development of labor unions. He expanded voting rights to citizens who formerly could not vote.

However, a disastrous war with Germany led to a humiliating defeat of the French forces. Napoleon III lost favor with the people. The army of the newly formed French Third Republic captured and deposed Napoleon III in 1870. He spent the rest of his life in exile in England.

Napoleon III

? Whom did European leaders put in power in France?

Anti-Semitism in Europe

Amid change in Europe, the ugly reality of **anti-Semitism** (hostility toward Jews) reemerged and became more and more prominent as the nations rushed toward the twentieth century. You may recall from Chapter 2 that the Jews were blamed for calamities. Animosity toward Jews had ebbed and flowed in intensity during succeeding centuries. However, it remained like a smoldering ember ready to burst into flame. The Jews had remained separate from the larger society so that they could retain their culture and beliefs. This separation made them an easy target.

Anti-Semitism in Germany

German composer Richard Wagner provided a glimpse into German anti-Semitism in 1850 when he wrote an essay attacking Jewish composers, including Felix Mendelssohn. He opposed the Jewish influence on German culture. Another glimpse surfaced in 1878 when the Lutheran court chaplain to Kaiser Wilhelm I formed the Christian Social Party to resist Jewish influence in Germany.

? What is anti-Semitism?

The cover of a French journal about the Dreyfus affair

Anti-Semitism in France

The **Dreyfus Affair** exposed a strong undercurrent of anti-Semitism in France. In 1894, the French army accused Alfred Dreyfus, a Jewish artillery captain, of passing military secrets to the Germans. Even though the French government had very little evidence against Dreyfus, they convicted and sentenced him to life in prison on Devil's Island in South America. In 1896 evidence was found that another man, Ferdinand Esterhazy, was the actual person who passed the secrets. Esterhazy was brought to trial but was found innocent and quietly fled to England.

When a popular novelist revealed all the details in a front-page newspaper article, the case divided the nation. Those who held to the ideals of the French Revolution supported Dreyfus, but Catholics and the military condemned him. Riots erupted in some French cities against Dreyfus, especially in French-occupied North Africa.

After a thorough investigation, the Supreme Court annulled (declared invalid) Dreyfus's conviction. But he was again tried by the military and found guilty. The French president offered Dreyfus a pardon if he confessed, which he did since he had suffered so much. Dreyfus later went on to serve heroically in World War I.

The Dreyfus affair is significant because it opened the eyes of a Jewish journalist, **Theodore Herzl**, to the anti-Semitism in Europe. He realized that the Europeans would not allow Jews to participate equally in society. He started a movement called **Zionism**, in which he fought for the reestablishment and development of a Jewish nation in the land of Israel.

What movement began because of the Dreyfus affair?

Anti-Semitism in Russia

Over the centuries, many Jews had fled to Russia to escape persecution in western Europe. The czars welcomed them because of their skills and strong work ethic. However, by the nineteenth century, more and more Russians began to view the Jews with jealousy and suspicion. As revolutionary fervor and violence grew in Russia, the Russians blamed the Jews for assassinations and other crimes. Russian authorities and citizens murdered Jews without regard for age or gender. The term **pogrom** was first used to refer to a sweeping, targeted, and repeated attack on Jews in Russia.

CRITICAL THINKING 13.2

Why did the temperance movement fail to solve the world's social problems?

13.3 Culture, Education, and the Christian Response

Culture in Europe shifted from an idealistic view of man to one that emphasized reality. Writers and artists created works that reflected what they saw rather than what they imagined. Leaders also realized that citizens required education to become a productive and informed society. Public education became more widely available as a result. As cultural change sped up dramatically, Christian leaders faced growing challenges but found that God's Word was just as relevant for the issues of the day.

GUIDING QUESTIONS

- Why did educational opportunities and literacy increase in nineteenth-century Europe?
- How did major movements in literature, music, and the visual arts shape social and cultural values in nineteenth-century Europe?
- How did Christian leaders respond to the challenges of the nineteenth century?

Cultural Movements

Throughout history, cultural movements (the way people see things and interact with others and the world) have come and gone. When people find the cultural movement does not adequately explain reality, they react and start a new cultural movement. Just like the change in the seasons, one movement changes into another. Since the pace of change was speeding up, the West went through three significant cultural movements from 1770 to 1960.

Romanticism

Romanticism dominated the first half of the nineteenth century. Several themes characterize romanticism. Romanticism emphasized emotion over reason and freedom over the rules of any system. As a result, romantics preferred nature to urban life. Truth was not a single thing to be found through science, but rather there were many truths, and they were found through multiple perspectives.

A replica of the Walden Pond cabin of Henry David Thoreau, a famous American romanticist

Romantic Literature

Romantic novels and poetry celebrated nature over industry and mysticism over the organized religion of the church. Novels exalted heroic lovers who followed their hearts or mystics who sought forbidden knowledge even if it led to their destruction. Romanticism taught that it was right for a person to do what his heart told him. In other words, it would be better to rise against impossible odds and do the heroic thing than to rationally weigh the possible outcomes.

? **Where would romantics prefer to live?**

Thomas Cole's romantic painting of the Oxbow, a loop in the Connecticut River, as viewed from Mount Holyoke, Massachusetts

Ludwig van Beethoven

Romantic Art and Music

Romantic paintings are often peaceful scenes of rural life or landscapes. Some artists also painted scenes from the revolutions. In music, composers reacted to the orderly, classical style by moving toward the full, emotion-filled romantic style. Ludwig van Beethoven is perhaps the best-known composer of this age. He mixed classical and romantic elements in his works.

Realism

By the middle of the nineteenth century, realism had replaced romanticism as a new art form. **Realism** reacted against romanticism's dreamlike quality by emphasizing, as its name suggests, what life is really like. In writing and painting, realists pictured everyday life in detail.

However, realism, like romanticism, failed to correctly portray the totality of life. Realism tended to show life as pessimistic and hopeless. Realists seemed to be suspicious of redemption, and their literature implied it would be dishonest to have a happy conclusion.

Realist Literature

Realist authors did not abandon emotion in their writings. Instead, they sought to describe events that occurred in everyday life. At times, the events they described were sad or unpleasant. For example, Charles Dickens wrote about the negative aspects of the Industrial Revolution, including the slums where many workers lived. He vividly described the terrible conditions in the industrial cities and provided the reader a glimpse into the British debtors' prisons. Another realist author, Leo Tolstoy, described the difficulties of life in Russia. In his novel *War and Peace*, he emphasized the struggles of all kinds of people rather than focusing on leaders such as Napoleon or the czar.

A realist painting of London

Realist Art

Realist painters produced works of art that portrayed everyday life. Scenes included common events, such as friends meeting and engaging in conversation. Photography developed during this period, and the reality captured by a photograph may have contributed to the appeal of realism in paintings.

What invention may have influenced realist painters?

Modernism

Modernism was a philosophy that began around the 1890s. It did not just want to describe reality but to change it. The theme of modernism was "the newer the better." It emphasized the new things that could be done through science and industry. It focused on the material world and rejected the existence of a spiritual world. Modernism saw the world as continually improving.

Modernist architects believed that new building materials like steel rendered old styles obsolete. They built buildings with straight lines that were functional rather than decorative. Gone were the columns and facades (decorative building faces) borrowed from the ancient Greeks and Romans. An early example of modernist architecture is the Eiffel Tower. Skyscrapers are another example; built of steel and glass and with straight lines, they are extremely functional.

What was the theme of modernism?

The Eiffel Tower

A modernist painting called "The Arrival" by Christopher Richard Wynne Nevinson

Children experience life in a Victorian school during a visit to Queen Street School in England.

Education

Opportunities for education were very limited in Europe prior to the nineteenth century. The Roman Catholic and Anglican churches still operated most schools and emphasized religious education. However, in Britain and France public education became a priority during the nineteenth century. The government established and financially supported schools. Literacy (the ability to read and write) and a basic education finally became available to most children in these countries.

Education in Britain

Early public education in Britain began with the Sunday school movement. Though we tend to think of Sunday school as a time for Bible training in church, it began as an effort to teach poor children how to read. The teaching occurred on Sunday, so it became known as Sunday school. By 1831 over one million British children had attended these sessions and learned to read. The goal for these students was to be able to read the Bible and learn God's Word.

The public school system began in 1833 when Parliament voted to spend money to build schools for poor children. The government became increasingly involved in education by determining the courses for grammar school in the 1840s. Britain required children to attend school during ages five through ten. In 1893 the government provided educational opportunities for blind and deaf children. By 1918 the British government required education for five- to fourteen-year-old children.

What was the earliest form of public education in Britain? What was its goal?

Education in Germany

During the eighteenth century, Prussia became one of the first European states to provide a free primary education that was required for all children. Improvements included certification for teachers and special schools to train people how to teach.

Shortly after achieving unification in 1871, Germany continued to make advances in education. For example, the new nation established one of the first separate secondary schools for girls in Europe. Continued improvements led to secondary schools that trained German students in ancient and modern languages. Students also received training in science and math. Those students who did not qualify for a college education could receive technical training in preparation for an industrial job.

By the end of the nineteenth century, Germany had developed one of the finest systems of education in Europe. The state regulated these schools and demanded the right to set educational standards.

What would German students who did not qualify for college study?

Education in France

Modern French education began near the end of the nineteenth century. Jules Ferry, the Minister of Public Instruction, created the first school system. It required all children to attend school until the age of fifteen. Ferry made public education free and secular. Prior to these changes, Roman Catholic clergy had played a central role in education. The system established by Ferry has continued with little change.

The Christian Response to Radicals and Reformers

As in any age, the only true answer to society's problems is Christ. During the 1800s, several revivals swept England and America. The preaching of **Charles H. Spurgeon** and Dwight L. Moody brought many people to the Savior. In England, Spurgeon preached Christ-centered messages and worked to confront the issues of his day. He was one of the first to understand and speak against the evils of socialism. At the same time, he built a ministry to meet the needs of the poor children and families of the city. Improved transportation allowed dedicated Christians to go to the mission fields of China, India, and Africa.

Other believers stayed in Europe to establish ministries at home. These Christians helped people by pointing them to Christ. The Salvation Army, the Young Men's Christian Association (YMCA), and the Young Women's Christian Association (YWCA) were started to meet both physical and spiritual needs. Orphanages, schools, hospitals, and Sunday schools provided for the poor and needy. The dedicated Christian men and women who ran these ministries touched many lives as they spread the love of God to those in need. Their works showed their faith by combining the Bible's commands to "preach the gospel" (Mark 16:15) and to "do good unto all men" (Gal. 6:10).

Charles Spurgeon

Men and boys at East End Mission in London, 1895

CRITICAL THINKING 13.3

How were the three cultural movements reactions to each another?

GUIDING QUESTIONS

- What were the major scientific and technological developments during the late nineteenth and early twentieth centuries?
- How did global communication and trade improve in the nineteenth and early twentieth centuries?

13.4 Progress in Science and Technology

Scientists continued to make important discoveries, and inventors came up with new machines to improve life. For centuries, scientific and technological discoveries in the West flowed from a culture that had accepted a biblical worldview. The scientists understood that the world was rational because it was created by a rational God. And if the world worked according to reason, a person could use reason to discover more about how the world worked. Some of the first inventors in Europe were monks who viewed time as a valuable gift from God that should be used to serve Him, so they invented ways to do everyday tasks in less time.

Scientific Discoveries

Major scientific advances occurred during this period, especially in the fields of physics, chemistry, and biology.

James Clerk Maxwell

James Maxwell, a Scottish scientist, made major contributions to the fields of physics and astronomy. Regarded by many as a scientific genius, he predicted the existence of radio waves before their discovery. Perhaps his greatest contribution was combining the sciences of electricity, magnetism, and optics into one model. Other great scientists, including Albert Einstein, built on the foundations laid by Maxwell. While others recognized Maxwell for his great intellect, he acknowledged himself to be but a humble sinner. Maxwell was trained by his mother. He was saved during his college years and matured into a devout man of God.

What did James Clerk Maxwell combine into one model?

James Clerk Maxwell investigating magnetism, light, and molecular spinning tops

Louis Pasteur

Louis Pasteur

Louis Pasteur, a chemist in France, made many important discoveries that prevented several diseases. He developed a method of heating milk and other liquids to slow the development of disease-causing microbes. Today we call this process pasteurization.

Pasteur also made an immense contribution to science by proving that spontaneous generation is a myth. He placed a mixture of sugar and yeast in a flask and heated it to sterilize the mixture. The design of the flask allowed air to enter but prevented dust and microbes from encountering the mixture. If the theory of spontaneous generation was correct, some basic life form should have developed from the sugar-yeast mixture. However, no life forms developed. This discovery struck at the very foundation of the emerging theory of evolution.

What theory did Louis Pasteur prove to be a myth?

Gregor Mendel experimenting with pea plants

Gregor Mendel

Gregor Mendel was a Czech scientist and Catholic church leader, and through his work he came to be known as the father of the study of genetics. By experimenting with pea plants, he proposed theories about how different traits are passed on through the genes. Eventually he formulated Mendel's Laws of Inheritance.

Other Scientific Discoveries

Scientists made other important discoveries concerning viruses, x-rays, the atom, radioactivity, and electromagnetism. They also discovered the laws of thermodynamics. These discoveries were the first steps into these fields that scientists continue to build on today.

Technological Advances

Inventive minds continued to develop improved methods of transportation, communication, and civilization. They also invented technology to make war more deadly. At the same time, society gradually came to replace faith in the God of the Bible with faith in science and human achievement. As a result, improvements in technology tended to increase man's self-confidence and reduce his dependence on God.

Transportation

Railroads

During the 1840s, the British combined their railroad routes into a national network. The railroad became an important method of transporting goods and people across Britain and, later, across Europe. While canals were frozen and unavailable in the winter, railroads could operate year-round. With continuing improvements, the railroads got faster and provided transportation at a reduced cost, benefiting the British economy.

America imported its first steam locomotives and steel rails from Britain and gradually developed rail lines along the east coast. Railroads proved to be strategic during the Civil War as they delivered supplies and troops. The nation quickly recognized the tremendous importance of the railroad, and workers completed the first transcontinental railroad in 1869. The railroad became a vital asset in settling the western United States.

Steamships

With the development of steam-powered engines, several inventors sought to power ships using this new device. For a time, wind-powered ships could travel faster than the early steamships. However, the use of Watts's steam engine, combined with improvements by other inventors, led to faster and faster steamships.

With continued improvements, steamships replaced sail-driven ships and traveled across the ocean. Soon ships carrying mail, other cargo, and hundreds of passengers traveled between Britain and America.

What two modes of transportation developed because of the invention of the steam engine?

Internal Combustion Engine

The steam engine received its power from the burning of wood or coal outside of the engine. The internal combustion engine, however, produced heat by burning gasoline or diesel fuel within the combustion chamber and could therefore be much smaller. This engine revolutionized transportation. Automobiles developed as a combination of many inventions after years of trial and error. Though Europeans developed the first working automobiles, the American entrepreneur Henry Ford designed a mass production process to produce cars cheaply. Ford made it possible for almost everyone to afford a car, and it became essential for transportation in America and around the world.

Henry Ford driving the first type of car he built in 1896

Flight

Man has dreamed of flying for centuries. Sketches by Leonardo da Vinci reveal his interest in human flight. However, the first successful flight did not occur in Europe. **Wilbur and Orville Wright**, two brothers who owned a bicycle shop in Ohio, built the first successful airplane. On a sandy beach in Kitty Hawk, North Carolina, the Wright brothers made their first successful flight on December 17, 1903.

The first flight of Orville Wright at Kill Devil Hills, Kitty Hawk, North Carolina, on December 17, 1903, with Wilbur Wright looking on

Communication

Inventions such as the telegraph, telephone, and radio laid the foundation for global communication. Messages that previously took days or weeks to be delivered could now be transmitted and received in a matter of minutes or seconds.

Telegraph

The telegraph enabled people to send messages to others who lived far away. Operators sent the first messages over wire lines using a code developed by Samuel Morse and his assistant. In 1837 Morse patented the first known machine to send these coded messages. By 1861 telegraph lines stretched across the country to the West Coast. Continued developments enabled operators to transmit many messages at the same time through the existing wire.

In 1866 James Anderson captained the SS *Great Eastern* to lay the first successful telegraph cable across the Atlantic Ocean. This cable enabled operators to send messages directly to Europe. By 1870 Britain had finished a submarine cable to India. Within a few years, operators could send messages around the world.

Telephone and Phonograph

While many men worked to develop the technology that resulted in the telephone, **Alexander Graham Bell** was the first to patent it. The great inventor **Thomas Edison** also worked to improve Bell's invention. Edison had lost most of his hearing as a child. When he first tried to use a telephone, he could not understand what he heard. As a result, Edison made improvements to the telephone that enabled him (and many others) to hear the caller clearly. In 1877 Edison invented the phonograph, which was the first machine to record sound.

?

Why could Edison not use Bell's early version of the telephone?

Samuel Morse with a telegraph machine

Thomas Edison with his phonograph

Radio and Motion Pictures

Guglielmo Marconi, an Italian, invented the radio in 1896. His invention was built upon the theory of electromagnetic radiation put forward by James Maxwell and the work of Heinrich Hertz. Initially the radio could only transmit signals, like a telegraph. But on December 24, 1906, Reginald Fessenden broadcast the first voice transmission over radio waves. The broadcast included a performance of "O Holy Night" and a reading of Luke 2:14. In 1889, William Friese-Greene, an English inventor, was issued a patent for his camera that could take up to ten photographs per second, the earliest motion picture camera.

Weapons

The tools of war became more deadly during this time. In 1803 the British army started using shrapnel shells that contained many bullets. In 1867, **Alfred Nobel** invented dynamite, a high-powered explosive that was one thousand times more powerful than anything before it. Although Nobel did not intend for dynamite to improve the destructive power of weapons, that is what it did. Hiram Maxim invented the Maxim gun in 1884, one of the first machine guns.

What three inventions made war more deadly?

Other Notable Inventions

During the second half of the nineteenth century, inventors devised many products and tools we take for granted today. Edison invented electric lighting that everyone could use, making it possible for people to work through the night. The invention of the safety brake elevator made it feasible to build very tall buildings. Everyday life was made easier with the invention of the refrigerator, the zipper, cellophane, and the vacuum cleaner.

CRITICAL THINKING 13.4

Evaluate one or two of the improvements in technology. How have they improved daily life? How might they have increased man's self-confidence and decreased his dependence on God?

Guglielmo Marconi with his radio

Hiram Maxim with his first machine gun

GUIDING QUESTIONS

- What were the successes and failures of Latin American governments?
- Why did many Latin American countries fail to develop into stable nations?
- How was Mexico affected by foreign interventions?
- How did Canada become an independent nation?

13.5 Latin America and Canada

While most of Europe and the United States benefited from stable governments and growing economies, Latin America searched for stability. Far to the north, Canada slowly advanced toward its goal of becoming a self-governing nation.

Central and South America

Latin America struggled for stability following its independence from Spain and Portugal. The countries faced many problems in governing themselves. The geography and border divisions isolated the nations from each other and caused conflicts over power and resources. The wealthy landowners took over the governments and continued many Spanish policies. The only difference in their rule was that the wealth went to them rather than to Spain. The common people still had no say in government. They were no better off under these leaders than they had been under the Spanish. Strong men called **caudillos** often overthrew the weak governments that had adopted constitutions modeled after those of Great Britain and the United States. Most of these caudillos ruled as dictators. Civil wars and revolts became a way of life in many of these new nations. Although this region is rich in natural resources, the people lacked the freedom and the means to develop those resources.

How did the wealthy landowners in Latin America rule?

Successes

Latin America initially saw little economic growth because it did not have much access to markets off the continent. But in the 1850s, Europe started importing products from Latin America. The wealth from Europe helped to stabilize many of these nations since they could build things like schools and roads with the income. The leaders who ruled responsibly gained the support of most citizens in the country.

Failures

Most of the countries in Latin America tried unsuccessfully to develop a sense of nationality for many years. Often the states warred with one another over territorial disputes and access to natural resources.

In the War of the Triple Alliance (1864–70), Argentina, Brazil, and Uruguay defeated Paraguay. Paraguay's population dropped from over five hundred thousand to two hundred thousand because of wars, disease, and migration. From 1879 to 1884 Chile fought and defeated Bolivia and Peru to gain control of mineral-rich areas.

The gap between the rich and poor in the struggling countries also remained great. By 1910 about 1 percent of the population controlled 85 percent of the land. Wealthy landowners controlled gold mining and food production. Wages for the average worker remained very low, and opportunities for improvement were rare. Rather than confirming the teachings of Marxism, which promised equality, these countries acted like feudal countries. However, when Chile opened its market to free trade, everyone in the country benefited, and Chile found peace and stability.

What caused Latin American nations to fail in developing?

Paraguay Territorial Disputes, 1864

Mexico

Mexico's struggle resembled the struggle of the other Latin American countries. This young country tried in vain to overcome economic and political instability. In addition, the Mexican American War (1846–48) resulted in Mexico losing a large section of its territory to the victorious United States.

In 1861 Napoleon III invaded Mexico under the excuse that Mexico had not paid its debt to France. Napoleon forced Mexico to accept Archduke Ferdinand Maximilian of Austria as its ruler. But he was a puppet of Napoleon III. This foreign rule ended in 1867 when the Mexican government regained power and then tried and executed Maximilian.

The execution of Maximilian

Mexicans elected **Porfirio Díaz** in 1876 based on his promises to form a constitutional democracy and provide prosperity. Once in power, Díaz maintained order and welcomed investments from foreign businesses. Under his leadership, Mexico became one of the most prosperous nations in the region.

Unfortunately, Díaz then transformed his government into a dictatorship and ruled for another thirty-one years. Over time, the people saw him as a pawn of foreign businesses. Many of these companies took advantage of Mexico's financial weakness. As a result, Mexicans developed a hatred for foreign influences.

Following a rigged election in 1910 in which Díaz was declared the winner, the people overthrew the dictator. The people of Mexico elected Francisco Madero in 1911, but an assassin killed him two years later. Civil war followed, and an estimated nine hundred thousand people died in the fighting. Assassinations and revolutions prolonged Mexico's struggle for democracy for another six years.

Mexican president Porfirio Diaz

What country invaded Mexico in the 1860s and set up a puppet ruler?

Canada

Canada began as a French colony. The British won this vast territory because of their victory in the Seven Years' War (1756–63). The British passed the Quebec Act in 1774 to keep the loyalty of the French Canadians. The act granted the French Canadians special rights by retaining French civil law and allowing the practice of Roman Catholicism. While this pleased the French Canadians, it alarmed American colonials and played a role in their eventual War for Independence.

Colonists in Canada were not satisfied for long. In 1837 rebellions against the British government occurred throughout Canada. British forces defeated the rebels and arrested hundreds of Canadians.

To establish a long-term solution, the British government sent Lord Durham to be Governor General of British North America and to investigate the problems of Canada. He returned to Britain six months later with a report. Durham advised that Parliament grant the Canadians the right to govern themselves in domestic matters while Britain would control foreign dealings. He also recommended that Parliament unite the Canadian provinces. Parliament accepted the second recommendation and made this official with the Act of Union in 1840.

The British North America Act in 1867 created the dominion of Canada with four provinces: Ontario, Quebec, New Brunswick, and Nova Scotia. The government established the province of Manitoba in 1870. British Columbia and Prince Edward Island became provinces in the 1870s. In 1905, Alberta and Saskatchewan also became provinces. Newfoundland and Labrador became the tenth province, joining the Canadian Confederation in 1949.

What act initially secured French Canadian loyalty to Britain?

CRITICAL THINKING 13.5

Contrast the British government's treatment of Canada with its treatment of the American colonies.

Canada, 1867

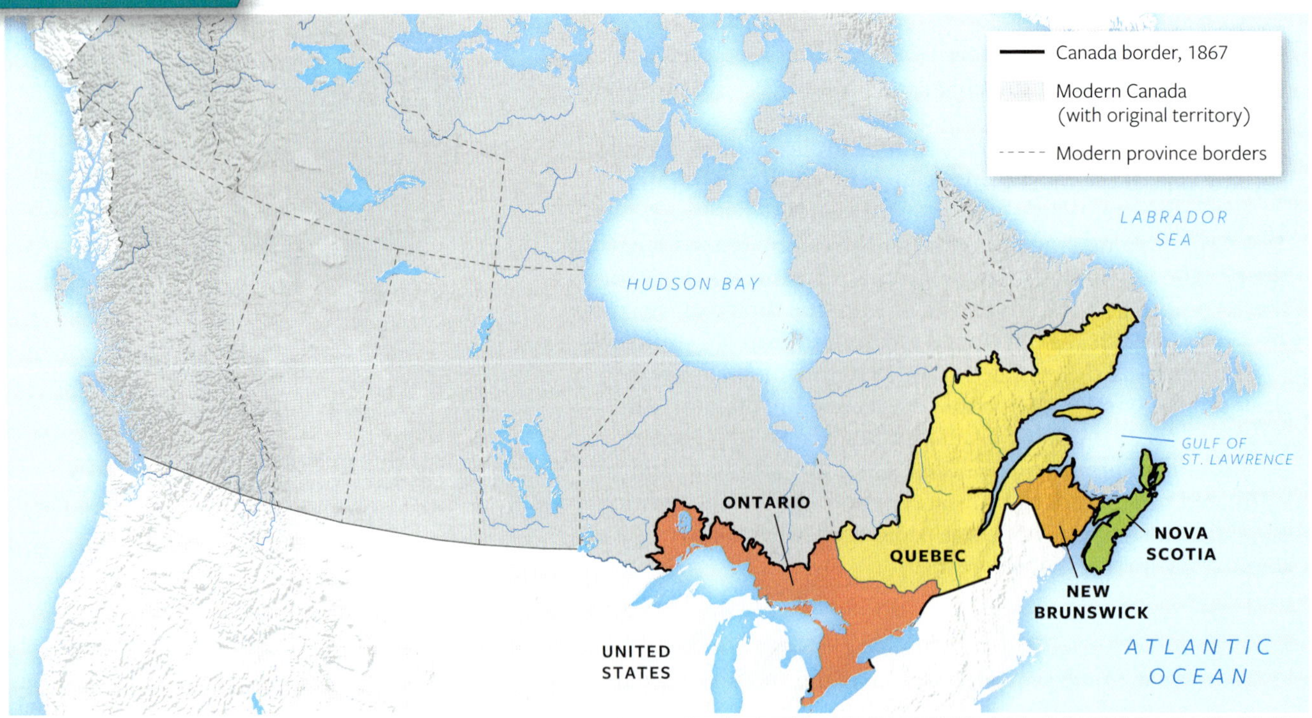

Making Connections

1. What is the central conflict in the world according to Marx?
2. Why did several European countries expel Karl Marx?
3. According to Darwin, where do humans come from?
4. Why are Christians unable to blend the Darwinist story with the Bible's account?
5. Why did legal efforts to ban drinking in Britain fail?
6. What was the result of Britain's shift toward a free trade economy?
7. How did German composer Richard Wagner demonstrate an anti-Semitic attitude?
8. How did education change in Europe in the nineteenth century?
9. Which type of painting would probably be brighter and more colorful, romantic or realist? Why?
10. What material did modern architects use to build their buildings?
11. How did Charles Spurgeon respond to radical movements?
12. Describe Louis Pasteur's contribution to science.
13. How did a biblical worldview inspire scientists and inventors?
14. Why did some Latin American countries succeed?
15. Why did France invade Mexico? What was the effect?
16. How did Canada become a nation?

Thinking Critically

1. Considering George Mueller and Karl Marx had a similar background, how did they try to solve social problems so differently?
2. What are the strengths and weaknesses of the philosophy of realism?
3. Based on the information in previous chapters and this chapter, describe the political reforms that allowed Britain to enjoy greater prosperity and political stability than France.
4. Compare and contrast the Latin American countries that succeeded in gaining stability with those that failed.

What to Know

DATES & EVENTS

Reform Act of 1867
Dreyfus Affair
British North America Act

PEOPLE

George Mueller
Karl Marx
Robert Owen
Charles Fourier
Charles Darwin
Benjamin Disraeli
William Gladstone
Napoleon III
Theodore Herzl
Charles Spurgeon
James Maxwell
Louis Pasteur
Gregor Mendel
Wilbur and Orville Wright
Alexander Graham Bell
Thomas Edison
Guglielmo Marconi
Alfred Nobel
Porfirio Díaz

TERMS

Marxism
communism
socialism
The Communist Manifesto
bourgeoisie
proletariat
suffrage
temperance
anti-Semitism
Zionism
pogrom
romanticism
realism
modernism
caudillos

14 COLONIAL AFRICA

1830 – 1914

ESSENTIAL QUESTIONS

- How was Africa affected by efforts to develop it in the mid-1800s?
- How did European imperialism progress in Africa?
- Is the policy of imperialism consistent with a biblical worldview?
- How did imperialism impact Africa?

The Battle of Adwa

Starting in the late 1800s, Europeans almost completely redrew the map of Africa. They took territory and established colonies throughout the continent. Only two states (political units) escaped colonization during this period: Liberia and Ethiopia. Liberia was established as a home for former slaves and free people of color from the United States. Its connection with the United States likely helped to protect it. Ethiopia, on the other hand, was the only African state that successfully protected its independence on the battlefield.

Ethiopia was a collection of small kingdoms in the region known as the Horn of Africa. Italy had gained access to a port in the region, and the Italians began pushing for more influence in the surrounding territory. When the Ethiopian emperor Yohannes IV died in 1889, a local leader, Sahle Maryam, gained power. With European help, he strengthened his military and dominated other kingdoms, eventually becoming Emperor **Menelik II** in November of 1889.

Earlier in 1889, Menelik had signed the Treaty of Wichale with Italy. Most of the treaty's terms seemed routine. They included an Italian loan for Ethiopia and the granting of coastal territory in eastern Ethiopia to Italy. (This territory became the Italian colony of Eritrea.) Article XVII of the treaty was a problem, however. Some said there were two versions of this article. There were certainly two opinions on its interpretation. The article talked about Italy's helping Ethiopia with diplomacy. The Ethiopians believed getting Italy's help was an option; the Italians believed it was a requirement. If the Italians were right, the Ethiopians would be giving up some of their independence to Italy. Menelik was not willing to do this. He rejected first the article and later the treaty itself. With tensions high, Italy prepared for conflict.

In 1895 Italy stopped an uprising in Eritrea and defeated the Ethiopians in a battle. Several months later, Ethiopia defeated Italy in a battle. As the months wore on, both sides ran low on supplies. Facing off in the Tigray province of northern Ethiopia, they each waited on the other to make a move. The Italian commander, General Oreste Baratieri, wanted to retreat in late February 1896, knowing that he was outnumbered and running out of food. However, the ruler of Italy insisted that he attack. The troops finally began moving out just after midnight on March 1. Italy had about 14,500 battle troops to Ethiopia's approximately 100,000.

The Italians seemed to have a workable strategy. Three of their brigades (units within an army) would march to the peaks of nearby mountains and attack from the high ground. Their strategy failed, though. Their maps were inaccurate, and the brigades had trouble communicating. In the meantime, the Ethiopian troops moved out. They engaged the Italian troops near the town of Adwa. After a few hours of fighting, 25,000 reserve forces joined the Ethiopian troops and overwhelmed the Italians. Eventually, all the Italian brigades were forced to surrender.

Surprisingly, Menelik was not severe in his peace demands. He achieved his main goal, which was the recognition of Ethiopian independence, with the Treaty of Addis Ababa (October 1896). Though Ethiopia was defeated and briefly occupied by Italy during World War II, the military victory at the Battle of Adwa brought the country significant prestige among the nations of Europe. It also stood as a proud symbol of African determination.

Colonial administrators and tribal messengers in Nigeria

GUIDING QUESTIONS

- How did the African states change following the end of the slave trade?
- Why did the African interior open to the outside world?
- What were some characteristics of nineteenth-century missions in Africa?
- How and why were the earliest European colonies in Africa established?

14.1 Africa after the Slave Trade

Newly freed from the influence of the slave trade, Africa made great progress in the second half of the 1800s. Many Africans modernized their states and improved their way of life. However, by the end of the 1800s, European powers began to interfere in Africa to take greater advantage of African resources. **Colonialism**, the conquest of one nation by another nation, became Europe's goal in its quest to control Africa. **Imperialism**, the dominance and power asserted by one nation over less powerful nations, became the accepted practice of the period.

Progress in the Continent

Economic Transition

The slave trade had ended along the coasts of Africa, thanks in large part to the efforts of the British navy. Much of the African economy changed from selling slaves to providing raw materials needed by industrial countries. Palm oil was a leading export because industrial nations used it to lubricate their machines. Other materials included ivory, beeswax, honey, cotton, and rubber.

(top left) Ivory tusks; (top right) Oil palm tree fruit; (bottom) Tapping a rubber tree

How did African states make money following the end of the slave trade?

Quality of Life

Warfare and raiding of enemy tribes had gone on before the slave trade. However, the demand for slaves in the New World had led to a great increase of both. When the slave trade ended, the warfare and raids declined significantly. Africa experienced a steady increase in population. Tribes also gained some stability. Peaceful conditions in many areas allowed them to settle rather than continue to migrate.

Powerful tribal leaders had controlled the slave trade and the wealth it generated. Once slavery ended, there was an improved distribution of wealth. Anyone could harvest the natural resources, and many Africans took advantage of new opportunities in this **gathering-based economy**.

gathering-based economy economy that sells things that are collected rather than grown or manufactured

Most important of all was the changed status of the Africans. After centuries of being treated as objects for sale, Africans instead established themselves as producers and important members of the worldwide trading network.

Why were African tribes able to settle in one place rather than be forced to migrate?

Unification

African commerce had been regional for centuries. There were separate markets for the coasts bordering the Atlantic Ocean, the Mediterranean Sea, and the Indian Ocean. During the 1800s, however, these commercial routes united. This unification expanded trade and brought great wealth to Africa and its people.

Modernization

African states began to modernize their economies by encouraging the development of industries. For example, Egypt built many factories. In them, workers produced textiles, processed wood, made glass, and produced paper.

Some African states also modernized their armies in anticipation of possible threats from European nations. Menelik of Ethiopia replaced his poorly trained volunteer army with well-equipped and well-trained soldiers. He built factories to assemble modern military equipment. General **Samori Ture** also developed a modern army with up-to-date weapons to defend the empire he built in West Africa, known as the **Wassoulou Empire**.

Educational and Political Development

Many Africans in the 1800s received schooling and demanded a voice in their governments. Some struggles led to violence, while others remained peaceful. For example, states on the west coast of Africa won representation without violence.

The **Fante Confederation** formed along the coast of Ghana in 1868. This organization, led by African pastors and teachers, was an excellent example of Africans working to maintain self-rule and to improve the lives of their people. The confederation produced a constitution that reflected a spirit of cooperation, promoted education for both males and females, and advocated the development of African resources to benefit Africans. The supporters of the confederation had worthy goals: technical training in addition to a basic education for all African children, the development of self-reliant citizens, and cooperation between educated Africans (who tended to abandon tradition) and those who maintained African traditions.

Sadly, conflict between the British and the Asante Empire (located in central Ghana) destroyed the possible attainment of the lofty goals of the Fante Confederation. The British were determined to gain control over portions of the Gold Coast in West Africa. To help achieve this goal, they purchased a Dutch fort along the coast. However, the Asante Empire had worked in cooperation with the Dutch and used this region to gain access to the coast. The British intrusion threatened Asante trade. The Asante responded by invading the region. British forces eventually forced the Asante to retreat. They seized control of this region of Ghana in 1873, forcing the Asante Empire to submit to British control and effectively ending the Fante Confederation.

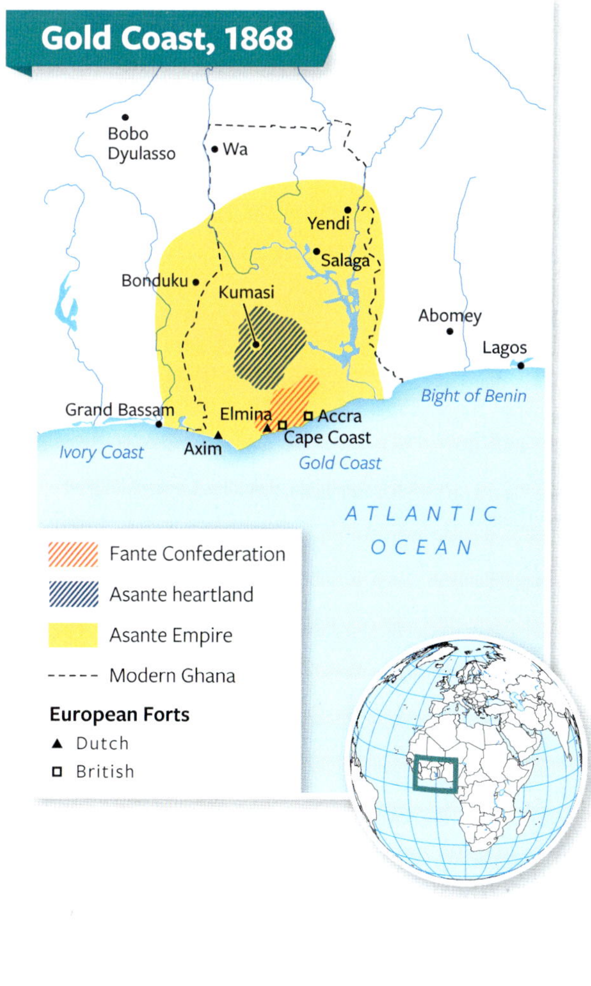

What were some goals of the Fante Confederation?

Opening the Interior

The interior of Africa (the regions not touching the coasts) had long been a mystery to the rest of the world due to its dense forests and difficult terrain. However, two developments in the second half of the 1800s drew attention to that part of the continent. First, tribes from the interior increased trade with tribes on the coast. Second, European exploration dramatically increased knowledge of and interest in the African interior.

Increased Trade

What prompted the growth of trade in Africa's interior?

The more demand increased for Africa's natural resources, the greater their value. Cash crops (crops that are raised to sell) provided a growing income for many Africans. Tribes that had not previously engaged in trade began to do so. As a result, economic opportunity spread into the interior of the African continent.

European Exploration

Many Europeans explored Africa to answer questions they had long had about the continent. For example, Sir Richard Burton searched for the elusive source of the Nile River. He and another explorer concluded that the Nile began in a lake called *Ukerewe* or *Nalubaale* by the Africans. Burton's associate later named the lake Victoria in honor of Queen Victoria.

The most famous European explorer in Africa during the 1800s was **David Livingstone** (1813–73). Born in Scotland, he arrived in South Africa in 1840 and traveled throughout Africa until his death in 1873. His few trips to Great Britain allowed him to set before Europe the need for missionaries in Africa.

Livingstone ventured inland to places no European had been known to visit. He followed the Zambezi River and discovered the falls that the Africans called *Mosi-oa-Tunya* (the Smoke that Thunders). Other Europeans named these falls **Victoria Falls**.

Livingstone also traveled to Lake Tanganyika. It was there in 1871 that **Henry Stanley**, a Welsh reporter, found him. The *New York Herald* newspaper had sent Stanley to find Livingstone after he had been out of contact for several months. Livingstone later died near this lake.

Livingstone's body was buried in Westminster Abbey (London), but his heart was buried in Africa.

Victoria Falls

Early Missionary Outreach

Scottish-born **Robert Moffat** became one of the earliest British missionaries to serve in Africa. At eighteen, Moffat met some Methodists and heard the gospel. After weeks of searching the Bible for answers, he trusted Christ for salvation in 1816. Shortly after his conversion, Moffat decided to serve abroad as a missionary. In 1817 Moffat landed in South Africa and began a ministry that lasted fifty-three years. His fiancée joined him in South Africa two years later. They were married in December 1819.

Moffat took the gospel to many tribes and established a mission that became a launching point for later missionaries. He established friendships with several tribal leaders and worked to bring peace to the area. He also translated the Bible and other works into one of the African languages. His work continued to the next generation when his daughter Mary married David Livingstone.

In response to the pleas for help from men like Moffat and Livingstone, more missionaries took up the work in Africa. In addition to sharing the gospel, missionaries established schools, provided medical care, and trained Africans in a variety of occupations.

? **How did Robert Moffat's mission help later missionaries?**

Robert and Mary Moffat with daughter Mary Livingstone

Samuel Ajayi Crowther

Samuel Ajayi Crowther, named Ajayi at birth, was born around 1809 in Nigeria. When Ajayi was about twelve, his whole village was captured by Muslim slave raiders. The Muslims sold them to Portuguese slave traders, but a British navy ship intercepted the traders and rescued the captives. The British took them to Freetown, Sierra Leone. There Ajayi received care from the Anglican Church Missionary Society and learned English. He converted to Christianity and, upon baptism, took the name Samuel Ajayi Crowther.

Crowther attended the Fourah Bay Institution, an Anglican missionary school, beginning in 1827. He developed a great interest in linguistics and mastered several languages. He soon advanced from student to teacher. In 1842, after further study in London, he was ordained to the ministry.

Crowther labored for many years to translate the Bible into the Yoruba language. He concentrated on this language because many of the Africans who had gathered at Freetown were members of the Yoruba tribe. When they returned to their original homes, they took the gospel and education back to their people. Crowther also promoted an African-led outreach to the Yoruba and, eventually, to all of Africa.

In 1864 Crowther became the first African bishop in the Anglican Church. That same year Oxford University recognized Crowther's great contribution to Africa by giving him a Doctor of Divinity degree. He served in various roles, including overseeing the production and refining of African translations of the Bible, until shortly before his death in 1891.

Early Coastal Settlements

Early Patterns of Colonization

Initially, European colonization of Africa involved setting up colonies on uninhabited islands to establish trade with mainland Africa. Over time, European nations began to lay claim to coastal territory on the continent. Portugal, Great Britain, and France established some of the earliest coastal settlements in Africa.

Portugal

In Chapter 5 you learned that Portugal was one of the first European nations to sail around Africa and visit port cities in East Africa. Though Portugal lacked the ability to develop into a major power, the Portuguese retained control of these coastal settlements and profited from the ongoing trade.

Great Britain

In Chapter 10 you learned that Britain expanded its exploration following the loss of the American colonies. In addition to major discoveries in the South Pacific, British explorers established trade colonies in West Africa. Early British trade with Africa involved slaves primarily. When the British ended this terrible practice, African raw materials grew into a large and profitable industry for British merchants. The expanding Industrial Revolution provided a growing demand for these items.

France

In the 1700s the British hindered and ultimately ended France's first colonial empire. However, the French viewed themselves as a world power, and they believed a world power needed colonies. As a result, they invaded Algeria in North Africa in 1830, beginning the **Second French Colonial Empire**. The Algerians resisted for several years before French forces defeated them. Another fifty years passed before France acquired additional territory in Africa.

What was the beginning of the Second French Colonial Empire?

CRITICAL THINKING 14.1

1. To what extent did African life improve following the end of the slave trade?
2. How would translation work, like that of Robert Moffat and Samuel Ajayi Crowther, help to strengthen African believers?

14.2 Partitioning of Africa for Imperialism

In 1879 several events triggered a rapid conquest and partitioning of the continent of Africa. First, the French sent three groups to determine routes for a trans-Saharan railway. Second, the French appointed a commander in North Africa to expand French interests farther inland. Third, King Leopold of Belgium and the French sent diplomats to secure treaties with tribes in the Congo basin (in west central Africa).

Since Britain and Portugal had previously laid claim to the Congo region, these moves created great alarm. Continued expansion by France and Belgium resulted in claims by Britain and other European nations. Soon, almost all of Africa came under European domination.

GUIDING QUESTIONS

- Were motives for imperialism consistent with biblical principles?
- What happened during the Scramble for Africa?
- How successfully did Africans resist imperialistic conquest?

Motives for Imperialism

It is sometimes hard to understand why the Europeans chose to colonize Africa. Making money was clearly a motivation. However, while some colonies promised financial gain, others seemed to be a financial drain on their mother countries. The reality is that Europeans had a variety of motives for imperialism. Understanding these motives gives the opportunity to evaluate the reasoning that prompted their behavior.

Economics

Because of the Industrial Revolution and free-trade policies, international trade grew rapidly in the 1800s. As more European nations developed industries, however, existing industries faced greater competition. To help their own industries, nations raised tariffs. This increased the price of foreign goods, but it also hindered trade between nations. The desire for new markets created a demand for colonies that could be forced to buy European products.

The increasing need for raw materials also made control of resources in Africa appealing to the European nations. Africa already supplied a growing quantity of raw materials to industrialized Europe. However, European powers thought they could better manage and profit from Africa's resources if they took direct control.

Finally, financiers who had profited from investments made during the Industrial Revolution sought new places to invest funds. Africa appeared to offer vast potential for economic profit.

How did the desire for new markets create a demand for colonies?

Nationalism

Europe in the 1800s displayed an exaggerated spirit of nationalism. This feeling was especially strong in Germany and Italy, which were each recently unified. They were barely a decade old when they set out to prove that they were worthy of being world powers. Taking colonies in Africa provided an opportunity for them to compete with the established European powers.

France had experienced several upheavals at home and defeats abroad in the 1800s. A humiliating loss to Germany in 1870 left the French desperate for a victory. French pride was at stake, and the conquest of African states provided France with a way to regain its standing in the world.

What two recently unified European powers quickly joined the race to colonize Africa?

Religion

Some Europeans claimed that colonialism was valuable for expanding evangelistic outreach in Africa. Of those, some used evangelization simply as cover for their sinful treatment of the Africans. Others genuinely saw colonialism as a way to spread the gospel but were blinded to the negative aspects of colonialism.

Some missionaries opposed colonialism. They were often in conflict with the colonial rulers. Because they lived among the Africans, these missionaries often developed close relationships with them and tried to understand life from the Africans' viewpoint. They protested the ill treatment of Africans by colonial rulers.

Whether colonialism was helping or hindering evangelism, the colonial era was a time of great missionary advance. By the end of the 1800s, almost six thousand British missionaries had traveled to foreign lands under British control. Many of these missionaries were in Africa.

Racism

Tragically, many Europeans used the lie that Europeans were superior to the African people to justify colonialism and imperialism. As Darwin's theory of evolution became more popular, it offered support for the idea that some people groups were more advanced than others. Using Darwin's theory of the survival of the fittest, Europeans concluded that they were part of a superior race. This attitude of superiority was reflected in some of the literature of the day, such as Rudyard Kipling's poem "The White Man's Burden," which asserted the white man's obligation to civilize the "heathen."

Many African scholars sought to challenge this prejudice against Africans. For example, **James Africanus Horton** disproved the claims that the black man was racially inferior. His work *West African Countries and Peoples: A Vindication of the African Race*, published in 1868, argued that different stages of civilization had nothing to do with race.

? **How was Darwin's theory of evolution used to justify colonialism and imperialism?**

▲ Africanus Horton was a doctor, a soldier, and an entrepreneur. He argued for African equality and self-rule.

The Scramble for Africa

In what is known as the **Scramble for Africa**, European nations advanced in three phases to control the continent. In the first phase, Europeans pressured Africans to sign treaties giving the Europeans exclusive trade and mining rights. In exchange, the Europeans often made promises they did not intend to keep, such as protecting the African peoples from enemy attack. In the second phase, representatives of European nations met with each other to work out agreements. They signed treaties that defined their regions of interest in Africa and agreed on boundaries to avoid conflict. They signed these treaties in Europe with no Africans present. The most significant event of the second phase was the **Berlin Conference of 1884–85**. In the third phase, European nations used military power to subdue African armies. By the end of the third phase, all but two African states had lost their independence. France, Portugal, Belgium, Great Britain, and Germany had taken possession of most of Africa.

Imperialism in Africa 1914

TURNING POINTS

Berlin Conference of 1884–85

The Berlin Conference was a series of negotiations designed to set rules and settle disputes about the colonization of Africa. The conference began November 15, 1884, and concluded February 26, 1885.

Officially, the conference's purpose was to settle the status of the lands around the Congo River in Central Africa. King Leopold II of Belgium had been secretly building up personal territory in that region, and the French, Portuguese, and British all wanted to limit his expansion. Portugal wanted to control the mouth of the Congo River, and that claim also needed to be considered. Then there was the entrance of Germany into the quest for African colonies. The presence of this powerful new competitor worried those with existing claims in the continent.

Otto von Bismarck, the political leader of the German government, called the conference. There were fourteen participants, mostly from Europe but also including the Ottoman Empire and the United States.

Conference decisions were confirmed by an agreement called the General Act. The act's provisions included the following: (1) No slavery would be allowed in Africa. (2) King Leopold II could keep the territory he claimed in Central Africa (denying Portugal's claim to the mouth of the Congo River). (3) European nations could trade freely in the Congo region. (4) Shipping would not be hindered on the Niger or Congo Rivers. (5) No European nation could claim African territory unless it established "effective occupation" there. Generally, this seemed to mean signing treaties with the local people and establishing some type of government. (6) Any new territory taken along the African coast must be reported to all conference participants. (7) Each nation was given a zone of influence in Africa. The boundaries for zones were set using lines of latitude and longitude or geographical features.

The Berlin Conference started a rapid colonization of the African continent. European nations controlled only 11 percent of African territory in 1875, but by 1902 they controlled 90 percent. For the European nations, the competition produced by their interactions in Africa helped lead them down the path toward world war. For Africa, the effects of the colonial period continued to be felt far into the future, even after the last African country gained its independence from European control.

1. What region of Africa was disputed by several European powers?
2. What were the provisions of the General Act?
3. How did European colonization of Africa change after the Berlin Conference?

France

France dominated the region of West Africa. To their original territory of Algeria, the French added French West Africa, Senegal, Tunisia, and most of Morocco. France also established a significant presence in Central Africa with the founding of French Equatorial Africa.

? **Where were most French African possessions located?**

Portugal

Portugal had two colonies in southern Africa: Angola on the west coast and Mozambique on the east coast. Like other African colonial territories, these had been exploited for the slave trade first but later provided natural resources.

Belgium

Leopold II of Belgium had first tried using his family fortune to purchase existing, undeveloped colonies in Africa from other European nations. However, his efforts failed. Leopold then took advantage of pleas from men like David Livingstone to "heal this open sore of the world," the "open sore" being damage done to Africa as a result of the slave trade. Leopold played the role of a humanitarian (one concerned for human welfare). His motives, however, were anything but noble, as later became evident.

Leopold hosted a convention of explorers in 1876 and offered to help pay for the cost of exploration. He also encouraged investments by other nations in an organization called the **International African Association (IAA)**, of which he was the president. Europeans initially saw Leopold as the leader of the crusade against slavery. The fact that he used his own money made him look even better. Leopold had finally gotten access to Africa.

By 1882 Leopold owned the company that resulted from the IAA. It was named the International Congo Society. The questionable actions of the company began to make the other European nations nervous.

Investors in the IAA later found that Leopold encouraged the harsh treatment and torture of African workers (slaves) on his plantations. Leopold's detestable actions caused an outcry that persuaded the Belgian government in 1908 to take control of the territory where Leopold had been operating. The territory was in the interior of Africa along the Congo River. It was renamed the **Belgian Congo**.

Leopold II

Why did the Belgian government take territory away from Leopold in 1908?

Africans were forced to provide grueling manual labor in Leopold II's Congo Free State.

Great Britain

South Africa

The British established Cape Colony at the tip of South Africa in 1806 when they were fighting Napoleon. At that time, controlling the southern tip of Africa was important because ships had to pass that way to get to Asia. After Napoleon was defeated, the British sent settlers and continued to develop the colony. This put them in conflict with the Boers, Dutch settlers who had come to South Africa starting in the 1600s. The Boers moved north and established two new territories of their own, the Orange Free State and the Transvaal. Conflict with the British in the late 1870s led to the recognition of Boer independence.

One of the most influential British imperialists in Africa was Cecil Rhodes. Rhodes was a businessman and politician. He started in the diamond business in 1871. He bought so many diamond mines that he eventually controlled most of the world's diamond trade. He also invested heavily in gold mines. Rhodes became the Prime Minister of Cape Colony in 1890. He established a new colony to the north that was named Rhodesia after him. Rhodes lost political favor when he sponsored a raid on Boer territory without the approval of the British government.

The Kimberley Mine in South Africa is the world's largest diamond mine.

The conflict caused by Rhodes's raid led to the **Boer War** (1899–1902), fought between the British and Dutch settlers in South Africa. Though the British eventually won the war, the costs were great. A few years after the war, the Boer territories were incorporated into a new state called the Union of South Africa.

Both British and Dutch citizens of the new state participated in its government, but black South Africans were left out (despite strong protests). Throughout this period, black South Africans at times were pushed out of their territory, used for their labor, or denied the rights to vote and hold office.

?

What European colonists fought each other for control of South Africa?

North Africa

Great Britain developed a strong interest in Egypt when the Suez Canal was completed in 1869. The canal connected the Mediterranean Sea to the Red Sea by way of the Gulf of Suez. The trading route between Europe and Asia was greatly shortened as a result.

Egypt was ruled from 1805 to 1848 by Muhammad Ali, an Ottoman governor of Albanian descent. Muhammad Ali did much to modernize Egypt. His work was continued by his grandson, Isma'il Pasha, beginning in November of 1848. Isma'il undertook many massive construction projects, including the Suez Canal. In the process, he put the country into deep debt. Because of the debt, Isma'il had to sell Egypt's shares of the Suez Canal Company to the British government. Great Britain used Egypt's shaky finances as an excuse to gain influence in the state, although Egypt was never officially a British colony.

? **Why did Isma'il have to sell Egypt's shares of the Suez Canal Company?**

In addition to its influence in Egypt, Great Britain established colonies in Sudan, Uganda, and Kenya. These colonies, together with the ones in southern Africa, gave the British control over much of the eastern side of Africa.

Germany

Germany had three scattered colonies. German Cameroon was in Central Africa. German Southwest Africa was along the southern Atlantic coast. German East Africa bordered the Indian Ocean.

Other Nations

After its failure to take Ethiopia, Italy invaded and conquered the Ottoman North African territory of Tripoli. The Italians renamed it Libya. The Spanish controlled a small slice of Morocco and a West African territory called Rio de Oro.

African Reactions to Imperialism

Reactions of Africans to imperialism can be classified under three general categories. Of course, reactions varied over time, depending on several circumstances.

Submission

Some African leaders chose to submit. They knew that the Europeans had better weapons and that they would not be able to protect their people through armed resistance. Some submitted with no thought of future resistance, while others did so either to buy time and seek a peaceful resolution or to prepare for a future conflict.

Alliance

Other African leaders saw European forces as a means of protection from hostile neighbors or internal forces that threatened their rule. They embraced alliances with Europeans with the hope that their governments would remain secure.

Samori Ture

Unfortunately, the Africans often discovered that these alliances offered them no protection at all. Sometimes a European power would make promises to the ruler of an African state while supporting his enemies at the same time. This treachery left some African leaders no option but to either submit or confront the European forces.

For example, Samori Ture had established a Muslim empire in West Africa. When the French attempted to take control of his land, he resisted and defeated them in many battles. However, he realized that he could not overcome the French completely, so he signed a treaty with them in 1886. Despite signing the treaty, the French continued to encourage resistance to Ture's authority among the people of his empire. Ture spent two years preparing for one major battle to defeat the French. Despite heroic efforts, Ture's men could not defeat the well-equipped French forces. Ture was eventually captured in 1898. He died two years later.

Why did alliances not protect African rulers?

Confrontation

Many African states chose to confront the European forces who demanded control of their land and resources. This confrontation took two forms. Some African leaders negotiated with the Europeans. They sent diplomats to try to seek a solution that would preserve African independence. The European powers often refused to meet with these diplomats or proceeded to invade a state even as they met with its diplomats. Diplomacy typically only slowed down the process of colonization.

Other African tribes turned to war as soon as they realized the Europeans' true intentions. Muslim rulers were determined not to submit to rule by the Europeans. They offered stiff resistance and died in large numbers because of the weapons they faced. With few exceptions, even the most advanced African forces still used flintlock weapons while the Europeans returned fire with rapid-firing weapons like the **Maxim gun**.

CRITICAL THINKING 14.2

How did Europeans use technology to gain control of Africa?

▲ Algerian man with a flintlock musket

◄ European soldier with a Maxim gun

GUIDING QUESTIONS

- To what extent did imperialism affect the future of Africa?
- Is imperialism consistent with biblical teaching on justice, power, and citizenship?
- How could justice, power, and citizenship be biblically applied in a current political conflict?

14.3 Consequences of Imperialism

Mixed in with the many negative results of imperialism were a few positive ones, though Europeans can take little or no credit for the positive results. It would not be an exaggeration to say that most of the positive results were accidental rather than intentional. However, the Christian should not be surprised to find that God can bring good things out of even the worst actions of fallen humans.

Political Consequences

Positive Consequences

European powers established **bureaucracies** in their colonies. Colonial bureaucracies varied in their efficiency, but the British system produced well-trained and effective civil servants (government workers). A bureaucratic structure proved helpful to African states when they gained their independence.

What were two helpful things that colonial governments set up for African states?

Another positive development for African states was the formation of modern judicial systems. These have undergone very little change since their formation and have been very successful.

Negative Consequences

Over time, European forces captured or killed the leaders of rebellions against colonial rule. Weapons were confiscated, and armed resistance declined. New African leaders had no choice but to work within the system to benefit their people. As long as these leaders submitted to European control, African states experienced a temporary peace and stability. However, Africans paid a great price for this peace: the loss of their freedom.

Gradually, over fifty new African states emerged from colonial rule. While this appeared to be an improvement over the hundreds of tribes that existed before, these divisions were artificial. Europeans often drew boundaries on maps with little regard for the actual location of tribes. As a result, they divided tribes or combined tribes at the stroke of a pen and without African input. Groups that had little in common and even spoke different languages suddenly found themselves fellow citizens. These differences led to unrest in several states, especially as they gained independence.

At the time of European colonization and imperialism, many African states were in the process of developing into modern societies. European conquest effectively ended this development. At least two generations of Africans grew up under the control of Europeans and had no experience in self-government. In addition, European nations limited their colonies' economic and political interactions with other countries. Therefore, Africans became isolated from the rest of the world.

What price did Africans pay for temporary peace and stability during the colonial period?

bureaucracies government organizations that oversee the details of managing a state

infrastructure network of facilities and structures needed for things like travel and communication

Economic Consequences

Positive Consequences

The Europeans built a modern **infrastructure** in Africa. They laid thousands of miles of track for railroads and built many miles of roads. In addition, they strung miles of wire for telegraph and, later, telephone communications.

The Europeans also introduced improved farming methods to Africa and greatly increased the production of many natural products. The railroads and roads allowed much larger harvests to be delivered to markets.

The traditional African barter-based economy was replaced with a money-based economy during the colonial period. Europeans introduced Africans to modern concepts of banking. This knowledge became a great asset to the African states as they gained freedom from European control.

? **How did the African economy change during the colonial period?**

Negative Consequences

The Europeans developed Africa in ways that best fit their own needs. As a result, some parts of Africa experienced greater development than others. For example, some areas experienced significant improvements in their infrastructure while areas that were of no interest to the Europeans received no improvements. In addition, when the Europeans drew boundaries for African states, they did not always divide resources evenly. Some regions had access to the coast, rich mineral deposits, and other natural resources. Others were landlocked and had access to few natural resources. These decisions left some African states with little opportunity to prosper.

Even though the Europeans brought industry and technology to Africa, they denied the Africans the opportunity to develop industry and technology on their own. This had a long-term effect of hindering natural African development in those areas. Also, significant progress had been made in the development of intra-African trade following the banning of the slave trade. European colonization effectively ended this progress.

Another problem developed as the Europeans forced the Africans to concentrate on growing cash crops rather than food to feed their people. As a result, Africans had to eat food imported from other parts of the world. Following their independence, African nations found it difficult to change their agricultural practices and continued to depend on other nations to provide food for their people.

Finally, European colonization resulted in great wealth for some European investors. These investors, however, often took their wealth back to Europe rather than reinvesting it in Africa. Africa was left with an underdeveloped and underfunded economic system.

? **How did the emphasis on growing cash crops become a problem for Africans?**

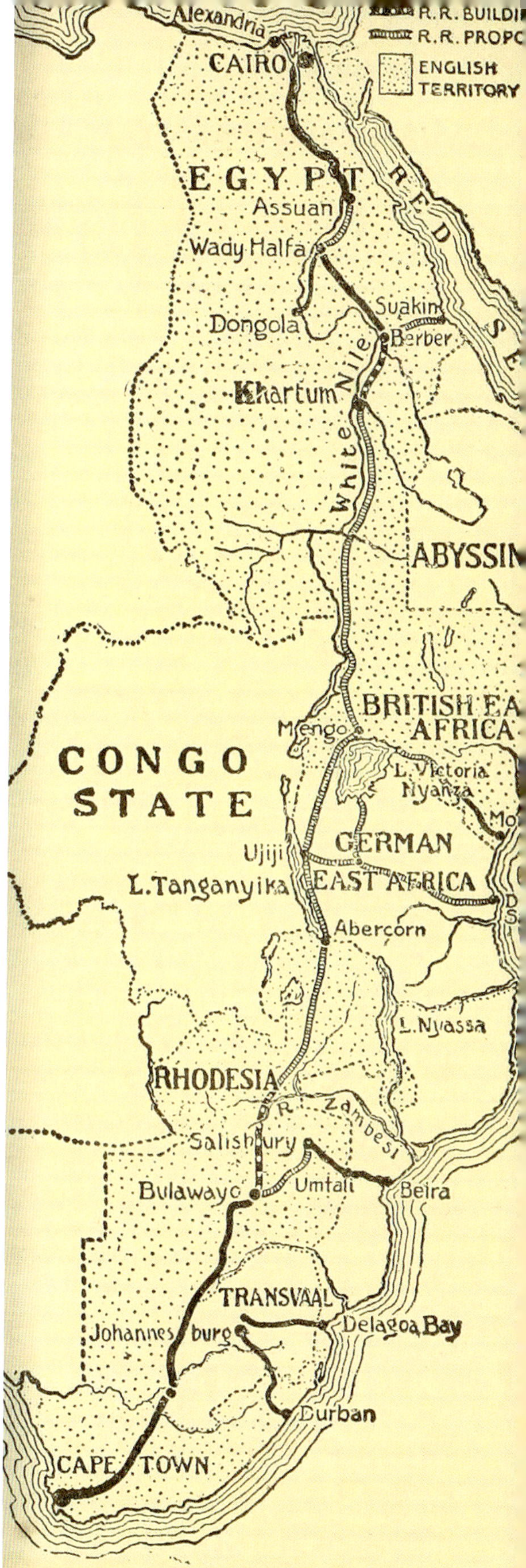

In 1874 journalist Edwin Arnold proposed the construction of a Cape to Cairo railway. The project was never fully completed.

NAIROBI

Environment

Nairobi, Kenya, was established in 1899 as a depot for the Uganda Railway. At that time, it was in the colonial territory of British East Africa. The Nairobi River runs through the region and explains the city's name (***Nairobi*** means "cool water"). Sir George Whitehouse, who worked for the railroad, chose the spot because of its pleasant temperatures, steady source of water, and elevation.

Justice

As was happening throughout Africa, peasant farmers in Kenya experienced an upheaval in their lifestyles during the early 1900s. Their land was taken, and they were unable to grow food to feed themselves as they had always done. When the Europeans introduced a money-based economy and imposed taxes, Africans had to look for jobs that would pay cash. They found these jobs on newly established European plantations. However, the Africans wanted to work only long enough to pay their bills. To try to guarantee a more regular workforce, plantation owners asked local officials to "draft" workers for them. Though the British government tried to put a stop to this system, forced labor continued to be a problem for some time in colonial Kenya.

Plantations commonly grew crops such as coffee, tea, and sisal (leaves used for making rope).

The flag of the Colony and Protectorate of Kenya had a British Union Jack and a red lion on a blue background.

Citizenship

Education is an essential element for informed citizen participation in government. Educated Africans laid the groundwork for more stable and democratic governments in the future.

Power

European nations were able to subdue African peoples because technology and organization gave the Europeans greater power. Possession of this power was not wrong. It was gained through living out the Creation Mandate. But in a fallen world, God-given abilities can be put to evil purposes. Sadly, many European nations claimed Christianity as their religion. In their colonial dealings, however, they failed to observe basic Christian ethical teachings: "love thy neighbor as thyself" (Matt. 22:39) and "whatsoever ye would that men should do to you, do ye even so to them" (Matt. 7:12).

Religion

Sociologist Robert Woodberry researched the long-term effects of Protestant missionary activity on a region. He concluded that areas that had experienced a strong missionary influence in the past now rank higher in many aspects of quality of life, including health and education. In addition, he found that missionaries of independent churches tended to oppose injustice practiced by colonial powers. For instance, missionaries smuggled pictures out of the Congo region to raise public awareness of horrible abuses taking place there, and missionaries in South Africa spearheaded an agreement that protected the peoples in what is now Botswana from further European land grabs.

Nairobi's elevation is around 5,500 feet, while the Ngong Hills to the southwest rise to more than 8,000 feet.

Social Consequences

Positive Consequences

After an initial decline, Africa began to experience significant population growth. The initial decline was due to contact with European diseases and armed conflict with European forces. But as violent resistance subsided, African population growth rebounded.

Villages grew into towns, and towns experienced significant urbanization. This development proved to be an important long-term contribution to Africa.

In some African states, especially those controlled by the British, Europeans encouraged the spread of religion and education. In addition to proclaiming the gospel, missionaries also provided most of the education for the Africans.

Finally, African historian Adu Boahen notes that European colonization created a new social order based on merit and achievement. Prior to European control, many Africans based their social order on birth. Under European management, Africans who worked hard and cooperated with the system could advance and gain promotion.

(top) Africans in traditional dress; (bottom) Street in Nairobi, Kenya, 2018

What new social order did the Europeans establish in Africa?

Negative Consequences

Although the Europeans urbanized Africa, they also created a large gap between the urban and the rural areas. The urban areas had access to most of the modern infrastructure, while the rural areas remained undeveloped. African cities also had most of the medical facilities and schools. The Europeans constructed few of these facilities outside the urban areas.

In addition, Europeans tended to downgrade the status of African women. Europeans built more educational facilities for boys than for girls. Lacking equal educational opportunities, women could not gain access to many professions, including medicine, law, and civil service. The colonial world favored men, while women were restricted to menial tasks.

Finally, Europeans, including many missionaries, condemned everything African. They opposed African names, music, art, and anything else that originated in Africa. They even forced the Africans to wear European-style clothing. These measures disrupted the cultural development of Africa.

How did Europeans disrupt the cultural development of Africa?

CRITICAL THINKING 14.3

1. Why did the European formation of new African states create many problems?
2. Why is it a problem when someone does too much for you, as when the Europeans brought industry and technology to Africa?

Making Connections

1. How did the end of the slave trade affect Africa's peace and prosperity?
2. What attempts did Africa make to unify and modernize following the end of the slave trade?
3. What did the Fante Confederation hope to achieve? Why did it fail to meet its goals?
4. What factors opened the African interior to the outside world?
5. In what ways did British missionaries help the African people?
6. What were the earliest European nations to colonize Africa? How did each begin its colonization efforts?
7. Using the map on page 303, identify the region(s) of Africa colonized by France, Portugal, Belgium, Great Britain, and Germany.
8. What reason did King Leopold of Belgium give for wanting to develop Central Africa? What was his true motivation?
9. How did Cecil Rhodes try to extend British influence in South Africa?
10. How was Great Britain able to gain influence over the government of Egypt?
11. Describe each of the three general African reactions to imperialism. Tell whether each reaction helped Africans keep their independence.
12. How did imperialism shape modern Africa both negatively and positively? Consider political, economic, and social influences.

Thinking Critically

1. Name four key European motives for imperialism. Evaluate each motive according to a biblical standard of justice found in passages such as Amos 5:11, 2 Corinthians 10:12, Matthew 28:19–20, and Luke 10:25–37. Explain whether you think each motive was just or unjust.
2. Did Europeans use power in a biblical way in Africa according to Matthew 7:12 and Matthew 22:39? Defend your answer.
3. Were interactions between Kenyan peasant farmers and plantation owners just? Give evidence to support your answer.
4. How well did European missionaries help prepare Africans for participating in their governments?

What to Know

Dates & Events

Scramble for Africa
Berlin Conference of 1884–85
Boer War

People

Menelik II
Samori Ture
David Livingstone
Henry Stanley
Robert Moffat
Samuel Ajayi Crowther
James Africanus Horton

Places

Victoria Falls
Belgian Congo

Terms

colonialism
imperialism
gathering-based economy
Wassoulou Empire
Fante Confederation
Second French Colonial Empire
International African Association (IAA)
Maxim gun
bureaucracies
infrastructure

15 NINETEENTH-CENTURY ASIA

1757 – 1914

ESSENTIAL QUESTIONS

- How did the Ottoman Empire respond to the challenges of lost territory?
- Why did Russian reform fail to address the nation's problems?
- What were the results of British power in India?
- How did the Manchu dynasty respond to economic and political crises?
- What was European and American colonization of East Asia like?
- How did Japan transform into a modern nation-state?

The siege of Sevastopol during the Crimean War

Boxer Rebellion

China's history with Christianity follows a pattern. The gospel is preached, the people respond, and the church grows significantly. A new dynasty or government takes over and feels challenged by the Christians, so it persecutes the church. This cycle has been repeated numerous times, even up to the present day.

One of the most brutal crackdowns on Christians in China that we know about happened in the summer of 1900. Over 32,000 Chinese Christians and 188 foreign missionaries were killed. A group of violent men called **Boxers** arose in reaction to what the European imperialists were doing in China. Christians served as the Boxers' easy target for revenge. The Boxers burned churches and tortured and killed Christians.

A British journalist reported what he saw and heard: "As darkness came on, the most awful cries were heard in the city. . . . the cries of the Boxers—*Sha kuei-tzu* [kill the devils]—mingled with the shrieks of the victims and the groans of the dying. For Boxers were sweeping through the city, massacring the native Christians." The missionaries were forced to flee for their lives. These missionaries and their children displayed amazing faith and courage as they faced certain death.

One group of missionaries "included two families with six young children and four single women. . . . Mobs followed them from one village boundary to the next, hurling sticks and stones, shouting, 'Death to the foreign devils!' Robbers stripped them of everything but a few rags. Emaciated from hunger and thirst, shoeless, barebacked in the scorching heat, desperately trying to hold up filthy, torn Chinese trousers, they staggered from village to village half alive.

"The young children displayed remarkable insight and faith. 'If they loved Jesus they would not do this,' seven-year-old Jessie Saunders reminded her parents."

Chinese Christians suffered much worse than the missionaries. A Chinese Christian leader known as "Faithful" Yen and his wife were tied to a pole to be burned, but they still did not deny Christ. The Boxers eventually untied Mrs. Yen. But they burned Mr. Yen even though Chinese soldiers tried to stop them.

In another instance, a Chinese family was taken in an open cart to be executed and was heard singing the hymn "He Leadeth Me." There are thousands more stories of Chinese and Western Christians remaining faithful to Christ in China despite extreme persecution during the summer of 1900.

Missionary families had to flee their homes in China in the summer of 1900.

Ottoman market

GUIDING QUESTIONS

- What did the French invasion of Egypt in 1798 reveal?
- Why did the Ottoman Empire leave the Balkans and the Black Sea region?

15.1 Ottoman Empire

By the nineteenth century the Ottoman Empire was showing definite signs of decline. The final symptom of the political and economic rottenness that had plagued the empire for centuries was the loss of large amounts of territory.

Wars reveal the strength of nations. When Napoleon invaded Egypt in 1798, he showed that European militaries were technologically and organizationally superior to the Ottoman forces. The French invasion also awakened the Ottoman citizens to the idea of self-rule.

Ottoman Empire, 1798

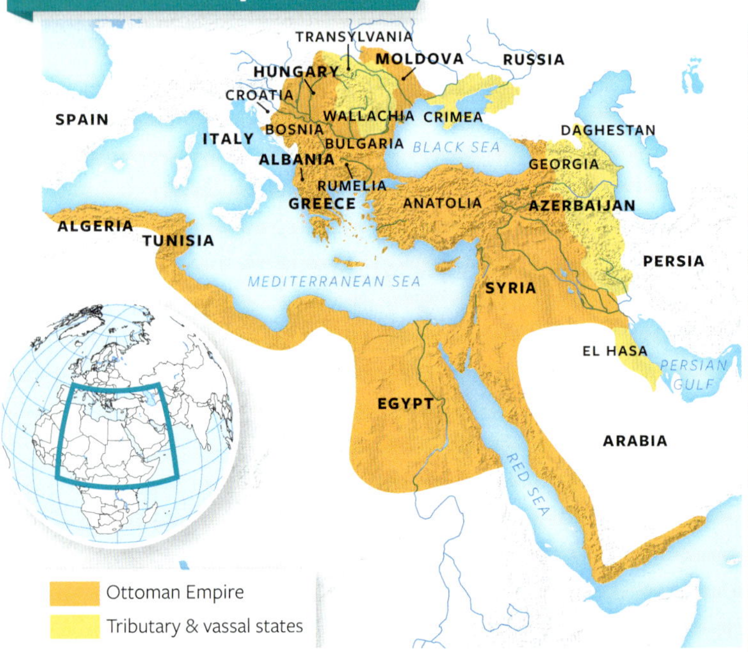

Failure to Reform Economically

After the Europeans discovered the Americas and a sea route to Asia, they gained more power and wealth. The Ottomans did not know how to respond to this challenge. They had depended on the income from being the middlemen between the Asians and Europeans. Rather than opening their markets, the Ottomans closed them. State officials required bribes from businesspeople in exchange for permission to do business. This corruption grew as the officials got their family members involved in collecting bribes. The practice of bribery drained the productivity of the empire since the bribe money did not go toward the growth of the economy. As real material wealth disappeared, the government printed more money, which caused inflation (a situation in which money loses its value).

What Ottoman territory did Napoleon invade in 1798?

Failure of Political Leadership

The central Ottoman government proved to be unable to respond to external and internal threats. The empire had started out as somewhat of a meritocracy (where the most qualified are promoted to leadership), but that had changed as the leaders realized they could gain power and wealth by promoting family and friends. The leaders failed to adequately modernize the military and found themselves outgunned by their rivals. From 1808 to the empire's end in 1918, eight sultans reigned, three of them for a short time. None of the sultans were able to halt the decline, although they tried.

What did the Ottomans require of businesspeople for them to operate?

Mahmud II

Mahmud II reigned from 1808 to 1839. His half-brother tried to murder him, but Mahmud barely escaped. During Mahmud's rule Greece gained its independence, Serbia gained some autonomy (self-rule), and other Ottoman lands were lost to Russia. In addition, Mahmud found himself powerless to stop the French in 1830 from seizing Algeria, an Ottoman province.

However, during the decline, Mahmud laid the foundation for a modern Turkey. He enacted social and legal reforms. He discarded the custom of wearing large turban hats and robes and instead adopted a more European fez hat and pants. Not everyone was happy with these reforms. The Janissaries, whom you learned about in Chapter 8, were an elite and corrupt military organization developed in the fourteenth century. They fervently opposed reforms and constantly revolted until Mahmud finally destroyed the Janissaries and replaced them with a more modern Ottoman army.

The Ottoman sultan's dress before and after Mahmud's reforms

What type of clothing did Mahmud introduce to the Ottoman Empire?

Abdulmejid I

Abdulmejid I reigned from 1839 to 1861. He tried to integrate the non-Muslim citizens of the empire into society and keep them from seeking independence, but he failed. As Russia took pieces of Ottoman territory, Abdulmejid made alliances with Britain and France for support; this led to the Crimean War (discussed in Section 15.2). Russia lost the war, but the Ottomans showed weakness since they needed to ask for help. Abdulmejid continued the reorganization of the army that Mahmud had started. He introduced a military draft (forced participation of citizens in the military). He reorganized the court system and established an Ottoman parliament. All along the way the reforms were met with opposition from those who depended on the old system for their wealth.

How did Abdulmejid reform the empire?

Artwork celebrating Abdul Hamid II and the Ottoman constitution

Abdulaziz

Abdulaziz reigned from 1861 to 1876. He continued to reform the empire. He built up the navy, but in doing so, he drained the treasury. He was interested in the arts. He composed music and studied literature. He did not lose territory during his reign, but because of his lavish spending Ottoman officials dethroned him. Abdulaziz died five days later.

Abdul Hamid II

Abdul Hamid II reigned from 1876 to 1909. At the beginning of his reign, he accepted a constitution. The reforms he put in place were ineffective to stop the disintegration of the empire. In 1877 the Ottomans had to fight a war with Russia, the Russo-Turkish War. The two empires fought in Romania, Georgia, and Armenia. The Ottomans performed poorly. In 1878 Hamid put the constitution on hold to allow him more power to put down rebellions in Bosnia, Montenegro, and Bulgaria. Russia had encouraged the rebellions. The British mediated a peace treaty in 1878 to end the war, but the Ottomans lost most of the land in dispute.

Hamid's biggest fear was that he would be in charge when the empire dissolved, which almost happened. By the end of his reign, Romania had gained its independence, as had the Balkan Peninsula countries of Serbia, Montenegro, and Bulgaria. The empire had shriveled and only included the Turkish Peninsula through the Holy Land and the lands along the Red Sea on the Arabian Peninsula.

Ottoman Empire, 1914

Why did Hamid suspend the constitution?

CRITICAL THINKING 15.1

How were the Ottomans trying to play catch-up with the West? What was the result?

15.2 Russia

By the mid-1700s, Russia had expanded to become the largest country in the world, controlling territory from the Baltic Sea to the Pacific Ocean. However, much of Russia suffered from a harsh climate, and the short growing season restricted the food supply. As a result, this vast state had a population of only about fourteen million people. Successive rulers moved west and south to seize new lands, gain access to warm-water ports, and increase Russian influence. While Russia expanded its control over neighboring countries, much of the Russian population remained in virtual slavery as serfs.

The czars assumed the right to rule without question and tolerated no criticism. They used several kinds of power to keep Russia firmly under their control. They wielded military power and suppressed rebellion through force. They exercised power through the Russian Orthodox church, which encouraged the people to submit to the state. The czars also retained power by promoting nationalism; they emphasized individual sacrifice for the good of the nation.

Uprisings increased as the Russian citizens grew impatient with the way things were. To survive, Russia would have to make major reforms to benefit its people. Failure to do so would provide fertile ground for the growth of violent revolution.

GUIDING QUESTIONS

- How did Napoleon's invasion affect Russia?
- How successful were Russian imperial reforms in the nineteenth century?
- Why were opposition movements popular in nineteenth-century Russia?

? **Why did Russia want to expand its territory southward?**

Catherine the Great

Russian imperialism continued during the reign of **Catherine the Great**. Catherine was a German princess who married a German heir to the Russian throne. Her husband proved to be a weak leader. He soon died under mysterious circumstances, and Catherine became the ruler of Russia.

Under her aggressive leadership, Russia continued to expand westward and southward. During her reign, Russia seized Ottoman land that lay between Russia and the Black Sea. Catherine also joined with other nations in taking land from Poland, the land now known as the countries of Lithuania and Belarus.

The Russian rulers continued to tolerate the oppression of over one-third of the population. Millions of serfs lived on land owned by nobles and spent most of their time working to support the nobility. As a result, they were little more than slaves and lived in terrible, impoverished conditions.

A Russian serf could change his owner on Yuri's Day.

Catherine the Great

In 1773 Catherine made life for the serfs even worse by making it legal to sell serfs separate from selling the land. Before that the serfs were attached to the land. In response, the peasants revolted and nearly entered Moscow before royal forces brutally defeated them. Succeeding Russian rulers tended either to work for reform or to react to violence and suppress the people.

How did Catherine become ruler of Russia?

Alexander I

Alexander I

Alexander I became the czar of Russia following Catherine's death in 1796. He continued Russia's expansion by seizing control of Finland from Sweden in 1809. In 1812, after the Russo-Turkish War, Alexander took the lands of Georgia and Moldova in Eastern Europe from the Ottomans.

The central event of Alexander's rule was the French invasion of his country. Despite Napoleon's capture of Moscow, the Russians would not surrender. Events in France and a lack of supplies forced Napoleon to return to France. As his forces were on their way out, 90 percent of them died from Russian attacks and the harsh winter.

Napoleon's invasion had disrupted much of Russian society and led those who suffered most to expect reform. The serfs had played a major role in defeating Napoleon. In return, they demanded reforms that would free them from their virtual slavery. While Alexander I discussed possible constitutional reforms and introduced a few minor changes, no significant reform followed.

Nicholas I

When **Nicholas I** came to power in December 1825, a group of well-educated Russian officers demonstrated against the czar in what was called the **Decembrist Revolt**. The officers hoped to establish a constitutional monarchy, something they had learned about while traveling in the West. The rebellion was quickly put down by the army.

However, such a threat led Nicholas to reject the westernization begun by Peter the Great and embrace "Orthodoxy, Autocracy, and Nationality," meaning a return to the old ways of the czar being a strict dictator. Because of this, opposition groups became more popular, and more people began to accept radical proposals to solve Russia's problems.

What kind of group led the Decembrist Revolt?

The Decembrist Revolt took place in Senate Square in St. Petersburg and was put down by soldiers loyal to the czar.

Internal Struggles: Anarchism

Michael Bakunin became one of the Russian radicals to emerge during this period. Known as the Father of Anarchism, Bakunin supported **anarchy**, or the concept of a society without government. In simple terms, *anarchy* means "without law" or "the absence of law." The French Revolution provides a clear example of the chaos that follows the overthrow of the government.

To escape imprisonment, Bakunin fled to western Europe. However, his participation in an uprising in Dresden, Germany, led to his imprisonment and deportation to Siberia. Bakunin managed to escape and return to Europe, where he worked with Karl Marx.

Russian authors, including **Fyodor Dostoyevsky** and **Leo Tolstoy**, provided their readers with a glimpse into Russian society. Their conclusions, however, were opposites. For example, Dostoyevsky embraced Eastern Orthodoxy and opposed the anarchists and atheists who were becoming popular in Russia.

Tolstoy, on the other hand, rejected Eastern Orthodoxy and emphasized the Sermon on the Mount. However, his interpretations of the Sermon conflicted with the rest of the Scripture. He interpreted the command to "turn the other cheek" to teach pacifism (not fighting wars) and the abolition of private property. Tolstoy played a key role in developing anarchist reasoning. In works such as *The Kingdom of God Is Within You*, he attacked the church, the state, and the principle of law in Russian society. Tolstoy imagined a theoretical state where there is simply no law or government and where man has the liberty of governing himself. Tolstoy dreamed of achieving this state without resorting to violence and disorder.

Even though Tolstoy envisioned peaceful anarchy, his vision of the world conflicted with the way God designed it to work. It is unrealistic to think that a fallen world could exist without government to ensure justice (Rom. 13:1–7).

◄ | Michael Bakunin

▲ Fyodor Dostoyevsky

▲ Leo Tolstoy

? What is Michael Bakunin known as?

External Struggles: The Crimean War

At the end of Nicholas I's reign, Russia and Greece fought a two-and-a-half-year-long war against the Ottomans, France, and Britain. This conflict was called the **Crimean War** (1853–56); the goal was control of the Ottoman territory surrounding the Black Sea. The Russians controlled the strategic warm-water port of Sevastopol on the Crimean Peninsula. But the port was useless without access to the Mediterranean Sea via the Ottoman-controlled territories around the Bosporus Strait in Turkey.

Russia's early success against the Ottoman navy alarmed Britain and France, who wanted to limit Russia's expansion. The Ottoman allies decided to invade the Crimean Peninsula and fought there for almost a year. The war was characterized by incompetence and disorganization on both sides. Cholera killed more soldiers than the fighting.

Crimean War

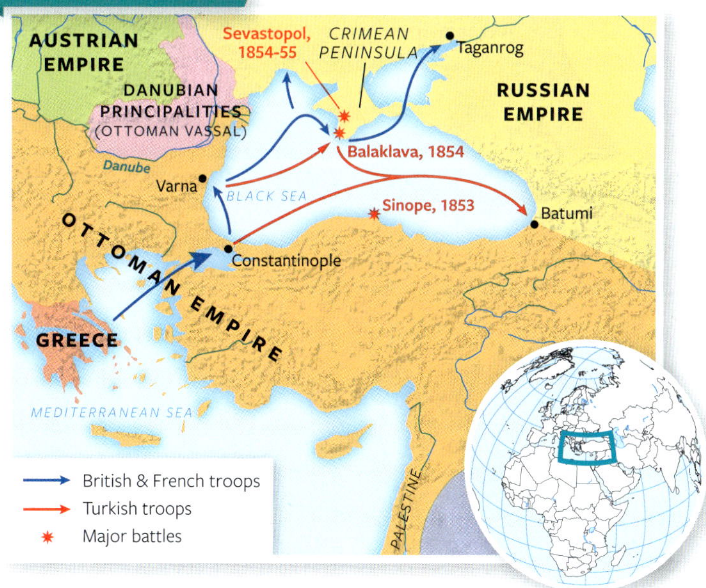

The British leadership lost support for the war at home as people saw photos of the results of the war and as telegraphs gave the people more immediate access to the events of the war. The Russians were finally defeated on the Crimean Peninsula but continued to fight in other locations. When Prussia threatened to join the war against Russia, Russia agreed to seek peace. The peace treaty returned everything to the way it was before the war. The war was a preview of the type of fighting and incompetent leadership that would characterize World War I. Twenty years later, after France and Britain had lost interest, Russia gained some of these same territories from the Ottomans, this time without a fight.

Who fought in the Crimean War?

Florence Nightingale

Florence Nightingale was born on May 12, 1820, into a wealthy British family in Italy. Soon after her birth, the family moved back to England. Florence's father allowed her and her sister to get a well-rounded education. They studied history, mathematics, foreign languages, literature, and philosophy.

Nightingale believed she was called by God to be a nurse. She decided not to get married. She traveled the world, learning and seeing the need for medical workers. Nightingale is most famous for her work during the Crimean War; in 1854 she brought a team of nurses to Crimea. They found that the soldiers were dying because the hospitals were unsanitary, and the medical staff was ill-supplied and overworked. She directed the reorganization of the hospital. She made the hospital staff wash their hands and began other cleaning practices. These improvements decreased the deaths of soldiers at the hospital from 42 percent to 2 percent. From that time on, she taught that sanitary conditions in homes and hospitals were vital for preventing disease. Nightingale later became known as "The Lady with the Lamp," based on a line from the tribute poem "Santa Filomena" by Henry Wadsworth Longfellow.

Lo! in that house of misery
A lady with a lamp I see
Pass through the glimmering gloom,
And flit from room to room.

Following the war, she set up a successful training school for nurses. She introduced nurses into the British workhouse system to help the people there. She was also a skilled statistician and one of the first to use statistics to improve hospital performance. Florence Nightingale died in her sleep on August 13, 1910, at the age of 90.

Alexander II

Alexander II sensed the growing demand for reform in Russia. Rather than wait for reform to occur through violent revolution, he made a bold move in 1861. Alexander II abolished serfdom and freed twenty-three million people out of a total Russian population of sixty-seven million. This emancipation created a great supply of free laborers to move to the cities and fill jobs created by developing industries.

However, freed peasants did not receive land along with their new status. Instead, the government required them to pay a huge tax to continue to farm the land. The government then used this money to pay the nobles large sums for the land the government had taken. The peasants often ended up with the least productive land, and this land belonged to the village community rather than to individual farmers.

▲ Alexander II freeing the serfs

In the end, simply abolishing serfdom did little to improve the lives of millions of Russians. Russia needed fundamental reforms to correct centuries of repression. Because the Russian government did not implement these reforms, conditions did not improve. Support for revolution continued to grow. Despite Alexander II's attempts to bring reform to Russia, his efforts proved to be in vain. In 1881 he died at the hands of assassins.

? What did Czar Alexander II decree in 1861?

Alexander III

Alexander III suppressed all real and imagined threats to the monarchy. He censored the press and persecuted many groups, including the Poles and Finns. Pogroms became a brutal tool of the government to terrorize those considered a threat.

The Industrial Revolution did not occur in Russia. So western Europe was far ahead of Russia economically. While Russia had the necessary natural resources, it lacked free and mobile laborers, stable government, and other ingredients needed to develop industry on a large scale.

Russia continued to expand its empire by seizing land from weaker states, but it lagged further and further behind economically. Western Europe became wealthy by expanding industry and trade, but Russia could not compete or catch up. Western success exposed the great weaknesses of the Russian Empire. Radical groups used these weaknesses to attract increasing support for their efforts to overthrow the existing system in Russia.

? Why did Western Europe surpass Russia economically?

? CRITICAL THINKING 15.2

Compare and contrast Dostoyevsky's and Tolstoy's views on anarchy. What would a more biblical perspective be?

GUIDING QUESTIONS

- How did Britain increase its power in India in the nineteenth century?
- What were the consequences of British control of India?
- How did Britain rule India?

15.3 India

The English initially came to India for trade. However, as the Mughal Empire declined, Britain gradually took control of most of the country. Britain was not the only European country to seek influence in India. France also labored to establish and maintain trade with this vast country.

From East India Company Rule to Crown Rule

The East India Company developed extensive trade relations with states in India. Over time, the British government became more involved and eventually took control of British affairs in India. However, Britain had to deal with its main competitor, France, before extensive trade could continue.

Britain soon ended the threat of French competition by winning the Seven Years' War (1756–63). At the **Battle of Plassey** in 1757, British commander **Robert Clive** defeated a much larger Indian force whose leader supported the French. With only three thousand men, Clive routed a disorganized Indian force of eighty thousand. This battle broke France's strength in India. Within three years, the British had ended all French influence in India.

British trade with India grew over the next hundred years. The British government began to exercise greater control over the East India Company in 1773 due to the company's financial mismanagement. As the British government became more involved, officials quickly realized the importance of stabilizing India to enhance British trade. British commanders such as Lord Cornwallis put down rebellions and enforced stability. In 1813 the Charter Act gave the British crown control over all that the company possessed.

Why did the British government exercise greater control in India?

Robert Clive meeting with Mir Jafar, an Indian military leader who helped the British achieve victory at the Battle of Plassey

The British Raj (1858–1947)

The final incident that led to the British government taking complete control occurred when Indian soldiers, called sepoys, revolted. The **Sepoy Mutiny** (1857–58) began because of a rumor that the cartridges for a newly issued rifle had been greased with either pork or beef fat. To use the cartridges, the soldiers had to open them, usually by biting them. The Hindu soldiers were offended because the cow was sacred to them. The Muslim soldiers were offended because they considered pork unclean.

When the British commanded the sepoys to load the new rifles, they refused, and the British stripped them of their uniforms and pensions. British forces arrested and imprisoned other sepoys when they also refused to obey this command. As news spread of the British actions, a mutiny arose. Before the British could restore order, both sides had massacred many innocent people.

The British suppressed this mutiny within a year. Queen Victoria proclaimed India under control of the British crown and said that the Indian people had the right to a voice in their own government. But the queen had effectively absorbed India into the British Empire without any input from the Indian people.

The British rule of India was called the Raj, which means "rule" in Sanskrit. The British faced many problems in ruling India. The country had over two hundred million inhabitants who spoke over a hundred different languages. In addition, they followed several religions.

British officials in India often misunderstood the Indians and had little desire to learn about Indian culture. The British rulers also tended to isolate themselves from the Indian population and assumed the role of master over their Indian subjects.

? **What rumor led to the Sepoy Mutiny?**

The cow was sacred to the Hindu soldiers in India, and the pig was unclean to the Muslim soldiers.

The British disarmed the Indian soldiers during the Sepoy Mutiny.

BRITISH INDIA

Power

The British ruled the more than two hundred million Indians with just about twenty thousand troops. Many took this as evidence that most Indians approved of British rule. The British encouraged the ancient Indian class system, which kept the people divided and maintained British control. The noble Indian classes were educated in English schools and served in the British army or the civil service. The Indian nobles ruled the lower-class Indians. The British viewed exercising their power in India as a charitable act, carrying "the white man's burden." But Britain also benefited greatly from its control of India, gaining wealth through trade, and the Indians provided the British army with soldiers.

Justice

The British East India Company established a civil and criminal court system in the 1770s. Ancient India had never organized their laws or established courts. The Rajas (rulers) had judged as they saw fit. When the British took over, they established a supreme court where people could appeal decisions made by lower courts. In the beginning, there were separate courts for Hindus and Muslims since religion influenced what was legal. This legal system slowly evolved to be more secular.

Environment

To improve agriculture, the British brought in better equipment, introduced fertilizers, and taught the Indians better farming methods. To increase production, they also built many miles of irrigation canals. The British also developed raw materials such as tea, cotton, and jute into products for export. British officials planted the first rubber trees on the island of Ceylon (Sri Lanka). These plants thrived, and Ceylon became a major exporter of rubber. Britain also set up a telegraph system, reorganized the postal system, and laid thousands of miles of track to construct a massive railroad system.

Citizenship

From 1858 to 1950, all people born in India were British subjects. The British did not discriminate based upon ethnicity but upon class. The higher castes were able to access English schools and get better jobs. Still, the British did restrict the Indian nobles from the upper tier of British society that ruled India. The British and Indian nobles excluded the lower castes from access to opportunities to raise their status.

Religion

Many British officials hindered missionary efforts to evangelize the Indians. They feared that this evangelism would lead to unrest and instability as the missionaries revealed the error of Indian religions. Queen Victoria proclaimed a policy of noninterference. This policy obstructed missionary efforts to spread the gospel and bring about reforms to protect women, children, and the outcasts of Indian society. British officials compelled **William Carey**, the Father of Modern Missions, to work on translating and printing the Indian Bible outside of India. William Carey was an English Baptist preacher and linguist who went by the motto "Expect great things from God; attempt great things for God." When the British government restricted direct evangelization, missionaries often used medical and educational outreaches to provide opportunities to witness.

CRITICAL THINKING 15.3

Do you think the British rule of India was generally positive or negative? Explain.

GUIDING QUESTIONS

- What caused the governmental and social collapse during the Manchu dynasty in China?
- What were the patterns of British trade that linked India and China with Europe?
- How did the Europeans force China to open its markets?
- What were the causes and consequences of the Taiping Rebellion?
- How did foreign countries influence Southeast Asia and Korea during this period?
- What were the Christian missionary efforts in East Asia during this period?

Why did the British have to pay the Chinese in silver?

15.4 Mainland East Asia

China came under the domination of the Europeans as the Manchu, or Qing, dynasty weakened. In addition, most of Mainland Southeast Asia became subject to French and British imperialism, while Island East Asia charted a different course.

China

China had remained isolated from the rest of the world for centuries. China continued to resist change, while the Europeans were advancing far past them technologically. The imperialist activities of European nations led to the collapse of the Manchu dynasty in the nineteenth century.

Europe-China Trade

Europeans could not get enough of the things China produced, like porcelain, silk, and tea. The British especially had an insatiable appetite for tea. Little did the early traders expect the first obstacle they met once safely in China—the Chinese did not care to trade with them. The goods of the West had little appeal to the Chinese. The British had developed cotton production and weaving in India. British ships transported goods, including cotton cloth and raw cotton, to Chinese ports. In exchange, the Chinese traded tea and silk. However, the goods brought from India were worth less than those offered by the Chinese merchants. As a result, British merchants had to pay the difference in silver. This situation created a negative balance of trade for British merchants.

China protected its treasures. Merchants would sell the tea leaves to Britain but not the plants, so the British had no way of producing the tea themselves. The British did grow an inferior tea in India in the early nineteenth century, but it was not the same as Chinese tea.

Europe-China Trade Routes

During the eighteenth century, foreign traders were mostly limited to the Chinese port of **Canton**. The British controlled most of the trade. British merchants lived in a specific section of the town and traded only through authorized Chinese agents. These agents set prices as high as they liked and could refuse to trade at any time.

British Opium Trade

The British merchants knew that the key to improving their unfavorable trading relationship with China was finding a product the Chinese wanted. They found that product growing in India—opium. **Opium** was a drug that users took to try to escape their problems. However, this feeling was only temporary and solved nothing. Once the effect of the drug wore off, the person still had his problems.

An opium warehouse in India

Opium had been used in China for several centuries before the British came, mostly to treat illness. When the British began importing large amounts of the drug, the Chinese began to use opium for its mind-changing effect. The demand for opium grew, and the British were happy to supply it. By selling this drug, the British slowly began to make more profit on their exports to China than they spent on their imports of tea and other goods. In the early 1700s, the British brought about 70 tons of opium a year into China. By 1838 the amount had increased to around 2,800 tons.

? **Why was there a demand for opium in China?**

Chinese Response

Millions of Chinese were addicted to opium. They would not work nor take care of their families. The British had turned the trade imbalance around; now China was paying the British the difference in silver. The emperor ordered all opium sales to stop and made it illegal to import it. However, greedy British and Chinese merchants smuggled the drug in.

Finally, the Chinese emperor appointed a man named **Lin Tse-Hsu** to solve the problem. On March 10, 1839, Lin went to Canton and demanded the British hand over all their unsold opium and stop bringing opium into China. He threatened decapitation for those who continued the trade.

Destruction of opium seized from British traders

How did the British respond after their opium was destroyed?

The British did not take Lin seriously; they assumed they could bribe him and continue the opium trade. But Lin was not corruptible. He ordered all transport to and from Canton to stop and for Chinese troops to surround the thirteen foreign trade houses. He ordered all Chinese workers to leave the trading houses and forbade the sale of food to the people inside. The British trading houses became prisons.

Captain Charles Elliot, the English Superintendent of Trade, made a decision that affected the negotiations later. Rather than having the merchants turn their opium over to the Chinese directly, Elliot took the opium, making it the property of the British government. Elliot gave all the opium to Lin, who destroyed it. Feeling that he had achieved a victory, Lin presented a document for Captain Elliot to sign. It was an agreement that the British would honor Chinese regulations. Elliot refused to sign.

Instead, the British sent their fleet. They blockaded (blocked trade from entering) Canton and then went north to capture the city of Tinghai. The emperor, angry with Lin for the situation, appointed a new negotiator, Ch'i-shan. When Ch'i-shan boarded a British ship and saw their weapons, he quickly realized that Britain outgunned China. Ch'i-shan suggested that the emperor adopt a policy of appeasement (to satisfy or calm) toward the British.

The Chinese offered to return to their former trading policy and to pay the British a small sum of money for their inconvenience. But the British saw the opportunity for gaining much more control in China. Since Captain Elliot had all the opium turned over to the British government, the British demanded payment for the destroyed opium. The British also insisted that China give them the city of Hong Kong and access to other ports of trade.

The Opium Wars

The Chinese refused, and war broke out. Called the **Opium War**, the fighting lasted three years (1839–42). British military power proved superior and easily defeated the Chinese. The Treaty of Nanking ended hostilities, and the Chinese gave in to the British demands.

A second opium war and British victory a few years later resulted in more open ports and the opening of inland China to trade and foreigners. Through these wars, the Western nations forced China to open. Although the Europeans obtained the trade rights they desired, they did not encourage good relations between China and the West. Resentment against foreigners grew and led to many problems.

The British navy capturing Chinese islands in a naval battle during the first Opium War

A painting depicting the Taiping Rebellion

Rebellions

Throughout China, more and more people rebelled to express their rejection of the Manchu government. The heavy taxation and government corruption especially angered the people. Famine became another serious problem for China. The Chinese population had rapidly increased, but the people had no additional farmland for growing more food. During some years, the farmers could not produce enough food to pay taxes and feed their families. Hungry and angry peasants often joined revolts against the government.

Taiping Rebellion

A frustrated Chinese student named Hong Renkun became the leader of one of the worst rebellions in Chinese history. Hong channeled his frustration into the development of a cultic political movement that attracted a huge number of roaming peasants. As his movement grew, he changed his name to **Hong Xiuquan** ("Heavenly King") to reflect his claims that he was the younger brother of Jesus.

The weakness demonstrated by the Manchu government during the Opium Wars caused more people to join Hong's movement. By 1851 he had a ten-thousand-man army with which he could attack the Manchurian forces.

The resulting **Taiping Rebellion** lasted from 1851 to 1864. Hong's movement quickly grew to over one million peasants who joined him in rebellion. At first, the rebels were difficult to suppress because they remained mobile. However, once the British and Chinese forces established a capital in Nanking, they were able to mount an attack and end this serious threat. During the many battles required to suppress this rebellion, between twenty and thirty million people died.

?

Who did Hong Xiuquan claim to be?

A horde of Boxers walk down the the street in Tianjin, China.

Boxer Rebellion

Unrest again erupted when the **Boxer Rebellion** broke out in 1899. The rebels were members of the Society of Righteous and Harmonious Fists, a society in which members were sworn to secrecy about the group's actions. The Europeans nicknamed members of this group Boxers because their martial arts practice looked like shadowboxing. Initially, this society opposed the Chinese government. However, they concluded that an alliance with the government against European imperialists would better represent Chinese interests. The **Empress Dowager Cixi** discouraged the imperial government from restraining this movement.

Foreign navies from eight countries expanded their presence on the northern China coast by the end of April 1900 after the Boxers had killed many European and American citizens. In addition to Britain, France, and the United States, Japan and Russia sent large numbers of warships and troops. Germany, Italy, and Austria-Hungary each provided a small force to complete the Eight-Nation Alliance. Initially, European commanders dispatched 435 soldiers to help put down the rebellion. However, the crisis deepened, and marine and army forces numbering over 49,000 were required to crush this violent and deadly rebellion.

How did the Boxer Rebellion end?

The Empress Dowager Cixi

Foreign Powers in China

As foreign nations saw the Manchu dynasty continue to weaken, they began to take advantage of China. The emerging state of Japan made the first move. Europeans quickly acted to limit Japan's access to Chinese territory. Fearing that Japan would gain control of more Chinese territory, several European nations sought ways to claim territory for themselves and establish "spheres of influence" in China. Like children eyeing a huge pie, each nation demanded a "slice" of China. Britain, France, Germany, and other European countries all chose areas they wished to control. The weak Chinese government could only watch as the land was taken.

The Last Emperor

A child born with the name Zaitian became the tenth emperor of the Manchu dynasty in 1875. He became the ruler at the age of four and was given the name **Guangxu**. Empress Dowager Cixi adopted Guangxu as her son, and she served as the actual ruler of China for the first fourteen years of his reign. She used her considerable power to oppose reform and change in China.

In 1889 Guangxu began to rule China officially. He worked to modernize China and develop a constitutional monarchy like the one in Japan. In June 1898, the young emperor started the Hundred Days' Reform to implement sweeping political, legal, and social changes in China. By September, the Empress Dowager had staged a coup d'état (a small group taking over the government by force) and imprisoned Guangxu. She issued an edict stating that Guangxu was not fit to be emperor and quickly reversed his efforts to reform China.

Guangxu remained under house arrest until his mysterious death at the age of thirty-seven. Empress Dowager Cixi picked a new emperor, two-year-old Puyi, to replace Guangxu. The next day she died.

Emperor Guangxu

Missionaries to China

Despite its many negative aspects, European imperialism did open China to missionaries. **Robert Morrison** became the first Protestant missionary to China, arriving there in 1807. He translated the Bible into Chinese. Morrison also produced an English-Chinese dictionary. He had to contend with Catholic missionaries who opposed his ministry.

James Hudson Taylor was another radical for Christ like George Mueller. He established the China Inland Mission in 1865. Over time, this mission guided hundreds of missionaries to China. Taylor changed how missions work was done. He humbled himself and adopted the neutral cultural practices of the Chinese, including their dress and hairstyle. Before this, British missionaries had stayed separate from those they were trying to reach. One of the key struggles in missions and ministry, in general, is deciding how much of the culture to adopt in order to reach the people.

James Hudson Taylor with his wife and a group of Chinese Christians

Jonathan and Rosalind Goforth

Canadian missionary **Jonathan Goforth** and his family got caught up in the Boxer Rebellion. The Chinese Christians at their mission urged them to leave. They knew that the Boxers had a special hatred for Chinese converts to Christianity. However, the Chinese Christians could blend into their villages or hide in the countryside, while the foreigners could not.

The Goforths fled their home in China on June 28, 1900, and walked for about twenty-four days through territory overrun with Boxers. On July 8, Boxers attacked Goforth and his group but failed to kill Jonathan, despite several blows with swords and a club. The Boxers soon became more interested in the goods in the missionaries' carts, and the missionaries slipped into the crowd to safety. Two years later, the Goforths returned to their work in China.

How did Hudson Taylor differ from other missionaries?

Korea

Emperor Kojong, last monarch of Korea, ruled from 1852 to 1919.

Korea is a peninsula that borders China and Russia in Northeast Asia. Up to the present day, Korea has been bullied by the larger nations in the neighborhood. For many years Korea was under Chinese control, but it was allowed some independence. In 1876, since China had weakened and Japan was gaining strength, Japan forced the Koreans to sign a treaty declaring their independence from China. The pro-Chinese king of Korea requested military assistance from China. The Japanese also sent troops, and in 1894 the **Sino-Japanese War** began. The Japanese easily defeated China and humiliated the Manchu government. The Japanese took possession of Korea and received Taiwan along with other Chinese territories.

Different world powers wanted to control Korea.

While Japan allowed Korea a form of independent rule, other world powers were eyeing the territory. In 1897 the Korean king declared the founding of the Korean Empire. The king began reforms to bring Korea up to speed with the rest of the world. Russia was trying to influence the empire, but in 1905 Japan defeated Russia in the **Russo-Japanese War**. At that point, Korea was firmly in the grasp of Japan.

By the early twentieth century, Japan established more direct control over Korea as Korean groups demanded greater freedoms. In 1910 the Japanese emperor made Korea officially part of the Japanese Empire, ending any charade of independence. The Japanese required the Koreans to speak Japanese and did not allow them to practice their traditions. The Japanese used Korea as a natural resource supplier, cutting down most of the trees.

What countries influenced Korea?

Mainland Southeast Asia

Mainland Southeast Asia consists of two large peninsulas, the Malay Peninsula and Indochina. Britain colonized the Malay Peninsula, which includes the countries of Malaysia and Myanmar (Burma), while France colonized the Indochina Peninsula (Laos, Cambodia, and Vietnam) after they won a war with China in 1885. Thailand on the Malay Peninsula was never colonized since it served as a buffer zone between the two rival European nations. Europeans seized control of many countries and islands in the area for strategic and economic reasons. For example, the Europeans exported many natural resources from this area, like rubber.

Adoniram Judson became the first foreign missionary from the United States, arriving in Burma in 1813. Despite various afflictions, including imprisonment and the deaths of his first and second wives, he completed a Burmese Bible translation so precise that it is still used today.

Adoniram Judson, first American overseas missionary

Which country colonized Indochina?

CRITICAL THINKING 15.4

Evaluate the British motives for selling addictive opium to the Chinese.

Judson translated the Bible into Burmese.

GUIDING QUESTIONS

- What caused the Meiji Restoration?
- Why did Japan modernize?
- How did Western ideas and reformed Shintoism influence Japan in the Meiji period?
- How did Japan's relation with China and Western powers change from the 1850s to the early 1900s?
- Who colonized the Philippines and Indonesia?

15.5 Island East Asia

Island East Asia includes Japan, the Philippines, and Indonesia. Each of these archipelago nations followed a different path during the nineteenth century.

Japan

Before 1853 Japan resembled medieval Europe with a feudal decentralized society. The people farmed the land, the shogun and samurai kept the peace, and Japan was closed to outsiders.

Before the Empire

When **Commodore Matthew Perry** led a fleet of American warships into Tokyo Bay, the United States forced Japan to open to foreigners. In 1854 the two countries signed the **Treaty of Kanagawa**. This treaty opened Japan to trade with other nations.

In a later visit, Perry brought several inventions that amazed the Japanese, including a telegraph system and a model railroad. The Japanese realized that they had much to learn if they were to catch up with the rest of the world.

Once Perry and his fleet had ended Japanese isolation, the Japanese had to decide how to respond to the West. Would they follow China's example of resisting change?

Commodore Matthew Perry meets with the Japanese.

Start of the Empire

Japan fought a civil war to decide if they should open relations with the West or continue to isolate. In the process, the victorious forces overthrew the shogun and recognized the Japanese emperor as the leader of Japan in 1868. The emperor was again ruling a unified Japan after centuries of being a figurehead (a leader in name only, without real power). The emperor used the title Meiji, meaning "enlightened rule," to describe his reign. Since he was restored to power, this period was called the **Meiji Restoration**.

Who forced Japan to open?

TURNING POINTS

The Meiji Restoration

Japan saw how the Europeans had colonized the rest of Asia. The Japanese had defeated the Mongols centuries before; they were not going to be defeated by the West either.

The Japanese did what few peoples have been able to do; they completely changed their culture. Emperor Meiji led the transformation of Japan into a modern state. Japan was the first nation in Asia to industrialize.

The Meiji Restoration succeeded because the emperor delegated power to a group of able men who earned their roles through success rather than by birth. These leaders traveled through America and Europe to educate themselves. They were particularly impressed with German culture. The orderly society, high-quality products, and cleanliness of Germany made the Japanese want to copy it. Their admiration for German culture was strange since Asian culture and German culture are so different. German military officers went to Japan to advise the Japanese on building an army, and German physicians advised on building hospitals. The Japanese learned how to build a modern navy from the Dutch, French, and Americans. Japan developed a constitutional form of government and later established a parliament. They also developed modern educational and judicial systems modeled after the West.

There was some continued opposition to change from the samurai class. In the Satsuma Rebellion of 1877, a European-styled Japanese army finally defeated the samurai. Internal opposition to reform ceased.

Despite a lack of raw materials, including coal and iron ore, Japan manufactured modern weapons and built a naval fleet that made Japan a powerful nation. Japan's navy was on par with Western navies by 1920; it was the third largest in the world.

The Meiji leaders inspired the people to accept and participate in all these changes by reviving Shintoism. While Buddhism had taken precedence as Japan's religion, it was Shintoism that taught the deity of the emperor. By renewing the people's belief in the emperor as a god, descended from the gods and goddesses that created Japan, the leaders could unite the nation behind the emperor and get them to obey him without question.

Japan before the Meiji Restoration

For Japan to finally sit at the table with the Western powers, it would have to prove itself in some real wars. The opportunity to do this came in three major wars. The 1894 Sino-Japanese War was explained in the previous section. Then in 1900, Japan supplied warships and thousands of well-armed troops to help suppress the Boxer Rebellion in China. But in 1905 Japan did what no Asian country of the era had; it defeated a European power. Japan astonished the European states by quickly and decisively defeating the Russian army and navy in the Russo-Japanese War. With this victory, Japan established itself as the power in East Asia.

In 1912 the emperor died, but with his leadership, Japan had done what no nation had ever done in so short a time, completely transforming its nation and culture. The Japanese now had a centralized, constitutional, parliamentary government. They had a modern transportation and communication system that rivaled any Western nation's systems. They had factories that could produce high-quality machines. They had a powerful army and navy. They had a public education system that stressed learning math and reading. The education system also included moral training on how to be a good citizen, obeying the emperor and one's family. The following chapters reveal the path that Japan took because of the Meiji Restoration. Whether this massive change was the right decision is still up for debate since, like individuals and nations, Japan continues to live with the positive and negative consequences of its choice.

1. What were some of the political, economic, and social changes that occurred during the Meiji Period?
2. Why was it effective to use the emperor as a symbol of unity?
3. What European developments did Japan study?
4. What was the West's response to Japan's military victories?

Japan after the Meiji Restoration

Missionaries to Japan

Samuel R. Brown founded China's first Protestant school at Canton. After a visit to America in 1847, he left for Yokohama, Japan, in 1859. Brown became one of the first Christian teachers in that city. During his years of ministry in Japan, he translated the Bible into Japanese and wrote a grammar book entitled *Colloquial Japanese*.

J. C. Hepburn served as a missionary-doctor in Japan. He spent many years producing an English-Japanese dictionary. Hepburn started a school that later became Meiji Gakuin University. The Japanese government recognized his contribution by awarding him the Order of the Rising Sun.

A Japanese Bible

The Philippines

The **Philippines** is an archipelago made up of 7,641 islands. By the 1570s, Spain had colonized and gained control over all the islands. In 1863 the queen of Spain established free public schools in which teachers used the Spanish language for instruction. As Spain lost its colonies in Latin America, it held onto the Philippines, but in 1870 it allowed the islands a certain amount of autonomy (self-rule). The Filipinos desired full independence. Jose Rizal was a talented writer who spoke out for Philippine independence. Rizal's ideas inspired a revolution in 1896 against the Spanish. Although not directly involved in the revolution, Rizal was wrongly accused and executed.

General Emilio Aguinaldo and his army during the Philippine-American War

The revolution continued, while on the other side of the world Spain and the United States fought in Cuba. Since the Philippines was a Spanish possession that the United States desired, the islands got caught up in the Spanish-American War. The United States asked **Emilio Aguinaldo**, the Philippine revolutionary leader, to return from his exile in Hong Kong and to rally the Filipinos to fight the Spanish. On June 12, 1898, Aguinaldo declared the independence of the Philippines. Meanwhile, Admiral Dewey used the American fleet to defeat the Spanish in the Battle of Manila Bay on August 13, 1898. Following the Spanish defeat, Aguinaldo declared himself president of the new Philippine Republic.

The United States, led by President McKinley, went against its tradition and character and decided to colonize the Philippines. McKinley attempted to justify the move by saying that the Filipinos were not ready to govern themselves. In 1900, the Philippines was the second-wealthiest Asian nation behind Japan. The Filipinos continued to revolt against their colonizers, this time the Americans. The **Philippine-American War** went on from 1899 to 1913. It was an ugly war in which both sides committed atrocities. The war turned out to be more costly to the Americans than the Spanish-American War had been, but it was devastating to the Filipinos. The United States lost 4,234 soldiers, while the Philippine Republican Army lost around 18,000 soldiers. At least 200,000 Filipino civilians died as an indirect result of the war because they were displaced; many died of cholera.

?

Who colonized the Philippines in 1898?

Indonesia

Indonesia makes up the majority of the Malay Archipelago, which has five main islands: Sumatra, Borneo, Java, Sulawesi, and New Guinea. The Dutch followed a similar model to the British in India. The Dutch East India Company established itself as the governing power on the islands early on, but by 1840 Dutch forces were fighting wars to maintain control.

The Dutch government took over direct colonial rule of Indonesia beginning in 1901. It took them until 1910 to defeat all the remaining Indonesian rulers who opposed colonization. Like the British in India, the Dutch felt they had a duty to bring Western knowledge and culture to Indonesia. They felt they were liberating the Indonesians from tyrants who enslaved them.

The Dutch East India Company's first coat of arms

?

What happened in Indonesia in 1901?

?

CRITICAL THINKING 15.5

How did Japan's transformation into an industrial nation differ from Britain's industrial revolution?

Making Connections

1. What were the two main failures of the Ottoman Empire in the nineteenth century?
2. What did Napoleon's invasion of Egypt reveal about the Ottomans?
3. What group opposed Mahmud II's reforms?
4. Why was Russia able to support only a small population?
5. In which geographical directions did Russia expand during Catherine the Great's rule?
6. What did the serfs do when Napoleon invaded?
7. Why did Europe side with the Ottoman Empire in the Crimean War?
8. Why did a small group of army officers seek to replace Czar Nicholas I?
9. Briefly define *anarchy*.
10. What happened at the Battle of Plassey?
11. How did the British affect Christian missions in India?
12. How did the British improve India?
13. Why did the Chinese effort to end the sale of opium lead to war with Britain?
14. Why did several European nations seek ways to claim Chinese territory for themselves?
15. What was the cause of the Taiping Rebellion?
16. What countries exercised influence over Korea in the nineteenth and early twentieth centuries?
17. Which missionary to China changed the way missionaries interacted with the host culture?
18. What treaty opened Japan to foreign trade?
19. How did Japan unify its people for radical change?
20. What country colonized Indonesia?

Thinking Critically

1. Did the abolition of serfdom accomplish its intended goal? Why or why not?
2. Contrast the British rule of India with European and Japanese imperialism in China.
3. How did the Chinese rebellions further weaken the Chinese government?

WHAT TO KNOW

EVENTS

Decembrist Revolt
Crimean War
Battle of Plassey
Sepoy Mutiny
Opium War
Taiping Rebellion
Boxer Rebellion
Sino-Japanese War
Russo-Japanese War
Philippine-American War

PEOPLE

Boxers
Mahmud II
Abdulmejid I
Abdul Hamid II
Catherine the Great
Alexander I
Nicholas I
Michael Bakunin
Fyodor Dostoyevsky
Leo Tolstoy
Florence Nightingale
Alexander II
Alexander III
Robert Clive
William Carey
Lin Tse-Hsu
Hong Xiuquan
Empress Dowager Cixi
Guangxu
Robert Morrison
James Hudson Taylor
Jonathan Goforth
Adoniram Judson
Commodore Matthew Perry
Emilio Aguinaldo

PLACES

Canton
Korea
Philippines
Indonesia

TERMS

anarchy
opium
Treaty of Kanagawa
Meiji Restoration

16 War, Instability, and Depression

1914 – 1939

ESSENTIAL QUESTIONS

- What were the major causes and developments of World War I?
- How did World War I affect nations?
- How successful were attempts at peace following World War I?
- What political and economic conditions did states experience between the wars?
- Why were people disillusioned after World War I?

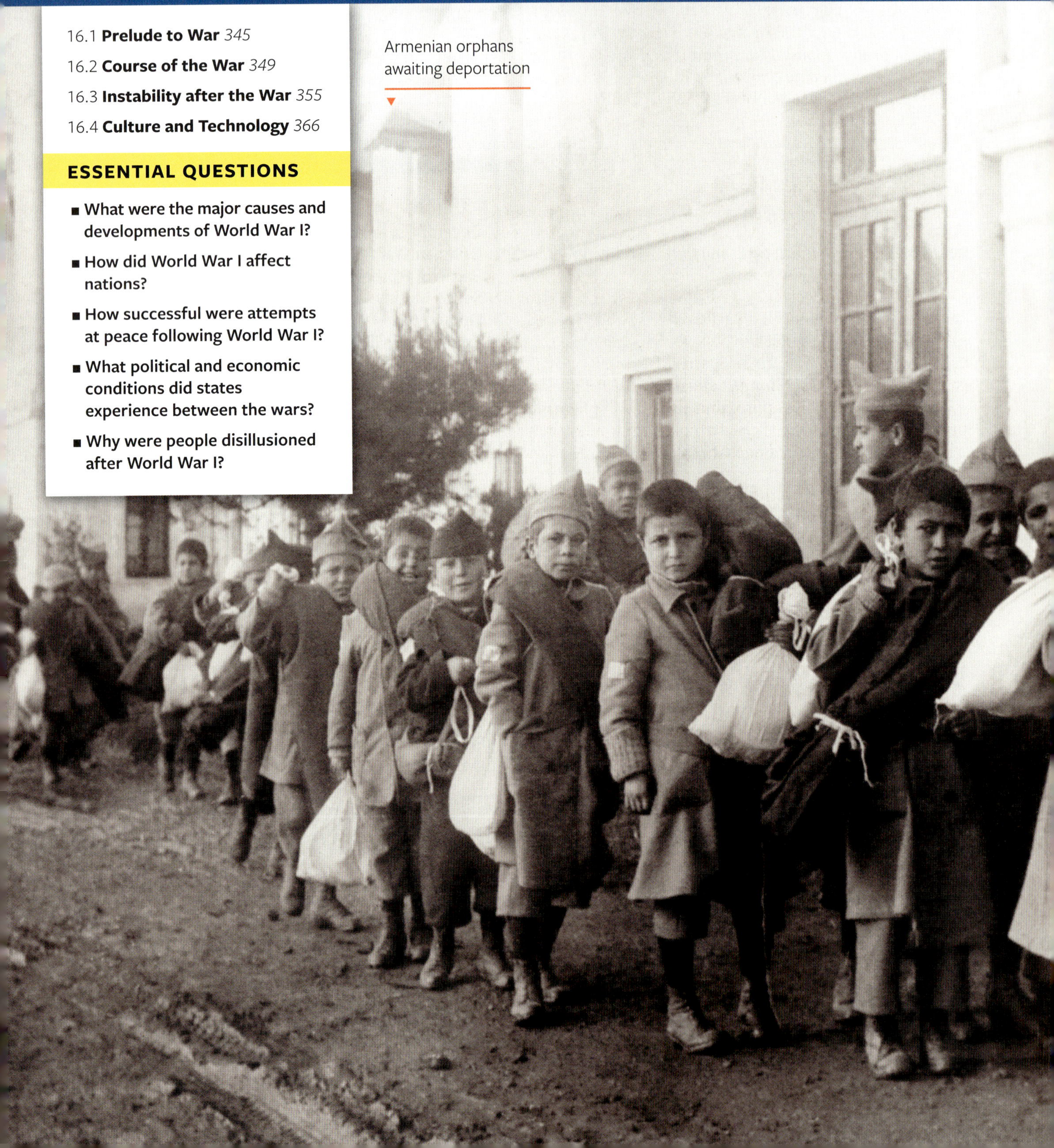

Armenian orphans awaiting deportation

Armenian Genocide

Modern Armenia is a small country in the region between the Black and the Caspian Seas (see map). It lies to the east of Turkey and the northwest of Iran. The modern country is a smaller version of a civilization that has existed in that region since ancient times.

Many Armenians came under the control of the Ottoman Empire in the 1400s. When the empire began to decay in the 1800s, the Ottomans began to view the Armenians as a threat. The Armenians were Orthodox Christian, whereas the Ottomans were Muslim. In addition, the Armenians in the Ottoman Empire had a natural connection with Russia because there were many Armenians living in Russian territory also. The Russians hoped to get Armenian help in their ongoing attempts to take Ottoman territory.

When the Armenian people began asking for political rights, the Ottomans responded violently. Over one hundred thousand Armenians died in a first round of killing in the 1890s. Another round of repression in 1909 resulted in the deaths of around thirty thousand more.

When World War I broke out, some Ottoman leaders feared the Armenians might side with the enemy. Others saw an opportunity to get rid of the Armenians permanently. At first there was the harassment, torture, and killing of various individuals. In 1915 the violence spread. Ottoman officials decided to eliminate all the Armenians living within their empire. Soldiers killed Armenians without restraint. Then the Ottomans marched the survivors over two hundred miles to detention camps in Syria and Palestine. Guards killed some on the march, and most of the rest died of hunger, abuse, or disease.

Estimates vary, but approximately 1.5 million Armenians died between 1915 and 1923. This attempted **genocide** (the planned killing of a people group) forced another five hundred thousand Armenians to live in exile.

Only a small population of Armenians remains in the nation of Turkey today. Despite a large body of evidence supporting the attempted genocide, Turkey denies that the slaughter ever took place and refuses to use the term *genocide*.

16.1 Prelude to War

Faith in Science and Technology

Faith in the ability of science and technology to bring about progress was a common viewpoint at the beginning of the 1900s. People began to believe that humans could solve any problem and cure all of society's ills.

Science

Scientists made several discoveries about the atom and its structure. For example, they learned that atoms contained negatively charged particles called electrons. Continued research greatly expanded understanding of the atom and its enormous potential.

Physicians developed processes to reveal and confirm the causes of certain diseases. In the 1870s German physician Robert Koch discovered the cause of a disease called anthrax. This disease spreads from animals such as cattle to humans and can be deadly. Koch's discovery helped others understand the spread of disease.

GUIDING QUESTIONS

- How did developments in science and technology affect events of the early twentieth century?
- What were four main causes of World War I?
- What led to the start of World War I?

How did Robert Koch's discovery of the cause of anthrax help other physicians?

This chemical plant in Oppau, Germany, produced nitrogen, used for fertilizer and for explosives during the war.

Technology

Inventors came up with new processes for producing steel, electricity, and chemicals. Developments in chemicals resulted in the mass production of paper, soaps, and fertilizer. Germany, the largest producer of chemicals, developed synthetic dyes and improved ways to refine oil. Technological advances such as these allowed European countries to build infrastructures, modernize their militaries, and multiply wealth.

What effect did technological advances have on European countries?

Causes of War

There are many theories about the causes of World War I. Here we will discuss four basic causes. They can be remembered using the word "MAIN" as an acronym (a word whose letters each stand for a word or part of a word).

M — MILITARISM

In the late 1800s and early 1900s, several European nations built up militaries that were much larger than what was needed for defense. A large army and navy became an expression of national glory and a symbol of power. In some nations the military dominated the government. Citizens often glorified war regardless of why nations were fighting.

A — ALLIANCES

Otto von Bismarck, the chancellor of Germany, made an alliance with Russia and Austria-Hungary in 1873 to protect Germany in case of a conflict with France. When this agreement fell apart, he made an alliance with Austria-Hungary and Italy in 1882 that was known as the **Triple Alliance**. In addition, he arranged a secret treaty with Russia in 1887.

When **Wilhelm II** became the emperor of Germany in 1888, he dismissed Bismarck and allowed the Russian treaty to expire. As a result, France convinced Russia to sign an alliance in 1894. Wilhelm also ordered the construction of a large fleet that challenged Great Britain on the seas. To defend against possible German aggression, Great Britain and France developed an *Entente Cordiale* (friendly understanding). In 1907 Russia joined this loose confederation, and the three nations formed the **Triple Entente**. This system of alliances led Europe into war.

I — IMPERIALISM

You learned about imperialism in Chapters 14 and 15. The push for colonies continued into the 1900s. Germany and Italy still sought to gain access to foreign lands to show their national importance. Rivalry for colonies led to tension and suspicion among the European powers.

N — NATIONALISM

The nationalism that swept across Europe in the 1800s, prompting uprisings in Greece, Belgium, Hungary, and Poland, continued into the next century. Rather than being simply a devotion to one's people, though, the nationalism of the late 1800s and early 1900s encouraged national groups to believe that they were superior to each other. This kind of extreme nationalism naturally led to competition. Competition between the nations of Europe could be clearly seen in the imperialism and militarism of the period. Inevitably, competition led to war or threats of war.

Who were the members of the Triple Alliance and the Triple Entente?

Upheaval in the Balkans

The Balkan region, located in southeastern Europe, has a long history of conflict. The Ottoman Empire took control of the region through a series of conquests in the 1300s and 1400s. However, a growing sense of nationalism in the 1800s prompted several Balkan states to seek independence. Russia supported these states because of common ethnic ties. (Russians are Slavic as are many in the Balkans.) Russia also hoped to gain territory as the Ottomans grew weaker. Austria-Hungary, on the other hand, opposed Balkan independence. The Austro-Hungarian Empire had many Slavic peoples. The Habsburg emperors were afraid of unrest in their empire based on the example in the Balkans.

In 1878 the Treaty of Berlin was signed. It recognized the independence of the Balkan states of Serbia, Montenegro, and Romania. To relieve Austria-Hungary's fears about Slavic influence, the treaty allowed Austria-Hungary to occupy but not annex the Balkan provinces of Bosnia and Herzegovina. In 1908 Austria-Hungary ignored the treaty and annexed the territories.

The Balkans and Austria-Hungary, 1914

With the many competing interests in the Balkans, conflict was likely. And with the system of alliances that had been formed, any spark of conflict in the Balkans could ignite a major war throughout Europe. For that reason, the Balkans were considered the "powder keg" of Europe.

The spark that led to World War I occurred on **June 28, 1914**. On that day, a Bosnian radical (with ties to Serbia) assassinated Archduke **Francis Ferdinand**, heir to the throne of Austria-Hungary. The Austrian government then made demands that the Serbian government could not meet. Germany responded by pledging its support to the Austrians, while Russia mobilized (got its troops ready to fight) to defend Serbia.

Germany demanded that Russia stop mobilizing within twelve hours. When Russia continued, Germany declared war on Russia. A rapid series of declarations of war followed. Germany, Austria-Hungary, and the Ottoman Empire formed the **Central Powers**. Opposing them initially were Russia, Serbia, and France. Great Britain soon joined this alliance. This side was known as the **Allies**.

?

Why were the Balkans considered the "powder keg" of Europe?

Archduke Francis Ferdinand

Archduke Francis Ferdinand was born on December 18, 1863, in Graz, Austria. He was the oldest son of Archduke Karl Ludwig of Austria and Princess Maria Annunciata of Bourbon-Two Sicilies. His father's brother, Franz Joseph, was the emperor of the Austro-Hungarian Empire. Francis was not first in line to be emperor, but when his cousin and then his father died, he became the heir.

Francis Ferdinand married Countess Sophie Chotek on July 1, 1900. Sophie was not from a royal family, so she was not given the same status as her husband. For example, she could not stand next to him at some official events, and her children were left out of the line of succession for the throne. Despite their differences, though, the couple had a happy marriage.

Francis Ferdinand entered the army when he was twelve and reached the rank of major general at thirty-one. In 1913 he was appointed inspector general of the army. Francis Ferdinand pressed for political change in the Austro-Hungarian Empire. He believed that the empire was in danger of collapsing if it did not allow its many minority groups to have more of a say in their governing. He was especially concerned about the Slavic peoples. With his harsh, blunt manners, Francis Ferdinand often clashed with his uncle on these ideas.

In the summer of 1914, Francis Ferdinand received an invitation to visit the Austro-Hungarian troops stationed outside the city of Sarajevo, capital of the Balkan provinces of Bosnia and Herzegovina. Sophie would accompany him. The visit was set for June 28.

After Austria-Hungary had annexed Bosnia and Herzegovina in 1908, a group of young Bosnian revolutionaries had formed to oppose Austro-Hungarian rule. With the help of a Serbian terrorist organization, the Black Hand, they made plans to assassinate Francis Ferdinand on his visit to Sarajevo.

Francis Ferdinand and Sophie arrived at the train station in Sarajevo around 10:00 a.m. A line of several cars, holding officials and staff, traveled together toward the City Hall, where a reception was to be held. Francis Ferdinand and Sophie traveled in the second car with the top down. Unknown to the local police, several potential assassins were stationed along the way. As the cars drove through the city, one assassin threw a grenade at Francis Ferdinand's car. It bounced off the back of the car and landed in front of the car behind him, injuring several people. Now alert to danger, the procession quickly drove on to City Hall.

After the planned ceremony, the cars left again. Instead of heading directly out of town to see the troops, though, Francis Ferdinand wanted first to go to the hospital and visit the injured. Confusion among the drivers about the planned route resulted in the need to turn around. When the car transporting Francis Ferdinand and Sophie briefly stopped and backed up, one of the assassins, nineteen-year-old Gavrilo Princip, was sitting at a nearby café. Seeing his target appear unexpectedly before him, Princip walked up to the car with a pistol and shot Francis Ferdinand and Sophie. Both died not long after.

CRITICAL THINKING 16.1

1. What alliances were created in response to the actions of Wilhelm II?
2. Why did independence movements in the Balkans cause conflict between Russia and Austria-Hungary?

◂ Princip was arrested immediately following the assassinations.

16.2 Course of the War

As Europe rushed to war, both sides were confident that they would win and that the war would be over quickly. However, the war dragged on, and casualties climbed into the millions, with little to show for the massive loss of life. After four brutal years, the war finally ended, but its conclusion laid the groundwork for another war twenty-one years later.

GUIDING QUESTIONS

- What was the Schlieffen Plan?
- What were some major battles of World War I?
- How did new weapons affect battlefield strategies and outcomes?
- How did changing alliances after 1917 affect the outcome of the war?
- How did peace plans differ from each other?
- How did World War I affect individuals and nations?

Initial Invasions

Germany

With France to the west and Russia to the east, Germany found itself fighting on two **fronts**. However, this did not take the Germans by surprise. Several years earlier a German general named Alfred von Schlieffen prepared a strategy for fighting just such a war. The **Schlieffen Plan** called for the Germans to send most of their forces west through Belgium (officially neutral by an 1831 treaty) and quickly surround Paris. Once France surrendered, the German forces would rush to meet the advancing Russian forces on the eastern front.

When the Germans demanded the right to travel through Belgium, the Belgians refused. However, the Germans forced their way through anyway, violating Belgium's neutrality. This violation brought Great Britain into the war on the side of the Allies.

front a location of battlefield activity during a war

The Schlieffen Plan

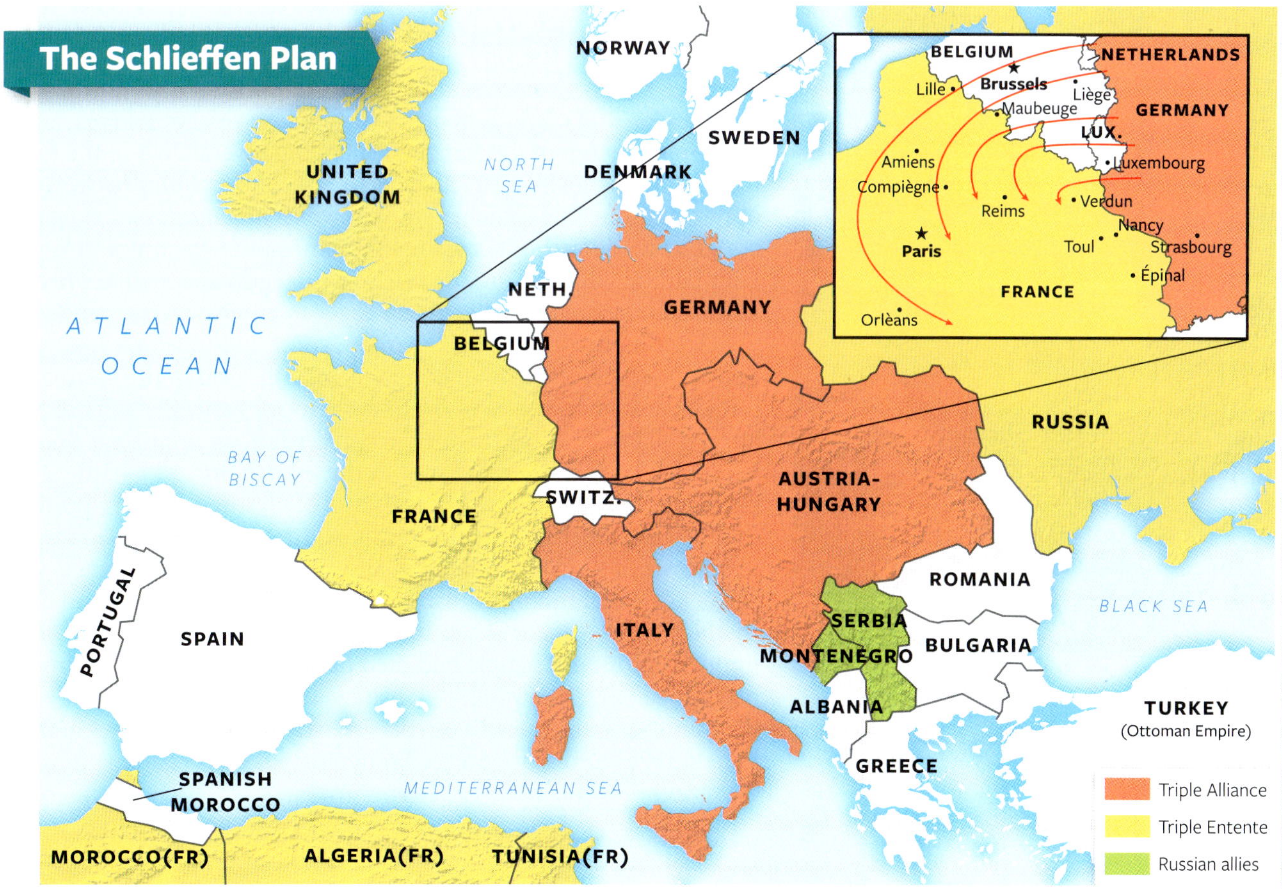

British troops move through a communication trench on their way to the front line.

France

The French stopped the German advance outside of Paris and reinforced their troops at the Marne River. Taxicabs from Paris helped to deliver troops to the battle. Despite the German push into France, the French held their position. British forces soon joined the French and helped to prevent German forces from advancing.

Russia

The Russian army surprised the Germans by mobilizing more quickly than the Schlieffen Plan anticipated. Russian forces enjoyed initial success against German and Austrian forces. However, under the command of Field Marshal Paul von Hindenburg, German troops defeated the Russians and seized more than two hundred thousand Russian prisoners. German victories discouraged the Russian troops, driving them back to Russia. Although the Germans ended the Russian threat, they had to keep troops on the border to prevent another attack.

What was the strategy of the Schlieffen Plan?

Stalemate

While Germans on the Eastern Front were halting the Russian advance, armies on the Western Front were sacrificing large numbers of troops without major gains on either side. Unable to move forward but unwilling to fall back, each side dug a series of trenches that eventually extended from the English Channel to the border of Switzerland. **Trench warfare** became the norm on the Western Front for most of the war.

Each side typically had three rows of trenches: front-line trenches, trenches for support, and trenches that housed reserve soldiers. Soldiers rotated in and out of the trenches, spending several days in the front lines before being given a few days to rest. The territory between the opposing front-line trenches was known as *no man's land*. No gains could be made without crossing no man's land, which was covered with barbed wire and guarded by machine gun and artillery fire. Understandably, no soldiers were eager to enter no man's land.

After many months of stalemate (condition in which two opposing forces have no major gains on either side), the German military leaders decided to try to force movement. They chose to attack the French near the fortress of Verdun, an important French landmark and a vulnerable spot in the French line. The battle started on February 21, 1916, with nine hours of German artillery bombardment. Then the infantry moved out. At first the Germans made good progress, but the French held on and stiffened their resistance. Over the next several months, furious engagements raged back and forth. By the time the Battle of Verdun ended in December, close to eight hundred thousand people had died or been wounded, with almost no change in territory held. The story was similar for the Battle of the Somme, a four-month offensive carried out mainly by the British to help relieve pressure on the French troops at Verdun.

trench warfare warfare in which specially dug ditches provide protection for troops

Industrialism and Innovation

Industrial developments of the late 1800s and early 1900s affected the course of World War I in several ways.

NEW WEAPONS

Machine guns
- fired hundreds of bullets per minute

Flamethrowers
- sprayed a deadly stream of burning liquid

Poison gas
- caused terrible burns and agonizing deaths

Soldiers were issued respirators to protect them from gas attacks.

AIRCRAFT

Airplanes
- monitored enemy activities, conducted bombing raids and aerial battles

Blimps
- bombed civilian areas, located enemy submarines

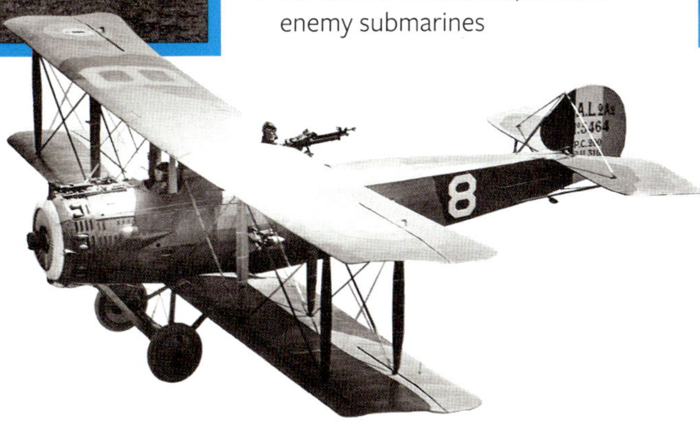

? Why was there so much destruction on the battlefields of World War I?

TANKS

- combined firepower and protection

SUBMARINES

- prevented the free movement of ships

Propaganda posters stirred up patriotism and encouraged people to support the war by buying government bonds.

Propaganda and Total War

Governments used mass communication to gain support for their side while demonizing the enemy. Propaganda emphasized national pride and the terrible acts (real and exaggerated) committed by the enemy. Religion became a tool of the government. Often, the war was presented as a moral crusade against a wicked enemy.

World War I was fought as a **total war**. In a total war, there are no limits on targets or the kinds of weapons used. Total war brought the war to civilians. Germans bombed civilian areas with zeppelins. They also fired artillery from great distances, and exploding shells often struck civilian targets. As the war took its toll, food became scarce. Civilian deaths from attack, disease, and famine climbed into the millions.

What happens during a total war?

Changes for the Allies

Russia's disastrous defeats at the hands of the Germans resulted in the collapse of central government in Russia. Czar Nicholas II was forced to abdicate (give up his throne) on March 15, 1917. In 1918 the new Communist Russian leader, Vladimir Lenin, signed a treaty with the Germans and took Russia out of the war. This freed the German forces to concentrate on the Western Front and possibly defeat the Allied forces.

The Germans had angered the United States on several occasions, especially with their policy of **unrestricted submarine warfare** (sinking of any vessel, military or civilian, without warning). Also, on March 1, 1917, the German foreign minister, Arthur Zimmermann, sent a telegram to the Mexican government. If the United States should support the Allies, Germany wanted Mexico's support. In exchange, Germany offered to help Mexico retake Texas, New Mexico, and Arizona. The British intercepted the telegram and shared it with the Americans, who were outraged. At the request of President Woodrow Wilson, Congress declared war on Germany on April 6, 1917. At first the American forces had little influence on the war. However, during the war's final months, America sent approximately ten thousand troops to France every day. The American forces provided the Allies with a much-needed advantage and helped defeat the German forces.

What were two factors that prompted the United States to enter World War I?

Aftermath

The Germans agreed to sign an **armistice** (truce or ceasefire) on **November 11, 1918**, because they believed the Allies would treat them fairly in peace negotiations. (Other Central Powers had signed armistices earlier that fall.) The outcome proved to be very different, however.

The Paris Peace Conference

Delegates from close to thirty nations attended the **Paris Peace Conference** in January 1919. The Allies excluded countries that had supported the Central Powers. They also excluded Russia because of its early withdrawal from the war.

Four empires were broken up because of World War I: German, Austro-Hungarian, Ottoman, and Russian. One of the crucial tasks of the conference was considering what to do with former territories of those empires. Eventually, eleven new nations were formed: Finland, Estonia, Latvia, Lithuania, Poland, Bulgaria, Yugoslavia, Turkey, Czechoslovakia, Austria, and Hungary.

TURNING POINTS

Treaty of Versailles

The Paris Peace Conference negotiations took place at the Palace of Versailles and other Paris locations. Three government leaders made most of the decisions: Prime Minister David Lloyd George of Great Britain, Prime Minister Georges Clemenceau of France, and President Woodrow Wilson of the United States. Treaties were signed with three of the Central Powers while the conference was in session. The Treaty of Versailles was the treaty signed between the Allies and Germany.

Before the war ended, Woodrow Wilson had given a speech to the US Congress presenting fourteen points he believed would help the world avoid more wars. Though his points dealt with specific situations, they generally followed these principles: (1) there should be free trade and open navigation on the seas, (2) people groups should be able to govern themselves, (3) diplomacy between nations should be open, and (4) a league of nations should be established to help keep peace in the world. Germany believed these points were reasonable and hoped the final treaty would be like Wilson's Fourteen Points.

Unlike the United States, though, France had endured great destruction during the war, having been the location of much fighting. The French wanted Germany to pay for the damages the war had caused. They also wanted to make sure Germany was too weak to attack in the future.

After months of negotiations, the Treaty of Versailles was signed on June 28, 1919, exactly five years after the Archduke's assassination. It included provision for a League of Nations, reduced Germany's military significantly, and made territory adjustments that cut Germany's population and land by about 10 percent. There were two parts of the treaty that Germany especially opposed. The first, often called the "war guilt clause," placed all the blame for the war on Germany. The second was the plan for Germany to pay reparations (payments for war damages) to the Allies.

TREATY SIGNED; WAR OVER

The Evening World. FINAL EDITION

NEW YORK, SATURDAY, JUNE 28, 1919.

WILSON LEAVES PARIS; SAILS SUNDAY

GERMANS PLEDGED TO ACT IN GOOD FAITH

CITY'S BELLS RING TIDINGS AS PEACE TREATY IS SIGNED; FLEET JOINS IN CELEBRATION

TREATY SEVERE ON GERMANY, SAYS WILSON, BUT IMPOSES NOTHING SHE CANNOT DO

GUNS BOOM, PLANES FILL AIR; FRENCH CROWDS CHEER PEACE

President in an Address to the American Public Says It Furnishes a Charter for a New Order and Ends Rule of Selfish Groups

GERMANS PLEDGED TO ENFORCE TREATY; NO RESERVATION

WILSON, STARTING FOR HOME, BIDS FRANCE GODSPEED

Mueller Signs for Germans at 3.12, Bell a Minute Later—Wilson's Name Comes Next, Followed by Lloyd George and Clemenceau.

Soldiers Break Ranks and Join in the Demonstrations of Joy—Chinese Refuse to Attend Ceremony and Gen. Smuts Signs Under Protest.

George

Clemenceau

Wilson

Few were pleased with the Treaty of Versailles. France doubted that the League of Nations was strong enough to prevent future German aggression. Some British believed that the Germans had been treated too harshly and that the reparations clause would cause economic problems for the continent. The United States never ratified the treaty because of some concerns in the Senate about the League of Nations. And Germany was bitter about the blame it received for the war, the territory it lost, and the reparations it was asked to pay. Resentment of the Treaty of Versailles became a cause that groups like the Nazis used to gain support.

1. What general principles did Wilson's Fourteen Points follow?
2. Why did France want a harsher peace settlement than Wilson proposed?
3. Which two parts of the Treaty of Versailles were especially unpopular with Germans?

▲

This French military cemetery contains the graves of 16,142 known soldiers. The remains of approximately 130,000 unknown soldiers are kept in the ossuary (building) in the background.

The Cost

The losses sustained by both sides in this terrible war were staggering. Estimates suggest that there were close to ten million military deaths and a similar number of civilian ones. Approximately twenty-one million were wounded.

In addition to the tremendous cost in human lives, the direct and indirect financial costs of the war may have exceeded three hundred and fifty billion dollars. Some believed that the cost had been so great that no nation would ever go to war again. They would tragically be proven wrong within a few years.

The Course of WWI

1914

June 28, 1914
Archduke Francis Ferdinand is assassinated, leading to World War I.

September 6–12, 1914
First Battle of the Marne

May 1915
Italy enters the war on the Allied side.

February 21–December 18, 1916
Battle of Verdun

July 1–November 18, 1916
Battle of the Somme

1917
Russian Revolution propels Vladimir Lenin into power as first Communist dictator of Russia.

April 6, 1917
America's Congress declares war on Germany.

1918
Lenin signs a treaty with Germany and takes Russia out of the war.

November 11, 1918
Germany signs an armistice, ending World War I.

1919
Paris Peace Conference

1919

CRITICAL THINKING 16.2

How did changes for the Allies in 1917 and 1918 affect the outcome of the war for Germany?

The Council of the League of Nations met in Geneva, Switzerland.

16.3 Instability after the War

Attempts at Peace

The League of Nations, established by the Treaty of Versailles, was supposed to promote international cooperation to prevent future wars. However, the League had power only to recommend action. It had no power to enforce its recommendations. The League soon proved to be weak and ineffective, especially when dealing with powerful nations.

Other efforts to prevent future wars included the signing of three pacts, or agreements. Several nations met in 1921–22 for the **Washington Naval Conference**. They agreed to limit the number of warships each nation could build. The participants assumed that nations could avoid war by simply reducing or eliminating weapons.

In 1925 European nations met in Locarno, Switzerland. At this meeting, Germany signed an agreement with France and Belgium recognizing its present borders with those two nations as permanent. The **Locarno Pact** briefly offered the promise of peace in Europe.

In 1928 the American secretary of state, Frank Kellogg, decided that the best way to prevent war was to get nations to agree to renounce offensive war. Those who signed the **Kellogg-Briand Pact** agreed to settle their disputes by negotiation rather than force. Kellogg naively believed that this agreement would prevent wars from being started. However, three years after signing this pact, Japan invaded Manchuria.

Conditions in the Democratic States of the West

United States

Following World War I, some nations seemed to recover and prosper financially. Others struggled and found themselves awash in national debt. The United States appeared to be able to absorb massive war debt and still prosper. However, that apparent prosperity faded, and the United States entered a period of severe economic decline. Many blame the stock market crash in 1929, but that was only a symptom of underlying problems. The costs of the **Great Depression** created a great burden for the world to bear, and the consequences endure to this day.

GUIDING QUESTIONS

- How did nations attempt to ensure peace after World War I?
- What was happening in the 1920s and 1930s in the democratic states of the West?
- What led to the rise of authoritarian governments in the 1920s and 1930s?
- How did conditions change in Africa and Asia following World War I?
- How did the Mexican Revolution compare with other revolutions?
- How should Christians respond to crisis?

How did the Kellogg-Briand Pact attempt to prevent war?

Causes of the Depression

There is much debate about the causes of the **Great Depression**. We can, however, identify two basic economic problems that the United States experienced leading up to the Depression.

First, there was the financial devastation of World War I. The United States had loaned the Allies over ten billion dollars during the war. While most of the Allies promised to pay back their debt, only Finland was able to do so entirely. In addition, there were the costs of America's own participation in the war. The result was stress on the American economy.

Second, there was the rise of **protectionism**. As the US economy weakened in the late 1920s, American companies pressured the government to pass tariff legislation that would raise the prices on foreign goods and protect American-made products. The result was the Smoot-Hawley Tariff Act, the highest tariff in US history. Many European nations responded with restrictive tariffs of their own. American exports dropped from seven billion dollars in 1929 to two and one-half billion dollars in 1932. The loss of trade damaged the American economy, and the damage spread throughout many nations.

How did the Smoot-Hawley Tariff damage the American economy?

Costs of the Depression

The United States and other nations had experienced financial panics and brief depressions many times prior to 1929. However, this time governments took a much more active role in trying to restore their economies. Therefore, natural economic corrections did not occur. The Great Depression endured for many years with little improvement, despite massive spending of taxpayers' money.

Widespread unemployment was one of the immediate effects of the Depression in the United States. Up to one-third of the country's workers lost their jobs. Since the Depression began during the presidency of Herbert Hoover, many blamed him for this economic downturn and pressured him to help those in need. Hoover, however, believed that most of the solutions to the nation's problems lay at the local level. He wanted federal funds to be used only after all voluntary (that is, private and religious) and local resources were exhausted. When federal money was used, Hoover thought it should be carefully managed.

protectionism the use of tariffs to support industries in one's country

The unemployed stood in long lines at soup kitchens to get a free meal.

Another effect of the Depression was a substantial increase in the size of the federal government. Even Hoover tried to offer Americans more help by establishing new government agencies such as the Federal Farm Board, which tried to raise the price of farm goods, and the Reconstruction Finance Corporation, which loaned money to industries and businesses. Franklin D. Roosevelt, who took office in 1933, called for a **New Deal** that would take more decisive action to try to end the Depression. The result was the creation of numerous federal programs and agencies that came to be known by their initials. Though Roosevelt's actions made people feel like something was being done to solve their problems, the New Deal failed to bring America out of the Depression.

How did Roosevelt try to bring America out of the Depression?

Men planted trees on the Nett Lake Reservation in Minnesota as part of a Civilian Conservation Corps (CCC) project.

Great Britain

Trade was damaged in Great Britain, first by the war and then by the introduction of protective tariffs in 1932. Foreign competition and the rising popularity of other energy sources hurt Britain's coal mining, resulting in layoffs and strikes by miners. To try to help the British people, the government created many new social welfare programs. The Labour Party, which was formed to provide a political voice for workers, took control of the government for the first time briefly in 1924 under the leadership of Ramsay MacDonald.

France

Initially, France had a greater economic recovery than Great Britain. New factories were built. Rich mineral deposits and valuable factories were gained in the territories of Alsace and Lorraine, transferred from Germany to France by the Treaty of Versailles. Unemployment was not as severe in France as in Britain because most French people were small businessmen or farmers.

Rise of Authoritarian States

Soviet Union

In Chapter 15 you learned about the conflict in Russia. Despite brutal suppression by the czar and the central government, unrest continued to grow. During the reign of Czar Nicholas II, many radical parties formed in Russia. One of the most radical, the Social Democratic Party, soon split. The more radical faction of the party took the name **Bolsheviks**, and the more moderate faction became known as **Mensheviks**. The Bolsheviks, who eventually became the Communist Party, supported violence, while the Mensheviks sought change through peaceful methods.

While many events contributed to the overthrow of the Russian monarchy, violent strikes and riots beginning on March 8, 1917, quickly led to Nicholas's abdication on March 15. (Later, the Bolsheviks executed him and his family.) Initially, a temporary government led by Menshevik Alexander Kerensky tried to stabilize the chaotic conditions in Russia. However, the Bolsheviks sabotaged these efforts and stirred up Russian workers to prevent the possibility of Menshevik success.

Vladimir Lenin (left) and Joseph Stalin (right)

Vladimir Lenin, who was living in exile in Switzerland, was the leader of the Bolshevik party. In a strategic move, the German government helped Lenin return to Russia from exile, anticipating that he would pull Russia out of the war. On November 7, 1917, Lenin's forces took over the government offices in St. Petersburg. With little effort, Lenin became the virtual dictator of Russia.

How did the Bolsheviks defeat the Mensheviks?

Lenin embraced Marxist teaching, but he disagreed with Karl Marx on several issues. First, Lenin rejected the possibility of peaceful change in favor of violent revolution. Second, Lenin believed that revolution would occur under the direction of strong leadership, not as spontaneous revolts by the working class. Third, Lenin believed a small, elite group of people should control the government, not the masses.

Lenin became a strong opponent of religion. He declared that atheism was a vital and inseparable part of Marxist teaching. He viewed religion and churches as tools used to take advantage of the working class. In 1918 when pastors and priests opposed Lenin's violent tactics and his orders to empty the churches of valuables, he ordered the military to put down their resistance with great brutality. Large numbers of religious leaders were executed.

When Lenin died in 1924, two of his followers, Leon Trotsky and **Joseph Stalin** (1879–1953), competed to replace him. Stalin quickly outmaneuvered Trotsky and became the second dictator of the Union of Soviet Socialist Republics (USSR), or **Soviet Union**, a new confederation of Russia and several of its neighbors established in 1922.

In 1928 Stalin introduced the first of several Five-Year Plans. With these plans, Stalin tried to build up industrial production and bring agriculture under central government control. However, many peasants, especially those in the agriculturally rich area of the Ukraine, opposed Stalin's plan to take land and set up collective farms. Stalin used the secret police and the army to burn the homes of defiant peasants. Authorities deported or executed those who resisted. Production plummeted; and when collective farms failed to reach the production goals set for them by the government, they sometimes had more food taken from them as punishment. It is estimated that five million people died in this manmade famine, close to four million of them from the Ukraine alone.

Stalin continued and intensified oppression of religion. The Soviet government closed thousands of churches and religious schools and executed an unknown number of pastors and priests.

The manmade famine that took place in the Ukraine in 1932 and 1933 is known as the Holodomor (killing through starvation).

Benito Mussolini

Italy

Italy had supported the Allies during the war and had suffered the loss of five hundred thousand men. However, Italy received no territory or colonies because of its efforts. Instead, the Italian economy suffered from a large war debt and strikes by discontented workers. The wealthy looked for protection from a possible Communist revolution, and the masses wanted a strong leader to restore Italy's national pride.

Benito Mussolini had been a member of the Socialist Party in Italy, but his support of World War I was unpopular with other Socialists. In 1921 he formed the **Fascist Party** and quickly gained popularity. In his writings and speeches, Mussolini promised order and stability. Sensing that the government was vulnerable, Mussolini led thousands of followers in a march on Rome in October 1922. King Victor Emmanuel III agreed to the Fascists' demand that he appoint Mussolini the premier of Italy.

Mussolini gradually transformed Italy into a dictatorship. While maintaining the image of a representative government, Mussolini and the Fascists sought to gain total control over the government. Within three years, they had achieved their purpose.

Mussolini worked to make Italy economically self-sufficient. To help accomplish this goal, he organized Italy's workforce into groups called syndicates. Each syndicate determined wages, prices, policies, and working conditions for its group.

To add the appearance of legitimacy to his rule, Mussolini ended Italy's long-standing dispute with the Catholic Church. In 1929 Mussolini and Catholic representatives signed the Lateran Treaties. These agreements ended the church's opposition to the unification of Italy that had continued since 1870. In exchange for money and a small independent region known as Vatican City, the pope recognized Mussolini's government and ended the papacy's prior claims to additional territory.

Communism vs. Fascism

Both Communism and Fascism resulted in totalitarian governments (governments that control every area of life), so sometimes it is hard to tell the two apart. However, here are some technical differences. (These are the ideal views of these philosophies. Things did not always work out this way.)

	Communism	Fascism
Economic Policy	Businesses owned and controlled by the government	Businesses privately owned but controlled by the government
Form of Government	Dictatorship by the workers	Military dictatorship
View of the Nation-state	International, teaches that state will wither away	Highly nationalistic (love for one's own nation), glorifies state

What was the purpose of the Lateran Treaties?

GERMANY

At the end of World War I, the last German kaiser (emperor) abdicated, and the German Empire that was founded in 1871 came to an end. To replace the empire, German leaders formed the Weimar Republic (named after the town in Germany where the republic was organized). Despite early optimism, this German government had little opportunity to succeed. Most Germans did not support it. In addition, the large number of political parties in Germany made it difficult for one party to win a majority in elections.

Political and economic instability in the country allowed radical groups like the National Socialist German Workers' Party (or **Nazi Party**) to gain support. Led by **Adolf Hitler**, the Nazis gained control of the German government in 1933. Once in power, they convinced the members of the Reichstag (German parliament) to suspend the republic and make Hitler the dictator of Germany. The Nazi government is often referred to as the **Third Reich**. The German word *reich* refers to a kingdom or empire. The first two German reichs were the Holy Roman Empire (800 to 1806) and the German Empire of 1871 to 1918.

The Nazis developed four-year plans for controlling the economy. The first plan put many Germans back to work rebuilding Germany's military and constructing public works, like a modern highway system. The second plan tried to prevent problems in industries by regulating conditions for workers.

Huge crowds came to Nuremberg, Germany, to hear Adolf Hitler speak at Nazi Party rallies.

LIFE IN

Berlin

Power

The Nazis tried to overthrow the government of the German province of Munich in 1923. When violence failed to put them in power, they switched to politics. Hitler was skilled at propaganda; he gained support by stirring up concerns about the economy, fears of communism, and anger at the Treaty of Versailles. Though the Nazis never gained a majority in the Reichstag, they used force and intimidation to push their way into total power.

Justice

Hitler and the Nazis believed that the Aryans (considered to be a racial group who settled Northern India, Iran, and Europe) were superior to other peoples. This belief prompted them to act with great prejudice against the Slavic people and, most especially, the Jewish people, who had experienced persecution in Europe since the Middle Ages. Germans were encouraged to boycott Jewish businesses. Jews were officially banned from many types of public work. And on November 9–10, 1938, there was the *Kristallnacht* (Night of Shattered Glass) tragedy. Using the excuse of the assassination of a German government official in Paris by a young Polish Jew, the Nazis encouraged attacks on Jewish people and property. Rioters burned synagogues, destroyed businesses, and killed at least one hundred people that night.

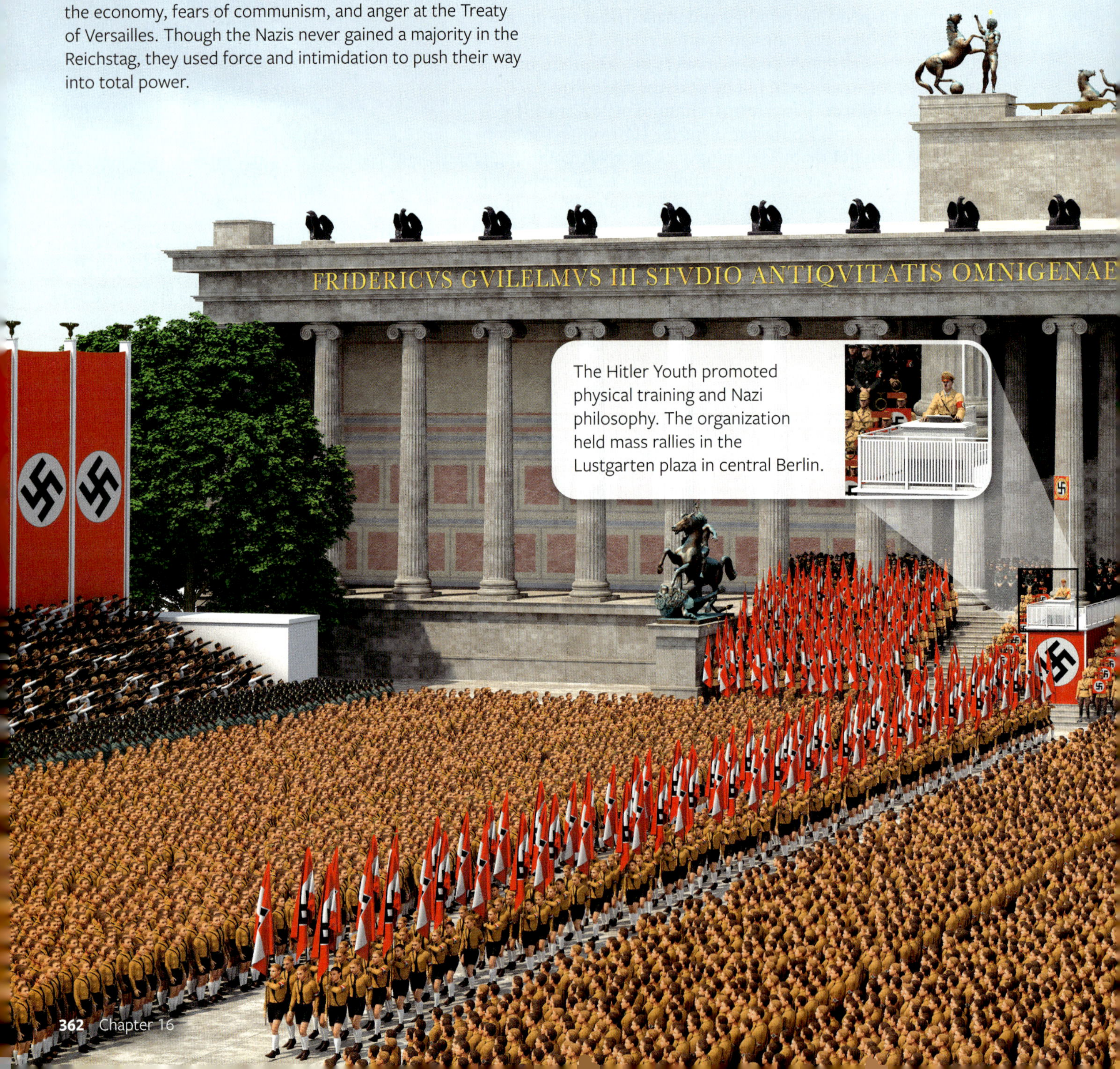

The Hitler Youth promoted physical training and Nazi philosophy. The organization held mass rallies in the Lustgarten plaza in central Berlin.

Citizenship

Hitler considered the Jewish people to be Germany's enemies and the source of its problems. He promoted the Nuremberg laws of 1935, which deprived Jews in Germany of citizenship and banned intermarriage with other Germans.

Religion

Though the Nazis used religion when convenient to maintain their power, they disliked what they saw as the weakness of Christianity. Under Nazi rule, church-run schools in Germany were closed, and many pastors were arrested.

Environment

Hitler believed that the German people needed more living space, or land. More land for farming could help Germany become self-sufficient (able to produce everything needed by the country). Self-sufficiency would limit the ability of enemy forces to cut off supplies in a time of war.

Changing Conditions in Africa and Asia

Mandate System

The League of Nations established a system that allowed some of the Allied powers from World War I (mainly France and Britain) to govern colonies previously owned by the Central Powers. Under this system, the Allied powers could oversee the former colonies but not annex them. The system was called the **mandate** system because the Allied powers were operating under a mandate, or formal assignment, from the League of Nations.

During World War I, Arabs working with British officer T. E. Lawrence (Lawrence of Arabia) helped the Allies defeat the Ottoman Empire in the Middle East. In return, they expected to receive their independence. Instead, the former Ottoman territories of Lebanon and Syria became French mandates, and the former territories of Iraq and Palestine became British mandates.

? **What former Ottoman territories became French and British mandates?**

Sun Yat-sen

Chiang Kai-shek

China

In Chapter 15 you learned about the decline of the Manchu dynasty and its continued resistance to change. By 1911 young Chinese officials, along with military officers and students, staged a revolution to replace the Manchu dynasty with a republic. Led by **Sun Yat-sen**, the Chinese worked to bring reform to China. However, others pressured Sun Yat-sen to postpone reform and allow Emperor Puyi to abdicate. He soon regretted agreeing to this compromise. Chinese president Yuan Shikai used his influence to dismantle the new republic before being forced to step down in 1916. A power vacuum developed, and Sun Yat-sen struggled to bring unity to China through the **Kuomintang,** or Nationalist Party.

Following the death of Sun Yat-sen in 1925, **Chiang Kai-shek** (1887–1975) assumed the leadership of the Kuomintang. In 1927 a radical element of this party split off into what became the **Chinese Communist Party**.

Led by **Mao Zedong** (1893–1976), the Communists stirred up peasant revolts to challenge the conservative government of Chiang Kai-shek. These two forces fought a civil war to gain control of China. The Japanese invasion of Manchuria in 1931 postponed this struggle until the conclusion of World War II.

Japan

Japan had demonstrated its military might with victories over China and Russia in the late 1800s and early 1900s. It had also aided the Allies in World War I. Therefore, Japan felt slighted by events such as the Washington Naval Conference, which restricted the Japanese navy to fewer ships than the British and American navies were allowed.

Another problem for Japan in the period between the wars was resources. With a growing population and a booming industrial economy, Japan needed more food and natural resources than were available in its home territory. Trade had slowed because of the Great Depression. Conquest of foreign territories (with needed resources) seemed to be an alternative.

? How did resources become a problem for Japan in the period between the wars?

Mexico

Mexico experienced revolution from approximately 1910 to 1920. Some of the issues that provoked the revolution were like those that prompted other revolutions of the period. Porfirio Díaz was the presidential dictator of Mexico for thirty-one years. Díaz organized the government to benefit himself and chose officials who would be loyal to him. Both peasant farmers and industrial workers were unhappy with their conditions and with the favoritism shown to wealthy landholders and business owners.

The revolution started with dissatisfaction with the 1910 presidential election. Though Díaz won, the election was clearly unfair. His opponent, Francisco Madero, took part in an armed uprising against Díaz's government. After Díaz was forced to resign, Madero was elected president and took office in November of 1911 (though he governed only until February 1913). Unlike other countries' revolutions, Mexico's was slow to establish a stable government. There were overthrows, assassinations, and shifting alliances occurring regularly throughout the next several years. A new constitution, passed in 1917, addressed many of the grievances that had started the revolution.

? What issues provoked the Mexican Revolution?

CRITICAL THINKING 16.3

? How did the Nazis adapt their tactics to ultimately gain power in Germany?

(top) Propaganda posters for Mao Zedong featured red, the color of the revolution, prominently. (bottom) General Pancho Villa played a prominent role in the power struggles of the Mexican Revolution. Though he failed to gain political power, Villa became famous through movies and books about his life.

GUIDING QUESTIONS

- How did innovations in science and technology affect society between the wars?
- How did the art and literature of the early twentieth century compare with a biblical view of society?
- In what ways did the rise of mass media impact American and world culture?

16.4 Culture and Technology

Science and Technology

French physicists **Pierre and Marie Curie** pioneered work in radioactive matter. They discovered that radioactive elements could be reduced to simpler elements. **Albert Einstein** developed theories on relativity and the relationship between matter and energy ($E = mc^2$). In addition, he theorized about the existence of black holes in space and other celestial concepts that helped humans realize the vastness of the universe.

Scientists used discoveries in fields such as mathematics, physics, and chemistry to develop many improved modes of transportation. Airplanes changed dramatically between the first flight and the end of World War I. Larger and more powerful engines were developed for self-propelled vehicles such as cars, trucks, and tanks. And railways continued to progress from slower wood-powered steam locomotives to faster coal- and then diesel-powered engines.

Transportation advances benefited society. Industries could get goods to market quickly. Workers could more easily travel to find work. And vacations could be more comfortable and frequent.

How did transportation advances benefit society?

Science also contributed to the rise of a mass consumption culture. Technological improvements made popular goods such as bicycles, refrigerators, and radios less expensive to produce and thus affordable to more people. The development of artificial (rayon and acetate) and synthetic (nylon) fibers gave consumers new choices in textiles.

Pierre and Marie Curie in their laboratory in Paris

Albert Einstein giving a lecture in Vienna

Santa Fe's Super Chief diesel streamliner ran a route from Los Angeles to Chicago.

Literature, Art, and Architecture

In the years between the wars, many Americans and Europeans found life to be empty and ultimately futile. To them, feelings became more important than facts. These feelings found expression in literature and art. Even architecture changed during this period.

Literature

Literature following World War I often reflected the despair and emptiness of modern life. T. S. Eliot (1888–1965) wrote an intricate poem entitled "The Waste Land" that attempted to describe this emptiness. German writer Thomas Mann (1875–1955) wrote works whose main characters were passive victims of forces beyond their control. Much of the literature from this period expressed misery and gloom.

Art

Two schools of art emerged during this period, **expressionism** and **cubism**. Expressionist painters created art that reflected how the artist felt about his subject rather than what he saw as he painted his subject. Cubist painters reduced their subjects to geometric shapes (often cubes). This school of painting attempted to depict the subject from several perspectives at once. Cubist painters often designed their works to astonish and to confront the observer's view of the world.

? What became more important than facts in American and European society?

T. S. Eliot won the Nobel Prize in Literature in 1948.

The Scream, by Norwegian Edvard Munch, is a classic expression of modern anxiety.

Portrait of Pablo Picasso, by Juan Gris, is a tribute to the co-founder of cubism.

Architecture

Using concrete, glass, and steel, architects designed open and functional buildings. American architect Louis Sullivan (1856–1924) developed the concept of skyscrapers. Walter Gropius (1883–1969) developed the concept of functional architecture in Europe. Frank Lloyd Wright (1868–1959), an American architect, added his own personal touch by designing buildings that blended in with their surroundings.

The Bauhaus (top left) in Dessau, Germany, was designed by Walter Gropius. The Prudential Building (right) in Buffalo, New York, was designed by Louis Sullivan. Fallingwater (bottom left) in the Bear Run Nature Reserve in Pennsylvania, was designed by Frank Lloyd Wright.

What advances lowered the cost of producing printed materials?

Mass Media

Improved printing presses and the mass production of paper lowered the cost of producing various forms of printed materials, including newspapers and magazines. Commercial advertising helped to finance these publications.

Moving pictures developed, and scientists soon found a way to add sound. Movies became a popular and inexpensive form of entertainment. Continued improvements to the radio led to mass production, and soon no home was complete without one. Mass media contributed to the development of common cultural ideas within nations and around the world.

CRITICAL THINKING 16.4

How do Jeremiah 17:9 and Proverbs 28:26 apply to emphasizing feelings over facts?

Making Connections

1. How did scientific and technological developments of the late 1800s and early 1900s affect society?
2. Identify and briefly describe the four main causes given for World War I.
3. What events in the Balkans created tension between Austria-Hungary and Serbia?
4. How did the Schlieffen Plan propose to win a two-front war?
5. What type of warfare was fought on the Western Front?
6. Describe the impact of new weapons, tanks, airplanes, and submarines on the fighting of World War I.
7. How did changes within the Allies in 1917 and 1918 affect the outcome of the war?
8. What costs did the world experience because of World War I?
9. Name and describe agreements made between the wars to promote peace.
10. How did the Great Depression affect the democratic states of the West?
11. How did totalitarian governments gain support in Russia, Italy, and Germany?
12. What was the mandate system?
13. What two forces fought a civil war in China?
14. What problems caused Japan to become more militant between the wars?
15. How were the complaints that prompted the Mexican Revolution like complaints that prompted other revolutions?
16. Why did the Mexican Revolution last for ten years?

Thinking Critically

1. How did Wilson's Fourteen Points compare with the final terms of the Treaty of Versailles? Which plan did Germany prefer? Why do you think the Germans preferred that plan?
2. How did science and technology change the way people lived and thought between the wars?
3. Evaluate the modern view of life as empty and meaningless. Is it a biblical view according to Jeremiah 29:11 and Romans 8:18? Explain your answer.
4. How has mass media shaped the modern world?

What to Know

Dates & Events

June 28, 1914
November 11, 1918
Paris Peace Conference
Washington Naval Conference
Great Depression

People

Wilhelm II
Francis Ferdinand
Vladimir Lenin
Joseph Stalin
Benito Mussolini
Adolf Hitler
Sun Yat-sen
Chiang Kai-shek
Mao Zedong
Pierre and Marie Curie
Albert Einstein

Places

Soviet Union

Terms

genocide
Triple Alliance
Triple Entente
Central Powers
Allies
front
Schlieffen Plan
trench warfare
total war
unrestricted submarine warfare
armistice
Treaty of Versailles
Locarno Pact
Kellogg-Briand Pact
protectionism
New Deal
Bolsheviks
Mensheviks
Fascist Party
Nazi Party
Third Reich
mandate
Kuomintang
Chinese Communist Party
expressionism
cubism

17 World War II

1939 – 1945

ESSENTIAL QUESTIONS

- What were the causes of World War II?
- How did World War II progress?
- What were the consequences of World War II?

American soldiers running into battle

The Roy Rickerson Story

The victory achieved by the **Allies** (Britain, USSR, and the United States) in World War II was largely the result of citizen soldiers stepping up to do their duty. These soldiers put their civilian lives on hold to fight fascist totalitarianism. They possessed the qualities of faith, personal initiative, and courage. One such soldier was Lieutenant Roy Rickerson.

Rickerson led a group of fifteen soldiers who parachuted deep behind enemy lines into southern France. At the time, the Germans still controlled most of France. Since Rickerson was from Louisiana, he happened to be fluent in French. The soldiers were tasked with stopping the Germans from moving to fight the Americans and British who were going to invade southern France on August 15, 1944. The second part of their job was to assist downed American air crews with getting home. Rickerson would sit in a café in his full-dress uniform to make himself known to the townspeople. They would know where to send the pilots or where they could give information to the Americans. Just one French person wanting to gain the favor of the Germans could have turned Rickerson in.

On August 31, 1944, the American operatives were fighting alongside French resistance fighters. They were trying to cause enough trouble to the German soldiers that the Germans would surrender. When they came up against a large group of Germans, the French fighters all went home. Rickerson and two of his sergeants found themselves all alone. The three men were able to capture a German captain. They asked the captain to tell the rest of his unit to surrender. The captain said he needed his major's permission to surrender, so the four drove an old car to the German camp to speak with the major. The major told them he could not surrender without his colonel's approval. Rickerson threatened that the Americans would bomb the German camp if they did not surrender. The Americans had been relentlessly bombing, so the Germans took the threat seriously, but Rickerson had no way of contacting the planes. The colonel told them that convincing his battalion commanders to surrender would be difficult. Rickerson repeated his threat, so the colonel left to call his commanders. Surrounded by Germans, the three Americans stood wondering what their fate would be if their bluff failed. Rickerson carried a pocket New Testament that he read whenever he had time. He opened it to Ephesians 4:1 and read, "Walk worthy of the calling with which you were called." After showing the verse to another soldier, they decided to trust the Lord and continue in their bluff. They were able to arrange the surrender of 3,824 men. Rickerson received the Silver Star for this action.

Rickerson said, "But we did not really do it [get the column to surrender]; the little black book did it. We do not take any pride in it. . . . We put that many people out of the war and saved their lives and many American lives as a result." A year later Rickerson found himself fighting the Japanese in China in much the same way that he fought the Germans. It was not common for a soldier to fight in both Europe and Asia during World War II. Roy Rickerson was truly a legend.

He retired from the army as a colonel after also serving in the Korean War. He worked as the vice president of a paper company. He was an active member in his church until his death on February 11, 2001.

GUIDING QUESTIONS

- What were the causes of World War II?
- What were the early aggressions of the Japanese Empire?
- How did Germany prepare to fight World War II?
- How did Western democracies respond to fascist aggression?

Most of the chapters in this book cover a period of hundreds or many hundreds of years. Yet this chapter covers only six years. Why? World War II was a war like no other before it and no other since. You are living in a world shaped by the events of this war; it resulted in the most dramatic reset of world power. Among other things, the United States became the key power in the world.

At the beginning of the war, only six nations were involved. By the end, only eleven of the world's countries remained neutral, and five of those neutral nations still served important purposes in the war.

17.1 Steps toward War

A great world event or war is like a volcano. The causes for it brew below ground until finally there is an explosion. In this case, many political, economic, cultural, and religious conflicts were bubbling under the surface. As a volcano releases steam before it erupts, the Axis powers telegraphed what was to come when they engaged in small wars that were overlooked at the time.

Causes

What were the three reasons for the war?

We can group the many causes of the war under three broad reasons. The first reason was imperialism. The **Axis powers** (Germany, Japan, and Italy) had imperialist tendencies that flowed from their fascist ideology. The second reason was revenge. The Germans, especially, felt they had been treated unjustly and wanted revenge. The third reason was the appeasement of (giving in to) the Axis by nations like Britain and France.

Imperialism

Germany and Japan believed not only that their cultures were the greatest but that they were a superior race of people. By conquering and subjugating (bringing under control) their neighbors, they would prove who was stronger. They also believed they would bring order to the lands they conquered. These newly acquired lands would also provide them with more space and resources.

One of Hitler's popular narratives was that German politicians were trying to satisfy Jews and socialists when they signed the Versailles treaty, thus betraying (stabbing in the back) the German army and Germany's people.

Revenge

In the last chapter you learned that the Allies treated the Central powers harshly following their agreement to stop fighting. Furthermore, the demand that Germany pay the Allied nations huge sums of money destroyed the German economy and led to the chaos that enabled the rise of the Nazi Party. Germany would not be satisfied until these injustices had been corrected.

Hitler placed the blame for the Versailles treaty on German politicians who "stabbed the German people in the back" by surrendering in World War I and agreeing to the harsh punishment Germany received. Fighting never occurred on German soil, and even though many families lost fathers and sons, German civilians were not killed in great numbers. As a result, Hitler convinced many that the nation should have continued fighting World War I.

Having fought on the side of the Allies in World War I, Japan felt it deserved to be treated as an equal by the Western nations. Yet the Western powers were trying to constrain Japan through agreements like the Washington Naval Conference.

Why did Germany seek revenge?

Appeasement

After World War I, most Europeans and Americans wanted nothing to do with war. They were still rebuilding their families and economies in the 1930s. Because the people did not want war, the leaders remained reluctant to resort to conflict. The empire-building fascist states took full advantage of this paralyzing fear and rushed toward another world war. The story of the 1930s was the democratic nations consistently giving in to the bad behavior of the fascist countries.

In 1935 Hitler first officially broke the Versailles treaty by beginning a draft. In 1936 he more openly defied the treaty by placing soldiers in the **Rhineland**, land west of the Rhine River. According to the treaty Germans were not allowed to put any military equipment or soldiers in this region. French soldiers occupied the land until 1930, when it was agreed no armies of any country would be on the land. On March 7, 1936, hundreds of German soldiers marched across the Hohenzollern Bridge cheered on by crowds of onlookers. Later it was discovered that Hitler had given the order that if the French army opposed them the German soldiers were to turn around and go home. But the French government did not have the will to oppose the remilitarization (return of soldiers) of the Rhineland. Germany fortified this region to protect against a future attack from France.

What was the first piece of land Hitler moved soldiers to?

German troops crossing the Hohenzollern Bridge to reoccupy the Rhineland

The Preparatory Wars

Adolf Hitler and Eberhard von Stohrer greeting General Franco, the Spanish dictator

The three Axis nations engaged in various wars during the 1930s that helped them perfect the tactics they would use in World War II. The only Allied groups to fight in these wars were the Soviet Union and small volunteer units from Europe and the United States.

Spanish Civil War

When the democratic government in Spain started to embrace socialism and communism, the church and other conservative groups opposed it. Finally in 1936 the political war turned hot. Those fighting for the Spanish government united under communism and were supported by the Soviet Union, while those on the other side united under fascism and were supported by Germany. The fascists were led by General Francisco Franco. Hitler supported Franco and used the **Spanish Civil War** to test his new weapons and tactics in preparation for future conquest. By March 1939 Franco and the fascists had defeated the Communists. This war served as a dress rehearsal for World War II.

Italian Invasions of Ethiopia and Albania

In 1935 Mussolini sent a well-equipped, modern army into Ethiopia and quickly conquered this poor African country. Despite pleas by the Ethiopian leader to the League of Nations, Europe made no serious attempt to stop or punish Italian aggression. Mussolini took advantage of this weak response and seized Albania in 1939. The Italians had been increasing their influence in this strategic country for several years. When the Albanian king refused to submit to Italian domination, Italian forces seized control of the country.

Members of the 29th Chinese army stand at attention, preparing to defend their country against Japanese invasion in 1937.

Second Sino-Japanese War

The Japanese had taken a progressively more dominant role in Manchuria. In 1931 someone destroyed a section of railroad in Manchuria that was controlled by the Japanese. The Japanese used this event as justification to invade Manchuria and seize additional land. China protested, but no European powers intervened to stop the Japanese aggression.

In early 1937 Japan became increasingly bold and staged a major assault on China. When the League of Nations protested this invasion, the Japanese simply ended participation in the league. Japan brutalized China and seized its many natural resources to build its military.

For six weeks beginning in December 1937, Japanese soldiers went on a rampage, murdering hundreds of thousands of Chinese civilians, including women, children, and unarmed Chinese soldiers in Nanjing. China estimates that three hundred thousand people perished in the attacks.

?

How did Germany take advantage of the Spanish Civil War?

Steps toward War in 1938 and 1939

According to the Treaty of Versailles, Germany and Austria were not allowed to form a political alliance. Despite this restriction, Hitler secretly planned to gain control of Austria; he was born there. In 1938 he arranged to have an Austrian Nazi selected as the chancellor. The Austrian chancellor then invited Germany to send troops and stabilize Austria; this union was called the **Anschluss**, an event portrayed in the movie *The Sound of Music*.

Prime Minister Neville Chamberlain meeting Adolf Hitler at the Munich Conference

Munich Conference

Hitler followed successive steps to enlarge German territory. His first major move was demanding an area called the **Sudetenland** from Czechoslovakia. To resolve this issue, British and French leaders met with Hitler at the **Munich Conference** in September 1938. Hitler promised he would take only the Sudetenland, no other land. Without even consulting the Czech government, the British and French leaders agreed to meet Hitler's demands.

British prime minister **Neville Chamberlain** led the European nations in a policy to avoid war through appeasement. Chamberlain used Britain's influence to pressure weaker nations to submit to Hitler's demand for territory. European leaders, including French prime minister Édouard Daladier, followed Britain's lead and sought to appease Hitler and Mussolini. Chamberlain famously declared he had achieved "peace for our time," holding up an agreement signed by Hitler.

What did the Europeans give to Hitler at the Munich Conference in exchange for a promise of peace?

Invasion of Czechoslovakia

Despite Hitler's promise not to invade Czechoslovakia, German troops marched into the Czech capital six months later, taking control of most of the country. The weak response of Britain and France led Hitler to conclude that he could continue to seize neighboring countries without fear of European interference.

The United States, under President Roosevelt, maintained a policy of isolation. Most Americans wanted to leave European conflicts to the Europeans and supported Roosevelt's neutrality. In addition, many Americans continued to suffer under the Great Depression and had little interest in foreign affairs.

Six months after the Munich Agreement, Hitler's army marched into Prague, Czechoslovakia.

Forming of the Axis Alliance

Initially, Germany had no allies in Europe after World War I. Even Mussolini had opposed some of Hitler's early attempts at conquest. However, in 1936 Mussolini and Hitler formed an alliance called the Rome-Berlin Axis. Later that same year, Germany and Japan formed an agreement known as the **Anti-Comintern Pact**. This pact allied Germany and Japan against the Communist Soviet Union. In 1937 Italy and Japan signed a similar agreement.

The alliance against the spread of communism provided Europe with a false sense of security. Many European leaders feared communism more than they feared fascism, since the Communists had been the main source of upheaval in their countries. But they were shocked in August 1939 when Germany and the Soviet Union signed an agreement to refrain from attacking one another for the next ten years. This accord protected Germany from a two-front war and encouraged German conquest. Japan signed a similar agreement with the Soviets, which paved the way for continued Japanese aggression. In September 1940 Italy, Japan, and Germany signed the Tripartite Pact. These pacts officially tied the three countries together to form the Axis.

Who were the members of the Axis alliance?

LIFE IN

1930s TOKYO

Citizenship

The Japanese were devoted to their family, their nation, and the emperor. They would not want to do anything to dishonor their family. Students were rewarded not only for good grades but also for their discipline, traditional worldview, and loyalty to the emperor. Students were required to read books about the divinity of the emperor and their duty to worship him.

Justice

The Western imperial powers held loosely to a rule of law based on tradition and written agreements for governing their colonies. But Japan made no pretense of following a rule of law with the governing of its colonies. For the Japanese, what was just was decided by the emperor or those who spoke for him.

Power

In the 1930s a group of military officers began to push back against the rule of the civilian parliament. In some ways, this was a renewal of the previous century's samurai rebellion. The officers admired the ideal of the selfless samurai in contrast to the Western-style self-seeking politician. When the Depression struck Japan, the people blamed the civilian leaders, and the young officers gained more power as the civilian government declined. In 1932 and 1936 someone assassinated the prime ministers, who were trying to halt the total military takeover of the government. Finally, a military-led government came to power led by generals and the emperor.

Environment

By the 1930s the Meiji Restoration was complete. Downtown Tokyo resembled a more orderly New York City or London, with tall buildings and with subway and automobile traffic. The Japanese garden exemplified a desire for harmony with nature. This principle, however, did not continue into Japan's colonies. The Japanese tried to transform Korea into a giant rice field by cutting down most of the trees. They turned Manchuria into their manufacturing region by rapidly building factories there.

Religion

Shinto priests taught the young people Shinto theology that supported the emperor's divinity and Japan's supernatural origins. Shintoism also became a tool to motivate improvements, such as industrial growth, in a way that would enhance extreme nationalism and promote militarism.

CRITICAL THINKING 17.1

What lessons can be learned from the democratic nations' practice of appeasement toward the Axis powers?

GUIDING QUESTIONS

- Where was World War II fought?
- What were the early Axis successes in World War II?
- What were the actions of the different world leaders during World War II?
- What was the Holocaust?

The Germans used blitzkrieg tactics, which involved tanks and Stuka dive-bombers, to conquer Poland in 1939.

17.2 The Axis on the Offensive (1939–42)

When war broke out, no one had any idea what it would turn into, but because both sides made missteps and miscalculations, the war grew. Except for the Pacific Islands, World War II's battlefields were not new. The lands around the Mediterranean Sea, Russia, the Balkan Peninsula, France, Belgium, North Africa, and China had been fought over since ancient times. But it was like all these old wars were being fought at the same time. Both sides ignored the historical lessons of fighting in these places; for example, Hitler ignored the lessons of Napoleon when he invaded Russia. The Americans ignored the lessons of Hannibal (who avoided invading Italy from the south), and the Japanese ignored the ancient cautions against fighting on the mainland of Asia.

Axis Advances in Europe: 1939–40

German Invasion of Poland

On September 1, 1939, over 1.5 million German troops marched across the border into Poland. Despite Hitler's confidence that Britain and France would continue to appease, these countries demanded an immediate end to the invasion. The Germans used the techniques they mastered while fighting in Spain. They called it **blitzkrieg** (lightning war). It involved coordinated air and tank units moving speedily to paralyze the enemy. One hallmark of blitzkrieg was the use of German Stuka dive-bombers blaring sirens to terrify their enemies. The Polish were ill-prepared. Their army was still largely dependent on horses.

France, Britain, and the countries that had been a part of the British Empire, including Canada, Australia, India, and New Zealand, declared war on Germany. Germany was already outnumbered. Although the determination of the Allies surprised Hitler, he resolved to fight and take control of Europe. The Allies had declared war, but they were in no position to provide Poland with any military assistance.

Poland faced invasion from both sides. The Soviet Union invaded Poland on September 17. Although it was motivated only by self-interest, the Soviet Union was helping the Axis cause for the first two years of the war. The Soviet nonaggression (no fighting) pact with Germany, signed in August of 1939, was an agreement to divide Poland between the two of them.

The Polish forces fought bravely against the German army in the west and the Soviet army in the east. Polish soldiers destroyed many German vehicles and nearly three hundred aircraft during the brief conflict. Although Poland ultimately fell, Polish forces continued to oppose German and Soviet occupation through a resistance movement.

? **What did the Soviets do after Germany invaded Poland?**

British and French Response

Britain quickly put itself on war footing by enacting a draft and spending large amounts of money on its military. Millions of children were evacuated from the cities to the countryside so they would be safe in the event of bombings. The first British action in the war was bombing German industry. Initially, both sides agreed not to bomb civilians.

France began mobilizing its army—five million soldiers in all, the largest European army in 1939. On October 6, Hitler declared his desire for peace with Britain and France. Meanwhile he was preparing to invade Belgium, France, Luxembourg, and the Netherlands. The Allies disregarded Hitler's calls for peace.

The Phony War

By October 11 there were an estimated one hundred and fifty-eight thousand British troops in France. The Allied armies stood behind a line of concrete fortifications and guns on the French-German border called the **Maginot Line**. There was no significant conflict on the French-German border for eight months, so this period was called the **Phony War**.

The Maginot Line had a big problem; its fortifications were much weaker along the Belgian border. The Allies thought that Belgium's neutrality and the thick Ardennes forest would prevent Germany from driving tanks through Belgium into France.

? **What was the phony war?**

Soviet and German Invasions of Scandinavia

On November 30, 1939, the Soviet Union invaded Finland with a far superior force. Despite their lack of numbers and equipment, the Finns fought bravely, causing unexpected losses to the Soviets. The war involved soldiers on skis having to survive the cold as well as the fighting. But by March, the outnumbered Finns were defeated and agreed to a peace treaty in which they gave up a large portion of their industrialized area to the Soviet Union. In addition to Finland, the Soviets seized the small countries of Latvia, Lithuania, and Estonia. These conquests provided the Soviet Union with control of territory from the Baltic to the Black Sea.

In the spring of 1940, Germany invaded Denmark and Norway. Even though Britain and France tried to help Norway, they were ineffective in stopping the Germans.

German Invasion of the Netherlands, Belgium, and France

During World War I, the Schlieffen Plan for Germany to invade France through Belgium had failed because it depended on battle speeds that Germany could not attain. In 1940 the plan was successful because Germany could quickly move through Belgium into France with its tanks and airpower.

On May 25, 1940, the Germans invaded the Netherlands and Belgium. The British and French responded by rushing troops into Belgium to stop the Germans. However, German forces anticipated this maneuver and slipped past French defenses south of Belgium. Then the German army swept into France, behind the Allied lines.

British soldiers wading into the English Channel to board ships and escape France in 1940

After a month of fighting, the Germans had done the unthinkable by conquering so much territory, but the army had suffered many casualties. Hitler decided to have the German air force (**Luftwaffe**) wipe out the remaining Allied force composed of more than three hundred and fifty thousand troops. These Allied troops were trapped near the English Channel on the beaches of **Dunkirk**. However, Hitler could not control the weather. While fog and clouds made it impossible for the Luftwaffe to launch air attacks, British citizens ferried the trapped Allies across the English Channel to safety in Britain.

It is difficult to understand the evacuation of Allied forces from the beach at Dunkirk as anything less than an act of God. Fog, rain, and low cloud cover prevented the Luftwaffe from bombing this area for nine days. In addition, the channel was unusually calm, and mild winds blew from the east instead of the north, as they often do. These conditions made it possible for more than eight hundred British vessels, everything from destroyers to fishing boats, to carry the soldiers to safety.

France quickly fell to the German conquerors and signed an armistice on June 22, 1940. The armistice was harsher on France than the Versailles treaty had been on Germany; Hitler had his revenge. Germany occupied more than half of France and allowed a puppet French government to represent German interests in the unoccupied regions of France. However, many French citizens rejected the puppet regime and actively resisted the German occupation.

Why were British soldiers able to escape France?

Battle of Britain

In July 1940 Hitler began a bombing campaign against Britain to prepare for a land invasion. After destroying many military targets, Hitler grew impatient with the resistance of the British and made a change in strategy that doomed the Third Reich to ultimate failure. The Luftwaffe began to bomb London and other British cities to kill civilians and destroy British morale. The bombing of civilian targets strengthened British resolve. The Royal Air Force (RAF) destroyed many German bombers and fighter planes. Germany was quickly losing its well-trained pilots. The British were able to use their new tool of radar effectively and send British pilots to meet German planes at a moment's notice. At the end of the battle, Churchill, referring to the young British pilots, said, "Never in the field of human conflict was so much owed by so many to so few." By September 17, 1940, Hitler ended his plans for Operation Sea Lion, the land invasion of Britain.

The Battle of Britain, between the German and British air forces, was the first battle to take place completely in the air.

Winston Churchill

Winston Churchill, at times, wanted to be a soldier, sometimes a writer, and sometimes a statesman. He eventually did all three and did them very well. If one had to credit a single person for defending the heritage of democracy (or representative government) against both fascism and communism, it would be Winston Churchill.

Churchill was born in 1874 to an English nobleman father and an American mother. Churchill graduated from Britain's leading military school and joined the army. He soon found himself fighting in the far reaches of the British Empire. Churchill fought against a Muslim uprising in Sudan in 1898. There he came under fire in one of the last great cavalry charges in history. Afterward he wrote a history of the campaign, *The River War*, one of his many books. While reporting on the Boer War in South Africa for a newspaper, Churchill was captured by the enemy. He made a daring escape that made him famous in Britain. Churchill then began a spectacular rise in politics.

When World War I broke out, he was head of the British navy. He risked his career supporting a dangerous attack on the Ottoman Empire. The British hoped the attack by the army and navy would knock the Ottomans out of the war. But the attack failed, and Churchill was blamed and forced to resign as head of the navy. Churchill's rise turned suddenly into a devastating fall. He wrote an excellent history of World War I, *The World Crisis*, but his political career seemed over.

In the 1930s, Churchill stood on the fringes of politics. As the dictators rose to power, he was alone in sounding the alarm. As Hitler became more powerful, more people began to listen to Churchill. After the Munich agreement, Churchill declared, "And do not suppose that this is the end. This is only the beginning of the reckoning. This is only the first sip, the first foretaste of a bitter cup."

Why was Churchill on the political fringes in the 1930s?

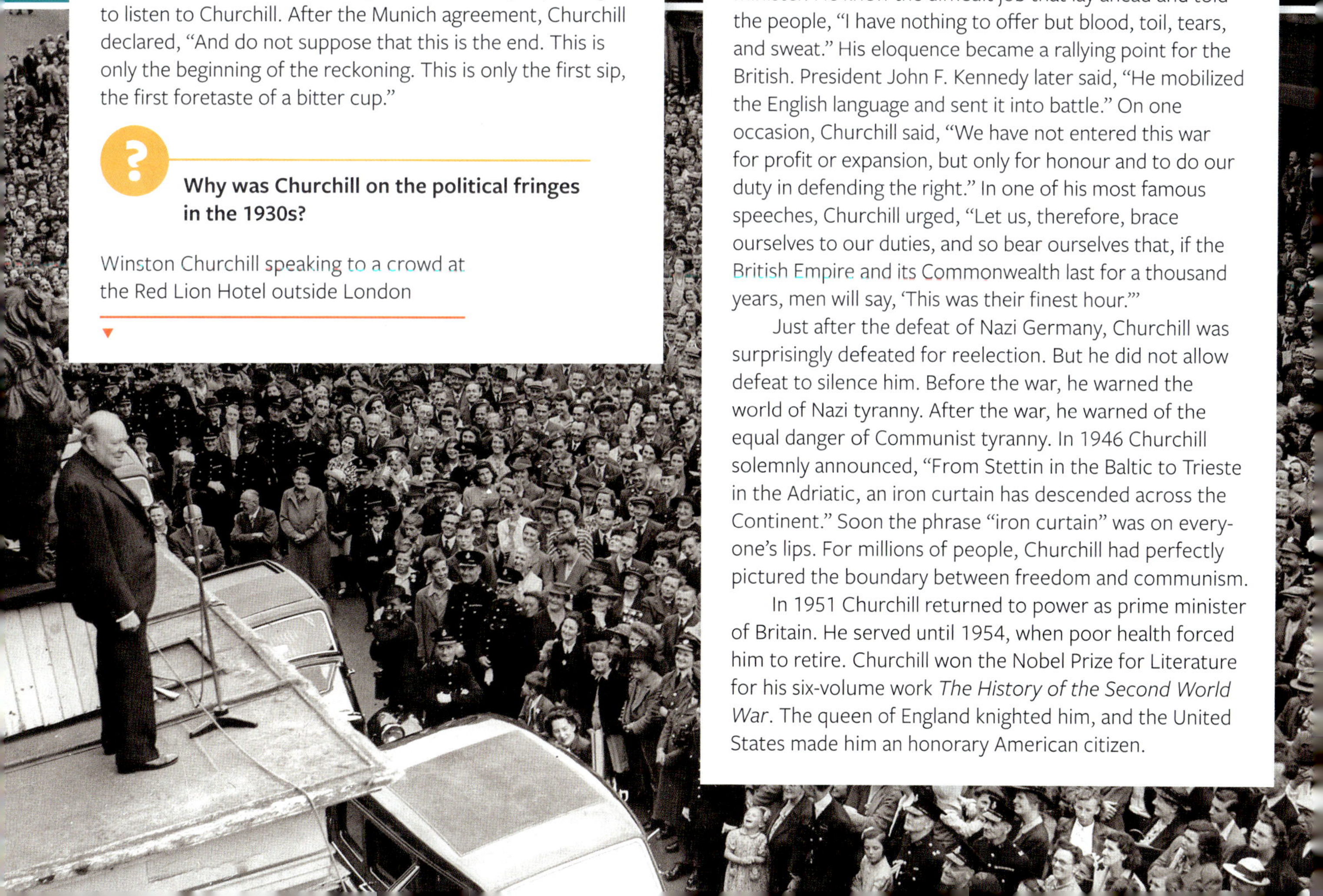

Winston Churchill speaking to a crowd at the Red Lion Hotel outside London

After war broke out, Churchill became the prime minister. He knew the difficult job that lay ahead and told the people, "I have nothing to offer but blood, toil, tears, and sweat." His eloquence became a rallying point for the British. President John F. Kennedy later said, "He mobilized the English language and sent it into battle." On one occasion, Churchill said, "We have not entered this war for profit or expansion, but only for honour and to do our duty in defending the right." In one of his most famous speeches, Churchill urged, "Let us, therefore, brace ourselves to our duties, and so bear ourselves that, if the British Empire and its Commonwealth last for a thousand years, men will say, 'This was their finest hour.'"

Just after the defeat of Nazi Germany, Churchill was surprisingly defeated for reelection. But he did not allow defeat to silence him. Before the war, he warned the world of Nazi tyranny. After the war, he warned of the equal danger of Communist tyranny. In 1946 Churchill solemnly announced, "From Stettin in the Baltic to Trieste in the Adriatic, an iron curtain has descended across the Continent." Soon the phrase "iron curtain" was on everyone's lips. For millions of people, Churchill had perfectly pictured the boundary between freedom and communism.

In 1951 Churchill returned to power as prime minister of Britain. He served until 1954, when poor health forced him to retire. Churchill won the Nobel Prize for Literature for his six-volume work *The History of the Second World War*. The queen of England knighted him, and the United States made him an honorary American citizen.

General Montgomery commanding the British army in Africa from a tank

North Africa

Italy had observed Germany's rapid conquest of Europe and decided to conquer North Africa. Since Britain was enduring German bombing and preparing against a possible Nazi invasion, Italy assumed it would have a free hand in Africa. However, the British troops in Africa proved to be more than a match for Mussolini's forces. The British expelled the Italians from Egypt and captured over one hundred thousand Italian troops.

In the spring of 1941, Hitler responded by sending **General Erwin Rommel**, the Desert Fox, with highly trained German troops to rescue the Italians. Despite inadequate forces and a lack of supplies, General Rommel advanced into Egypt and nearly defeated the British. In 1942 British commander **General Bernard L. Montgomery** finally defeated the German forces that threatened British control of Egypt.

The North African Front, 1941–42

The Atlantic and Mediterranean Naval War

Britain had naval supremacy in the Atlantic Ocean. The Germans hoped to counter this supremacy by producing hundreds of **U-boats** (submarines). In March 1941, the passage of the **Lend-Lease Act** gave the US president authority to offer vast military and material aid to the Allies. But the material had to cross the Atlantic by ship in waters filled with German U-boats. At the start of the war, the Nazis were causing major losses to merchant shipping in the Atlantic. To better survive the U-boat attacks, the Allied ships went across the Atlantic in convoys (groups of ships) guarded by destroyers. Later the Allies used aircraft with radar to fight the U-boats more effectively.

? **What did the Germans use to stop merchant shipping across the Atlantic?**

One of the most important naval battles in Europe included a convoy. The island of Malta in the middle of the Mediterranean Sea was controlled by the British. The Germans needed to conquer Malta to move freely in the Mediterranean region and supply Africa and southern Europe. For two years the Germans had tried to take the island. In the summer of 1942, the Maltese were on the verge of surrender. They lacked food and gasoline for the fighter planes. The Germans were bombing them many times during the day. The British put together a convoy of eighty-seven ships to save the island. The most important ship was the SS *Ohio*, an American tanker carrying fuel for the fighters. The planes needed the gas so they could defend the island against the German bombers. As the convoy crossed the Mediterranean Sea toward Malta, German submarines and planes sank many British ships, but the convoy continued. A German submarine torpedoed the *Ohio*, and German planes bombed it; one plane even crashed onto the ship, yet it continued to sail. The British wanted to abandon the tanker, but the captain and crew nursed it on. Finally, the tanker got close to Malta and was towed into the harbor. The *Ohio* delivered its cargo of fuel and then broke into two pieces. Without the rescue of Malta, the war would have lasted much longer.

A painting depicting the *Ohio* being attacked as it tried to reach the island of Malta

Axis Advances in Asia and the Pacific: 1939–42

Japan declared neutrality after Germany invaded Poland, but throughout 1939 Japan continued to expand its holdings in China. In 1940 Japan further expanded its territory in Asia with an invasion of Indochina (Vietnam, Cambodia, and Laos). Japanese forces also seized several islands in the Pacific and heavily fortified them. The United States and Great Britain objected to this expansion and blocked shipments of oil to Japan. This move threatened to cripple Japan's fleet and end Japanese imperialism.

Pearl Harbor

The Japanese developed a two-track policy for dealing with the United States. Japanese diplomats continued to negotiate to arrange an end to the oil embargo. However, the Japanese military, with the consent of the emperor, also prepared for war against the United States. When the Japanese concluded that war presented their best option for conquest of the Pacific region, they planned a major assault to end the American naval threat.

On December 7, 1941, the Japanese launched a surprise attack on the American naval base at **Pearl Harbor**, Hawaii. During this unprovoked assault, the Japanese air forces killed more than two thousand Americans, destroyed most of the aircraft, and sank several battleships. Providentially, the American aircraft carriers were away on maneuvers and escaped destruction. This brutal attack turned the previously neutral United States into a key Allied power.

What happened on December 7, 1941?

The US Congress quickly declared war on Japan. Roosevelt, however, was more concerned about Germany and wanted to focus on defeating Hitler before defeating Japan. On December 11, Hitler obliged Roosevelt by declaring war on the United States; without that declaration the United States would not have been able to fight a Europe-first war.

A photo of the Japanese attack on Pearl Harbor

Japanese Capture of the Philippines and Singapore

Following the attack on Pearl Harbor, the Japanese military staged attacks on many islands throughout the Pacific. The Philippines became one of the victims of Japanese aggression. American soldiers in the Philippines concentrated their defenses on the Bataan Peninsula and the fortress island of Corregidor in Manila Bay. They withstood Japanese attacks for several months. Finally, President Roosevelt ordered the American commander, **General Douglas MacArthur**, to leave the Philippines to escape capture. The Japanese treated captured American forces with great brutality. Japan also conquered several Dutch and British colonies with little resistance; the loss of Singapore was especially disheartening for the British.

The Japanese forced over 70,000 captured Filipino and American soldiers to march 85 miles with little food or water; approximately 10,000 died on the journey.

Battles of the Coral Sea and Midway

The first major naval battle between the United States and Japan occurred in the Coral Sea, northeast of Australia. The Americans lost an aircraft carrier, but they stopped Japanese advancement toward Australia. One month later, American forces discovered that the Japanese planned to attack **Midway Island**, west of Hawaii. Although the Japanese forces far outnumbered American naval forces, the Americans found the Japanese first, and American pilots sank several Japanese aircraft carriers, forcing the Japanese to retreat. From that point on, Japan was on the defensive.

When the Americans sank four Japanese carriers in the Battle of Midway, they turned the tide of the war.

Operation Barbarossa

Why were the Germans unable to conquer Moscow?

Axis Advances in Europe: 1941–42

German plans for **Operation Barbarossa**, the invasion of the USSR, began in 1940. Despite a peace treaty with the Soviets, Hitler determined to overrun this vast country and take advantage of its many natural resources, including its great oil reserves.

On June 22, 1941, the Germans launched Barbarossa, with three million troops attacking along an eighteen-hundred-mile front. German forces quickly captured thousands of Soviet prisoners and seized half a million square miles of Soviet territory. Hitler had caught Stalin completely off guard.

By December, the Germans had advanced to within ten miles of Moscow but were stopped. The severe winter saw temperatures that fell to forty degrees below zero. German forces could not advance, and most German equipment would not function in these extreme conditions. The Soviet army was able to counterattack since the Germans could not move and lacked supplies.

Hitler ordered his army to attack the city of Stalingrad in the south to gain access to the oil fields. **Stalingrad** proved to be a graveyard for the German army. From July 1942 to February 1943, they fought for this one city, losing eight hundred thousand soldiers. The Soviet army had even heavier losses, some 1.1 million soldiers, but did not give up. Stalin had ordered them to stand their ground. By February 1943, the surviving German army, with no more food or ammunition, surrendered. The Battle of Stalingrad was a decisive victory for the Soviets and ensured the Allies' inevitable victory.

The Battle of Stalingrad involved brutal urban fighting during the winter of 1942–43.

The Holocaust

Adolf Hitler led the Germans to commit crimes against civilians in ways previously unimagined. His goal of ridding Europe of Jews, Romani (Gypsies), and the weak and disabled was as important to him as gaining territory for Germany. He only wanted "perfect" people of the so-called Aryan race to live in Europe.

Jewish people waiting to be deported to a concentration camp by train

Throughout the 1930s the Nazis stripped Jews of their rights and segregated them. Hitler forced the Jews in Germany and the lands he had conquered to relocate to ghettos (slums). Relocation to concentration camps followed soon after. As German armies marched into the Soviet Union, the Nazis sent along special mobile killing units to hunt down and kill people. Later the Germans developed centralized killing locations in Poland and Germany. In July 1941 they authorized what they called the *Final Solution*, the mass murder of Jews and those the Nazis saw as unfit. They constructed six death camps in occupied Poland to kill thousands of these victims. It was industrial-scale murder using gas chambers disguised as shower rooms.

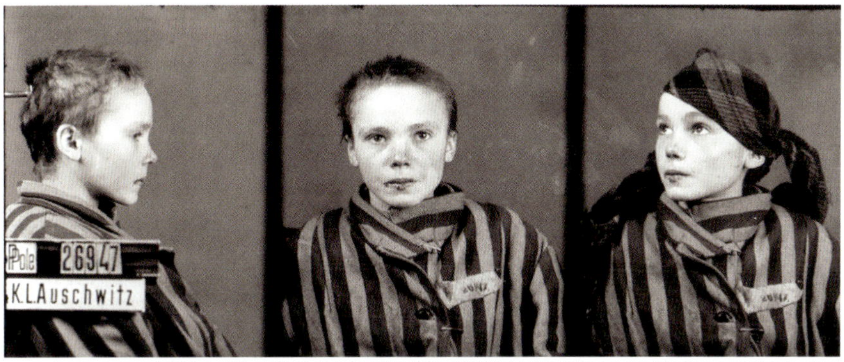

A Polish girl's identification photos, taken at the Auschwitz concentration camp

The German camp at Auschwitz gained the terrible distinction of killing more people than any other concentration camp. At least one million two hundred thousand Jews died at this camp. The officials at Auschwitz also murdered one hundred thousand others whom they saw as unfit. The killing continued until American and Soviet troops liberated these centers in the spring of 1945.

Many use the word **Holocaust** to refer to the genocide of the Jews. However, many Jews prefer the Hebrew term *Shoah*, which means "calamity." Regardless of the term used, the Nazi attempt to destroy the Jewish population in Europe remains one of the worst atrocities in history.

? CRITICAL THINKING 17.2

How did the Axis nations commit injustice?

The entrance to the Auschwitz concentration camp

GUIDING QUESTIONS

- What were the Allies' offensive actions and victories against the Axis powers?
- Why did the Allies insist on the unconditional surrender of the Axis powers?

17.3 The Allies on the Offensive (1942–45)

In 1942 Germany and Japan together controlled almost half the globe. But they had made serious miscalculations and were destined to lose once the Allies decided to fight in 1939. While the outcomes of previous wars had been dependent on who could produce the most, World War II took this principle to new levels. US industrial power compared to that of the Axis powers was shocking. But even the island of Britain was outproducing Germany during the Battle of Britain. Germany's industrial sector was minuscule compared to that of the Allies', and its factories were under constant threat from bombs. United States and Canadian factories worked unabated, with no fear of being destroyed.

Not only did the Allies produce more, but they coordinated their efforts. For example, the Americans had a great fighter airplane in the P-51 Mustang, but it had a poor engine. The British offered their Rolls Royce engine, making the P-51 the best fighter of the war. The Germans and Japanese would not work together in that way because they mistrusted each other. The Soviets did not waste any effort on building a navy or a large air force since the British and Americans provided those.

WWII Weaponry

T-34 TANK

The Soviet main battle tank. Almost 200,000 were built. It required little maintenance and was faster than German tanks since it was lighter.

SHERMAN TANK

Was the main American battle tank. Although it was smaller and had less armor than the German tanks, it could go faster and needed less maintenance.

PANZER IV

German tanks had the most destructive power of all tanks in WWII, but they were slower and required a lot of maintenance.

U-BOAT

In World War II the Germans had 1,162 submarines, which was their primary warship; they sank 2,779 Allied ships in the war.

AIRCRAFT CARRIER

The aircraft carrier replaced the battleship as the most powerful and important warship.

B-17

Was the American four-engine bomber used to bomb German factories and cities. The Germans had no equivalent.

ME-109

It was the main German fighter. It was a superb fighter in the late '30s and early '40s but was inferior to newer Allied fighters.

SPITFIRE

This British fighter showed its superiority over German planes in the Battle of Britain.

AMERICAN 2½ TON TRUCK

Although not a flashy military weapon, this truck was a key to victory in Europe for the Allies.

Allied Offensives against the Germans

In 1942, under General **Dwight D. Eisenhower**, later the Supreme Allied commander, US troops landed in North Africa. They moved east while the British moved west from Egypt. The Allies defeated the Axis troops in Africa within a year. Then, in 1943 the Allies invaded Sicily, the island to the south of Italy. As the Allies advanced into Italy, the Italian government surrendered. However, large numbers of German troops continued to resist the Allied advance northward through Italy, and it became clear that it was impossible to invade Germany from the south.

Casablanca Conference

Why did the Allies want an unconditional surrender?

In January 1942 President Roosevelt and Churchill met in Casablanca, Morocco, to discuss all aspects of the war. They were also in contact with Stalin in the Soviet Union and Chiang Kai-Shek in China. The two agreed that they would not accept a negotiated surrender by Germany or Japan. The only choice the Axis nations had was to surrender unconditionally, meaning putting themselves under the total control of the Allies. **Unconditional surrender** was essential because the Allies did not want to leave a half-defeated Germany or Japan to fight a World War III twenty or thirty years later. Roosevelt and Churchill had learned the lessons of World War I and the Munich Conference.

French general Henri Giraud, President Roosevelt, French general Charles de Gaulle, and British prime minister Winston Churchill at the Casablanca Conference

Invasion of France

The Soviets demanded that the Americans and British invade France to ease the German pressure on the Soviets in the east. The Americans wanted to invade France early in the war, but the British were hesitant. Finally, in 1942, they started planning an invasion of France across the English Channel. After much planning, on June 6, 1944, the Allies launched a massive invasion of France. It was the largest amphibious (landing troops from the sea) invasion ever. One hundred and seventy-five thousand men landed and established a beachhead on that first day, which was known as **D-day**. Within three weeks, one million Allied soldiers, five hundred thousand tons of supplies, and nearly two hundred thousand vehicles had landed in France. The Allies lost thirty-seven thousand soldiers during the invasion, from June through August 1944. The fighting in Europe would continue for another year, but this successful landing sealed the fate of Germany.

With the massive infusion of troops and military equipment from the United States, the Allies steadily regained territory from the Axis powers. British and American forces pushed German forces out of France and Belgium. While the Allies were more united than the Axis, they were not in total agreement. The British under Montgomery wanted to attack along a very narrow front in the north, while the Americans under Generals Bradley and Patton preferred a wide front in the south. General Eisenhower masterfully balanced the demands of the strong personalities around him and kept the alliance together. The Allies were also having trouble getting supplies to the front; so in September 1944 Montgomery got his wish, and Operation Market Garden (the invasion of the Netherlands toward Germany) went forward. It involved airborne soldiers parachuting behind enemy lines and capturing territory while tanks caught up to them. However, the operation failed to get the Allies into Germany.

A reenactment of the Operation Market Garden paratrooper landing in the Netherlands

Final Push

By December 1944 the Allies in the west had reached the border of Germany. Hitler ordered an attack (**the Battle of the Bulge**) to break through a lightly protected section of the Allied line. The battle was called the Bulge because the attack created a bulge in the Allied lines. This last German offensive completely surprised the Americans and sent inexperienced soldiers running in fear. But slowly the veteran soldiers fought back, and as the skies cleared the air force was able to support the troops. Germany had consumed much of its remaining military strength.

In March 1945, the Americans approached the Rhine River and were surprised to find the Ludendorff Bridge still standing. The Americans crossed into Germany nine years to the day from when Germany violated the Versailles treaty by crossing the same river. The Americans and British stopped west of Berlin and allowed the Soviets to fight their way into Germany's capital from the east. Hitler killed himself on April 30, and on May 7 the Germans unconditionally surrendered. The Allies declared May 8, 1945, **V-E Day** for the victory in Europe.

A crowd in London, England, celebrating V-E Day, the German surrender

What was the final German offensive of the war?

Allied Offensives against the Japanese

The Americans came at the Japanese from two directions. In New Guinea, General MacArthur led the army coming from the south. In the Central Pacific, American Admiral Chester Nimitz commanded the navy and marines who "island-hopped" toward Japan from the east. They captured important islands that the Allies could use for air bases. They bypassed other islands and left the Japanese troops there stranded to await the end of the war.

By the end of 1944, the two forces met in the Philippines, which General MacArthur had promised to return to. In 1945 American forces captured the Japanese territorial islands of Iwo Jima and Okinawa, with terrible loss of life on both sides.

The Japanese fought with fierce determination, and few lived to become prisoners of war. Most died in battle or committed suicide rather than allowing themselves to be captured. However, the Japanese zeal proved to be no match for superior air and naval power. At a great cost of life for the Allies and the Japanese, the Americans continued to close in on the Japanese home islands.

Despite the massive bombing of Japanese cities with explosives and incendiary bombs (designed to start fires), the Japanese emperor and his military council refused to surrender. An estimated one hundred thousand people died in one night during the firebombing of Tokyo. While the death toll continued to rise, the Americans assembled thousands of planes and other war supplies for the invasion of the Japanese home islands.

? **Who promised to return to the Philippines?**

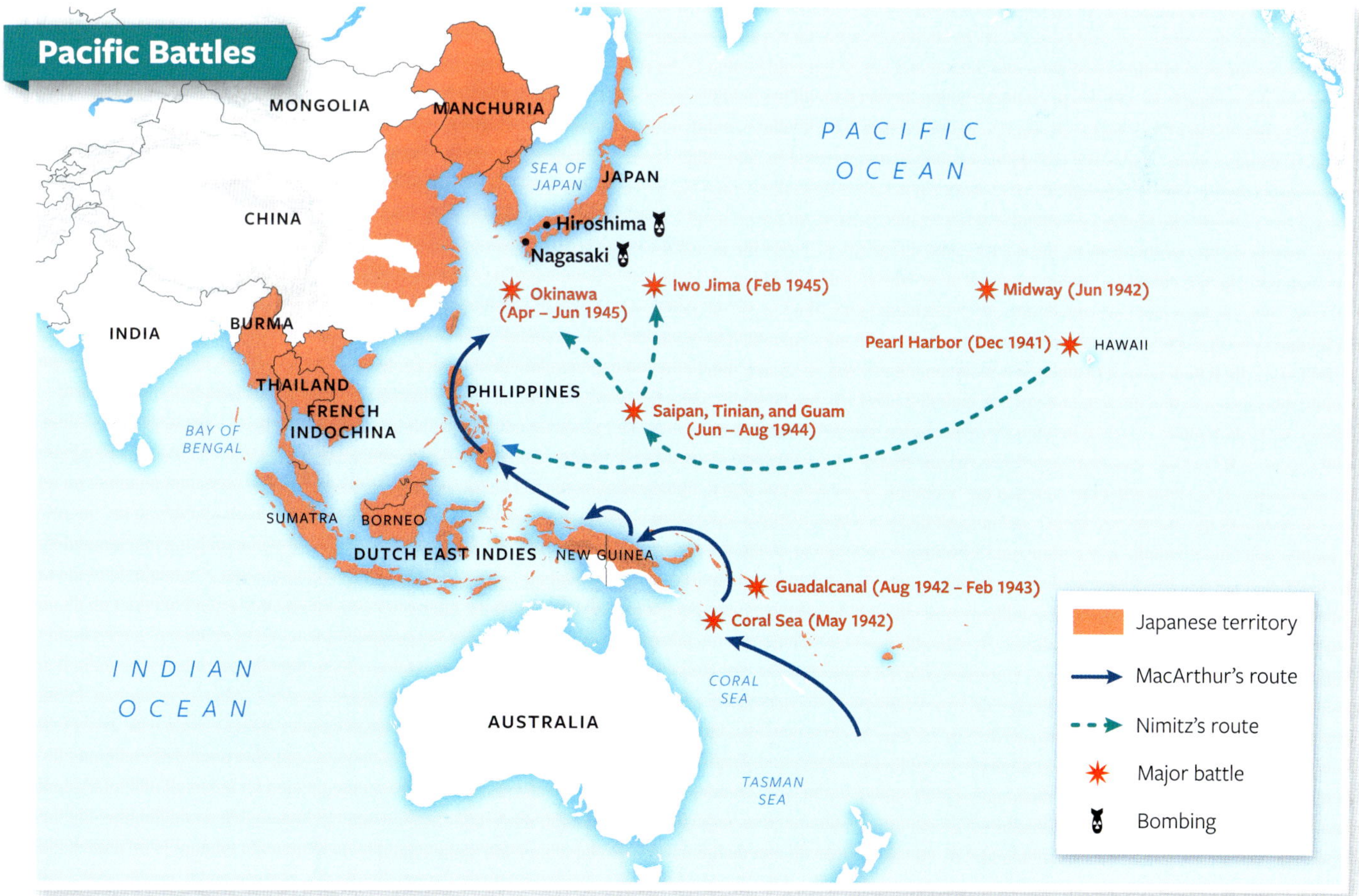

TURNING POINTS

Beginning of the Nuclear Age

In April 1945, President Roosevelt died, and his vice president, Harry Truman, became president. When Truman became president, he learned of a top-secret project to create a nuclear bomb. To him fell the great responsibility of deciding whether to use the secret weapon that American scientists had developed.

In the summer of 1945, the Allied leaders met in Potsdam, Germany, to discuss the end of the war and various postwar issues. They insisted that Japan surrender or suffer terrible consequences. Japanese officials rejected this demand. President Truman responded by ordering that an atomic bomb be dropped on the Japanese city of Hiroshima on August 6. The blast destroyed nearly five square miles of the city and immediately killed an estimated seventy thousand people. Another seventy thousand people suffered terrible injuries from the blast.

Truman again demanded the surrender of Japan and threatened additional destruction if they failed to do so. However, the Japanese leaders refused to surrender. In response, on August 9, an American bomber dropped a second atomic bomb on the Japanese city of Nagasaki. This blast immediately killed about forty thousand people, with another forty thousand injured, who died after the blast.

Many today look back and criticize the decision to drop the nuclear bombs on Japan because the bombs killed civilians. They say a demonstration bomb in the desert would have been sufficient for the Japanese to surrender. They also characterize the introduction of nuclear weapons as a terrible thing.

But historians must evaluate the decision in the context of when it was made. Truman was dedicated to one single purpose, ending the war. If the American people had later found out he had access to a weapon that could have ended the war but continued to let American troops die, he would have been forever condemned. Before dropping the bomb, the Americans did drop leaflets on Hiroshima, warning the people of the coming disaster.

Hiroshima, Japan, after the atomic bomb was dropped

Others have made the case that dropping the bombs saved not only American but Japanese lives. Japanese soldiers almost always fought to the death, even after it was obvious that they had lost the battle. Just a couple of months prior, the Japanese had committed unspeakable atrocities on the Filipino civilians in Manila, even after the Americans had certainly defeated the Japanese in the Philippines. Americans knew that if they invaded the Japanese home islands they would receive the same kind of deadly resistance from the entire Japanese population. The Allies felt that Japanese emperor worship had to be proven a failure, just as Hitler and Nazism had been proven failures months before. The atomic bomb was seen as the best way to end a war already immensely costly in human lives.

It could also be argued that, in addition to saving lives, the atomic bomb prevented future wars. The destructive power of this weapon caused leaders to hesitate in engaging in all-out war again for fear their nation would be destroyed; that is why the world has not experienced World War III.

1. Why did Truman order the atomic bomb to be dropped on Japan?
2. Do you think a demonstration bomb in the desert would have been successful at ending the war? Why or why not?
3. Evaluate the morality of dropping atomic bombs on Hiroshima and Nagasaki.

On August 14, the Japanese government finally surrendered. On September 2, 1945 (**V-J Day**), the Japanese and Allied representatives signed the documents that formally ended Japanese involvement in World War II.

CRITICAL THINKING 17.3

How would the Allied demand of unconditional surrender be a step toward preventing World War III?

17.4 Consequences of the War

GUIDING QUESTIONS

- What were the long-term consequences of the total war?
- How did economic and political alliances change following the war?
- What was the result of the Holocaust?
- What were the philosophical and religious consequences of the war?

World War II resulted in loss of human life and destruction of property on a scale not previously witnessed in human history. Statistics alone fail to provide an adequate description of the horrific losses. The war transformed the world politically, philosophically, and economically.

Loss of Lives

It is unlikely that anyone could have imagined a more destructive war than World War I, with about twenty million deaths. However, World War II resulted in more than seventy-five million deaths. Populations of nations in Europe suffered significant decline. Countries like Belarus, Poland, and Ukraine lost close to 25 percent of their population; they are still recovering from this loss today. Still, in World War I it was mostly soldiers who died, but in World War II almost 80 percent of the people who died were civilians.

Did the war kill mostly soldiers or civilians?

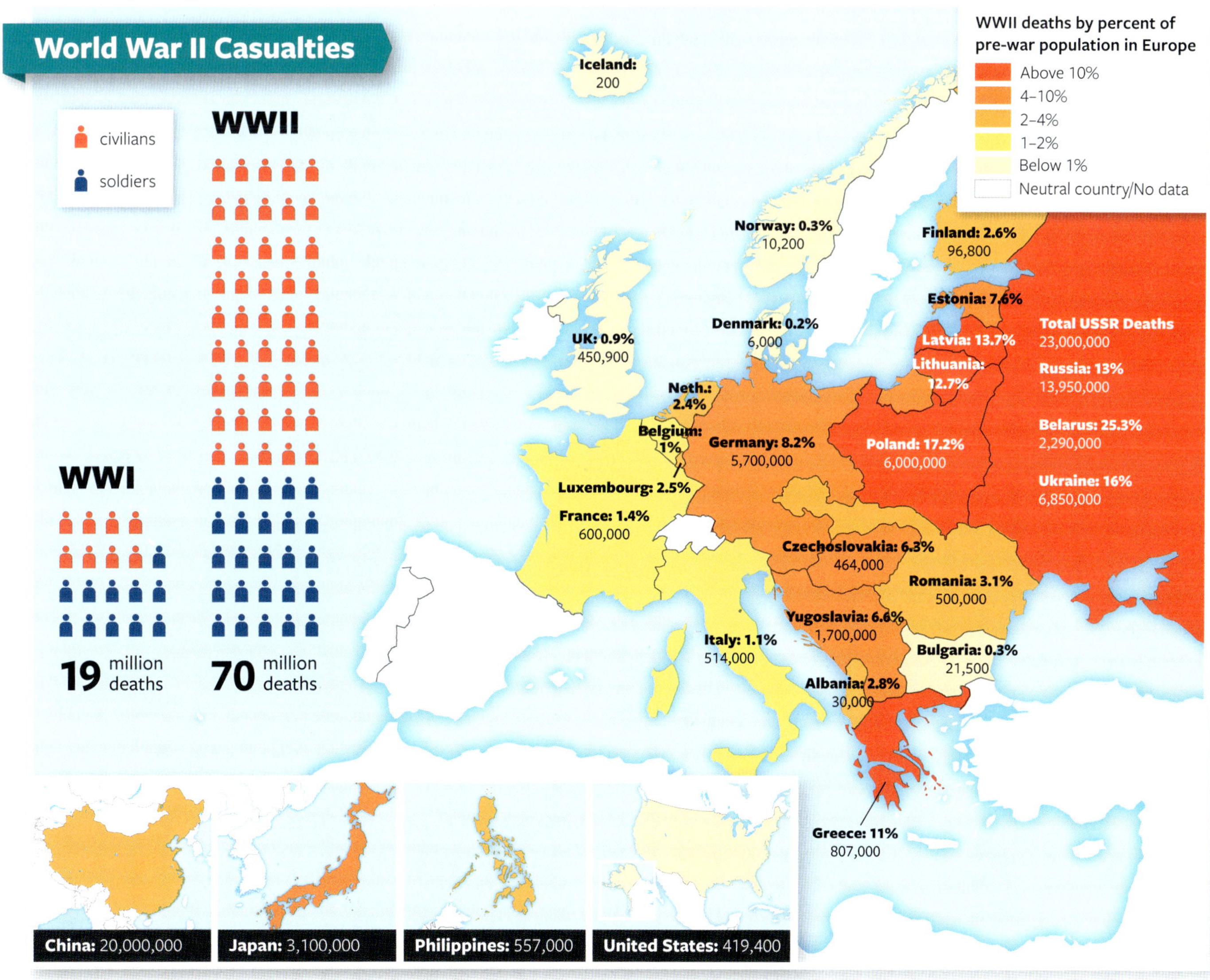

Massive Destruction of Property

Entire cities were bombed into rubble or firebombed into ashes. Europe and Japan lay in ruins. Their industries and infrastructure suffered almost complete destruction. While the cost of the war had been incredible, the cost of rebuilding would tax the resources of the free world.

Economic Changes

Few escaped the consequences of rigidly controlled national economies. Total war resulted in widespread affliction due to a rationing of food, medicine, and anything else that would contribute to the military effort.

World War II led to dramatic economic changes for countries such as France and Britain. They lost most of their colonies. The few colonies still under their control demanded freedom. Within a few years, the Europeans granted freedom to these remaining colonies. They could no longer lay claim to world power status.

Dresden, Germany, and many other European cities were left in ruins following World War II.

Transformation of Germany and Japan

The Allied treatment of Germany following the war was much harsher than after the Versailles treaty, but no one complained this time. Each major Allied power was given a section of Germany to govern. America, Britain, and France together ruled West Germany, while the Soviet Union charted a different path in East Germany.

Following the Japanese surrender General MacArthur led Japan. He dictated a new constitution, which restructured Japanese society once again. The army was dismantled, the emperor was officially made a figurehead, and women were given greater rights.

▲ This photo of General MacArthur and Emperor Hirohito was significant in proving to the Japanese that they were truly defeated. In addition to being noticeably shorter, the emperor stood to MacArthur's left, as the less-powerful person always did in that culture.

Results of the Holocaust

Many Jewish people struggled with the idea of God after the Holocaust since He had allowed them to suffer so much. But one earth-shaking result of the Holocaust was the establishment of a Jewish state. The Jewish survivors of the Holocaust still faced closed doors for immigration. Because no one would let them in, they made every effort to migrate to Palestine. After the people of the world learned the full extent of the horror of the Holocaust, sentiment turned in favor of the establishment of Israel in a portion of the British mandate of Palestine.

Political Reset

Following the war, the Soviets tightly controlled the European countries they occupied, despite their promises to allow these nations to have free elections. Stalin installed Communist regimes in these countries.

World War II ended Europe's domination of the world. Both wars had resulted, in part, from exaggerated nationalism and the illusion that one nationality enjoyed superiority over other nationalities. These errors had been disproved at an incredible cost. Political change emerged as one of the consequences of these wars. Rather than many strong political powers, only two remained. Following the war, power shifted to the United States and the Soviet Union. Europe would merely side with one or the other of these political camps.

? How did General MacArthur change Japanese government?

? Who were the two world powers following the war?

Disillusionment and Material Pursuit

Postwar literature and art reflected the view that life has no meaning or purpose. For example, American painter Jackson Pollock developed a form of painting known as abstract expressionism. He created many of his paintings by randomly splashing wet paint on the canvas with brushes.

Other artists expressed their hopelessness by writing stories or plays that demonstrated the meaninglessness of life. For example, Albert Camus, a French philosopher, wrote stories dealing with absurdity. He reasoned that people value what is meaningless since all people value their life even though all die.

Many people had thought they would never survive the war. When they did survive, they vowed to live life to the fullest. They did this by raising a family, having a fulfilling career, and accumulating material possessions.

Philosophical Change: Existentialism

The world wars devastated the illusions upon which most philosophies had been founded. The wars disproved the fantasy that man is born without a sin nature. Philosophies and religions could not explain the outpouring of animosity and hatred that led to the deaths of multiplied millions. They found themselves unable to provide answers for the past or hope for the future.

The horrors of World War I followed by the intensified horrors of World War II altered the thinking of most Europeans. They abandoned the idealism that prevailed in the nineteenth century. This collapse of idealism led to relativism, the idea that truth and moral values are not absolute but rather vary with each person or group.

The philosophy known as **existentialism** became popular during this period. This philosophy stresses a person's uniqueness while encouraging free choice and accepting the consequences of that choice. Existentialists deny that an all-powerful God rules over the affairs of humans. In fact, many leading existentialists were atheists. They also denied the existence of a moral code defining what a human being is or should be. Instead, they believed that humans are free to determine their own values and their own meaning in life. Humans are not obligated to obey the dictates of a government or a church. They are to choose a course of action that seems right to them and then strive to be faithful to that selection.

Besides failing to explain the atrocities of the world wars, human philosophers had not predicted the devastation of the twentieth century. This level of destruction contradicted man's high view of himself and left men without hope or answers. But Christians understood that God was still on the throne and accomplishing His will.

?

Define existentialism.

Religious Changes

The world wars discredited religious teaching that assumed humans are basically good. Gone were the dreams of a perfect society. As a result, the churches of Europe began to empty. Atheism grew more popular, and eventually even some prominent theologians concluded that God was dead.

Nevertheless, Christianity also grew during this period. In the United States, many men returned home from war and attended Christian colleges. These men had seen the world and had seen death. They were prepared to sacrifice to spread the gospel around the world. Many of them returned to minister in places they had been during the war.

?

CRITICAL THINKING 17.4

What do you think was the most important consequence of World War II? Why?

Making Connections

1. What did the Versailles treaty do to Germany's economy?
2. How did Germany's support of General Franco in Spain prepare German forces for war?
3. Why did Japan become increasingly confident that no nation would come to China's defense?
4. How did France respond to the German seizure of the Rhineland?
5. What tactics did Germany use to conquer almost all of Europe except for Great Britain?
6. Why did Hitler invade Russia in 1941?
7. Where did the Japanese commit a surprise attack on the United States?
8. What did Churchill do before and during the war to sustain Britain?
9. What battle in Russia ended German advancement? What battle in the Pacific ended Japanese advancement?
10. What does unconditional surrender mean?
11. What was the Holocaust? Why did it happen?
12. How was World War II a total war?
13. How did people's outlook on life change following the war?

Thinking Critically

1. Respond to the following statement: "The refusal of the United States to lift the oil embargo against the Japanese forced Japan to attack American naval forces."
2. Why did the influence of European nations decline following the Second World War?
3. Suppose that you are a Christian historian responding to the denials of an unbeliever regarding God's providence at Dunkirk. Specifically respond to the charge that the events at Dunkirk cannot demonstrate the providence of God because the Germans' conquest of France has its own equally remarkable series of events. Use Genesis 50:20 and Daniel 4:34–35 to prepare your answer.

What to Know

Dates & Events

Spanish Civil War
Munich Conference
Anti-Comintern Pact
September 1, 1939
attack on Pearl Harbor
Battle of Stalingrad
D-day
Battle of the Bulge
V-E Day
V-J Day

People

Neville Chamberlain
Winston Churchill
Erwin Rommel
Bernard L. Montgomery
Douglas MacArthur
Dwight D. Eisenhower

Places

Rhineland
Sudetenland
Dunkirk
Midway Island
Hiroshima
Nagasaki

Terms

Allies
Axis powers
Anschluss
blitzkrieg
Maginot Line
Phony War
Luftwaffe
U-boats
Lend-Lease Act
Operation Barbarossa
Holocaust
unconditional surrender
existentialism

An RAF pilot with his Spitfire

18 THE COLD WAR

1945 – 1991

ESSENTIAL QUESTIONS

- How were Communist and Western states different?
- What were major events of the Cold War?
- How successful were independence movements among former colonies?
- Why did the Soviet Union and its satellite states fall?

Georgi Vins

Georgi Vins was born on August 4, 1928, to Peter and Lydia Wiens (Vins in Russian). Georgi's father, Peter, was born in Russia but emigrated with his family to the United States when he was a teenager. Peter's father, Jacob, was a minister in both the United States and Canada. Like his father, Peter became a preacher. In 1926 he moved to the Russian territory of Siberia to preach the gospel there. Peter got married while living in Siberia, and Georgi was born there.

Ministry was dangerous in Siberia. The Soviet Union targeted believers. Peter was put in prison three times. The last time, his family never heard from him again. Years later Georgi learned that his father was executed in 1936.

Georgi and his mother moved to the Ukrainian city of Kiev. Georgi trained to be an electrical engineer and got married. Despite the persecution his father had faced, Georgi had a burden for ministry. Churches in the Soviet Union were required to register with the state. Registered churches could not witness or disciple believers. Georgi opposed state control of churches; he started a congregation that joined an underground (secret) organization known as the Council of Churches. Because they could not worship openly, members of this organization met in homes or in secret places like forests. Sometimes they were arrested. Georgi's work with this organization led to his arrest in 1966. He spent three years in prison and a labor camp.

After his release, Georgi continued his ministry. In March 1974 he was again arrested. He was sentenced to ten years but served only five. On April 26, 1979, he was unexpectedly taken to Moscow. There he learned that his Soviet citizenship had been canceled. Together with four other dissidents (people who oppose government policies), he was sent to the United States. Unknown to Georgi, Jimmy Carter, the president of the United States, and Soviet officials had agreed to trade two Soviet spies in the United States for the five dissidents. In New York City, the dissidents exited the plane while the spies entered it.

Soon after his arrival in the United States, Georgi's family joined him. They settled in Elkhart, Indiana. Georgi devoted his time to supporting the underground church in the Soviet Union. In 1990 Georgi's citizenship was restored because of reforms in the Soviet Union. He made several preaching trips to his homeland before his death in 1998.

18.1 Postwar Conditions

Beginnings of the Cold War

By the end of World War II, a different sort of war had begun. The United States and the Soviet Union emerged from the conflict as the clear world leaders. Although they had been allies in the war, their differences were so deep that their relationship quickly declined. Over the next four decades, the Americans and the Soviets fought what has been called the **Cold War**. Though they were not officially at war, their relationship was not peaceful either. Each side tried to dominate the other through the development of new weapons or through involvement in conflicts between other nations.

How did the United States and the Soviet Union try to dominate each other during the Cold War?

GUIDING QUESTIONS

- What is a *cold war*?
- How did the philosophies and goals of the Soviet Union and the United States differ?
- What economic and political developments occurred in Western Europe following World War II?
- How was Japan successfully rebuilt following World War II?
- What role does the United Nations play in world affairs?

Philosophical Differences

There were major philosophical differences between the United States and the Soviet Union. For example, they disagreed on economics. The United States promoted a capitalist approach. Privately owned businesses could serve customers and pursue profits. The Soviet Union pursued a command approach. The state owned all businesses. It decided what would be produced, how much would be produced, and what would be charged.

They also disagreed on government. The United States practiced a democratic form of government. It stressed the role of the individual in the political process. The Soviet Union was controlled by the Communist Party. Most citizens had no say in their government.

Finally, they disagreed on religion. The United States considered itself a Christian nation (though not all practiced true biblical Christianity). The Soviet Union believed that religion is evil because it encourages people to be submissive when they need to be stirred up to support Communist revolution.

? How was the American economy different from that of the Soviets?

Differences in Goals

The United States and the Soviet Union had different goals following World War II. The United States wanted to fix the problems that had caused previous wars. It hoped (1) to establish a more effective peacekeeping organization than the League of Nations had been, (2) to allow people to choose their own governments, and (3) to promote economic cooperation in Europe.

The Soviet Union, on the other hand, wanted security. It also wanted to encourage the spread of communism. Soviet leaders still believed, as Marx had said, that capitalism would ultimately destroy itself and that communism would be left to rule the world.

The goals of the two sides help to explain many developments of the Cold War. Each side pursued policies that either promoted its own goals or hindered its opponent's goals.

Eastern Europe and Germany

Germany had invaded the Soviet Union (or Russia) by way of Eastern Europe in both world wars. After the Soviet army freed the nations of Eastern Europe from Nazi control at the end of World War II, the Soviets wanted to keep some control over the region. They believed it would be a helpful buffer from any future Western aggression. Therefore, they supported the rise of governments that would be friendly to the Soviet Union and support its interests.

After the war, Germany had been divided into four zones of occupation, one each for the Soviets, the French, the British, and the Americans. Though the Soviet zone was only about one-third of Germany's total land area, the Western powers worried that the Soviets wanted control over the entire country. They considered plans to unify the three Western zones of occupation.

Post-WWII Europe, 1945

The Mediterranean Region and Containment

Another region that was important to the Soviets was the Mediterranean. They already controlled territory bordering the Black Sea. Gaining access to the Mediterranean would help them with trade and military protection. The Soviets demanded to share control of the waterways connecting the Black and Mediterranean Seas. They also wanted to establish naval bases in the eastern Mediterranean.

The United States, having received requests for help from nations in the region, refused to give in to the Soviets. Discussions of how to deal with Soviet aggression led to the policy of **containment**. George Kennan, who worked for the American embassy in Moscow, proposed the idea. Under containment, the United States would not go to war but would just try to keep the Soviets from expanding their influence. The hope was that the Soviets would eventually see that aggression did not help them.

How was containment supposed to work?

The Truman Doctrine

Politically, containment was promoted by the **Truman Doctrine**. In 1947 President Truman offered aid to Greece and Turkey to fight against Communist aggression in their countries. This offer became the basis of a general American policy that offered help to any nation threatened by communism.

The Marshall Plan

Economically, containment was promoted by the **Marshall Plan**. World War II had left most of Europe in ruins. The United States was concerned that communism, which promised better economic conditions for workers, would appeal to devastated Europeans. To avoid that possibility, Europe needed to be completely rebuilt.

The European Recovery Program, more commonly known as the Marshall Plan (for US secretary of state George Marshall), began sending massive economic assistance to Europe beginning in 1948. The Marshall Plan achieved its purpose. By improving conditions for common Europeans, it made Communist revolution less attractive. Marshall Plan assistance was offered to all of Europe, but the Soviets refused it and forced their allies in Eastern Europe to follow their lead. By doing so, they drew a clear division between the two regions of Europe.

Cold War Alliances

The division of Europe was further fixed by the establishment of rival military alliances. Fearing Soviet aggression, several nations of Western Europe asked the United States for military protection. This request led to the creation of **NATO** (the North Atlantic Treaty Organization). In response, the Soviet Union and its Eastern European allies created the **Warsaw Pact**. NATO members and other nations that identified with the United States and democracy were sometimes described as the "Western bloc," or "first-world countries." Nations that were part of the Soviet sphere of influence, on the other hand, were described as the "Eastern bloc," or "second-world countries." (A *bloc* is a collection of states or organizations that have similar goals.)

What military alliances divided Europe?

(top) German poster promoting the Marshall Plan, (middle) NATO flag, (bottom) Warsaw Pact emblem

Developments in Western Europe

Economic Growth in West Germany

The German capital of Berlin lay entirely within the Soviet occupation zone of Germany. As with the country, the Allies had divided the city into four zones. In 1948 the Soviets blocked all traffic through East Germany, testing the determination of their former allies to maintain the freedom of their zones. This **Berlin Blockade** forced the Western powers to make a difficult decision. To deliver much-needed supplies to their zones by road or rail, they would have to use military force. But if they allowed the Soviet blockade to succeed, West Berlin would face starvation or fall under Soviet control. Ingeniously, they devised an alternative plan that avoided both going to war and giving in.

For eleven months, the United States and Britain delivered everything from coal to milk in a massive airlift. Unarmed cargo planes loaded with supplies landed every ninety seconds, twenty-four hours a day. The Soviets finally backed down and lifted the blockade. This struggle between the Western powers and the Soviets ended without a shot being fired.

(left) Berlin airlift: planes being loaded with milk, (middle) children waiting as planes fly into West Berlin, (right) planes lining up to unload supplies

Konrad Adenauer

On May 23, 1949, eleven days after the blockade was lifted, the British, French, and Americans combined their zones of the country to form the Federal Republic of Germany, or West Germany. (The Soviets established the German Democratic Republic in the East German territory they controlled. They built a wall around West Berlin in 1961 to prevent East Germans from fleeing to the West.) Under the leadership of Chancellor **Konrad Adenauer**, West Germany experienced an incredible economic recovery. Adenauer rejected socialism and embraced the principles of the free market. National income tripled, and the small nation produced more goods by 1955 than a larger Germany had produced prior to the war. Germany quickly became a major economic force in Europe.

How did the Western powers manage the crisis of the Berlin Blockade?

Struggle for Stability in France

France struggled with instability following the formation of the Fourth Republic in 1946. It tried to demonstrate that it was still a world power by retaking its colonial empire. However, French forces suffered a crushing defeat to Vietnamese Communist forces in 1954. France gained some stability when **Charles de Gaulle** became the president in 1958 and established the **Fifth Republic**. This government provided the French with a constitution and strengthened the office of president.

Like many nations of Europe, France developed elements of a welfare state following World War II. In welfare states, governments sponsor a variety of programs to help meet citizens' physical and financial needs. For example, France has a national healthcare system and a tax-subsidized retirement plan.

Charles de Gaulle

Decline in Great Britain

Great Britain emerged from the war in decline. The British Empire began to crumble as former colonies gained their independence. No longer did Britain play a leading role in the world.

The economic devastation caused by the war led to demands for more government involvement in the British economy. Under the Labour Party, the government created the National Health Service and took control of key industries, including coal and railroads. By the late 1970s unemployment and inflation had crippled the British economy. The British voted out the Labour Party and elected the Conservative Party in 1979.

Beginnings of European Integration

European leaders believed that some form of European unity was needed to prevent future wars. The Marshall Plan promoted this idea by calling for economic cooperation among participating nations. This cooperation became a reality in the 1950s through two organizations.

In 1952 six European nations (France, West Germany, Italy, Belgium, the Netherlands, and Luxembourg) officially established the European Coal and Steel Community (ECSC). The purpose of the organization was to allow coal and steel to be bought and sold freely throughout the six nations. The ECSC sought to promote peace and support economic growth.

Encouraged by the success of the ECSC, its members established the European Economic Community in 1957. Also known as the **Common Market**, the organization expanded economic cooperation to include many other products. Removing trade barriers led to lower prices and increased sales. Over the next forty years, the Common Market grew to include nearly thirty countries.

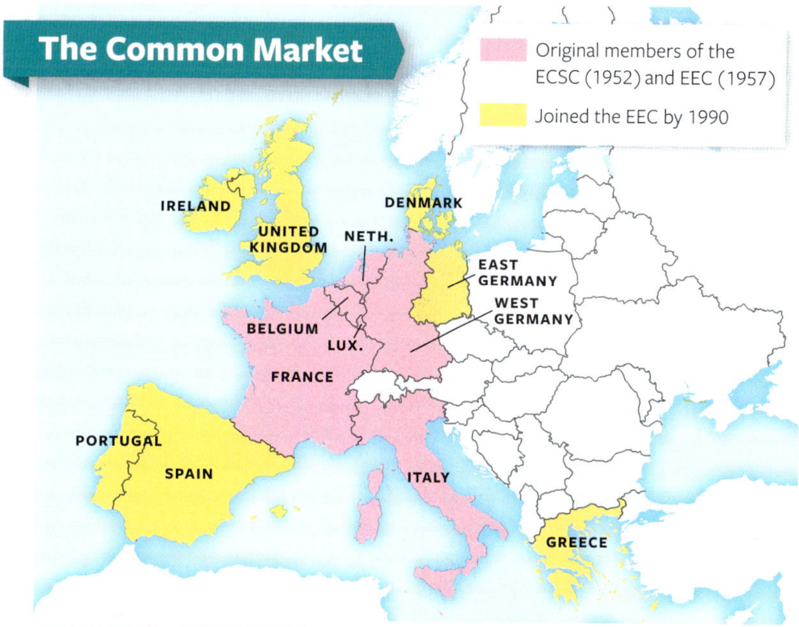

? What was the Common Market?

Toyota Motor factory, 1957

Recovery in Japan

Japan made an astonishing political and economic recovery following the war. General Douglas MacArthur supervised the occupation and directed the drafting of a new constitution. In 1955 the Japanese voted the **Liberal Democratic Party** into power. This party ruled Japan until 1993, when political scandals led the Japanese to replace it with a coalition government.

American financial and technological aid helped Japan become strong in industry. Japanese automakers gradually became world leaders. By the 1980s, Japan had also developed a world market in high-quality electronic equipment.

? **What was the result of American financial and technological aid to Japan following the end of World War II?**

Organization of the United Nations

When Allied leaders met to discuss strategy during World War II, they agreed to form an international peacekeeping organization after the war. In 1945 diplomats representing fifty nations organized the **United Nations** (UN). The UN's original goal was to promote international peace. Later, it expanded its role to address social, economic, and humanitarian problems.

Because the United Nations eventually included most of the world, the nations who caused problems were usually participating in the discussions of solutions. For instance, during the Cold War the Soviet Union caused major problems in the world while at the same time holding a permanent seat on the UN Security Council (fifteen-member organization within the UN that has final authority on many issues).

The United Nations tries to address great moral issues that arise in the affairs of nations. However, because of the diversity of nations and moral viewpoints represented, its approach to these problems is mixed. While the UN condemns atrocities like genocide, it supports the right of mothers to kill their unborn children.

(top) meeting of UN General Assembly, 1946, (bottom) UN peacekeeping operation in Democratic Republic of the Congo, 1960

WORLDVIEW DILEMMA

Should an international organization try to achieve world peace?

A Yes, an international organization should try to achieve world peace because human progress has made it possible to have world peace.

B An international organization may create a peaceful atmosphere for sovereign nations to discuss global issues without assuming the role of creating world peace.

C No, an international organization is an obstacle to world peace because nations would naturally achieve world peace on their own if there were no outside interference.

18.2 Cold War Developments

Proxy Conflicts

The United States and the Soviet Union engaged in a series of **proxy conflicts** during the Cold War. Communism was on the rise in many parts of the world, sometimes as the result of World War II peace negotiations. Communist and non-Communist forces fought for control of several countries. In these conflicts the Soviets and Americans were not engaged in open warfare with each other but gave economic or military help to the side that furthered their goals. For the Soviets, that meant supporting the spread of communism. For the Americans, that meant containing the spread of communism.

Chinese Civil War

In Chapter 16 you learned about the power struggle in China between Chiang Kai-Shek and Mao Zedong. After World War II, this struggle resumed. Chiang Kai-shek received aid from the United States, and Communist leader Mao Zedong received support from the Soviet Union (although later the Chinese and Soviets would become hostile toward each other). Mao promised the peasants a better life. He gradually gained enough popular support to drive Chiang's forces to an island off the coast of China in 1949. There Chiang established the **Republic of China**, which has governed the island of Taiwan to the present.

Mao developed a Five-Year Plan in 1949 to try to increase agricultural and industrial production. Small farms were combined into large collective units, and industrial development was controlled by the government. In 1958 Mao announced a new economic plan known as the **Great Leap Forward**. He intended to double the production of steel and agricultural products from that of the previous year. The results were disastrous. Communist authorities forced peasants to produce steel without proper equipment or training. The steel they manufactured was often impure and useless. Poor management and unfavorable weather resulted in reduced harvests for the farm collectives. Famine swept across China, but Mao continued to export grain to convince other nations that communism had produced a great bounty. The devastation caused by the famine and Mao's exportation of much-needed grain led to the deaths of twenty to thirty million people.

proxy conflict conflict in which parties are not directly involved but support opposing sides

GUIDING QUESTIONS

- Was the policy of containment successful in proxy conflicts?
- In what ways did the United States and the Soviet Union compete for technological supremacy during the Cold War?
- How did the Soviet Union try to maintain current conditions in Eastern Europe in the 1950s and 1960s?
- Why and how was the policy of détente implemented?

China and Taiwan

? Who won the Chinese Civil War?

Peasants working on a collective farm

The Korean War

By the mid-1960s, Mao became convinced that the Chinese people had been influenced by ideas that would cause capitalism to spread. To remove these influences, Mao unleashed a social and political purge in 1966 known as the **Cultural Revolution**. During that period Mao's young Chinese followers formed gangs called Red Guards. They carried out violent attacks against anyone considered a threat to the Communist revolution. By 1969 Mao had to withdraw his support for these zealous followers and allow authorities to suppress them. The Cultural Revolution continued, however, until after Mao's death in 1976. It targeted reform-minded members of the government and others. In the end the Cultural Revolution weakened support for communism among the Chinese people.

Korean War

The Allies had divided the Korean Peninsula, previously a Japanese possession, between the Soviet Union and the United States at the end of World War II. A boundary was set at the **38th parallel**. The Soviets supported the rise of a Communist government under Kim Il Sung in the north. Anti-Communist Syngman Rhee was elected president in the south.

Following many border skirmishes between the two sides, the North Korean army invaded South Korea in June 1950 to try to unite the entire peninsula under communism. Despite assistance from UN (mostly US) forces, much of South Korea was overrun in a few months.

Changing to a more offensive strategy, UN forces under General Douglas MacArthur made a daring attack at **Inchon** in September. MacArthur's forces pushed the Communists back deep into North Korea. The entry of thousands of Chinese troops into the country, however, preserved North Korea from total defeat. UN troops were again forced back across the 38th parallel, and the South Korean capital of Seoul changed hands for the third time. (It would go back to South Korea before the end of the war, changing hands for a fourth and final time.)

Fighting continued until July 1953, when both sides signed an agreement to stop fighting. Neither side had won or lost. The border was restored close to the 38th parallel, and a demilitarized zone was established that divides the two countries to this day.

What was the outcome of the Korean War?

Cuban Missile Crisis

During the fall of 1962, the United States discovered that the Soviets had placed nuclear missiles in Cuba. With Cuba only ninety miles away from the southern tip of Florida, these missiles posed a serious threat to American security. The United States demanded the removal of the missiles and imposed a naval blockade to prevent access to Cuba.

The United States and the Soviet Union came dangerously close to nuclear war during a two-week period in October. Complicating an already tense situation, a Soviet commander in Cuba launched a missile and shot down a U-2 spy plane flying high above the island. The crash killed the American pilot, and tensions peaked on October 28. Following secret negotiations, the Soviets agreed to remove the missiles. In exchange, the United States removed recently installed missiles from Turkey and promised not to invade Cuba.

What were the results of the secret negotiations between the United States and the Soviet Union during the Cuban missile crisis of 1962?

Relative ranges of nuclear weapons on the island of Cuba, delivered either by bomber or by surface-to-surface missile

Helicopters performed many functions in Vietnam, from troop and medical transport to battle support.

Vietnam War

Following World War II, the French tried to regain control of their colonies in Indochina, including Vietnam. However, a Communist leader named **Ho Chi Minh** resisted French efforts. Vietnamese Communists destroyed the French army at the Battle of Dien Bien Phu in 1954. At the peace conference, diplomats divided Vietnam into a Communist north and a non-Communist south. However, Communists in the north began working with Communist agents in the south (the **Viet Cong**) to seize control of the whole country.

The United States and other countries provided financial support to South Vietnam to prevent its fall to communism. Presidents Eisenhower and Kennedy also sent military advisors to train Vietnamese forces.

The American presence increased dramatically under President Johnson beginning in 1964. The government eventually sent over five hundred thousand troops. Although US forces won every battle, many troops died, and many Americans grew tired of the war. Critics questioned Johnson's motives for increasing American involvement and America's reasons for intervening in Vietnam in the first place. In addition, the media convinced many Americans that the United States was losing. As a result, the war became very unpopular.

Richard Nixon became the president in 1968. He began a general trend of "Vietnamization," which gradually withdrew American forces from Vietnam and trained the Vietnamese to defend themselves. Following the final evacuation of American forces in 1973, the South Vietnamese slowed the Communist advance until 1975. Congress voted to reduce aid to the South Vietnamese during this critical period. Soon the well-supplied Communists conquered South Vietnam, creating a unified Communist country.

The cost to Americans had been high, with the deaths of more than fifty thousand soldiers. In addition, the United States had spent one hundred and forty-six billion dollars to pay for the war. Following the failure to contain communism in Vietnam, the United States returned to a policy of isolation, and communism rapidly spread to nations in Southeast Asia and Central America.

Vietnam War demonstration in New York City, 1969

What was the outcome of the United States' return to a policy of isolation following the Vietnam War?

(top) Russian Air Force MiG-31, (bottom) American B-2 Spirit stealth bomber

Rivalry for Technological Supremacy

Warfare in the twentieth century was dominated by technology. This was true of both world wars, and it was true of the Cold War. The importance of technology was clear to both the United States and the Soviet Union. They competed to see who could develop new technologies and refine old ones. Many assumed the winner of the technology race would become the dominant world power.

Military

Both sides refined technologies for traditional warfare. There were improved versions of tanks, planes, submarines, and ships. There was also more advanced radar that could detect enemy vessels at greater distances.

Since the United States initially had a technological edge, it had to guard against spies. Soviet military advances often looked suspiciously like those developed in the West.

Nuclear

Though the United States was the first country to develop nuclear weapons, the Soviet Union was not far behind. It tested its first atomic bomb in 1949. The United States responded by developing the much more powerful hydrogen bomb. However, the Soviets soon developed their own hydrogen bomb.

This ongoing struggle to match or exceed each other's weapons was known as the *arms race*. During the Cold War, the United States and the Soviet Union developed and stockpiled more than enough weapons to destroy each other. Ironically, some viewed the existence of these weapons as a guarantee against war. The policy of mutually assured destruction (**MAD**) said that enemies who were equally capable of destroying one another would never risk an attack. One side might destroy the other, but it would itself be destroyed by a strike back. (There are different explanations of how the second strike would be launched.)

What was the arms race?

Schoolchildren hiding under their desks during an A-bomb drill

Space

The Soviets took an early lead in the race to conquer space. In 1957 Soviet scientists launched ***Sputnik 1***, the first manmade satellite. While the American government hurried to catch up, the Soviets took another leap forward by launching the first human into space. From this point on, Americans determined not to be left behind. On July 20, 1969, they were the first to land humans on the moon. Abandoning their own efforts to travel to the moon, the Soviets concentrated on building a space station.

Satellites were one of the more far-reaching results of the space race. Though the Soviets had launched the first satellite, the Americans launched a satellite of their own by 1958. Satellite technology had a variety of uses. The first American satellite, *Explorer 1*, measured radiation levels. *TIROS 1*, launched on April 1, 1960, was designed to track weather. *Echo 1*, launched on August 12, 1960, was used for communication.

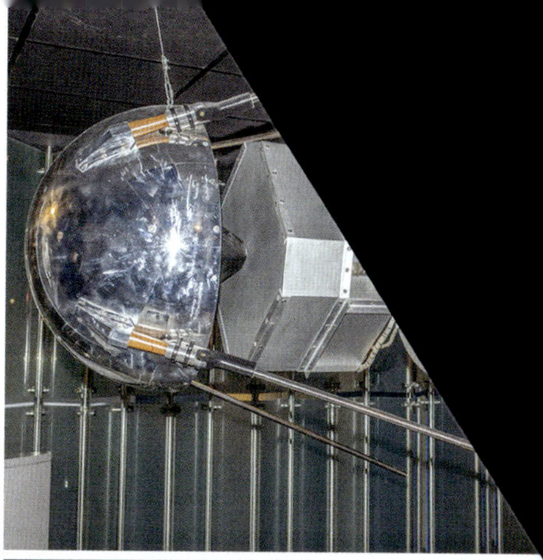

(top) Sputnik satellite, on display in Moscow Space Museum, (bottom) Apollo 15 Lunar Module pilot, James Irwin, saluting the US flag

? **What firsts did the Soviets achieve in the space race?**

Suppression of Reform Movements

Joseph Stalin died in 1953. Nikita Khrushchev, the new Soviet leader, initially moved away from the repression of the Stalin era. He allowed people some freedom in what they read, made the secret police less powerful, and shut down some forced-labor and prison camps. He even gave a speech in February 1956 in which he condemned Stalin as a tyrannical dictator. The movement away from Stalin's policies and legacy was known as "de-Stalinization."

Khrushchev's rejection of Stalin, however, had some unintended consequences. The people of Eastern Europe were motivated to consider the harsh conditions that Stalin had caused in their own countries. Some rebelled against their Communist authorities and pushed for reforms. Concerned that he had gone too far, Khrushchev toned down his anti-Stalin campaign and tightened control over the Soviets' Eastern European allies.

Poland and Hungary

Dissent in Poland led to reforms by Polish Communists and a statement of Polish economic independence. To avoid confrontation with the Soviets, the Poles agreed to remain loyal members of the Warsaw Pact.

Unrest was worse in Hungary. Many Hungarians were dissatisfied, not just with repression but with communism itself. Imry Nagy became the new Hungarian leader on October 26, 1956. He announced his determination to give the Hungarian people more freedom and independence. Part of this new course would be withdrawing from the Warsaw Pact. The Soviets were not prepared to allow this kind of independence, however. They sent troops into the capital city of Budapest on November 4, 1956, and crushed the rebellion.

Czechoslovakia

After the unrest of 1956, some Eastern European nations had experienced limited reforms. Czechoslovakia had not been among them, however, and discontent was mounting. Alexander Dubček became the leader of Czechoslovakia in January 1968 and began to restore rights to the people. This reform concerned the Soviets, who feared that allowing too much dissent in Czechoslovakia would be a bad example for other parts of the Eastern bloc. Therefore, the Soviets and their allies sent a large armed force to crush resistance in Czechoslovakia in August 1968.

? **Why were the Soviets concerned about reforms in Czechoslovakia?**

GUE

Justice

The complaints that the people of Czechoslovakia had with their government were like those of other Eastern European nations. Strict Communist controls had hindered the economy. Freedom to publicly express oneself was forbidden. And secret police were used to crush dissent. When Alexander Dubček came to power, he gave more economic control to individuals. He loosened control of the media, allowing free speech. And he put restraints on the secret police. Though these reforms did not last, they produced optimism and hope, leading people to call this period the "Prague Spring" (for the capital city of Prague).

Warsaw Pact tanks and troops rolled into Prague's Wenceslas Square on August 21, 1968, to crush the "Prague Spring."

Environment

Communist governments in Eastern Europe wanted to increase industrial production in their countries. They built many factories and mines to accomplish this. Industrial pollution caused problems for the air and water in these nations.

Religion

As in other Communist-controlled countries, churches in Czechoslovakia had to be licensed by the government. The government regulated the leadership of churches and banned evangelization. Atheism was officially encouraged. These strict controls over religious practice led to the establishment of underground churches in many Communist countries.

Power

Nikita Khrushchev was replaced by Leonid Brezhnev in 1964. Brezhnev was not interested in reform. He wanted to keep the Soviet Union and the Eastern bloc as they were. His intervention in Czechoslovakia established the **Brezhnev Doctrine**. This doctrine said that the Soviet Union would intervene anytime an existing socialist government was threatened.

The invasion of Czechoslovakia resulted in more than a hundred deaths, thousands of refugees, and the rejection of any further reform.

Détente

The 1970s were a new era for the Cold War. Many opposed the arms race. It was tremendously expensive. More importantly, people feared that someday nations would use their weapons of mass destruction. The Cuban missile crisis had brought that concern frighteningly close.

Both sides wanted **détente**, or a relaxation of tensions. They met to try to solve difficult issues. In 1972 the SALT (Strategic Arms Limitations Talks) Treaty was signed. It limited the number of nuclear weapons each side could possess. In 1975 the Helsinki agreement was reached. The Americans agreed to recognize Cold War boundaries as permanent, and the Soviets promised to consider human rights complaints.

Détente lasted only a few years. The Soviets were not following the weapons restrictions or considering human rights. Their invasion of Afghanistan in 1979 (see page 418) effectively ended détente.

What is détente?

CRITICAL THINKING 18.2

Do you think the policy of containment worked well for the United States during the Cold War? Explain your answer.

US president Richard Nixon and Soviet general secretary Leonid Brezhnev signing the SALT 1 Treaty

18.3 Nationalism in the Third World and the Middle East

GUIDING QUESTIONS

- Was it reasonable for former colonies to want to be independent?
- How did colonies differ in their approaches to gaining political independence?
- How stable were new nations established in Asia and Africa?
- What were some causes and outcomes of conflicts in the Middle East?

World War II helped many colonial powers realize that the citizens of their foreign empires had the right to be free. After all, the colonial powers themselves had fought to remain free of fascist control. In addition, the African colonies had contributed men and materials in support of the Allied cause. Following the war, the European nations gradually granted independence to their colonies. Over the next thirty-five years, nearly one hundred and twenty nations emerged from the **third world**.

India

Indians had pressed the British government for independence for many years. Britain responded by gradually granting India some self-rule through provincial councils. Not satisfied, the people continued to push for full independence.

Several Indian revolutionaries clashed violently with the British. However, **Mohandas Gandhi** (1869–1948) rejected violence. He supported a strategy of **passive resistance**. His followers took part in strikes, refused to pay taxes, and pursued other nonviolent strategies. After years of Indian resistance, the British finally granted India full independence in 1947.

Mohandas Gandhi

Independence did not end the turmoil in India, however. To minimize the growing hostility between Hindus and Muslims in India, the British had partitioned India into two nations in 1947. India was for the Hindu population, and Pakistan was for the Muslim population. Despite the efforts to avoid violence, rioting broke out between Muslims, Hindus, and Sikhs, and about half a million people died.

What did the strategy of passive resistance involve?

Africa

Many African colonies gained their independence in the decades following World War II. Some transitioned to independence peacefully. For example, in Ghana the British announced a general election in which Africans could vote and run for offices in a national assembly. In 1951 Kwame Nkrumah and his Convention People's Party captured the national assembly in a landslide victory. On March 6, 1957, Ghana was officially recognized as an independent nation.

Decolonization of Africa

third world regions that remained neutral and did not ally themselves with the Western or Communist powers (also used of nations with less technological development)

Some independence struggles, however, involved armed conflict. In Southern Rhodesia European settlers dominated the colonial government but were a minority within the colony. They feared that Britain would force them to accept majority rule, and they knew that they would lose power to the larger native-born population if that happened. Therefore, to preserve their power, the members of the colonial government declared independence from Britain in 1965. In the early 1970s, some native Africans within the country began a guerilla war against the European-dominated government. Finally, a settlement reached in 1979 gave all Africans the right to vote. On April 18, 1980, Southern Rhodesia officially became the Republic of Zimbabwe.

Why did Southern Rhodesia experience a violent struggle for independence?

At first, many of the new nations seemed to prosper. However, several factors hindered growth. First, most Africans had no experience with a free-market economy. They had traded only with their mother countries. Second, many African leaders believed that socialism could bring their people out of poverty. They set up some policies that hindered economic growth, like collective agriculture. Finally, some leaders were corrupt and channeled wealth into their own pockets rather than using it to benefit their people.

One notable exception to these trends was the country of Botswana. Seretse Khama, the first president, worked diligently to avoid the problems other post-colonial nations encountered. He strengthened the economy by promoting free markets and developing Botswana's mineral resources. He chose government workers for their ability and worked to get rid of corruption. And he emphasized personal freedom and respect for all. The result was a prosperous, stable country.

African nations often found themselves caught between the United States and the Soviet Union. The Soviets took advantage of the weakness of young nations and tried to spread communism. The United States responded by trying to contain communism, sometimes even temporarily supporting dictatorships if the dictators stood with the West against the Soviet Union.

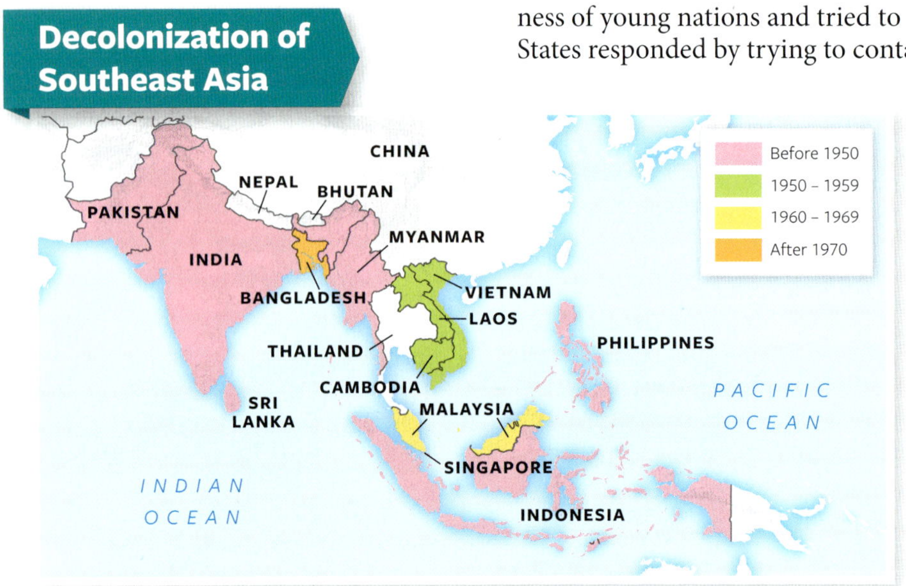

Southeast Asia

Several regions of Southeast Asia that had been colonized during the 1800s achieved independence following World War II. For example, the United States had prepared the Philippines for eventual independence, and this occurred in 1946. Native peoples across Southeast Asia formed national governments and regained their independence over the next twenty years.

Middle East

Israel

The Zionist movement, which began in the late 1800s, had the goal of reestablishing a homeland for the Jewish people in Palestine (the ancient land of Israel). There was always a Jewish presence in Palestine, though many Jews had been exiled to other nations after Roman legions destroyed Jerusalem in AD 70. Centuries of persecution of Jewish people in their lands of exile convinced many that the Jews needed their own land again. The first official recognition of this idea was the **Balfour Declaration**, a statement issued by British Foreign Secretary Arthur Balfour in 1917. It said that the British government favored the idea of a homeland for the Jewish people in Palestine.

The British governed Palestine as a mandate starting in April 1920. After World War II, large numbers of Jewish immigrants, fleeing Europe and the horrors of the Holocaust, tried to enter Palestine. Not wanting to provoke conflict with Arab residents, the British tried to restrict this immigration. However, by 1947 British forces realized they could no longer balance the two sides. They decided to divide Palestine into a Jewish state and an Arab state.

The British Mandate expired on May 14, 1948. On May 13 Jewish leaders announced their independence and named their new country Israel. The United States immediately recognized Israel as a country and provided military aid. Stalin and the Soviet Union also recognized the nation of Israel.

Surrounding Arab nations, however, did not want a Jewish state in Palestine. Forces from Egypt, Syria, Jordan, Lebanon, and Iraq attacked Israel on May 14 and started the **1948 Arab-Israeli War**. After a year of fighting, both sides signed a ceasefire, but tensions remained.

In June 1967 Egypt, Jordan, and Syria prepared to invade Israel with the assistance of several other Arab countries. The Jewish forces struck first and quickly destroyed most of the tanks, planes, and other weapons that were waiting to invade from Egypt and Syria. In what is known as the **Six-Day War**, Israel smashed the imminent threat. As a result of the war, Israel took control of several new pieces of territory: the Sinai Peninsula, the Gaza Strip, the West Bank, and the Golan Heights.

What new pieces of territory did Israel take control of after the Six-Day War?

Pan-Arabism

A significant movement in the Arab world during this period was **Pan-Arabism**. It was an effort to unify all Arabs under one government. The movement began to grow as Arab states gained their independence in the twentieth century (first from the Ottoman Empire in 1918 and then from European mandates in the mid-1900s). Two steps toward unification took place in the 1940s. First, the Ba'ath Party was founded in 1943 to promote a single Arab state. Members of the Ba'ath Party gained control in Syria and Iraq. Second, the Arab League was founded in 1945 to increase cooperation among Arab states. In 1958 Egypt and Syria joined together to create the United Arab Republic, the first union of Arab states. Syria withdrew from the union in 1961, however.

Gamal Abdel Nasser was the most significant figure of Pan-Arabism. He was an Egyptian army officer who participated in the overthrow of the Egyptian monarchy in 1952. He officially ruled Egypt from 1956 until his death in 1970. Nasser created a socialist state and tried to modernize his country. His broader goal was to rule a unified Arab people. After Nasser's death, Pan-Arabism declined in popularity, and new Islamic groups became political forces in the Middle East.

CRITICAL THINKING 18.3

What role do you think religion might have played in the conflicts of the Middle East?

THE PALESTINE POST

STATE OF ISRAEL IS BORN

Most Crowded Hours in Palestine's History

JEWS TAKE OVER SECURITY ZONES

Egyptian Air Force Spitfires Bomb Tel Aviv; One Shot Down

U.S. RECOGNIZES JEWISH STATE

Proclamation by Head Of Government

2 Columns Cross Southern Border

Etzion Settlers Taken P.O.W.

Special Assembly Adjourns

2 Villages Taken In Road Battle

EMERGENCY

EGYPTIAN INVASION BEFORE U.N. SECURITY COUNCIL

Sir Alan Sails From Palestine

ACRE CAPTURED

(top) May 16, 1948, edition of the Jewish newspaper *The Palestine Post*, (middle) destroyed Egyptian aircraft at the El Arish airport in the Sinai Peninsula, (bottom) arrival of fresh troops at Port Said during the Suez Crisis of 1956

GUIDING QUESTIONS

- Why did unrest develop in the Soviet Union and its satellite states?
- What role did key leaders play in ending the Cold War?
- Where did revolutions occur in 1989?
- How did the Soviet Union dissolve in 1991?

18.4 Collapse of the Soviet Union

Few predicted the rapid demise of the Soviet Union that occurred in the late 1980s and early 1990s. In hindsight, however, it seems that the Soviet Union was destined to fall. Like other empires from the past, the Soviets and their allies had seized more territory than they could successfully rule. In addition, the Soviet Union was composed of many ethnic groups with little in common. In the end, a combination of internal unrest and contributions by key leaders brought the entire system crashing down.

Internal Unrest

Economic Weakness

The Soviet Union was crumbling from within. The Communist system had failed to produce prosperity. Economic planning by the government was inefficient and too focused on expensive military equipment. The people had no incentives to work hard, so production fell in factories and on collective farms. And equipment was old and in need of updating.

The one form of private enterprise that was allowed was the *household plot*. This was a small plot of land that a family used for growing food, either for its own use or to sell. Though covering a tiny portion of the Soviet Union's total land area, the household plots produced a significant amount of food.

(top) Lech Walesa, (bottom) Afghan soldier aiming an American-made Stinger missile at enemy aircraft

Dissatisfaction within the Soviet Bloc

Dissatisfaction and unrest continued to build in Soviet-dominated countries of Eastern Europe. Poland and the Solidarity Free Trade Union clearly demonstrated this unrest. Led by an electrical technician, **Lech Wałęsa**, Polish workers formed an anti-Communist movement that combined labor interests, the Roman Catholic Church, and Polish nationalists. Wałęsa endured job loss and imprisonment to lead the **Solidarity** movement and work toward Polish independence. Pope John Paul II lent his support to the movement in 1987. In 1989 Poland achieved its independence.

What was the purpose of the Solidarity movement?

Failed Ventures

The Soviets engaged in aggression again when they invaded Afghanistan in 1979. On the excuse of bringing stability to the country (whose young Communist government was under attack), the Soviets sent over one hundred thousand troops to seize control. However, the Afghans vigorously resisted the Soviet occupation. With the United States providing weapons and financial support, the Afghans fought the Soviet troops to a stalemate. Facing growing losses, the Soviet forces withdrew in 1989.

Key Leaders

Margaret Thatcher

In 1979 **Margaret Thatcher** led the Conservative Party in Great Britain to victory. She returned many nationalized industries to the private sector and tried to reverse many of the socialist programs that had weakened the British nation. In addition, she forged a strong anti-Communist alliance with the United States during her eleven years as prime minister of Great Britain.

Margaret Hilda Roberts was born on October 13, 1925, to Alfred and Beatrice Roberts. Her father was a shopkeeper and a local politician. Margaret was a hard worker and prospered at school. She won a scholarship to the all-women's Somerville College, Oxford, in 1943. She studied chemistry while at Somerville, but she was already showing an interest in her true passion, politics. In 1946 she became the president of the Oxford University Conservative Association. She read books by conservative authors and developed the philosophy that would shape her political career.

After graduating Margaret worked for four years as a research chemist and then became a barrister (a type of lawyer). Margaret met businessman Denis Thatcher at a political dinner in 1949. They were married in 1951 and had twins, Carol and Mark, in 1953.

Margaret ran for a seat in the House of Commons as a member of the Conservative Party for the first time in 1951, but she did not win an election until 1959. Once in office, she drew attention for her firm opposition to big government. She was given a cabinet post in 1970.

Margaret was chosen to be the leader of the Conservative Party in 1975. When the Conservatives won a majority of Parliament seats in 1979, she, as leader of the party, became the prime minister. Margaret was prime minister from 1979 until 1990. Not only was she the first woman prime minister, but she was the only one in the 1900s to be elected three times in a row.

Margaret transformed British politics through her policies and personal character. Her influence became known as "Thatcherism." It included things such as individual responsibility, smaller government, and an aggressive pursuit of the policies she believed in. In foreign relations she proved to be as strong a leader as she was at home. She was concerned about Soviet influence in Europe, and she worked together with the United States to maintain a strong military defense. A Soviet journalist called her the "Iron Lady." It was a reference to remarks she made about the Iron Curtain, but it was a good description of her strong, no-nonsense approach to government.

Margaret resigned from the leadership of the Conservative Party in 1990, but she continued to be a public figure for many years. She died on April 8, 2013, at 87 and was the first prime minister since Winston Churchill to be given a state funeral (public funeral held for an important national figure).

Margaret Thatcher

Ronald Reagan

Ronald Reagan became the fortieth president of the United States in 1980. His strong leadership turned a struggling America into a political, social, and economic force that influenced the world. Reagan was determined to bring an end to Communist domination. Through alliances with other conservative leaders, such as Margaret Thatcher, he led an effective campaign to plant or restore democracy in many countries.

TURNING POINTS

"Evil Empire" Speech

The presidency of Ronald Reagan produced a change in direction for the Cold War. The key to the change was Reagan's unwillingness to accept things as they were. Many had concluded that the Soviets were valid and permanent partners on the world scene. Furthermore, they believed that détente was the only way to protect themselves from nuclear war. Ronald Reagan challenged these assumptions through a series of well-constructed speeches.

One of Reagan's most famous speeches was delivered in Orlando, Florida, on March 8, 1983, to the National Association of Evangelicals. In it, Reagan denied that the Soviet Union was America's moral equal and that both sides were responsible for nuclear tensions. Instead, he placed the blame fully on the Soviets. Criticizing their totalitarian control of their people and their aggressive desire for world domination, he described them as "the focus of evil in the modern world" and an "evil empire."

This speech and other speeches by Reagan were significant because they convinced people that the Cold War did not have to go on forever. It could, and should, be won by the United States through military strength and technological advancements. For example, in another speech Reagan called for a space-based defensive system (**SDI**, or Strategic Defense Initiative) that would protect the United States from foreign missile attacks.

More important even than the effect of his speeches on Americans was their effect on the Soviets. Though outwardly scoffing at Reagan, the Soviets were privately fearful of a military buildup that they could not match without financial ruin. This fear contributed to the unraveling of the Soviet Union and ultimately brought an end to the Cold War.

Ronald Reagan delivering the "Evil Empire" speech

1. What was Ronald Reagan unwilling to do?
2. How did Ronald Reagan describe the Soviet Union in his speech on March 8, 1983?
3. Why did the Soviets fear Reagan's words?

Mikhail Gorbachev

Leonid Brezhnev was succeeded briefly by two aging Soviet leaders, Yuri Andropov and Konstantin Chernenko. Meanwhile, a younger leader rose through the ranks of the Kremlin. Upon Chernenko's death in 1985, **Mikhail Gorbachev** emerged as the leader of the Soviet Union. He assumed power without violence or opposition.

Gorbachev tried to revive the Soviet Union by introducing two new policies. ***Perestroika*** was a restructuring of the economy and the political system. For example, Gorbachev allowed some private ownership of businesses. He also moved the Soviet Union closer to democracy by calling for multi-candidate elections. In 1990 the people elected him as the first president of the Soviet Union.

The other policy Gorbachev introduced was ***glasnost***. *Glasnost* was an openness about problems in Soviet society. Gorbachev released thousands of political prisoners. He allowed people to discuss policy and give their opinions freely without fear of punishment.

Perestroika did not work because economic reforms were not always well thought out. But *glasnost* worked remarkably well. When given the chance to freely express themselves, the Soviet people expressed opposition to the entire Soviet system.

? **Describe the policies of *perestroika* and *glasnost*.**

Revolutions of 1989

The dissatisfaction with communism and Soviet repression that had been building for years in Eastern Europe finally boiled over in the fall of 1989. The most dramatic evidence of this new era was the opening of the Berlin Wall for free passage on November 9, 1989. In the weeks surrounding this event, the countries of East Germany, Bulgaria, Czechoslovakia, Hungary, and Poland all broke away from Soviet influence and ended Communist rule. Revolutions in Eastern Europe occurred peacefully except in Romania, where the tyrannical dictator Nicolae Ceaușescu was overthrown and later executed.

Symbolic tearing down of the Berlin Wall

Dissolving of the Soviet Union

In August 1991 several Soviet leaders, believing that reforms had gone too far, tried to remove Gorbachev. Boris Yeltsin, who had been elected president of the Soviet republic of Russia in June 1991, took part in a mass uprising to prevent the attempted coup. Having no desire to return to the old system of repression, the republics of the Soviet Union began declaring their independence. By the end of 1991, the Soviet Union ceased to exist.

With the fall of the Soviet Union, religious freedom returned to Eastern Europe. Christians could worship in public and witness without fear of arrest or harassment. Missionaries from the West obtained visas to minister in former Communist nations. The light of God's Word began to shine across this vast region.

CRITICAL THINKING 18.4

How did the household garden plots in the Soviet Union demonstrate the failure of the Communist system?

The Fall of Communism

1989

November 9, 1989
The Berlin Wall is opened for free passage.

November 10, 1989
Leader of Communist Party in Bulgaria is forced to resign.

November 17, 1989
Velvet Revolution begins in Czechoslovakia with a peaceful transfer of power away from Communist Party.

December 1989
Dictator Nicolae Ceausescu is forcibly overthrown in Romania.

1990

October 3, 1990
East Germany reunites with West Germany.

1991

June 1991
Boris Yeltsin is elected president of the Soviet republic of Russia.

August 1991
Soviet leaders attempt coup of Mikhail Gorbachev.

December 1991
Soviet Union is officially dissolved.

1992

States emerging from the former Soviet Union

Making Connections

1. What were key economic, political, and religious differences between the United States and the Soviet Union?
2. Describe how the Japanese government and economy developed following World War II. Tell whether these developments were helpful for Japan.
3. State whether the United States was successful in containing the spread of communism in each of the following proxy conflicts: the Chinese Civil War, the Korean War, the Cuban missile crisis, and the Vietnam War.
4. Name and describe three areas of technological competition during the Cold War.
5. How did the Soviets respond to uprisings in Hungary in 1956 and Czechoslovakia in 1968?
6. Why did both sides of the Cold War want détente? What agreements were reached because of détente?
7. Compare methods to gain political independence in India, Ghana, and Southern Rhodesia.
8. How did religious differences prevent stability in India following its independence?
9. What factors hindered progress toward African development following the end of the colonial period?
10. What economic and political complaints did the people of the Soviet Union and its satellite states have?
11. Which Eastern European nations experienced revolutions in 1989?
12. Describe the events that led to the dissolving of the Soviet Union in 1991.

Thinking Critically

1. Why is it difficult for a secular organization like the United Nations to resolve moral issues between nations?
2. Based on Habakkuk 2:9, how was the gaining of political independence for former colonies of Asia and Africa a just outcome?

WHAT TO KNOW

DATES & EVENTS

1948 Arab-Israeli War
Six-Day War

PEOPLE

Konrad Adenauer
Charles de Gaulle
Ho Chi Minh
Mohandas Gandhi
Lech Wałęsa
Margaret Thatcher
Ronald Reagan
Mikhail Gorbachev

PLACES

Republic of China
Inchon

TERMS

Cold War
containment
Truman Doctrine
Marshall Plan
NATO
Warsaw Pact
Berlin Blockade
Common Market
United Nations
proxy conflict
Great Leap Forward
Cultural Revolution
38th parallel
Viet Cong
MAD
Sputnik 1
Brezhnev Doctrine
détente
third world
passive resistance
Balfour Declaration
Pan-Arabism
Solidarity
SDI
perestroika
glasnost

Ronald Reagan's critics called his SDI plan "Star Wars," comparing it to the movie series.

19 GLOBAL GROWTH AND CULTURAL CHANGE

1963 – 2000

ESSENTIAL QUESTIONS

- How did world population, material prosperity, and technology grow in the twentieth century?
- What happened in Europe and the Americas in the late twentieth century?
- What happened in Africa, Asia, and the Middle East in the late twentieth century?
- What were the cultural, religious, artistic, and philosophical movements during this period?

Mumbai, India

A Century of Change

When Beth Snyder was born in 1903 in Nevins, Wisconsin, the fastest a person could travel was around 45 miles an hour by train, not much faster than a galloping horse. When Beth died in 1997, a person could travel in a Boeing 747 jetliner at speeds exceeding 650 miles an hour. When she was born, people were still dreaming of soaring with the eagles. When she died, men had already gone to the moon and back many times.

When Beth was three, her family moved to eastern Montana. When they first arrived, they lived in a cave dug out of the hillside. There was no indoor plumbing or electricity. Even as late as 1940, only 55 percent of Americans had indoor plumbing, but by 1990, 99 percent did.

Even before the Great Depression, most Americans were materially poor. Beth's father and two uncles had to hitch a ride on a train and travel to North Dakota to work in the coal mines to earn livings for their families. Her father would do many different jobs during his life. He ran a sawmill and later a flour mill; he also built houses. Eventually, he was able to make a living at the job he loved best, raising honeybees. He started the Blue Star Honey company. He also built a community church, the Log Chapel, because he was concerned about the lack of biblical teaching in the area.

In 1927, Beth married Glenn Snyder. Glenn had dreams of being a farmer, but the Great Depression shattered those dreams. Glenn had to find work anywhere he could. Eventually he was employed building roads across Montana, but that meant being away from his family.

In 1920 a phone call from New York City to Los Angeles would cost $15 ($200 today) for the first three minutes. By 1997 that same call would cost 45 cents. Up until the 1990s, to get a little information on any subject, a person had to find a printed set of encyclopedias. A set of encyclopedias was expensive, and they were out of date immediately after publication. But in 1997, although the internet was still new, it already contained up-to-date information many times that of the encyclopedia.

The movies of the 1930s were relatively tame and innocent, yet as Christians, the Snyder family chose to avoid the movie theater. Even long after it was common for families to own a television, the Snyders did not. Like many Christians of their generation, they desired to stay separate from the world system. By the 1960s Glenn and Beth were managing an apartment building close to downtown Seattle, Washington. In Seattle, the Snyders encountered young people who had rejected the cultural standards of their parents.

On June 28, 1997, Beth Snyder entered her heavenly home. She left behind a more prosperous and advanced world but also one that was more chaotic and accepting of sin.

A bookmobile served as a library during the Great Depression in rural Montana.

- Why did the world population increase so rapidly in the twentieth century?
- Why did the number and size of cities grow during this time?
- Why did literacy, wealth, and leisure time increase throughout the world?
- How did scientific and technological advances impact the world?

19.1 Worldwide Growth

It is impossible to exaggerate the number of changes and the growth in the world during the twentieth century. World population, city sizes, literacy rates (the number of people who can read), and personal wealth all exploded during this time.

More People

From 1887 to 1977 the world population doubled two times. Before that it had taken over three hundred years to double three times. The populations of Asia and Africa by far outpaced every place else. The countries of India and China had the largest and fastest-growing populations. The reasons for the population growth are large families, efficient food production, and better sanitation. If a couple has more than two children, then they have not only replaced themselves but added to the growth of the world population. Families were generally very large from the period after the Flood to the beginning of the twentieth century. For most of that time, many of the children would die as infants or at a young age because of disease or poor sanitation, and adults would also live shorter lives. When food production became more efficient and sanitation methods improved, infant deaths declined dramatically; and couples continued to have many children, so in turn, world population increased dramatically in the twentieth century.

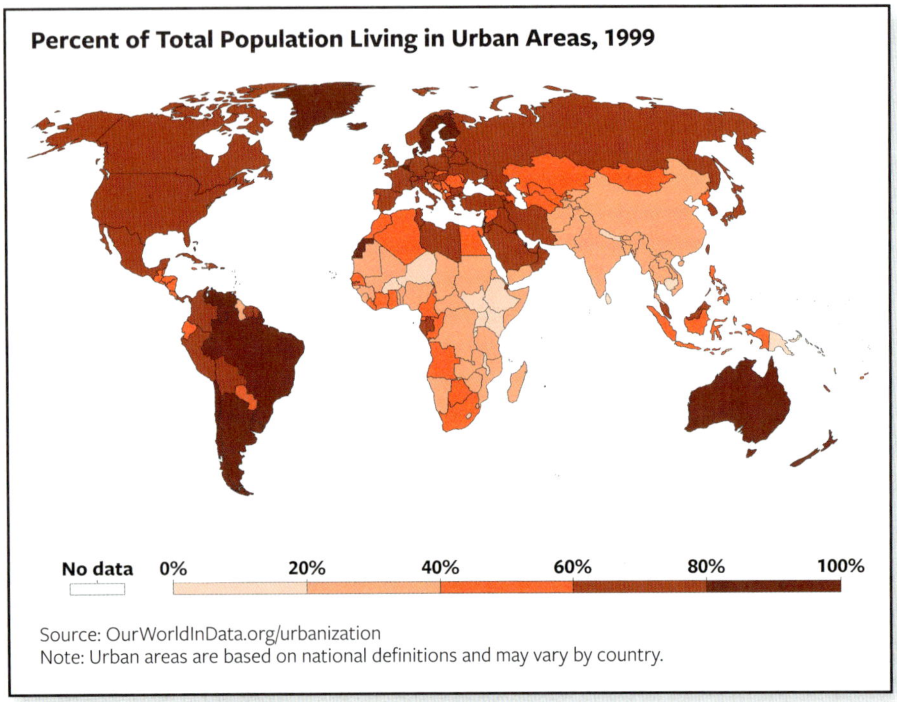

Percent of Total Population Living in Urban Areas, 1999

More Cities

Not only were there almost four times as many people in the world at the end of the twentieth century as there were at the beginning, but thousands more cities had been built, and old ones had been expanded beyond recognition. More and more people moved to urban centers to find employment. In 1900 the world's largest cities were in Europe or North America. By the end of the century, the largest cities were in East Asia and Latin America. For most of human history, the majority of people had lived in rural areas. *Rural* can be defined as a place with fewer than 500 people per square mile. But by the end of the twentieth century, the number of people living in urban areas was about the same as the number living in rural areas. The process of people moving to the cities is called **urbanization**. Because of growing cities, nations struggled with worsening air pollution as the use of coal and oil increased.

Why were populations growing in the twentieth century?

A ship loaded with containers

More Wealth

The world economy doubled almost four times following World War II. In general, everyone in the world was wealthier than they had ever been, although those living in non-Communist nations held a greater proportion of that wealth. With a larger world population, there were more people to produce material wealth. This goes against the belief that the earth cannot support a larger population.

The increase in global trade has also made nations wealthier. By the 1990s there was a truly global economy. Global trade agreements and improvements in transportation made it possible to ship products across many national boundaries. In addition, new technology like **containerization** contributed to the efficiency of global trade. Containerization refers to containers of uniform size and shape, filled with goods, that are stacked on ships, transported over oceans, and then put on semitrailer trucks or railroad cars after arriving at port. Finally, the sustained peace that most nations experienced after World War II allowed global trade to flourish.

With more wealth people had more leisure time. They did not have to work all the time. Growing numbers of people watched and participated in sports. Soccer and basketball were very popular, along with the Olympics. Movie theaters provided entertainment for many people around the world.

World GDP over the Last 2000 Years

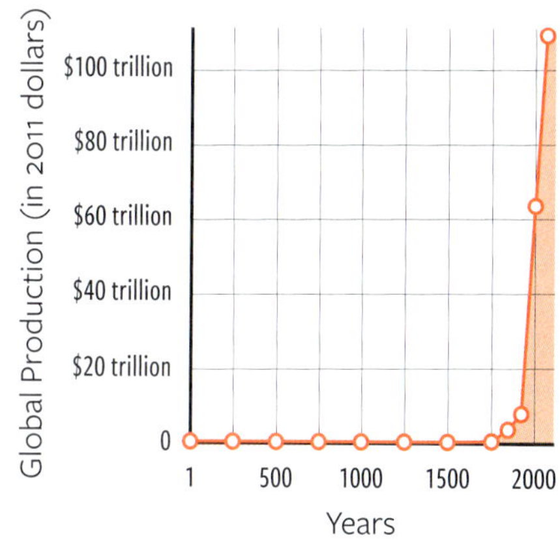

Source: OurWorldInData.org/economic-growth

More Literacy

At the start of the twentieth century, 78 percent of people in the world could not read, but by the end of the century only 18 percent could not read. The increased literacy was a result of countries requiring children to go to school. And with the increase in wealth, families no longer needed to have their young children working, so the children were free to attend school.

? What was the literacy rate at the end of the twentieth century?

More Scientific and Technological Achievements

The scientific and technological achievements of the twentieth century vastly improved people's lives.

The Microchip

The key invention of this period was the computer chip, or **microchip**. It can be said that almost every other technological and scientific advancement since the 1960s was a result of this one invention. Simply speaking, a microchip is made up of thousands of switches or transistors that can be in either the on or off position. In other words, the chips send signals of 1 (on) or 0 (off). Before microchips, computers used vacuum tubes the size of a light bulb to produce these signals. Even a very simple computer would fill a whole room! But as scientists learned how to put more switches on the chip, computers improved and got smaller and smaller. Now microchips can contain millions of transistors, which means they are millions of times more powerful than the earliest computers.

A microchip

? What did the microchip replace?

A representation of DNA

Medical Advances and New Challenges

In 1953 James Watson, Francis Crick, and Rosalind Franklin discovered the structure of DNA. This discovery provided further evidence of the complexity and design of the human body. DNA studies have helped scientists to understand diseases and to develop drugs to overcome several of them.

The invention of antibiotics to fight infections dramatically decreased the worldwide death rate. In addition, researchers developed vaccines to prevent or eradicate diseases such as polio and smallpox. Advances in medical technology included laser surgeries and other procedures to destroy tumors or repair injured organs through tiny incisions. These procedures protect the patient from many surgery-related infections and enable more rapid recovery. By the 1990s, people had a greater understanding of the negative health effects from smoking cigarettes. Because of this knowledge, the practice of smoking decreased. Also during this time, inventors developed X-ray and magnetic resonance imaging (MRI) machines. These machines allowed doctors to diagnose and treat diseases much earlier than before, thus saving millions of lives.

What did DNA studies enable?

While doctors were wiping out old diseases, new diseases were appearing, affecting millions of people. In 1981 a disease called the Human Immunodeficiency Virus (HIV) arose in Africa and spread rapidly, killing millions of people throughout the world. HIV leads to an illness called acquired immunodeficiency syndrome, or AIDS. By 1997 doctors were successfully treating AIDS using a mixture of medicines; they decreased death rates from AIDS by 47 percent.

In 1906 Doctor Alois Alzheimer discovered a disease caused by plaque buildup in the brain. The disease resulted in increased memory loss for those who had it. Alzheimer's disease became one of the leading causes of death in the United States.

The space shuttle *Atlantis* lifts off on September 9, 2006.

The Space Age

In 1981 the United States launched *Columbia*, the first **space shuttle**. The space shuttles were the first mostly reusable rockets (everything but the shuttle's large fuel tank) flown by any country. Their job was to carry cargo into space, such as satellites and space probes, and to supply a future space station. They were also used to extend the time people could be in space so that, among other things, they could perform science experiments. In 1986, however, a tragedy occurred. The second shuttle built, *Challenger*, blew up minutes after it was launched. It was the twenty-fifth space shuttle mission, and everyone had taken the safety of space flight for granted. In 1988 shuttle flights resumed, and in 1998 NASA began building the International Space Station. Space flights provided invaluable benefits for life here on earth. Satellites launched via shuttles and other rockets greatly increased worldwide communication and weather forecasting. The Global Positioning System (GPS), a series of satellites that allow those with receivers to know their position on the earth, is the key element for tools that show your location and how to reach your destination. Unmanned space probes have visited almost every planet in our solar system, sending back stunning photos. In 1990 NASA launched the Hubble Space Telescope. It sent back the clearest images ever captured of the Milky Way as well as other galaxies. In 2003, *Columbia* exploded as it was coming back to earth, again reminding everyone of the dangers of space flight and demonstrating the need for a new space vehicle. In 2011 the space shuttle was retired after flying 135 missions.

What was the space shuttle used for?

Advances in Energy

As the century progressed, many ways of producing electricity were developed. Hydropower was producing almost 20 percent of the world's electricity by the end of the century. Hydropower is produced when river water is stopped by a dam and channeled through tubes to turn turbines connected to generators.

Nuclear energy is used to heat water, making steam, to produce electricity. The nations of the world hoped nuclear energy would be a cost-effective solution for their energy problems. It has the potential to supply all the world's electricity. But nuclear accidents in Pennsylvania and Chernobyl, Ukraine, put a stop to the growth of using nuclear energy. As a result, the United States gets only 20 percent of its electricity from nuclear energy. Nuclear power is also used to power submarines and some ships, such as aircraft carriers.

Throughout the twentieth century, oil, coal, and natural gas continued to be the primary energy sources. Oil can be processed into many products, including gasoline or heating oil. Gasoline is most often used for automobiles. Diesel is used to power cars, trucks, and locomotives. Oil and natural gas are used to heat homes or produce heat in power plants to turn water into steam and produce electricity.

In the latter part of the century, technology to harness energy from the sun became more effective. Light and heat from the sun are used to produce electricity through two methods: heat engines and solar panels. Solar heat engines use the sun's heat to turn water into steam and produce electricity. Solar panels turn the sun's light directly into electricity.

Advances in Communication

People and businesses were making connections worldwide more than ever. Long-distance telephone service was so much cheaper than earlier in the century. Satellites enabled radio and TV signals to be broadcast all over the globe, and email use was more common. Missionaries could communicate with their supporting churches in real time and rapidly share their needs, prayer requests, and answers to prayer. Families could converse over long distances easily and economically.

▲ The Roznow Dam on the Dunajec River in Poland

Nuclear Energy Use Entering the 21st Century

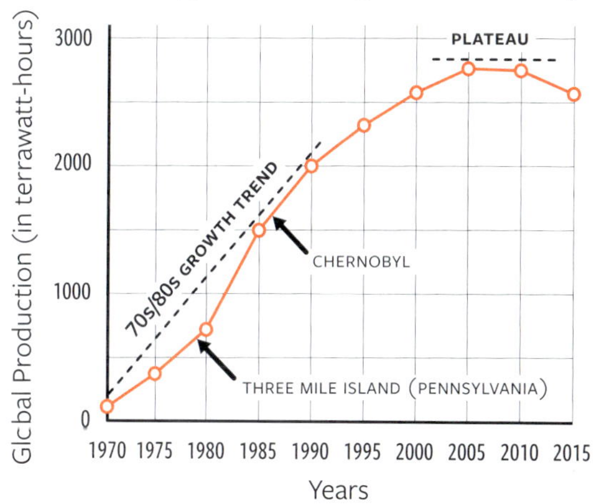

? **Why did nuclear energy not grow in popularity as an energy source?**

TURNING POINTS

Invention of the Internet and the World Wide Web

It is hard to imagine a world without the internet, apps, or the **World Wide Web** (the "www" preceding internet addresses; the system of linking various documents through clickable text or buttons). But it was not that long ago that none of those things existed.

In 1969 the first form of the internet, called ARPANET, was developed for the military. At first, it connected only four Pentagon-funded universities, but it quickly grew. ARPANET looked nothing like today's internet, but it did the same core task, connecting different computers in different cities so that people could share information and write to each other via email.

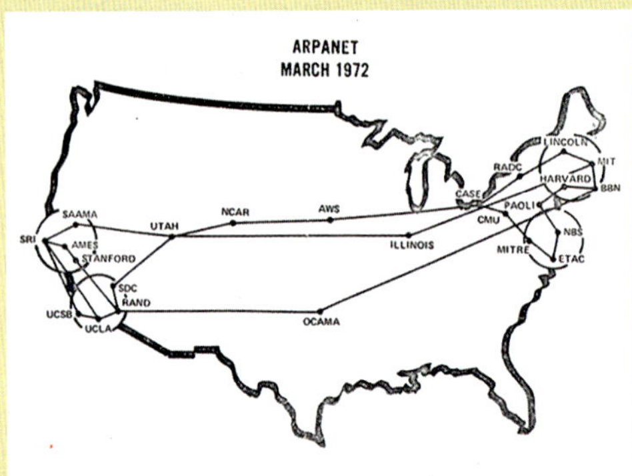

A 1972 map of the ARPANET-connected universities

In 1978 Robert Kahn developed the framework of the modern internet, which is still being used today: IP (internet protocol) addresses. The goal was for the internet to be a place that was open for everyone to share information and communicate.

By 1989 average people were beginning to access the internet using services like America Online (AOL). People would get online through their landline phones. Initially, people were limited to the network they subscribed to and could only share text since speeds were so slow. By 1990 the beginnings of the World Wide Web were being imagined when the HTTP (Hypertext Transfer Protocol) address framework was invented. HTTP gradually made services like AOL irrelevant.

In 1995 the internet we know today came on the scene. That year schools and companies developed websites and began to promote them as something special. Yahoo, Amazon, eBay, and Internet Explorer all had their start in 1995.

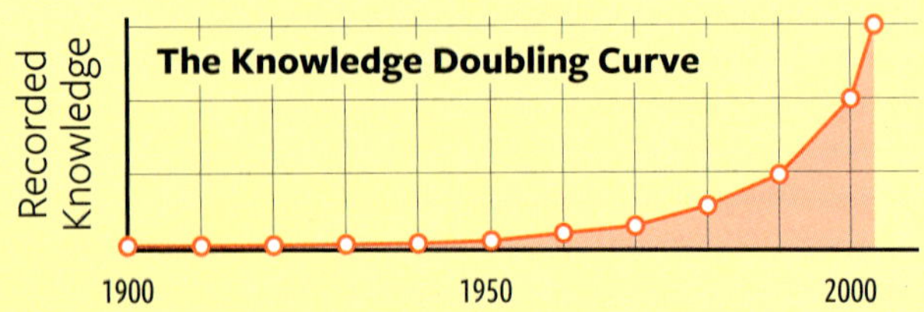

While the internet has made buying products and communicating easier, its main effect has been astounding growth in the amount of information and the storage of that information. In 1982 Buckminster Fuller proposed what he called the knowledge doubling curve. He said that up to the year 1900, the collective amount of recorded knowledge was doubling every one hundred years. After 1945 it was doubling every twenty-five years. After the internet was invented, recorded knowledge was doubling every thirteen months. It is said that when the internet takes its next form (with everything connected, not just phones and computers) knowledge will be doubling every twelve hours! This kind of growth is hard to fathom.

But with the doubling of knowledge, there has not been a doubling of wisdom. Wisdom is necessary for determining what information is important and true. It seems ironic that despite all this information, people still cannot find answers to life's deeper questions. Proverbs 9:10 says, "The fear of the Lord is the beginning of wisdom: and the knowledge of the holy is understanding." James 1:5 says, "If any of you lack wisdom, let him ask of God, that giveth to all men liberally, and upbraideth not; and it shall be given him." People may be able to collect and store vast amounts of information, but God and His Word are still the only sources of wisdom and understanding.

1. Describe the different phases of the internet's development.
2. How does the internet improve our lives?
3. How is wisdom different from information or knowledge?

CRITICAL THINKING 19.1

1. In 1968 Paul Ehrlich wrote in the book *Population Bomb* that by 1985 England would not exist because of mass starvation. He predicted that because so many people would starve, the world population would be only 1.5 billion. How has he been proven wrong, and what can we conclude about other scientific prophecies?
2. Write a brief paragraph describing what you imagine life would be like without the microchip.

19.2 Europe and the Americas

The United States found itself as the leader of the free world at the end of World War II. Rather than returning to a policy of isolation, it accepted the role of world leader, so much so that the twentieth century has been called the American Century.

In the Bretton Woods Agreement of 1944, the economic leaders of the Allied nations, including the Soviet Union, met to decide what the postwar world financial system would be like. They decided that all currencies would be linked to the US dollar. This meant that, in effect, the US Federal Reserve Bank would oversee the world's money supply. With this agreement, they created the **International Monetary Fund (IMF)** to lend to financially troubled developed countries, and they created the **World Bank** to help less developed countries. The agreement made the United States the financial leader of the world. It also moved the world further toward the idea that governments can successfully manage their economies. This was also the beginning of a new globalization movement in which countries made themselves economically dependent on each other so they would not attack each other militarily.

GUIDING QUESTIONS

- How did the European Economic Community grow during the latter half of the twentieth century?
- How did the Eastern European nations progress following the fall of communism?
- What were the ethnic conflicts in former Yugoslavia following the Cold War?
- What were the civil and women's rights movements in Europe and the United States?
- How did the environmental movement start?

What is the purpose of the IMF?

Representatives from the USSR, the UK, and Yugoslavia at the Bretton Woods Conference

Europe

In the previous chapter you learned that post–World War II, Europe was divided between the West (free) and East (Communist). The division of Europe kept it weak for much of the century, but after the Iron Curtain lifted, European leaders hoped to form a strong continental union that could rival the United States.

The European Union

In Chapter 18 you learned that Western Europe set up a Common Market in 1974. In 1986 this group of twelve European nations ended tariffs with each other. In 1992 the twelve members signed the **Maastricht Treaty**, which created the **European Union**, an economic and political alliance. The Maastricht Treaty eliminated border checkpoints between member countries and made the crossing of national borders equivalent to the crossing of state borders in the United States. EU member nations have standardized laws and a common currency, the euro (€).

The EU seeks to be a community of nations that can compete on the world stage economically and politically, providing a counterbalance to the United States. The EU government is complex. It includes a parliament consisting of representatives from each member nation. The number of representatives allotted is based on population. The European Commission includes a president, a vice president, and a representative from each member nation; this group fills the role of the executive branch.

When was the European Union established?

The European Court of Justice is the judicial branch. The EU enforces many regulations that seem burdensome to individuals and businesses. Extensive rules regulate everything from the quality of fruits and vegetables to how much electricity a certain appliance can use.

The EU does not have a military but relies on each nation for defense. Most EU members are also members of NATO. By the end of the century, there were fifteen EU member nations and many more nations waiting in line to join.

The euro is the currency of the EU.

Northern Ireland Conflict

One major conflict in Europe that was not part of the Cold War happened in Northern Ireland. In 1922 most of the island of Ireland achieved its independence from the United Kingdom, but Northern Ireland remained a part of the UK because it had a Protestant majority. For many years two groups fought for power in Northern Ireland. The Nationalists were Roman Catholic and fought for independence, while the Unionists were Protestants who fought to remain part of the United Kingdom. The conflict became heated from the 1960s to 1998. The Irish Republican Army (IRA), the military arm of the Nationalists, made terrorist attacks on British security forces in Northern Ireland. Many civilians got caught in the middle. On the other side was the Ulster Volunteer Force, which fought back against the IRA. (Ulster was the province in Ireland with a Protestant majority.) In 1998 both sides signed the Good Friday Agreement, a compromise in which both sides got a little of what they wanted. But most importantly, it ended the violence.

A 1981 riot in Belfast after an IRA leader died while on a hunger strike during his imprisonment

War in the Balkans

The country of Yugoslavia was a group of different republics held together by a Communist dictator, Josip Broz Tito. After Tito died in 1980, tensions began to rise between the Yugoslav republics. The problem was that the republics were divided by different religions. Bosnia and Kosovo were close to 50 percent Muslim. Slovenia and Croatia were majority Roman Catholic, while Serbia, Montenegro, and Macedonia were majority Eastern Orthodox. These divisions had existed for many years. In World War II the divisions determined which side the different republics would support. Croatia, Slovenia, and many Bosnian Muslims supported Germany, while the Eastern Orthodox republics supported the Soviets. World War II left a lot of unresolved anger among the Yugoslav peoples. As early as 1986 there were calls to expel all non-Serbians from Serbian lands. A Serbian, **Slobodan Milošević,** rose to power in Yugoslavia by standing up to perceived injustices done to Serbians living in Kosovo.

What was the IRA fighting for?

Yugoslav President Slobodan Milošević giving a speech in 1999

With the fall of communism in 1990, Slovenia voted overwhelmingly for independence; almost 89 percent of Slovenes supported separation. Croatia soon followed Slovenia in trying to achieve independence. Since Slovenia had few Serbians living there, Serbia was willing to allow that republic to leave Yugoslavia. But Croatia had a greater number of Serbians living within its borders, so Croatia would have to fight for its independence. In September 1991 war broke out. The people of the world were shocked to see war in the Balkans so quickly after communism fell. They seemed to think ethnic wars in Europe were a thing of the past. In January 1992 EU and US diplomats negotiated a treaty in which Croatia would be granted independence. During this time, Macedonia was also able to become independent.

But in April 1992 an even bloodier war broke out when Bosnia and Herzegovina tried to obtain its independence. Bosnia had a slight Serbian majority, so what was left of Yugoslavia was not going to let Bosnia just wander off. The war went on for three years. Eventually, the Serbians were accused of genocide for killing Muslim Bosnian civilians. All told, over sixty thousand Bosnian soldiers and civilians died, and over twenty thousand Serbian soldiers died. The United States and Europe entered the conflict in 1995, bombing Serbian targets. Recognizing that world opinion was firmly against them, the Serbs finally agreed to peace after the ethnic borders with Bosnia and Herzegovina were more solid.

Breakup of Yugoslavia

In 1998 the final republic, Kosovo, sought independence, and Milošević sent troops to hold onto the land. In 1999 NATO forces stepped in to keep the peace. As of 2022 a NATO force is still there, with no plan for withdrawal. Kosovo is independent, but the UN does not yet recognize it as an independent nation. In 2000 Serbia voted Milošević out. In 2001 he was put on trial by the World Court for genocide, but he died in 2006 before the trial ended.

What Yugoslav republic suffered the most in the 1990s?

Mart Laar

Mart Laar was born in the Soviet Union, but he was Estonian. Estonia is a small Baltic country that became independent when the Soviet Union dissolved. Laar, a politician and historian, was one of the young leaders trying to bring Estonia out of the shadow of communism.

In 1991 the quality of life in Estonia was worse than it had been in 1989 when it was still part of the Soviet Union. The Estonians had thought that just getting rid of communism would be the ticket for success, but, as Laar noted, "Nobody actually understood how backward and underdeveloped the Communist economies really were. As a result, the return to the free world was harder and more painful than anybody could have predicted."

Laar studied countries that had the most success in growing their economies. He found that the common factor among successful nations in the twentieth century was that they followed the teachings of Milton Friedman, an American economist. Friedman believed that governments should have a limited role in controlling the economy, that the government should step out of the way and give people the chance to dream and work hard to fulfill those dreams. Two aspects of Friedman's economic system were free trade (no tariffs on goods traded between countries) and a flat tax (everyone paying the same percentage of their income no matter how much they earned).

The United States had followed many of Friedman's principles in the 1980s and 90s and had experienced economic growth. Chile, Hong Kong, and New Zealand also followed Friedman's policies and experienced prosperity. But as the prime minister of Estonia in 1992, Mart Laar implemented Friedman's economic policies to a greater extent than any other leader had before.

Laar passed a balanced budget so that Estonia did not spend more money than it received. The budget meant making unpopular cuts in spending. Laar and other Estonian leaders were honest with the people, explaining that at first things would be painful. But after the pain would be the reward of a strong economy. It did not take long; Estonia started seeing results in 1993.

Following these hints of success, Laar moved on to phase two, which was creating business opportunities for the citizens. This was a major change since under communism people did not suffer when they failed in their business or their work, nor did they reap the rewards of their success. The Estonian leaders passed laws that guaranteed property rights. They reduced trade barriers, making the nation a free trade zone. Because of these new freedoms, investors opened new companies and factories. The Estonians told the rest of the world, "Give us no aid, but more trade." Laar also understood that any corruption among Estonia's leaders would limit the country's success. They had to follow the rule of law.

All these policies set Estonia up for success. Laar introduced a flat tax. The simplified tax system made it easier for both taxpayers and tax collectors. As in other countries that simplified and lowered taxes, money coming to the government increased. This surprised many people who assumed government funds would decrease when the tax rate decreased.

Laar stated, "The flat tax reform also supported a rapid increase in economic activity. The Estonian people saw that if they worked more, they could earn more without the government punishing their success through higher tax rates." Estonia was the first former Communist country to achieve the status of "free" by the Heritage Foundation.

The Americas

Central and South American countries endured conflicts between Communist guerrillas and government forces. They also suffered violence fueled by the drug trade. Argentina and Colombia saw great change in the late twentieth century and serve as examples of the upheaval that occurred throughout Latin America. In the United States, movements for change arose beginning in the 1950s and 60s.

Colombia

Colombia suffered through intense violence from 1964 onward. Many different groups were responsible for the violence. Communist guerillas known as the FARC were fighting to establish a Communist government in Colombia. The government, along with private armies, fought these rebels for over fifty years. Another source of violence was the drug cartels (groups of illegal drug manufacturers). Americans and Europeans bought more and more cocaine, so these cartels became wealthy and powerful by providing the drugs.

What was FARC's goal?

The FARC claimed to be fighting for the poor of Colombia. Instead, they brought misery to the people living in the jungle and terror to those living in the city. They also captured and killed several Christian missionaries. The height of the violence came in 1985, when M19, another Communist group, took over the Colombian Supreme Court building in Bogotá, the capital. They took the justices and many others hostage. M19 killed eleven of the justices. When the army stormed the building, they accidentally set it on fire, resulting in the deaths of other civilians. During the many years of the conflict, over two hundred thousand Colombians were killed.

The leader of the Medellin cartel, the most dangerous of them all, was Pablo Escobar. He was the wealthiest criminal in history. He survived by bribing officials. In 1993 the government had had enough. The police tracked Escobar to his home, and in the resulting gunfight, the cartel leader was shot and killed. Ironically, Escobar was loved by the poor, and twenty-five thousand people attended his funeral.

The Colombian army uses an armored vehicle to break down the door of the Supreme Court to retake the building and rescue the hostages.

Argentina

In 1900 Argentina was one of the richest nations in Latin America. Its wealth came from exporting grain and beef. Argentina prided itself on being European in its culture and tastes. After World War I Argentina found that its farm exports no longer brought in enough money to maintain prosperity.

Democracy was one of the first victims of the hard times. In the 1930s the military toppled the government, and in the 1940s a military officer named **Juan Perón** earned the support of the people. His wife, former actress Eva "Evita" Duarte Perón, increased his appeal. Evita was beautiful and at least as magnetic in personality as her husband. The Peróns identified themselves with the *descamisados*, the poor factory workers who crowded into Argentina's cities. In February 1946 Perón was easily elected president of Argentina.

Perón led a social reform program, and incomes began to rise. But in 1952 Perón's regime began to fall apart. Evita died of cancer, and the economy took a downturn. Perón had spent the money in the treasury to keep his followers happy, but now there was no more money. When discontent began to grow, he responded harshly. The dictator became increasingly unpopular. Finally, in 1955 the military ended his rule, and Perón fled the country.

In the nearly twenty years that followed his departure, not a single president of the nation finished out his term of office. Each time, the armed forces forced the president out of office. Finally, Perón returned to Argentina and was elected president in 1973. His second wife, Isabel, was elected vice president. Perón died less than a year after taking office, and Isabel Perón tried to rule. But the military toppled her after only two years. Under military rule, Argentinians suffered repression and economic hardship.

The military rulers tried a desperate gamble to increase their support among the people; they went to war with Great Britain. For years the two nations had been arguing over who should control the **Falkland Islands**. The Falklands are a group of barren islands in the South Atlantic, about three hundred miles off the coast of Argentina.

In 1833 the British established a permanent colony. One hundred and fifty years later, the Falkland residents still desired to be British despite living closer to Argentina. However, Argentina also claimed the Falklands. The Argentines said that the early Spanish claims and the islands' closeness made them part of Argentina. They demanded that Britain leave. Great Britain refused to surrender the Falklands.

In 1982 Argentina invaded and quickly took the Falklands. Angrily, Great Britain sent a fleet of warships to retake the islands. The war lasted less than three months, but it drew worldwide attention. British bombers destroyed the airstrip on the main island so the Argentines could not use it. A British submarine sank an Argentine cruiser, causing Argentina to pull back its warships for fear of losing even more. Argentina's air force was able to sink some British ships and shot down several planes.

In the end the superior discipline of the British army won out. Landing on the west side of East Falkland, the British troops spread out rapidly and pushed back the inexperienced Argentines. Despite being outnumbered, British paratroopers were able to capture the main island.

In 1983 free elections were again held in Argentina—and this time the president was allowed to finish out his term. The new government brought members of the old dictatorship to trial and punished them for their abuses of power.

(top) Juan and Eva Perón, (bottom) British commandos in the Falkland Islands in 1982

Why did Argentina invade the Falkland Islands?

LIFE IN San Francisco

Citizenship

Americans who survived the Great Depression and won World War II tried to provide their children with everything they had lacked as children growing up in the 30s and 40s. But these parents largely failed to pass on biblical values or a reason for living other than the pursuit of wealth. Many young people in the 1960s saw an emptiness in the pursuit of education and material goods, so they rebelled against their parents and society. They found acceptance among their peers who believed the same things and shared their tastes in music and their rejection of the cultural norms of how youth should act. They were called hippies. Hippies demonstrated their identity by having long and uncombed hair and wearing casual clothes.

Justice

Hippies advocated the old ideas of anarchy. Like the French Revolutionaries, hippies opposed the established government and systems. They called those who maintained these systems "the man," and they would not obey "the man." Hippies talked about nonviolence and love. They promoted openness and tolerance.

Environment

Many hippies lived in New York City and California, especially San Francisco. Hippies were the ones to begin the environmental movement. One of the later focuses of the hippie movement was to live on communal farms and get back to nature. These places resembled the New Harmony and La Reunion, utopian communities of the past. And like those communities they were short-lived. Many hippies became vegetarians and ate all-natural foods.

Power

College-aged youth of the 1960s used their numbers to protest US involvement in the Vietnam War. They were able to change popular opinion in the country.

Religion

Hippies rejected Christianity in their search for spiritual truth. They sought answers to their spiritual questions in Hinduism and other Eastern religions. They also used drugs in an attempt to find spiritual revelation. None of these methods were adequate. Some hippies abandoned the lifestyle and went back to following their parents' example in seeking material gain. But surprisingly, in the early 1970s, some hippies realized that all the religions considered Jesus a good man. So these hippies began to pursue Jesus. They were known as Jesus People. Many were genuine Christians, but they did not see a need to give up their style of music or hair. As a result, both they and the traditional church largely did not accept each other. The Jesus People started their own denominations and missed an opportunity to be discipled by older believers, while the established church missed out on the Jesus People's energy and zeal for the Lord.

Martin Luther King Jr. gives his "I Have A Dream" speech in Washington, DC, in 1963.

Cultural Movements in the United States and Europe

Civil Rights Movement

From the 1950s to the end of the 60s, African Americans in the southern United States pursued equal rights. They wanted to end segregation and legal discrimination; this was the **civil rights movement**. The protesters engaged in nonviolent civil disobedience to end the discrimination, and they won the admiration of many observers. Examples of their civil disobedience included sitting at whites-only lunch counters, marching, and sitting on bus seats reserved for whites.

The civil rights movement saw success in 1954 when the US Supreme Court ended segregation in schools with the *Brown v. Board of Education* decision. In 1963, at the national mall in Washington, DC, **Martin Luther King Jr.**, the leader of the movement, gave a speech in which he envisioned a nation where people were judged by their character and not the color of their skin. The Civil Rights Act of 1964 explicitly banned all discrimination based on race, color, religion, sex, or national origin in employment practices. It also ended unequal voting laws.

Women's Rights Movement

In the 1960s and 70s, some women fought for the right to be treated as equal to men and to have equal opportunities. This was called the women's rights movement, or the women's liberation movement. It was the "second wave" of feminism, as the "first wave" came in the nineteenth and early twentieth centuries when women fought for the right to vote. This second movement included the pursuit of equality in areas like politics, work, and the family. Sadly, one of the results of this movement was the legalization of abortion across the country in 1973.

Environmental Movement

Concern over the danger of nuclear weapons and industrial pollution grew to new levels in the late twentieth century. Groups like Greenpeace even tried to force the ending of activities like offshore oil drilling and commercial fishing. In Europe, political parties arose whose main purpose was to fight for the environment. They were called Green parties. In 1970 the first Earth Day was celebrated on Vladimir Lenin's one hundredth birthday.

CRITICAL THINKING 19.2

How were the 1960s a time of major change for the United States?

19.3 Africa, Asia, and the Middle East

During this time Africa suffered as the leaders of the newly independent countries fought over how they should govern their nations. Asia saw unprecedented growth as East Asia became the manufacturing center of the world. The Middle East became a focal point of world conflict in the late twentieth century.

GUIDING QUESTIONS

- How did Asian nations grow in economic and political influence during the late twentieth century?
- What were the challenges faced by African nations following their independence?
- What was the proliferation of nuclear weapons during the late twentieth century?
- What were the conflicts in the Middle East during the latter half of the twentieth century?

Africa

The twentieth century was not a positive time for Africa. As the African nations became free of their colonizers, many of the countries experienced serious growing pains.

Ethiopia

Ethiopia suffered greatly in the 1980s, and this suffering gained the world's attention. The country went through a civil war that displaced people and caused shortages of food and material goods. The civil war combined with a drought doomed almost a million to death by starvation and disease. The height of the crisis came in 1984, when media attention brought the famine into the living rooms of Americans and Europeans. The tragedy prompted celebrities to use their fame to fight for causes. Many pop musicians worked together to produce a song and a concert to aid the Ethiopians.

(left) Starving Ethiopian refugees, (right) The Live Aid concert at Wembley Stadium in London to raise relief funds for Ethiopia

Libya

In 1969 **Muammar al-Qaddafi** became the dictator of Libya in North Africa. He set up a Marxist government and called it "Islamic socialism." Qaddafi also wanted to be seen as the leader of all the Arabs. To achieve this leadership role, he supported terrorist attacks against the United States. Libyans attempted to assassinate Americans at various African embassies. In 1986 Libyan terrorists successfully bombed a nightclub in Germany that American soldiers attended. In response to this attack, President Reagan launched airstrikes on Libya. In 1989 Libyans blew up an airliner traveling from Scotland to New York City, killing all 259 onboard. But after witnessing the American, British, and Arab coalition forces oust Iraq from Kuwait in 1991, Qaddafi changed his tune. He did everything he could to please the United States. He paid the United States money and handed over terrorists to face justice.

?

How did Qaddafi try to make himself the leader of the Arab world?

(top) The wreckage of a 747 jetliner brought down by Libyan terrorists, (bottom) Nelson Mandela and F. W. de Klerk in 1994

South Africa

Following World War II, the southern African countries of Rhodesia, Namibia, and South Africa, which were ruled by white minorities, were pressured to grant power to their black majorities. In 1950 the ruling white South Africans determined the best way forward was to impose a policy of segregation called **apartheid**, meaning "apartness." In Rhodesia, black rebels fought the white rulers until they won control in 1979. They changed the name of the country to Zimbabwe.

But South Africa clung to white rule until 1994. The Afrikaners (white South Africans) contended that each ethnicity was culturally different from all others. Thus, it was best to keep all ethnic groups separate so that each could develop. Apartheid severely regulated life for nonwhites. They could not vote in national elections, could not own land, and, after 1959, had no representation in the South African Parliament. Because opposition groups were banned, the oppressed groups had no organized voice.

Under apartheid, the leaders segregated every area of life: restaurants, stores, buses, trains, and so forth. The apartheid government also forced black people to live in reservations called "homelands." Homeland citizens had to carry identity documents. The government brutally stopped any protest. As a result of apartheid, the international community imposed embargoes and sanctions on South Africa.

In 1989 President **F. W. de Klerk** responded to the international criticism and pressure by easing the apartheid restrictions. In 1990 he released the jailed opposition leader, **Nelson Mandela**. De Klerk and Mandela began negotiations to make a smooth transition away from apartheid. In 1993 de Klerk and Mandela shared the Nobel Peace Prize. Mandela was elected president of South Africa in 1994. The number of official languages rose from two to eleven, and a new constitution went into effect in 1997.

?

How did the world respond to apartheid in South Africa?

Somalia

In 1992 another African country was suffering a massive famine caused by civil war. World attention focused on the plight of the people of Somalia in East Africa. President Bush responded by sending in the marines to stabilize the nation and provide food aid. The different factions fighting the civil war used food as a weapon to control the people. While the US military was present, the people had food. In 1993 President Clinton wanted to expand the mission of the US personnel and directed them to capture the leader of one Somali faction. But Clinton also withdrew many US forces from Somalia that were needed to accomplish this mission. On October 3, 1993, eighteen US Army soldiers were killed while trying to capture Somali leaders. Not long after this tragedy, the United States left Somalia. Another terrorist leader, Osama bin Laden, took note that the deaths of eighteen men caused the US withdrawal from Somalia.

A Somali girl plays on the wreckage of an American Blackhawk helicopter eleven days after the battle.

How did President Clinton change the mission in Somalia?

Rwanda

Rwanda is a small country in Central Africa that was colonized by Belgium. To better control its colony, Belgium intensified the divide between the two main tribes in Rwanda, the **Hutus** and the **Tutsis**. The Belgians issued Rwandans with identity cards according to their tribe. The Belgians gave the minority Tutsis the leadership positions. Then, just before Rwanda got its independence, the Belgians switched the roles and put the Hutus in charge, causing more division.

In 1993 it seemed things were on a more peaceful track as the Hutu Rwandan president was pursuing a power-sharing agreement with the Tutsis. But on April 6, 1994, the president's plane was shot down, and he was killed. Although the Hutus blamed the Tutsis, the Tutsis had the most to lose from the president's death. A short time after the assassination, the Hutus started killing Tutsis. The killing went on for one hundred days and resulted in almost one million deaths. When a Tutsi rebel force retook the Rwandan capital, the genocide ended. Genocides were supposed to be a thing of the past after World War II, but the world experienced two genocides just in the 1990s. The United States, still stung from its experience in Somalia, would not get involved in the Rwandan conflict.

What incident triggered the violence in Rwanda?

Three hundred skulls outside a chapel in Rwanda, November 6, 1994

Asia

Communist China

The "Goddess of Democracy" stands amid a crowd of pro-democracy demonstrators in Tiananmen Square.

What happened in China in 1989?

Following Mao's death in 1976, the Chinese Communist Party (CCP) realized it would have to allow the people some economic freedom for the party to remain in power. President Nixon had opened relations with China to cause a division between the Soviet Union and Communist China. But renewed China–US relations also meant new trade opportunities. In 1980 the Chinese government began allowing people to own property and businesses. The government also privatized some state-owned industries. In 1987 the CCP allowed Western fast-food restaurants like KFC to open.

The general thinking in the West was that these economic freedoms would lead to personal and religious freedoms in China. While house churches did flourish in the 1980s and 90s, they were still illegal. In 1979 China imposed a "**one-child policy**" to control population growth. To enforce this policy families were fined for having more than one child, or women were forced to have abortions.

In the spring of 1989, Chinese college students held a protest for over a month in **Tiananmen Square** in Beijing. The students wanted the government to allow more personal freedoms, including freedoms of speech, press, and assembly. On May 20, the CCP stationed as many as 250,000 troops along with tanks outside the square. On the night of June 4, the soldiers entered the square. The soldiers killed hundreds, perhaps thousands, of students. Following the crackdown, President Bush made it clear to China the incident would not hamper Chinese and American relations. He believed in a policy of engagement with Communist China despite their brutality.

In 1997 the United Kingdom handed over control of the city of Hong Kong to Communist China. Since 1841 Hong Kong had been under British rule. In 1898 the United Kingdom signed a ninety-nine-year lease of Hong Kong with the then Nationalist Chinese government. Hong Kong and the island of Taiwan had thrived as examples of democracy in China, but now Taiwan was alone. The CCP promised to leave Hong Kong alone for fifty years, but it was quickly evident they were not going to keep that promise.

The Hong Kong handover ceremony, July 1, 1997

Japan

Japan began to have a major debt problem in the 1990s, and the problem had become even worse by 2022.

General MacArthur's reforms and the Japanese work ethic set the nation of Japan up for economic success. The period from 1952 to 1989 was called the **Japanese economic miracle**. During those years, Japan became the leading manufacturer of cars and electronics. Eventually, it was the second-largest economy behind the United States. It seemed Japan was set for economic dominance of the world. The Japanese were buying up property all over the world. They owned more land on the Hawaiian Islands than any other foreign nation.

But all of that ended in the 1990s as Japanese banks took on more and more debt. This resulted in inflation. Food and other necessities became very expensive. The 90s were called the "lost decade." As people struggled economically, they had smaller families or chose not to have children at all, which further weakened the economy.

Why is the 1990s called the "lost decade" in Japan?

Korea

Following the Korean War, both South and North Korea suffered extreme poverty. South Korea was one of the poorest countries in the world, while North Korea slowly improved. In the 1960s, South Korean general Park Chung-hee took over the government in a coup. He began a period of rebuilding the nation. Park led a dictatorial government in which South Korean freedoms were limited but economic growth was prioritized. The economic plan included land reform, in which farmers were given the right to own the land they worked. Park also required the people to work for any material aid they received. Park's government also emphasized education and fought corruption. In 1979 Park was assassinated, but he had set South Korea on a path of economic growth. The change in South Korea was called the "miracle on the Han River." By the end of 1995, South Korea had the eleventh-largest economy in the world. In 1997 many Asian nations suffered when their money lost its value because weakened Japanese banks pulled their money out of foreign Asian banks. The crisis hit South Korea and Thailand especially hard. Prices doubled in a matter of months. The IMF stepped in with loans. To pay off these debts and return to economic growth, over three million South Korean citizens donated gold to the government.

What was the status of South Korea after the Korean War?

(left) South Korea, 1952; (right) Seoul, South Korea, more than fifty years after the war

Israeli soldiers during the Yom Kippur War

How did Israel's conflicts with Egypt end?

The Middle East

In the late twentieth century, for religious and economic reasons, Middle Eastern conflicts required the blood and focus of the Western world.

Israel

Israel faced continued threats to its existence; the Arabs did not want a Jewish state to exist. Following the Six-Day War, Israel controlled the Sinai Peninsula, and Egypt wanted it back. A war of attrition (sustained attacks to weaken an enemy) went on until 1970, when both sides agreed to a ceasefire. In 1973 Egypt and Syria launched a surprise attack on Israel on Yom Kippur, a Jewish holiday. Syria attacked from the east and Egypt from the south. The **Yom Kippur War** ended with an Israeli victory. In March 1979, Israel and Egypt signed a historic peace agreement that ended the conflict between the two nations.

In 1982 Israel invaded and occupied southern Lebanon. Lebanon was in the midst of a civil war that had begun in 1975. Palestinians (Arabs living in Israel) took advantage of Lebanon's instability and used it as a base to attack Israel. In 1983 President Reagan sent a force of marines to keep the peace in Lebanon. But they were withdrawn when a terrorist bombed the marine barracks in Beirut, Lebanon, killing 241 Americans.

In 1987 the First Intifada began, six years of intensive Palestinian uprisings. These uprisings occurred in the regions of the **West Bank** and **Gaza Strip**. The Israelis responded by putting over eighty thousand soldiers in these territories and filling prisons with those who committed hostile acts.

Israel and its Occupied Zones

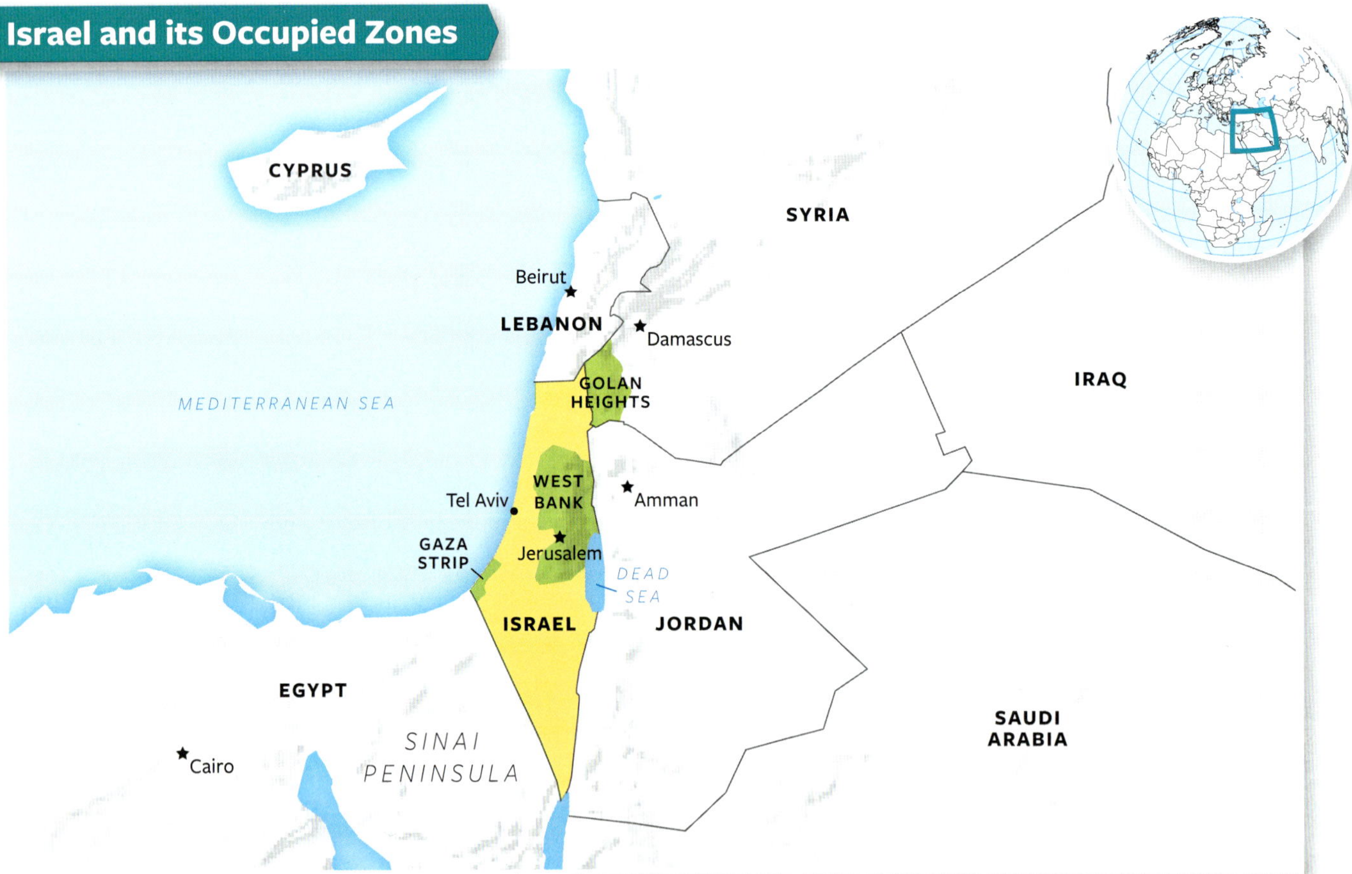

Iranian Revolution

In 1953 Shah Mohammad Reza Pahlavi became the monarch of Iran. He aligned Iran with the United States. The Shah became known for his lavish lifestyle and authoritarian rule. Slowly he lost the support of the people. **Ayatollah Khomeini**, an Islamic cleric who was exiled in France, led the opposition against the Shah.

In 1979, following two years of demonstrations, strikes, and acts of civil disobedience, the Shah went into exile in the United States. The Ayatollah was invited back to the country, and in April 1979 the Iranians voted to become the first Islamic state, meaning it would be a **theocracy** led by Muslim clerics. Because the United States had assisted the Shah, Iranian students retaliated by taking fifty-two American diplomats and citizens hostage at the US embassy in Tehran. The hostages were held for over a year.

Barry Rosen, the American embassy's press attaché, is taken hostage by Iranian students.

The Iran-Iraq War

Saddam Hussein, the dictator of Iraq, feared that the revolutionary fervor from a powerful Shia Islam state in Iran would spill over into his country. Iraq had a Shia majority, but Hussein and his ruling party were Sunni. Hussein also saw Iran as weak following the revolution and saw an opportunity to make Iraq the most powerful country in the Persian Gulf. On September 22, 1980, Iraq invaded Iran. After three months of success, the Iraqi advance came to a standstill. The war began resembling World War I, with trench warfare and the use of chemical weapons. The war lasted eight years. The United States did not get seriously involved as it saw two of its enemies weakening each other. The war ended in 1988, with the border lines virtually the same as they had been before the war.

? **What form of government did Iran adopt in 1979?**

? **Who started the Iran-Iraq War?**

theocracy a system of government in which clerics rule in the name of God or a god

Iraqi soldiers behind sandbags, during the Iran-Iraq War, 1984

Desert Storm

Heavily in debt after the Iran-Iraq War, Saddam Hussein looked for new sources of wealth. He saw tiny, oil-rich Kuwait to his south as easy to conquer. On August 2, 1990, Iraq invaded Kuwait. Hussein gambled that the rest of the world would do nothing and simply accept his acquisition of Kuwait. But the United States quickly condemned the invasion. Saudi Arabia, another major US ally, felt threatened. In response, the United States sent thousands of troops from posts in Europe to Saudi Arabia since they were no longer needed to defend against the Soviet Union. It was unheard of for "Christian" soldiers (as the Muslims saw the US soldiers) to be stationed in the Islamic holy land.

The mission to defend Saudi Arabia against Iraq was called Desert Shield. As diplomatic pressure failed to remove Hussein from Kuwait, a coalition force (a temporary alliance of nations for a specific purpose) led by the United States began **Desert Storm** with six weeks of airstrikes on Iraq. Saddam Hussein responded by firing missiles at Israel, hoping to bring Israel into the war and in turn anger America's Arab allies. But Israel remained patient and absorbed the attacks. Hussein also set the Kuwait oil fields on fire.

In February 1991, the American-led coalition launched a ground attack, quickly forcing Iraq out of Kuwait. The culmination of the hundred-hour ground war was a massive tank battle resembling those of World War II. In the Battle of 73 Easting, American tanks found the majority of Iraqi tanks. The battle revealed just how capable the American tanks were. During the twenty-three-minute battle, the Americans destroyed 160 Iraqi tanks as well as over two hundred other vehicles. The Americans lost only one personnel carrier. The war demonstrated how advanced America's "smart" weapons were. The coalition declared victory since Kuwait was again free, but Saddam Hussein remained in power in Iraq.

American Abrams tanks travel across the Kuwaiti desert during Operation Desert Storm.

Why did the United States fight Iraq in 1991?

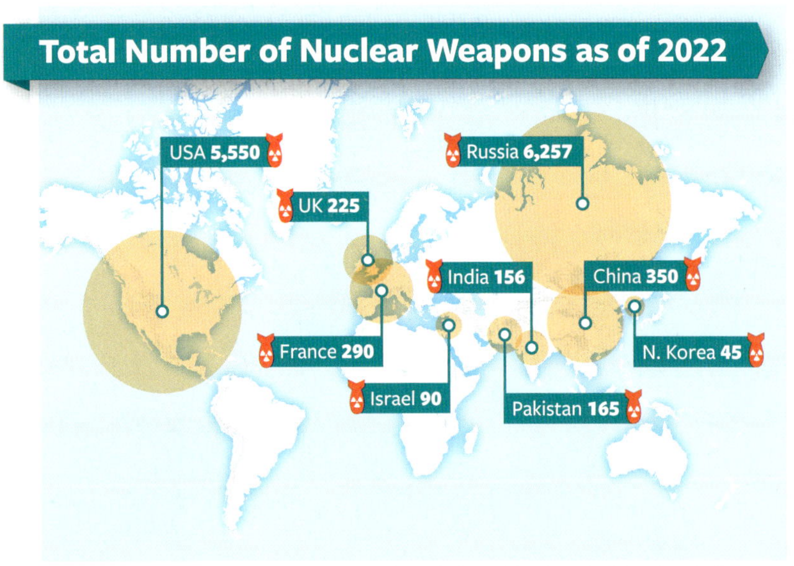

Spread of Nuclear Weapons

The spread of nuclear weapons technology and the material for making the weapons is called nuclear proliferation. Following the Cold War, many people hoped that no more countries would obtain nuclear weapons and that the ones that already had the weapons would destroy them. But by the end of the century, most realized the world would never be nuclear weapons–free. Before 1964 four nations had nuclear weapons: the United States, the Soviet Union, the United Kingdom, and France. In 1964 Communist China developed them, and ten years later, India did as well. Israel has nuclear weapons but is very secretive about them. In 1981 Israel launched an airstrike on Iraq, destroying Iraq's nuclear reactor, thus preventing it from developing the bomb. When the Soviet Union dissolved, many of the newly independent republics found themselves to be nuclear powers. Fortunately, the new nations were willing to return their weapons to Russia and limit the spread. In 1998 Pakistan developed nuclear weapons to counter India. In the 1990s, Russia began helping Iran with nuclear research, but as of 2022 Iran has been prevented from producing a bomb.

CRITICAL THINKING 19.3

Should Christians agree with how the world responded to apartheid? Why?

19.4 Cultural Change

The worldwide culture change in the past one hundred years is like no other time in history.

Cultural Diffusion

Cultural diffusion is the term for the spreading of one culture to different places. In the twentieth century, cultural diffusion happened throughout the world via increased global communication and trade. In general, the dominant culture that was spread was American culture. It is easy to take this spreading of American culture for granted, but it is still remarkable. McDonald's and Coca Cola could be found in most countries. American sports stars, celebrities, movies, and television shows spread American styles all over the world. It is interesting to compare early 1990s family photos from around the world and note the similarities in style.

Postmodernism

Postmodernism was the philosophical movement that followed modernism. The world today is largely ruled by postmodern thought. People began to reject the teachings of modernism as they failed to find their answers in science. In fact, their studies only resulted in more questions. Instead of turning to the Word of God for answers, they concluded that there were no answers.

The key idea of postmodernism is that there is no absolute truth. Postmodernism teaches that everyone has a story and each person's story is valid. For example, if a person claims to be a deer, according to postmodernism, that person needs to be accepted as a deer, even though he or she is not a deer. Postmodernism is very similar to Marxism. Both philosophies teach that the meaning of words should be destroyed and that institutions like governments and churches should be changed or destroyed.

Postmodernism can seem workable in theory, but in the real world it falls apart. For example, you can sincerely believe that 2 plus 2 equals 10. But if you build a house based on that idea, it will not stand. More dangerously, you can believe that the traffic lights are a societal construct to enslave you and that according to your truth red means go. But if you live by that principle, you will eventually be involved in an accident.

Art, Literature, Music, and Movies

In keeping with the American Century, the center of arts and culture moved from Paris to New York City in the latter part of the century. Movies came on the scene and overwhelmed all other forms of art. Rock-and-roll music became the most popular music style, and rock groups like the Beatles had a lasting influence on music styles and culture. The purpose of art, literature, music, and movies was to relentlessly cross perceived moral boundaries and shock society. As the century passed, it became harder to shock people. The new genre of science fiction became popular with the advent of the Space Age. Many became engrossed in science-fiction movies and literature since it provided them with an escape. When *Star Wars* premiered in 1977, the world was enthralled. The *Star Wars* movies of the twenty-first century made less of an impression.

GUIDING QUESTIONS

- How did cultural diffusion happen at an extraordinary rate during this period in history?
- Why did postmodernism become the mainstream worldview?
- How did art, literature, and music reflect the great change in culture during the late twentieth century?
- In what ways did Christianity grow during the second half of the twentieth century?

Forty-six percent of the world's countries have a McDonald's, including this one in Fujian, China.

What is the key idea of postmodernism?

Spread of Christianity

From 1800 to 2000, there were three significant Christian missions movements. From 1800 to 1865, the focus was on reaching the nations of the world. But because of logistics, manpower, and local governmental control, the missionaries could only reach the peoples living on the coasts of these nations.

From 1865 to 1980, foreign Christian missionaries focused on reaching the people in the interior of the countries who had not heard the gospel. After World War II, Christian missions organizations became specialized as they sought to use every tool at their disposal to spread the gospel. Some organizations focused on Bible translating, some on radio broadcasting, some on medical services and relief, some on aviation, and the list goes on.

In 1989 missionaries launched a plan to bring the gospel to every ethnic group in the world by the year 2000. This initiative was called the **AD2000 movement**. It represented another change in strategy, as the missionaries went from thinking in terms of reaching countries to reaching the different people groups living within those countries. The year 2000 served as a motivational mark. Although they did not meet the goal, Christians made significant progress toward reaching every people group for Christ.

CRITICAL THINKING 19.4

Evaluate the positives and negatives of cultural diffusion.

Making Connections

1. What happened to the world population in the twentieth century?
2. Why did cities grow in the twentieth century?
3. What was the most significant invention of the twentieth century?
4. How did Mart Laar set Estonia up for economic success?
5. What was Martin Luther King Jr.'s dream?
6. Why did Yugoslavia break apart in the 1990s?
7. Why was the EU formed?
8. Why was the CCP able to stay in power in China?
9. What happened to the Japanese economy from the 1950s to the end of the century?
10. Which countries had nuclear weapons at the end of the century?
11. Why did Arab countries keep attacking Israel?
12. What was the West's response to Saddam Hussein's invasion of Kuwait?
13. How did the emphasis of Christian missions change over the century?

What to Know

EVENTS

Yom Kippur War
Desert Storm

PEOPLE

Slobodan Milošević
Mart Laar
Juan Perón
Martin Luther King Jr.
Muammar al-Qaddafi
F. W. de Klerk
Nelson Mandela
Hutus
Tutsis
Ayatollah Khomeini
Saddam Hussein

PLACES

Falkland Islands
Tiananmen Square
West Bank
Gaza Strip

TERMS

urbanization
containerization
microchip
space shuttle
World Wide Web
International Monetary Fund (IMF)
World Bank
Maastricht Treaty
European Union
civil rights movement
apartheid
one-child policy
Japanese economic miracle
theocracy
cultural diffusion
postmodernism
AD2000 movement

Thinking Critically

1. Defend the claim that conserving the environment and opposing radical environmentalism are compatible agendas.
2. How are the governments of South Africa, Iraq, and Rhodesia similar?
3. How do the crises in Ethiopia, Somalia, and Rwanda all relate to each other?
4. Why was nonviolence important for the civil rights movement to succeed in the United States?

20 THE TWENTY-FIRST CENTURY

2001 – present

ESSENTIAL QUESTIONS

- What were the effects of terrorist and reform movements of the Middle East and North Africa?
- Has globalism become stronger or weaker in the twenty-first century?
- How have natural disasters and pandemics affected land and people?
- Why have population shifts occurred?
- How effective is the Christian church in the twenty-first century?

The twin towers of the World Trade Center burn following the crashes of the hijacked airliners.

9/11 Terror Attacks

September 11, 2001, like December 7, 1941, was a day of infamy for the United States. On both days the United States was attacked on American soil during a time of peace, with great loss of life. In 2001, however, instead of an ambitious empire, the enemy was radical Islam. Instead of a military attack on American armed forces, it was a terror attack on American civilians. And instead of being in the Pacific Ocean, the targets were in the nation's capital and its largest city.

The 9/11 attacks were related to American policy in the Middle East. Radical Islamic groups objected to America's support of Israel. They also opposed the Persian Gulf War and America's continued presence in the Middle East following the war. They believed that applying pressure would cause the Americans to retreat, as had happened in Lebanon in 1983.

Many people played a role in the attacks. Three especially stand out. **Osama bin Laden** led the terrorist organization **al-Qaeda**, which organized and carried out the attacks. Al-Qaeda member Khalid Sheikh Mohammed proposed the idea of hijacking planes and using them as weapons. And Mohammed Atta, originally from Egypt but later part of a terrorist cell (unit) in Hamburg, Germany, was the lead hijacker.

Nineteen hijackers settled in the United States in preparation for the attacks. Some took flight lessons. They planned to hijack four planes from East Coast airports. They chose planes that were headed to the West Coast so that fuel tanks would be full.

Once in flight, the hijackers took control of the planes using box cutters and knives as weapons. The events that followed shocked the nation. The World Trade Center was a set of two towers that were the tallest buildings in New York City. At 8:45 a.m., American Airlines Flight 11 from Boston crashed into the north tower. About eighteen minutes later, United Airlines Flight 175, also from Boston, crashed into the south tower. Both jets burst into flames. Less than an hour later, American Airlines Flight 77 from Washington, DC, crashed into the side of the Pentagon, the headquarters of the US military. Meanwhile, back in New York City the intense heat of the burning fuel dangerously weakened the twin towers. People standing on the streets and watching on television were stunned when first the south and then the north tower collapsed.

United Airlines Flight 93 from Newark, New Jersey, was the only plane that missed its target. In fact, it is not known what the target was supposed to be. Suggestions are the White House, the Capitol, or a nuclear power plant. Flight 93 was delayed, so it was the last of the four flights to take off. Passengers began to get calls telling them about the earlier attacks. The passengers attacked the hijackers to keep them from carrying out their mission, and the plane crashed in a field in Pennsylvania, killing everyone onboard.

Almost three thousand people were killed because of the 9/11 attacks, and many more were injured. The city of New York set up a park with a memorial and museum at "Ground Zero," the site of the attacks. A new building, One World Trade Center, was built in place of the twin towers. To preserve the memory of the events of that day and the people who lost their lives, September 11 was declared Patriot Day.

Osama bin Laden

GUIDING QUESTIONS

- Is terrorism a just political strategy?
- What were major events of the war on terror?
- What led to the Arab Spring, and did the movement achieve its purposes?

Who would be targeted by the war on terror?

US soldiers return to base after searching for Taliban fighters and weapons.

Why did the United States lead a coalition to challenge the Taliban?

20.1 Events of the Islamic World

War on Terror

On September 20, 2001, US president George W. Bush appeared before a joint session of Congress and declared a "**war on terror**." The war would target not only terrorist groups like al-Qaeda but also countries that helped or protected terrorists. Activities of the war would range from military conflicts to the gathering of information on suspected terrorists to security operations. The war on terror would dominate international relations in the early twenty-first century.

Military Action in the Middle East

Afghanistan

The Communist government of Afghanistan fell in 1992. Following that, the country was in upheaval. Several anti-Communist groups fought for control of the country. Mullah Mohammed Omar formed a group called the **Taliban**. His group, made up mostly of religious students, defeated several potential rivals. The Taliban took control of the capital city, Kabul, in 1996 and set up a strict religious government.

The al-Qaeda terrorist organization had its beginnings in Afghanistan during the Soviet occupation, but it moved its operations to the African country of Sudan around 1991. Al-Qaeda members returned to Afghanistan when the Taliban took power. The Taliban allowed al-Qaeda to set up training camps in the country. After al-Qaeda carried out the 9/11 attacks against the United States, the US government demanded that the Taliban turn over all al-Qaeda terrorists to international authorities. When the Taliban refused, the United States put together a coalition with Great Britain and other allies to challenge the Taliban. The coalition carried out airstrikes, and the Northern Alliance (a group of anti-Taliban forces within the country), together with some US special forces, attacked on the ground. Kabul fell on November 13, 2001, and the Taliban and al-Qaeda retreated.

Despite early allied successes, though, the conflict continued. Elections in Afghanistan did not produce a strong government. The Taliban recovered and pushed back against the new government and the Western nations that supported it. NATO led an international security force in the country starting in 2003. Support for the effort weakened over time, with many pushing for Afghan forces to take over all security. The United States decided to withdraw its remaining troops by September 2021. Much of the Afghan resistance collapsed, and the Taliban returned to power.

Iraq

In 2002, George Bush announced a new foreign policy for the United States. The policy would involve striking against potential threats before they had a chance to attack the United States. The first application of this new policy was **Operation Iraqi Freedom**, which began March 20, 2003.

The goal of the operation was to take out the brutal government of Iraq's dictator, Saddam Hussein. There were two main arguments for the action. First, Hussein was not cooperating with UN inspectors who were supposed to guarantee that Iraq did not have any weapons of mass destruction. Second, it was believed that Hussein supported terrorists. It was later concluded that Iraq did not have any weapons of mass destruction in 2003. No evidence was found of a link to the 9/11 attacks either. However, at the time the situation appeared threatening.

The conflict occurred in two stages. The first was a military action to remove Hussein's government, carried out mostly by the United States and Great Britain. This stage involved airstrikes and ground troops. Most of the country was under the control of coalition forces by the end of April, and Hussein was captured in December. The second stage was a military presence to help keep order while Iraq worked to transition to democratic rule. As in Afghanistan, the new government was hindered by violence and unrest within the country. The United States did not stay as long in Iraq as in Afghanistan. Troop withdrawals began in 2007 and were completed by December of 2011.

What were the main arguments for Operation Iraqi Freedom?

Operations against Terrorist Organizations

A second aspect of the war on terror was working to break up terrorist groups. The United States worked with other nations to cut funding for suspected terrorists. They used organizations like the CIA (Central Intelligence Agency) to gather intelligence (military or political information) that would help them find terrorists. And they sponsored secret operations to capture terrorists.

One of the key events of this phase of the war was the operation that targeted Osama bin Laden. On May 2, 2011, several Navy SEALs raided a compound (group of buildings surrounded by a wall) in Abbottabad, Pakistan. Based on surveillance and intelligence gathering, US forces believed that bin Laden was living there with his family. Power was cut to the compound in preparation for the raid. The SEALs came in on helicopters. Using night vision goggles, they found bin Laden on the third floor of one of the buildings. Bin Laden was killed in the struggle, and his body was later buried at sea.

How did Osama bin Laden die?

Security in the United States

The United States made changes to try to fight terror at home. Congress passed the Patriot Act in 2001. The act gave government agencies greater power to search for evidence and to monitor the activities of suspects. Though many powers were designed to be temporary, there were concerns that the act ignored constitutional rights.

In November 2002, Congress passed the Homeland Security Act, which created the **Department of Homeland Security**. The Department of Homeland Security combined several existing government agencies into one department that would be part of the president's cabinet. The Department of Homeland Security would oversee activities such as airport and border security, enforcement of immigration and customs laws, and disaster relief measures.

What activities would the Department of Homeland Security oversee?

(top) An Iraqi soldier trains for taking over the defense of his country; (middle) SEAL Team Six carried out Operation Neptune Spear, the raid on Osama bin Laden's compound; (bottom) The Transportation Security Administration, part of the Department of Homeland Security, oversees security screening at US airports.

LIFE IN Kabul

Environment

Afghanistan is dominated by mountains, most notably the Hindu Kush range. The tallest mountain in Afghanistan is Mt. Nowshak at 24,446 feet. Afghanistan's rugged terrain made it an ideal place for terrorist groups to train without attracting attention. As coalition forces attacked Afghanistan in 2001, al-Qaeda members held out in Tora Bora, a region of caves in the eastern part of the country. Eventually, they were forced to retreat to Pakistan.

The city of Kabul experienced extensive damage during the civil war of the 1990s.

Justice

Women experienced severe restrictions under Taliban regulations from 1996 to 2001. They could not work or attend school. They could not leave their houses unless they were accompanied by male relatives. They were required to wear the burqa, a garment that completely covers a person except for a small opening for the eyes. And they were forbidden care from many doctors. Women who disobeyed the rules were severely punished.

Power

Terrorism uses force to try to achieve goals. Typically, the goals are political. In other words, terrorists want governments to change their actions in some way. Terrorism is different from warfare because it usually involves unprovoked attacks on civilians by independent groups (not governments). Organizations like al-Qaeda exist for the sole purpose of supporting terrorism. They do not exercise the legitimate use of power that God assigned to governments. Instead, they promote violence and hurt innocent people.

Religion

Sharia is Islamic religious law. It is based on the Qur'an, other words and actions of Muhammad, and decisions made by Muslim scholars. The Taliban operated according to their own interpretation of sharia. Their laws included such things as the banning of photography, regulations for dress and men's facial hair, and prohibitions on most forms of entertainment.

Open-air markets in Kabul sold goods ranging from produce to meats to clothing.

Arab Spring

In 2010 and 2011 a movement that became known as the **Arab Spring** swept across North Africa and the Middle East. Like the Prague Spring of 1968, the movement offered the hope of more individual freedom. Many governments in the region were controlled by oppressive dictators. During the Arab Spring, the people in several countries tried to replace their governments with democracies. Some of these attempts were successful, while others resulted in bloodshed and chaos.

Who controlled the governments of many countries in North Africa and the Middle East?

New Governments in Tunisia and Egypt

The Arab Spring began in the North African country of Tunisia with protests by a street vendor named Mohamed Bouazizi. He was upset over economic hardship and government corruption. Others rallied to the cause, taking to the streets in mass demonstrations. The government of Tunisia tried different tactics to suppress the movement. They ordered violent crushing of protests while at the same time trying to introduce some reforms to keep the rest of the people calm. The government's efforts ultimately failed, and President Zine al-Abidine Ben Ali left the country in January 2011. The people were able to elect a president and prime minister in December of that year. A new constitution went into effect in January 2014.

How did the Arab Spring begin?

A revolution in Egypt was inspired by the one in Tunisia, and the events were similar. Economic and political complaints led to street demonstrations starting in January 2011. The government tried to suppress the demonstrations while granting some reforms. Again, the strategy failed. Having lost the support of the military, President Hosni Mubarak stepped down on February 11. Egypt failed to produce a stable government immediately following its revolution. Its first government, led by Mohamed Morsi of the Muslim Brotherhood (an organization that promotes Islamic government and opposes Western influence), was overthrown by the military in 2013 after more protests by the Egyptian people. Military leader Abdel Fattah al-Sisi won the presidential election of May 2014.

What happened to President Ben Ali of Tunisia and President Mubarak of Egypt?

Demonstrators in Egypt call for reforms in July 2011.

Civil War in Libya, Yemen, and Syria

Though uprisings occurred in several other countries around this time, most failed to produce new governments. In Libya, Yemen, and Syria, unrest led instead to civil war. Government and rebel forces in Syria engaged in a multiple-year conflict. Foreign nations and organizations got involved at various points to protest conditions in Syria and to try to secure a peaceful end to the conflict. President Bashar al-Assad remained in power.

Complicating the situation in Syria was the emergence of a new Islamic group in the region. Known as ISIS (Islamic State in Iraq and Syria), ISIL (Islamic State in Iraq and the Levant), or the **Islamic State**, this group tried to establish a caliphate (Islamic empire) in part of western Iraq and eastern Syria. The Islamic State was at its strongest in 2014. The movement weakened for a time as it lost leaders and territory, but it gradually renewed strength, shifting its focus to other parts of the world.

▲ The Syrian city of Homs was a battleground between Syrian military and opposition forces.

What was the outcome of the Syrian civil war?

CRITICAL THINKING 20.1

Do you think America's immediate response to the 9/11 attacks was similar to or different from the response the terrorists were hoping for? Explain your answer.

The War on Terror and the Arab Spring

2001

September 11, 2001
Al-Qaeda carries out terrorist attacks in the United States.

November 13, 2001
US-led coalition captures Kabul, Afghanistan.

March 20, 2003
Operation Iraqi Freedom begins efforts to remove Saddam Hussein from power.

January/February 2011
Presidents of Tunisia and Egypt step down in response to reform demonstrations.

March 15, 2011
Civil war begins in Syria with government crackdown on protests.

May 2, 2011
Osama bin Laden is killed.

2021

September 2021
United States withdraws remaining troops from Afghanistan.

GUIDING QUESTIONS

- How has globalism been challenged in the twenty-first century, and how has it moved forward?
- How does a global economy affect individual nations?
- How has global culture been shaped by technology?
- How can a person use technology wisely?

20.2 Globalism in the Twenty-First Century

As you learned in previous chapters, the trend toward globalism following World War II resulted in the creation of several new organizations. The goal of these organizations was to increase economic and political cooperation among nations. The world continued to move in a global direction in the twenty-first century, but globalism also faced challenges.

Political Developments

Challenges for the European Union

The European Union (EU) added new members in the early twenty-first century. By 2013 it included twenty-eight nations. At the same time, Europe experienced an economic downturn and a refugee crisis. EU leadership had to try to respond to those problems. In addition, the EU lost a member in 2020.

Economic Problems

The EU faced a crisis of sovereign (national) debt for several of its members in 2008. The countries in trouble were Iceland, Ireland, Portugal, Spain, Italy, and Greece. The basic problem was that the countries were spending much more than they were taking in through taxes. They had to borrow more and more money to cover their expenses. Eventually, lenders became unwilling to give them any more loans. Because the states of the EU were tied so closely to each other, this problem affected the entire organization.

To prevent the economies of troubled countries from collapsing, the EU gave them bailouts, or emergency loans. A condition for receiving the loans was that the countries must revise their budgets. They had to raise taxes and cut spending significantly. In Greece, the new conditions put many out of work, and thousands of people left the country. For a time, there was concern that the Eurozone (states that use a common currency, the euro) would collapse. But eventually there were signs of some economic recovery.

Migration

One of the main purposes for the creation of the EU was to avoid the kind of national competition that had caused so much destruction in Europe during the world wars. Therefore, a key goal of the organization was to reduce border restrictions within Europe. It was

The Schengen Area is the territory of European states that have eliminated all border controls.

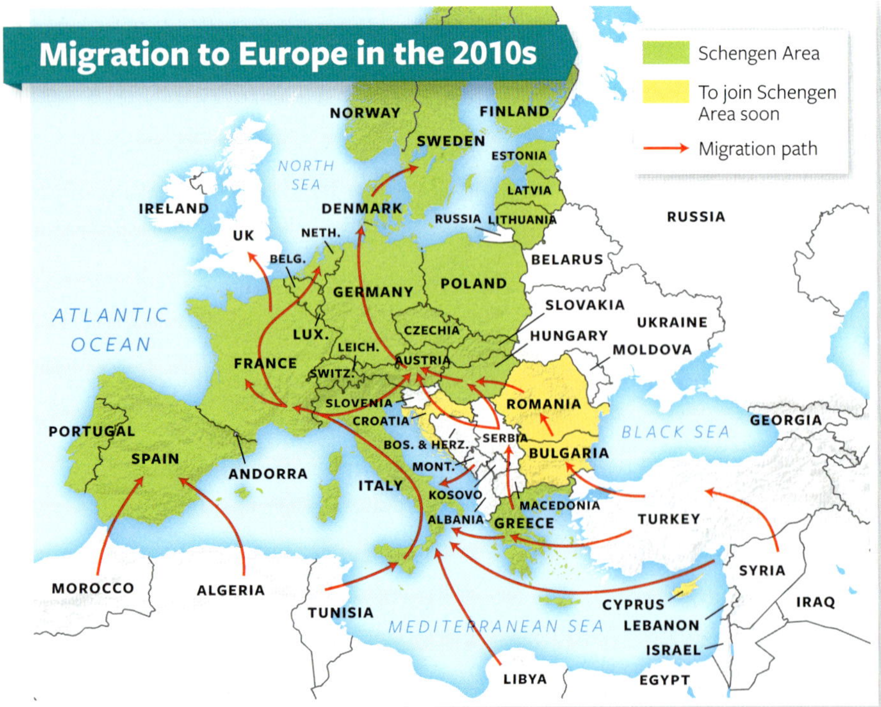

Syrian refugees cross from Turkey to the Greek island of Lésvos.

hoped that allowing more freedom of movement would encourage cooperation among different countries. Without as many restrictions, migration (movement between countries) became more common in Europe. Circumstances of the twenty-first century caused migration to become a challenge for the EU.

First, several states of the former Eastern bloc joined the EU in 2004. These states were not generally as prosperous as the states of Western Europe. It was natural, then, that some of their citizens would want to travel to the West to find new financial opportunities. This migration put some strain on the economies of Western states.

Second, the Arab Spring caused a tremendous flood of refugees from North Africa and the Middle East. For example, the civil war in Libya pushed thousands of desperate people out of that country. Many more fled from war-torn Syria and the terror that people were experiencing in the Islamic State.

As thousands of migrants flooded Europe in the second decade of the twenty-first century, the EU faced a dilemma. The organization was supposed to establish a cooperative, open society. Therefore, leaders like German chancellor Angela Merkel believed there should be no limits on immigration. However, not all EU states shared her position. Some states that especially struggled with this issue were those closest to the conflicts, places like Greece and Italy.

One problem was that it was hard to tell which of the migrants were truly in danger and in need of protection, which were coming to look for better jobs, and which might be criminals. Another problem was the greedy boat captains, who made money while placing refugees in danger by transporting them in unsafe boats across the Mediterranean Sea. Then there was the problem of what to do with the migrants once they got to Europe. Many were placed in camps for lack of a better immediate solution. European economies struggled to incorporate thousands of new workers. The unity of the EU continues to be tested by this ongoing crisis.

BREXIT

The UK, or United Kingdom (Great Britain and Northern Ireland), joined the European Communities (EC) in 1973. At that time, most European cooperation was economic. There were always some in the UK who opposed EC membership, but more than 60 percent of the British people voted to continue that membership in a referendum (special vote) in 1975. Voters were never given a chance, however, to vote on the later treaties of Maastricht or Lisbon, which created the European Union. These treaties established a European government that had the power to control immigration, establish justice, and set social policies for its member states. Increased opposition to UK membership in the EU led to calls for another referendum to allow the British people to vote on the issue. That vote finally took place in 2016, and the people chose by a small margin to leave the EU.

It took a few years to work out the terms for the UK and the EU to separate. The separation, known as **BREXIT** (for "British exit"), occurred officially on January 31, 2020. According to the final terms, the UK would continue to trade freely with members of the EU and cooperate in various other areas but would handle its own policing and judicial matters.

UK prime minister Boris Johnson signs the EU-UK Trade and Cooperation Agreement.

What member did the EU lose in 2020?

Shifts in Power

Rise of China

China transformed from an isolated nation with a mainly agricultural economy to a rapidly growing world power in the late twentieth and early twenty-first centuries. From 1952 to 1978, China's GDP (gross domestic product) failed to grow. At that time, Communist leaders began to adopt economic reforms that encouraged some free enterprise. As a result, China's GDP rose dramatically, from around nine billion US dollars in the 1970s to over nine trillion dollars in 2013.

Another step that was likely to increase China's standing in the world was the One Belt, One Road Initiative, or simply the **Belt and Road Initiative** (BRI). Introduced in 2013 by Chinese president Xi Jinping, the BRI is a huge infrastructure project. Through this program China offers loans with low interest rates to help other countries improve their infrastructure. The project was at first focused on two areas in particular: (1) Central Asia and (2) the seas ranging from Southeast Asia to South Asia, the Middle East, and Africa. The goal of the project was to increase trade and economic cooperation in the region. Eventually, the project expanded to other parts of the world, and by early 2021 around 140 countries had joined the initiative. Structures that have been completed as part of the BRI include roads, railroads, dams, tunnels, pipelines, ports, airports, and buildings. Concerns over Chinese influence and the heavy debt in some participating countries led the United States and the EU to consider alternative infrastructure programs.

?

What is the goal of the Belt and Road Initiative?

China's Belt and Road Initiative

Globalism vs. Nationalism

Though globalism continued to thrive in the twenty-first century, there was some dissent from the ideals of globalism. The election of President Donald Trump in the United States in 2016, the exit of the United Kingdom from the European Union in 2020, and opposition to European Union policies from countries like Poland and Hungary signaled a renewed support for some aspects of nationalism. Among other things, nationalists of this period wanted to control who came through their borders and to pursue fair trade deals.

Whose election signaled a renewed interest in nationalism?

Economic Developments

Today a person can go almost anywhere in the world and find a favorite soft drink or fast food. In addition, products previously available only in distant markets can now be purchased locally. Both developments have come about because of a global economy.

Causes

The global economy, which began to develop following World War II, expanded in the twenty-first century. The fall of communism in Eastern Europe provided new trading partners. Trade agreements allowed products to be shipped across many national boundaries. Technology contributed to the efficiency of trade. Finally, peace among many nations allowed global trade to flourish.

Evaluation

A global economy has some advantages. Companies can stay competitive by building factories in countries where the costs of production are relatively low. In addition, small companies increase their potential for growth by offering their products to customers around the world. Finally, mass production for a global customer base gives consumers access to more products at lower costs.

For Christians, global trade has also historically provided an opportunity for missionary outreach. Many nations allow Christians to work in businesses located in their countries. In this setting, Christians can witness to coworkers and neighbors.

Coke bottle in Iran

Sporting goods factory in India

However, there are also disadvantages to a global economy. Many companies close factories in their own countries to take advantage of cheaper production costs in other places. When that happens, people lose their jobs. Complicating the situation is the fact that some governments offer subsidies (grants of money to help keep costs low) to manufacturers in their countries. Factories whose governments do not offer subsidies have a harder time competing.

What do subsidies do for manufacturers?

Another disadvantage to a global economy is the potential for safety problems. Some governments may not supervise their manufacturers as carefully as others do. Consumers may be concerned whether products made overseas are safe to use or safe to eat. They may also wonder whether the workers who made the products had unsafe working conditions.

Social Developments

Developments in Technology

Society in the twenty-first century became more and more global. Much of that change was due to developments in technology.

TURNING POINTS

A Digital Age

One of the most significant developments of the twenty-first century was the entrance of the world into a digital age (the period that has been characterized by the use of computers and the availability of large amounts of information). Across the globe, digital technology changed the way people worked, learned, socialized, and shopped.

The increased use of robots meant that factories required fewer workers with different skill sets. More people started their own online businesses and began working for themselves. Some companies began allowing employees to work from home, using high-speed internet connections to communicate with coworkers and customers. The ability to work from home became especially important during the COVID-19 pandemic of 2020, as many more workers shifted to home offices.

Schools too were significantly affected by the digital age. Use of the internet transformed the research process for students. Much communication between schools and families switched to online. And teachers were able to give online assignments that could be automatically graded. As with work, school was radically affected by the COVID-19 pandemic. As schools closed for in-person learning, many students switched to online learning from home, a format that many homeschooled students were already familiar with.

Much social interaction went digital with the rise of social media. Though the earliest network, Six Degrees, was created in 1997, it was the launch of the Myspace (2003), LinkedIn (2003), and Facebook (2004) sites that guaranteed social media would become a long-lasting success. These sites were followed by the creation of the Twitter (2006), Instagram (2010), and Pinterest (2010) sites and the Snapchat (2011) app. Research in 2019 revealed that 72 percent of American adults used some form of social media. Worldwide, the total number was more than 3.2 billion people (out of the more than 7.7 billion people in the world).

Though social media interaction was originally intended to build online communities, companies caught on to its huge potential for marketing. They targeted potential customers with ads and raised awareness of their products by establishing their own social media presence.

Buying and selling continued to be influenced by the digital age in the twenty-first century. Amazon, which was founded in 1994, grew into one of the largest companies in the world. Through Amazon and many other online commerce sites, online shopping brought in almost $4 trillion in revenue in 2020.

1. What changes did the COVID-19 pandemic cause for workers and students?
2. How did companies use social media?
3. Why might online shopping have brought in so much revenue in 2020?

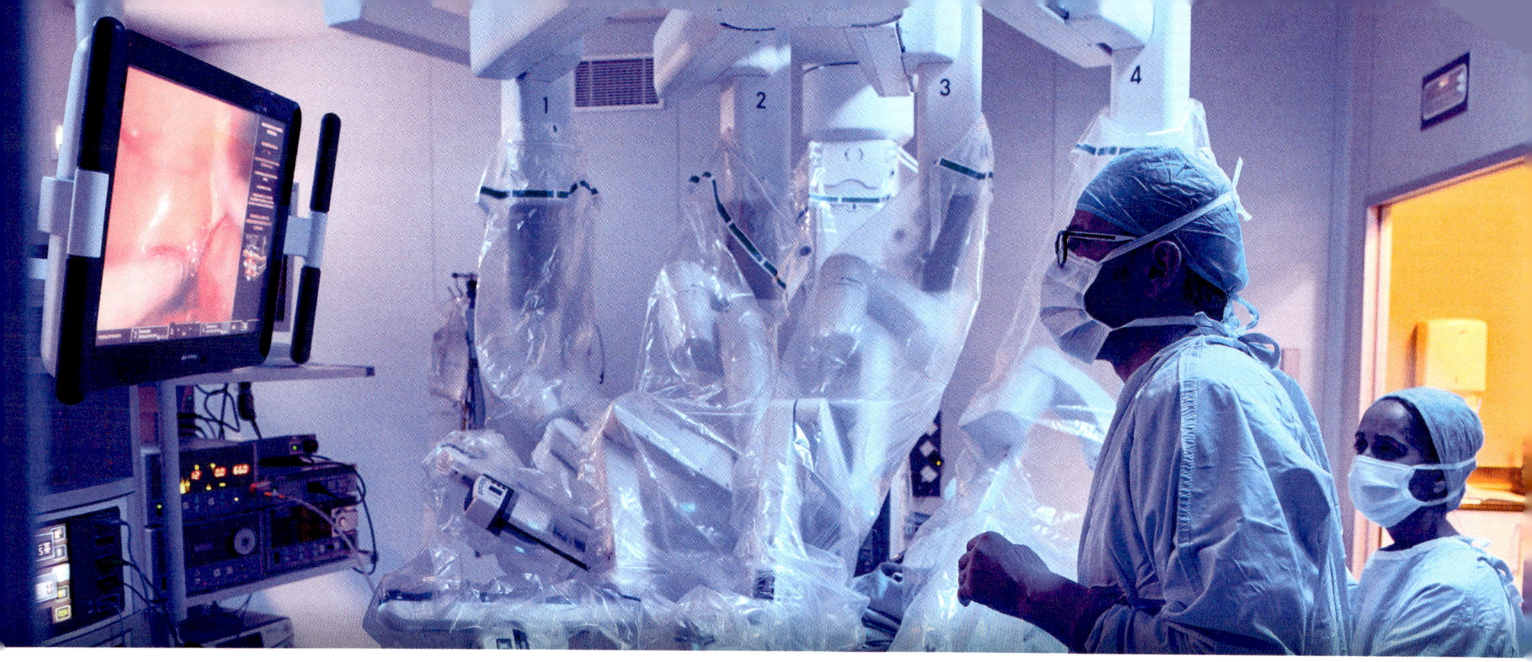

▲

Surgeons in Spain use a surgical robot to perform cancer surgery.

Wise Use of Technology

Technology has many benefits but also many potential dangers. The wise person will learn to use technology as a helpful tool without being controlled by it.

Medical Advances

People live longer and have a better quality of life because of medical technology, and that is a blessing. A potential problem, however, is that people who expect to live a long time may not think about the reality of death and the need to be prepared for eternity. Technology can affect the doctor-patient relationship if doctors rely more on technology than on interaction with the patient. Sometimes medical technology is even used for unbiblical purposes, such as abortion.

Communication Advances

New communication technologies have allowed people to keep in contact with family and friends, learn helpful information, and share biblical truth. However, there are cautions to communicating in a digital age. Constant communication interrupts work. It also prevents people from being quiet and thinking thoughtfully through issues and problems. Online communication can easily become unkind and even destructive. The same biblical standard that directs speech (for example, Colossians 4:6) should be applied to online communication as well.

Information Explosion

Christians should be concerned about the abundance of information they receive from the internet. It can be difficult to judge what is helpful and worth spending time on. It can also be challenging to determine what is accurate. Of special danger is the easy access to harmful and sinful materials. For all these reasons, it is important to use great caution when spending time online.

? CRITICAL THINKING 20.2

What personal goals can you set for using technology wisely?

GUIDING QUESTIONS

- What effects have natural disasters had on the physical environment and on people?
- What have been some significant pandemics of the twenty-first century?
- How have population trends changed in the twenty-first century?
- What challenges and opportunities has Christianity faced in the twenty-first century?

20.3 Science and Culture

Natural Disasters

Every century has its share of natural disasters, and the twenty-first century has been no different. From floods to droughts to earthquakes to wildfires, natural disasters caused loss of life, injuries, and tremendous property damage. Disaster relief agencies, some run by governments and some independent, worked to meet the challenges caused by these events. Some countries were more affected by disasters than others because buildings were not constructed as solidly, insurance was not as readily available, and there were fewer resources to provide basic needs like food and clean drinking water. However, victims of natural disasters in every country suffered hardships and faced challenges.

Earthquakes

The century began with an earthquake in India's Gujarat district on January 26, 2001. It measured 7.7 on the magnitude scale used by scientists for measuring earthquakes. That is considered a major earthquake. It is often difficult to get exact numbers for deaths and damage from natural disasters, but there were thousands of deaths and homes lost. Two more earthquakes occurred in that part of the world within the next few years: a 6.6 magnitude earthquake (strong) in Iran on December 26, 2003, and a 7.6 magnitude earthquake (major) in the region of Kashmir (by India and Pakistan) on October 8, 2005. The Sichuan State of China experienced an 8.0 magnitude earthquake (great) on May 12, 2008. Finally, a 7.3 magnitude earthquake (major) hit Haiti on January 12, 2010.

The National Palace of Haiti sustained significant damage from an earthquake in January 2010.

Earthquakes that occur under the ocean cause even more devastation because they often create huge waves known as **tsunamis**. Two locations experienced tremendous loss from tsunamis during this period. On December 26, 2004, a 9.0 earthquake (great) occurred in the Indian Ocean near the island nation of Indonesia. The earthquake lasted between eight and ten minutes and caused a tsunami that had waves of up to one hundred feet. The waves hit the coasts of surrounding countries. It is estimated that more than two hundred thousand people died during this event. A similar situation occurred in Japan on March 11, 2011. A 9.0 magnitude earthquake occurred in the Pacific Ocean east of the Tohoku region of Japan. The earthquake set off a tsunami there as well, with waves reaching up to 130 feet. Besides the loss of life and property damage caused by the tsunami and earthquake, there was a meltdown of nuclear reactors at a local power plant. The resulting release of radioactive materials created further danger for people living in the area.

A fire at the Fukushima nuclear power plant released radioactive material into the air.

HURRICANES

The twenty-first century has also had devastating tropical storms. One of the most devastating for the United States was **Hurricane Katrina** in 2005. Katrina hit states along the Gulf Coast from Florida to Louisiana. Hurricane Katrina was labeled a Category 4 storm (out of five categories). Category 4 storms have winds between 130 and 156 miles per hour. The heavy rain and high winds cause significant property damage. Complicating the situation during Hurricane Katrina was the failure of levees in the city of New Orleans. (Levees are barriers that prevent flooding. Levees are necessary in the city of New Orleans to keep the Mississippi River and Lakes Borgne and Pontchartrain from flooding the city.) With up to 80 percent of the city flooded, residents had to be rescued from rooftops by boats and helicopters. Many people were displaced to surrounding communities and states.

Tropical storms in the South Pacific and Indian Oceans are called cyclones. Cyclone Nargis hit the coast of Myanmar in May of 2008. The rising of the sea produced flooding in heavily populated areas, causing approximately 138,000 deaths and leaving 55,000 more missing.

How were the people of New Orleans affected by Hurricane Katrina?

A rescue boat saves a New Orleans resident from his flooded home.

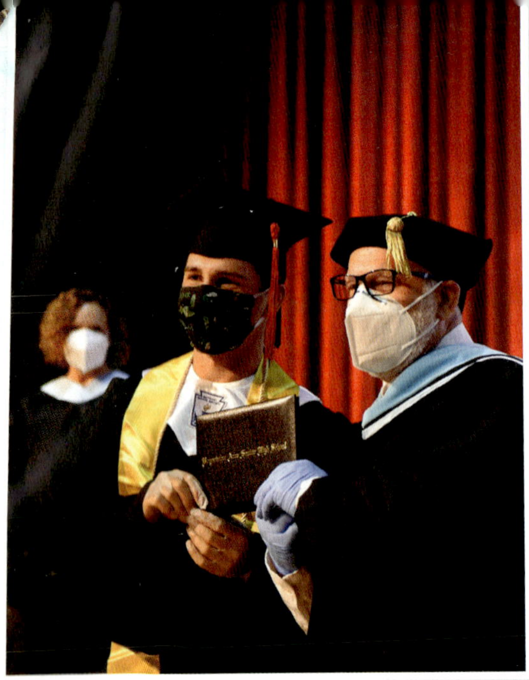

Graduation ceremonies in 2020 faced many challenges in adjusting to the COVID pandemic.

Pandemics

New diseases and the challenges of how to deal with them have been a major concern of the twenty-first century, particularly with the outbreak of **COVID-19**, a global **pandemic**. Two earlier pandemics of the century were the SARS (severe acute respiratory syndrome) outbreak of 2003, which affected more than eight thousand people, and the H1N1 influenza virus of 2009. H1N1 was different from most of the viruses of its time, and few young people had immunity to it. Estimates range from 151,700 to 575,400 for the number of deaths caused worldwide by H1N1.

The impact of these earlier diseases, however, was greatly overshadowed by the emergence of COVID-19. COVID-19 is a respiratory disease that is caused by the SARS-CoV-2 virus. SARS-CoV-2 is a new coronavirus (a group of viruses that can cause respiratory, stomach, intestinal, or nervous system problems) that first appeared in the Wuhan, Hubei, province of China. COVID-19 soon spread across the globe. By the summer of 2021, 220 countries and territories had been affected by the disease, with more than 180 million cases and close to 4 million deaths reported worldwide.

The economic and social effects of COVID-19 were significant as well, as countries tried to keep the virus from spreading. Travel was severely restricted within and between countries. Schools closed for in-person classes, and many students had to switch to online learning. Many workers had to work from home or lost their jobs entirely as shutdowns caused businesses to close. Many churches were also required to stop meeting in person, and congregations joined together for worship online.

How many cases and deaths had been reported for COVID-19 by the summer of 2021?

Population Shifts

The twenty-first century has experienced a significant population shift. Across the globe, populations are getting older on average. For example, the percentage of people aged 65 or older was approximately 6.8 percent of the world's population in 1999. By 2050, it is expected to be almost 17 percent.

Causes of this population shift are easy to see. Medical advances have helped people live longer. At the same time, families in almost every part of the world are having fewer children. Several countries now have more citizens over 65 than under 14. It is expected that this trend will affect the entire world at some point in the twenty-first century.

Living longer is good news for the citizens of the world. However, aging populations can present some economic challenges. Many countries offer retirement programs that are funded through contributions by workers. When there are fewer workers but the number of retirees keeps growing, retirement programs face financial strain. Some countries also sponsor healthcare programs. Because aging populations typically require more medical attention, healthcare may need greater funding. Considering how best to take care of their senior citizens and, at the same time, encourage the growth of families will be important steps for governments in the twenty-first century.

Why is there an aging trend in the world population?

pandemic a disease that affects a large area

Christianity

Challenges for Christianity

Postmodern philosophy, which you learned about in Chapter 19, created serious challenges for Christianity in the twenty-first century. Because postmodernism considers truth to be relative to each person, postmodernists clashed regularly with those who insisted that the Bible is absolute truth. This clash showed up in many cultural issues, ranging from abortion to same-sex marriage to transgender issues. Bible-believing Christians hold to the truth of passages such as Isaiah 45:5, which denies the existence of any god but the God of the Bible, and John 14:6, which identifies Jesus as the only source of truth and the only way to God the Father.

Another rising problem for many twenty-first century Christians is persecution. Persecution has often come from either Communist governments or other religions. Sometimes the persecution from other religions is prompted by a government, whereas other times it comes from private militias or family and neighbors. Persecution ranges from physical and financial attacks to imprisonment or even execution.

What groups have persecuted Christians in the twenty-first century?

The Redeemed Christian Church in Nigeria was attacked by a suicide bomber in July 2015.

Asia Bibi

Aasiya Noreen, often called Asia Bibi, is from the country of Pakistan. She and her family were the only Christians in the small village where she lived. In 2009 Noreen got into an argument on the farm where she worked. During the argument, she defended her faith against the statements of her Muslim coworkers. In response to this incident, Noreen and other family members were beaten by a mob, and Noreen was arrested.

Noreen was charged with breaking Pakistan's law against blasphemy. Under the law, no one may speak disrespectfully of a recognized religion within Pakistan. The law has been used at times by Pakistani citizens to cause trouble for people with whom they have conflict.

Noreen was found guilty of the charge in 2010 and was sentenced to death. Many leaders and human rights groups from around the world protested the conviction. Noreen was finally acquitted (declared innocent) by the Pakistani Supreme Court in October 2018. The court stated that there were doubts about the reliability of the witnesses' testimony. Noreen was prevented from leaving the country for some time longer, with pressure being put on the government by extremist groups to change the ruling of the Supreme Court. Finally, however, the last challenges were lifted, and Noreen left for Canada in May 2019. As of 2021, the government had not put anyone to death under the blasphemy law, but people accused under the law had been killed by private individuals or groups.

Opportunities for Christianity

Despite philosophical challenges and persecution, biblical Christianity has continued to grow in the twenty-first century. One area of rapid growth is Latin America. Distinct from Roman Catholic and traditional Protestant churches, Evangelical and Charismatic congregations grew and multiplied in many Latin American countries.

The expansion of Christianity in Africa provides another clear example of growth. There were an estimated ten million Christians in Africa in 1900. By the year 2000, the number had increased to around 360 million, and the growth continued.

China provides yet another example of the phenomenal growth of Christianity. Some estimate the number of Christians in China in 1949 to have been between three and five million. By 2010 the Christian population was estimated to have increased to sixty-eight million, though precise numbers are impossible to obtain.

Significantly, these places where Christianity is growing once received missionaries. Now, however, they are sending missionaries out. The willingness of believers to respond to the call of the Great Commission (Matt. 28:19–20) is exciting evidence that churches in these areas are maturing and that God is continuing to do a work in the world.

? Critical Thinking 20.3

How would you respond to the statement that no one can know absolute truth?

Worship service in São Paulo, Brazil

Making Connections

1. Describe the purposes and outcomes of the wars in Afghanistan and Iraq.
2. What strategies did the United States use to break up terrorist groups?
3. What steps did the United States take to increase security at home?
4. What was the goal of the Arab Spring movement? In which countries was the goal achieved? What happened in other countries?
5. What challenges did the European Union face in the twenty-first century?
6. How did China attempt to increase its standing in the world in the twenty-first century?
7. What evidence was there of a renewed interest in nationalism in the twenty-first century?
8. What are some advantages and disadvantages of a global economy?
9. What were significant pandemics of the twenty-first century, and how did they affect people around the world?
10. What population shift occurred in the twenty-first century?
11. How has postmodern philosophy challenged Christianity?
12. Who persecuted Christians in the twenty-first century? Where did Christianity grow?

Thinking Critically

1. Explain biblical problems with terrorism, considering Genesis 9:6 and Romans 13:4.
2. How can you use technology without letting it control you?
3. What challenges would you expect for the people and environment of a region that experienced a natural disaster?

WHAT TO KNOW

DATES & EVENTS

September 11, 2001
war on terror
Operation Iraqi Freedom

PEOPLE

Osama bin Laden
al-Qaeda
Taliban

TERMS

Department of Homeland Security
Arab Spring
Islamic State
BREXIT
Belt and Road Initiative
tsunami
Hurricane Katrina
COVID-19 pandemic

Technology allowed families to work and learn together at home.

Atlas

World: Physical

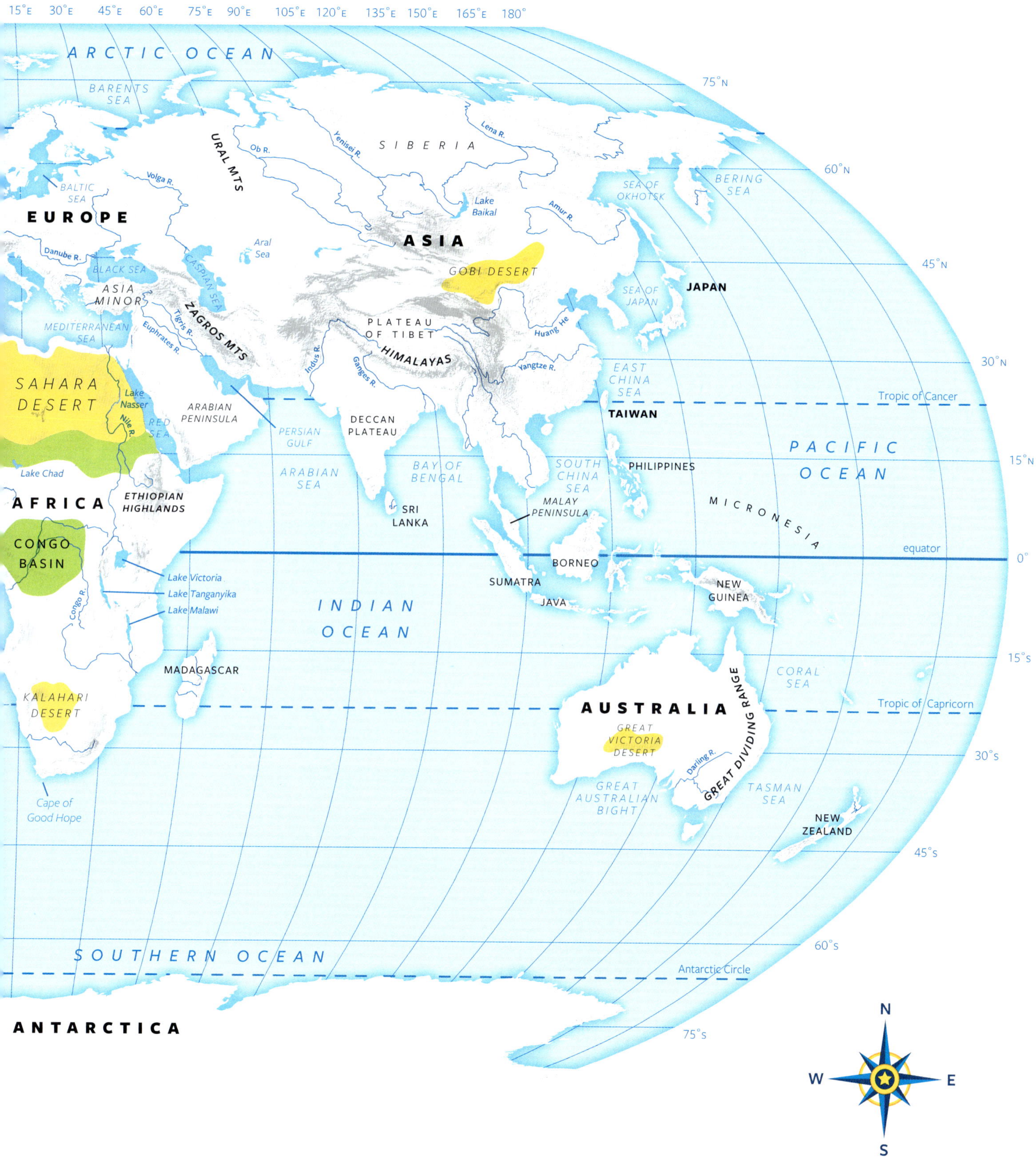
15°E
30°E
45°E
60°E
75°E
90°E
105°E
120°E
135°E
150°E
165°E
180°
ARCTIC OCEAN
BARENTS SEA
75°N
URAL MTS
Ob R.
Yenisei R.
SIBERIA
Lena R.
60°N
BERING SEA
SEA OF OKHOTSK
BALTIC SEA
Volga R.
Lake Baikal
Amur R.
EUROPE
ASIA
Aral Sea
Danube R.
BLACK SEA
CASPIAN SEA
GOBI DESERT
45°N
ASIA MINOR
ZAGROS MTS
SEA OF JAPAN
JAPAN
Tigris R.
Euphrates R.
PLATEAU OF TIBET
Huang He
MEDITERRANEAN SEA
Indus R.
HIMALAYAS
Ganges R.
Yangtze R.
EAST CHINA SEA
30°N
SAHARA DESERT
Lake Nasser
Nile R.
ARABIAN PENINSULA
Tropic of Cancer
RED SEA
PERSIAN GULF
DECCAN PLATEAU
TAIWAN
PACIFIC OCEAN
ARABIAN SEA
BAY OF BENGAL
SOUTH CHINA SEA
PHILIPPINES
15°N
Lake Chad
AFRICA
ETHIOPIAN HIGHLANDS
SRI LANKA
MALAY PENINSULA
MICRONESIA
CONGO BASIN
equator
0°
BORNEO
Lake Victoria
SUMATRA
NEW GUINEA
Lake Tanganyika
Congo R.
JAVA
INDIAN OCEAN
Lake Malawi
MADAGASCAR
15°S
CORAL SEA
KALAHARI DESERT
AUSTRALIA
GREAT DIVIDING RANGE
Tropic of Capricorn
GREAT VICTORIA DESERT
Darling R.
30°S
Cape of Good Hope
GREAT AUSTRALIAN BIGHT
TASMAN SEA
NEW ZEALAND
45°S
SOUTHERN OCEAN
60°S
Antarctic Circle
ANTARCTICA
75°S
N
W
E
S

Atlas

World: Political

ARCTIC OCEAN
EUROPE
ASIA
RUSSIA
Moscow
SWEDEN
NORWAY
FINLAND
POLAND
GERMANY
UKRAINE
ROMANIA
ITALY
GREECE
Algiers
KAZAKHSTAN
Astana
MONGOLIA
Ulaanbaatar
AZERBAIJAN
GEORGIA
ARMENIA
UZBEKISTAN
TURKMENISTAN
KYRGYZSTAN
TAJIKISTAN
CHINA
Beijing
NORTH KOREA
Pyongyang
Seoul
SOUTH KOREA
JAPAN
Tokyo
Nagasaki
TUNISIA
Tripoli
ALGERIA
LIBYA
Cairo
EGYPT
LEBANON
ISRAEL
SYRIA
JORDAN
IRAQ
Baghdad
IRAN
AFGHANISTAN
KUWAIT
SAUDI ARABIA
BAHRAIN
QATAR
UNITED ARAB EMIRATES
OMAN
YEMEN
PAKISTAN
NEPAL
New Delhi
BHUTAN
BANGLADESH
INDIA
MYANMAR
Naypyidaw
LAOS
Hanoi
Vientiane
THAILAND
CAMBODIA
Phnom Penh
VIETNAM
SOUTH CHINA SEA
GULF OF TONKIN
Manila
PHILIPPINES
PACIFIC OCEAN
NORTHERN MARIANA ISLANDS (U.S.)
GUAM (U.S.)
PALAU
FEDERATED STATES OF MICRONESIA
AFRICA
NIGER
CHAD
SUDAN
Khartoum
ERITREA
DJIBOUTI
BENIN
Abuja
NIGERIA
CENTRAL AFRICAN REP.
SOUTH SUDAN
ETHIOPIA
Addis Ababa
SOMALIA
TOGO
CAMEROON
EQUATORIAL GUINEA
GABON
UGANDA
KENYA
Mogadishu
DEMOCRATIC REPUBLIC OF THE CONGO
CONGO
RWANDA
BURUNDI
TANZANIA
SÃO TOMÉ & PRÍNCIPE
Luanda
ANGOLA
ZAMBIA
MALAWI
MOZAMBIQUE
COMOROS
Antananarivo
MADAGASCAR
MAURITIUS
RÉUNION (FRANCE)
ZIMBABWE
NAMIBIA
Windhoek
BOTSWANA
ESWATINI
SOUTH AFRICA
LESOTHO
INDIAN OCEAN
SRI LANKA
Kuala Lumpur
MALAYSIA
BRUNEI
SINGAPORE
INDONESIA
Jakarta
EAST TIMOR
PAPUA NEW GUINEA
Port Moresby
SOLOMON ISLANDS
SAMOA
VANUATU
FIJI
TONGA
NEW CALEDONIA (FRANCE)
AUSTRALIA
Canberra
NEW ZEALAND
Wellington
SOUTHERN OCEAN
ANTARCTICA
N
W
E
S

Glossary

A

Abbas Strong leader of the Safavid Empire who was regarded as the second founder

Abdulmejid I Ottoman emperor who reigned from 1839 to 1861

abolition Movement in Europe and America to end and outlaw the African slave trade

Aborigines Indigenous Australians

AD2000 movement Christian movement to reach every people group with the gospel by the year 2000

Adenauer, Konrad German chancellor under whose leadership West Germany experienced an incredible recovery

Afonso King of Kongo when the Portuguese arrived

Age of European Exploration Time period when Europeans sailed the world, exploring

Age of Reason Period of the 1600s and 1700s in Europe when people were supposedly guided by reason and not by superstition and religion

Aguinaldo, Emilio Philippine revolutionary leader

Akbar The most effective Mughal emperor

Albuquerque, Afonso de Portuguese explorer, admiral, and statesman who made several expeditions to India and one as far as the Persian Gulf

Alexander I The czar of Russia following Catherine's death in 1796

Alexander II Russian ruler who abolished serfdom and freed twenty-three million Russian serfs

Alexander III Russian czar who suppressed all real and imagined threats to the monarchy

Alexander VI Spanish pope who decided the location of the Line of Demarcation

Alexander the Great Greek general who conquered most of the known world in the 300s BC

Allies (World War I) League formed by Russia, Serbia, and France

Allies (World War II) League formed by Britain, France, and (later) America

Alopen The first Christian missionary to China in 635

al-Qaddafi, Muammar Dictator of Libya

al-Qaeda A terrorist organization led by Osama Bin Laden

Anabaptists A group that rejected infant baptism and rebaptized each other

anarchy Radical concept of society without government

Anatolia The Asian portion of modern-day Turkey

anatomy The science of muscle and bone connections, studied by Renaissance painters to make portraits and paintings more realistic

Anschluss Union between Austria and Germany

Anti-Comintern Pact Alliance between Germany and Japan against Communist Russia

anti-Semitism Hatred and violent acts against Jews

apartheid South African policy of segregation

aquaculture The practice of farming fish

Arab Spring A protest movement that spread across the Middle East in 2010 and 2011

Arkwright, Richard Entrepreneur who used patents to control the sale of inventions and thus eliminate competition in sales

armistice Truce or ceasefire

astrolabe An instrument used by sailors to measure the angle between the sun or a star and the horizon to determine latitude

Atahualpa Emperor of the Inca Empire who was defeated by Francisco Pizarro

atolls Low islands made of coral

audiencias High-level courts that helped to carry out laws coming from Spain

Australasia Region that includes the continent of Australia, the island of Tasmania, and the smaller islands to the north and south of the continent

Axis powers Group made of Germany, Japan, and Italy during World War II

B

Babur Founder of the Mughal Empire in India

Baibars The Mamluk emperor of Egypt and Syria

Bakunin, Michael Russian radical who became the Father of Anarchism

Balfour Declaration Document stating the British government's desire for a Jewish homeland in Palestine

Bastille A French fortress-prison formerly used to house political prisoners

Bastille Day July 14, celebrated as France's day of independence

Battle of Ain Jalut 1260 battle in which the Mongols were defeated in the Holy Land

Battle of Austerlitz Pivotal battle in which Napoleon defeated the combined armies of Austria and Russia

Battle of Liegnitz A battle in Eastern Europe between the Mongols and a combined force of Poles, Czechs, and Germans

Battle of Plassey Conflict in the Seven Years War in which Robert Clive fought an Indian army and ended France's strength in India

Battle of Stalingrad A decisive victory for the Soviets that ensured the Allies' inevitable victory

Battle of the Bulge Hitler's last push to break through the Allied line in World War II

Battle of Trafalgar Naval battle off the coast of Spain in which France suffered a crushing defeat by the British

Battle of Waterloo Battle in Belgium in which the combined European forces finally defeated Napoleon and ended his rule

Batu Khan A grandson of Genghis Khan who led a Mongol invasion into Eastern Europe

Belgian Congo Territory in the interior of Africa along the Congo River

Bell, Alexander Graham Inventor who patented the telephone

Berlin Blockade The Soviets' blocking of all traffic through East Germany into West Berlin in 1948

Berlin Conference of 1884–85 Assembly of European countries in 1885 that carved up the continent of Africa

bin Laden, Osama A Saudi terrorist who formed and led the al-Qaeda organization

Bismarck, Count Otto von Chancellor of Prussia who led the German states to political unification

Black Death A plague during the Middle Ages that killed perhaps as many as twenty-five million Europeans

blitzkrieg Germany's strategy of lightning war

Boer War War fought between the British and Dutch settlers in South Africa

Bolívar, Simón Liberator of Venezuela and Colombia from Spanish rule

Bolsheviks Radical Russian political group led by Vladimir Lenin that supported violence

boomerang Australian throwing stick

Bougainville, Louis Antoine de French explorer who colonized Tahiti

bourgeoisie Communist name for the middle class against whom the working class rebels

Boxer Rebellion A period of violent attacks against foreigners and Chinese Christians

Boxers A Chinese group that attacked foreigners in 1900

BREXIT British separation from the European Union

Brezhnev Doctrine Doctrine that said the Soviet Union would intervene anytime an existing socialist government was threatened

British North America Act British Parliamentary decision in 1867 to create the dominion of Canada, incorporating Ontario, Quebec, New Brunswick, and Nova Scotia

bureaucracies Government organizations that oversee the details of managing a state

C

cabinet A committee in English government that made it more answerable to the people

Cabot, John Explorer who led the first English expedition to North America

Caesar, Julius The popular first dictator of the Roman Empire

Calvin, John Leading figure in the Reformation who wrote *Institutes of the Christian Religion*

Canton Chinese port where foreign traders were allowed to trade

capital Money given on loan by bankers to entrepreneurs and inventors

capitalism An economic system in which businesses try to make money as they compete in a marketplace

caravel A ship used for European exploration and capable of travel on open seas

Carey, William British missionary to India who was known as the Father of Modern Missions

Castiglione An Italian Renaissance author who wrote *The Courtier*, a book on proper conduct for a Renaissance man

Catherine the Great Eighteenth-century Russian queen who made Russia a strong power in Europe and increased Russian territory

caudillos South American leaders who overthrew weak governments and established dictatorships

Cavour, Count Camillo di Prime Minister of Sardinia who led the Italian unification movement in northern Italy

Censorate An office of the Ming government that supervised the activities of government officials

Central Powers League in World War I formed by Germany, Austria-Hungary, and the Ottoman Empire

Chalmers, James Missionary to New Guinea in the nineteenth century

Chamberlain, Neville British Prime Minister who tried to prevent World War II by appeasement

Champa The central and southern kingdom in Vietnam

Charlemagne The first emperor of the Holy Roman Empire

Charles I King of England who asserted the divine right of kings

Charles V Habsburg emperor of the Holy Roman Empire crowned in 1519

charter A legal document issued by the king that listed privileges of the town's inhabitants and freed them from most feudal duties

Chartism Movement in England in the 1800s among the working class that called for universal male suffrage and elections by secret ballot

Chaucer The writer of *The Canterbury Tales*

Chengzu Third emperor of the Ming dynasty

Chiang Kai-shek A leader of China's Kuomintang Party

Chinese Communist Party Radical political party led by Mao Zedong that challenged the conservative government of Chiang Kai-shek

chivalry A code or strict set of rules and expectations for a knight

Christian humanism Philosophy that wanted to return Christianity to the simple values of its early days

Church of England The established church in England, which was Protestant in doctrine and practice but took steps to avoid offending Catholics

circuit courts A group of judges who traveled within a particular province to hear cases

city-states Cities that had their own governments, independent of those of other cities (even those within their own nation)

civil rights movement Movement to end both segregation and legal discrimination in the United States

Cixi, Empress Dowager Chinese empress in the 1800s who resisted modernization and westernization in China

Clan In Africa, the largest family group, whose members can trace their ancestry to a common relative

Cold War Political rivalry and conflict of ideas that stops short of actual war

colonialism Conquest of one or more nations by another nation

Columbian Exchange Exchange of plants, animals, and diseases between Europe and the Americas

Columbus, Christopher Explorer for Spain who discovered America in 1492

Committee for the Abolition of the Slave Trade Quaker and Anglican society that prompted Britain's Parliament to end the British slave trade

Committee of Public Safety French Revolutionary government during the Reign of Terror

common law Uniform laws set up by Henry II that applied to all of England and overruled differing local laws

Common Market An organization that promotes economic cooperation in Europe; also known as the European Economic Community

communism Economic system in which property is commonly owned, not privately owned

Communist Manifesto The book in which Karl Marx and Friedrich Engels outlined their philosophy

Congress of Vienna Meeting of kings to restore Europe to the condition it had been in before the French Revolution

conservatism A desire to maintain the old institutions of the kings and the church to ensure social stability

containerization System in which containers of uniform size and shape are filled with goods, stacked on cargo ships, and then put on trains or tractor-trailers after arriving at port

containment American policy of trying to keep the Soviets from expanding their influence

Cook, James English explorer and sea captain who discovered Australia and New Zealand

Copernicus, Nicolaus Astronomer who discovered that the earth revolves around the sun rather than the sun around the earth

Corday, Charlotte French woman who assassinated Jean Paul Marat

corporation A business that receives a legal charter and sells stock to individual investors

corps system A division of the national army into smaller self-contained armies

Cort, Henry Inventor of the puddling process, which removed impurities from iron

Cortés, Hernando Spanish explorer who conquered the Aztec Empire

cottage industries Small-scale businesses, usually owned and operated by one family

council A meeting of church leaders to resolve conflict over doctrine

Council of Trent A meeting of Catholic leaders during the Reformation that produced the first written statement containing all Catholic doctrines

COVID-19 A respiratory disease that arose in 2019, caused by the SARS-CoV-2 virus

Creation Mandate God's command for humans, stated in Genesis 1:28

Creoles People of pure Spanish or Portuguese descent who were born in the Americas

Crimean War Conflict between Russians and United European forces in 1854 to stop the increase of Russian influence in this region

Cromwell, Oliver Englishman who led Parliamentary forces during the Civil War and who established the Protectorate

Crowther, Samuel Ajayi African church leader who translated the Bible into the Yoruba language

crusade A Roman Catholic effort to liberate the Holy Land from "infidels"

Cuba Large island in the Caribbean that was the first substantial Spanish colony in the New World

cubism Art style after World War I that portrayed subjects in geometric shapes and from several perspectives at once

Cultural Revolution Attempt by Mao Zedong to purge capitalism from China

Curie, Pierre and Marie Physicists who pioneered work in radioactive matter

Cuzco The capital of the Incan civilization

czars Monarchs of Russia

D

da Gama, Vasco Portuguese explorer who sailed along Africa's west coast to India and started Portuguese colonization in those areas

Dai Viet The northern kingdom in Vietnam

Dante A medieval Italian writer famous for his work *The Divine Comedy*

Darwin, Charles English naturalist who taught evolution and man's natural origin in his works *Origin of Species and The Descent of Man*

da Vinci, Leonardo Italian Renaissance humanist who is known for painting the Mona Lisa

D-day Name for June 6, 1944, when the Allies made successful (though costly) amphibious landings on several beaches on the French coast

dead reckoning Sea navigation using estimation and few instruments

Decembrist Revolt Failed attempt by officers to replace Nicholas I with his brother as Russia's ruler

Declaration of the Rights of Man Document of the French Revolution signed by the National Assembly supporting liberty and humanism

de Gaulle, Charles French president after World War II and founder of the Fifth Republic

deism Philosophy that views God like a clock-winder who made the world but left it to run according to the natural laws that He set up for it

de Klerk, F. W. South African president who ended apartheid

Department of Homeland Security Agency that oversees airport and border security, enforcement of immigration and customs laws, and disaster relief measures

Descartes, René Philosopher and mathematician who developed the philosophy of rationalism

Desert Storm Military operation to force Iraq out of Kuwait

détente A relaxation of tensions

Dias, Bartolomeu Portuguese explorer who discovered a trade route to India by rounding the tip of Africa

Díaz, Porfirio President and then dictator of Mexico who was overthrown in a civil war

didgeridoo Musical instrument played by Australian Aborigines

Dien Bien Phu Battle in 1954 in which Vietnamese Communists fought and ended French rule

Directory French Revolutionary government that replaced the Committee of Public Safety and consisted of a five-man committee

Disraeli, Benjamin British prime minister who succeeded in doubling the number of men who could vote

doctrines Beliefs of the church

donatário Title given to a nobleman to whom the Portuguese government had granted total control of a section of land

Dostoyevsky, Fyodor Russian writer who embraced Eastern Orthodoxy and opposed anarchy and atheism

Douglass, Frederick American abolitionist who was born a slave in Maryland

Dreyfus Affair A demonstration of anti-Semitism in France in which Alfred Dreyfus, a Jewish captain of the French army, was mistreated and falsely accused of treason

Dum Diversas Pope Nicholas V's declaration that gave the Portuguese authority to put pagans and unbelievers into perpetual servitude

Dutch Republic Protestant provinces in Northern Europe

E

Easter Island Island in the eastern corner of Polynesia

Edict of Nantes A written guarantee of religious toleration to Huguenots during Europe's religious wars

Edison, Thomas Inventor of the phonograph and the light bulb

Edward VI Protestant king of England

Egypt Eyalet Egypt's name when it was part of the Ottoman Empire

Einstein, Albert Father of Modern Physics who studied the relationship between matter and energy

Eisenhower, Dwight D. American World War II general who was the supreme commander of the Allied forces in Europe

electoral district Section of the country that voted for one or more members of Parliament to represent it

Elizabeth I Half-sister of Mary I and queen of England for almost forty-five years

empiricism Belief system founded by John Locke stating that man can find knowledge only through experience

encomienda A system in which the indigenous peoples of the Americas paid tribute and provided labor for the Spanish in return for the promise of protection, wages, and spiritual care

English Bill of Rights Document signed by William and Mary that limited the monarch's power

English Civil War War between King Charles I and Parliament that resulted in limiting the king's royal power

entrepreneur A person who sets up and operates a business for financial gain but with a risk of personal loss

Erasmus A Dutch Renaissance linguist and scholar who published a Greek New Testament and advocated church reform

Ericson, Leif The first European to set foot in North America

Estates-General An assembly in pre-Revolutionary French government that had financial authority

etiquette Good manners that were considered essential to members of the growing middle class during the Renaissance

European Union An economic and political alliance in Europe

excommunication A dismissal from the Roman Catholic Church denying the expelled any chance of salvation

existentialism Philosophy in the 1900s that stressed a person's uniqueness, free choice, and consequences of those choices

exports Goods taken out of a country or colony

expressionism Art style after World War I that focused on how the artist felt about his subject

F

factory Building where entrepreneurs brought together machines and workers to produce goods on a large scale

Falkland Islands British-held islands off the coast of Argentina

Fante Confederation African organization formed in 1868 by African pastors and teachers to maintain self-rule

Fascist Party Italian political party founded by Benito Mussolini

Federal Reserve American organization that controls the money supply and protects the banking system

Ferdinand II King of Spain who, with his wife Isabella, financed the explorations of Christopher Columbus

Fez A city with stone towers that serves as one of Morocco's two capitals

First Estate Highest level of French society besides the king before the French Revolution; contained French Catholic leaders

First Fleet The first English ships that brought convicts to Australia

flying shuttle Invention of John Kay that wove strands of cotton into cloth more quickly

Fourier, Charles A French utopian socialist

Francis Ferdinand Archduke of Austria-Hungary who was killed on June 28, 1914, prompting the start of World War I

French and Indian War Part of the European Seven Years' War fought in North America

fronts Locations where the battles are occurring in a war

G

Gaínza, Gabino General who led Central America to independence

Galilei, Galileo Astronomer whose observations using the telescope supported the heliocentric theory

Gandhi, Mohandas Indian nationalist leader who used passive resistance to achieve India's independence from Britain

Garibaldi, Giuseppe Italian nationalist who led the unification movement in southern Italy

Garrison, William Lloyd American abolitionist who edited the newspaper *The Liberator*

gathering-based economy Economy that sells things that are collected rather than grown or manufactured

Gaza Strip Israeli land along the Mediterranean Sea that has a Palestinian majority

Genghis Khan A Mongol title meaning "Great Ruler" that was given to the Mongol Empire's founder

genocide The planned killing of a people group

gers The movable houses used by the Mongols

Gladstone, William British prime minister who stressed domestic English reforms

glasnost Soviet policy of openness

Glorious Revolution The change of power in England from James II to William and Mary without any war

Goforth, Jonathan Nineteenth-century missionary to China

Gold Coast A name for Western Africa due to the gold trade that occurred at its coasts

Golden Horde A Mongol empire based in Western Asia and founded by Batu Khan

Gorbachev, Mikhail Soviet leader and first president that allowed private ownership of property

Gothic Architectural style of the late Middle Ages used in cathedrals

Gran Colombia Area that included the Spanish colonies in northwestern South America, Venezuela, Colombia, and Ecuador

Grand Canal Chinese canal enlarged and completed by Ming ruler Chengzu

Great Depression Financial and economic downturn in the early 1900s

Great Famine of 1315 A natural disaster in Europe caused by heavy rains and ruined crops

Great Leap Forward Failed Chinese attempt in 1958 to double agricultural production

Great Schism Division within the Roman Catholic Church in 1378 that involved having a French pope and an Italian pope at the same time

Great Wall A defensive wall over 13,000 miles long in western China

Great Yasa A Mongolian law code written by Genghis Khan

Great Zimbabwe City state along Africa's eastern coast that developed its own surrounding empire

Gregorian chants Monophonic music (just one melody line) that went along with the mass and daily prayer routines of the Catholic Church

griots African storytellers

Guangxu Nineteenth-century Chinese emperor who worked to modernize China

guild People of the same occupation (e.g., cloth-makers) who work together to set up rules for their occupation and to protect themselves from competition

guillotine The machine used to behead people during the French Revolution

H

Habsburgs One of the most powerful families in Europe, known for its strong support of the Catholic Church and its rule over the Holy Roman Empire

hacienda A large country estate in Latin America

Halley, Edmond Astronomer who developed a theory about the orbit of comets and accurately predicted the next appearance of the comet that was later named for him

Hamid II, Abdul Ottoman emperor who reigned from 1876 to 1909 and accepted a constitution

Hargreaves, James Inventor in the Industrial Revolution who made the spinning jenny

Harvey, William English physician who studied medicine and the blood's circulatory system

Hawaii Chain of islands in northern Polynesia

Hawaiians Native people from the Hawaiian archipelago

Henry II English king during the Middle Ages who strengthened royal authority by using royal circuit courts

Henry VIII King of England from 1509 to 1547

Henry of Navarre A member of the Huguenot Bourbon family who became king of France and issued the Edict of Nantes

Henry the Navigator A ruler of Portugal who founded a school for Portuguese navigation

Herschel, William Astronomer who discovered the planet Uranus and the moons of Saturn

Herzl, Theodore A Jewish French journalist who started the Zionist movement

Heyerdahl, Thor Norwegian explorer who theorized that the first Polynesians came from South America rather than Asia

Hidalgo y Costilla, Miguel Priest who began the independence movement in Mexico

high islands Pacific islands whose height enables agriculture to grow and humans to reside there

Hiroshima Japanese city that was the site of the first hostile use of nuclear bombs on August 6, 1945

Hispaniola Island in the Caribbean

history The inquiry into what happened in the past and why it happened

Hitler, Adolf Leader of Germany's Nazi Party before and during World War II

Hobbes, Thomas English philosopher who believed that people should agree to be governed by an absolute ruler who had enough power to keep them from hurting each other

Ho Chi Minh Leader who established communism in Vietnam

Holocaust The German attempt to destroy all the Jews in Europe

Holy Roman Empire An association between the German and Italian states

Horton, John Africanus African scholar who disproved the claim that black men were racially inferior

Huguenots French Protestants during the Reformation

Hundred Years' War The war fought from 1337 to 1453 between England and France to settle the issue of English control of land in France

Hurricane Katrina Category 3 hurricane that struck New Orleans in 2005

Huss, John A pastor in Bohemia who was influenced by Wycliffe's teachings and was burned at the stake

Hussein, Saddam Dictator of Iraq who invaded Kuwait in 1990

Hutus Majority tribe in Rwanda that was put in charge of the government by Belgium

I

Imperial City Royal section of Beijing, China, built by Ming rulers

imperialism Dominance and power asserted by one nation over less powerful nations

imports Goods brought into a country

Inchon Place where UN forces made an amphibious landing to begin an attack against North Korea during the Korean War

Index of Prohibited Books A list of books and Bible translations that were forbidden and declared heretical by the Catholic Church during the Counter Reformation

indulgence A paper issued by the Roman Catholic Church granting pardon from the punishment of sins

Industrial Revolution Movement in eighteenth- and nineteenth-century Europe and America that changed manufacturing and increased inventions

infrastructure Network of travel and communication in a land area

Inquisition A Roman Catholic Church court set up to find and punish heretics

International African Association (IAA) A society of explorers and others that was established in 1876 and sponsored by King Leopold II for the purpose of developing Central Africa

International Monetary Fund (IMF) A fund for lending to financially troubled developed countries

Isabella (queen) Ruler of Spain who, with her husband, Ferdinand II, financed the explorations of Christopher Columbus

Islamic State A group that tried to establish a caliphate (Islamic empire) in part of western Iraq and eastern Syria

Ismail I Founder of the Safavid Empire and its dynasty in Eurasia

Istanbul The name of Constantinople after the Ottomans took it over

Iturbide, Agustín de First emperor of Mexico following independence

J

Jacobins The radical group in the French Revolution that advocated violence

Japanese economic miracle A time period when the Japanese economy boomed and Japan became the leading manufacturer of cars and electronics

Jenner, Edward Scientist who discovered a vaccine to protect people from getting smallpox

Jesuits A new Catholic monastic order founded during the Reformation to stop the spread of Protestantism

Joan of Arc A French peasant girl who led the French to victory during the Hundred Years' War

John (king) King of England who ruled from 1199 to 1216 and signed the Magna Carta in 1215

joint-stock company An early version of the corporation

Judson, Adoniram The United States's first foreign missionary

June 28, 1914 Date on which Francis Ferdinand was killed, beginning World War I

justice To be treated rightly

K

Ka'ahumanu (queen) Led the revolution against the old Hawaiian religion

kapus Laws that regulated every aspect of life in ancient Hawaii

Kay, John Inventor in the Industrial Revolution who made the flying shuttle

Kellogg-Briand Pact Agreement among nations to settle disputes by negotiation rather than force

Keōpūolani (queen) Hawaiian ruler and mother of the second and third kings of Hawaii

khanate A division of the Mongol Empire ruled by a khan

Khmer Ancient empire in Cambodia

Khomeini, Ayatollah The Islamic cleric who led the revolution in Iran

Kilwa Key port through which Zimbabwe's gold was transported north

King, Martin Luther, Jr. American civil rights leader

Kingdom of Guatemala Kingdom which included the countries of Costa Rica, El Salvador, Honduras, Nicaragua, and Guatemala

Kingdom of Kongo An independent African kingdom that lasted until 1857

Kublai Khan The Mongol emperor of the Yuan dynasty in China

Kuomintang Nationalist Chinese Party in the early 1900s

L

Laar, Mart Prime minister of Estonia following the fall of communism

landscapes Paintings that feature nature scenes

Las Casas, Bartolomé de Roman Catholic missionary to Latin America who defended the Indian people from slavery and abuses

Lavoisier, Antoine French scientist who became the Father of Chemistry and who worked with chemicals

Lend-Lease Act American act to provide weapons and material aid to the Allies in World War II

Lenin, Vladimir First dictator of Russia, who took Russia out of World War I

Leonin and Perotin French composers who introduced harmony in music

liberalism Political philosophy that stressed freedom and equality for all

Lili'uokalani (queen) Ruler of Hawaii who was overthrown by the Hawaiian Reform Party

Line of Demarcation The boundary in South America that divided the land claims of Spain from those of Portugal

Livingstone, David Nineteenth-century British explorer and missionary to Africa

Locarno Pact Agreement after World War I in which Germany recognized France's and Belgium's boundaries

Locke, John English philosopher who argued in favor of empiricism, the belief that the best way to find true knowledge was through experience rather than through human reason

Louis XIV King of France who became the most successful absolute ruler

Louis XVI King of France who was killed during the French Revolution

low islands Pacific islands that have little fresh water and few places where humans can live

Luddites Skilled craftsmen who had lost business as a result of the Industrial Revolution and pursued change violently

Luftwaffe Name for Germany's air force in World War II

Luther, Martin German reformer who wrote the Ninety-Five Theses and translated the whole Bible into German

M

Maastricht Treaty Treaty that created the European Union

MacArthur, Douglas Supreme Allied commander in the Pacific during World War II

Machiavelli An Italian Renaissance author who wrote *The Prince*

MAD (Mutually Assured Destruction); the Cold War practice of stockpiling weapons to ensure that each side was capable of destroying the other

Magellan, Ferdinand Spanish explorer whose crew sailed around the world

Maginot Line French defensive line during World War II

Magna Carta A document signed by King John of England that assured rights for the nobility and limited royal power

Mahmud II Ottoman ruler who laid the foundation for a modern Turkey

Malintzin Cortez's translator

Mamluks Slave soldiers in Egypt

Manchu dynasty Chinese dynasty during the nineteenth century that witnessed European imperialism

mandate A formal assignment

Mandela, Nelson First black president of South Africa

manor A nobleman's self-supporting estate found in a feudal society

Maoris Native people of New Zealand

Mao Zedong Leader of the Chinese Communist Party

Marat, Jean-Paul Radical leader of the French Revolution

Marconi, Guglielmo Inventor of the radio in 1896

Marco Polo The most famous European to witness the Mongol Empire and the Mongol rule of China

Marie Antoinette Queen of France who was killed during the French Revolution

marketplace A location where goods and services are bought and sold

Marrakesh The "red city," which was one of the two capitals of Morocco

Marshall Plan America's financial help to Europe to help it recover from World War II

Marx, Karl Philosopher and historian who founded communism and cowrote *Communist Manifesto* with Friedrich Engels

Marxism A political, economic, and religious theory that strives for global, stateless (no countries) communism

Mary I Catholic queen of England

Maxim gun Rapid-firing gun that European colonists used to conquer Africa

Maxwell, James Scottish scientist in the 1800s who contributed to the studies of physics, astronomy, electricity, magnetism, and optics

Mayflower Compact An agreement of self-government signed on November 11, 1620

Mazzini, Giuseppe Italian nationalist who formed a group called Young Italy

Mehmed II Ottoman ruler who united the empire and defeated the Byzantines

Meiji Restoration Time period in which the Japanese emperor was restored to power

Meikle, Andrew Inventor in the Industrial Revolution who developed the threshing machine

Melanesia Group of Pacific islands that includes Papua New Guinea, the Solomon Islands, and Fiji

Mendaña, Alvaro de Spanish explorer who discovered and named the Solomon Islands

Mendel, Gregor Father of the study of genetics

Menelik II A descendent of the son of Solomon and the Queen of Sheba (according to Ethiopian tradition) who began the line of Ethiopian kings and who used modern military equipment to defend Ethiopia from European colonizers

Mensheviks Moderate Russian political group that sought change through peaceful methods

mercantilism Economic system in which a country was considered wealthy if it had a large supply of gold and silver

Methodists Congregations with laymen (church members other than pastors) serving as leaders

Michelangelo An Italian Renaissance artist who painted the ceiling of the Sistine Chapel in Rome

microchip An integrated circuit made up of millions of switches

Micronesia Group of Pacific islands that are small and low

Middle Kingdom Translation of Chung Kuo, a name the Chinese gave to their country

Middle Passage The trip the African captives were forced to take between West Africa and the Americas

Midway Island Pacific island near where American pilots sank several Japanese carriers and forced Japan to retreat

Milošević, Slobodan President of Yugoslavia during the 1990s

Ming dynasty Chinese line of rule established after Mongol rule in China was overthrown

modernism Philosophy which had the theme, "the newer the better"

Moffat, Robert Nineteenth-century British missionary to South Africa whose daughter married David Livingstone

Montesquieu French political philosopher who supported a separation of powers in government

Montezuma II Ruler of the Aztec Empire who was defeated by Hernando Cortés

Montgomery, Bernard L. British World War II general who fought in North Africa

More, Thomas An official under Henry VIII who wrote *Utopia* and advocated church reform

Morrison, Robert First Protestant missionary to China

Mueller, George British reformer who led a faith-based ministry to house the orphans of Bristol, England

Mughal dynasty A Mongol empire and dynasty in India founded by Babur

Munich Conference Meeting before World War II that gave Hitler the Sudetenland

Musa, Mansa The ruler of Mali who became famous for bringing a large offering of gold to Mecca

Mussolini, Benito Fascist leader and dictator of Italy after World War I

Mutapa Kingdom East African kingdom that followed Great Zimbabwe

N

Nagasaki Japanese city where the second atomic bomb was dropped

Napoleon III French president of the Second Republic who declared himself emperor and founded France's Second Empire

Napoleonic Code System of laws in France organized by Napoleon Bonaparte

National Assembly of France Members of the Third Estate in the French Revolution who convened and signed the Tennis Court Oath and the Declaration of the Rights of Man

National Convention Group that replaced the National Assembly in 1792 in Revolutionary France

nationalism Intense devotion and loyalty to one's own people and country

NATO (North Atlantic Treaty Organization) International league founded in 1949 to give its members protection from the Soviet Union

Nazi Party German radical political group founded after World War I and led by Adolf Hitler

Nebuchadnezzar The king of Babylon who finally realized God's greatness and the foolishness of his own pride

Nestorians Religious group which taught that Jesus was both God and human but was not a single person

New Deal US government program that created numerous federal agencies to lessen the effects of the Great Depression

New Guinea Largest Melanesian island

New Holland Name given to Australia by Dutch explorer Abel Tasman

New Laws of 1542 Laws in Spain's colonies that were issued to protect native peoples from abuses

New South Wales England's first colony in Australia, founded by James Cook

Newton, Isaac Scientist whose discoveries include the laws of gravity and motion, advanced forms of calculus, and the reflecting telescope

Newton, John Captain of a slave-trade ship who became a Christian and supported abolition; author of the hymn "Amazing Grace"

New Zealand Set of islands near Australia that were inhabited by Maoris and explored by Abel Tasman and James Cook

Nicholas I Russian ruler who resisted westernization

Nightingale, Florence British nurse who modernized nursing techniques

1948 Arab-Israeli War First attack on Israel after it received independence from Britain

Nobel, Alfred Inventor of dynamite

November 11, 1918 Armistice Day, when the Germans stopped fighting World War I

Nubia Present-day Sudan

O

Oceania Large geographical region in the Pacific Ocean

Ögödei The son chosen to be Great Khan after Genghis Khan

one-child policy A policy imposed in China in 1979 that limited couples to one child

Operation Iraqi Freedom Military operation to remove the brutal government of Iraq's dictator, Saddam Hussein

opium An addictive drug that the British brought to China in order to create trade for Britain and make China financially dependent

Opium War Conflict in China when Britain and other European imperialists forced China to trade opium with them

Orient A name for the countries of Asia, especially East Asia

Ottoman Empire Turkish Islamic empire that defeated the Byzantine Empire in 1453 and made Istanbul the capital

Owen, Robert A British textile manufacturer and early socialist

P

Pan-Arabism Movement among Arabs to unite under one government

Paracelsus Scientist who stated that the body is made of **chemicals** and should be treated with chemicals

Paris Peace Conference Allied meeting in 1919 that ended World War I

Parliament A group of advisors of the English king who were eventually divided into the House of Lords and the House of Commons

passive resistance The practice of resisting foreign rule by nonviolent means (strikes, not paying taxes)

Pasteur, Louis French chemist whose discovery of pasteurization made it possible to slow the development of disease-causing microbes

patent Set of government-issued rights to an inventor stating that no one can legally copy and sell his invention

Paton, John Missionary to the New Hebrides islands in the Pacific

Pax Mongolica A period of stability and trade caused by Mongol rule

Peace of Augsburg Agreement that gave each German prince the right to choose the religion for his territory

Peace of God A church decree making church property out of bounds for fighting among knights

Pearl Harbor Site of America's naval base in Hawaii that Japan attacked on December 7, 1941

Pedro I The first emperor of Brazil after gaining independence from Portugal

penance Certain deeds to help earn forgiveness of sins

peninsulares Spaniards who were born in Spain and then moved to the New World

perestroika Soviet policy of restructuring the economy and the political system

Perón, Juan President of Argentina

Perry, Commodore Matthew American naval leader who convinced Japan to trade with America and end its isolation from the world

perspective The technique Renaissance artists used to give depth to paintings by adjusting the size of objects in relation to the observer's viewpoint

Peter the Great Czar who led the westernization of Russia

Petrarch A pioneer of Renaissance humanism, a central figure in Italian literature, and the Father of Humanism

Philip II A Capetian king of France who developed a strong monarchy

Philippine-American War A guerilla war between Filipinos and Americans that lasted from 1899 to 1913

Phillip, Arthur Captain who brought the First Fleet to Sydney Cove and served as Australia's first governor

philosophes French Enlightenment philosophers

Pizarro, Francisco Spanish explorer who conquered the Incan Empire

pogrom An attack on Jews living in Russia

Polynesia The group of Pacific islands located among and including Hawaii, Easter Island, and New Zealand

pope The bishop of Rome, who became an especially powerful member of medieval society

porcelain Product developed by the Chinese through the process of shaping kaolin clay into objects and then using heat to harden them

postmodernism Philosophy that teaches there is no absolute truth

power An essential ingredient for the rule of any civilization

prayer book Liturgical book of the Church of England

proletariat Communist term for laborers who rebel against the bourgeoisie (middle class) to make a classless society

protectionism The use of tariffs to support industries in one's country

Protestants Reformers who protested certain doctrines and practices of the Roman Catholic Church

proxy conflict Conflict in which parties are not directly involved but support opposing sides

purgatory A place where, according to Catholic doctrine, people go after death to finish atoning for their sins before being allowed into heaven

Puritans An English religious group that founded Massachusetts Bay Colony

Q

Qin Shi Huang Ti Founder of the Qin dynasty in China

Quebec Act Granted the French Canadians special rights by retaining French civil law and allowing the practice of Roman Catholicism

R

Rapa Nui People who lived on Easter Island

rationalism Belief popularized by René Descartes which stated that the path to truth is through human reason

Reagan, Ronald American president who opposed communism and tried to spread democracy to other countries

realism The movement in art and literature that replaced romanticism and focused on everyday life

Reconquista Roman Catholic campaign to take back Spain and Portugal from Muslim control

Reform Act of 1867 British law that granted voting privileges to all male homeowners

Reign of Terror The period in the French Revolution of mass executions by the guillotine

Renaissance A time period in Europe following the Medieval Era that was characterized by a revival of literacy and education

Renaissance humanism Philosophy of the Renaissance based on the writings of the classical world that focused on human interests and experiences

Republic of China Country founded by Chiang Kai-shek on the island of Taiwan near China's coast

Requerimiento A document used by Spanish explorers which said that God made Saint Peter and his heirs, the popes, rulers over all the earth

Rhineland Land west of the Rhine River

Robespierre, Maximilien Leader of France during the Reign of Terror

Romanesque An architectural style of the early Middle Ages that used elements of Roman styles of architecture

romanticism A movement in art, music, and literature that was characterized by an emphasis on the mysterious and supernatural, a longing for the Medieval Age, and a love for freedom, nationalism, personal emotion, and nature

Rommel, Erwin German general who fought in North Africa during World War II

Rousseau, Jean-Jacques Philosopher who believed that humans were happy in their primitive condition but needed government once private ownership was introduced to society

Russo-Japanese War War in which Japan defeated Russia and proved that Japan had developed into a world power

S

Safavid dynasty Safavid Empire's line of rulers that began with Shah Ismail I

Sahel A narrow strip of land in Africa between the Sahara Desert and the rainforests

San Martín, José de Liberator of Chile and Peru from Spanish rule

San Salvador Caribbean island where Columbus first landed

savanna Flat grasslands in Africa

Schlieffen Plan Germany's two-front war strategy in which Germany would quickly conquer France and then fight Russia

scientific method A series of steps scientists use to answer questions about the physical world

Scientific Revolution A period from the sixteenth through the eighteenth centuries when many scientific advances and discoveries were made

Scramble for Africa Nineteenth-century rush for European conquest of Africa

scurvy Disease that many sailors had because of a lack of vitamin C in their diet

SDI (Strategic Defense Initiative) satellite system that would protect America from missile attacks

Second Estate Second-highest level of French society before the French Revolution, consisting of the aristocracy

Second French Colonial Empire French colony of Algeria in 1830

seed drill Invention of Jethro Tull that planted seeds in even rows to enable the growing of more crops with less seed

separation of powers Division of government into three parts that can put helpful checks on each other's power

Sepoy Mutiny Rebellion in British India by hired Indian soldiers because of a rumor that the cartridges for a newly issued rifle had been greased with either pork or beef fat

September 1, 1939 Day on which Germany invaded Poland and triggered World War II

September 11, 2001 Day on which Islamic terrorists used hijacked jetliners to target buildings in New York City and Washington, DC

serf A farmer bound under the feudal system to work on his lord's estate in slave-like conditions

shading A technique used by Renaissance artists to give dimension to their paintings

Shia Islam The sect of Islam that insists that the right of rule was limited to a descendant of Muhammad

Shoah The name many Jews use to refer to the Holocaust; means "calamity" in Hebrew

Sikhism An Indian religion that believes in just one god but teaches that god is in everything and everything is in god (pantheism)

Silk Road An overland trading route from China to Europe

Sinan, Mimar Ottoman architect who designed hundreds of buildings and other structures across the empire

Sino-Japanese War A war between Japan and China in 1894 that resulted in Japan taking over Korea and Taiwan

Sistine Chapel A building in Rome whose ceiling was painted by Michelangelo during the Italian Renaissance

Six-Day War A war in 1967 between Israeli and Arab forces that resulted in Israel's quick victory

Smith, Adam Scottish economist who challenged the ideas of mercantilism, teaching that countries should trade freely with each other, that a country's greatest asset was the labor of its people, and that governments should not interfere in the economic activities of their people

social contract An agreement by a group of people to place themselves under the authority of a government

socialism Economic system in which the government owns a nation's businesses

Solidarity Polish anti-Communist labor movement led by Lech Wałęsa

Solomon Islands Pacific island chain discovered by the Spanish in the sixteenth century

Song dynasty A Chinese dynasty of the tenth century under whose rule China split into Northern and Southern Kingdoms

Soviet Union A confederation of Russia and several of its neighbors established in 1922

space shuttle A mostly reusable rocket used to carry payloads and people into space

Spanish Armada A powerful Spanish fleet that attacked England in 1588 but was defeated

Spanish Civil War A war between the socialist Spanish government and the fascists led by Franco

spinning jenny Invention by James Hargreaves that could spin spools of cotton thread into yarn

Spinoza, Benedict de Philosopher who doubted anything in the Bible that he thought was contrary to reason

Spurgeon, Charles Minister who preached Christ-centered messages in nineteenth-century England and worked to confront the issues of his day

Sputnik 1 First manmade satellite, launched by the Soviet Union in 1957

Stalin, Joseph Soviet Union's second dictator, who oppressed freedom and religion

Stanley, Henry British reporter who found David Livingstone after Livingstone was missing for several months

steam engine Invention of the Industrial Revolution that was improved by James Watt and became a reliable source of power

Stephenson, George Inventor and engineer who helped make railroads common in Great Britain

Sudetenland Area of Czechoslovakia that Hitler took before World War II

suffrage The privilege to vote in elections

sultan Muslim king

sultanate Islamic kingdom

Sunni Islam The sect of Islam which teaches that any worthy Muslim could become the ruler of Islam

Sun Yat-Sen Chinese leader who struggled to bring unity to China through the Kuomintang Party

Swahili A Bantu-based trade language along the Southeast African coastline

T

Tahitians Natives of the Polynesian island of Tahiti, who also settled Hawaii

Taino People group living on the island of San Salvador when Columbus landed there

Taiping Rebellion A thirteen-year-long uprising of Chinese peasants led by Hong Xiuquan against the Manchu government, resulting in many deaths

Taizong A Tang dynasty emperor who welcomed Christian Nestorian missionaries

Taizu Chinese ruler who founded the Ming dynasty

Taliban A strict Islamic sect that ruled Afghanistan from 1996 to 2001 and returned to power in 2021

Tang dynasty A Chinese golden age, one of the longest Chinese dynasties following the time of Christ

tariffs Taxes on goods coming into a country

Tasman, Abel Dutch explorer who discovered Australia, Tasmania, and New Zealand

Taylor, James Hudson Missionary who established the China Inland Mission in 1865

technology Advances that put scientific knowledge to effective use

temperance The practice of drinking alcohol in moderation

Temujin The son of a Mongolian tribal chieftain, born around 1162, who became Genghis Khan

Tennis Court Oath French Assembly's pledge to continue meeting until a constitution guaranteeing basic rights to all French citizens was written

Tenno, Jimmu The mythical ancestor of Japanese emperors

Tenochtitlán Capital of the Aztec Empire

Thatcher, Margaret Prime minister of Great Britain in the 1980s who tried to reverse socialism in the country

theocracy A system of government in which clerics rule in the name of God or a god

Third Estate Lowest level of French society before the French Revolution, which contained the middle class, artisans, and peasants

Third Reich Name for the German empire founded by Hitler before World War II

third world Regions that remained neutral during the Cold War

38th parallel Point to where North Korean and Chinese troops fought back UN troops

Thirty Years' War A major conflict of Catholic and Protestant forces involving many European nations

threshing machine Invention of Andrew Meikle that enabled farmers to separate wheat from its husks and stalks

Tiananmen Square Scene of a 1989 political protest in Beijing, China, against communism

Timur A Mongol leader in the fourteenth century who founded an empire in central Asia

Tlaxcalans The people who lived on the eastern side of the Mexico Valley and were victims of the Aztecs

Tolstoy, Leo Russian realist author who described the difficulties of Russian life in his book *War and Peace*

total war A war in which all the resources of a country are devoted to destroying the enemy

trade unions Organizations that consist of people who worked in the same industries

trade winds The winds blowing from east to west that brought European explorers across the Atlantic Ocean

transubstantiation Catholic doctrine stating that the bread and wine of the Lord's Supper become part of the very body and blood of Christ

Treaty of Kanagawa Agreement between America and Japan in 1854 that opened Japan to trade with other nations

Treaty of Paris Treaty after the French and Indian War that required France to give England its Canadian land and to surrender its claims to the Mississippi and Ohio River valleys

Treaty of Tordesillas Final agreement between Spain and Portugal that moved the line dividing the countries' land claims in South America about 600 miles west

Treaty of Versailles The treaty that ended World War I and blamed Germany for the war

Treaty of Waitangi A treaty between the British and the Maoris

trench warfare A defensive strategy during World War I in which opposing sides built systems of trenches and made very few gains

triangular trade Trade pattern that involved guns, textiles, and wine from Europe being sold in Africa, slaves from Africa being sold in the Americas, and crops like sugar and coffee from the Americas being sold in Europe

Triple Alliance The 1882 alliance of Germany, Italy, and Austria-Hungary

Triple Entente Loose confederation between Russia, England, and France

Truce of God A church decree restricting fighting among knights to certain days of the week

Truman Doctrine Truman's policy of containment

Tse-Hsu, Lin Chinese administrator charged with stopping the opium trade

tsunami A massive wave created by an earthquake

Tull, Jethro Inventor during the Industrial Revolution who developed the seed drill

Tupou I Christian king of Tonga

Ture, Samori African ruler of the Wassoulou Empire who used a modern army with military equipment to resist European colonization

Tutsis Minority tribe in Rwanda

U

U-boats German submarines

unconditional surrender A demand that a defeated nation submit to the total control of the victors

United Nations International peacekeeping organization formed after World War II

unrestricted submarine warfare A policy of sinking of any vessel, military or civilian, without warning

urbanization The process of people moving to the cities

V

vaccine A weakened form of a disease exposed to a person on purpose to prevent a more serious form of the disease

Valle de Mexico The fertile valley in Mexico where Mexico City is located today

Van Leeuwenhoek, Anton A scientist who made developments in microscopes

V-E Day Victory over Europe day, May 8, 1945

Velazquez, Governor The Spanish governor of Cuba

vernacular A common spoken language

Vesalius, Andreas Physician who improved understanding of human anatomy by dissecting human bodies

viceroy A ruler of a Spanish colony who represented the king of Spain

Victoria Falls Waterfall at the Zambezi River discovered by David Livingstone

Viet Cong North Vietnamese Communist agents who tried to take over South Vietnam

V-J Day Victory over Japan day, September 2, 1945

Voltaire Pen name of François-Marie Arouet, French philosopher of the Enlightenment

W

Wałęsa, Lech Leader of the Polish anti-Communist Solidarity movement

War of Jenkins' Ear War between England and Spain that resulted from the Spanish boarding an English ship in the Caribbean in 1731

War on Terror American war that targeted terrorist groups like al-Qaeda as well as countries that helped or protected terrorists

Warsaw Pact Military alliance of the Soviet Union and the countries of Eastern Europe

Washington Naval Conference The 1921 meeting in which several nations agreed to limit the number of warships each could build

Wassoulou Empire Empire in Africa led by Samori Ture that resisted European colonization with modern weapons and an army

Watt, James Englishman during the Industrial Revolution who improved the steam engine

Wesley, John Popular preacher in England during the Industrial Revolution and a supporter of the Great Awakening

West Bank Region of Israel with a Palestinian majority

Whitefield, George Popular preacher in Britain, Wales, and England's American colonies and a supporter of the Great Awakening

Wilberforce, William Christian supporter of abolition who led British Parliament to end the English slave trade

Wilhelm II German ruler who allowed the Reinsurance Treaty to expire

William and Mary Rulers of England who replaced Charles II during the Glorious Revolution

Winston Churchill Prime minister of Great Britain during World War II

World Bank A bank to help less developed countries

World Wide Web The internet system that links various documents through clickable text or buttons, indicated by "www" in front of an internet address

Wright, Wilbur and Orville Two brothers who made the first successful airplane and flight

Wu Zetian The only legitimate empress in Chinese history

Wycliffe, John A pre-Reformation pastor, teacher, and theologian in England who produced the first Bible in the English language

X

Xavier, Francis Jesuit missionary to Japan

Xiuquan, Hong Chinese leader who started the Taiping Rebellion

Y

Yom Kippur War The 1973 attack on Israel by Egypt and Syria

Yuan dynasty Chinese dynasty ruled by the Mongols

Z

Zheng He Admiral of a large fleet sent by Ming rulers to enhance China's reputation among other Asian and African countries

Zionism Movement devoted to the reestablishment and development of a Jewish nation in the land of Israel

Zollverein Economic union of German states in the nineteenth century that resulted in German unification

Zwingli, Ulrich Swiss reformer who studied and accepted Martin Luther's teachings

Index

D

E

N

O

P

Q

R

S

T

U

V

W

X

Y

Z

Photo Credits

Key: (t) top; (c) center; (b) bottom; (l) left; (r) right (bg) background; (i) inset

Cover

front tl Gilmanshin/Shutterstock.com; **front** tr Tar Pichet/Shutterstock .com; **front** bl Stanislav Fosenbauer/Shutterstock.com; **front** br OY/iStock /Getty Images Plus via Getty Images; **back** Ivan Cholakov/Shutterstock.com

Front Matter

vi l Christie's Images Ltd. / SuperStock; **vi** r The Picture Art Collection / Alamy Stock Photo; **vii** Katiekk2/iStock/Getty Images Plus via Getty Images; **vii** i iannomadav/iStock/Getty Images Plus via Getty Images; **vii** (typography) Adobe Stock/Patrick; **viii** Danny O'Leary illustrationX; **viii** (small people) KostiantynL/Shutterstock.com

Chapter 1

2 Renata Sedmakova/Shutterstock.com; **3** ViDI Studio/Shutterstock .com; **6** Ollyy/Shutterstock.com; **7** Fandorina Liza/Shutterstock.com; **9** penfold/iStock/Getty Images Plus via Getty Images; **10** Gary Hincks /Science Source; **11** (border) Kozyrina Olga/Shutterstock.com; **12**t INTERFOTO / Alamy Stock Photo; **12**b Lanmas / Alamy Stock Photo; **13**l adventtr/iStock/Getty Images Plus via Getty Images; **13**tr Neirfy /Shutterstock.com; **13**br Morphart Creation/Shutterstock.com; **14–15** (border) svetolk/iStock/Getty Images Plus via Getty Images; **14** graziano /Moment via Getty Images; **16–17**l Transia Design/Shutterstock.com; **17**tr RavindraJoisa/iStock/Getty Images Plus via Getty Images; **17**br saiko3p/Shutterstock.com; **18–19** (border) John Lock/Shutterstock .com; **19**t The Metropolitan Museum of Art, New York, Munsey Fund, 1931; **19**b bjdlzx/E+ via Getty Images; **21**l Heritage Image Partnership Ltd / Alamy Stock Photo; **21**r THP Creative/iStock/Getty Images Plus via Getty Images; **22** (border) valeriya_sh/Shutterstock.com; **23**t Julia Reschke/Shutterstock.com; **23**b Jane Rix/Shutterstock.com; **24** Asar Studios / Alamy Stock Photo

Chapter 2

26 Christie's Images Ltd. / SuperStock; **27** The Picture Art Collection / Alamy Stock Photo; **29** CPA Media Pte Ltd / Alamy Stock Photo; **34** (typography) Adobe Stock/Patrick; **36** Photos.com/Getty Images Plus via Getty Images; **37** Sammy33/Shutterstock.com; **38, 42**tl North Wind Picture Archives / Alamy Stock Photo; **40** Milkovasa/Shutterstock.com; **42–43** (banner) vectorkat/Shutterstock.com; **42**tc S. Greg Panosian/E+ via Getty Images; **42**ttr Bruce Yuanyue Bi/The Image Bank via Getty Images; **42**tbr Svetlana Beleacov/Shutterstock.com; **42**blt mary416 /Shutterstock.com; **42**blb Zvonimir Atletic/Shutterstock.com; **42**br SlavkoSereda/iStock/Getty Images Plus via Getty Images; **43**t, **45** Album / Alamy Stock Photo; **43**bl The Metropolitan Museum of Art, New York, Gift of Louis L. Lorillard, 1896, transferred from the Library; **43**br, **44** Chronicle / Alamy Stock Photo; **46** (small people) KostiantynL /Shutterstock.com

Chapter 3

49 Providence Collection / GoodSalt.com; **50** ViewStock via Getty Images; **51** CPA Media Pte Ltd / Alamy Stock Photo; **53**t © cherry lv | Dreamstime.com; **53**i xyom/iStock/Getty Images Plus via Getty Images; **53**ct akg-images; **53**cb "Yuan Bronze Cannon" by Gary Todd /Flickr/modified/Wikimedia Commons/Public Domain; **53**b Alan Kolnik / Alamy Stock Photo; **54**t © Nastypenguin | Dreamstime.com; **54**c agefotostock / Alamy Stock Photo; **54**b The Metropolitan Museum of Art, New York, Gift of Stanley Herzman, in memory of Gladys Herzman, 1997; **55**bg Katiekk2/iStock/Getty Images Plus via Getty Images; **55** iannomadav/iStock/Getty Images Plus via Getty Images; **56** Danny O'Leary illustrationX; **61** Candida Slater / Alamy Stock Photo; **62** (typography) Adobe Stock/Fuadi Alhusaini; **64**bg Reed Kaestner/The Image Bank Unreleased via Getty Images; **64** Jimmy Tran/Shutterstock .com; **65** Pakawat Thongcharoen/Moment via Getty Images; **66** Pavel Sukhov/iStock/Getty Images Plus via Getty Images; **67** PRISMA ARCHIVO / Alamy Stock Photo; **69** Science & Society Picture Library /SSPL via Getty Images

Chapter 4

71 Ian Dagnall / Alamy Stock Photo; **74**l SPCOLLECTION / Alamy Stock Photo; **74**c "Baldassare Castiglione" by Raffaello Sanzio/modified /Wikimedia Commons/Public Domain; **74**r "Portrait of Niccolò Machiavelli" by Santi di Tito/modified/Wikimedia Commons/Public Domain; **75** Lebrecht Music & Arts / Alamy Stock Photo; **78** "Printing Press" by Jon Augier/Copyright Museums Victoria/modified/CC By 4.0, https://collections.museumsvictoria.com.au/items/404914; **79**t VladyslaV Travel photo/Shutterstock.com; **79**b "The Small Cowper Madonna" by Raphael/National Gallery of Art/modified/Wikimedia Commons/Public Domain; **80**tl Dover Publications/Public Domain; **80**tr PictureLux / The Hollywood Archive / Alamy Stock Photo; **80**b savcoco/123RF; **81**l pchoui /iStock/Getty Images Plus via Getty Images; **81**rt Circumnavigation /Bigstock.com; **81**rc Timur Kulgarin/Shutterstock.com; **81**rbl gionnixxx /iStock/Getty Images Plus via Getty Images; **81**rbr Sergieiev/Shutterstock .com; **82**t OscarCatt/iStock/Getty Images Plus via Getty Images; **82**bl Vaara/iStock/Getty Images Plus via Getty Images; **82**br incamerastock / Alamy Stock Photo; **84**t Photos.com/Getty Images Plus via Getty Images; **84**b GeorgiosArt/iStock/Getty Images Plus via Getty Images; **85** Luciano Mortula - LGM/Shutterstock.com; **86** DeAgostini / Superstock; **87** Stock Montage/Archive Photos via Getty Images; **89**t Three Lions/Hulton Archive via Getty Images; **89**b Album / Alamy Stock Photo; **90** Heritage Image Partnership Ltd / Alamy Stock Photo; **91** Science History Images / Alamy Stock Photo

Chapter 5

92 Private Collection / © Look and Learn / Bridgeman Images; **93** Private Collection / Photo © O. Vaering / Bridgeman Images; **94** Dmitrlch /Shutterstock.com; **97**t "Astrolabe (PSF)" by Pearson Scott Foresman /modified/Wikimedia Commons/Public Domain; **97**c Sueddeutsche Zeitung Photo / Alamy Stock Photo; **97**b "A Naval Encounter between Dutch and Spanish Warships" by Cornelis Verbeeck/National Gallery of Art/modified/Wikimedia Commons/Public Domain; **99**t Hulton Archive via Getty Images; **99**b Peter Hermes Furian/Shutterstock.com; **100** (typography) Adobe Stock/struvictory; **100** (icon) Sidhe /Shutterstock.com; **104**t TonyBaggett/iStock/Getty Images Plus via Getty Images; **104**bl Pictorial Press Ltd / Alamy Stock Photo; **104**br Niday Picture Library / Alamy Stock Photo; **105** "Columbus Taking Possession" by L. Prang & Co., Boston/Library of Congress/modified/Wikimedia Commons/Public Domain; **107** Smith Archive / Alamy Stock Photo; **108** Archivart / Alamy Stock Photo

Chapter 6

110 Bashar Shglila/Moment Unreleased via Getty Images; **112–13**bg tellmemore000/iStock/Getty Images Plus via Getty Images; **112** Gilles Paire/Shutterstock.com; **113**t helovi/iStock/Getty Images Plus via Getty Images; **113**c Dewald Kirsten/Shutterstock.com; **113**b EcoPrint /Shutterstock.com; **114** Katiekk/Shutterstock.com; **115** MicheleAlfieri /iStock Editorial/Getty Images Plus via Getty Images; **117** Stefano Ravera / Alamy Stock Photo; **118**t kevin snelling / Alamy Stock Photo; **118**b TDway/Shutterstock.com; **119**t simplerdesign/Shutterstock.com; **119**b © Serafima Manekina | Dreamstime.com; **120** Eddie Gerald / Alamy Stock Photo; **121**t National Museum of African Art, Smithsonian Institution, Purchased with funds provided by the Smithsonian Collections Acquisition Program, 89-13-7; **121**b, **130**t Everett Collection /Shutterstock.com; **123** Edwin Remsberg/The Image Bank Unreleased via Getty Images; **124** (typography) Adobe Stock/didik; **126** © Blossfeldia | Dreamstime.com; **127**t Hemis / Alamy Stock Photo; **127**b Suzuki Kaku / Alamy Stock Photo; **129** "Ten Views in the Island of Antigua ... - caption: 'Slaves cutting the sugar cane'"/British Library/Flickr/Public Domain; **130**b Arterra Picture Library / Alamy Stock Photo

Chapter 7

134 (smile) Vector bucket/Shutterstock.com; **134** (frown) Studiobrand /Shutterstock.com; **135**t MPI/Archive Photos via Getty Images; **135**b "Giorgio vasari, seconda storia della notte di san bartolomeo, 1573, 03" by Sailko/modified/Wikimedia Commons/CC By 3.0; **137** Peter Righteous / Alamy Stock Photo; **138** ZU_09/DigitalVision Vectors via Getty Images; **142** Division of Work and Industry, National Museum of American History, Smithsonian Institution; **143** Album / Alamy Stock Photo; **148** "A Map of the Inhabited Part of Canada. Frontispiece by William Faden 1777"/Library of Congress/modified/Wikimedia Commons/Public Domain; **149** Richard Cummins / Alamy Stock Photo; **150**t AF Fotografie / Alamy Stock Photo; **150**b Granger, NYC; **151**t Kenneth Wiedemann /iStock/Getty Images Plus via Getty Images; **151**b CPA Media Pte Ltd / Alamy Stock Photo

Chapter 8

154 Lester120/Bigstock.com; **156, 171**t CPA Media Pte Ltd / Alamy Stock Photo; **157**l The Metropolitan Museum of Art, New York, Gift of Robert E. Tod, 1937; **157**r agefotostock / Alamy Stock Photo; **158**l "Fishing under Chinese Sweet Gums" by Qiu Ying/modified/Wikimedia Commons /Public Domain; **158**r Universal History Archive/Universal Images Group via Getty Images; **159**t cowardlion/Shutterstock.com; **159**b Chu Yong via Getty Images; **164** UPI / Alamy Stock Photo; **165** RudyBalasko /iStock/Getty Images Plus via Getty Images; **166** (horse) agrino /Shutterstock.com; **167** Private Collection / © Keith Rocco. All rights reserved 2022 / Bridgeman Images; **169** 1688671507/Shutterstock.com; **170**t Valery Rokhin/Shutterstock.com; **170**b Alex. Shevchenko /Shutterstock.com; **171**b Lukas Bischoff Photograph/Shutterstock.com; **173** R.M. Nunes/Shutterstock.com; **174** Dima Fadeev/Shutterstock.com; **175** Robert Preston Photography / Alamy Stock Photo

Chapter 9

176 Portrait of The Honourable Robert Boyle (1627 - 1691), Irish natural philosopher. Wellcome Collection. CC By 4.0 (modified); **177** Hulton Archive via Getty Images; **178** DEA PICTURE LIBRARY/De Agostini via Getty Images; **179** walter_g/Shutterstock.com; **180** "Frederick the Great" by Christoph Friedrich Reinhold Lisiewski/modified/Wikimedia Commons/Public Domain; **181**bg World History Archive / Alamy Stock Photo; **181** GL Archive / Alamy Stock Photo; **182** (typography) Neuevector/Shutterstock.com; **184** Peter Horree / Alamy Stock Photo; **185** Historical Images Archive / Alamy Stock Photo; **186** The Picture Art Collection / Alamy Stock Photo; **186**i Michael Nicholson/Corbis Historical via Getty Images; **189**t Album / Alamy Stock Photo; **189**b Photos.com/Getty Images Plus via Getty Images; **190**t The National Trust Photolibrary / Alamy Stock Photo; **190**b Akademie / Alamy Stock Photo; **191** Album / SuperStock; **192** Buyenlarge/Archive Photos via Getty Images; **193** Tetra Images via Getty Images; **194**t IanDagnall Computing / Alamy Stock Photo; **194**c "Portrait of John Locke" by Godfrey Kneller /Hermitage Museum/modified/Wikimedia Commons/Public Domain; **194**b Pictorial Press Ltd / Alamy Stock Photo; **196**t Science History Images / Alamy Stock Photo; **196**b eurobanks/Shutterstock.com

Chapter 10

198 Nature Picture Library / Alamy Stock Photo; **201**t CampPhoto/E+ via Getty Images; **201**it VectorMine/Shutterstock.com; **201**b bradlifestyle /Shutterstock.com; **201**ib USGS/Public Domain; **202**bg Ryan Rossotto /Stocktrek Images via Getty Images; **202** Dusan Vainer/Shutterstock.com; **203**t From The New York Public Library; **203**ct Avalon.red / Alamy Stock Photo; **203**cb MarTata/Shutterstock.com; **203**b Robert Harding / Lynn Gail / MediaBakery; **205**t The Picture Art Collection / Alamy Stock Photo; **205**c imageBROKER/Frank Schneider via Getty Images; **205**b Holger Leue/The Image Bank Unreleased via Getty Images; **206** (typography) Adobe Stock/Syaid; **209** Print Collector/Hulton Archive via Getty Images; **211** Asar Studios / Alamy Stock Photo; **214** "The Founding of Australia. By Capt. Arthur Phillip R.N. Sydney Cove, Jan. 26th 1788" by Algernon Talmage/State Library of New South Wales/modified /Wikimedia Commons/Public Domain; **215** Taras Vyshnya/Shutterstock .com; **217** "Reconstruction of the Signing of the Treaty of Waitangi, Marcus King (16044258961)"/Archives New Zealand/modified /Wikimedia Commons/CC By-SA 2.0; **218** INTERFOTO / Alamy Stock Photo; **219** Alpha Historica / Alamy Stock Photo

Chapter 11

222 DE AGOSTINI PICTURE LIBRARY/De Agostini via Getty Images; **223** Masterpics / Alamy Stock Photo; **224–25**bg Photo taken by Kami (Kuo, Jia-Wei)/Moment via Getty Images; **224**t Archivart / Alamy Stock Photo; **224**b, **237** Album / Alamy Stock Photo; **226**t The Picture Art Collection / Alamy Stock Photo; **226**b pidjoe/iStock Unreleased via Getty Images; **227**t, **240** Heritage Image Partnership Ltd / Alamy Stock Photo; **227**b IanDagnall Computing / Alamy Stock Photo; **228, 235** Chronicle / Alamy Stock Photo; **230**l DnDavis/Shutterstock.com; **230**r vectorissimo /Shutterstock.com; **231**t "Napoleon I of France by Andrea Appiani"/The Yorck Project/modified/Wikimedia Commons/Public Domain; **231**b CTK / Alamy Stock Photo; **234** "Europe 1812 map en" by Alexander Altenhof/modified/Wikipedia/CC By-SA 3.0/Map Resources; **236** Bettmann via Getty Images; **241** Signal Photos / Alamy Stock Photo

Chapter 12

246, 251tc, **255** Heritage Image Partnership Ltd / Alamy Stock Photo; **247, 264**tr Pictorial Press Ltd / Alamy Stock Photo; **249**t, b, **250**br Science & Society Picture Library/SSPL via Getty Images; **250–51** (banner) aleksandarvelasevic/DigitalVision Vectors via Getty Images; **250**tl Elchin Javadov/Shutterstock.com; **250**tr Colin Waters / Alamy Stock Photo; **250**c Ivy Close Images / Alamy Stock Photo; **250**bl Adobe Stock /Ossie; **251**tl Ricky Blakeley via Getty Images; **251**tr George-Standen /iStock Unreleased via Getty Images; **251**b Our Wild Life Photography / Alamy Stock Photo; **252** Nikolaus Löwe via flickr; **253**t Stephen Barnes / Northern Ireland / Alamy Stock Photo; **253**b Library of Congress, LC-DIG-nclc-01342; **254**t Division of Cultural and Community Life, National Museum of American History, Smithsonian Institution; **254**b Print Collector/Hulton Archive via Getty Images; **256**t "Bibb Mill No. 1, Macon, Ga. Many youngsters here. Some boys and girls were so small they had to climb up on to the... - NARA - 523148" by Lewis Hine /National Archives/modified/Wikimedia Commons/Public Domain; **256**b Private Collection / © Look and Learn / Bridgeman Images; **260**l ANEK SANGKAMANEE/Shutterstock.com; **260**r Photo 12 / Alamy Stock Photo; **261**t, **264**tl Classic Image / Alamy Stock Photo; **261**c Chronicle / Alamy Stock Photo; **261**b National Portrait Gallery, Smithsonian Institution; **263** Niday Picture Library / Alamy Stock Photo; **264** (banner) ChrisGorgio/iStock/Getty Images Plus via Getty Images; **264**bl Photos.com/Getty Images Plus via Getty Images; **264**br Album / British Library / Alamy Stock Photo

Chapter 13

266, 284 Hulton Archive via Getty Images; **267**t, **283** Chronicle / Alamy Stock Photo; **267**b © Mary Evans/Peter Higginbotham Collection/Mary Evans Picture Library Ltd/age footstock; **269** Don Smetzer / Alamy Stock Photo; **270** ullstein bild Dtl./ullstein bild via Getty Images; **271** Jimlop collection / Alamy Stock Photo; **273** "Darwin's finches by Gould" /modified/Wikimedia Commons/Public Domain; **274** Archive Pics / Alamy Stock Photo; **275** Everett Collection Inc / Alamy Stock Photo; **276**t Private Collection / © Look and Learn / Bridgeman Images; **276**b whitemay/DigitalVision Vectors via Getty Images; **277** "Napoleon III" by Alexandre Cabanel/modified/Wikimedia Commons/Public Domain; **278** Print Collector/Hulton Archive via Getty Images; **279** Adobe Stock /anemone; **280**t The Metropolitan Museum of Art, Gift of Mrs. Russell Sage, 1908; **280**c Keith Lance/DigitalVision Vectors via Getty Images; **280**b–**81**bl Roman Sigaev/Shutterstock.com; **281**t Lanmas / Alamy Stock Photo; **281**br Asar Studios / Alamy Stock Photo; **282** Sean Spencer / Alamy Stock Photo; **285**t incamerastock / Alamy Stock Photo; **285**b Bettmann via Getty Images; **287**t Classic Image / Alamy Stock Photo; **287**b Apic/Hulton Archive via Getty Images; **288**l Stock Montage /Archive Photos via Getty Images; **288**r National Portrait Gallery, Smithsonian Institution; transfer from the Smithsonian American Art Museum; gift of Eleanor A. Campbell to the Smithsonian Institution, 1942; **289**l Photo 12 / Alamy Stock Photo; **289**r Lordprice Collection / Alamy Stock Photo; **291**t History and Art Collection / Alamy Stock Photo; **291**b DEA PICTURE LIBRARY/De Agostini via Getty Images

Chapter 14

296t Hulton Deutsch/Corbis Historical via Getty Images; **296**cl Svetlana Foote/Shutterstock.com; **296**cr dolphfyn/Shutterstock.com; **296**b Mohd Haniff Abas/EyeEm via Getty Images; **298**t © Jgaunion | Dreamstime .com; **298**b guenterguni/E+ via Getty Images; **302**bg Unknown / Alamy Stock Photo; **302** Granger, NYC; **304** Chronicle / Alamy Stock Photo; **305** Photos.com/Getty Images Plus via Getty Images; **306** Pump Park Vintage Photography / Alamy Stock Photo; **307** "Canal de Suez, el-Kantara LCCN2017656987"/Library of Congress/modified/Wikimedia Commons/Public Domain; **308** Roger Viollet via Getty Images; **309** ND/Roger Viollet via Getty Images; **311** The Reading Room / Alamy Stock Photo; **314**t Africanway/iStock Editorial/Getty Images Plus via Getty Images; **314**b Billy Miaron/Shutterstock.com; **315** Ken Gillespie Photography / Alamy Stock Photo

Chapter 15

316, 325 Album / Alamy Stock Photo; **318, 336**b World History Archive / Alamy Stock Photo; **320, 323**t Chronicle / Alamy Stock Photo; **321** Artexplorer / Alamy Stock Photo; **322**t, b, **326** The Picture Art Collection / Alamy Stock Photo; **323**c, b Nastasic/DigitalVision Vectors via Getty Images; **324** Pictorial Press Ltd / Alamy Stock Photo; **327** Dinodia Photos / Alamy Stock Photo; **331** A busy stacking room in the opium factory at Patna, India. Lithograph after W. S. Sherwill, c. 1850. Wellcome Collection. Public Domain; **332**t Everett Collection Inc / Alamy Stock Photo; **332**b, **333** CPA Media Pte Ltd / Alamy Stock Photo; **334**t Everett Collection Historical / Alamy Stock Photo; **334**c History and Art Collection / Alamy Stock Photo; **334**b Signal Photos / Alamy Stock Photo; **335** Thomas Fisher Rare Book Library, University of Toronto;

336t Alpha Historica / Alamy Stock Photo; **337**t The History Collection / Alamy Stock Photo; **337**b dourleak/iStock/Getty Images Plus via Getty Images; **338** Private Collection / © Look and Learn / Bridgeman Images; **340** liebre/iStock/Getty Images Plus via Getty Images; **341** Bettmann via Getty Images; **342** Science History Images / Alamy Stock Photo

Chapter 16

344, 352r Everett Collection/Shutterstock.com; **346**t, **348**b, **364**t ullstein bild Dtl./ullstein bild via Getty Images; **346**b National Archives; **348**t, **366**r Bettmann via Getty Images; **350** Trinity Mirror / Mirrorpix / Alamy Stock Photo; **351** (banner) Photos.com via Getty Images; **351**tl DEA PICTURE LIBRARY/De Agostini via Getty Images; **351**tc "Australian infantry small box respirators Ypres 1917" by Captain Frank Hurley/Australian War Memorial/modified/Wikimedia Commons /Public Domain; **351**tr Gavran333/Shutterstock.com; **351**bl "Lot 3619-3 (LC-USZ62-15800)"/Photograph Curator/Flickr/Public Domain; **351**bc "1st Aero Squadron Salmson 2A2"/Air Service, United States Army /modified/Wikimedia Commons/Public Domain; **351**br Library of Congress, LC-DIG-ggbain-17781; **352**l Shawshots / Alamy Stock Photo; **353**t Library of Congress; **353**bl Archive Pics / Alamy Stock Photo; **353**bc Photo 12 / Alamy Stock Photo; **353**br "28 Woodrow Wilson" /GPA Photo Archive/Flickr/Public Domain; **354** Lionel LOURDEL /Photononstop via Getty Images; **355** colaimages / Alamy Stock Photo; **356** Sueddeutsche Zeitung Photo / Alamy Stock Photo; **357** MPI/Archive Photos via Getty Images; **358** Heritage Image Partnership Ltd / Alamy Stock Photo; **359** CPA Media Pte Ltd / Alamy Stock Photo; **360** Print Collector/Hulton Archive via Getty Images; **361** GK History Images / Alamy Stock Photo; **364**b Pictorial Press Ltd / Alamy Stock Photo; **365**t Album / Alamy Stock Photo; **365**b Science History Images / Alamy Stock Photo; **366**l API/Gamma-Rapho via Getty Images; **366**c History and Art Collection / Alamy Stock Photo; **367**l AF Fotografie / Alamy Stock Photo; **367**c "The Scream" by Edvard Munch/modified/Wikimedia Commons/Public Domain; **367**r "Portrait of Pablo Picasso" by Juan Gris /modified/Wikimedia Commons/Public Domain; **368**lt Leo_tronico /Shutterstock.com; **368**lb Richard T. Nowitz/Media Bakery; **368**r © Atomazul | Dreamstime.com

Chapter 17

371 WorldWarTwoVeterans.com; **372** akg-images / Alamy Stock Photo; **373, 374**b, **380** ullstein bild Dtl./ullstein bild via Getty Images; **374**t Shawshots / Alamy Stock Photo; **375**t, **390, 396** Bettmann via Getty Images; **375**b, **378**t, b Sueddeutsche Zeitung Photo / Alamy Stock Photo; **381** Keystone Press / Alamy Stock Photo; **382** "General Bernard L. Montgomery watches his tanks move up. North Africa, November 1942."/National Archives and Records Administration/modified /Wikimedia Commons/Public Domain; **383** ©Imperial War Museum /Norman Wilkinson (Art.IWM ART LD 6005); **384** Science History Images / Alamy Stock Photo; **385** National Archives; **386** Vintage_Space / Alamy Stock Photo; **387**t Photo 12/Universal Images Group via Getty Images; **387**c FLHC / Alamy Stock Photo; **387**b Stefano Zaccaria /Shutterstock.com; **388**t pzAxe/Shutterstock.com; **388**c bieg/123RF; **388**b © Oleg Bogutskyy | Dreamstime.com; **389**lt Kao Jung Chou /Shutterstock.com; **389**lc, rb Martin Spurny/Shutterstock.com; **389**lb Innershadows Photography/Shutterstock.com; **389**rt Dario Lo Presti /Shutterstock.com; **389**rc Stocktrek Images, Inc. / Alamy Stock Photo; **391** digitalimagination/iStock/Getty Images Plus via Getty Images; **392** Photo 12 / Alamy Stock Photo; **394** World History Archive / Alamy Stock Photo; **397**t Everett Collection Historical / Alamy Stock Photo; **397**bl grebeshkovmaxim/Shutterstock.com; **397**br mabesadze /Shutterstock.com; **398** CALVIN AND HOBBES © 1991 Watterson. Reprinted with permission of ANDREWS MCMEEL SYNDICATION. All rights reserved.

Chapter 18

401 Keystone Press / Alamy Stock Photo; **403**t Album / Alamy Stock Photo; **403**b Roman Babakin/Shutterstock.com; **403**i "Logo The Warsaw Pact" by Dmitry Tretiakov/modified/Wikimedia Commons/CC By-SA 3.0; **404**tl FPG/Archive Photos via Getty Images; **404**tc, **406**c Everett Collection Historical / Alamy Stock Photo; **404**tr "C-47s at Tempelhof Airport Berlin 1948"/U.S. Air Force/modified/Wikimedia Commons /Public Domain; **404**b, **405** dpa picture alliance / Alamy Stock Photo; **406**t The Asahi Shimbun via Getty Images; **406**b INTERFOTO / Alamy Stock Photo; **408** PJF Military Collection / Alamy Stock Photo; **409** Universal History Archive/Universal Images Group via Getty Images; **410**t Daniele Faccioli/Stocktrek Images via Getty Images; **410**c "B-2 first flight 071201-F-9999J-034"/USAF/modified/Wikimedia Commons /Public Domain; **410**b jdb collection / Alamy Stock Photo; **411**t Aleks49 /Shutterstock.com; **411**b NASA; **414** Hum Historical / Alamy Stock Photo; **415** Dinodia Photos / Alamy Stock Photo; **417**t John Frost Newspapers / Alamy Stock Photo; **417**c, b Hulton Deutsch/Corbis Historical via Getty Images; **418**t Wojtek Laski/Hulton Archive via Getty Images; **418**b Robert Nickelsberg/Hulton Archive via Getty Images; **419** (art reference) Jean GUICHARD/Gamma-Rapho via Getty Images; **420** "41st Annual Convention of the National Association of Evangelicals"/U.S. National Archives and Records Administration /modified/Wikimedia Commons/Public Domain; **421** Justin Leighton / Alamy Stock Photo

Chapter 19

424 Catalin Lazar/Shutterstock.com; **425** PAc 89-38.F5 WPA Bookmobile, Fairfield, Montana Historical Society Photograph Archives (edited); **426** Our World in Data/CC By 4.0/modified; **427**t tcly /Shutterstock.com; **427**b Lucie Lang/Shutterstock.com; **428** Stocktrek Images via Getty Images; **429** Nahlik/Shutterstock.com; **430** "ARPANET Maps"/Roberts (L. G. (Lawrence G.)) Papers/CC By 4.0/modified; **431** Hulton Archive via Getty Images; **432** Anton Starikov/Shutterstock.com; **433**t Keystone Press / Alamy Stock Photo; **433**b, **442**t AP Photo; **435** (art reference) ullstein bild via Getty Images; **436** AP Photo/Carlos Gonzalez, File; **437**t Bettmann via Getty Images; **437**b IWM/Imperial War Museums via Getty Images; **438** (typography) Mott Jordan/Shutterstock .com; **440** Geopix / Alamy Stock Photo; **441**l Keystone/Hulton Archive via Getty Images; **441**r Georges De Keerle/Hulton Archive via Getty Images; **442**i Barry Iverson / Alamy Stock Photo; **442**b Star Tribune via Getty Images; **443**t, b Scott Peterson/Hulton Archive via Getty Images; **444**t Peter Charlesworth/LightRocket via Getty Images; **444**b KIMIMASA MAYAMA/AFP via Getty Images; **445**l Sidney M. Schaer, M.D./Archive Photos via Getty Images; **445**r Bohemian Nomad Picturemakers/Corbis Documentary via Getty Images; **446** William KAREL/Gamma-Rapho via Getty Images; **447**t Alain MINGAM/ Gamma-Rapho via Getty Images; **447**b peter jordan / Alamy Stock Photo; **448** Everett Collection/Shutterstock.com; **449** xiaoke chen/iStock Unreleased via Getty Images; **450** brainmaster/iStock/Getty Images Plus via Getty Images

Chapter 20

452 Laperruque / Alamy Stock Photo; **453** Getty Images News via Getty Images; **454** "US 10th Mountain Division soldiers in Afghanistan" by Staff Sgt. Kyle Davis/U.S. Army/modified/Wikimedia Commons /Public Domain; **455**t "Live Fire Exercise" by Staff Sgt. Luke P. Thelen /DVIDSHUB/modified/Flickr/CC By 2.0; **455**b Scott Olson/Getty Images News via Getty Images; **456** (frame) Hassan Haider/Shutterstock .com; **458** Claudia Wiens / Alamy Stock Photo; **459, 470** REUTERS / Alamy Stock Photo; **461**t Michael Honegger / Alamy Stock Photo; **461**b PA Images / Alamy Stock Photo; **463**t Lebazele/iStock Unreleased via Getty Images; **463**b PradeepGaurs/Shutterstock.com; **464** (Myspace) Mehaniq/Shutterstock.com; **464** (LinkedIn, Pinterest), (Facebook) rvlsoft/Shutterstock.com; **464** (Twitter, Instagram, Snapchat) Rose Carson/Shutterstock.com; **464** (Amazon) sdx15/Shutterstock.com; **465**t agefotostock / Alamy Stock Photo; **465**b Maskot via Getty Images; **466** christian kober / Alamy Stock Photo; **467**t DigitalGlobe/Maxar via Getty Images; **467**b JAMES NIELSEN/AFP via Getty Images; **468**t MediaNews Group/Reading Eagle via Getty Images; **468**b Phanie / Alamy Stock Photo; **469** AP Photo/Adamu Adamu; **469** (art reference) Antoine Gyori - Corbis/Corbis News via Getty Images; **471** 10'000 Hours /DigitalVision via Getty Images

All maps from Map Resources